Books by Elizabeth Bishop

Poems

NORTH & SOUTH

A COLD SPRING

QUESTIONS OF TRAVEL

THE BALLAD OF THE BURGLAR OF BABYLON
with woodcuts by Ann Grifalconi

THE COMPLETE POEMS (1969)

GEOGRAPHY III

THE COMPLETE POEMS: 1927–1979

Prose

THE COLLECTED PROSE
edited by Robert Giroux

THE DIARY OF ''HELENA MORLEY''
translated from the Portuguese

BRAZIL
with the editors of "Life"

Anthology

AN ANTHOLOGY OF
TWENTIETH-CENTURY BRAZILIAN POETRY
edited with Emanuel Brasil

ONE ART

Elizabeth Bishop

ONE ART

LETTERS, SELECTED AND EDITED

BY ROBERT GIROUX

Farrar · Straus · Giroux

NEW YORK

Frontispiece
Elizabeth Bishop on the steps of the Square Roof brothel in Key West.
Photo by James Laughlin

Contents

Introduction

BY ROBERT GIROUX

I

In a tribute to Elizabeth Bishop after her death, poet James Merrill cited her "instinctive, modest, lifelong impersonations of an ordinary woman," an acute and witty observation about an extraordinary woman who is regarded as one of the major poets of our century. Richard Wilbur called her poems "inexhaustibly fresh." Harold Bloom said her poetry stands "at the edge where what is most worth saying is all but impossible to say." Octavio Paz wrote: "The enormous power of reticence—that is the great lesson of the poetry of Elizabeth Bishop . . . To hear it is not to hear a lesson; it is a pleasure, verbal and mental, as great as a spiritual experience." Frank Bidart—a close friend of Elizabeth in her last years (to whom she left her library)—has shown that her poetry also has a "dark side" since "too often she has been considered 'cool' and 'perfect,' and not the profound, even tragic artist she is."

She once described her younger self as "painfully—no, excruciatingly—shy." Only at the urging of her friend Robert Lowell, who recognized her genius early on, did she reluctantly agree to accept the post of Poetry Consultant at the Library of Congress, succeeding him and Léonie Adams in this office, known today as that of the Poet Laureate. Her sad and humorous letters around this period show that it was a lonely and difficult time for her.

During her life she wrote several thousand letters, from which the selection in this book has been made. The letters here cover fifty years —from 1928, when she was seventeen (and already a poet), to her death in 1979—and they represent only a fraction of her output. "When Elizabeth Bishop's letters are published (as they will be)," Lowell predicted, "she will be recognized as not only one of the best, but also one of the most prolific writers of our century." In a sense the letters constitute her autobiography, though they were not intended as such: she was *not* recording her life but was simply keeping in touch with her friends and correspondents. Inevitably, the details of her little known private life emerge in these pages. As one would have expected from "so honest a nature as hers" (the phrase is Richard Wilbur's), she was explicit about the great love of her life, which lasted fifteen years and ended in tragedy.

When accepting the Neustadt International Prize for Literature in 1976, she revealed in her biographical notes that "for some fifteen years . . . [I] shared a house in the mountains near Petrópolis and an apartment in Rio de Janeiro with a Brazilian friend, Lota Costellat de Macedo Soares." Part Four of this book covers their life in Brazil, beginning late in 1951 and ending with Lota's suicide in New York in 1967. Elizabeth describes her years in Brazil, before Lota's illness, as the happiest of her life.

One Art, the title of this book (taken from her villanelle), stands for the art of poetry, to which she devoted her life. William Butler Yeats believed that "The intellect of man is forced to choose / Perfection of the life, or of the work," and Elizabeth chose the latter. Her meticulous striving for perfection in her verse is legendary, immortalized by Robert Lowell in his poem "For Elizabeth Bishop 4": "Do / you still hang your words in air, ten years / unfinished, glued to your notice board, with gaps / or empties for the unimaginable phrase— / unerring Muse who makes the casual perfect?" She started to write one of her most famous poems, "The Moose," in 1956, promising her Aunt Grace she would dedicate it to her when it was ready; she mailed her the finished poem sixteen years later. The natural, unstrained language of this long, subtle, and marvelous poem, describing an interrupted bus trip from Nova Scotia, reads as if it had been written in one sitting. (Elizabeth was asked to read "The Moose" at the Harvard commencement in 1972 as the Phi Beta Kappa poem, and considered it a great compliment when a student who was asked what he thought of it said: "Well, as far as poems go, it wasn't bad.")

One Art also stands for the art of letter writing, which she practiced more casually and with more prolific results than composing poems. She was not only a good letter writer herself, she enjoyed reading other people's letters. Her library contained scores of books of letters—the Elizabethans, George Herbert, Lady Mary Wortley Montagu, Jane Austen, Sydney Smith, Gerard Manley Hopkins, Oscar Wilde, Virginia Woolf, etc. Not many people know that she gave a seminar at Harvard on letter writing as an art. Limited to fifteen students, the course was listed in 1971–72 as *"English 2902. Conference Group: Letters—Readings in Personal Correspondence, Famous and Infamous, from the 16th to 20th Centuries."* She told a friend that the kind of letters and letter writers she had in mind for her class were "Mrs. Carlyle, Chekhov, my Aunt Grace, Keats, a letter found in the street, etc."—not only literary or formal letters, that is, but human and eloquent (even perhaps illiterate) ones, like those sent to her by Jimmy O'Shea of Fall River, aged seventy, when she briefly worked at a correspondence school after leaving Vassar (see her memoir "The U.S.A. School of Writing").

She said that once, while staying with her friend the atomic physicist

Jane Dewey, she wrote forty letters in a single day. This was the exception, of course; she usually complained of being behind in her correspondence. She wrote her close friend Mrs. Kit Barker: "I am sorry for people who can't write letters. But I suspect also that you and I, Ilse, love to write them because it's kind of like working without really doing it." Some letters are more carefully composed than others, like those to Marianne Moore and Robert Lowell—especially the one written in response to his recollected near-proposal of marriage. Her most spontaneous letters always display her "famous eye" for interesting or unexpected details—of birds (like her beloved toucan, Uncle Sammy), animals (her cats' antics), flora and fauna, and the behavior of children. There are a few *cris de coeur*, whose recipients were asked to burn or destroy them, but since the letters have remained extant, they are here. Letters like the one she wrote Robie Macauley (who had just moved into her Boston neighborhood and asked her about local stores), and the letter she wrote John Frederick Nims on the day she died (objecting to too many footnotes explaining words in her poems for students who could look them up and learn their meaning for themselves) are Elizabeth at her most characteristic as a letter writer.

I first met her in 1957 at the Cosmopolitan Club in New York, when we were drawing up a contract for her translation of *The Diary of "Helena Morley"*; I published this book and all her subsequent books of poetry. She was reserved and formal at the beginning, and also attractive and intelligent. Our mutual interests in poetry and music (especially opera; occasionally she was my guest at the Met), and the fact that for years I had known Marianne Moore and Robert Lowell, two of her closest friends, helped our publishing relationship deepen into a friendship that lasted until her death twenty-two years later. Her delightful poem "Manners" tells a great deal about Elizabeth: she always cherished, as well as practiced, good manners. Though highly sophisticated, she possessed at the same time a down-to-earth quality which perhaps came from her early upbringing in Nova Scotia. She not only had common sense and a superlative sense of humor, but enjoyed calling herself "a country mouse," which made it easy to impersonate an ordinary woman. Among her many domestic gifts was that of being a superb and inventive cook (Lota's nickname for her was "Cookie"). She knew a great deal about painting, and excelled at watercolors, as the exhibit of thirty-seven of her drawings and sketches at the Key West Literary Seminar in January 1993 proved. When depressed she had trouble with drinking, but in all our years I never once saw her drunk. There are degrees of alcoholism, as any editor or publisher quickly learns. Despite books by writers (who never knew her) labeling her an "addicted alcoholic," the letters show she was at times a heavy drinker, with a serious but not an all-consuming problem. After she took on her first teaching job (at age fifty-five), a professor wrote her, "You are the soberest poet we've had here yet." Only an understanding of the whole cycle of her life provides the key to her character and genius.

I I

"When you write my epitaph, you must say I was the loneliest person who ever lived," she told Robert Lowell in 1948, on an occasion he never forgot. The most significant fact of her biography seems to be that early in life she became an orphan. She was born in Worcester, Massachusetts, on February 8, 1911; her father, William Thomas Bishop, died when she was eight months old. He had been an executive of Bishop Contractors, a New England construction firm founded by his father at the turn of the century. Her mother, Gertrude Bulmer of Great Village, Nova Scotia, never recovered from the shock of her husband's sudden death; it seriously affected her mental health. After 1916 Elizabeth, a child of five, never saw her mother again; Mrs. Bishop died in an asylum in 1934. Elizabeth was raised in Great Village by her Bulmer grandmother and went to primary school there. "I used to ask Grandmother, when I said goodbye [for school], to promise me not to die before I came home." She had an unhappy interlude of nine months living with her well-to-do paternal grandparents in Worcester (see her memoir "The Country Mouse"), and felt she was "on the same terms in the house" as their Boston bull terrier, Beppo, and she became asthmatic and developed eczema. Her health improved when she went to live near Boston with Aunt Maude, her mother's sister.

Her excellent education was financed by a legacy from her father, which dwindled over the years through inflation, so that she was more and more dependent on grants, fellowships, awards, magazine and book royalties, and finally teaching. After attending the Walnut Hill boarding school, where she met Frani Blough and published her first poems in the student magazine, she followed Frani a year later to Vassar College. Among her other college friends were Mary McCarthy, Louise Crane, Margaret Miller, and Eleanor and Eunice Clark. She graduated in 1934, the year in which she met Marianne Moore and the year in which her mother died. Worried about the choice of a career, she first thought of becoming a composer (she studied music at college and later was a pupil of Ralph Kirkpatrick, the noted harpsichordist and musicologist), and then a doctor ("I got myself enrolled at the Cornell Medical School . . . Marianne Moore discouraged me from going on with that"). In 1935 her poems were published for the first time in a book, *Trial Balances*, an anthology introducing new poets, in which she was "presented" by Marianne Moore.

Not until four years after they started corresponding did she address "Dear Miss Moore" as "Dear Marianne," and only at the latter's invitation. She genuinely admired, deferred to, and delighted in the friendship of the older poet. "I never left Cumberland Street [Moore's Brooklyn address]," her memoir "Efforts of Affection" reveals, "without feeling happier: uplifted, even inspired, determined to be good, to work harder, not to worry about what other people thought, never to try to publish anything until I thought I'd done my best with it, no matter how many years it took—or never to publish at all." David Kalstone's brilliant posthumous book, *Becoming a Poet: Elizabeth Bishop with Marianne Moore and Robert Lowell* (1989), has analyzed Miss Moore's role as her early mentor. He also noted their inevitable point of artistic departure—that moment of liberation which came on October 17, 1940, over Elizabeth's ambitious war poem "Roosters." Miss Moore and her mother had rewritten it, changing the language, the triplet rhyme scheme, and even the title (their choice was "The Cock"). Elizabeth firmly rejected their revisions; in capital letters she humorously proclaimed "ELIZABETH KNOWS BEST" and published "Roosters" in *The New Republic* as she had originally written it. Fortunately, despite this literary disagreement, their friendship lasted until the older poet's death in 1972.

After leaving Vassar, Elizabeth in July 1934 rented an apartment in Greenwich Village at 16 Charles Street, where her classmate Margaret Miller was briefly her roommate. But it was another classmate, Louise Crane, who became her closest friend and lover in these years. Louise was not an intellectual and had flunked her freshman year, despite tutoring by Elizabeth and Margaret Miller; she attended classes for three years but never graduated. She came from a distinguished family, her father, Winthrop Murray Crane, having been governor of Massachusetts and a U.S. senator. Her mother, who moved to New York after her husband's death, was a founder of and a leading spirit at the new Museum of Modern Art, as well as founder of the Dalton School (also in New York) named after their hometown in Massachusetts. The family fortune came from Crane Paper, a company which produced not only superior notepaper but the silk-threaded paper (invented by Mr. Crane) on which U.S. currency is printed.

Though Mary McCarthy claimed that Louise "was a comic butt" at Vassar, with big blue eyes and a tendency to be overweight, other classmates admired her generosity, her sense of humor and adventure, and her intuitive good taste in modern art. She loved jazz and made friends of the best Harlem musicians; that's how Elizabeth met Billie Holiday, for whom she wrote her poem "Songs for a Colored Singer." At college Louise drove a Dusenberg and was known as a fast driver; when Margaret Miller was injured in a car accident in France (see the letter of August 9, 1937), Louise was at the wheel and escaped injury, as did Elizabeth. Some of these early trips abroad were partly financed by Louise. On one occasion she and Elizabeth stayed in Paris at the commodious apartment of Mrs. Crane's friend, the Comtesse de Chambrun (born Clara Longworth and a sister-in-law of the famous Alice), where Elizabeth wrote "Cirque d'Hiver," her first poem to appear in *The New Yorker*, as well as "Paris, 7 A.M." Louise was generous to artists of all kinds, including Marianne Moore, who gave readings at Mrs. Crane's salons at 820 Fifth Avenue. It was through Louise Crane and Monroe Wheeler of MoMA that Elizabeth first met Lota, during the latter's New York visit in 1942. Elizabeth's discovery of Key West can be attributed to Louise, who loved fishing; they jointly bought a house there at 624 White Street in 1938. Elizabeth lived in Key West for nine years, with frequent trips to New York. Though their affair ended before the war, Louise and Elizabeth always remained good friends.

After the war in June 1945 Elizabeth submitted her first book, *North & South*, for the Houghton Mifflin Literary Fellowship. Her sponsors were Edmund Wilson, Marianne Moore, and Dr. John Dewey, and her manuscript was chosen from 800 entrants for the prize of $1,000. Published in August 1946, the book was greeted with an extraordinary review by the best (and toughest) poetry critic in America, poet Randall Jarrell:

The best poems in Elizabeth Bishop's *North & South* are so good that it takes a geological event like *Paterson* to overshadow them. "The Fish" and "Roosters" are two of the most calmly beautiful, deeply sympathetic poems of our time; "The Monument," "The Man-Moth," "The Weed," the first "Song for a Colored Singer," and one or two others are almost or quite as good, and there are charming poems on a smaller scale, or beautiful fragments—for instance, the end of "Love Lies Sleeping" . . .

The poet of *North & South* . . . is as attractively and unassumingly good as the poet of *Observations* and *What Are Years*—but simpler and milder, less driven into desperate straits or dens of innocence, and taking the Century of Polycarp more for granted. (When you read Miss Bishop's "Florida," a poem whose first sentence begins, "The state with the prettiest name," and whose last sentence begins, "The alligator, who has five distinct calls: / friendliness, love, mating, war, and a warning," you don't need to be told that the poetry of Marianne Moore was, in the beginning, an appropriately selected foundation for Miss Bishop's work.) . . . Her work is unusually personal and honest in its wit, perception, and sensitivity—and in its restrictions too; all her poems have written underneath, *I have seen it.*

In 1947 Jarrell introduced Elizabeth to Robert Lowell, who, for the remainder of their lives, was her most important literary friend and colleague. During the summer of 1948 she vacationed in Maine with Lowell and Mrs. Carley Dawson, a widowed Washington socialite who thought Lowell was going to marry her. It was Elizabeth he wanted to propose to, he later confessed in a letter (see page 344). "I suppose we might almost claim something like apparently Strachey and Virginia Woolf," he wrote

Elizabeth, and her reply of December 11, 1957, is a poker-faced masterpiece.

After she accepted the Library of Congress appointment at Lowell's insistence, in 1949, her letters to her good friend the painter Loren MacIver, during the summer preceding her stint in Washington, record the anxiety attacks and near-hysteria she suffered as the starting date approached. Even after completing her term at the Library, she was uneasy and plagued with doubts. She wrote Dr. Anny Baumann, her physician in New York, who became her close friend and confidante:

> I get myself into a fine state of discouragement and panic, sleeplessness, nightmares, etc.—and why, I don't really know . . . When I went to the hospital for five days I had not been drinking so much, but I was afraid I was going to . . . I am exactly the age now at which my father died, which also might have something to do with it.

At this juncture Bryn Mawr awarded her their Lucy Martin Donnelly Fellowship of $2,500. It changed her life. She was allowed to travel and decided on "a crazy trip," circumnavigating the continent of South America. Her ship *Bowplate* took seventeen days to reach the Brazilian port of Santos, where she arrived in late November 1951. At Rio, her train was met by her friend Pearl Kazin, as well as by Mary Stearns Morse, a former dancer and lover of Lota's. Elizabeth expected to resume her voyage after two weeks or so, but she stayed in Brazil fifteen years.

Soon after her arrival, while living in Lota's penthouse apartment on Copacabana Beach, Elizabeth took two bites of the fruit of the cashew and had a violent reaction. "That night my eyes started stinging," she wrote Dr. Baumann, "and the next day I started to swell—and swell and swell . . . I couldn't *see* anything for over a week." The doctor diagnosed her affliction as the "Quincke Edema." Elizabeth believed that this illness endeared her to Brazilians, because Lota's relatives and friends brought her *their* pills and smothered her with the kind of affectionate attention she was not used to but loved. When she moved to the modern and elegant house Lota was building on her estate in the mountains above Petrópolis—the old imperial summer residence, more than one hour's drive from Rio—she learned that Lota had fallen in love with her. On December 20, 1951, Lota not only asked Elizabeth to stay and live with her but said she would take care of her and build a studio next to the house in which the poet could concentrate on her work. Later Elizabeth, through tears, told friends: "It was the first time anyone ever offered me a home, or so much. Lota's gesture meant—just everything." In her notebook Elizabeth wrote: "Sometimes it seems . . . as though only intelligent people are stupid enough to fall in love & only stupid people [meaning herself] are intelligent enough to let themselves be loved." She dedicated her next book of poems, *Questions of Travel*, to Lota with the words of Luis de Camões, the sixteenth-century Portuguese poet: "O to give you as much as I have and as much as I can, / since the more I give you the more I owe you." As she wrote Lowell in the second year of her stay, "I am extremely happy, for the first time in my life."

What was Lota like? Her full name was Maria Carlota Costellat de Macedo Soares, the daughter of an aristocratic and wealthy family that had come to Brazil with the Portuguese settlers. Convent-educated, Lota had been born in Paris and spoke fluent French as well as Portuguese, with English as a weaker third language. Her father, owner and editor of one of the largest newspapers in Rio, the *Diario Carioca*, had long opposed the dictator Getúlio Vargas, who had taken over in 1930. (Even when he left office in 1945, Vargas maintained control through his strong political machine and returned to public power as President in 1950; he died by his own hand in 1954.) Lota's father—exiled several times, imprisoned, and also shot at (the family treasured his straw hat with a bullet hole)—was honored "at a tremendous banquet" on Freedom of the Press Day in 1953. Lota and her father had been estranged for years; unlike her attractive sister, Marietta, who married and had a family, Lota was the ugly duckling, the intellectual, unconventional and lesbian. On their mother's death she and her sister had inherited the large and ancient *fazenda* or plantation of Samambaia, officially designated "a national monument"; they divided the land, Lota choosing the higher mountainous part. Elizabeth said that Lota "kept a couple of square miles here at the top where we live, so it will always be protected from neighbors." For income Lota depended on the sale of parts of her estate; several relatives and friends, including the young up-and-coming politician Carlos Lacerda, had houses on her land.

Elizabeth Hardwick, who had been a guest at Samambaia, described Lota as "not tall. She had a lot of lustrous black hair which she wore in a bun. She was witty indeed, civilized—and yet different from the women I had known. She had wonderful, glistening dark eyes and glistening dark-rimmed glasses. You felt, or I felt, in her the legacy or curse of the Spanish-Portuguese women of the upper classes . . . Her English was fluent, fractured and utterly compelling. Lota was talkative, amusing and very sophisticated, and yet somehow melancholy too, the Iberian strain . . . [She] was very intense indeed, emotional, also a bit insecure as we say, and loyal, devoted and smart and lesbian and Brazilian and shy, masterful in some ways, but helpless also. She adored Elizabeth in the most attractive way, in this case somewhat fearfully, possessively, and yet modestly and without any tendency to oppress."

Another friend of Lota's, Robert Fizdale of the duo-piano team Gold & Fizdale, who in the 1940s had met her in New York through Louise Crane and harpsichordist Sylvia Marlowe, described Lota as "one of the most charming, original, remarkable women I've ever known. She was small, volatile, outgoing and thoroughly artistic. Do *not* underestimate

Lota." Whenever Elizabeth wrote to the pianists, Lota usually added her own comments; see their jointly written letter of May 5, 1953, for an example of Lota's writing style. The only occasion on which I met Lota was at the small dinner party Robert and Elizabeth Lowell gave for the recently married T. S. and Valerie Eliot in New York. The occasion was congenial and Eliot's marital happiness and good humor were noticeable, but I failed in efforts to get Lota to talk. She had intelligent eyes and mannish looks and smiled pleasantly and seemed at ease, but owing either to shyness or faulty English, she hardly opened her mouth.

Elizabeth's friend Pearl Kazin, who in this period was living in Brazil, called Lota "shrewd and generous and wise, full of strong and irrepressible opinions about everything," fully convinced that what Elizabeth needed "for her health and her sanity and her writing was . . . the affectionate protection of a home, a sense of belonging, the orderly consolations of habit and dailiness, the will to stay put. They became lovers, even if Lota more often acted the mother to Elizabeth the child."

Before Elizabeth's arrival, Lota had adopted a son named Kylso. He was a poor and bright young man she had discovered in the garage where her car was being repaired. A neglected victim of polio, Kylso could scarcely walk. She sent him to the hospital for treatment, purchased a motorscooter for him, and got him a job in an architect's office; by the time Elizabeth met him, Kylso was married and had a family. Mary Stearns Morse, whom they called "Morsey," moved to her own house nearby, after Elizabeth's arrival, and also adopted several children. Later Elizabeth wanted to adopt a twelve-year-old boy, a painter, but his parents would not consent. Elizabeth paid so much attention to the cook's baby girl that one of the workers on the estate complained that something was wrong with the child because it "laughed too much." (Lota agreed with Elizabeth's theories of child-raising; they talked about translating Dr. Spock's books into Portuguese, until they realized that the parents most in need of advice would never read his books. They referred to themselves as "maternal old maids" and Elizabeth wrote her Aunt Grace: "Now I know why poor children cry more than rich ones: their parents are so dumb.")

After she moved in with Lota, they were known to their Brazilian neighbors and servants as Dona Elizabetchy and Dona Lota. The house they occupied at the top of Samambaia, designed by Sergio W. Bernardes, was a prize-winning (with Gropius one of the judges) architectural marvel. Elizabeth in 1952 drew a pen-and-ink sketch of the unfinished split-level, horizontal building, with ramps, sliding glass walls, and what was to be an aluminum roof. Her one-room *estudio* was high up and apart from the house, situated to the left above a boulder, with a stream falling down beside it, one section of which they dammed up as a swimming pool. The grounds were spacious, very steep, dotted with granite, and had a fine view of the mountain peaks across the valley. In Elizabeth's new studio a solid wall blocked out this view, to prevent any distraction from her creative work. The main house had two maid's rooms with baths, and there was a separate house for the cook and gardener and their families, a tool shed, and sheds for Mimosa the horse and Mimoso the donkey.

The security of a real home, combined perhaps with the liberating "foreignness" of Brazil, seemed to free Elizabeth to write about her earliest years. Her long story from this period, "In the Village," about her mother's insanity and her childhood in Great Village, is one of her finest prose creations. When *The New Yorker* published it in 1953, paying her the then large sum of $1,200, she bought a black MG with red leather seats, though she had no driver's license (she later sold the car for a large profit). "Gwendolyn" was another Nova Scotia childhood story written during her first years at Samambaia. Poems with Brazilian themes soon followed, including "Arrival at Santos," "The Mountain," and "The Shampoo," her love poem addressed to Lota, with the lines "you've been, dear friend, / precipitate and pragmatical; / and look what happens."

In 1954, nine years after *North & South*, Elizabeth had her second book ready, *A Cold Spring*, whose final poem was "The Shampoo." When Houghton Mifflin, concerned that the book's twenty poems were too few, suggested that she combine *North & South*, long out of print, with the new poems, she wisely agreed. *Poems*, as the combined volume was called, came out in July 1955 and won the Pulitzer Prize for poetry the following spring. This brought overnight fame to Dona Elizabetchy throughout Brazil, where poets are honored figures. This book found her an English publisher, Chatto & Windus; she was also awarded a *Partisan Review* Fellowship of several thousand dollars.

Two demanding prose works now occupied her time. The first was a translation, *The Diary of "Helena Morley,"* the journal of a twelve-year-old girl in a mining town in the 1890s. It was a Brazilian classic, but Elizabeth's expectations for it in English, inspired by her enthusiasm and perhaps her self-identification with the young heroine, were unrealistic. On its publication in 1957 it sold well and received good reviews, but it was not a best-seller. She was soon disenchanted with the complaints of the elderly "Helena Morley" (now the wife of a banker) about the small royalties. Another prose work was later commissioned by *Life* magazine, which offered her ten thousand dollars, more than she had ever earned in a single year, for a book about Brazil, half text and half photos. She would doubtless have done much better on her own, but her co-authors by contract were "the Editors of *Life*," a powerful and impersonal corporation. When the book came out in 1962 she wrote Pearl Kazin: "I am horribly and idiotically distressed by the book—absolutely everything seems wrong." The photos chosen by *Life* had "not a single bird, beast or flower—in Brazil!" As for the text, she claimed it had "not a *trace* of what I tried to say." However, the income enabled her to treat Lota and herself to a trip to Italy, and also helped her to buy the run-down eighteenth-century house in Ouro Prêto, later named the Casa Mariana, that she wanted to restore.

In 1960 Carlos Lacerda, Lota's friend, ran for governor of the state of Guanabara, whose capital is Rio—and won. Lota had fought hard for his election, rounding up voters and driving them to the polls. Now she and Elizabeth were not only invited to dinners at the Governor's Palace but Lota persuaded Lacerda to convert an undeveloped stretch of landfill along the Rio coast on Guanabara Bay into a "People's Park." She offered to work out the park's design and supervise the enterprise, without salary. Lacerda not only agreed to her proposal but gave her control of the project and an important title, Chief Coordinatress of Flamingo Park (Parque do Flamengo)—the colorful name he decided to give the new area. In publicity releases Lota was given an engineer's title of "Doctor," though she had never been to university. It was the opportunity of a lifetime for her; she could now put into practice the progressive city-planning concepts of architects like Le Corbusier, whose work she had admired for years.

Elizabeth estimated that the area in question was "as big as Central Park." In a country where men never took orders from women, Lota proposed to transform the reclaimed area into a landscaped network of cafés and restaurants, playgrounds with carousels, a children's railroad, museums, libraries and reading rooms for kids, a dance pavilion, gardens, a boat pond, and, of course, beaches. She would use the newest lighting methods to illuminate the park at night. Elizabeth was impressed by Lota's courage and praised her for "using her brains and helping poor dirty dying Rio at the same time." They moved to the apartment in Rio, nearer to Lota's work, with only an occasional weekend at Samambaia. "Lota has been admirable," Elizabeth wrote Pearl Kazin, "clear, succinct, quiet—directives like Napoleon's!" Lota expected and experienced resistance from entrenched male bureaucrats, and the work progressed slowly but unrelentingly under the firm direction of the Coordinatress. As Elizabeth wrote Dr. Baumann, Lota "comes home from work every evening looking so pale and exhausted that I get very worried about her." By February 1961 she was writing Pearl Kazin: "The job is enormous— I went 'on location' with her and about a dozen engineers last week— and so far I think she's doing marvelously—just the right tone—but I don't trust these gentlemen . . . they are all so jealous of each other, and of a woman, naturally."

Three years later, writing to Loren MacIver, Elizabeth confessed to ambivalent feelings: "Lota is getting so famous and powerful it is frightening. If our friend [Lacerda] gets elected President (he's running, but a lot can happen here in the next few months), I'm afraid she'll be an ambassador or something—an awful prospect. But she's thriving on it and is too energetic, almost, for my taste—a combination of Lewis Mumford and Fiorello La Guardia." Yet early in 1965 Elizabeth reported real success on the day the trains for children began operating: "[The park] is looking really lovely—the first Sunday of the 'trains for children' there were over 3,500 passengers, and that first week 17,000. There is so little for the poor and the 'middle class' to do in Rio." On another occasion Elizabeth wrote: "Perfect strangers passing us on the road lean out of their cars and shout, 'Bravo for the new park, Dona Lota!' Really, it is very nice."

Later in 1965—Lacerda's term as governor ended in December—things began to go sour. Oddly enough, it was Lacerda himself who was causing Lota's problems. Elizabeth wrote Dr. Baumann: "Lota is more or less 'on strike'—I don't know how it will turn out. She is fighting with Carlos. For some reason or other he will not sign the papers necessary . . . for the libraries for children, in the playgrounds . . . The park is by far his most popular project and the one that will last longest, too—and yet he seems to enjoy making things complicated . . . It is *hopeless*." She predicted that if "Carlos gets elected [President], I think I'll leave rather than live any longer in the hysterical atmosphere he creates around him." She wrote Lowell: "It has been a hideous stretch. I am utterly sick of Brazilian politics, big and little. [Lota] is a fighter, after all, and in some ways enjoys all the bloodshed, I think. A while ago I was afraid it would really kill us both before the thing got finished." A few of Lota's colleagues now began to attack *her*, including the landscape expert, Roberto Burle-Marx, one of her closest friends; Elizabeth called his attacks "indecent." Perhaps to escape the pressures of Lota's problems and her constant scolding of Elizabeth, the latter found herself going more often to Ouro Prêto, to work on restoring the old house.

When the new governor set up a "Foundation" to supervise the completion of Flamingo Park, naming Lota as its head, they saw through this political ploy. The project had such a low financial priority in the new administration that Lota knew the park and her role in it were doomed. Meantime the University of Washington, in Seattle, had renewed an offer to Elizabeth to serve two terms as writer-in-residence (she followed Theodore Roethke). The offer was so attractive financially that she decided to embark on her first teaching experience. "I wish Lota would go along with me for part of the time," Elizabeth wrote Dr. Baumann, but Lota would not leave Brazil. Yet it was a relief to get away from the hectic political turmoil as well as from Lota's complaints to Elizabeth about "drinking and laziness." (When visiting American friends stayed up late with Elizabeth, Lota embarrassed and annoyed her by pounding on the wall, ordering them to go home.) Elizabeth was also worried about Lota's health, informing Dr. Baumann that she was having "dizzy spells and even falls down." During the first term at Seattle, Elizabeth assured her doctor: "*Of course* I am going back [to Brazil], and of course I mean to live there, and with Lota, forever and ever." She did go back, and when a small legacy from an aunt enabled her to travel, she took Lota abroad that summer to Holland and England. Unfortunately they had to cut the trip short, because Lota "was not up to it."

The medical truth emerged in January 1967—Lota had arteriosclerosis. After resigning in despair from the Flamingo Park foundation, she suffered a nervous breakdown and went into hospital. In a shaking hand, she added a short and sad postscript to Elizabeth's letter of March 18, 1967, to Gold and Fizdale, and seemed to blame Elizabeth for all their troubles: "E.B. is undertaking a cure for all the nonsences [*sic*] and alcoholism she had this horrible year of '66." Lota's doctor, a psychiatrist, advised Elizabeth to get away temporarily ("He thought he could treat Lota better without me"), so she left for New York and stayed at Loren MacIver's home at 61 Perry Street, while the painter and her husband (the poet Lloyd Frankenberg) were in Paris.

Elizabeth and Lota had both agreed to make new wills. Elizabeth left everything to Lota; outside the will, she arranged through Dr. Baumann for $15,000 to be paid in case of her death to "X.Y." (as I will refer to her), a young divorced woman she had met in the West who served as her "secretary." Lota's will left Elizabeth the apartment in Rio, as well as several offices she owned. The house at Samambaia went to Mary Stearns Morse, to whom Lota owed a long-standing debt. Much later Elizabeth learned that Lota had clearly indicated she was planning suicide—by inserting into her will a quotation from Voltaire: *"Si le bon Dieu existe, il me pardonnera, c'est son métier."* ("If God exists, he will forgive me, that's his business.")

More than once that summer Lota cabled Elizabeth that she wanted to come to New York, and Elizabeth sought the doctor's approval by cable or phone; he never replied. Finally in September Lota cabled that she was flying to New York and asked Elizabeth to meet her plane. When Lota disembarked at Kennedy Airport on Saturday, September 16—the plane was three hours late—Elizabeth said she looked "very sick and depressed." They arrived at Perry Street "extremely tired and went to bed early." Around 6 a.m. on Sunday Elizabeth phoned Dr. Baumann that Lota was in a coma, having swallowed a bottle of pills. The doctor immediately called nearby St. Vincent's Hospital for an emergency rescue crew and then called architect Harold Leeds, Elizabeth's friend who lived across the street, for help. He and filmmaker Wheaton Galentine rushed there at once and helped the paramedics and policemen to carry the comatose figure of Lota down the narrow curving staircase on a kitchen chair, since the rigid stretcher could not round the curves. Leeds urged Elizabeth to get into the ambulance with Lota and later walked over to the hospital to join her. When Dr. Baumann arrived, they learned that the pills Lota had taken were Valium. Lota remained in a coma for a week, and Elizabeth delayed informing the family in the hope that Lota would recover and the attempt at suicide would never be known. On Monday, September 25, Lota's heart stopped beating. Elizabeth cabled the news to Brazil.

Lota's body was shipped to Rio, where it was met by a military guard of honor. Several officials, including Carlos Lacerda and the former head of the Supreme Court, as well as a crowd of two hundred, were on hand for the plane's arrival. Elizabeth, who remained in New York, asked that Lota be buried in the Macedo Soares tomb with her father, "because she loved him in spite of everything, I know."

I I I

Elizabeth's return to Brazil in late November—to settle her share of Lota's estate and reclaim her books, manuscripts, and other personal posses-sions—was, she wrote Dr. Baumann, "one of the most disturbing expe-riences of my life, and it will take a long long time to get over it." Not only was she treated badly, and even shunned, by many of Lota's relatives and friends, who blamed her for Lota's suicide, but some of her posses-sions had disappeared. Hurt and depressed, she moved to her house at Ouro Prêto. "I just couldn't seem to start living alone right away," she wrote Frani, "and couldn't bear New York just now, and certainly not Brazil." She decided to start a new life in California with her young friend "X.Y.," the divorcée from the West who now had a baby boy; they would "try keeping house together for a while."

At her publisher's suggestion, Elizabeth's next book was a collected edition of her poems, published in April 1969, with typography by Cynthia Krupat, Frani's daughter. A year later, when the news broke that *The Complete Poems* had won the National Book Award for poetry, Elizabeth was living in the Casa Mariana at Ouro Prêto with "X.Y." and the child. In the spring of 1970 life there began to become unpleasant. Local hood-lums threw stones at the Americans and tossed garbage into the gardens of the Casa Mariana. Elizabeth realized she would soon have to put the house up for sale. She then reported a new medical crisis to Dr. Baumann: "X.Y." had fallen ill. After being treated at the Belo Horizonte hospital, her friend was flown home to the United States and her son was returned to his mother's family. As Elizabeth admitted, "I should have realized much, much sooner that [X.Y.] was really extremely sick."

That summer Harvard asked Elizabeth to take over Robert Lowell's courses for the 1970 fall term, during his absence in England, and she accepted. She moved into Kirkland House on the campus, where she met the young house secretary, Alice Methfessel, "a very friendly woman," who became her close friend and companion. After another visit alone to Ouro Prêto that summer, to arrange for the sale of the house, Elizabeth came down with severe amoebic dysentery and had to return to Cam-bridge for medical treatment. Fully recovered by August 1971, she was ready to take a trip to the Galápagos Islands with Alice before classes resumed. (It was a trip she had long wanted to make: the Galápagos were the site of important discoveries by Charles Darwin, her "favorite hero.") That fall at Harvard she conducted her new seminar in "Personal Correspondence, Famous and Infamous." Marianne Moore died in February 1972. Joining Elizabeth at the memorial service in Brooklyn were Dr. Baumann, Louise Crane, Margaret Miller, Harold Leeds, and many others including myself; we all intoned the sonorous hymns whose familiar words Elizabeth relished. The opportunity arose for her to acquire an apartment at 437 Lewis Wharf in 1974; it had a fine view of Boston harbor, whose maritime activities she loved to watch.

The last book issued in her lifetime was *Geography III*, dedicated to Alice. The format designed by Cynthia Krupat was one that Elizabeth preferred over all her books. Its publication in 1976 was not only a literary event; it brought her work to a wider circle of readers than she had previously known and won the National Book Critics Circle Award. Poet Anthony Hecht wrote in *The Times Literary Supplement* that "In *Geography III* all the virtues of ear and eye, of speech and reticence, and of lonely courage are superbly, beautifully in evidence . . . [It] contains only ten poems, none unusually long. But ten new poems by Elizabeth Bishop are enough to make a good-sized readership in the United States rejoice in gratitude and pride. Hers is about the finest product our country can offer the world . . . It beats our cars and films and soft drinks hollow."

Robert Lowell's sudden death in September 1977 came as a shock to Elizabeth, inspiring her memorial poem, "North Haven." After the funeral for Lowell in Boston, she invited many guests—poets, writers, publishers—to her apartment at Lewis Wharf. When they crowded onto her balcony for a view of the harbor, she was heard to murmur, "If the balcony breaks, a big part of literary New York will disappear." After completing a teaching assignment at New York University in 1978, she wrote a friend, "My one desire is to retire," but her financial situation would not allow this.

She accepted a teaching job at M.I.T., scheduled to start late in September 1979. Because she was ill and in hospital (see her letter to her students, page 637), she was unable to meet her first class, but she recovered sufficiently to be discharged from the hospital before the next class. There never was a class. At home that weekend, after writing what was to be her last letter, she suffered a cerebral aneurysm. Alice found her body on the floor of the Lewis Wharf apartment early in the evening of Saturday, October 6, 1979.

•

In addition to her genius, Elizabeth had two gifts—wit and good manners—that typified her life. James Merrill has recorded one occasion (when he visited the Casa Mariana) on which both qualities were displayed with brilliance. Elizabeth was particularly glad to see Merrill because she had not been able to speak English with anyone for weeks. "Late one evening," he wrote, "over Old Fashioneds by the stove, a too recent sorrow had come to the surface; Elizabeth, uninsistent and articulate, was in tears." At that moment a young Brazilian painter entered the room and, seeing her weeping, stopped dead in his tracks. "His hostess almost blithely made him at home," Merrill wrote. "Switching to Portuguese, 'Don't be upset, José Alberto,' I understood her to say, 'I'm only crying in English.'"

Chronology

1911 Born February 8 in Worcester, Massachusetts, to William Thomas Bishop and Gertrude Bulmer. Father died from Bright's disease eight months later.

1914 Lived in Boston with widowed mother. Swan-boat ride with mother in the Boston Public Garden, at age three, vividly remembered.

1916 Lived in Great Village, Nova Scotia, with the Bulmers, her mother's family. Attended primary school. For the last time saw her mother when she entered a mental hospital.

1917 The Bishops, her paternal grandparents, brought her back to Worcester. During her nine months' stay, EB suffered from asthma, eczema, and other illnesses.

1918 Three days before her seventh birthday EB accompanied her Aunt Florence Bishop to the dentist, which later inspired "In the Waiting Room." EB moved into Aunt Maud Sheperdson's Boston home and attended local public school.

1923 At age twelve EB won a prize for her essay on "Americanism" in a contest sponsored by the American Legion.

1924 Enrolled at Camp Chequesset on Cape Cod (Wellfleet) every summer until 1929. EB excelled at swimming, sailing, and sea chanteys.

1925–30 In 1925–26 enrolled at Saugus (Massachusetts) High School. Transferred to the North Shore Country Day School at Swampscott and published poems and stories in *The Owl*. In 1927 entered Walnut Hill boarding school at Natick, graduating in 1930; published poems and other writings in school magazine, *The Blue Pencil*; classmate Frani Blough became lifelong friend.

1930–34 Four years at Vassar College in Poughkeepsie, New York. Mary McCarthy, Frani Blough, Margaret Miller, Louise Crane, Eunice and Eleanor Clark, and Muriel Rukeyser among her Vassar contemporaries. Walking tour in Newfoundland in summer 1932. Launched *Con Spirito* magazine with other students in 1932. Editor of senior yearbook, *Vassarion*. Received honorable mention for poems in *Hound & Horn*. Met Marianne Moore on March 16, 1934; mother died on May 29.

1935–36 First book publication in the anthology *Trial Balances*, introduced by Marianne Moore. First trip abroad in summer 1935, spending winter in Paris with Louise Crane. In March 1936 traveled to London, Morocco, Spain. Lived in New York in summer and fall.

1937 Winter fishing in Florida with Louise Crane; discovery of Key West. Spent six months in Paris; car accident in France on July 19. Returned to U.S. by way of Italy in December.

1938–41 In January settled in Key West for nine years, buying house at 624 White Street with Louise Crane. Through Loren MacIver met Dr. John Dewey and family. *Partisan Review* published her story "In Prison" in March 1938. *The New Yorker* accepted her poem "Cirque d'Hiver" in November 1939 (published January 1940).

1942–43 During World War II at Key West, EB worked briefly for the U.S. Navy in their optical department. Traveled in Mexico, where she met poet Pablo Neruda and painter David Siqueiros.

1945–46 Received the Houghton Mifflin Literary Fellowship Award for her first book of poetry, *North & South*, published on August 20, 1946.

1947 Randall Jarrell introduced her to Robert Lowell, their friendship continuing until his death. Received Guggenheim Fellowship.

1949 Summer at Yaddo, Saratoga Springs, N.Y. Consultant in Poetry at Library of Congress, Washington, D.C., September 1949 to September 1950. Visits with Ezra Pound at St. Elizabeths Hospital.

1950 American Academy of Arts and Letters award; at Yaddo in autumn and early winter.

1951 Awarded the first Lucy Martin Donnelly Fellowship by Bryn Mawr College. In November voyaged to South America; became ill in Rio de Janeiro; stayed on in Brazil for fifteen years, living with Lota de Macedo Soares.

1952 Shelley Memorial Award.

1953 Two autobiographical stories, "In the Village" and "Gwendolyn," in *The New Yorker*.

1954 Inducted into the National Institute of Arts and Letters.

1955 Second book, *Poems* (including *North & South* and *A Cold Spring*), published by Houghton Mifflin on July 14.

1956 Pulitzer Prize for poetry; *Partisan Review* Fellowship; editing and translating of Henrique Mindlin's *Modern Architecture in Brazil*.

1957 Amy Lowell Traveling Fellowship. *The Diary of "Helena Morley,"* translated by EB from Portuguese, published by Farrar, Straus and Giroux on December 16.

1961 Trip down the Amazon and, with Aldous Huxley, to Matto Grosso to see Indian tribes.

1962–63 *Life* World Library published *Brazil*, co-edited by EB and "considerably altered" by the editors of *Life*. Two months in New York, 1963.

1964 Academy of American Poets Fellowship; traveled during summer to Italy and England.

1965 *Questions of Travel*, her third book of poems, published on November 29 by Farrar, Straus and Giroux. Paperback edition of *Poems* (Houghton Mifflin). EB acquired and restored colonial house at Ouro Prêto, the Casa Mariana.

1966 First teaching experience, January to June, at the University of Washington in Seattle.

1967 Stern-wheeler trip down the Rio São Francisco. Visit to New York; Lota's illness and suicide.

1968–69 Lived for a year in San Francisco; received the Merrill-Ingram Award; stay at Ouro Prêto. *The Complete Poems* (Farrar, Straus and Giroux) received the National Book Award; Brazilian government awarded EB the Order of Rio Branco.

1970 Living in Ouro Prêto. To Cambridge, Massachusetts, in September to teach at Harvard University.

1971 Fall term at Harvard; several months in Ouro Prêto.

1972 Fall term at Harvard; trip to Ecuador, the Galápagos Islands, and Peru. With Emanuel Brasil co-edited *Anthology of Twentieth-Century Brazilian Poetry* (Wesleyan University Press).

1973 Fall term at Harvard; spring term at University of Washington at Seattle. Trips to Sweden, Finland, Leningrad, and Norway; from Bergen by mail boat to North Cape and back.

1974 Both terms at Harvard. Harriet Monroe Poetry Award. Summer at North Haven, Maine (Sabine Farm). Moved to Boston waterfront (Lewis Wharf).

1975 Both terms at Harvard. St. Botolph Club (Boston) Arts Award. July in North Haven, Maine.

1976 Awarded Neustadt International Prize for Literature by an international jury; ceremony at University of Oklahoma on April 9. In June attended Poetry International Congress in Rotterdam; travel in Portugal in July; summer at North Haven, Maine. *Geography III* (Farrar, Straus and Giroux) published on December 28.

1977 *Geography III* awarded National Book Critics Circle Award. Death of Robert Lowell in September. Fall teaching term at New York University.

1978 Consultant at Bryn Mawr for Marianne Moore Collection. Honorary degree from Princeton. Summer at North Haven, with visit by Kit and Ilse Barker.

1979 Visiting professor of poetry at M.I.T. for fall term, but illness prevented classes. Died on October 6 at Lewis Wharf.

1980 *Elizabeth Bishop: A Bibliography 1927–1979*, edited by Candace W. MacMahon with EB's help, published by the University Press of Virginia.

1983 *The Complete Poems: 1927–1979*, edited by Robert Giroux (Farrar, Straus and Giroux), published on March 20. *Elizabeth Bishop and Her Art*, edited by Lloyd Schwartz and Sybil P. Estess (University of Michigan Press) published.

1984 *The Collected Prose*, edited by Robert Giroux (Farrar, Straus and Giroux), published on January 20.

[O N E]

1928 - 1936

SCHOOL, VASSAR, NEW YORK, EUROPE

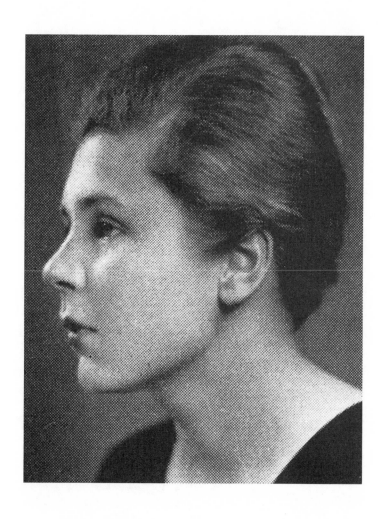

Elizabeth Bishop in Vassarion 1934, *her senior yearbook.*
Courtesy Vassar College Library

To Frani Blough

Frani Blough (later Mrs. Curt Muser) first met EB in 1927 at the Walnut Hill boarding school in Massachusetts, where she was one year ahead of EB. Frani went on to Vassar in 1929 and EB followed a year later. They remained lifelong friends. EB mailed this letter from Nova Scotia, enclosing a Christmas note from one of her teachers (see footnote), as well as her early poem "Imber Nocturnus [Night Rain]," published in the school magazine The Blue Pencil, *December 1928, and in* The Complete Poems: 1927–1979 *(1983).*

Great Village, Nova Scotia
December 31, 1928

Thank you for the helpful little card. Of course I realize that you could never quite realize the full significance of all this [the "love letter" from their teacher*] but isn't it too sweet for words, anyway? Auntie [Grace] read it and said our friend had an "aching void." Alas, all she needed was a little snow. And *what* do you suppose she didn't dare say? Oh, Miss Talbot told me a mystery that will appeal to your romantic soul. I'll tell you when I get back, if I ever do—

and *my* love†
BISHOP

Having become an expert swimmer and sailor during summers at Camp Chequesset on Cape Cod, EB successfully copes with a tipped-over sailboat.

[Harwich Port, Massachusetts
August 30, 1929]

I arrived at the [summer] home of my fathers scarce three hours ago with a suitcase, a coat, a hat, a bathing suit, a paper hatbox and three books—oh yes, and a can of powder. Such a nice drive—and after our Chesterfields my aunt's Camels are very tame animals indeed. I think I'm being here until Tuesday . . . Lord! There were letters here from you and Judy—thank you. Besides being my warmest welcome, they rather impressed the two females [EB's paternal Aunts Florence and Ruby].

I have news of greatest importance: I've tipped over in a sailboat!

* *Teacher's note:* "Elizabeth my dear, Come up the path through the fir trees and white birches to my little cottage by the sea and there by the fireside, where nothing is 'developed' save friendliness and poems and contentment, I would tell you that this was meant to be a wee book to slip into your pocket and to say 'Merrie Christmas' for me . . . ¶There are fairy colors in the driftwood blaze in my fire. I picked up the stick down in the rock cave at low tide; and now it is dry it flames a tale in emerald and turquoise and copper-red. *I think you would understand it* [underlined by EB in wavy lines]. Outside there is a Christmas moon of clear silver beauty. Shall I tell you things that can only be told here—ah well, someday when you come! ¶Meanwhile Christmas joys, and the star-shine of a poem, and my love."

† EB drew a line from her teacher's three final words to her own closing.

1 9 2 9   [*3*

Tuesday afternoon there was a violent wind—a good one—and Louise [Crane?] and I wanted to have a good long sail so we started out as soon as the boats were afloat—bearing heavy sweaters and cigarettes and wearing bathing suits. The tide and the wind were both against us—we should have had a reef and the boat bounced like a bottle. We got out past shirttail all right and kept being pushed into shore. I was heading for that little white house down in the cove. All of a sudden a saltwater apple tree appeared right behind the stern and caught the main sheet. The boat swung right around—away from the wind. I couldn't reach the rope and I was scared stiff for fear we would jibe or Louise would drown or something. I yelled *"Pull down the sail!"* But she couldn't get there quickly enough. It went so slowly—the water was a long, bright line all around the combing—then it poured over and the sail settled on the water. I thought Louise might get caught underneath—she was sort of on the centerboard box and I told her to jump out from the boat. She gave a big jump and landed right in the middle of the sail in the most graceful sitting posture. She might have been a Turk taking a siesta, if you can combine such things. I climbed up on the side and pulled her up—then dove in and captured the floorboards and oars that were floating away. Then I swam into the dock with the boat—very simple, because the wind and waves were so strong they fairly pushed us along. Louise lay on the top and waved our sweaters—it was so silly. I laughed so hard that I kept sinking and I quite surprised Barb and Betty, who came frantically splashing in a rowboat to rescue us. They thought my sailing reputation was ruined, I guess. It took us about two hours to fix the boat up—and I didn't have a chance to go out again. The poor *Kut Up* is still tied to the dock —her sail all muddy . . .

Perhaps I shall omit reunion. Reunions are exactly like eating spaghetti and finding the ends left outside, anyway. I cannot seem to rake up the yeast and breathe the spirit of life into it—even yesterday's . . . I'm inhabiting a *comfy* place called the *pink room* [at her aunt's]. I feel about as much at home as an elephant in negligée. Ah me! I'm going to begin to pine—feature me as pale green lolling between my pink sheets. I do wish my dear Aunt Ruby made the various shades harmonize at least.

I am enjoying very much your essay on "Comus." Perhaps if I study it hard, and you send me a few pointers on my handwriting, I'll get into Vassar. Tell me when your address changes so I can get going with the night letters. Don't you think "double-barreled idiot" is a nice term? I miss you greatly.

[Boston, Massachusetts
September 5, 1929]
Wednesday afternoon
. . . Harwich Port is not my future summer home, I'm afraid. I got the asthma so badly from poor Major [a dog] that I had to leave Saturday

morning. Of course my uncle [Jack] and aunt [Ruby] couldn't bear to give me up—and Kay, it broke her heart! She kissed me as I crudely counted the change left from buying my ticket. But it all began poorly, anyway. You see, Aunt Ruby had to sit on my suitcase, and I suppose that wasn't a very tactful thing to have her do, and then just as we emerged from the Lookout she bumped the shutter and it fell down on her head. It made an awful thud . . .

Since then I have been doing absolutely nothing but read, and compose wholly imaginary Life-Saving essays. I've gone through everything now except Shakespeare and the Bible and I'm halfway through *Cymbeline*. I had no idea it was so good—I never thought of Shakespeare except in terms of *Macbeth* and *Hamlet*, but don't you like this?

Fear no more the heat o' the sun,
  Nor the furious winter's rages;
Thou thy worldly task hast done,
  Home art gone and ta'en thy wages.
Golden lads and girls all must,
As chimney-sweepers, come to dust.

Do you remember that erstwhile book report about Lafcadio Hearn? Well, I bought a little book of his called *Some Chinese Ghosts* and I'm getting quite interested in him. He was *walleyed*, whatever that may be, and he married first a Negress and then a Japanesess. (At that point Louise called me up and informed me that walleyed is the opposite of cockeyed, so picture the gentleman for yourself.) . . .

The other day I got for myself out of the attic a patchwork quilt, one that my great-grandmother made. It's the *Sunflower Pattern*—big orange wheels on a white ground, and so many thousands of little white stitches that it pains one to look at it. I'd love to hang it on the wall of my room at school—a spur to conscientiousness, you know—but then I'm afraid it might make it rather like a padded cell. Well, I shall huddle under it in January and bless my great-grandmother. It should look well placed artistically near a bowl of calendulas.

I gathered up the bathing suits you left and left one to charity and packed the other in my duffel bag. I'll send it to you if the duffel bag ever gets to me. Somehow I see Jolly seated upon it in an Oriental attitude—reaching Nirvana. I keep remembering things I left behind—towels, my music, and just this minute I recollect my white shoes.

Lives of great men all remind us
We can mold life as we choose
And departing, leave behind us
Towels, safety pins and shoes.

. . . You know, that's what you and I noticed in Kay this summer—
"jealously" the "graceful development of beautiful girlish bodies," and
"*womanly* pride in crafts"—a few of their "products of happy industry
are shown at the right" certainly reminds me of rest hour.

Methinks that Frani needs refreshing, so let us repair to the farewell
or closure. Taps—after the fleeting shades of purple, blue marigold, and
burnt henna have given way to deep, deep night blue. The sunsets are
glorious. Oh, and here is a sample of female correspondence from *Diana
of the Crossways.** (Just as I went to get the book, Judy called up—we're
going to be in the poorhouse with these long-distance calls. And it's
Saturday, not Friday, and she was about to go to the movies with Peggy):
"I am shattered, and I wait panting for a reply. I have no more time
(space), it is my life I cry for. This is your breast," my Frani! Come!!

> [Hotel Lincolnshire
> Boston, Massachusetts]
> August 9, 1932

. . . Ev [Evelyn Huntington Halpin] and I are sailing Saturday . . .
[for Newfoundland on a walking trip]. The boat takes from then until
Thursday to get there and we're going second-class, so heaven knows
what *shape* we'll be in when we arrive. I've collected a small knapsack,
a small flashlight, a small flask . . . Barbara [Chesney Kennedy] wanted
to buy me a money belt, a khaki thing about a foot wide with innumerable
flaps and two or three buckles, supposed to be worn *next to the skin*. She
bade me farewell today on Beacon Street as if forever and ever—and
someone told me the insects up there would eat me alive. And even a
trip to Hell could be talked about afterwards. "Oh, why yes, I've been
there," and everyone turns to look. But we still think it may be fun.

It's these awkward in-between days—like measuring your paces over
and over on a diving board before the final spring. I envy you a certain
security your summer must possess. I never learned what became of Mary
[McCarthy, their Vassar classmate]. Did she go home or stay in New
York? But I suppose it is useless to ask questions now—and I'm sorry I
couldn't seem to do it sooner. When does college open? for example.

> [POSTCARD]
>
> St. John's, Newfoundland
> August 20, 1932

This place is far beyond my fondest dreams. The cliffs rise straight
out of the sea 400–500 feet (this picture is really very tame). I wish, and

---

* EB was writing a story about a balloon ride, "A Flight of Fancy," published in the
school's literary magazine (*The Blue Pencil*, December 1929, pp. 22–26), in which she cites
these words from George Meredith's novel: "It is my life I cry for . . . Come! This is your
breast, my Tony."

not just conventionally, that you could see them. The streets and houses all fall down toward the water—apparently supported on the masts of the sealers and schooners below. The penetrating stink of fish and the after-effects of a sea voyage and floating and up-tipping all combine to make it very strange and frightening . . .

Wellfleet, Massachusetts
July 17, 1933

. . . I suppose you know all about Mary [McCarthy]'s wedding by now. I wanted to get up to it, but I couldn't make it in time—they only run one train a day down here now. From Margaret [Miller]'s description, though, it sounds like a very emotional affair, although she said John [the bridegroom, Harold Johnsrud, an actor and would-be playwright nicknamed John] managed to keep one eyebrow raised pretty nearly to the end of the ceremony . . .

It is one of those awful foggy days here when your clothes practically mildew on you, and I am all alone . . . Peggy, however, may show up in an hour or so, please god. At least I took a bath for her sake in the dishpan with terrible difficulty, and gave the milkman the surprise of his life, and scalded my foot, so she'd better come . . . The trouble is, I can't get anything done when there are people here, but neither can I get anything done alone. After the first few days, I sink into melancholia: "As for myself, I walk abroad o' nights / And kill sick people groaning under walls; / Sometimes I go about and poison wells." [Marlowe, *The Jew of Malta*, II, iii] . . . My old friend Louise Crane is coming—with her *tutor*—this week to stay a few days.

Since you are so careful to assure me that you are working, I must tell you that I am too. The writing market looks quite hopeful. I did send a couple of things to that *Hound & Horn* contest, and they're both still going and I feel quite encouraged about them. One Mr. dudley fitts (spelt just like that) and I have been carrying on a lively, flippant kind of cor-respondence. It seems that he took the poem to a boat to show to a friend who was sailing to Spain, and somehow (I can imagine) the poem got sent along to Spain too. Mr. Fitts requests another copy, also one for Mr. [Lincoln] Kirstein [the editor-founder], who's gone to Europe, pre-sumably by mistake too. Altogether I've copied everything for them about four times, and I do wish that Mr. Kirstein and the Virgin (for it is she) [EB's poem, "Hymn to the Virgin," published in *Con Spirito*] would meet in Spain and that she would ravish him completely. I have hopes too—probably false—about this magazine called *Story*. And let's see, one chorus of [EB's translation of Aristophanes'] *The Birds* is done . . .

It really isn't bad here if there were only a little more society. The surf at the back shore has been wonderful and, well, the beer is nice. I wish to hell I did have enough money to get over there [Europe] somehow, but I'm balancing my budget in a very risky way even to get back to college, and this is cheap. Also no such fine place as that [Conservatoire Américain, Fontainebleau, where Frani was studying music] seems to be catering to my chosen *art*.

To Eleanor Clark

The rebel literary magazine at Vassar, Con Spirito, *was started by EB, Mary McCarthy, Margaret Miller, and the Clark sisters, Eunice and Eleanor, because they were dissatisfied with the stodgy official* Vassar Review, *which rejected their writings. After three issues,* Con Spirito *ceased publication. This letter to Eleanor Clark (who became a well-known author and married Robert Penn Warren) explains why.*

Wellfleet, Massachusetts
September 10, 1933

Aside from making all my guests sit down at once & read the two extant issues of *Con Spirito*, I'm afraid I've just been gloating all about its possible future. But I'm awfully glad you wrote me & started me to wondering again. I'd rather go on with it than anything else I can think of doing at college—& I haven't a doubt but what a campaign such as you describe would fix us financially—but as to the Magazine itself, I have a lot of doubts. Well, I'll tell you what I think:

With your sister & Mary & Frani gone [they graduated in June], I think we'd have a very hard time keeping the quality of the writing up to what it was. (Before I wrote that, I took another look at the [two issues] & I am as amazed as usual to see just how good that quality was.) I am quite sure now that we never ought to try to get "outside" contributions. The only people who could write or who were interested in writing were on the board & the college has practically no buried treasure. I think what we did get out was through just a happy combination of circumstances & people. We'd have a very hard time duplicating them. If we did duplicate, then it means a sort of one-ring circus trying to sell itself over & over to the college—which (with the exception of, say, three faculty) is *not* interested.

. . . What I should like would be to carry *Con Spirito* quite away from college next year & set it up in New England somewhere . . . If you think there's anything to my idea of making it an *outside* magazine why let me know & I'll write to Frani and Mary . . . Please call on me in the tower, won't you, with all the news . . .

To Frani Blough

Vassar College
Poughkeepsie, New York
October 22, 1933

I've been meaning to write you every day since your visit, because when you were here I don't think I had time enough to thank you properly for the wealth of gifts you heaped on me. And now that half the cigarettes are smoked and all the poetry, etc., is read, I'm beginning to feel quite guilty about it. I wish you could have stayed longer . . .

[The last number of] *Con Spirito* is coming out shortly . . . I'm feeling pretty encouraged. There's a lot of mediocre verse, of course, but there are really some quite interesting things and a very nice little illustration. The *Review* seems to have died completely.

Margaret [Miller] is standing up in front of a window with her hair flowing back, looking as if she expected the Dove to fly in. It's one of those dark, steam-heated Sunday mornings, and I feel completely gorged, having just put in an hour on the Sunday paper. I had a very nice letter from Mary [McCarthy]. I want to get down to New York soon and see her. Did *The New Republic* send you a decent book [to review]? When do you appear?

Let's see: we all had our [senior] pictures taken last week . . . The Alumnae have been trotting around all week, coming to classes and fussing about things. The new board have all been given passes to the movies. I've been over to dinner in Blodgett with Jean Pieper a couple of times and it is good fun: they live on 36¢ a day apiece and the food is wonderful . . .

How is Pittsburgh? I suppose you are practicing music all the time & writing book reviews, and tearing them up and writing more. I have done a couple of stories this last week that rather please me. Margaret and I are mutually inspiring each other to an exchange of arts, I think. At least I caught her writing a story the other day—a very good one too —and I lean more and more toward watercolors . . . I wish you were around. I keep expecting to see you in the English section—it wouldn't surprise me in the least . . .

To Donald E. Stanford

At the suggestion of Yvor Winters, a regional editor of Hound & Horn, *under whose supervision he had written poetry, Donald Elwin Stanford began an exchange of letters and poems with EB while he was in graduate study at Harvard. His lively account of their correspondence appeared in* Verse *(vol. 4, no. 1, November 1987). Co-editor of* The Southern Review, *he served on the faculty of Louisiana State University, where he is professor emeritus. This is EB's first letter to him.*

I had been forewarned by Mr. Winters that you were going to write
to me. Perhaps I ought to explain how it all came about: Last spring I
contributed a poem and a story to the *Hound & Horn* undergraduate
contest (so you see I am acquainted with the magazine) and managed to
rate the honorable mention. Mr. Kirstein asked me to send him some
more things, and I did recently and he, I guess, must have handed them
along to Mr. Winters. Anyway, I had a very kind letter from Mr. Winters
offering to criticize some poetry for me, and mentioning you. I remembered your name from the poems in the summer number, particularly
the one "For the Audience." But the poems you have sent me are, well,
I like them so much more . . .

I'm a senior here, taking mostly what we wrongly call "independent
study" in English and also in Greek. The nicest thing I'm doing, I guess,
is a translation of Aristophanes' *The Birds* into English verse. As the old
lady who superintends this believes that the ideal translation should be
halfway between Gilbert Murray and T. S. Eliot, and with nothing
"cheap" in it, it's rather hard. I'm also writing a long paper on Cotton
Mather—partly because it gives me a chance to find out more about old
Boston. Do you like it? Compared with your strenuous list of professors
this sounds very genteel. Who is La Piana? The only comparison I can
think of there is the fact that I have a melodeon in my room. I too am
chiefly interested in the seventeenth century, although I know little about
it except for some of the poets.

"A First Valentine" I like extremely, also the "Country Church" and
most of "On a Child in the Woods." It is very strange the way you give
the same feeling to a thought that Donne does—a weird clearness—and
yet without his directness—the same thing obliquely. And yet the first
verses of the child in the woods are direct enough. I wonder if it is perhaps
because your rhythms are so well in hand. That's what rather spoils the
sonnets for me—although I'm afraid I'm incapable of thinking that well
of graduation besides. I should like to say some more—and about "Wedding Wine"—but perhaps I had better wait until you see if you want to
bother to listen.

I have never thought of myself as writing poetry purposely until the
last two years. I have very little to show for myself, and as you can see in
the sonnets, I feel as if I had undertaken to solve the most hopeless of
problems. I am sending you the copy of them that Mr. Winters returned
to me—with his comments. I think it is in them, and they're the recentest
of these, that I have tried to say more the kind of thing you seem to be
interested in than in the others.

It was awfully nice of you to write that letter (which must have been
very difficult) and to send me those things. I hope you'll feel it's to some-

one's advantage, anyway, to go on. I should like very much to see some more of your poetry and to have you see some more of mine—those I am working on at present. Where is Neebish?

November 20, 1933

I sometimes wish here that I had nothing, or little more, to do but write letters to the people who are not here. But be that as it may, I am determined to finish a letter to you this afternoon. First I guess I shall take up, in order, your remarks about my poems, and then go on to what I think about yours. I am sending you a carbon copy of the first couple of pages of *The Birds*. I am using different kinds of meter for the different parts and letting my fancy run wild on the bird songs themselves. I wanted to send you a bit of prose, too, but the teacher still has the one I had in mind.

In the sonnets [her "Three Sonnets for the Eyes"], I realize that "sickening rupture" and "awful socket" [in "Tidal Basin"] are, as you say, crude—but at the same time I think they "go." After all, the idea behind that sonnet is not a very pretty one, and "sickening rupture" is its introduction. "Awful socket" has been prepared for by it, and the following line, which you liked, closes the unpleasant incident. They are the perceptions which give rise to the whole thing, so I don't see how they could very well be left out or smoothed over. In the last one I'm afraid I didn't intend to suggest the machine age at all—as I remember it, I had just brought two clocks back from the jeweler's—and surely clocks are ancient enough to appear with dignity. The fault is mine, though, if you thought I was talking about a canning factory.

Why do you dislike the "Virgin" ["Hymn to the Virgin"] so? It isn't sacrilege, you know—it's really supposed to be quite sad. I agree with you, but I was writing of the people who can't leave things to retire peacefully, who "know a thing or two." Raising one's eyes airplane-wise means simply upwards. You can say sidewise, why not up-wise, and so on to what's up there?

I agree with you more on the subject of rhythm than would probably seem to be the case from the poems I sent you. I can write in iambics if I want to—but just now I don't know my own mind quite well enough to say what I want to in them. If I try to write smoothly I find myself perverting the meaning for the sake of the smoothness. (And don't you do that sometimes yourself?) However, I think that an equally great "cumulative effect" might be built up by a series of irregularities. Instead of beginning with an "uninterrupted mood" what I want to do is to get the moods themselves into the rhythm. This is a very hard thing to explain, but for me there are two kinds of poetry, that (I think yours is of this sort) *at rest*, and that which is in action, within itself. At present it is too hard for me to get this feeling of action within the poem unless I just go ahead with it and let the meters find their way through. I really think, though, if you read the sonnets carefully, there are some spots where everything stays together. The line, "And filléd blue this full to the horizon" is one, perhaps . . .

The other day I ran across a very good description of what I mean about poetry in a book called *Studies in English Philology*, in the article "The Baroque Style in Prose" by M. W. Croll. He is talking of the "curt period" and he says:

> We may describe it by observing that the first member is likely to be a self-contained and complete statement of the whole idea of the period. It is so because writers in this style like to avoid prearrangements and preparations . . . The first member therefore exhausts the mere fact of the idea; logically there is nothing more to say. But it does not exhaust its imaginative truth or the energy of its conception. It is followed, therefore, by other members, each with a new tone or emphasis, each expressing a new apprehension of the truth expressed in the first. We may describe the progress . . . as a series of imaginative moments occurring in a logical pause or suspension.

Further on he calls it "a progress of imaginative apprehension, a revolving and upward motion of the mind as it rises in energy" and a "spiral movement." But the best part, which perfectly describes the sort of poetic convention I should like to make for myself (and which explains, I think, something of Hopkins), is this: "Their purpose (the writers of Baroque prose) was to portray, not a thought, but a mind thinking . . . They knew that an idea separated from the act of experiencing it is not the idea that was experienced. The ardor of its conception in the mind is a necessary part of its truth."

. . . Quite a small percent of Hopkins's poetry deals with his "Excruciating" experience. He may have learned his technique from attempting to deal with it, but at the same time many of his poems which are most successful contain nothing of passion, agony, etc., and all the things so mistakenly connected with his name. I don't believe that the third of my sonnets, for example, involved any less "passion" than, say, "Morning Midday and Evening Sacrifice"—though of course it is crude presumption for me to compare them in any way.

And one thing more—what on earth do you mean when you say my perceptions are "almost impossible for a woman's"? "Now what the hell," as you said to me, "you know that's meaningless." And if you really do mean anything by it, I imagine it would make me very angry. Is there some glandular reason which prevents a woman from having good perceptions, or what? . . .

November 29, 1933

I think I shall write you a short letter before I start off on my Thanksgiving holiday. Yes, I think "Don" is much better, "Mr. Stanford" was getting to sound almost sarcastic to me. However, you will be the first person ever to call me Elizabeth—excepting a couple of aunts. I'm always called just Bishop or Bish or Bysshe—all of them very ugly, so perhaps I'd like being thought of as Elizabeth for a change . . .

I am quite surprised that you have been hearing a lot about poems "at rest" and "in action." I thought it was my own unique way of putting it. The division is a very rough one, of course, and far from an equal one, the "at rest" sort occupying properly almost the entire history and field of poetry. Only Donne occasionally, a few stray poems in his century, and Hopkins have done the kind of thing I mean—yes, and strange to say sometimes Chatterton. I made a point of it because I wanted to tell you what I am trying to do, and I think if I have any talent at all it is along these narrow lines. What I meant about Shakespeare: it was he who gave that beautiful, slightly sad lilt to the sonnet form, the impressiveness of first lines and the importance and finality of last lines—an atmosphere easy to crawl into without really having the right to be there, and a pillow for any number of weary ideas.

What you say of variation holds true for me—oppositely. I become very intent upon what I *must* say, the series of ideas being built up in my head, and "I tend to exaggerate in my own mind" the ease with which the series piles up, and forget that the reader will not have my excitement to carry him over the awkward spots which seem simple and even necessary to me at the time.

I should very much like to know what you think about subject matter—a rather foolish-sounding expression. Recently I have been working out my own ideas on the proper things for me to write about.

December 10, 1933

. . . I have just decided to send you the two copies of Con Spirito that came out last year. It was a little magazine about six of us started in an attempt to startle the college and kill the traditional magazine—which kept turning down everything we wrote. Of course it was a total failure financially, and this year after getting out one very poor issue, we gave it up as a bad job and joined the old magazine, which was eager to have us by that time. There are some very poor things in them—but for college writing, particularly women's college writing, I think they're pretty good. Also, you see, we decided to get rid of another curse of women's colleges—the awful emphasis on personality—and have it anonymous. I think I have sent you already the poems of mine which are in it—except "The Flood," another of those poems "I think we shall forget." But the story in the first number ["Then Came the Poor"] is by me, the same one I sent to the *H&H*, only I think I improved it a bit then. Also the "Seven-Day Monologue" is mine, two or three years old. I think the little story "The Bite" is quite good. And I'm very fond of the format of Con Spirito. I'm afraid I'll have to ask you to send them back to me eventually, because they're the only ones I have and there are only a few copies in existence . . .

It is a wonderful cold night here. I live up in a tower (that isn't a figure of speech) and so have a fine view of the stars and the smokestack of the power plant. A ladder goes up out of our living room or lobby onto the roof and once up among the elaborate Victorian iron railings, it's a very nice spot to smoke a dishonest cigarette. We are gradually filling the gutters with butts.

I wish I had some more of *The Birds* typed to send you, but it is way after midnight and I guess I'd better get off to bed. I'm spending part of vacation here [at college], though, to work on it, as there is a faint chance of its being given, and I want to get it done . . .

To Frani Blough

[Vassar College]
December 12, 1933

. . . How is your job coming? Has the debutante returned yet? Mary [McCarthy]'s doing awfully well, I think. In fact all the people I knew who graduated seem to be making their way. I went down to visit Mary and John the weekend of Thanksgiving vacation and read all their latest productions. But I am so worried about their finances just now; the account they gave me sounded rather desperate. Has Mary told you about their movie? It's really pretty funny, about a set of gangsters who go into the art-gallery business. I read it, and I really think it would make a much better story—sort of on the lines of that "Rackety-Rax" one—than movie. Also I read Mary's review of *Charles I* [by Hilaire Belloc], which is extremely good. Mary held a breakfast party for Mrs. Miller, Margaret, and me and supposedly Nat, though of course she [Nat] never turned up. We had quite a time with the popovers, and at one point before the Miller family came, John and I both retreated to the living room and looked at each other helplessly over the tops of our newspapers, while Mary wept into the batter in the kitchen. But they turned out beautifully in spite of the lumps.

Con Spirito after another very poor number decided (1) to die, then (2) to join the *Review*, which seemed to show signs of coming to life and wanted us. Eleanor Clark and Margaret, the only people who had any census points, were put on the *Review* board, and things looked very hopeful. But they've been having a terrible time, it seems, and the first joint number promises to be awful. I wrote a poem celebrating the match, before the battle began:

> *Hymen, Hymen, Hymenaeus,*
> *Twice the brains and half the spaeus.*
> Con Spirito *and the* Review
> *Think one can live as cheap as two.*

Literature has reached a deadlock
Settled now by holy wedlock,
And sterility is fled . . .
Bless the happy marriage bed.

Last night Margaret and I took [Vassar librarian] Miss [Fanny] Borden to dinner. We were a little worried beforehand about the conversation, but Miss Borden was apparently very excited by the attention and she kept up a wonderful flow of wit and anecdote . . .

I'm pretty sick of college and the things I'm doing don't make good letters, and then I know you must be occupied with your own problems rather deeply. This awful cloud that hangs over senior year, thinking all the time where shall I be next year this time, for heaven's sake. Christmas vacation begins Friday, but I'm planning to stay on for most of it and try to write a few of those innumerable papers. There is just the faintest chance of their considering giving *The Birds* for third hall, so I want to get it done. I think you'd like it; it goes very fast and in spots is really very entertaining. Perhaps I'll send you our famous intruder scene when I get it done. Mr. [T. S.] Eliot's vituperous attack ["Euripides and Professor Murray"] on Mr. [Gilbert] Murray still rankles in Miss McCurdy's breast. Have you seen that book of his Harvard lectures [1933 Norton lectures, *The Use of Poetry*]? Very dry, but there are some pretty good spots. Miss McCurdy has changed her rooms to downstairs on the other side, and she also has a new cat named Mau—which means cat in Egyptian, I believe . . . In a few days I'm to read what's done of *The Birds* to the Classical Society—what glory. I think those two old ladies just wait till I translate the obscene parts . . .

I hear that you are trying to break into *The New Yorker*, and I've kept my eye open. Mary said it was about people boring you by telling you their dreams, and that makes me feel pretty awful when I consider how many of mine I've made you listen to. Sometime too I think you might write a funny article on the girl who kept *smelling* things and insisted on asking you if you didn't smell them too. Personally I find that *The New Yorker* sends things back quicker than any other publication, quicker than the twinkling of an eye, so quick it's quite painless.

I may possibly spend Christmas with Mary. Then I guess I'll go to Boston to see if I can find any prospects—in case you're going to be in those parts.

To Donald E. Stanford

Vassar College
January 21, 1934

It is interesting that the two things in *Con Spirito* you picked out to comment on are by my two—well, best friends. "The Experiment in

Objectivity" is by the same girl [Frani] who wrote the take-off on D. H. Lawrence (we were both studying the *Bacchae* at the time)—a person whom I went to boarding school with, and camp, and three years of college. She graduated last year, as did all the people who could set pen to paper in a respectable way. The Surrealist article is by my present roommate [Margaret Miller]. I think perhaps I shall send you a copy of the next *Review* when it comes out. It's a very poor affair, but this number will have another and much more interesting article on the same subject by said roommate, and also my contribution in praise of G. M. Hopkins—though I may think better of this and resolve not to lay myself open to an attack from you on the subject.

Some mysterious person sent me a copy of the second number of *The Magazine*. I like it much better than the first—I like the story by [John] Conley very much. Also some of Mr. [Richard] Blackmur's eight poems, perhaps best number V. Surely there must be a misprint in the last line of VII? I've just been reading the article on Pound he has in the last *Hound & Horn*. I think he is very good. Do you remember the one on Wallace Stevens a couple of years ago? He manages to go into things deeply without getting into that horrible life & death hysterical tone that marks a lot of the *H&H* criticism. (Now I must accept an invitation to go "off campus"—as we euphemistically call getting a ten o'clock cup of coffee.)

Mrs. [Janet Lewis] Winters's poem is nice—and I like the fact that there are no editorial remarks of any nature. But Baker still leaves me rather cold, I am sorry to say.

You see that I have nothing lively or new to tell you about or send you. This is the long and dreary stretch. I should be interested to hear what you think of Stephen Spender—and Auden—who are objects of discussion here just now . . . Just now I am very proud because I recently acquired a wonderful edition of Sir Thomas Browne . . . very elegant, once selling for $36 and now remaindered at $12. It's edited by Geoffrey Keynes and has a lot of charming portraits. I should like to do nothing but sit all evening and copy off such sentences as "That wee call a bee bird is a small dark gray bird," or "What word you give our knotts or gnatts, a small marsh bird, very fatte and a daintye dish." But Cotton Mather still awaits me with his prayers and groans . . .

To Frani Blough

[March 2, 1934]
Friday morning
. . . Getting out of college seems to be about the worst step one can take. Tell me some more about the play. I'm positive you could write a

better one than John [Harold Johnsrud], Frani. You are willing to work harder than he is and, ye gods, you have more taste.

Don [Stanford] tells me that there are whole apartments behind the State House in Boston for as little as $20 a month, which cheers me up some. Will you come and visit me next year? I shall undoubtedly have a large circle of witty and interesting friends by then and life will be on a very high plane—elegant, literary, and in perfect order. I'm even considering chartering the swan boats for a summer's evening and giving a party. On the roofs of the brick houses and on the island in the pond there will be all sorts of romantic musicians, and supper will be served on the island too—strung with lanterns. It will be very pleasant, reminiscent of Venice, and the Last Days of Rome and the Chinese Emperors, with a bit of Coney Island thrown in. Well, I'll write you when the time comes. Oh, we would have the musicians sing the Purcell songs from *The Tempest*.

Hallie Tompkins [Vassar classmate] met and talked with Dudley Fitts the other day, and it seems that he is not going to purchase my poems [for *Hound & Horn*] after all. I am "too mannered," "too clever," and also I remind him of Hopkins and—of all people—Hardy. (Having read practically none of Hardy's poems, and those I have read being either descriptions of funerals or the complaints of seduced milkmaids in Devonshire dialect, I'm pretty mad.) I know they're not wonderful poems but· even so I think that to try to develop a manner of one's own, to say the most difficult things, and to be funny if possible (which is what he means by "too clever," I imagine) is more to one's credit than to go on the way all the young *H&H* poets do with "One sweetly solemn thought" coming to them o'er and o'er. Oh Hell—I thought I might get myself a new hat with the money at least.

I found out last week to my great surprise that Miss Borden, Miss Fanny Borden, is a friend of Marianne Moore. I started a sort of paper on [Moore] and Miss Borden has the only copies of her books at college. She also offered to write me a letter if I wanted to go to see her and I think I shall some weekend soon. I'm so surprised at Miss Borden. She first met M.M. when she was a little girl and was so fascinated with her that she's kept knowing her ever since. She [MM] had brilliant red hair and called everyone she knew by the names of animals. Now she lives in Brooklyn, is quite poor, I gather, and has to devote herself entirely to taking care of her mother. She can't even go out for an hour, Miss Borden says. I want very much to go see her. She can talk faster and use longer words than anyone in New York.

This weekend we're going to the [Gertrude] Stein opera. I notice all the critics are beginning to have their doubts now—I suppose it's getting too popular to be praised—but I want to hear Virgil Thomson's music. . .

Didn't you once have to make a speech at Alumnae House? Well, I did last Saturday, a sort of advertising turn in between courses of a luncheon for the *Vassarion* [the 1934 college yearbook, edited by EB]. I was introduced as *Eleanor* Bishop and people kept shouting "Louder" and I think I got four subscriptions out of it, so I guess I'm not much of a public speaker. However, the *Vassarion* is coming pretty well. It's almost done, and Harriet just went out to dinner with a man from Liggett's drugstore and got a full-page ad. It's a very demoralizing piece of work.

[Contemporary] press class is unendurable and I know Miss Lockwood is going to prevent my graduation at the last minute. Why don't you come to Boston and write your play next year—your next play? They speak of the cocksure college graduate who thinks she knows everything. I've never seen such an uncertain, modest group of people. Well, I guess I'll stop and eat a sandwich.

I'm expecting to see Mr. Stanford pretty soon, only by that time we'll be so mad at each other we'll spring at each other's throats. He sent a picture, and he has it all over me as far as looks go, unfortunately.

To Donald E. Stanford

March 5, 1934

. . . You tell me to watch out for unpleasant phrases like "meditate your own wet"—when I have watched out for them and put them in deliberately. It has a lot to do with what I am attempting to write, so I guess I shall try to explain it to you. "Meditate your own wet" is unsuccessful, I see now, because it has such unpleasant connotations and it's liable to carry the point rather afield. But—if you can forget all your unpleasant associations with the words—I think possibly you'll admit that the phrase does for a second give you a feeling of intense consciousness in your tongue. Perhaps even that is unpleasant, but I think that momentary concentration of sensation is worthwhile . . . Have you ever noticed that you can often learn more about other people—more about how they feel, how it would feel to be them—by hearing them cough or make one of the innumerable inner noises, than by watching them for hours? Sometimes if another person hiccups, particularly if you haven't been paying much attention to him, why you get a sudden sensation as if you were inside him—you know how he feels in the little aspects he never mentions, aspects which are, really, indescribable to another person and must be realized by that kind of intuition. Do you know what I am driving at? Well, if you can follow those rather hazy sentences—that's what I quite often want to get into poetry . . .

You know I really am fairly well-read! I have studied *The Bridge* rather carefully, and I have also read [Robert] Bridges and Shakespeare. I dislike [Hart] Crane's romanticism. And I still think you are being a little unfair to Mr. Porter [Vassar teacher]. I think some of the lines you accuse of being "tripe" you have not appreciated—you've confused them with the more ordinary sort of love poem. It isn't great—but it is extremely witty and well done . . .

I just got back from N.Y.—hearing the Stein opera. It has some beautiful Negro singing and the sets are ravishing. Gertrude had very little to do with its success, however, the words being mostly unintelligible and then ignored as far as the characters, moods, etc., went. It was awfully nice. Oh dear, I wish Virgil Thomson would begin taking an interest in *The Birds* . . .

March 15, 1934

. . . My roommate got to taking pictures by lamplight the other night—mostly very arty time exposures of coils of copper and typewriters, etc. I'm sending you the only one of me that came out. The things on my shoulders are not wings or epaulettes but a pair of egg cups, one of my prized possessions. I don't ordinarily look that solemn, but it's the only expression one can keep up for two minutes with three howling people making remarks about you.

In the same mail which brought me your "last poem on the theme of lust" I received one of the circulars advertising a full and illustrated book on sex with which the college mails are always flooded. I thought the coincidence rather funny. I was on my way to the hairdresser's and when I got there I noticed that one of the canaries that decorate the place was behaving very strangely. He hopped up and down and shrieked and stretched his neck out through the bars to a horrible length. Finally I asked the hairdresser what the matter was. "Well," she said, getting a little embarrassed, "we just took his wife away from him and he's sort of peeved." Poor canary with his "private heat." I don't know about the poem—do you mean it as very much more than an exercise? As such I find it interesting—but it is, I believe, too unrestrained in tone for the height of feeling you manage to produce. Your Hamlet is a disgusting romanticist who remains disgusting because he can't show his own horror without ranting and half-boasting about his own virility. The word "green-house" has a strangely Victorian feeling about it when used in such a poem—it strikes me as being out of place. And so has "charms"—my god, how loathsome an expression that is. It represents surely one of the worst sides of masculinity—to sum up three or four more exciting features of female anatomy and label them all with one convenient word. I think Ophelia quoting at such length is a little odd.

You know Ophelia doesn't mean a word of it when she goes on about "reverence, honor, beauty, charity," etc. She has already hinted that she wants to be kissed again. The whole thing is messy, Don (and so are my remarks on it) and Hamlet leaves me convinced that he just wanted to impress his Ophelia with the strength of his passion and that he's the kind of a man who enjoys creating scenes and then brooding about them. Now maybe that's the impression you wanted to give, but I don't think so.

My vacation is from the 23rd to the 3rd. Possibly I could see you on the 1st or 2nd—would that be all right? I don't know where I'll be staying, possibly visiting a friend, but I can let you know. You'll probably come with an Elizabethan dagger in hand and slay me on the spot.

To Marianne Moore

This letter inaugurates a very important exchange of correspondence in EB's life— with Marianne Craig Moore (1887–1972). When EB discovered her poems, Miss Moore was far from being the legendary figure she became. She had published only two books, Poems *(1921) and* Observations *(1924), and from 1926 to 1929 she had edited* The Dial. *Not until 1952, when her* Collected Poems *won three major prizes—the National Book Award, the Pulitzer Prize, and the Bollingen Prize—did Miss Moore attain full national recognition.*

[Vassar College]
March 19, 1934

I think you said you had not read the life of [Gerard Manley] Hopkins by Father [Gerald F.] Lahey [S.J.] so I am taking the liberty of sending you my copy of it. If you have read it, or if on reading it you think it is another book one shouldn't bother to own, why don't hesitate to get rid of it. The portrait is very strange.

I can't thank you enough for talking so long to me—and for coming into New York for the purpose. I'm amazed at my good fortune. I hope that I didn't tire you and that you weren't late for your dinner. The party was as bad as I expected but I went calmly through rehearsing our conversation, and I have been taking notes ever since.

Are you interested in tattooing? A wonderful book on it just came out and I am trying to get a copy.

April 4, 1934

Thank you very much for sending me "Camellia Sabina" [a new poem in Miss Moore's forthcoming *Selected Poems* (1935)]. I like it extremely. I have loaned it to Miss Borden, who also likes it. I was in Boston for my Easter vacation and at O'Brien's (the florist) they had large shallow tubs filled with Camellias all along the sidewalk. I'd never seen any before. They were lovely, all the way from white to quite a deep red. I liked best the white ones with red markings—exactly as you have described them.

I am wondering if you have been to the circus yet this year? Ringling Brothers is in town and I want to go and I thought perhaps you might let me take you. However, you have probably gone already, or have plans for attending it with someone else—or you may be too busy for such things . . . If there is any chance that you might care to go, won't you let me know and I can get tickets and meet you any place you prefer. It begins at two, I think.

To Frani Blough

[Hotel Lincolnshire
Boston, Massachusetts
April 1, 1934]
Easter Sunday

Having a couple of hours before I meet my Uncle [Jack], and not feeling able to stay in bed and sleep as I intended, I shall answer your last letter. I spent Thursday evening last with Mary and John, who were in the process of writing you a letter too; John, I believe, had written the first half and Mary was planning to go on from there. Isn't it fortunate about his play [being optioned by producer Frank Merlin]? Margaret and I went down to the celebration and everyone agreed that you should have been there. All debts paid and a beautiful new dress for Mary. Idleness seems to have set in again, though.

Are you serious about working this summer—because I think it's an excellent plan. The only trouble is that any place which would satisfy you might be too expensive for me. And then it is difficult to find a locale where the days might be uninterrupted, yet the evenings sufficiently entertaining . . . I like to be able to get at a decent library . . .

I have met the poet [Donald E. Stanford], who is very sweet but extremely young [two years younger than EB]. I think he is spending all the money he has made on poetry this winter on me and I feel rather guilty about it. If he were five years or so older, he'd be very nice.

Much more important: a couple of weeks ago I met Marianne Moore. I think I told you that I found Miss Borden had known her all her life. Frani, she is simply amazing. She is poor, sick, and her work is practically unread, I guess, but she seems completely undisturbed by it and goes right on producing perhaps one poem a year and a couple of reviews that are perfect in their way. I have never seen anyone who takes such *"pains."* She is very impersonal and she's a little like Miss Borden—speaks just above a whisper, but at least five times as fast. I wish I could tell you about her—I will sometime in person—she really is worth a great deal of study (but this damned hotel pen scratches so, every sentence is getting worse and worse) . . .

Your activities impress me very much. I haven't your letter here or I'd comment more particularly, but I'm glad there's something interesting to do. I really think we might get a lot done, Frani, if we concentrated our determination and working hours in one place. I am trying to interest Bill Ricketts in some music for *The Birds*, and succeeding fairly well so far. I want to get that done, and polish up the sections of the "novel" to sell to the magazine as stories. I have to earn enough money to buy a new coat next winter somehow . . .

Just now I have an unreasonable desire to think about a new drama *in poetry*. Perhaps it isn't so unreasonable after all, as Eliot seems to be working that way. And the Stein opera made me feel cheerful about the return of the masque-like entertainment. Lord, I'd like to attempt that sort of thing. Now I remember that Eliot has just written a masque, too —a liturgical affair for one of his English churches [*The Rock*, 1934]. I suppose it would take years of theatrical training to get anywhere with it . . .

To Donald E. Stanford

Vassar College
April 5, 1934

. . . I had a beautiful time in Boston. I feel as if I should write you a regular bread & butter letter, as to a host. You were so nice to do all those things with me and for me. It has rained here ever since I got back, but everyone persists in wearing their spring clothes anyway. The chimney pots here (my exclusive view from one window) are shaped rather like a merry-go-round and all winter long the birds have come and sat in them to warm themselves. First they sit with their tails inside, then they switch around and warm their heads. It's a very amusing sight. I'll even draw you a picture of it:

I am so eager to go to the circus. I wrote and asked Marianne Moore to go with me, but it seems that her mother has been dangerously ill again, and she can't leave her this week. Now I guess I must stop and get on with my work. I wrote nothing but poetry for two days after I came back, but none of it is fit to be seen yet. I hope you are feeling equally inspired.

April 26, 1934

. . . The most interesting thing I've been doing lately is taking Marianne Moore to the circus. We went last Wednesday and had a perfectly beautiful time. She arrived carrying two large bags or satchels. One of them contained two paper bags, one for each of us, full of stale graham bread to feed the elephants with. They like it even better than peanuts and we were uncomfortably popular with them. All up and down the line of elephants they were pushing and writhing their trunks and trumpeting. I was mystified as to the other bag until halfway through the performance, when Miss Moore produced from it a large green glass bottle and some paper cups and napkins. It was orange juice. I became so impervious to the public that I even ate a large juicy pear on the train coming back. In the circus the seals were particularly good, especially the ones that can play "My Country 'Tis of Thee" on pipes. Marianne Moore really is so nice—and the most interesting talker; I've seen her only twice and I think I have enough anecdotes to meditate on for years . . .

To Frani Blough

[May 27, 1934]
Sunday morning

These are such trying times up here [at college]—as you well know. I am writing in one of those intervals when all thought has ceased, all thought that can be turned into some sort of paper, anyway. Clover said she'd been having a good time with you in N.Y. and reported minutely on all your new clothes . . .

I've decided to live in New York instead of Boston. There'll be more chances for reviewing, etc. Hallie and I have plans for driving across the country this summer and seeing America, wearing small American flags and singing national anthems all the way . . . We've neither of us even been further west than Albany, so we expect to be all exclamations and patriotism all the way to California. Please come.

The *Vassarion* came out yesterday at last. I have been in a state of rage and despair since it appeared, because of the mistakes, careless presswork, etc., but I guess no one else notices such things except Margaret, and most of the class reassures us it's "the nuts," so I guess it's all right. Now at last I can clean up that corner of my room. I've been reading a "Physiologus" trying to find some wise things to say about Marianne Moore and I discover:

"It is written, 'As a turtle-dove did I chatter, and as a dove did I mourn.' " "So is this bird like to Christ our very wise and talkative turtle-dove." "The Centaurs have the upper part as of a man, and from the breast down the form of a horse. So has every man two souls, and is unstable in his ways." It is all very edifying, and quite nice. I notice particularly that every time they direct you to take a medicine they say to take it in wine.

Oh, I suppose I might tell you about the wonderful housing scheme Margaret and I have. We think it would be highly practical to rent a whole house in N.Y.—Margaret and her mother, perhaps Mary and John, you (i.e., if you will be in New York as we hope), me, Louise Crane (who wants a studio or something), and a few nice ladies and gentlemen. If there were enough nice people, the idea is that a bad locality wouldn't be so bad, even a sort of industrial district . . .

June 4, 1934

Hallie's parents objected to the trip, and as I am very eager to work anyway, I guess I shall be in New York all summer, except for a couple of trips to Cuttyhunk . . . When I leave here, I think I'll go and stay at the Brevoort [Fifth Avenue hotel, in Greenwich Village] until I have found an apartment. I see that rooms there are very cheap, and I rather like it. So after the 11th [of June, graduation day], why if you want to, address me there.

I guess I should tell you that Mother died a week ago today. After eighteen years, of course, it is the happiest thing that could have happened.

To Donald E. Stanford

June 6, 1934

. . . I am afraid that by now you are through in Boston and are off in some other part of the country, and that this will not reach you. I'm so sorry not to have written for so long—but probably you have been just as busy so will understand the situation. I am all through now except for a little more Greek and all the packing. The heat has been so bad it has retarded us all. I am not sure what I shall be doing after college at first, but I guess I shall be in New York for most of the summer except for a couple of trips to Cuttyhunk. I want very much to work hard all summer and also I'd like sometime soon to begin a sort of study of metaphor and contemporaneity in poetry—an idea that's been bothering me for a long time . . .

I've been doing quite a lot with [Richard] Crashaw lately—particularly "Musicks Duell." Do you like that? I'm translating the Parabasis of *The Birds* and the imagery and lightness of the whole thing is so like it that I am making use of it. Have you read any of one William Saroyan's stories—in *Story* & the *Mercury*? Or perhaps you know him. He sent me a letter the other day and I think he sounds like a very interesting person. I like particularly the *motion* to his stories—they make the rest of *Story* look very feeble. Have you been on the swan boats yet? Please let me hear from you, won't you.

To Frani Blough

[Hotel Brevoort, New York]
June 30, 1934

. . . Once out of college, some kind of instant degeneration seems to set in and I've scarcely set pen to paper since. I went visiting: Louise Crane, Barbara [Chesney Kennedy], and Aunt [Florence] for a week and since then I've been at the above address, house hunting, redecorating, etc. . . .

I found an apartment, or rather Mary and John found one for me, on Charles Street . . . There's one large long room, 14′ × 22′, with a beautiful brick fireplace, and then there's a bedroom, bathroom, and kitchenette. The walls are a sort of rough plaster, which I'm having painted a lead white, and a gray blue in the bedroom. Margaret is of course full of ideas for decoration and I think it's going to be pretty nice in a modest way. Your present is going to be invaluable. I think it would look well holding a mixture of oranges, lemons and limes—or with five red and white camellias floating in it, if anyone ever sends me some. Margaret and her mother and Mary and John and I have been entertaining each other at supper all week long and have had a very nice time . . .

An awful row is taking place at the Brevoort this morning, or has been going on since 5 a.m. A man is wandering around the halls announcing in front of every door, "Open that door or I'll kick it open. You dirty swine, you bastard," etc. How I'm ever going to make my exit I can't quite see . . .

Tomorrow night I'm leaving for a few days at Harwich Port with Uncle Jack. My address until the 12th of July will be Cuttyhunk Island, Mass., Bosworth House. Perhaps being there will inspire me to a better letter than this one.

16 Charles Street
New York City
July 29, 1934

. . . I've been back since last Wednesday, camping out in an apartment devoid of furniture, gas, ice, and hooks to hang things on. Telephone and ice are supposed to arrive this afternoon, but I see no signs of them and losing one's temper to make people do things is too much to expect in this weather. Margaret and her mother feed me now and then, otherwise

I'd dry up & starve. I saw Mary & John at Margaret's the night I came back, and then they went off for a most mysterious weekend in Yonkers. Margaret and I believe that they are visiting the shady Mr. Russek in his hideaway—he's wanted by the police just now on two or three different charges. Mary wouldn't say where she was going, just feebly excused herself with "Oh, it's so *comic.*"

Ah, the telephone man just arrived and is now taking off his coat and rolling up his sleeves to get to work. The prospect of actually getting in touch with anyone by such a simple and civilized expedient will be a little too much for me, I'm afraid . . . I have to buy a piece of furniture a month and the problem is, which is more necessary to my hospitality, two chairs or a table? I hope you'll come to see me often. The telephone man is running up against all sorts of difficulties—he can't find the spot where the telephone is meant to come into the place. He's crawling in the closet with a flashlight just now. Now he's gone over to see the landlord, leaving me to guard his discarded clothing.

I'm glad you mentioned Paul Brooks [editor at Houghton Mifflin] again, because it reminded me to get to work. I've spent the entire morning typing and sending things off to their ill-fated destinations. I think this is going to be a very nice place to work in. Any time you want to write your play (which seems to have turned to a novel since I last heard of it) and can't get solitude at home, why come on down . . .

Margaret has been doing some painting . . . I want her to print for me in beautiful letters:

> But as for one which hath a long taske, 'tis good,
> With the Sunne to beginne his business . . .

to hang at the foot of my bed.

New York is rather nice in the summer if you don't try to be active. I like the park life particularly, and just riding around aimlessly on trollies and buses. I saw in the paper this morning that Mr. Merlin is giving some other play in September, and John's is just announced for *later.* I am so afraid that means disaster for the Johnsruds—they live under the worst strain all the time. Judith Anderson refused to play the lead—or did you know that? I wish to goodness they'd have a sudden stroke of some sort of luck.

Now the man is back putting on a pair of overalls. The janitor, William, accompanies him, and they are soon to be joined by the carpenter, Eric. It is all a little distracting and I guess I'll have to give up writing letters completely for the time being and stand around childishly and stare at them . . .

To Marianne Moore

August 14, 1934

I am sending to you today the copy of the little book about printers you kindly loaned my roommate [Margaret Miller] quite a while ago. She says she likes it very much and she wants me to thank you and apologize for its being kept so long. But I've been away and just came back a few days ago and she didn't know how to send it except through me.

Last week I received a letter from Mr. [Ted] Wilson of the *Westminster* magazine, about the Poetry Number of it. He said that you had given him my name. I think that was extremely nice of you. The embarrassing thing about it is that I haven't any poetry—some very light things which I do just for fun are the only ones I have any success with. But he says the issue will not appear until spring—so maybe by that time I shall have improved a bit.

I hope that you and your mother have not been minding the heat too much. I have taken a very small apartment here on Charles Street . . .

To Donald E. Stanford

September 7, 1934

You must be thinking that graduation determined the end of all my activities, intellectual or social, and that I am one of the ten thousand, or whatever it is, who are lost each year . . . [My] very small apartment here for the winter is still mostly unfurnished, but I think it will begin to look quite well shortly. I have just supervised the installation of another bookcase—two shelves running along the wall and forming a right angle with the desk—and painted them white. In a minute or two I know I shall forget and put my feet down in the wet paint.

I am wondering if you managed to get a position worthy of you. I am getting so distressed about all my friends who can't find anything to do and who hang around the city getting more discouraged every day. And when I think that a butler, say, earns more in a week than they can ever hope to! It even makes me feel personally doubly useless, first because I'm not doing "anything," and second because I wouldn't be if I were . . .

Isn't it too bad about *Hound & Horn* [ceasing publication]? However, let's hope the ballet will in some measure help culture along too. I've never seen much ballet, but a couple of weeks ago I saw Fokine's *Les Sylphides* and I think I could easily get to be one of those people who go every night. There is a sort of review of the American Ballet's first appearance this summer in *Vogue*—but it praises only their "youth and vigor" and says nothing about their skill. Mr. Kirstein came and gave us more or less an advertising talk about [the new ballet company] at the end of college . . .

I am reading, reading all the time now, but rather illogically, I guess. I went through *The Bridge* all very carefully again, and like it less—particularly with the addition of his other poems which I had not read. I also rather disliked the appeal to Mr. [Otto] Kahn. My former roommate and her mother [the Millers] are taking an apartment way downtown right beside Brooklyn Bridge, so that they can see it and another bridge and all the traffic on the river. It's a wonderful view. I go walking across it every now and then . . . Miss Moore is away just now, but I'm hoping to be able to see her again when she comes home.

To Frani Blough

November 1, 1934

. . . I suppose you know all about Mary [McCarthy] and her appendix by this time. I think she went home Monday. I went to see her a couple of times in New York Hospital, and I think she was enjoying herself very much. The last time I almost envied her. It was a dark cold day and Mary sat up in bed in a pink knitted jacket, with a wonderful view of the Queensboro Bridge, her lunch on a tray, and everything else the heart could desire. I saw John for just a minute. I spent a long time reading his late play (*Uneasy Lies the Head*, they finally called it), trying to decide why, with such a good idea, it was such a terrible play. When he writes about businessmen, etc., for some reason he's fairly good, but the minute he begins on his favorite "whores," "panhandlers," etc., he gets too much like Eleanor Clark. [Producer] Jed Harris has vanished, it seems, leaving him [John] jobless again . . .

Gertrude Stein is lecturing [at the New School] next Tuesday and, of course, we are to be in the audience. Her first lecture is tonight. Mrs. Crane [Louise's mother], being chairman at the Museum of Modern Art, has the honor of driving her from wherever she's staying to the Colony Club for the [first] lecture. Louise and I were with Alec, the chauffeur, the other day and we asked him if he knew Gertrude Stein. It appeared that he had never heard of her, so we decided to describe her to him as a simply ravishing young lady, a sort of movie star. He will be considerably disappointed this evening.

Uncle Jack [Bishop] died very suddenly two weeks ago, and I went to Worcester. My affairs are all very much up in the air. I finally thought of Larry as the person to turn to, he being a lawyer as well as a bank president, so last week I went up to Pittsfield—visiting the friend he lives with, to the probable horror of all Pittsfield. Aside from these trips, I spend my time reading "good books," I guess, and worrying about poetry. It hangs and droops, particularly my own. Really, one would so much rather starve than do some of the things people do, or the things one apparently has to do, to get a job . . . Every day I start out firmly to ask someone to let me review poems for them. I get so scared that I have to stay at home with diarrhea. (I looked that up in the dictionary and discover that it is defined as "a *morbid* purging.")

January 1, 1935

. . . On Christmas Day I was completely overcome by a mixture of flu and asthma and had to leave Mrs. Miller's hospitality and come home to bed. Margaret came the next morning to take care of me and since then she has done everything from holding my head to scrubbing my back with a large brush, which she thought would do me good. She has gone home now, quite exhausted, I'm afraid, and I'm practically cured, but so full of adrenaline, morphine, and a particularly drugged and poisonous kind of cough syrup, that I am light-headed and giggle all the time. It is a strange sensation—almost pleasant, like being partly tight. The doctor procured for me a hypodermic syringe of my own, a very flashing one, all red and chromium, and I play with it every now and then, feeling too decadent for words.

I suppose you had a masquerade ball or something like that last night. Mary [McCarthy] just called up to tell me all the gossip of Eleanor Clark's party . . . As for me, I took a hot bath and went to bed. However, at midnight I had a curiosity as to what Meridian 7–1212 would have to say [about the arrival of the New Year] so I called up. Without even a flicker in her [phone operator's] voice, she said, "When you hear the signal, the time will be twelve o'clock." Bzzz. "When you hear," etc. So that's what mechanization does . . .

To Marianne Moore

EB in her memoir of Miss Moore writes: "It was because of Marianne that in 1935 my poems first appeared in a book, an anthology called Trial Balances. *Each of the poets in this anthology had an older mentor . . . and Marianne . . . had offered to be mine. I was much too shy to dream of asking her." This letter concerns MM's introduction.*

January 25, 1935

. . . I enjoyed the new version of the "introduction"* very much, and I'm sorry I was so obtuse about the first one so that you had to change it. Miss [Ann] Winslow [editor of *Trial Balances*] is getting more and more

---

* The introduction, entitled "Archaically New," said in part: "The rational considering quality in her work is its strength—assisted by unwordiness, uncontorted intentionalness, the flicker of impudence, the natural unforced ending . . . Her methodically oblique, intent way of working is auspicious."

agitated all the time. I scarcely know what to expect from her next. I have just decided, after yesterday's Air Mail–Special Delivery, to adopt a course of silence . . .

I am wondering if you have seen Martin Johnson's moving picture *Baboons*? It *looks*, from the previews, as if it might have in it a few very nice animals, and I am planning to go and see it. If you haven't seen it already, I wonder if you would care to go with me one afternoon this week? It is so cold that going out is very uncomfortable, but I should like so much to take you if you could consider it. I could meet you at the theatre any afternoon except Thursday, at any time convenient for you. I have had my eye on another animal film called, I think, *Sequoia*, but it doesn't sound quite as promising as *Baboons*.

Do you know—I am sure you must—that medieval falcon cut from rock crystal in one of the medieval rooms at the Metropolitan? I was admiring him on Saturday, and hoping that you had seen him, too. I also always go to take a look at the little Egyptian jerobas—or gerobas, as the Metropolitan spells it. Some of their inscriptions baffle me—a perfectly sensible crystal fish, for example, something like a perch, labeled "Porpoise." And a young man on a Greek vase who is obviously cutting the ends of his hair with his sword, called "Boy Washing Hair (?)."

I hope your work on the biography is progressing satisfactorily, and the book [*Selected Poems*] as well . . . When I first read your letter, I misread "over-exertion" as "over-exhaustion," and for a whole day I went about reproaching myself for laziness, if you could consider exhaustion as a comparatively normal state—but I hope that you are guarding against both.

To Frani Blough

January 30, 1935

It must be almost time for you to come if you have not given up your idea of becoming our new music critic. Margaret [Miller] received her scholarship at New York University—isn't that splendid?—and is at present working on an amazing exposé of Picasso and Gertrude Stein. So you will both add many significant letters to your names in time, I suppose. I think I shall work with an eye to receiving a simple ladyhood from England. "Dame Bishop" would sound well. I've had music on my mind entirely the past couple of days, and you along with it. Do you know anything (maybe you know a good deal) about *Bruckner*? I heard his Fifth Symphony last night and I thought it very interesting. I'd like to know a lot more about him . . .

A couple of days ago a rather large check just came to me as a gift from the gods [inheritance from Uncle Jack] and I've spent the last two days in a delightful deliberation: shall I spend some of it for traveling next summer, buy myself a new coat and lots of beautiful dresses, invest it in something or other, give everybody handsome presents? This morning I made up my mind. I'm going to buy a clavichord, if I can get a secondhand one. I think I can, and take some lessons from Mr. [Ralph] Kirkpatrick—also attending his lectures on ornamentation, etc. I have an appointment with him for tomorrow morning. You don't think much of the clavichord, as I remember, but it's quite suited to my needs. Then, as Ezra Pound says somewhere, "The further poetry departs from music, the more decadent it gets," etc., and I want to learn whatever I can about the periods when it hadn't yet departed—which is approximately up to the end of the clavichord days . . .

The New School sent me their catalogue the other day and I find they have a course in *Improvisation*, which I think is a damned good idea, don't you? To sum up my ideas on modern music, have I ever referred to you an article in the last *Hound & Horn* called "Jazz and Music"? (I haven't spoken to anyone all day, so all my random forces are coming out.)

We [the Millers] went to a movie, *Romeo and Juliet* [with Norma Shearer, Leslie Howard, and John Barrymore], and liked it very much. Afterwards I saw Mary [McCarthy] and she said she'd seen it too. Then came a silence. It seems she had liked it extremely, and so had I, but we were each afraid to say so for fear the other hadn't. One of those peculiarly feminine conversational problems. I went to Mary's house to meet the famous Miss [Margaret] Marshall of *The Nation* and her husband. It was fun to see Mary so thoroughly scared by someone, and so worried that it "went."

I have just cooked and eaten the most beautiful artichoke it has been my privilege to see . . . Sometime when you're in New York I'll cook you a couple, with Hollandaise, which I have now mastered. This one had purplish tips and seemed particularly well arranged.

Tuesday morning I'm taking Miss Moore to see *Baboons*. It looks as if it ought to contain a great many animals. I'm going to try to inveigle her into having lunch with me and going to see the new zoo, but I'm afraid she'll scurry back to Brooklyn. Her volume of poems ought to appear next month. She has just been having her picture taken by George [Platt] Lynes, in order to be "honorable" with the reviewers, and not send them a younger one . . .

To Marianne Moore

April 2, 1935

I have it on good authority that the circus is coming to town on April 11th. I wonder, if you have no other plans, if you would consider going again with me? This year, from the posters, there is to be something new:

a Chinese family who do things (such as playing cards, eating, etc.) while hanging from hooks by their hair. Also some new acrobats. I saw one performance of the American Ballet and decided that after all there was nothing better for that kind of thing than acrobats . . .

I've been having some trouble finding a clavichord in good condition in this country and now I am getting one straight from the Dolmetsches. They are making very nice ones now, with beautiful tone, and small so that you can take them with you wherever you go. I didn't know until Mr. Wilson told me last night that Ezra Pound plays some early instruments himself, and has written about Arnold Dolmetsch.

It has been very strange finding in the Hopkins letters that he grew more and more absorbed in music, and mentions some of the very things I have been studying. His own ideas about composition seem almost to forecast some of Schönberg. I wonder, if I rewrote my paper on Hopkins, if it would be asking too much for you to look at it again? There is much more that should be said, and better said—but I feel very uncertain . . .

[P.S.] You once said something to me about being interested in handwriting. Have you seen those books on English handwriting by Roger Fry and Robert Bridges? I imagine that you have, but I mention them because if you haven't, they seem rather interesting.

April 13, 1935

I have two friends whose birthdays come about now, and on Wednesday morning I went into Macy's to send them each a copy of your new book [*Selected Poems*]. (I hope you won't mind such a heavily complimentary reference, but I thought you might like to hear this.) There were two on the shelf and when I gave them to the clerk she said, "This book is certainly selling well. These are the last two copies of our whole first shipment." And it was then only about eleven-thirty in the morning. So now I am quite confident that you are going to make a large American Fortune. I haven't had a chance to examine my copy carefully yet, and read all the Preface [by T. S. Eliot], but I do think the poems look so well in that larger type, don't you? I am eagerly awaiting the appearance of the George Lynes photograph . . .

Next week I am going to begin some hours of reading and translating French with a tutor up at Columbia. I am very poor at it and feel my ignorance, particularly in regard to modern French poetry . . . I have a general idea of the poets' names, at least up to about 1920, but that's about all. It will be so hard to get a tutor who knows as much as she or he ought to. The French graduate students I have known have usually been doing work in Edith Wharton and Robert Frost . . . I hope the trip to Bryn Mawr was highly satisfactory. [In this letter EB enclosed "Britannia Rules the Waves," her occasional poem included in *The Complete Poems: 1927–1979*.]

. . . I brought back some swan feathers, much superior to the one I sent you, which I shall give you. The swans were sitting on their eggs. Do you know—you probably do, but I never had before—that they turn them over every half hour, exactly? We went.to watch them do it—with their feet—and it is the nicest thing afterward to see the mother swan stretching her neck all around to see that all the eggs are underneath . . .

The friend I have been visiting [Louise Crane] is coming to the city this weekend, and she has a very large safe car. We wondered if possibly we could persuade you and your mother to permit yourselves to be driven to Coney Island for supper, on Monday night? We went down last Sunday, and it was really very nice, although a weekday is probably better. We thought we could start about four-thirty or five, which would give us time for a merry-go-round ride or two before supper. I have found a merry-go-round there which I hadn't noticed before, one with particularly pleasing horses, I think you might like. My friend is an awfully good driver and I shall request her to go just as fast or slow as you prefer . . .

I was so pleased to see the George Lynes photograph appearing in last Sunday's [Herald] Tribune. I think it is very nice. Have you heard of the work of Miss Margaret Washburn of Vassar in Animal Psychology? I knew she was a famous psychologist but I had never met her until my last trip up there, when I had the opportunity to talk to her for quite a while. Her books are not very well written but wonderful, I think. I thought perhaps you might be interested in her *The Animal Mind* . . .

To Frani Blough

[POSTCARD]

[Aboard S.S. *Königstein*]
August 3, 1935

. . . This picture [of a big steamship and a sailing vessel] is terribly flattering, I think. Give me that schooner off to the right, any time. The German tourists have so tramped on my person and intellect that I'm afraid I haven't much to say. I just hide away and moan and sail to Antwerp. They are simply IMPOSSIBLE * * @ @ ! !

To Marianne Moore

Hôtel de l'Europe
Douarnenez [Brittany]
August 21, 1935

You see, I did get abroad after all . . . I came over with a friend from college, landing in Antwerp, where we stayed a couple of days, then to

Brussels, Paris, and down here five days ago. There was an Exposition going on at Brussels which we thought we should see, but aside from the wonderful collection of early Northern painting, it seemed to be mostly the dregs of the World's Fair, including Dillinger in effigy, etc.

We spent four or five days in Paris—one with an American family who now live in one of Madame Pompadour's hunting lodges outside Versailles. The place is exquisite, rather neglected, with pools, fountains, goats and cows around in the fields, among hundreds of weatherbeaten statues, and apple and pear trees that have been trained to grow on the ground, or in spirals, or like candelabra. The Americans are just like people out of movies, so it wasn't as pleasant as it should have been.

Douarnenez is a fishing town on the coast of Brittany. We have settled here for about a month, I think (with a small library of French books), and I shall stay here until I am joined by Louise Crane. I am trying to decide whether to go to a university here next winter, the Sorbonne or some smaller one somewhere in France, or to go to a hot place which would be good for asthma, or to come home. With so many possibilities, and all of them looking equally delightful, it is very hard to decide. Douarnenez is too PICTURESQUE for much longer than a month. The picturesqueness is just like the water in Salt Lake, you simply can't sink in it, it is so strong . . . The fishnets (it's a center of sardine fishery) are an aquamarine blue, so the fish can't see them when they sink in deep water. There are such nice things for sale in all the stores—beautiful baskets, one species of which I simply must bring you, espadrilles, a kind of butterfly net of the same blue to catch crabs with. We just missed the Fête of Blue Nets they hold every year at Quimper. A small circus came to town last night; the acrobats and the woman who trains little ponies stayed here. It was very artistically done, and everyone in town, in full Breton costume, attended. I particularly liked it when one of the seals climbed his stepladder carrying a lighted lamp with a red silk shade and bead fringe, on his nose . . .

To Frani Blough

Hôtel de l'Europe
le 27 Août 1935
Douarnenez

You don't know what a blessing it is to have you be one, *the* one, friend who has been here, so I don't feel dutybound to—or maybe, I can't possibly let myself—DESCRIBE everything. I was so sorry to hear that you'd been sick and in the hospital—with your letter came one from Margaret, who announced very calmly: "I've been to see Frani in the hospital." Imagine my feelings if there hadn't been a letter from you with a little explanation in it. Her description of the golden oak, you, etc., made you sound very much like a small gold coin in an elaborate purse. Well, I hope you're all safely over it now, no enfeeblement, etc. I don't know whether you'll still be [in EB's apartment] at Charles Street or not—I wonder where you're going to live next year.

We've been here a week. Maybe I'd better go back beyond that and make a few comments on the TRIP. We were pretty much trampled underfoot by those German tourists—but somehow the intense discomfort of train trips, boat trips fades out as soon as you get wherever you're going. Have you ever heard of an *Atlantic Monthly* writer—a perfectly mummified specimen—named Albert Jay Nock? . . . He helped me and Hallie [Tompkins Thomas] to pass the time away considerably . . .

One reason this letter is such a mess is because I am not up yet. We have just eaten that magnificent breakfast you may remember, and repose in our crumby beds . . . We have been to Point Ray, to the Fête at St. Anne, to seven or eight churches in the vicinity, to a little place called, as nearly as I could make out, Le Juque . . . It is a beautiful walk back over the hills. I am getting rather fond of all these dirty little churches— also the *calvaires* [wayside crosses] around on all the hills. It is interesting to discover, in Rimbaud, this (*"armoricaine"* means Brittany, I think): *"Me voici sur la plage armoricaine . . . L'air marin brûlera mes poumons; les climats perdus me tanneront. Nager, broyer l'herbe, chasser, fumer surtout; boire des liqueurs fortes comme du métal bouillant."** Not of course to *fumer surtout*—with the cigarettes as they are, but the rest is all right, and these strong drinks are wonderful . . .

How is your harmony coming? Is Mr. Kirkpatrick returning to the New School? I have so many things in mind now—the Sorbonne, Grenoble, other universities, *travel*, etc. . . . Excuse my disconnectedness— why don't you try a music article on the English magazine *Life and Letters*? It's been started all over again with some very good people, so Miss Moore tells me, and they want "criticism." Margaret has the address, also that of another American magazine which sounds promising: *Contemporary Review*. We must all burst, blossom, and burgeon in print from now on.

Do you remember the slab of cement behind this hotel which they sometimes call the "terrace"? It is very nice out there in the morning, lots of sun and several cats, and I sit out there with a bottle of ink and a pen from breakfast till lunch every day. My French remains backwards, although I can now ask for rather complicated things like "white thread," "no starch in this blouse," etc., and be understood. Did you ever have any laundry done here? The laundryman's name is M. Le BASTARD. He lists everything as *"chemisettes,"* so we have no way of telling each other's

* "Here I am on the Brittany beach . . . The sea air will burn my lungs; the bad atmosphere will hurt me. To swim, to flatten the grass, to go hunting, above all to smoke; to drink drinks as strong as boiling metal."

relative bills at all. Only an exception or two—my step-ins are *"culotte* (f.),"* my pajamas *"py-* (m.)." I hope you are completely recovered, *chérie* . . .

58 rue de Vaugirard
Paris VIᵉ
October 20, 1935

Europe, until you get used to it, is TIRING. I'm sure I've been needing much more sleep, and I just realized that undoubtedly in a country where everything has to be *observed*—just to make sure it isn't different from what you're used to—of course you get tired. However, that period's over now. Louise and I decided to begin a new regime this morning. We told the maid about it, asking to be awakened at 8 a.m. henceforward. She giggled a little and then we realized that *régime* probably means "diet" in French. She giggles every time I open my mouth, in French that is— drops plates, rushes to the kitchen with her shoulders shaking, etc. But she is really very cute and I must tell you a lot about her later on. At this minute she is polishing the floor by putting a cloth down, running and sliding on it . . .

I was so pleased to get your letter, and it really made me feel kind of queer and isn't it STRANGE, because I came away with a large pad of paper, and Ben Jonson's *Masques* to study, with the express purpose of writing something like that. The only unpleasant aspect is that ultimately all that sort of thing, I'm afraid, has to DEPEND ON THE DOWAGER.* But maybe not. And, even if it does, I suppose that doesn't matter much. Is your idea to compose it yourself? I think, as you say, an American Pastoral might be excellent—something a little fantastic, anyway . . .

Last night we went to an extremely nice concert here. First the boys' choir of St. Thomas's Church of Leipzig (Bach's, isn't it?) sang a Bach Cantata—No. 67, I think the name is "Remember the Lord"—perfectly beautiful. Then the Paris Philharmonic played the Suite in D, then there was a Motet for double choir. The second half of the program was Mozart—three church songs, then the Symphony in D Major . . . Altogether it was one of the nicest evening's music I've ever heard. I went to the opening Philharmonic and, except for the same Bach Suite, it seemed very poor. They give such poor programs, mostly Ravel and Saint-Saëns, who's having some sort of anniversary this year. However, we have tickets now for Yehudi [Menuhin] when he comes, and next week we're going to the ballet. It makes me awfully mad that the movies are so expensive—scarcely ever less than a dollar—but they seem to take the cinema much more seriously, which is something . . . If Louise and I ever

---

* This cryptic phrase seems to refer to the widowed Mrs. Crane, mother of Louise, on whom she (and EB, partially) depended for financial help.

come to understand the catalogue of the Sorbonne, we're taking some courses there. I'll take one French literature course, 16th–18th centuries, and maybe something in Art.

This sounds as if I was settling down here for life, which is not the case. In fact my conscience gnaws badly all the time, and I find that I LOVE New York, etc.—particularly as one meets a few of the kind of Americans who do live here. But the city itself is so nice, don't you think?—and we are situated so *pleasantly*, and I'm gradually beginning to see through French poetry a little. But it's only for three months, or one semester at the Sorbonne.

Let's see. We might begin with the front door, I suppose. I found a lot of these postcards [showing the street entrance of General de Chambrun's apartment where they were living] in the desk. Comtesse de Chambrun (who's supposed to be a great authority on Shakespeare, I think— a homely, horse-faced, blunt woman, the bossy type, with all kinds of decorations in her lapels) is our landlady, and this apartment is furnished with her wedding presents, I guess—though it isn't so bad. In fact, having gone through about thirty French furnished apartments, it seems beautiful. She's Nicholas L[ongworth]'s sister, and dear Mrs. [Alice Roosevelt] Longworth and the famous Paulina were put up in this apartment this summer. I think all the dirty fingermarks we find on the white woodwork are Paulina's. In spite of the fact that we have *seven* rooms, five fireplaces, and a cook, it will not cost me as much as living on Charles Street did. Hallie is visiting us right now but she leaves tomorrow, and if you feel inclined to come aboard, you are of course invited to come and stay. We have three bedrooms. The house is right at the corner of the Luxembourg Gardens, where we walk and look at the fountains and dahlias and babies—and the violent croquet matches going on among cabdrivers and professors of the Sorbonne, I think, from appearances. The trees are all yellow now, and the effect is too antique for comfort, but very pretty nevertheless.

Please tell me what numbers of *The Nation* Mary [McCarthy]'s things [a series of articles, co-authored with Margaret Marshall, attacking the New York drama critics] are going to appear in, will you? . . . As you once told me, the subways here are very nice, except that for several days I failed to realize the difference between "Port" and "Pont" Something- with-the-same-name, and so got carried all over Paris . . . If we have enough money we may go over [to London] just long enough to buy a lot of secondhand books. If you see a book called *The Invaders* by William Plomer, read it . . . At present I am very deep in the poems of—D. H. Lawrence! Oh dear, but they're very good, all the same . . .

I am not, never, never, an EXPATRIATE. We went to a tea at Comtesse de Chambrun's and I met a few men—so languid, so whimsical, so *cultured*—youthfully middle-aged, and reminding me of nothing so much as a flourishing fuzzy gray *mold* . . . Some of the French Army lives in this house, and I am always squeezing into the elevator with a dashing young thing all spurs, swords, epaulets, and a headdress of red, white and blue feathers (honestly) about 18 inches high.

ENOUGH. I do wish if you have time you'd call up my dear Margaret and give her my love . . . Did you drink Pernod when you were here? It is not a lady's drink, but I like it, I'm afraid. We are heartily tired of the eternal vermouths and Dubonnets here. Louise went out and bought a cocktail shaker the other day, and since then we have had an excellent Side Car before our excellent dinner every night. She wishes to be remembered to "Frannie," although I correct [this pronunciation] carefully all the time.

To Marianne Moore

February 4, 1936

. . . Thank you so much for writing to Mr. [Edward] Aswell [editor at Houghton Mifflin]. I did send him a few things and now I think he remains "interested," etc. And it was so kind of you to offer to type for me—so more than kind, so headlong! But I found that an acquaintance here had a typewriter I could use, after all.

I am sending two pictures we managed to get of the doves the other day; one . . . shows Mr. Dove bowing to his wife with stiff knees and his throat puffed out. They are presenting quite a problem just now, as the mating season is coming on just as we are about to start traveling again. We have provided a small raffia nest and are urging them to line it with pink cotton, for the pleasing color effect, but I am afraid it may be very difficult to travel around Spain with a cage of young doves.

I was so pleased when I found that my friend Margaret [Miller] had chosen to send me as part of a Christmas present a copy of your [poem] "Pigeons," not realizing I could get it [*Poetry* magazine] here. She also copied out and sent me parts of your review of Wallace Stevens. The last paragraph, particularly what you said about the "experts," pleased us both enormously* . . . I liked Mr. Stevens's article in *Life and Letters Today*; it was the first of his prose I had seen. And most of all, in spite of what you say in your letter, I liked "Virginia Britannia."

All these things have been an extra consolation to me, since I have been rather ill, too (or I should have answered your letter sooner). I went to the American Hospital here just before Christmas for a mastoid op-

* MM's review of Stevens alluded to the "wild boars of philistinism who rush about interfering with experts."

eration and just got home about a week ago. It is a very slow affair, but really very interesting, involving all the physics of sound and balance, such fancy bones, and *tuning forks*. I am quite recovered now, except for a half-shaved head and a turban which I hope makes me resemble A. Pope a little. But all those poems and articles went along to the hospital with me, and the *Oxford Book of Seventeenth Century Verse*, so I got along very nicely. I remember you once spoke of William Empson's *Seven Types of Ambiguity* and I wonder what you think about it. I have been reading it again and following with his new book, *Some Versions of Pastoral*, some of which I think is excellent—the parts where I'm familiar with what he's talking about, that is . . .

I wasn't able to get very far with the clavichord before I became sick, but I hope I'm going to be able to take some lessons with Ralph Kirkpatrick next year. I studied some of the simplest of Bach and Purcell. I have a beautiful set of Preludes and Suites of his, really for harpsichord, but I am afraid I am not a purist.

We should have liked nothing better, Miss Moore, than your being able to go to Spain with us. We are leaving here about the 15th and going first to Morocco, which we think may be nice and hot, then we shall go North through Spain very slowly. We are going by way of London in order to see the Chinese exhibition, it sounds very good. I have been given a book to prepare me: *Chinese Art* by Leigh Ashton and Basil Gray— really just a book of photographs . . .

There is nothing like a hospital for making one despair of health and energy, etc., and I do wish you would tell me how you are. I have decided to enclose another picture—a little advertisement for VICHY WATER, which you may not think funny at all, though it is supposed to be.

To Frani Blough

[POSTCARD OF PICCADILLY CIRCUS]
[Aboard *paquebot*
March 1936]
Since last week your fondness for England has made me feel a little suspicious of you. However, it *is* nice to be able to trust yourself to a taxi driver. Did you ever go to the music halls [in London]? We are now en route to Gibraltar, and it is *freezing*. No heat, no hot water except a tin cup full once a day. The ship resounds with sneezes. Take bile beans. We lie in bed with two sweaters on, drinking excellent grogs, which cost sixpence.

[Taroudant, Morocco
March 25, 1936]
This man, in common with other Arabs, has a sweet tooth. He makes a Martini by squeezing a lemon and an orange, and then dropping in a little from *all* the bottles—there are more under the bar: anise, gin, bitters, vermouth (three kinds), cherry, kirsch, and so on. It is such a nice hotel, though—the small-sized palace of a Pasha, a few rooms around a court-yard of orange and lemon trees. We have one room half a block long, very narrow, all marble, and with enormous beds set at either end. This is a tiny walled village. A native wedding (perpetual singing for seven days) has been going on for two now. I shall be humming the tune when I come home.

[Ronda, Spain
April 1936]
I am afraid I have you branded hopelessly now as "musical." I tried and tried to get some Moorish records for you and may yet. Also some Spanish Flamenco singing, which is very strange. But I have a *flute* for you. This place is by far the nicest yet. The picture says "detail," which means it's only about half the drop. The cliffs run right through the middle of town. I saw my first bullfight and feel altogether too Hemingwayish.

To Marianne Moore

Hotel Venecia
Seville [Spain]
April 6, 1936
. . . Morocco was so nice—in spite of Moorish architecture, which is so awful, and the rather unfriendly atmosphere which has been caused by the French occupation (one immediately sympathizes with the Moors)—that we stayed probably longer than we should have. There are camel trains everywhere and we saw lots of baby camels. In spite of the disagreeable nature of their elders, the little camels seem quite affec-tionate. I saw one almost knocking his driver down with his demonstrations—rubbing and leaning against him. All the houses and city walls in Marrakech are covered with storks' nests—they are very "familial," as a French lady said to me, and wander around with six-foot sticks in their beaks building their houses exactly as well as the natives. But the nicest of all were the little owls we saw out in the country—stubby and almost tail-less, about six inches high, and very soft looking. They would sit right by the side of the road, sometimes in the road, and stare

quietly back at us as we went up to them, then just as we got quite close, the eyes would blink once and the face would seem really to change expression—becoming surprised, and annoyed with itself for being surprised—and the owl would fly off.

. . . The musicians are really quite good and we liked the music, too. We went to several cafés to see the singing and dancing with our guide, and one of the best things I saw were two very large Negroes, very black, one dressed in lavender and one in pink, one playing a large lute with a long feathered quill and the other a violin which he held upside down—the neck on his shoulder—while they both sang as loudly, or shouted as hoarsely as they could. It looked very much like a parody of the angels in an Italian painting I saw in London. The dancing is of course very improper but sometimes extremely amusing—as, for example, when the lady, to show how still she keeps the top of her head, dances with a tray on it, holding a teapot and glasses full of tea. Without spilling any she even lies down and rolls over, and at the end sits on the floor and takes a glass of tea off the tray and offers it to you, with her toes.

I saw the advertisement for *The Pangolin and Other Verse* [Miss Moore's new book of poems] in *Life and Letters Today*. It sounds very fancy and very nice and I am eager to see it.

Oh dear—I am worried by your speaking of my "leisurely" life. My conscience is troubling me so badly these days that it takes it for a confirmation of the very worst. And it is particularly bad since so many people I know are having such a difficult time. We are coming home at the end of June and I am going to try to work and study much more seriously and thoroughly than I ever have before. Not that that in any way has anything to do with the people's difficulties . . .

[P.S.] Do you think that the *Southern Review* contest might be a good thing to enter?

[P.P.S.] The Holy Week processions are not being held in Spanish towns because of the Communist troubles—but here they draw so many tourists that the government has ordered them to go on—well interspersed with police—whether the Church wants to or not. A Spanish monk in Tangier, when we asked him whether they were going to be held or not, said "Yes—but not for *God*."

Hotel Costa Brava
Puerto de Sóller, Mallorca
May 21, 1936
. . . I don't believe I told you that when we spent a week in London, before getting the boat to Gibraltar, we went to see *Murder in the Cathedral* and *The Dog Beneath the Skin*. I think the W.P.A. [Orson Welles] pro-

duction of *Murder in the Cathedral* must have been much better than the London one—although it [the latter] was such a success, and ran such a long time. I thought it was AWFUL—the general effect was that of a very shabby church pageant; the actor who played Thomas could not seem to avoid giving the impression of being, even when he was denying it, a spiritual snob (and reflecting the character onto Mr. Eliot). But the women of Canterbury were the worst—as you say, too. They *moaned* their lines and made us almost weep with embarrassment. *The Dog Beneath the Skin* was a little better theatrically, I think—but it was very poorly put on, too, and acting brought out the difference between the overprettiness of the in-between "poems" and the horseplay of the story rather too much. Ten times as much as either we liked the old Eisenstein movie *Potemkin* that we happened to find in London. I wonder if you have seen it?

One of the most delightful days of my life occurred about a week ago: one morning in the freezing cold of Toledo Louise and I confronted each other—mutual sufferers from a severe rash and severe indigestion —and confessed that we were tired of being "tourists," that we wanted nothing more than a week's rest in some sunny place. So we caught the bus back to Madrid, and after a very strange drive through miles of deep oily-blue-colored flowers, with a radio playing loudly in the ceiling of the bus, I arrived feeling very light-headed and went to the Poste Restante, where I found the *Pangolin*! It was quite safe and there was no duty, perhaps because, as I was horrified to see, the sender [Miss Moore] had written "Value—$1.00" on it. (I noticed and despaired of the *real* price in the advertisements.) I think that only one or two Christmas presents have ever pleased me so much . . .

For some mysterious international reason (I suppose to injure the Italian Lines) France is offering a ticket from Madrid to Paris, from Paris to Havre, and a passage home third class on any French line, for $90. We could not resist this wonderful bargain, as it seems to be, and at present we expect to come back third class on the *Normandie* on June 15. [They took an earlier boat, arriving in New York on June 10.]

Until we tired of being "tourists" we had planned to extend our trip to Burgos, León, etc., but instead we have been staying at this little fishing village in Mallorca . . . I am enclosing a couple of pictures of Baroque things we admired in Valencia—the doorway was best of all and I wish the "detail" of the lolling lion were clearer . . . I am torn between sending you [a postcard of] the bullfighter embroidered in silk and the bullfighter embroidered with sequins . . .

820 Fifth Avenue
[New York, June 11, 1936]

. . . I am staying here at Louise's home for two days, then I shall visit another friend for a few days until I have decided where to stay for the summer. If you are not too busy just now, or unwell, or any of the things that make "reception" unwelcome, I should so much like to see you for a little while before I leave the city, and to give you a small present from Morocco . . . I am leaving here tomorrow and my only sure address will be c/o Margaret Miller . . .

To Frani Blough

West Falmouth, Massachusetts
July 9, 1936

It has been a very exciting evening here. During most of it I have done nothing but comfort and reassure the kitten and rush around trying to find candles, etc. I think my house was struck by lightning, but I'm not quite sure, because I didn't see any balls of fire and I couldn't find any black scars, etc., when I looked with a flashlight. But there was a horrible crash which really blew me out of the chair, and a sort of ripping noise, and a blaze in the "orchard"; and then the lights went out. The poor little kitten rushed round and round the room crying, and ever since it has remained with its head under my arm or a pillow. I wonder if this is because cats have some special relation with the mysteries of electricity. But now the lights have at least come on again and the storm seems to be over.

The kitten is very sweet, about two months old, I think; gray semi-angora with white markings. Louise and I went out to Cuttyhunk Island for a visit a while ago and the landlady of the Inn gave her to me. She is nameless so far, so if you have any ideas. All I can think of is Sappho, because she comes from a small island. By August I'm afraid her charm will be mostly gone, however . . .

A Mr. Wagenar (I don't know who he is, but Louise seems to think he has some connection with you) is here. In Woods Hole they have a large choir of young and old, led by the Smith College leader. It is sup-posed to be quite good, I think. I am considering, slightly, joining. Then there are several quartets under formation that you could probably get in on, if you wanted to—or do you want to escape from it all? I have been sailing already three or four times with Louise in Woods Hole. One could probably rent a boat there. They have a class of boats that are amazing, completely unsinkable. We went out the other day in a very rough sea—terribly rough, really, through all kinds of tides and cross-rips. I should never have dreamed of going out in a camp boat or the Duck.

Thank you for offering to send some things from Macy's—but do you know that liquor cannot be sent from one state to another? I shall probably ask you to bring something large and heavy when you come, though. I baked some apples this afternoon which turned out wonderfully. I hope you will bring some books along. The books I really like to read best are always those I take away from someone else who is halfway through them . . .

To Marianne Moore

West Falmouth, Massachusetts
August 21, 1936

Just before I received your letter, the kitten had been christened MINNOW. The markings on her sides are pale gray over deep gray, an effect like light splotches on gray water. When she rolls over, she shows off a pure white stomach with gray spottings, like some variety of fish—closest to a mackerel, I think, but that name would not do, so it had to be MINNOW. I'm sorry we did not wait, because I think that PTERRY is very nice, but the necessary psychological training with dishes of milk, etc., had just been successful, and she had learned to answer to MINNOW, so we did not change . . .

Have you ever been to Cape Cod? I'm afraid the scenery lacks the refinement of Virginia, but I've always liked it very much and found it very *soothing*—bayberry, blueberry, sweet fern, scrub pine, scrub oak. A great many Portuguese Negroes live near me and come around in very high-set, polished old Fords selling blueberries and raspberries that go beautifully with their black faces and blue denim clothes. Louise Crane, at Woods Hole, has a wonderful sailboat (an S. boat, if you know about chassis), 20-something feet long, narrow, with a sail as high as a cathedral. I am sure I remember reading somewhere that you are fond of sailing. I do wish I could have you here to sail in this boat to the little island called "Cuttyhunk." It is a very pretty little place with about twenty houses on it, a church and schoolhouse—sassafras and catnip grow there. I once spent a month out there, and went swordfishing with the men. I think it must be the most exciting industry there is. It's supposed to be the island Shakespeare had in mind for *The Tempest*. The woman who runs the boarding house gave me Minnow.

Margaret Miller is living with me now—she has gained several pounds and looks infinitely better. She is working away at four or five canvases at the same time and is making some very nice things, I think. I was delighted with what you said about her looks. She once remarked desperately herself into the mirror that she feared she was a little Pre-Raphaelite-ish. But I always insisted it was more the early Picasso—those starved tumblers and clowns. It is very funny to find the intersecting point of Burne-Jones and Picasso in Margaret. Her mother was here for about three weeks; she has just sent me as a present Wallace Stevens's *Ideas of*

Order. I am so pleased to have it—but isn't the print dreadful?—and the price?

We play croquet every morning after breakfast, which we eat out-doors, and the cat goes wild with pleasure trying to stand on the balls and squeeze through the wickets. When we shove her off with a mallet, she rushes into the interior of a large perfectly round bracken bush that stands in the yard, like an igloo. (I am inclined to call it the BETTER BUSH, from your letter.) The ideality of this existence has been somewhat marred for me in the last two weeks. I have been a melancholy and superbly marked Job with poison ivy—but it is going away now.

The war in Spain is frightful. I wonder if you saw the amazingly pathetic pictures in the *Times* a few days ago—the wooden and plastic statues and crucifixes, all periods and quantities, dragged out of a church in Barcelona, lying so that at first one thought they were dead soldiers. There was something suspiciously dramatic about the arrangement, which makes it even truer to what I've heard about the Spanish character.

I have sent a poem to Roger Roughton's magazine [*Contemporary Poetry and Prose*] and some to the *Southern Review*, but now I regret both. I am reading St. Augustine's *Confessions*, Amiel's *Journals*, and Words-worth's *Prelude*, and this heaped-up autobiography is having extreme results, maybe fortunate. I cannot, cannot decide what to do. I am even considering studying medicine or biochemistry, and have procured all sorts of catalogues, etc. I feel that I have given myself more than a fair trial, and the accomplishment has been nothing at all. I had rather work at Science, at which I was fairly good at college, or even something quite uncongenial for the rest of my days, than become like one of my con-temporaries. But this is a great imposition. My only foundation is that your interest in behalf of POETRY will lead you to be very severe . . .

[P.S.] I must admit the temptation to return to N.Y. and take some clavichord lessons with Ralph Kirkpatrick is very strong.

820 Fifth Avenue
September 29, 1936

I do hope that you have not been suffering any ill effects from our jaunt [to Coney Island]. The food was so poor, and I'm afraid you weren't in the proper aggressive condition to fight it off well. I am also sorry that our farewells seemed so abrupt. I must tell you that we were going to the theatre that evening; we wanted to ask you to go with us, but it was a play just opening that we knew nothing about and hated to ask you to take the risk. It was so fortunate that we did not . . . because it was very bad, barely endurable—*Horse Eats Hat* [a Mercury Theatre/Orson Welles production]. But I am awfully sorry if it made us seem to rush off, and if I have left you encumbered with too much of my property. Louise says that she will be glad to drive me over at any time to get anything you may want to get rid of.

I have read Mr. [Morton Dauwen] Zabel's article and enjoyed it very much. It seems to me that in spite of his rather mystifying, in spots, style, he has attempted and managed to express a great deal that has never been touched on before. I like very much the part at the first: "—and other sleights of hand demanded by public success or moral insecurity," and "the banalities of allegory." And "When they present a thought, they do so in terms of all the accidents, analogies and inhibitory influences that went into its formulation." But I wish he would not say things like: "consolation and stimulus" and "amusing and provoking." I also wish that sometime someone would actually bring out, with examples, etc., what he hints at—that is the effect, YOUR effect, on one's interpretation of other poetry . . .

I am enclosing a slightly corrected version of "Paris, 7 A.M." I do not know whether you will think it fit to send to *Poetry* as it is now or not, or whether you had rather wait until I have finished one or two more— to which I am bending my efforts now. I am sorry I am being so obstinate about "apartments." To me the word suggests so strongly the structure of the houses, later referred to, and suggests a "cut-off" mode of existence so well—that I don't want to change it unless you feel it would mean a great improvement . . .

I hope Coney Island was not a disappointment, Miss Moore. I continue to see that beautiful sky and the fantasies of Luna Park and the deserted side streets. Louise would like to be remembered to you.

Hotel Chelsea, New York
October 18, 1936

. . . I had my first lesson from Ralph Kirkpatrick yesterday. One has to play with the windows closed in the city, and the clavichord has to be put in the closet every night to keep it from the drafts. He is a most remarkable young man. He lives without steam heat, so his various instruments won't warp, and very seriously he gave me all sorts of exercises to do which I feel to be a little overmystical, almost yoga-ish.

This story ["The Baptism"] is so untidy. Worse than that, I am afraid it is a little CHEAP. But after reading those in *Life and Letters Today* I felt a little encouraged. I was trying to produce an effect like Hans Andersen, but I'm afraid I haven't succeeded in this one. If you don't care for it, please don't bother to send it back but throw it out the window or down the elevator shaft . . .

P.S. I have just this minute received word from Roger Roughton that he will not accept "The Weed" this time either. Now I am so sorry that I ever caused you to be connected with it in any way.

Hotel Chelsea
October 27, 1936

Thank you so much for all your, and your mother's, trouble with my story. It is very sad to be capable of such mistakes—even in grammar and spelling! I sent off a copy to *Life and Letters*.

Two days ago I bought *The Nation* with your review in it of Miss Stein. I find it so interesting that I am on the point of buying the book, although I decided quite a while ago that I had bought quite enough, too much, of Miss Stein. I find the Wallace Stevens poem very confusing. I am not at all sure how personified "life" is. Please will you tell me when your review of his poems is to appear in *Poetry*? . . .

You helped me so much with "The Baptism." I'm afraid I was quite ungracious in that I accepted most of your suggestions but refused some—that seems almost worse than refusing all assistance. I have almost finished now a second story ["The Sea & Its Shore"], which I feel is much, much better—although I suppose that is just a "phase." I am hoping that you will think it worth sending to *The Criterion* . . .

Last night was so cold that the cat very affectionately got into bed with me—and brought along, in three trips, my fountain pen, a shell, and a button.

P.S. I must add my gratitude for all the time you have spent on "The Weed." I don't see how you could bear to copy it, the way you did, and I am extremely grateful . . .

Hotel Chelsea
December 5, 1936

I am so sorry we were late last evening [for the poetry reading by MM and William Carlos Williams]—sorry both to have interrupted you and to have missed that much of your talk. We thought we had timed the subway [to Brooklyn] carefully, but I'm afraid we hadn't. You looked so nice down there on the platform: the black velvet is overwhelmingly becoming, and you should not have apologized for the shoes. They looked extremely small, shiny and elegant, to me. I enjoyed everything you said and blamed the IRT for being so slow and the audience for not laughing more—as I thought they should have—at your many excellent jokes. And we were really quite baffled with admiration when you had to make those impromptu answers.

I enjoyed every moment except the one in which my own name struck me like a bullet [MM greeted her by name from the platform], and I felt myself swelling like a balloon to fill the auditorium. Dr. Williams is even nicer than I had imagined. The woman who conducted is wonderful too—I should love to have a photograph of her. The usher insisted that the third member of the party come in FREE.

. . . I had had a few "ideas" about [Wallace] Stevens, but I had been wandering around them in the dark. Things like [MM's] quotation from *Coriolanus*, the "spinnaker," and Mercury—but particularly the "spinnaker"—provide the most perfect and sudden illumination. Really they leave me completely wordless, but your remarks on "bravura," and *"the general marine volume of statement"* have kept me in an almost hilarious state of good cheer ever since the letter arrived . . .

I am afraid my own idea of *Owl's Clover* is much more simple and "popular." I took it as a defense of his own position, and the statue— dear me—I felt, and still cannot help feeling, is ART—sometimes the particular creation, sometimes an historical synthesis, sometimes his own work—but always his own conception of such art. In the first section I thought he was confessing the "failure" of such art (I don't like to use these words but they seem to be the only ones) to reach the lives of the unhappiest people, and the possibility of a change—of something new arising from the unhappiness, etc.

> *as if the black of what she thought*
> *Conflicting with the moving colors there*
> *Changed them, at last, to its triumphant hue*

"Mr. Burnshaw" I thought was a sort of mock-elegy for such art, and so on. However, what strikes me as so wonderful about the whole book —because I think there are a great many rough spots in it, don't you?— and I dislike the way he occasionally seems to make blank verse *moo* —is that it is such a display of ideas at work—making poetry, the poetry making them, etc. That, it seems to me, is the way a poet should think, and it should be a lesson to his thicker-witted opponents and critics, who read or write all their ideas in bad prose and give nothing in the way of poetry except exhortation or bits of melancholy description . . .

Have you seen the film *Son of Mongolia*? There is a review—quite inadequate, though—in the same issue of *The Nation* as your review. I feel so sure that you would like it that I wish I could urge you to come and see it. It is taken in Mongolia, with a native cast, and set in the most beautiful scenery—great icy plains, and ruined palaces, with many fat little horses (like Ming horses) running around, and there are some very strange sights: a native wrestling match mingled with queer dancing, and gorgeous painted palace doors opening to reveal a tank bristling with guns, etc. I find it's only going to be here three more days and I am planning to see it on Monday afternoon. I am afraid that such short notice is impolite, but I should be so glad if you felt you could come to see it with me then. It is taken without artificial sets, and it is almost entirely spontaneous—and very funny, too.

I am enclosing a poem that Mr. Zabel [of *Poetry*] has accepted ["From the Country to the City"]. I wanted to know if, as I feel, it may possibly be an example of "rainsoaked foppishness." In the last part I am referring to the peculiar effect of the headlights on the telephone wires ahead, driving at night . . .

[T W O]

1937 - 1945

KEY WEST, EUROPE, NEW YORK

In Key West around 1940.
Photo by Lloyd Frankenberg

To Marianne Moore

Keewaydin [Fishing Camp]
Naples, Florida
January 5, 1937

From the few states I have seen, I should now immediately select Florida as my favorite. I don't know whether you have been here or not—it is so wild, and what there is of cultivation seems rather dilapidated and about to become wild again. On the way down we took a very slow train from Jacksonville here. All day long it went through swamps and turpentine camps and palm forests and in a beautiful pink evening it began stopping at several little stations. The stations were all off at a tangent from the main track and it necessitated first going by, then stopping, backing up, stopping, starting again—with many puffs of white smoke, blowings of the whistle, advice from the loiterers around the station—all to throw off one limp bag of mail.

Louise enjoys fishing more than anything else in the world, I think, so until she left yesterday we have been doing chiefly that—and it is very good here. At Naples a long pier runs out in the water and the entire village seems to spend its time fishing off it. The pelicans gather there, too, and wait to take the fish off the hook before you can pull it in. They are very tame—on the beach you can walk right up to them, and then they just *walk* away.

The other day I caught a blowfish, who began to puff up as I pulled him in. Three pelicans immediately rushed over, holding up their tremendous bills, and by chance the blowfish, who was just snagged, fell off the hook right into one's mouth. By that time he was as big as a large-sized balloon and the poor pelican was very puzzled as to what to do with him. He paddled off with the other two after him; then he dropped the fish and another snatched him. They kept it up for quite a while—it was really like a basketball game. The fish was clever enough to keep blown up all the time. Finally he chose the right moment, deflated, and disappeared like a wink—the pelicans hurried back to watch our lines again. Most of them have brown heads, but once in a while you see one with what looks like a fine wig of peroxide blond. There is a place up the river here where they nest; I am going to row up someday soon and try to get some pictures.

We crossed to Miami on the road through the Everglades and saw all along the way the strangest and most beautiful birds. I am ashamed that I do not know more about them; they are mostly different kinds of herons, blue and white, and some small, pinkish doves. There are little chameleons all around and I am going to keep some in my room to eat the mosquitoes. The shells I have sent by Louise I'm afraid may be duplicates of those sent by Monroe Wheeler, but I think there may be a few new ones. And I am afraid you probably had to get the janitor with his axe to open the coconut.

This morning I have been working on [the story] "The Sea & Its Shore"—or rather, making use of your and your mother's work—and I am suddenly afraid that at the end I have stolen something from [MM's poem] "The Frigate Pelican." I say: "Large flakes of blackened paper, still sparkling red at the edges, flew into the sky. While his eyes could follow them, he had never seen such clever, quivering maneuvers." It was not until I began seeing pelicans that my true source occurred to me. I know you speak of the flight like "charred paper," and use the word "maneuvers." [MM, in fact, does not use the word.] I am afraid it is almost criminal. I haven't the book here and I wonder if you will tell me just how guilty I am and forgive what was really unconscious. When I think of the care and time that you and your mother have taken with that poor story, I feel that you should both be quite out of patience with me. I only hope that from now I shall be able to notice my own roughness and lack of natural correctness better. I have taken over, or gobbled up like a pelican, everything you suggested except one: "It is an extremely picturesque scene . . ." You say you feel it to be too "automatic." In a way, that was what I meant it to be—I was, I suppose, making fun of an automatic reaction to the scene I was describing and I wanted, as the only "moral" to the story, to contradict, as quietly as possible, the automatic, banal thing that one might have said: "How *picturesque*—He looks like a Rembrandt!" That is, the conclusion of the sentence, "but in many ways not," is really thought of as being spoken in a different tone of voice. However, if this oversubtlety (and, I'm afraid, superiority) on my part did not make itself plain to you, there must be something very wrong and I'm going to try to change it and convey the idea a little more clearly.

You are no comfort to me, at all, Miss Moore, the way you inevitably light on just those things I knew I shouldn't have let go. I must be unusually insensitive to be able to bear being brought face to face with my conscience this way over and over. I mean in [EB's poem] "A Miracle for Breakfast." I knew I should not let the "bitterly" and "very hot" in the second stanza go. It is as yet unsolved. The boisterousness of "gallons of coffee" I wanted to overlook because I liked "gallons" being near "galleries." And the "crumb" and "sun" is of course its greatest fault. It seems to me that there are two ways possible for a sestina. One is to use unusual words as terminations, in which case they would have to be used differently as often as possible—as you say, "change of scale." That would make a very highly seasoned kind of poem. And the other way is to use as colorless words as possible—like Sidney, so that it becomes less of a trick and more of a natural theme and variations. I guess I have tried to do both at once. It is probably just an excuse, but sometimes I think about certain things that without one particular fault they would be without the means of existence. I feel a little that way about "sun" and "crumb"!—

but I know at the same time it is only justified about someone else's work.

I am glad you approve of the quotation. I am reading [Pascal's] *Pensées* for the first time and I find them so full of magnet-sentences that accumulate strayed objects around them that I shall be very much ashamed if I do not return with a sort of poetic-calendar or birthday book of my stay here. Or it may be just a happy correspondence of the book to the scenery—the French *clarity* and the mathematics fit in so well with the few, repeated natural objects and the wonderful transparent sea! I feel as if I were made from the new Du Pont bendable glass . . .

I am sending a little literature from a peculiar sect that has a village near here. They took the measurements that prove the world to be concave on this very island, I think . . .

To Horace Gregory

American poet, critic, and editor Horace Gregory (1898–1982) co-authored A History of American Poetry: 1900–1940 *with his wife, the Pulitzer Prize–winning poet Marya Zaturenska.*

> Naples, Florida
> January 14, 1937

I sent you a postcard two weeks ago, but maybe it was lost, to ask if you had been able to use my poem "A Miracle for Breakfast" in the *Forum [and Century]* group or not. If it didn't get in that, I wonder if I can have it returned to me here. I have since made several corrections in it. Perhaps you never even received the poem—I don't think I ever heard. I wonder if you could send a card here and tell me if you received it, and if so what you've done with it, etc. I'd like to prevent its appearing anywhere in the present condition.

> Friday [undated]

I wish I knew more about the ethics of these things. Is there any book on the subject that you could recommend? "The Weed" is the poem that Mr. Zabel has, but does not like much and is keeping "provisionally." I'm sure that if you happen to like it, it could be withdrawn. Miss Moore likes it very much, but no one else seems to.

"From the Country to the City" I sent to Mr. Z. over a week ago and haven't heard from him yet. If you happen to like it best, *maybe* I could withdraw it—and of course it may get sent back any moment. I think it's probably the best, but I'm not at all sure. Anyway I should like to have you see it . . .

I don't know who the other poets you are gathering are, or what the material is likely to be like—but in case it's all "social consciousness," etc., and you'd rather keep up a united front, I am sending "War in Ethiopia." Of course it is very out-of-date, and I am not sure whether my attempts at this kind of thing are much good, but I should like to have you see it, too, and tell me what you think. It's completely free. [This poem apparently has been lost.]

I guess "The Weed" is the best bet—if only you like it. I may have some more finished in a day or two if you don't like these at all. Please remember me to Mrs. Gregory.

[undated]

I think you had better not count on me for anything more than "The Weed." I'm sorry I am so unprolific, but I don't seem to get anything else finished.

About the picture—I think I said to Mrs. Gregory on the telephone that I should think the best way would be for Mr. [René d'] Harnoncourt (if that is the name) to write to Mrs. Crane and ask for an interview, etc.

I'm sorry about the poems. I'm afraid I'm not doing much except work on the long one now. I'd like to be able to publish a volume fairly soon.

To Marianne Moore

January 19, 1937

. . . I didn't know, until Louise wrote me, that you had made a trip *yourself* to get [Minnow] the cat—she is so heavy—and Miss Mack, whom I've never seen, must be an undesirable person to have forced her on you that way—I am so sorry. Minnow's bites and scratches made me realize once more her savage character, and although you say "my omission" beside the poem, I am sure *that* is Minnow's, too. I think you have "caught" her hairiness very well, particularly on December 23rd. Louise also told me about the nine clams, and remarked that she felt Minnow had you "completely at her mercy." Oh dear! I hope that sometime you will quarter an elephant with me, or a bushmaster.

I had been baffled by the *Periodical*, but admiring the vulture's head, for several days. It would look so well as a mask in Aristophanes' *The Birds*, don't you think? To wind up my tedious thanks: I put a little of the pablum powder on my tongue every once in a while and savored every one of its minerals and vitamins. I had never realized how much was "in" the Sunday supplement to the [*Brooklyn Daily*] *Eagle*—but of course I like what you have to say of Dr. Williams best: "Temperament does not change," and "Dedications . . ." The English have a very "classy tone," I think, but they sound like phonograph records, cracked ones, of Auden. I was interested to see that he used, I think, the "Ode to Evening," because

I am trying to finish something in the same shape. I have just finished reading *The Ascent of F-6* ([reviewer] Day-Lewis is wrong on every point). I find much en- and dis-couragement in it.

. . . Could you tell me where and when what you are writing on Cocteau and the Surrealist Exhibition will appear. Please just *tell* me, and I can get copies—I insist on this . . .

[P.S.] I have changed, very feebly, the second line of the second stanza of "A Miracle" etc. to:

> *In the bitter cold we hoped that the coffee*
> *Would be very hot, seeing that the sun—*

I wonder if perhaps you could also *tell* me where I could read *The Infernal Machine*—I mean who published it, etc. I never said how wonderful I thought your remarks on Cocteau in the review of *New Directions* [anthology] are.

February 4, 1937

I am very grateful for the pages from the *Sun*—the picture of Oedipus and the Sphinx and the beautiful flower arrangements, although it rather upsets me that they insist Roanoke is the island of *The Tempest* and not Cuttyhunk, as I dearly believe. The Museum of Natural History magazine came yesterday and I am so glad you had it sent to me. It is really strange, I have been angry with [them] for years because they don't make a good photograph of that wonderful exhibit of the man's and horse's skeletons together. And now I have it, as well as that of the 'possum and beautifully compact horned-frog skeleton, which reminds me of the large crabs I found along the beach here—the enormous claws, bright red and blue, fit in around the body like parts of a puzzle together. Thank you so much . . .

I had a letter from Louise in which she was very pleased because you had gone to [Orson Welles's] *Faustus* with her, and worried because of the poor seats. She said you had been having a difficult time buying a *hat*. I do hope you have succeeded in finding one that comes up to your (extremely high) standard of chic.

The purpose of my trip to Fort Myers was to see Ross Allen wrestle with his alligator and give a lecture on, and exhibit of, snakes. I do wish you could have seen it, Miss Moore. I am so sure you would have liked it. He had two tremendous diamond-backed rattlers; they popped balloons with their fangs, and you could see the venom springing out—it was in a floodlight. Then he extracted venom in a cocktail glass set on a little white table. The rattling sounded like a sewing machine. He had some other beautiful snakes, especially one, a long shiny "chicken snake" vertically striped black and yellow. The Harlequin Coral snake is too small to exhibit that way, but I have seen some lovely ones, and some puff adders. Did you know—I didn't before—that when the puff adder plays dead and rolls on his back, a little blood actually trickles from his mouth? The part of the show devoted to the alligator was memorable chiefly because Mr. Allen wanted to creep up on it (in a big swimming pool) unnoticed, and yet go on with the lecture. So he slid into the water, and went right on talking. It was quite a sight to see his large solemn baby face apparently floating bodiless on the surface of the water, while from it came his imitations of the alligator's calls: the "bellow," the love call, the warning, and the social call. Alligators are very "love-like" according to him, and he described how the female runs away from the male looking coyly over her shoulder; they touch noses and hug each other with those stubby arms. Then Mr. Allen grew embarrassed and his head vanished momentarily under the water. When he gave the "social call," the alligator came right toward him. Afterwards he put it on its back and hypnotized it with two strokes on its stomach; it relaxed completely and its eyes shut . . .

I was with a young woman [Charlotte Russell] who is a teacher here and her husband [Charles "Red" Russell], who is in charge of the pool, the lectures, etc. (one of those men who go off shooting panthers with bows and arrows), and afterwards we had dinner with Ross Allen, whose table conversation consists of imitations of animals and birds. "Now this," he would say, "can be heard for seven miles," and we would all murmur, "Pretty." In spite of my extreme danger of being tedious, I should like to tell you where we ate: on the porch of a little tumbled-down white-washed shanty, owned by Aunt Seline, who serves chicken, rice, beautiful rose-red tomatoes, etc., salad bowls of raw oysters. She is 77 years old, a Cuban Negress; there are two rooms to her house, decorated in the Spanish way with nothing but palm-leaf fans and straight chairs set against the walls. She has one lantern to cook by, and one for people to eat by; sometimes she brings things out on the porch, sometimes she hands them through the window. "Heah's your cream," she said, handing out a little tin of condensed milk. Green glowworms crawled all over the porch screens as we ate . . .

I am sorry I let "The Weed" appear in the *Forum* [*and Century*]. I don't like the other poems at all, and even my own, there, although I am sorry for such conceit. Do you think Mr. Zabel would care for "The Miracle" sestina when it is repaired? I shall send him that, I think, and two others I am finishing now. I have written a [lost] story ["The Labors of Hannibal"] here; I am uncertain about it. I am afraid it is tedious and needs more apologies than "The Sea & Its Shore." I was going to send it to you, but I shall do so only with your permission . . . The enclosure you may find even worse than my bad "sparrows" [which Miss Moore referred to in *Trial Balances*]. I have written quite a few small sketches [including "The Hanging of the Mouse"] of this sort and I thought just possibly, if it does not offend, it might interest you. I once hung Minnow's artificial mouse on a string to a chairback, without thinking what I was doing—it looked very sad . . .

If you can think of any object native to Florida that you might want—from alligators to grapefruit—please let me know, won't you?

February 25, 1937

. . . The story was all ready to mail and I became dissatisfied with it. I was repairing it when my story "The Sea & Its Shore" came back from *The Criterion* with *two* rejection slips enclosed, which seemed unnecessarily cruel, don't you think?—and that made me have even more doubts. However, I have added a little and think I shall send it now to you. It is, I'm afraid, not "serious" enough. "The Sea & Its Shore" in the revised version I think I should send somewhere else, if I could think of a place. I have sent "The Miracle" poem and another to Mr. Zabel, quite a while ago, but have not heard from him. I received a letter from James Laughlin IV saying that he would be interested in "making a book" of poems for me this spring. I haven't seen anything he has done excepting the little story "Peonies of Sympathy," in paper, which I rather liked; I haven't written to him yet, but somehow feel like NO. Don't you think, Miss Moore (although I hate to fire these foolish questions at you), that a publisher like Random House, if possible, would be better, *if* I ever had enough worth publishing, of which I have the blackest doubts . . .

Louise Crane sent me this page torn from *Town & Country* [listing socially acceptable female dinner guests, with Miss Moore under the heading "Intellectuals"]. I hope you don't mind if I send it on to you. The red pencil is hers, and I think it is rather funny. I hope you aren't being besieged with too many dinner invitations!

. . . I shall send the story today and possibly enclose a review I've been trying to do—my first—of Auden's *Look, Stranger!* The reviews I have seen I thought were so poor. When I remember your review of Wallace Stevens in *Poetry*, however, my very pen shakes. Once more I am overcome by my own amazing sloth and unmannerliness. Can you please forgive me and believe that it is really because I want to do something well that I don't do it at all? . . .

To Rolfe Humphries

Poet and translator Rolfe Humphries (1894–1969) was in the class of 1914 at Amherst. His books include Europa and Other Poems *(1929) and a translation of Lorca's* The Poet in New York. *He co-edited the anthology* And Spain Sings *(1936).*

April 11, 1937

I have just read your announcement in the *Times* and should like to volunteer my services for the translation of Spanish War poems into English. I have had poems in *Direction, New Directions, Life and Letters Today*, etc. I can read French, also a very little Spanish, and I should be very glad to attempt verse translations to the best of my ability.

May 24, 1937

After having puzzled long and thoroughly on "Francisca Solana," I have come to the conclusion that the poem is not really worth the time and the work of putting it into English ballad form. It could be done as you suggested, but I feel that the dullness of the original would only be increased by the translation. In fact, I feel that a simple obituary notice would be more moving. I am very sorry to be of no more assistance than this, but please believe me, I am as interested and should like to help as much as when I first wrote.

To Marianne Moore

May 26, 1937

. . . Thank you so much for your letter, which lightened my sensation of being AN EXILE very much, and for the wonderful photographs. I had scarcely dared hope you would send the one with the long fingers leaning on the "manuscript" and the typewriter to one side. I shall treasure them all, even though I fail to find a trace of you among the sand dunes . . .

I am so sorry to have been so glum over the telephone. I am so glad you spoke of Louise and perhaps sometime you would be willing to read some of her letters, which I think are quite remarkable for their humor and selection of detail, without being at all descriptive . . .

Hôtel Foyot, Paris
August 9, 1937

. . . All the way through Ireland Louise and I told each other how much this or that reminded us of you, how we wished you were along, how well you would go with the Irish countryside, etc. Now I only wish I had written to you, as I should have, while we were still there. I wish much more that I could see you for a few minutes. I can't think of anything that would be more of a consolation. As it is, I'm sorry to be writing a letter that I know will cause you much distress.

Louise, Margaret Miller and I were in a very bad automobile accident, the 19th of July, coming back to Paris from a trip through Burgundy.

Louise and I were quite uninjured, but poor Margaret's [right] arm was completely amputated, between the wrist and the elbow [*sic*]. She is recovering very well now, in the American Hospital here, but you can imagine what she has suffered and has still to suffer and what the past three weeks have been like.

It was the most freakishly cruel accident I have ever heard of. We were forced off the road by a much larger car, on a curve, and the car skidded in the *sand* at the side. There was nothing Louise could do. The car overturned and then righted itself, throwing us all out, and we suppose that Margaret's arm must have been caught for a second as it turned— of course it all happened so quickly no one can say.

What has helped more than anything else is Margaret's courage. — She began to write with her left hand the second day after the accident. There is a wonderful surgeon here, and although it takes a very long time—a month longer at least—she is doing very well. Mrs. Miller arrived last week. We didn't want her to come until Margaret was stronger, but she is very brave and calm.

Margaret had a student insurance which will cover the medical expenses, Louise's car insurance will provide a very large "compensation"—so one does not have to worry about that side of it at least.

We feel it will probably be much better if Margaret can keep right on traveling when she is well again, instead of going home. To keep "going" is the main thing—not to let her feel that there has been the slightest interruption in her work, once she is out of the hospital. (The surgeon says she will be able to draw and paint eventually, too.) I imagine we'll go to Italy in the fall, and then I don't know where. [Before continuing, EB drew a line.]

I think you will like the pictures from the Dublin Zoo. It's the nicest, most informal zoo I have ever seen. Did you know that they raised lions there? Sometime I want to tell you about Merrion Square, the wonderful flowers, the beautiful things we saw at Trinity College and in the museum. I hope you didn't mind my two examples of Primitive Art—one found at the Orphanage yard at Montargis (part of the hospital where we first took Margaret after the accident), and [the] other my own naïve version of a Foyot room.

Mrs. Macpherson [the writer, Bryher] is expected to be at this hotel sometime soon. She has been writing to me urging me to be psychoanalyzed because of the asthma!

Thank you so much for sending me *Poetry* [July 1937], Miss Moore . . . I think my contributions ["A Miracle for Breakfast," "From the Country to the City," "Song"] looked rather weak—and I didn't realize they would use your name in that way in the Notes. I do hope you don't mind and I'm sorry. I have been doing quite a lot of work lately. Do you think that *New Writing* would be a good place to send a story? (Which I should like very much to have you see first sometime when you are not too busy.) . . .

[P.S.] My aunt writes that Minnow is *enceinte*. I'm afraid she will make a very severe mother.

September 7, 1937

Before your letter came I had tried in vain to semaphore myself back into normalcy by putting one of your pictures in the mirror frame (the one with the fingertips resting on the little heap of "work" —the eyes have the same look as they do in pictures where it says underneath "The third from the right in the group of spectators is the artist himself," or "The artist's favorite child") but, probably because Louise has a very languorous picture of Proust on the other side, it wouldn't work. Proust appeared in my "primitive," and I feel that I must tell you, because I am sure that one would interpret him as a picture on the wall by my bed instead of something tucked in the mirror frame. But your letter, which I can never properly thank you for —it represents so much thoughtfulness and actual *work* as well—has been such a consolation. Things are gradually resuming temporal proportions.

Margaret is recovering very well. They did the skin grafting two weeks ago and it has been completely successful; she has not lost a single graft, which is quite exceptional, I guess. It is a fascinating process—they take specks, a little larger than a pinhead, from the thigh, and transplant them and after a while they begin to grow and spread together—about 200 of them. (I hope I didn't tell you this before.) She is writing very well, but slowly, with her left hand, copying Ronsard as an exercise, and yesterday she had done a really remarkable drawing, all colored, of the view from the window—the Eiffel Tower, etc. The lines were perfectly clear and firm. So we are not worrying so much about whether what resides in the right hand is in the left too, or not. But of course she is so thin and weak—looking more than ever like one of those half-starved acrobats of Picasso. It is heartbreaking.

It was so kind of you to want to send a present. I have several things in mind I think she might like, but I thought I would wait until Saturday when Louise gets back. She was finally persuaded to go—much against her wishes, but she needed a change very badly—and visit her mamma a few days and drive back with her to Paris—and have her help me decide. The franc is so low now that we shall be able to get something extremely nice for that check's worth. But I shall tell you the particulars. Margaret will probably be out of the hospital in ten days—so we hope —then when she can travel we may go on to Italy, but everything is unsettled.

Your reassurance and *illumination*—I enjoy the "carp's evolution"* very much—in the matter of psychoanalysis were extremely welcome. I am so afraid I may have been rude to Bryher in the notes in which I tried to escape making an immediate appointment at the Freudian clinic. I am still hoping to see her here sometime soon—it might be easier to explain verbally. She says, "Psychoanalysis makes one write better and more easily"—and if that were true of course one would want to reap its benefits whether one had asthma or whooping cough—but everything I have read about it has made me think that psychologists misinterpret and very much underestimate all the workings of ART! "Psychoanalysts do not see the poet playing a social function, but regard him as a neurotic working off his complexes at the expense of the public. Therefore in analyzing a work of art, psychoanalysts seek just those symbols that are peculiarly private, i.e. neurotic, and hence psychoanalytical criticism of art finds its examples and material always either in third-rate artistic work or in accidental features of good work." That is from *Illusion and Reality* by Christopher Caudwell—have you seen it? It is a very confused, uneven kind of book, but nevertheless very worthwhile, I think. I am now reading *The Meaning of Meaning*, which I like much better than the other [I. A.] Richards books, but I find that kind of reasoning very hard to concentrate on and remember, anyway.

I have no typewriter with me and I am waiting until Miss [Sylvia] Beach [of the Shakespeare & Co. bookstore] gets back from vacation (the 6th) to copy some things. She has spoken to me of a place near here where one can go and do typing. You don't mention the *Dictionary*. I am wondering if you are too depressed by the weight of obscenity that seems to keep language going . . . I am so sorry about the Murray Hill [Hotel]'s ungracious attitude. We shall put it down to the "American tempera-ment." We are so tired of having things explained to one as the "French temperament"—and Margaret's nurse, the same one I had, a Russian, and extremely nice, is always explaining her Dostoevsky moods by saying, "It's the Russian temperament." (We have decided to make "American temperament" cover all deficiencies.)

Mrs. [Dorothy] Norman has written to me. She lives in Woods Hole in the summertime and Louise knows her—once upset her husband in a rowboat, I believe. She wrote me that the magazine [*Twice a Year*] would pay, "but less than commercial magazines." Thank you for mentioning me to her, and I do hope that the magazine will turn out well.

I am very distressed at present because I have received a note from Edward O'Brien saying that "The Baptism" was "quite high on his list"

* This may refer to Miss Moore's note for her poem "The Plumet Basilisk," which cites a source on Chinese dragons: "There is a 'legend of the carp that try to climb a certain cataract in the western hills. Those that succeed become dragons.' "

of [*Best*] *Short Stories of 1937*. It makes one feel like "Miss Wisconsin," and I am sure it means nothing but THE END . . .

Hôtel d'Angleterre
Rome, Italy
November 24, 1937

. . . Paris (and the Île Saint-Louis in particular) does not suit me very well, so I began to develop a fine case of asthma. Louise and I went to Arles for a week (I think, if you received the cards, that some were of Arles and Les Baux) but it didn't work at all, and I rushed back to the American Hospital for a week or ten days. (I hope I never see the place again.) Then came the ordeal of the French trial.

We all, including Mrs. Crane and her chauffeur, and two lawyers and an insurance man, had to go to a little French town, the seat of the county in which the accident occurred, and stay at one small hotel. The French court procedure is very interesting, but it is a very delicate affair because Louise, in Margaret's interest, had to be judged guilty—yet without having her sent to jail. It was an awful moment when we watched her back, very chic in a new Paris *tailleur*, as she stood up before the old judge and he said, "Guilty!" But a small fine was imposed, so everything turned out very well.

The asthma got worse and worse until my limbs were quite sievelike with needle punctures, and so when the lease on the apartment ran out, Louise and I came here—two weeks ago—where for over a week now I have been perfectly all right. Margaret and her mother are in Paris, as she still has to be near her doctor and the masseur . . . She had been talking and talking about writing to you, so you may have heard from her now, but in case she hasn't written yet, I must tell you what we did with your present. We finally decided on the "Editions Tel"—do you know them?—those big folders of excellent reproductions. They are very expensive in America, but in Paris you can get three of them for your very generous gift. I bought the *Sistine Chapel* set, when she was still sick, because it was one I was sure of, and she was delighted. Now she has *Giotto*, and I don't know what the third is to be.

. . . Minnow—I don't know whether you received my ode on hearing of the nativity or not—had five kittens, two males and three females of all possible styles and colorings. At present Louise and I are planning to sail for New York with from two to eight owls. I think I described to you the kind we saw in Morocco—stubby, fluffy, placid little owls that sat along the side of the road. They sell them in a shop here for a horrible purpose—to be used to attack other birds, for the hunters. They are very tame and friendly, although when we asked the man what they ate, he replied "Hearts!"

I saw the enormous bronze pinecone in the Vatican. It must have made a beautiful fountain. It is in a courtyard, with the peacocks on each side (you probably have a photo already, of course), but visitors can't get into the courtyard. I became quite frantic hunting for it, and then a guard took me to a window, opened it, and there it was right below. We have been sightseeing strenuously and systematically and I should like to describe many infinitely described things to you . . . But in the words of a fascinating guidebook we have, composed mostly of quotations from 18th- and 19th-century travelers, "My presentiment of the emotions with which I should behold the Roman ruins has proved quite correct."

To Frani Blough

On board S.S. *Exeter*
December 10, 1937

I was very glad to get your letter yesterday morning before we left, and so glad to hear that the reason why I haven't heard from Margaret is because they have left the hotel where my telegrams went. Now, of course, I am worried for fear I may be inconveniencing her by leaving— but then I guess she has had enough time to tell me definitely if my staying was really important. I hate to leave Italy, but it is necessary to get back to get to work, I think—and if I manage to get a book under way soon, as I rather hope I may, I shall certainly have to be there. But I'm going to come back to Italy just as soon as I possibly can; it is a wonderful country—or was . . .

This boat is so *silly*. But our manner of making it was a little undignified too—the night before leaving Florence we all ate oysters. They have the *quaintest* system there, my dear. The restaurants themselves don't sell fresh seafood, but a few old men go around with little trays and buckets of ice and a couple of lemons. They wander in and out of the bars and restaurants with all kinds of ancient and decaying shells on their trays. The sweetest old man served us—and wore three vests and a woolly sailor's coat, and long black fingernails which he used to flip the oyster over in its shell before serving. The result was that Louise and Nina were horribly sick all night, and I was not quite myself. We started off, very pale and hollow-eyed, in a taxi with eight pieces of luggage, two paper parcels with loose strings, an umbrella, and the owls in a cage—and poor Nina was sick in the taxi. At Genoa it was pouring. We were the only people getting on the boat and even we weren't expected, I guess—and we staggered down long slippery docks, no porters, no signs, no gangplank. Then it immediately grew rough (much rougher than the oysters) and from seven last night till this morning we have clung in agony to our very hard narrow beds. The owls have retained their composure . . . They balance beautifully, but as Louise says, "They are probably used to branches."

We are now at Marseilles for a day. We reach Boston the 23rd, New York the 24th. It [the Export Line] is all very American, and they seem to be keeping up so much "tradition" about their exclusive services, etc., that it is in some ways like visiting at Mt. Vernon. It is half freighter and 37 passengers—supposed to be 125—mostly consuls going home for Christmas. We are the *youngest*, we have been told, and so I suppose we are expected to be the life of the other 35, but if this weather keeps up — The cabins are very grand: showers, beds, couches, etc., and it is a very nice little boat.

Now I have just been warned by the clean, young, gum-chewing purser (everyone is awfully "clean-cut") that, if we go ashore, to take a taxi immediately and not to go over there to the right because it's the toughest part of Marseilles. Of course we can hardly wait. They have a list of *21 Rules*, one of which is "Please don't indulge in horseplay or rough games." It's a little like Walnut Hill: we dress *twice* in the course of the trip, but it isn't *compulsory*, and you mustn't wear high heels for any of the games. The food is also similar to Walnut Hill, but the waiters are such agreeable young football players, who also chew gum.

Now we are going to go ashore to buy some wine to take back with us, try bouillabaisse, etc. I'd send you a bottle of champagne only I think there's a high duty in Switzerland. The lute and the flute sound awfully nice—you might write me the names of some pieces to practice on the clavichord so I'll be ready for you. Is your report *oral?* Perhaps the "*Lux et Tenebris*" window at Les Baux would interest your Lutheran class-mates . . .

To Horace Gregory

Murray Hill Hotel, New York
December 27, 1937

I have returned to my native land and as usual I am very ignorant of "literary" affairs. I wonder if you could tell me when material is supposed to be sent in for the next *New Letters*, and whether I am permitted to try again? I guess I haven't said yet what an excellent piece of editing I think you did . . .

To Marianne Moore

Key West P.O.
Florida
January 20, 1938

It is very nice here; I wish so much that you and your mother could come here sometime, I am so sure you would like it. The sea is so beautiful—all spotted and striped, from dark black-blue to what my aunt calls "lettuce" green. And there are such wonderful plants and trees. For some reason, all the trees in the Key West front yards are labeled, just like in a museum, so it is all very instructive. The landlady just presented me with a "Devil Rose," and some "Heavenly Beans." I have found a nice large room for $4 a week, so you see how inexpensive it is.

Just before I left town I found that poor Louise had had to go to the hospital—where I think she still is, although I had a note from Mrs. Crane that she was improving.

I am enclosing two poems and a sort of joke (made out of a sentence in Dostoevsky's *House of the Dead:* "Money comes and goes like a bird"). I think that [number] 1 is the only possibility—or have I become too trivial for words—or tears? It is an awful dread, but please tell me what you think; I find it awfully hard to drop to the rear, or rather from the rear, *out.*

I like [Wallace Stevens's] *The Man with the Blue Guitar* [1937] more and more . . .

January 31, 1938

I have just been re-reading as "conversation" (it is so frightfully lonely here) your three forwarded and re-forwarded letters that reached me in New York, and I have decided that my skimpy notes are *shocking*—besides my having put you "on the spot" with those bad poems. Here are my best snapshots, so far, of Key West. I tried to take [the statue of] the Elk so that the front of the "lodge" or "temple" would show too, with the result that I tipped the camera. Also three elderly "elks" were watching me from the verandah in a rather unfriendly way. I want to take a great many pictures of the wooden houses with their scrollwork verandahs, and the sweet little Negro children too.

My landlady, Mrs. *Pindar*, is a very nice person. She and her husband also run a grocery store. They are very devout people and sing hymns all day long and on Sundays they sit rocking on the verandah outside my window and have long solemn conversations about "willpower," etc. There is another "roomer," a Mr. Gay, whom I am gradually writing a story about. His room is filled with what he calls "novelties," which he keeps in cigar boxes; they are all leaves and seed pods, etc. They all seem to have such violent names: he just gave me a "Rose of Hell," and there are "Woman's Tongue," "Crown of Thorns," etc.—the last is a very strange plant; I shall try to bring one back with me to show you. I am very much tempted to send *you* a cigar box full of dead leaves and assorted seed pods—it seems to be the thing to do—but my own room is beginning to look so unhealthy with them that I shall spare you.

I finished a story a few days ago which I wanted to send to you to see what you thought of it—but I had just received a letter from the

Partisan Review asking for a story by February 1st, if possible. I sent it to them and now of course regret it very much and hope they will send it back. My motives were doubly corrupt: they are going to have a $100 "contest" and I thought I should like to try. It is called "In Prison" and is another of these horrible "fable" ideas that seem to obsess me. Perhaps Mr. Gay will make me more Katherine Mansfield-ish! I am working very hard on a great many "projects" all at once but it is like running up and down in front of a stone wall.

The houses here, with all their scrollwork that looks as if it were cut from paper, are very pretty, and everyone has rows of magnificent plants all across the railings of the lower verandahs. The little cottages where the Negroes live have the most gorgeous plants of all. The plants appear to have "sapped the strength" of everything else in town. Down the street is a very small cottage I can look right into, and the only furniture it contains beside a bed and chair is an enormous French horn, painted silver, leaning against the wall, and hanging over it a pith helmet, also painted silver. The Negroes have such soft voices and such beautifully tactful manners—I suppose it is farfetched, but their attitude keeps reminding me of the *tone* of George Herbert: "Take the gentle path," etc.

My "family" seems to like it very much. Louise is still in the hospital, I think, but she will be leaving soon . . . Mrs. Pindar just came in to say she had heard over the radio that the barometers had "dropped 40 degrees in two hours," "up North," and tonight it will be doing the same thing here. Her eyes were so big that I think we are about to barricade the house for a hurricane. I hope nothing of the sort is happening to *you*.

To Frani Blough

February 7, 1938

. . . [I have] an awfully nice room—very large, and all boards painted yellow, and four long windows. In Key West they keep the shutters closed all day long while the sun is hot. Two of them open onto the upstairs verandah—all scrollwork, and a big tree. Also the landlady's pink bloomers, which she hangs on the tree every morning . . . It is right across from the courthouse and every day I can watch the convicts in their black-and-white stripes, at work. They are allowed to be "at large" here during the day, and they have to "report back" to the jail at nine o'clock—otherwise they're *locked out*! I saw a woman who lives around the corner washing her husband's convict pants in the back yard. It is such a nice town—I hope you'll come here sometime. I just purchased a history of it, written in 1908 by a retired judge, who threw in everything he could remember or had been told . . .

I had lunch, in New York, with Mary [McCarthy], [Frederick] Dupee and [Philip] Rahv (it is Rahv that's Mary's friend, isn't it?) [editors of

Partisan Review]. It was at a horribly crowded Schrafft's, and I'm afraid Mary and I rather monopolized the conversation—until the two gentlemen got into an argument about whether it is all right to tell a lie. (Is there any such *thing* as a lie? etc.) I thought we made an awfully tough-looking group. Dupee is so pale and scrawny, and his eyes were very bloodshot, and he has scars on his face. The other man hadn't shaved for a long time, and Mary looked rather white and raffish. And oh dear, what we didn't say about the Communists! I really think the three should announce themselves honestly as Trotskyists, because that's what they are, I think. I received the last number [of *Partisan Review*] a few days ago—it isn't very interesting except for an excellent article on the N.Y. Shakespeare productions by our Mary. They almost forced a story from me before February 1st, and now I wish I had it back ["In Prison," published March 1938]. Dupee used to be friendly with Ted Wilson, and now they despise each other, of course—and first I heard one side, then the other. I really don't think they're very *bright*—except Mary. This morning Ted sent me some Lenin pamphlets and he has underlined *every* emotional passage and written the most amazingly childish comments in the margin. I am thinking of joining the Anarchists, only I can't seem to locate headquarters where I can find out exactly what their *platform* is . . .

I'd love to travel with you some more, but I guess this is the best place for a while. I am doing absolutely nothing but work, scarcely ever read, and the results, for quantity anyway, have been quite satisfactory so far. I have my aunt and uncle here, you know. I eat dinner with them every night—they seem to like it very much, fortunately . . . I am thinking of renting a catboat—$25 a month.

To Marianne Moore

529 Whitehead Street
[Key West, Florida]
February 14, 1938

I cannot imagine *why* I left without leaving you the picture of the Temple of Paestum. I often become slightly confused at the very point of bestowal and feel that perhaps, after all, it is inadequate or unwanted—but I'm sure I thought you admired the Temple as much as I did! I am glad that you liked the leaves and I do hope they arrived wearing something of the original coloring. They fade fairly slowly, but they do fade. It was a "Sea Grape" . . . I am enclosing another—the front side is yellow marked with a marvelous blurred (as if done on blotting paper) cerise, at the moment, I'm afraid it will be faded, but you will still be able to see the peculiar linings on the back . . .

You mustn't mock my simple fancies about the Negroes, George

Herbert, etc. I will try to surprise you with a poem about them soon. The *Partisan Review* accepted the story, but I hope I shall be able to make several changes before they print it. I am so afraid you will not like it. I have just had another letter from Miss Norman, and I am wondering if you think that to send the two little "sleeping" poems ["Sleeping on the Ceiling" and "Sleeping Standing Up"] to her would be all right.* I have another story, though, that—if you are not too busy (but please tell me *truly* if you are)—I should like to have you see. *Twice a Year* might possibly like it.

Louise was so delighted with your visit; she wrote me about it—in fact, her illness has been very nice in that way—I have received quite a few letters! Margaret Miller sent me a book of *Atget*'s photographs of Paris—I had been wanting them for a long time. I hope I can show them to you someday, they are really marvelous. But perhaps you know them already . . .

We have a Carnival here now, set up on the vacant lot beside the burnt-out deserted cigar factory. It is quite a thorough little Carnival with a high-diving tower, a merry-go-round, trained apes, etc., and I hope to be able to make some photographs of it worth sending to you.

Louise sent me *Literary Opinion in America* and [William Carlos Williams's] *White Mule*. I am so glad to have your articles on Henry James and Wallace Stevens in permanent shape; also to have Mr. Zabel's article on *you*, although I have a strangely horns-in attitude about it! I enjoyed *White Mule*, but it does seem to have more weight than energy, don't you think?

Thank you so much for your "extenuation" on my behalf to Mrs. Macpherson [Bryher]. And thank you too for the picture of the child desiring the elk stickpin. And "unleavened bread"—that is *exactly* what the Sea Grape's leaf's edge is like. There are whole books of leaves here I wish you could see, only most of them, I'm afraid, are too perishable. My "family" gave me a "Crown of Thorns" plant (I talked about it so much, I guess) for my birthday, in a pot. The flowers are very small and brilliant scarlet, with a clear, glue-like drop in the middle that makes them look like little carelessly put-together artificial flowers.

P.S. I've decided I can include a leaf called "Woman's Tongue" (the one that rattles). Also some castor-oil beans, which may be squashed, but are very pretty if they aren't.

P.S. 2. This is about my landlady, whom I am really very devoted to: "*Sunday at K[ey] W[est]*. The rocking-chairs / In rapid motion / Approach the object / Of devotion. / Rock on the porches / Of the tabernacle: / With a palm-leaf fan / Cry Hail, all Hail!" I am going to try to get a picture of the Elk at night, illuminated.

* Both poems were published in *Life and Letters Today*, October and November 1938.

Louise came down about two weeks ago and we were both so sorry to hear that you are still not entirely recovered . . . Louise received *American Stuff* [anthology of stories] here. I'd ask her for a detailed comment only she's gone fishing—but we've both been enjoying it. I thought that almost every one of the stories had something very interesting about it, didn't you?

I am sending you (although it may easily break) the "sting" of a Stingray Fish or Stingaree. Of course it isn't a "sting" at all, and is properly called the "danger bone," I think. You probably know that the Stingaree looks like a long gray skate, and the sting lies out along its tail. Last year at Naples I saw a fisherman do an impromptu dance on the beach after a fish haul—holding a Stingaree by this bone, between his teeth, and twirling round and round. I wish I could provide you with an equally vicious weapon against all these marauding ills.

I shall also send the March *Partisan Review* with my story ["In Prison"] in it, if you will please not try to see a word of good in it or say a good word for it . . .

To Frani Blough

May 2, 1938

The beautiful scarf, kindly forwarded by Mrs. Miller, has just arrived. I admired them all last summer, displayed in Hermès' window, but always felt they were quite out of my class. Thank you *so* much. I shall do the Rumba with it at Sloppy Joe's—with a tight white satin evening dress—Saturday nights, and in between times keep it draped on the wall. Saturdays and Wednesdays are Rumba nights there. One of Joe's "girls"—there are six of them—is the Key West champion, and she is really wonderful, very very Latin, and fat, really more exactly like a Lachaise in the flesh than anyone I have ever seen, with very small feet and hands, and legs that taper in an almost isosceles triangle from the knees—five dimples in each, down. The last time I saw her she wore baby-pink satin, skin tight, no undergarments, and used a small raspberry-colored scarf . . .

I wonder how you liked Arles, and Les Baux, which has become a recurring dream with me—and the countryside in general, which I thought was wonderful . . . I begin to wish I weren't where I am, but I'm just going to stay here for a long, long time, I'm afraid. Lately I've been doing nothing much but reread Poe, and evolve from Poe—plus something of Sir Thomas Browne, etc.—a new Theory-of-the-Story-All-My-Own. It's the "proliferal" style, I believe, and you will shortly see some of the results. There was an indication of it in the March *Partisan Review*. But now I have an idea that quite a nice little operetta, very slight, could be made out of the scene witnessed here every week when the fortune-teller comes to "cut the cards" for the landlady, Miss Lula. The landlady is very deaf, and she sits up holding her little apparatus, which gives her a rather ecclesiastical look—the instrument is always going wrong, which might allow some effects of that wonderful loud *harshness* they have. (I've been listening to Bessie Smith records recently.) And a lot of nice songs could be made out of a book I'm (and everyone else in Key West's) reading, *Aunt Sally's Dream Book* . . .

I have a little Victor record player that attaches to the radio. It is quite good; and a lot of records I got from Sears, Roebuck, hoping to do an article on "modern American Ballads"—the Negro ones are the best: "That Bonus Done Gone Through," "Riding to Your Funeral in a Ford V-8," and I may be able to do something with them, but it is almost impossible to find anything about who is composing them (they appear all over the South within three days of any major news event, it seems) . . . Ted Wilson sent me a record he thinks is "marvelous"—Duke Ellington's "I've Got To Be a Rug Cutter." Well, it sounds all right to me but I'm afraid there must be a *double entendre* to "Rug Cutter"—it just says it over and over. Do you know of one?

Louise and I engaged a Negro woman to be our cook, etc. (taking for granted that you know we bought a house)—very tall, very black. She looks forty to me but she says she's a great-grandmother. Well, I find she is the leading contralto or something with "The Island Singers Choir." She has pictures of herself singing in it, so perhaps when you come to visit us we can have concerts. I'm afraid I probably appear at least a grandchild to her, and she's begun to call me "chile" already . . .

I wonder if you could tell me the edition, etc., of William of Aquitaine? I could order it through the French bookshop in New York. Also any other such things you feel I should know. I hope sometime you will loan me *The Mediaeval Mind*. If I get as much done in the next two months as I hope, I may come North this summer. It is frightfully lonely here, of course, but I seem to get quite a lot done. I think we'll rent a little catboat and I remember you like to fish. (If you are with Margaret, I think I extended the invitation to her and, as I remember her fishing with the greatest pleasure, she *must* come.)

To Marianne Moore

May 5, 1938

I had been postponing answering your letter about having received the crabs because I wanted to enclose in it a poem I had been working on. Now, of course, your extreme thoughtfulness has again outdistanced my industry, and I am very sorry and embarrassed. I am so glad to hear that you are much better, and to have it fortified by Louise, who on one occasion even said you were "very peppy."

Between Louise's helpfulness and my vanity I'm afraid you received two copies of *Partisan Review*. Thank you infinitely for what you say about my story—you can read my mind so well. Of course a flaw goes all the way through. I've been having some meditations this morning on the theme of the criticism you imply so gently. I was curious to hear what you thought of the story, because it is the first conscious attempt at something according to a *theory* I've been thinking up down here out of a combination of Poe's theories and reading 17th-century prose! I am writing another one now which I hope you will like better. It does attempt to be a little more "important." If only I could see half as clearly *how* I want to write poems. I wish sometimes you would tell me quite frankly if you think there is any use—any real use—in my continuing with them.

Have you seen Louis MacNeice's *Poems*?—that's the kind of spotted, helter-skelter thing it seems so easy to fall into. Some people can do it and nevertheless say what has to be said by them. I can't seem to. The "tentativeness" you object to is partly my bafflement by, and fear of, such shortsighted and, I think, ignorant views—not in general, but in application—as say, Ted Wilson's . . .

That's why I was so glad you mentioned Dr. [Reinhold] Niebuhr, the only living "minister" I've ever thought of at all that way. Where did you hear him in New York? I bought his last book last spring, but never had time to read it . . .

It is spring here now and the Royal Poinciana trees are in bloom all along the streets—brilliant flame color or dark red. Also a large tree—Spanish lime?—that sheds in some places fine green powder all over the streets, very pretty. Jasmine makes the whole town smell sweet at night —and all the cats have kittens. There has been the ugliest mother cat I have ever seen, and two kittens, in the yard of the little house we're buying, for five days. I don't want them—they are crosseyed, mangy, and mixtures of white, black, orange, gray and tiger—but they are growing so thin I couldn't stand it, so I took over a bottle of milk, and now they obviously consider themselves *mine*. The mother looks just like Picasso's *Absinthe Drinker*.

My chief delight at present is the Negro—mulatto, rather—carpenter we have working on the house, Milton Evans. He looks Miltonic—epic, at least—a "chieftain" type, with an enormous head (he must wear a size 25 straw hat), long bony features and deep-set eyes. He is by far the smartest, most conscientious person I have talked to here yet. He catches on to my most "modern" ideas right away, and yields to them with great dignity. He has ten children—the two oldest are working their way through college. Today he is wearing a pale blue shirt with a 6-inch-high, flourishing monogram "E" on his heart. His only fault is that he can't pronounce "v," and when I took him a bottle of Coca-Cola he said I was "wery, wery kind."

. . . Ted loaned me [Dr. Williams's] *In the American Grain*. I was rather disappointed in it, but I did think some of the remarks about Negroes were very good, and mean so much more than any of the novels, etc., I've read about them. I want very much to attempt something about them myself—those I have anything to do with here are all so *good*. Their cheerfulness is amazing—as Cootchie, the maid here, said to me the other morning, "That why I like colored folks—they never commit suicide."

I knew there were some bad spots in "In Prison." Perhaps sometime when I come North and you aren't too busy, you could check them with a pencil—no, it would be better if I fix them all myself, I suppose. I impose on you too much, besides these endless letters.

624 White Street
Key West, Florida
June 2, 1938

. . . I'm afraid you spent much too much time on my wretched story. When I look at your corrections I'm amazed at how naturally awkward I am. And thank you for sending on the other letter too. I remember in the 5th or 6th grade, in *précis* writing, the teacher confounded me by saying that there actually were people to whom a description "of a forest" meant more than the "forest" itself. I never believed her, but now I know that to send you a postcard is to get back something worth a thousand of them!

The house seems perfectly beautiful to me, inside and out. In the yard we have 1 banana tree, 2 avocados, 1 mango, 1 *sour-sop*, 1 grapevine (1 bunch of acid-looking grapes) and 2 magnificent lime trees, one loaded with large limes. They are such thorny trees, but all the different shades of green are very pretty. We have all sorts of insects and lizards, of course. I have just read a terrifying tract called "The Truth about Termites." Someone leaving town presented me with a homely little half-grown cat called "Sister." Her only charm is the way she runs up the window and door screens, suddenly looking at you to attract attention while she perches way up in the air spread out like a spider. My other part-time companion is a pleasant, plump black girl called *Mizpah*. Milton Evans, I discovered, is also a lay preacher on the side (I'm afraid dear Milton is a little priggish).

There are a great many questions I should like to ask, but I am coming North this Sunday, I think, so I shall postpone them . . .

To Frani Blough and Margaret Miller

June 3, 1938

Here is an envelope of odds and ends, most of them requiring some explanation. This week's *Life*, my dears, is devoted to the subject of

"American Youth," and two whole pages are labeled *Vassar* and consist of the drawings of Jean Anderson and Anne Cleveland (University Coop Bookshop, 75¢). I was going to send you the whole thing, but decided it would be too much of a shock—you'd probably both go and jump off the top of the Colosseum in embarrassment.

The enclosed photographs aren't much good but will give you an "idea." I think I'm looking awfully suave. The group includes Charlotte ["Sha-Sha" Russell], the girl I met last winter, married to the man who shoots with a bow and arrow. He's making one of those Grantland Rice Sports Movies now, so she came to visit me to get away from it all. They have five cameramen whose names were Rem, Rod, Russ, Ron and something else like that, and an *airplane* to take pictures from. Her husband's name is Red.

Also Mr. [Gregorio] Valdes, our new Key West Rousseau. Did Louise tell you how we got him to do a big painting of the house? It's awfully nice—he put in a parrot and a monkey, several types of strange palm trees, and the sky "all pinkee," as he says. So when we hung it on the wall we had a *vernissage*. Mr. Valdes had a wonderful time, I think. It was rather exhausting for us, though, because he speaks scarcely any English, and he stayed from four till seven. We had sherry, which he seemed to regard as just "wine." He kept saying "More wine" and he finished off the bottle, while Charlotte and I became sicker and sicker. The high point of the affair was when he and Charlotte imitated mosquitoes and buzzed around the room. I'm afraid I may be the serpent in the Rousseau "Garden of Eden," because the book he is holding is that *Art in America*. But it was so hard to talk to him, and he was enchanted [with the book] and took it home with him. Since our patronage he has changed his sign (a palette stuck on the front of his cottage) from "Sign Painter" to "Artistic Painter" . . .

I'm going North on Sunday the 5th, and *flying* to Miami, my first flight. I'm scared to death but they say it's so beautiful—all the Keys that I want to see . . .

I'm reading Emma Goldman, etc., and have just about decided to sign up with the Anarchists—or jump in with them, I think, is a nicer way of putting it. Why not join me? It's marvelous—all you have to do, apparently, is read Emerson's *Essays*, Whitman, and other equally dated and unpleasant works, and advocate "free love." Emma: "Then I met that grand old sex-rebel, So-and-So." A few page headings, in consecutive order, from her autobiography: "I meet Fedya / I, too, loved beauty / Fedya objects most to ugliness / Johann Most: preceptor / I dedicate myself to Most's happiness / I advocate free love / I am drawn to Sasha / I go to the opera with Most / Most proposes public speaking for me / Commemoration of the Chicago martyrdoms / Sasha makes love to me / I give myself to Sasha / I respond to Fedya / I belong entirely to Sasha"—and so it goes.

One of the reasons why I like Key West so much is because everything goes at such a *natural* pace. For example, if you buy something and haven't any money and *promise*, in the most New England way, to bring it around in half an hour and then forget for two weeks, no one even comments. And as soon as anyone has worked for a week, they "knock off" for two or so, and drunkenness is an excuse just as correct as any other. We bought a palm tree from a man who said it would be, planting and all, $20. Last Sunday he reeled to the door—I had to keep pushing him up by the shoulder to explain that when he said $20 he was drunk and I could have had it for $15—and he said, "Or $10, it doesn't make any difference."

Were you in Rome during the reception of Hitler [by Mussolini]? I think the band breaking into the wedding march (as reported in the papers here) was very funny. Louise writes me *appalling* stories of Margaret's mother's gay life. Has she confessed to you about her trip to the [Harlem] Savoy? Don't *overdo*, children.

To Marianne Moore

Finally asked to address Miss Moore by her first name (more than four years after their correspondence began), EB celebrates the occasion by drawing the name large and as if lit in electric lights.

La Residencia
523 West 113th Street
New York, New York
[July 12, 1938]

DEAR MARIANNE : *(electric light)*

Thank you very much for your note, which proves again how unnecessary my explanations always are and how adept you are at "getting" people. I am enclosing the poem I showed you the other night just to show you that I have attempted to fix it . . .

This [dormitory] seems to be a very good place to work. I have done a lot the last four days, and it is certainly amusing—the animation at mealtime is quite overwhelming. I am even saying "Pass me the sugar" and "The boy has my pen" in Spanish. The book about animals in Rome is really wonderful—I'm sure you must want it back. I also like some of the Merrill Moore sonnets—in bits, never a whole fourteen lines . . .

This place [La Residencia] is very battered, and has a slight madhouse air, but I don't mind it at all. Everyone is very friendly and the food—Spanish, which I prefer to the same class of American food, at least—very good. Everyone sings all the time. The cook and the housekeeper meet on the stairs and have a duet. The boy brings up the suitcase to a wild folk song. For a few weeks, as a gangster hideaway, it is all right, I think. This is not a letter.

c/o Loren MacIver
Box 333
Provincetown, Massachusetts
September 10, 1938

This house here has proved to be so nice, I am sure you would like it. The man who built it was a woodcarver, so it is very well made, with slightly arched beams so that it looks like either a ship's cabin or a freight car. There is one long window facing the ocean and the table, which I guess was his workbench, runs along under it. I have a Chinese keg to sit on, found on the beach. They are much more elegantly shaped than our barrels, with Chinese letters, painted in red, carved on one stave. There is a footstool made from a piece of driftwood with pegs stuck in it. Then there is a stove which looks slightly like some of Picasso's sculpture. It was made from an iron oil barrel from Japan, and has lettering all over it in white paint.

The house is right on the edge of the beach. There has been wonderful surf, and lots of *dulces*—have you ever eaten it?—which is the most beautiful color of purple and green. [Painter] Loren [MacIver, her hostess] said a large Irish family used to come here to gather it every year, and the grandmother always referred to it as "the lovely dulces."

The kite was a great success until I put it up in too strong a wind the other day and broke the cross arm—but I'm getting it fixed. I actually had it up a *mile* one day. It looks wonderful that high up over the ocean and gets rather wasp-waisted, but I blistered my hands pulling it in. One evening several barn swallows (the pink-breasted ones) tried to light on the string, and seagulls have flown right at the kite itself several times.

There seems to be something stupefying about living this close to the ocean. I am ashamed to think I have been away from New York this long and haven't written to tell you how much I enjoyed my last evening with you, and to see how well you and your mother are. I'm sending a sort of jingle about the white horse and if you think it "worth her while" perhaps you could give it to her. I think it should be called something like "Spleen."

[*Continuing the same letter*]   September 21, 1938

Oh this is really frightful. I shall be glad to get back to the South, where time seems to pass more slowly. I kept this letter open all this time because I wanted to enclose two poems I have been working on, but they still do not quite satisfy me, and all I can enclose is this cloudy photograph of Louise and me sent me by one of those N.Y. companies that take your picture unawares on the sidewalk.

My friend Frani Blough brought me a whole collection of little books of Provençal poetry. I had never read any except the quotations in Pound's essay, and I have been reading it a great deal, and also "Mother Goose," which I brought along too. Between Peire Vidal and "The House That Jack Built," I have enclosed some rhyme schemes that I hope will impress you—or *amaze*, anyway. I do hope you are well, and that you will forgive my seabound silence.

[Key West, Florida]
January 14, 1939

It is one of the rare rainy days in Key West and I'm sitting in the magnificent "studio" we found for Loren MacIver, rather sadly watching the leaks begin and the rain trickle down over the newly whitewashed walls. They [Loren and poet Lloyd Frankenberg, her husband] are coming the end of the month. It is an abandoned grocery store just around the corner from our house—one huge room. We put in a sort of skylight and had it whitewashed. I am writing at what was the counter, pushed against the wall. It is an awfully nice place—I hate to give it up! Last week I found such a nice little house to "work" in; a tree on one side and a vine on the other almost hid it. The walls were lemon-pie yellow, and the doors were white with raspberry-pink panels. The woman who was going to rent it to me had it all fixed so nicely—a green table and three chairs, a whatnot with a bunch of wax roses on top, and lots of pictures of movie stars on the walls. But of course she didn't tell me there was a *machine shop* just across the lane.

I put off writing originally because I wanted to send you "something"—a sample, at least—when I did, but I have done NOTHING although I try hard every day, honestly. Then the many things to thank you for began to mount—not that it is a chore to thank you, but my discomfort grew and grew. Then I wanted to write before the Cuban products got there, to say that you mustn't be conscientious about eating everything—they were really for the labels, and I'm so glad you liked the musical-instrument side, which I placed uppermost on purpose. The olives taste violently of garlic: WARNING. I think you would like our Cuban coffee bags, too—*Brazo Fuerte*, or something like that, with a strong arm and fist printed in red, but I thought I remembered that you don't drink coffee. If you do, we'd love to send some; it is quite different from the American kind.

The ASHTRAY—that is what we use it for—is so nice and goes so well with everything. We keep it on a "modern" table that we had a local cabinetmaker build for us—it looks very well. I must thank you for sending the horse, too, who now stands on a cupboard with our shells—and for the books. I have just started to read [Niebuhr's?] *Beyond Tragedy*— just the first chapter, which I like, but it is a little more popular than his other books, isn't it? And then I must thank you for giving *Vogue* my address—in an awful rush of worldly ambition I *wired* them my birthday, etc.—but now I think the plan, whatever it was, has been given up.

Key West is nicer than ever. I don't believe I have ever told you about Mrs. Almyda, our wonderful housekeeper. She is very solemn, gentle, and *good* as gold, and a very good cook for all the exotic local dishes that we eat—turtle, conch-shell chowder (the inside of those beautiful conch shells), etc. What I like best about Mrs. A., though—aside from her character—are her exclamations, which are almost *heavenly*. "Oh my precious love!" (that's for breaking a dish, or any catastrophe), "Oh my blessed hope!" etc.—and at anything you tell her that surprises her, and so much that we say seems to, she says "Oh hush!"

I'm sending a snapshot of the back of the house—showing one lime tree—and one of Mr. [Gregorio] Valdes's paintings of the front. Even the angle of taking it hasn't rectified his perspective, but we were so proud when Mr. Cahill, who is the head of the W.P.A. Art Project, was here and saw it. He said it was very good and wanted the local W.P.A. Art Project to give a *Valdes Show*. We were delighted because of course no one here pays any attention to little Mr. Valdes, who is very poor and sick, too—and they all used to make fun of our pictures by him.

The other day I caught a parrot fish, almost by accident. They are ravishing fish—all iridescent, with a silver edge to each scale, and a real bill-like mouth just like turquoise; the eye is very big and wild, and the eyeball is turquoise too—they are very humorous-looking fish. A man on the dock immediately scraped off three scales, then threw him back; he was sure it wouldn't hurt him. I'm enclosing one [scale], if I can find it. Mrs. A. is confronting a huge fish in the kitchen right now—Red Snapper, but it is gilt-rose. Oh how I wish that you and your mother too would sometime visit us, in the two-month Jane Austen style. There are so many things we'd like to show you—only of course we'd be *shown* so many more. I'd like to go on but I must divide items of interest with Louise, I feel. I was so glad to hear about Margaret from you. She has been typing us some wonderful long letters lately . . .

February 13, 1939

Perhaps Louise will have been able to see you before you receive this and will give you the news from this newsless bit of the world. I had a letter from Margaret in which she said that Key West has "such a beautiful cartographic presence the way it flies off the state like the arm of a spiral nebula." It sometimes makes one feel just as remote—which is not supposed to be an excuse for the awful way I did not write before. Loren and Lloyd are here now and it is all very quiet and hardworking, particularly since Louise has gone North for a couple of weeks. She seems to be a magnet for all odd people, animals, and incidents. Loren is painting a large picture of the red kite just now, I think. We have [the kite] here and intend to go flying it—on the town dump—as soon as there is the proper breeze. It is very warm. Every day we go swimming about noontime. The water is so calm we look as if we were dipping ourselves through a sheet of milk glass—very pretty—with those wonderful scissor-tailed man-of-war birds hovering up above . . .

I shan't say any more about "working" or not working to worry you. Things are really going better now, though. I have had such bad habits. Loren is a consolation in that way—she just goes right ahead. Please tell me if I haven't missed something of yours this fall or winter—I feel sure that I have, but I see so few magazines, etc. . . . . Well, I shall "tell you goodbye," as Mrs. Almyda says.

Sunday morning
[February 19, 1939]

Louise wrote and told me that you were still rather worried about your mother. I do hope she is completely recovered by now. Is it the cold weather, do you think? Is it an "allergy"?

Yesterday we had the great thrill of seeing our PRESIDENT [Franklin Roosevelt]. All Key West stood on the curb all dressed up, holding little flags and clapping respectfully. He is much better-looking than I had thought. In his speech he made the awful mistake of referring to Key West as "this pleasant village"—and the Key West *Citizen* reported him as saying "this pleasant *city*."

When I wrote before I forgot, or avoided, I guess, saying that a while ago I sent what I thought were my best poems to Random House, and they refused them. Do you think that James Laughlin would be a good person to try next?—he might possibly still be interested. I am trying to take it as an indirect blow at my laziness rather than a judgment on the poems themselves—oh dear. I wish I had told you before.

Last night we had the honor of having Dr. [John] Dewey to dinner. Did I tell you that he stays here with his daughter [Jane]? He likes Loren's pictures and came to see her after she arrived. He is such a wonderful old man, and *so cute*. The dignity of dinner was interrupted by Mrs. Almyda's rushing in, wild-eyed, and crying, "Where's Baby?" We had let him [the cat] out, to continue his flirtation with the beautiful gray Persian next door. They have been making eyes at each other all week, through the shutters, in real Persian style, except that Baby was on the inside and the gray cat was on the outside, mincing around on the lawn. —I think I should like to read one of Dewey's books—is there any one that you would recommend in particular?

March 29, 1939

. . . It seems so unfair to have us all here brown and fat and bicycling around in the sunshine and to have you in what must be a dreary, slushy New York, and your mother so sick. I wish I could think of something nice to send you both. There is never really anything but the baskets of oranges, but maybe I shall try some of the local green turtle consommé out on you . . . Mangoes are coming in pretty soon, though—the trees are loaded—and you must have some of those—they are marvelous.

There has been an almost-epidemic of kites in Key West this month. All the mommas seem to know how to make the prettiest ones, very tiny, out of tissue paper and three crossed sticks. Most of them have fringes. I have seen such pretty ones, pale pink covered with dark blue hearts and blue fringes; yellow and green and blue, etc. Every evening there are dozens up, over the palm trees, with long tails, not the kind we know, but a single strip of cloth that sways slowly, like a serpent. I asked Mrs. Almyda where they get the tissue paper, and she said, "All the stores keep tissue paper because of the paper roses." The Cubans make wonderful bunches of paper flowers to decorate their little blue sitting rooms, and they keep paper streamers up all the time to decorate the ceilings, like a children's party.

I have been painting tin cans and wooden tubs robin's-egg blue all week, to plant ferns, begonias, carnations and caladiums in. Baby [the cat] is so interested, and I can see him now out walking from can to can sniffing. We have a hummingbird that I wish I could send you . . .

To Charlotte Russell

The Russells—Charlotte, whom EB usually addressed as "Sha-Sha," and her husband, Charles, an Olympic athlete nicknamed "Red," were Floridians from Fort Myers who became lifelong friends of EB and Louise Crane.

418 West 20th Street
New York City
July 15, 1939

I came North—flew—rather unexpectedly about ten days ago and since I got your letter telling me about your father's death, Louise and I have been sending telegrams to various places we thought you might be at. We got so worried, and we were so glad to receive your letter two days ago. Oh Charlotte, I am so terribly sorry. I know how badly you must feel. I can't say more.

Louise and Loren found this apartment just before I came up. It's just two big rooms in a very quiet part of town, with a kitchenette, etc. If you and Red do come up, *please* stop and see us. I think we might manage to put you up, too, though—yes, I just lay down on the sofa and find I am not too long. Louise has gone to Woods Hole for the weekend; she has to go every weekend. I think I'll be going to visit my aunt next weekend, otherwise I'll be here for the next two months. Lloyd and Loren are in Provincetown till September. I spent yesterday in the Museum of Modern Art, where I've almost lived since I came back, seeing all the old movies, etc.—and saw the "horrible" *Shock* for the first time. It is awfully nice. Lloyd [Frankenberg]'s book [of poems] is to be called *The Red Kite* and has a picture of it on the cover.

Oh please plan to arrive in the middle of a week when we'll both be here, although I'll probably be here every weekend except next. Louise has bought a *case* of Scotch and one of wine. We keep them in one corner of the living room since there's no other place for them, and since just to look at them makes me feel ill, I think they will have a very good effect on my life and work. That and the fact that General Theological Seminary is right across the street and I hear their bells to prayers every hour or so.

I liked your story about Freud very much. Would you care to hear a simple sort of dream I had the other night? Someone handed me a watch—one of those black ones with luminescent figures, and said, "This is a Negro watch." I said, "Oh, I get it! *Blackface!*" and it seemed so extremely funny that I woke myself up laughing . . . Anna B. just told me over the telephone that last night she dreamed someone at her office asked her how big her apartment was and she answered, "Oh just a birdcage and bath." She is rapidly becoming a Radio Big Shot, I think. She writes a daily program of *News for Women* which comes at 9:15 a.m. I think. I've forgotten the station. She's had quite a hard time making ends meet since Queen Elizabeth left, though.

We have Louise's Victrola here and *Les Sylphides*, which I play several times every day, and sort of moon around the room. If you and Red really come, I promise you some more Chopin—there.

Darling Sha-Sha, please don't feel too badly. You can certainly "stand on your own feet" if anyone can. Take care of yourself. Please come and see us and we'll have some mild form of fun—the World's Fair, maybe? I haven't seen it yet . . .

c/o Lindsey
137 East 28th Street
New York City
[October 11, 1939]

Louise has just finished hurriedly reading me your letter on the telephone, and by now, I suppose, she is halfway to [the town of] Dalton—to witness Judy's wedding, or rather the wedding reception, because Judy is marrying a Catholic—all her New England family are horrified. I was so glad to hear from you. I'd been wondering and wondering if my last postcards had been too strong meat, or what. I am so glad you are going to start building the house—and I'd *adore* a trip through the islands—do you suppose I could paddle my own weight? The lease of the apartment was up on the 1st of the month and I moved to the Murray Hill [Hotel], but the air was so mid-Victorian there that it gave me asthma. Fortunately, the Lindseys decided to go to North Carolina for a week, so I'm here at their apartment until the 18th, when I have a reservation for chair, bed (and jolly good fellowship, I'm afraid) on the *Silver Meteor*. I might stay a week longer, but I don't think so. Please do come to visit me in Key West, and please let's take a trip of some sort—we might see a submarine and Red could shoot it with his bow and arrow. Mrs. King—remember our speaking about her—the one who hated Naples so—is probably coming to Key West this winter, and Loren & Lloyd are coming back, we hope.

Two of our [Gregorio] Valdes pictures—the big one of the house and the little one of the road & the palm trees—are now at the Museum of Modern Art. An exhibit of "Unknown Painters" for the trustees, etc.

The little schoolchildren in the school across the way are down on their knees saying their last prayers for the afternoon. Now they're up again saying some more, with their hands pointed together. I am carrying on a correspondence of waves and giggles with a little girl beside the window who will undoubtedly be moved tomorrow. It is *horrible*. They are memorizing the same awful old poems I did at Public School—you know the one that goes:

> *The snow had begun in the gloaming,*
> *And busily all the night*
> *Had been heaping field and highway*
> *With a silence deep and white.*

And then goes on with:

> *But I thought of a wood in sweet Afton,*
> *Where a little headstone stood,*
> *How the snowflakes were covering it gently,*
> *As the robins the holes in the wood*

And comes to the finish—that warped me emotionally for years:

> *—and I kissed her,*
> *But little did she know,*
> *My kiss was given to her sister,*
> *Buried deep 'neath the drifting snow . . .*

I have the clavichord here and am taking a few lessons—that's really why I stayed on—before I bring it to Key West. The Lindsey house is amazing—absolutely *everything*, à la *Good Housekeeping*. I just polished a silver mug, and now I'm going to polish my shoes—complete equipment for both. All that bothers me is the crumbs I make and can't get out of the carpet . . .

To Frani Blough Muser

The marriage of Frani Blough and Curt Muser had taken place in December 1938.

Key West, Florida
[November 1939]
. . . I got the clavichord here all right and have it in one of the bedrooms. I decided the living room was too large, at least with all the windows open the way it always is. Now I am frantic because I know it *must* be a little out of tune here and there, and I can't tell, and I'm afraid any local tuner would have worse ears than my own. What do you suggest? I practice in the evenings to the sound of palm branches waving over my head—very strange. I got that Kirkpatrick album—and don't you like the Rameau things? But I like the Scarlatti best. Kirkpatrick has been giving concerts in New York. Oh I'd give anything to hear that *Leçons des Ténèbres*! It is such a marvelous title—but Couperin has such marvelous titles, and then I never like the music so much—like Max Ernst. I feel a little foolish about the whole thing. I know Ralph K. thought I was an idiot and he was simply humoring me.

Louise is coming down next week, and then, my dear, we are going on *a canoe trip*. Red and Charlotte Russell . . . and another man who is a photographer. We're going down through the "10,000 Islands"—from island to island for about ten days (not a hundred islands a day, I trust). They're supposed to be very beautiful, all kinds of birds, shells and fish, and some beaches. A few are inhabited by poor whites who will probably rush out and shoot us. Never mind, we have two shotguns, a harpoon, and a bow and arrow along. I simply loathe canoeing, but you can sail a lot of the time . . . My idea is to make an article out of it, also advertising for Red, because he hopes to take several trips this winter with wealthy sportsmen, etc.

I realize I must have picked up that expression "simply loathe" from our very British friend, Mrs. King, who arrived a few days ago. She's terribly cute, about sixty, I suppose, although so well preserved it's hard to say, with a habit of referring to her divorced husbands as "my American-ex" and "my English-ex." She is staying at a hotel here, and we fell into the pleasant habit of spending the afternoons first in a Cuban café, then in a bar for a "spot" of Scotch, while she told me various secrets of international divorce and high life. She simply terrorizes the natives with her very English Panama hat, her stick, and her flow of English English. How she makes herself understood I don't know. I find it much more expedient to say to Mrs. Almyda, "No, I don't want none of them tomatoes today" than to say it right.

Oh dear, it is such a *beautiful* Sunday afternoon. I wish you and Curt were here to take in the baseball game, go swimming, have a frozen Daiquiri, etc. Is there any possible chance of your getting down?

I'm having a very minor poem ["Cirque d'Hiver"] in *The New Yorker* next week, I think [it appeared January 27, 1940]. They've asked me for more and I hope I'll be able to supply them because they pay one dollar a line. Otherwise I'm working on some long poems I hope to sell to *The Nation*—and a little book Loren and I hope to do together this winter— in fact, we hope to do two. They [Loren and Lloyd] are coming in a few weeks, bringing another painter friend. I sometimes feel just like Aeneas.

I have a lettuce bed, radishes, carrots, mint, parsley, etc. Also a trowel and a pair of gloves—exactly like a Helen Hokinson. Nothing ages one more than gardening, I'm sure.

To Marianne Moore

> 624 White Street
> Key West, Florida
> November 20, 1939

I have now heard from four separate sources that you were the most ravishing of the personages at Louise's tea party the other day. You and the opening of the Picasso show [at MoMA] fill every letter, until I'm beginning to wonder why I left New York. I wish at least I had written to you right away when the impact of all this greenery, this *beautiful* house, Mrs. Almyda's saintliness, etc., were freshest. I kept thinking that in a day or two I'd have so many wonderful poems to enclose, but of course I still haven't . . .

Now that the weather is nice, I've embarked on a great planting plan. There is an old, old Negro with white hair and a large white mustache here this morning "budding" a rosebush. I thought it would be spectacular to have white, red, pink, and yellow roses all on the same bush. He has tied it up in little rags like curl papers. I have also planted a ravaged-looking palm tree, and I *hope* to get a ten-foot Night Blooming Cereus planted in the front yard to make Louise open her eyes when she arrives. Mrs. Almyda had a permanent wave this summer and when I got here both she and the yard presented the same appearance of baroque abandon.

Viking sent my works back, too. I am now hesitating between trying Knopf and Simon & Schuster. Mr. Laughlin [of New Directions] wrote me about his latest anthology idea—five or six poets at a time—but I'm afraid I didn't like that idea very much either . . . *The New Yorker* took the little poem about the toy horse—only I changed the title to "Cirque d'Hiver." They want some more . . .

December 15, 1939

We came back from the canoe trip over a week ago, and found your nice long letter here waiting . . . Our trip through the 10,000 Islands was a great success. I wish I could have had you in the bow of our canoe, instead of Louise, who did not do her share of the paddling. She lent a very civilized note to the expedition, however, by holding a portable radio on her knees most of the time, and twirling the dials when I frantically begged her to backwater or look out for breakers, etc. etc. She was also the *only person* to tip over. She was out fishing by herself when it occurred. At first she was too proud to shout for help, but she finally gave her famous Pekinese call and Red went to her rescue. We were gone five days . . . I wrote an account of the trip day by day. It's not very good but there are some things in it I think you might enjoy . . .

In a wild moment I sent my mss. to Simon & Schuster. They had written to me several times, ever since I was in college, but I imagine they want a novel. I haven't heard from them yet, but when they return the mss. I am thinking of writing to Mr. Charles Pearce [poetry editor of *The New Yorker*], since I have learned that he and two other people are starting a new publishing house [Duell, Sloan and Pearce] . . . I haven't answered [James Laughlin] yet, but I somehow feel one should refuse to act as Sex Appeal [as the only woman poet with four males], don't you? . . .

I've never seen W. H. Auden, although I've always wanted to. Thank you so much for mentioning me that way.

To Frani Blough Muser

January 26, 1940

. . . That apathetic after-holiday mood has set in. It was all very trying here. Louise came down the day before Christmas, and *three* Spaniards—it was a little too much Latinity for me. Spanish seems to make so much noise when spoken by more than one. However, they all left in a few days, except Louise, who just went back last week. Her career as [musical] impresario is getting more and more impressive, and she is now "professional," I believe, and about to have an office on Broadway.

The chief problem is to think of a name for the whole business and the records that are to come later. I think and think but can't seem to surpass "Victor" or "Columbia."

I haven't any news about myself at all except that work progresses as slowly as ever and gets harder and harder. Did I tell you that a poem of mine called "Roosters" is to be in *The New Republic* in February in a literary supplement, I think? Hope you like it. Its presence there, and a large check for it, were due to Mr. [Edmund] Wilson, who has been extremely nice to me—writing letters of advice about publishing, etc. The literary highlight of the Key West season at present is James Farrell, who *looks* tough, maybe, but is just like a lamb that can swear—no, a sheep would be more accurate. I am utterly disgusted with "social-conscious" conversation—by people who always seem to be completely unconscious of their surroundings, other people's personalities, etc. etc. I am going to take him to church to see if I can instill a little respect.

Key West is as beautiful as ever. I'm beginning to think it has a sinister "hold" on me . . .

To Marianne Moore

February 5, 1940

The controversy about the colors of the rosebush has been settled—the grafts turned out to be another of Mrs. Almyda's "rascals." And *all* the roses are nothing but ordinary Rock Roses, pale pink . . . [The gardener] doesn't dare come back now, and has cut off his income of stray dimes and quarters . . .

I have one Key West story that I must tell you. It is more *like* the place than anything I can think of. The other day I went to the china closet to get a little white bowl to put some flowers in and when I was rinsing it I noticed some little black specks. I said to Mrs. Almyda, "I think we must have mice"—but she took the bowl over to the light and studied it and after a while she said, "No, them's lizard" . . .

I am so much hoping to see some of your new poems. I am sending you a real "trifle" ["The Fish"]. I'm afraid it is very bad and, if not like Robert Frost, perhaps like Ernest Hemingway! I left the last line on it so it wouldn't be, but I don't know . . .

February 19, 1940

What I think about *The New Yorker* [rejecting a poem by MM] can only be expressed like this: * ! @ ! ! ! @ ! * ! !

I have been re-receiving and re-rereading your letter ever since it came . . . And thank you for the marvelous postcard, and the very helpful comments on "The Fish." I did as you suggested about everything except "breathing in" (if you can remember that), which I decided to leave as it was. "Lousy" is now "infested," and "gunwales" (which I had meant to be pronounced "gunn'ls") is "gunnels," which is also correct according to the dictionary, and makes it plainer. I left off the outline of capitals [for the first word of each line], too, and feel very ADVANCED.

I am enclosing another poem ["Jerónimo's House," originally called "José's House"] that I'm afraid isn't very good—I just can't tell any more—perhaps if I think about your maxim for Key West I may be able to improve it in some way. I thought something *jiggledy* would suit the Cuban houses, but now I don't know. They pay from $1 to $2 a week rent, and Mrs. Almyda says, "Poor things, they have to move every month or so, and when they go they clean out even the electric wiring."

. . . Thank you so much for the "Glass Eye and Supplies." I think I remember hearing Louise telling you how fond I am of glass eyes. It is a story I'm afraid you will think a little indelicate. I used to have relatives with glass eyes when I was small and for some reason I worried because I thought they wouldn't go to Heaven. I don't think I was ever fully reassured until I read in [George] Herbert something about

> *Taught me to live here so, that still one eye*
> *Should aim and shoot at that which is on high . . .*

I am so sorry I am going to miss hearing you speak to Mrs. Crane's class. I always miss the nicest things that happen in New York. I hope you have a success *fou* and that the weather is right and you feel well.

[P.S.] James Laughlin now wants me to be #3 in some sort of monthly pamphlets he is getting out. That might not be so bad because it would be only about 30 pages, I think, and everything could be used again in a book after thirty days. I am eager to see your poem and the one, too, especially, that *The New Yorker* * @ !!!

February 24, 1940

. . . I want to do what a young man here calls a "tript-itch" of Key West poems. I am enclosing another one ["Cootchie"] that may be banal, I can't decide. Maybe you will remember Cootchie. I don't know what Miss Lula is going to do without her. She had lived with her 35 years. I am so eager to see your poems—and to have heard your talk. I am expecting Louise's *report* today, but I wonder—perhaps this is too much to ask—if I could *see* it?

Yesterday we went to see the goats again and Mrs. Almyda was telling me about a baby lamb she had as a child. I said was it a ram? and she said, "No, it was an EVE." She and I went to the Flower Show together yesterday and had such a nice time, and this morning she arrived on her bicycle with a mass, about three feet high, of the most beautiful branches of some wild shrub she'd found along the way. We don't know what it is—like a long, pale, raspberry-colored mimosa, with thorns.

March 14, 1940

. . . I simply can't understand *The New Yorker*—or yes, perhaps I can, they want all *New Yorker* poetry to sound like *New Yorker* poetry, on and on. When I think they'd print that monstrosity by Horace Gregory last week . . . One's blood boils and not because this is the subtropics. The first stanza of [MM's poem] "What Are Years?" must be what W. H. Auden has been trying to say for years. We have had such a busy week here I haven't had time and composure enough to read "Four Quartz Crystal Clocks" [MM's poem] properly. Just reading it through gave me the sensation of a wonderful long iced drink—and of course I am extremely proud of the buoy-ball line [EB supplied MM with this word in "the bell-boy with the buoy-ball"] . . .

Thank you for writing so much of your "lecture" for me—and thank you, of course, for the consoling remarks about ME. I hope the ladies all put my name down in their notebooks! I like very much what you say about Auden. I like the poem called "Schoolchildren" too—and the one on Spain has been improved just the right way, I think. But the "cabaret songs" I want to try to better myself. I changed the poem about Cootchie to "The skies were [eggwhite] . . . and the faces sable," but I am afraid you still can't be forced to admire it!

Partisan Review has asked me to write them a "Florida Letter" . . . They are printing "The Fish" this month, I think . . . Mr. [Alfred H.] Barr [Jr., of MoMA] and his wife are in Key West and have been here. He was so nice and appreciative about the [Gregorio] Valdes picture and the house, etc. The two boys who run the poetry magazine called *Furioso*—have you seen it? I just saw the first number with Wallace Stevens, E. E. Cummings, etc., in it—are here now and are "coming to call." I didn't like the number I saw, though, at all. Wallace Stevens was here too at the "fancy" hotel, and Robert Frost. I went to lunch there with Louise's aunt, almost provided with opera glasses, but the only person I saw of any importance was John L. Lewis chewing a cigar.

May 21, 1940

. . . Louise came down a week ago today, full of New York news, but also fatigue, so that she slept most of the time since arriving, on the sofa, under the trees, etc., and we are just beginning to get the benefits of her New York experiences now. She gave me your poem "A Glass-Ribbed Nest" [later entitled "The Paper Nautilus"], which I have just been reading over again. There are so many things in it I'd like to thank you for and praise you for. I admire especially from "wasp-nest flaws / of white on white," to the end. The whole poem is like a rebuke to me, it suggests so many of the plans for things I want to say about Key West and have scarcely hinted at in "José's House" for example. But I will try very hard, and won't write again until I have something of the proper length and depth to send you.

We have been over to see the Hemingways' paintings several times. Have you ever seen that wonderful Miró *Farm?*—with everything in it, trees, hens, fences, etc., and a dog barking at footprints. Mrs. [Pauline Pfeiffer] H[emingway, divorced wife of author] and her little boys play a game with it at mealtimes, the "I'm thinking of something beginning with the letter——" one. We are having a swarm of small, pale gray butterflies in the yard. They are lovely but they are laying little yellow eggs all over everything and I hate to think what new scourge will come from them—although the *termites* seem to have missed us this spring. I want to write some more but Louise says the mail goes in ten minutes . . .

To Charlotte Russell

May 24, 1940

What AGONY!! Is this the Age of Ice, or the End of the World? I hope you have your fireplace in. There's not a single sort of heater to be got in Key West and for the last four days we have huddled in the kitchen and dining room with the gas stove going full blast. The house smells of stale cigarette smoke, rum, food, and *us*, I suppose. It is too, too Russian. Cold seems to bring about a certain physical attraction with an accompanying mental repulsion, if you get what I mean . . .

Lloyd and Loren came about two weeks ago and Louise about ten days ago. I'm not sane, it's all been such a nightmare. Yes, the Laubers came by and we invited them for cocktails last Sunday, with niece. Isn't she amazing? And they also brought along an equivalently fat boy, "Larry"—very effeminate. As Miss Lula says, I can't imagine where they picked him up. *Then* it appeared in the Key West *Citizen* under "Casa Marina Notes," and *then* it appeared in the Miami *Herald* that I had entertained *at* the Casa Marina, causing much consternation of course in the Sheperdson family, etc. Oh how I wish you were here, Sha. Only you, I think, could cheer me up. Mrs. A. says she's never seen nothing like it since she had Eve-ull . . .

To return to the Laubers—I think he is very cute, don't you? The niece had on a wonderful bright blue hat and looked exactly like a Russian doll. She didn't say a single word except "Goodbye." Mrs. L. raved about your house—I wish I could see it . . .

To Marianne Moore

June 8, 1940

About a week ago I received a letter from a Mr. Stanley Young, of Harcourt Brace and Company, asking me to submit a volume of poetry to them. No, the letter is so nice I think I'll enclose it for you to read. I'm not sure quite how, but I am sure that you are entirely responsible for it all, and I want to thank you all over again, and more than ever, for all the things you do for me. If only the poetry were better! I sent it off last Tuesday and I hope so much that something will come of it this time. I, probably unwisely, said that I was afraid the general impression was one of slightness of subject matter, but that I felt that in the work I am doing now I am "finding myself" and that it is more serious, etc. I also sent him the stories.

Louise is here now, being "the life of the party," as Mrs. Almyda says. She comes just at the time of my sudden complete recovery from the flu and pyelitis, which was the real trouble all the time, it seems. But it all disappeared, almost overnight. It is the "rainy season" and we have had the most magnificent thunderstorms almost every day. I have taken a little room in our favorite hotel here to work in in the mornings. The hotel is rather like a ship—all white paint, shutter doors, long red carpets, and views of the ocean, and almost deserted at this time of year. It is very nice. On the third floor (very high for Key West) is a little balcony with a flagpole, and two benches where one can sit and watch the palm trees wave all over town and see the ocean on three sides. It is so pretty—but more and more Navy ships keep coming, and they are building a tremendous airplane hangar. I am very much afraid that this is the last season we'll be able to live here for a long time.

Yesterday morning while we were eating breakfast three very tiny little girls came by, pushing a toy baby carriage. In the carriage sat a very young puppy, almost like a little bear cub. He was so fat he could scarcely move, and he looked so solemn and sure of his position. His name was "Princey." Louise took some photographs and I'll send one if they come out well. My aunt and uncle left yesterday and left their canary with us. We all like him fairly well except Louise, whom I caught insulting him with "Dry up!" He sings almost automatically from dawn till dark, stretched out like the bird in your poem.

I am planning to stay on here until I get the things I am working on finished—probably until the middle of July. Then Louise and I are planning to take a trip of about a month through Nova Scotia. Of course we want very much for you to come on this trip with us. Would you possibly consider it? We shall probably take the boat to Yarmouth overnight, to avoid the long trip through Maine, and then drive around to Cape Breton, where I've never been but always wanted to go, it's supposed to be so

1 9 4 0 [*91*

beautiful. But Louise is going North in about ten days, I think, and she will give you all the details.

c/o Charles Russell
Brevard, North Carolina
September 1, 1940

There are so many things here you would like that if I could only write them properly I know it would give me more courage to write to you—after this other letter from Harcourt Brace which you see is not too encouraging, after my failure with the story I wrote, and after the wretched "ballets." Louise sent me the letter you wrote to her mentioning them, and I can't tell you how much I thank you for the things you said in it— whether I was meant to see it or not! I have just skipped the "ballets" and gone on to what you said about my using rhyme, etc., and that encouraged me more than anything I have heard or done in a long, long time. It has helped me decide how to go about these "serious" poems I always seem to be talking about . . .

This very primitive mountain cabin [belonging to the Russells] had nothing to read in it except all the magazines of the year 1926—on which I now feel myself to be an authority—and one number of *The Dial*, April 1928, which was very nice to see. Margaret wrote me a long time ago that you were writing an article on *The Dial*—I hope we shall see it very soon. Since I came here I have managed to get a few books: Rilke's *Wartime Letters*, which I think are terrifying, but full of wonderful things, and Yeats's *Last Poems*. The thing I like about them best so far being to be able to place the quotation "I must lie down where all the ladders start / In the foul rag and bone shop of the heart," which I had seen somewhere and admired, but I didn't know what it was from.

I should like to let myself go, Marianne, and give you masses and masses of Nature Description, but I am afraid that you may be *displeased* with me because of my recent laziness and miscalculations. So I shall confine myself to just my favorite items: we have the most beautiful spring, cut in the rock, with a big slab of rock laid across the top and covered with moss and vines. The spring runs into another square hole cut in the rock with a huge stone crock, brown and white, standing in it, to keep our milk and butter, etc., in. In this spring lives a bright pink salamander about six inches long, with black freckles. Red brought him up to the house one night and he crawled around on the table under the oil lamp—he is very clumsy. Then there are skinks that occasionally crawl down my bedroom wall. They are all black except for four white stripes down the back, and the tail is a brilliant iridescent purple-blue—like lightning. The woods—we are right in them, almost on the top of a mountain—are filled with Warblers, and Charlotte and I feed them every day—black-and-white Warblers, Black Hooded Warblers—the prettiest

—etc., and several varieties of Woodpeckers. Red said he saw a Pileated Woodpecker, the kind with the tall red crest, but I haven't seen him yet. At night the owls and whippoorwills come right up to the house. We went to see a deer farm in Pisgah National Forest, where they bring up all the baby deer found in the woods on nursing bottles, weigh them, etc. They had about twenty there, all about five months old, quite bright red with lines of white spatters. They are quite tame and *so* beautiful. I wish you could have seen them. And then one more thing—in our privy there is a large bag of white lime, and all the big crickets who live there have got into it and go hopping around all pure white, like clowns, leaving big white hieroglyphics on the walls. But all this kind of nature seems so unsophisticated compared to Key West. [There] it is much, much better, and I am hoping so *hard* that quite soon you will come and visit Louise and me and give us your opinion.

. . . I want to come to New York, but first I think I shall probably stay a few weeks someplace—maybe Beaufort, South Carolina—to see if I can't get something done that will make me feel better able to face my friends. The [war] news seems to fill me with such frantic haste and I am so worried about what may become of Key West.

To Frani Blough Muser

September 1, 1940

I don't believe I'd feel I had the right to write you a letter were it not for the fact that I dreamed about you last night. Louise wrote and told me that you are expecting a baby in February (I'm so glad you stuck to that month and hope you manage to make it the 8th [EB's birthday]). Last night I dreamed that you were wandering around a large open space, a sort of public square, blowing bubbles on one of those bubble pipes, and explaining it to me from time to time by saying, "A bubble within a bubble." Louise also wrote me about your weekend at Woods Hole, which sounded a little strange, I thought, although the thing that seemed to impress her most was Libby Holman doing a *crossword puzzle* in the evening—instead of what? I wonder.

As maybe she told you, I'm staying in a *very* primitive cabin here for a month now, with my friends Red and Charlotte Russell. The "Great Smokies" are really beautiful. We are very high up and often see the clouds floating around below us—and the neighboring "hillbillies" are almost beyond belief, *almost* like *Tobacco Road*. One little girl comes in every morning to help us clean; her name is *Walterine*, her father is a moonshiner. She is 14 and very pretty and is going to get married this winter to a boy 16. She has eight brothers and sisters . . .

Yesterday we took a walk about two miles through the woods to call on the local "crazy woman," Cordie Heiss. She lives all alone in a little cabin, and *walks* to town, about 8 miles, once a week to get 50¢ relief money . . . She always refers to herself in the third person as "poor Cordie" . . . If you still want songs, I think I'll have to send you a sort of imitation hillbilly song about "Poor Cordie." I should think something could be made of that awful monotonous music by changing the keys around, etc., don't you?

I have been staying here on purpose to work, and have done a fair amount. It is finding things that takes so long, though. I want to get back to New York sometime soon, but first I'm thinking of going to Beaufort, S.C., for a couple of weeks. Have you ever heard of that place? It is supposed to be a beautiful pre–Civil War Southern town, now almost entirely deserted. They call it "Bew-fort." Louise said you were going to Tiverton, so I shall send this there . . .

To Marianne Moore

September 11, 1940

. . . All the other salamanders here I've seen have been of the black or brown variety; the one in our spring is the only pink one. He is a real coral-pink, which looks so well on the gray-green moss and the dead brown oak leaves.

Thank you again, Marianne, for all the first part of the first letter. It seems to me that I make such demands on your thought and time and almost never give anything in return. I scarcely know why I persist at all. It is really fantastic to place so much on the fact that I have written a half-dozen *phrases* that I can still bear to reread without too much embarrassment. But I have that continuous uncomfortable feeling of "things" in the head, like icebergs or rocks or awkwardly placed pieces of furniture. It's as if all the nouns were there but the verbs were lacking—if you know what I mean. And I can't help having the theory that if they are joggled around hard enough and long enough some kind of electricity will occur, just by friction, that will arrange everything. But you remember how Mallarmé said that poetry was made of words, not ideas—and sometimes I'm terribly afraid I am approaching, or trying to approach it all, from the wrong track.

I wish so much that you could have been with us yesterday. There is the most beautiful waterfall I ever saw about two miles away . . . Rather it's a succession of waterfalls and cascades dividing and coming together again around rocks and trees. We spent several hours at the prettiest fall of all, in a sort of pit of huge trees—cedar trees with gray-green moss, birch, maples, etc. We caught several salamanders and tiny rainbow trout. What I like best are the little caves under the falls. Sometimes you can crawl through them—filled with a wonderful green light, dripping vines, and one or two pale blue flowers. I don't know what they are. I'm afraid we desecrated this particular spot by taking baths and shampoos and then *sliding* down the falls themselves. Just below, the water went through a deep corner under rhododendron roots and then spread out over a huge slab of black and white stone, like a fan, running very fast and evenly, without a ripple. These places must be really Heaven when the laurel and rhododendron are in bloom. But I prefer the Florida landscape—all this dampness and leafiness is a little oppressive, I think. Oh you *must* come to Key West! (I'll keep right on saying it until you say "yes" or "stop.")

We are entertained—or we entertain, I guess—a constant stream of mountaineer callers . . . But my favorite is a little boy, about five, named Grady, with platinum-blond curls. He uses expressions like "peart" and "tol'able." He watched me brushing my teeth the other day very sympathetically and then he said, "I ain't lost nary a tooth yit." Once he brought us a large bouquet which he called a "flower pot" and charmed Charlotte and me by saying, "I bet you can't guess which is the purtiest of them flowers."

I hope to get to New York fairly soon, but I feel that I can't face any of my friends, particularly you, without packages of manuscripts under my arm. Well, dear Dorothy Dix, I guess that is all. Thank you for mentioning Purcell and [George] Herbert and I shall try very hard to do something worth sending on to you . . .

September 20, 1940

This is what I have written to Mr. Young: "I have liked everything you have written to me about my work very much, and agreed with it very well, and cannot thank you enough for your letters and interest. Perhaps for the present it would be better if you would return the manuscript to me, and I hope that I shall feel that it is more or less complete in the near future" . . . I really feel that his letters are exactly what I deserve for my pretentious laziness, anyway, but I hope you will feel I have put it correctly.

I wish you could *see* Grady—he looks exactly like anyone's idea of a baby angel, and today he is wearing a pair of his brother's overalls, much too big, with nothing else under them, and is in his bare feet. Across one side of the [overall] seat is a large white trademark label that says in red, "Super-Bloodhound," and on each side of the suspenders is a bloodhound's head in red with the words "Blood" and "Hound" above and below it. At the post office yesterday I saw a little black boy on his way to school with a large book under his arm, the title of which was *Fun with English*.

Grady's brothers and sisters—the "younger set," that is (there are eight of them)—brought me a present of a can of snuff and wanted to teach me how to "dip" it. I tried, without much success, and Grady apparently felt that I had been embarrassed because he came back after they left and sat down and told me how if I "tried" I could "get used to it." I also had to let Charlotte Anne, aged five months, whom he "totes," bite my finger with her first tooth, to please him. She gave quite a nip . . .

We expect to leave here in about a week, and I may come straight to New York with Charlotte and Red, or I may go to Charleston or some-place to "concentrate" a little . . . And then it will be no time at all until I see you blindfolded, tied hand and foot (but not gagged) across the seat from me on the *Silver Meteor* to Miami . . .

Murray Hill Hotel
New York
October 17, 1940

What I'm about to say, I'm afraid, will sound like ELIZABETH KNOWS BEST. However, I *have* changed [the first words of each line of "Roosters"] to small initial letters! and I have made several other of your corrections and suggestions, and left out one of the stanzas . . . But I can't seem to bring myself to give up the set form, which I'm afraid you think fills the poem with redundancies, etc. I feel that the rather rattletrap rhythm is appropriate—maybe I can explain it.

I cherish my "water-closet" and the other sordidities because I want to emphasize the essential baseness of militarism. In the first part I was thinking of Key West, and also of those aerial views of dismal little towns in Finland and Norway, when the Germans took over, and their atmo-sphere of poverty. That's why, although I see what *you* mean, I want to keep "tin rooster" instead of "gold," and not use "fastidious beds." And for the same reason I want to keep as the title the rather contemptuous word ROOSTERS rather than the more classical THE COCK; and I want to repeat the "gun-metal." (I also had in mind the violent roosters Picasso did in connection with his *Guernica* picture.)

About the "glass-headed pins": I felt the roosters to be placed here and there (by their various crowings) like the pins that point out war projects on a map—maybe I haven't made it clear enough. And I wanted to keep "to see the end" in quotes because, although it may not be generally recognized, I have always felt that expression used of Peter in the Bible to be extremely poignant.

It has been so hard to decide what to do, and I know that esthetically you are quite right, but I can't bring myself to sacrifice what (I think) is a very important "violence" of tone—which I feel to be helped by what *you* must feel to be just a bad case of the *Threes* [EB wrote "Roosters" in triplet form]. It makes me feel like a wonderful Klee picture I saw at his show the other day, *The Man of Confusion*. I wonder if you could be mesmerized across the [Brooklyn] bridge to see it again with me? . . .

October 20, 1940

I've kept this [foregoing] letter the last two days while I pondered some more over the poem, and now when I reread it, I think it sounds decidedly *cranky*. But you know I'm not and that you are the one who should be very cranky and cross with me for being so mulish. May I keep your poem? It is so interesting, what you have done—almost what Louise would call a "swing" version, I think. I'm about to go up to Pittsfield for the concert there and I'll be coming back sometime tomorrow. Could you be persuaded to the Klee show sometime in the week?—that is, if your cold is entirely cured. I'll send a copy of the poem as I *think* it is now— or is that adding insult to injury? . . .

To Charlotte Russell

November 9 or 10, 1940

I waited till after the [presidential] election so that I wouldn't have to answer all your embarrassing questions—now everything is settled for us both. I went up to Louise's [in Massachusetts] last Sunday . . . The Spanish concert was a success, too, although naturally not quite as over-whelming as the swing one. I've been staying at Windsor since then—I can't stay in Dalton [the Crane summer residence]—the "pest house," as I call it—because of all the [asthma-inducing] dogs. It was marvelous but terribly cold . . . Mrs. [Pauline] Hemingway and her sister and a gentleman friend came and amazed us very much by being tight and slightly insulting everybody. I can't think of any other real tidbit except that the Spanish bagpiper proved to be stone-deaf and could only be *stopped* by the entire company screaming at him in chorus. It seems that you have to be deaf to be a bagpiper—isn't that an interesting thought?

I have been working here most of the time, and I sold my long poem called "Roosters" to *The New Republic*, which pleases me very much. It all depends on how many things I get done before December 15 whether or not I have a book in the spring, so I have decided (since I've been having so much asthma in this awful cold weather) to go straight back to Key West, probably leaving Wednesday. *If* I get enough done and make enough from the things I have sold, I'll come up by train for the last days of Loren's show [at MoMA] and then drive back with Louise—and then we'd all come to see you and Red. I want to very much, you know . . .

Louise's birthday is Monday and I'm trying to think of a present. Her mother is giving her a recording machine, but what I want to know is, is there an attachment to catch people unawares? . . .

To Edmund Wilson

Edmund Wilson (1895–1972) was an editor at The New Republic *when EB wrote him asking his advice about book contracts and about the publication date of her poem "Roosters." He had married Mary McCarthy in 1938.*

624 White Street
Key West, Florida
December 22, 1940

I tried to get a sample contract from James Laughlin before I left [New York], but I finally received a letter from him here saying that I could make out my own contract from paragraphs in the chapter on contracts in Wittenberg's *The Protection and Marketing of Literary Property*. He said, "You can just about write your own ticket." "A royalty of straight ten percent," etc. I'm having the book sent here, to study, but so far I am completely undecided, and having heard absolutely nothing from Harcourt Brace [Wilson's publisher at the time], I guess I shall just let it go a while longer.

I am sorry to trouble you more in this way, but do you suppose you could tell me when in February "Roosters" is to appear? [It appeared on April 21, 1941.] If it will be around the 15th, Oscar Williams would like to have it later in his anthology called *New Poems*—which is to appear shortly after the 15th, he says. It really doesn't matter to me very much, and of course there is no question about my wanting it to appear in *The New Republic*. I don't care anything about the anthology—however, I thought if it would not conflict, that is if *The New Republic* used it first, you might not mind Mr. Williams using it later. I'm sorry to make such a nuisance of myself.

Will you give my best regards to Mary? I wish I could have seen her again.

P.S. I shall send the review of Willa Cather in one week. [EB's review of the novel *Sapphira and the Slave Girl* was never published.]

January 17, 1941

I prefer to have the poem in *The New Republic* [Spring] literary supplement and not to bother about the [Oscar Williams] anthology at all. It is impossible to get any information from them as to when the anthology is going to appear, except "probably sometime in February," so I shall just write to them and say that you are using it and that if they care to use it too, they can—*if* the anthology comes out after the supplement, and let them find out for themselves. I've written to them several times already, and it seems to get more and more awkward to explain— and more boring . . .

To Frani Blough Muser

The Musers' daughter, Cynthia, was born on February 9, 1941.

March 11, 1941

I was so glad to hear about Cynthia from all quarters—it is a very elegant name, I think . . . I am sending a minor token of my esteem this morning. All the babies in Key West are dressed straight from the 5 & 10, but I hope to send a more accurate clue to what I consider you have done for yourself and the race soon now. (In fact, one of the town jokes last summer was when Kress's 5 & 10 put on a huge window display of baby's clothes with the question across the window, "Have you a baby in your house?"—because of course everyone has at least five.) . . .

Today, my dear, I am entertaining [artist] Grant Wood, who wants to see the Valdes picture. He is too depressing, very much like one of his D.A.R. matrons . . . Under the magic spell of all this I have started to paint myself, and yesterday I presented Mrs. Almyda with a picture . . . Of course what Mrs. A. really wants me to produce is a child so she can take care of it—she's insane about them—but alas . . .

To Charlotte Russell

To save money, EB rented her White Street home and moved in at this new address with her new companion, Marjorie Carr Stevens, who was separated from her Navy husband. EB and Marjorie (whose letters from EB were destroyed) later traveled together to Mexico and elsewhere.

623 Margaret Street
Key West, Florida
Monday morning [June 1941]

I was so touched by your offer of a LOAN. Thank you very much, but I guess it is good for all of us to go through these penitential periods, like France, once in a while. I'm gradually getting out of the red now, although I have a bill collector . . . on my trail. I hope to be able to get North sometime this summer.

I rented the house [on White Street] to Navy people—they moved in Saturday. They have two children, but I think that Navy people *without* children are probably harder on furniture, etc., than Navy people with them. Anyway, they seem very nice and resigned about the lack of conveniences and even asked me to come to have a drink with them.

Mrs. Almyda and I packed and moved *in one day*. I would have given up in the first half hour, if it hadn't been for her. Everything is stored except a few clothes and books I brought to Marjorie's, and I've settled down for a heat-endurance-economic race with her. She is broke, too, so it all works out quite well. The trees here are perfectly beautiful now and it's much quieter than my house—but I hate to leave White St. and can't bear to bicycle by it even.

You remember Mrs. (Blueberry Pie—or "Bundles," as Mrs. King called her) Barker? She has just left for the summer. She came to call last evening and couldn't keep her eyes off my (dirty) bare feet. It seems that in the middle house there are real Gangsters—the man had to leave town a while ago because he was trying to start a new "house," a rival to the Reid house, where the three murders took place. Now six barkeepers seem to be living there, in one bedroom, because the living room is filled to the ceiling with the roulette tables, etc., that they had to store away when they were raided. They come in all drunk, at four every morning. I'm sure something lurid will happen before long. You can imagine Mrs. B. telling all this.

Sloppy Joe died very suddenly while he was visiting [Ernest] Hemingway in Havana. They closed the bar for a few days, and hung those awful palm branches and purple ribbons on the doors. Now young Joe is running it, but they say he's fired Skinner . . .

Thank you for the photographs. I'm so impressed with the house and tell Red I think it looks wonderful. How is your planting coming along? I can see the Crotons. I wish I could have had Red build my new screened porch—or Louise's rather, because I just supervised. It is *beautiful*—the cistern has a tin roof, and is all screened in, and is going to have shutters all around. The floor is dark green, the shutters gray like the house, and the ceiling a heavenly pale blue. Then, when the tenants have left, if the children haven't crashed through—there will be lots and lots of plants in tubs and pots. It will be [a] nice [porch] to eat on. I wish it were fall already and you were paying a visit.

Louise's concerts were certainly a great success. I think she wants me to come up, but never again until I have some money saved ahead. I'm still paying for last November now. I feel so depressed about Key West, too, that I almost think I should enjoy it while one still can. The Navy has bought all the land as far over as Whitehead St. except the Courthouse itself, and old Penn's Garden of Roses—which is beautiful now. Mr. Penn, so René told me, "cries and cries." There has been a "schism" in the Church. I'm not quite sure of the details yet, but I'll tell you more next time. But you see how everything seems to be cracking up. Only the heat remains constant. I'd like very much to come to Brevard [N.C.] again for a while. When do you plan to be there? Maybe I could stop on my way North, whenever it will be . . .

To Marianne Moore

July 1, 1941

I had told Lottie, the colored woman here, to wake me up as soon as she came in, *because* I wanted to get up early to write to you, but when she did call me, I said, "Oh Lottie, just let me finish this dream," and she said, "I sure will, because maybe you'll dream a good number for me to play" (in the Havana Lottery). I dreamed about an island with cabbages and pine trees growing on it. Pine trees mean "fire," but cabbages aren't in *Aunt Sally's Dream Book*. I really think I should send you a copy, although I think Freud calls dream books the lowest perversion of the dream, or something like that—but it is very poetic. Lottie says, "I like Aunt Sally's numbers." She likes them whether they win or not, I think. She'll stop and look at a number in the newspaper and say, "Now that's a *nice* number." She told me the other day about someone singing "at the tip of her voice." Mrs. Almyda had such a sweet dream the other night. It began, "It seems like there was a lot of soldiers in Key West—French, German, and all kinds—and I'd been asked to make limeade for them."

I like "Spenser's Ireland" [poem later included in *What Are Years*] so much—did I say this before? I'm glad there's to be another stanza where you say, because the first stanza is the only thing that bothers me. I also like "The Student" very much, "The Mottoes," and "With knowledge as / with the wolf's surliness" / etc. Well, it is wonderful, I think, and why don't all these other people who are supposed to be poets ever say anything new? Margaret wrote me about "Ireland" also; she thought it so "spirited." I may have said this before, or may have the feeling I have, because I've thought it so many times.

Thank you for the [Vassar] *Miscellany*. I used to be an editor of it. I should love to have seen the "flowers bombarded with cathode rays." Have you seen those articles that have been running in *The New Republic* about the miracles of science, etc.? The last one on "atom smashing," June 16th, was fascinating—the atomic energy in a half-pint of water could send the *Normandie* to France and back, says the article. I've been reading a wonderful book that I gave to Margaret for Christmas and have finally got away from her, by the Dr. Kasner who gave the course in mathematics we took at the New School—*Mathematics and the Imagination*. I should like very much to send it on to you, if you think you'd like to see it. The parts about the fourth dimension, infinity, riddles, etc., are awfully good. Every day I make another attempt at mastering infinity. I get it for two minutes and then it slides away as if on ice . . .

I have moved in with a friend of mine [Marjorie Stevens on Margaret Street] for a while. Her house is one of the little ones set in one of the most beautiful, largest yards in Key West. I think I'll send you some pictures of it. There are wonderful trees and vines, Spanish Lime, Sea Grapes, Sugar Apple, etc. The warblers left in a few days, but there are lots of grackles who take baths in the sprinklers, and whom my little kittens stalk all day long.

I've had two letters from a William Roth, at Mr. [Edmund] Wilson's suggestion, I think. He runs The Colt Press in San Francisco and wants to publish a book for me. His letters are very nice, and James Laughlin writes too, but I still hope I'll hear from Harcourt Brace, at least . . .

You have mentioned chameleons several times. I wish I could send you some. They are so plentiful here and I watch them up in the Chinaberry tree puffing out their throats like little red balloons. There are lots in the house; some less than an inch long are adorable, with pink tails with black freckles.

Lottie was pressing a silk dress for herself and told me it was to wear to "Lodge"—"I sure enjoy my Lodge." So I asked her what kind of a Lodge it was and she said, "The Pallbearers' Lodge." But it isn't as bad as it sounds, because they get dressed up in white, the men with white sashes, and white and gold banners, and parade just like angels.

July 26, 1941

I *love* the poem about the ostrich ["He 'Digesteth Harde Yron' "]. I think it is one of the wittiest and most "interesting" I've ever read. I love "The egg piously shown," and "the ostrich-plume-tipped tent / and desert spear, jewel- / gorgeous ugly egg-shell / goblets," etc. It just isn't fair to prostrate me with these marvelous things when I am struggling along in the heat, trying to squeeze out a few of the dullest lines you'll have ever read. How do you do it? I get so *overexcited* and then angry because there is no one to show them to. How soon will I see the book? I will never forgive *Partisan Review* for almost everything else in the number, though. It is incredible what they'll print, including that tasteless bit by Williams.

It was so nice to hear from you from New London and I hope you're both enjoying your visit with your brother. If only I could just hand you over Mrs. Almyda. The thought of all your packing, book problems, etc., makes me feel so unjustly pampered. She and I packed and moved everything in one day [from White Street], not a safety pin left in a bureau drawer, and all the linen marked and counted and so on—and several little sit-down periods for limeade and conversation as well. Well, as I guess I've boasted before, I am trying to compose something about her, and then you'll see the full value of the personality, perhaps . . .

It has been so frightfully hot here that, following the example of the Army and Navy, everyone is taking salt pills. Have you ever tried them? I really think they do help keep one energetic, but maybe only if you're moving around in the sun and perspiring a lot. (And I don't know why I should seem to imply that you're *not*.) I learned about them from my new tenants, who, strange to say, just came from the submarine base at New London. He is Captain of the 0–12, sister-submarine to the one that sank a little while ago—very stolid and cheerful about it all. They are not the best of housekeepers, I'm afraid, but quite uncomplaining. In fact, they almost seem to like adversities like broken pumps, clogged drains, etc., and of course I am piling up rent money. I hope to be able to get up to

New York the first part of September. How long will you stay in New London?

I apologize for the dream book, which I'd already sent when your letter came warding it off. But you can just throw it away quickly, without a glance. And I *am* sending you some fruit, tomorrow or the next day, depending on the ripeness of the mangoes . . . I can't resist having you see some Sugar Apples. They have been the "theme" of the week here. We have a large tree that grows right beside the verandah—in fact it is almost flattened out beside me, loaded with the queerest, most Chinese, blue-gray-green fruit, the closest to fruit trees one might dream of and I've ever seen. Beside them is a guava, so that the air smells like strawberries all the time. I shall also include a specimen of Sapodilla (very nasty) and Spanish Lime (even nastier) and mango. Mangoes and Sugar Apples are the only pleasantly edible ones. The Sugar Apples should be chilled very cold, and eaten with a spoon, like a dish of vanilla ice cream. They are regarded as a great delicacy here . . .

We've been reading Henry James's *Letters* (the autobiographic ones) all week, a very good hot weather influence. I am particularly impressed with the War letters—and do you remember when he had shingles? Those letters at last made me properly sympathetic with your mother's troubles two years ago. The cats are splendid, but you will regret to hear that Gloria eats chameleons. I have done a few short poems, but I'll wait and send them to you, if I may, with the longer one I hope to finish soon. It is so peaceful here, and quiet, that there should be nothing in the way of my getting things done in order to assault Harcourt Brace again— nothing but myself, that is.

Holly House
Brevard, North Carolina
[September 1941]

. . . The mountains and the mountaineers here have all the charms they had last year. I think I told you how the people here call a bouquet a "flower pot." I heard the nicest use of it the other day when I said to a neighbor that it was a nice day and he said, "Yes, as purty as a flower pot." In back of Holly House is a very steep narrow valley, just like my idea of Switzerland. On one side of it lives an old, old white horse named Joe. We take him apples every evening and he is so lonesome and so affectionate that he almost sniffles one's clothes off, and whinnies loudly when we leave. On the other side is a very pretty small-sized tan cow named Betty. Her owner is very fond of her. She stands at the bottom of the pasture in the evening and as soon as Betty sees her, she comes *running* down the side of the mountain with her cowbell jangling. I said I thought she was very intelligent and the mistress said, "She's the damn pettedest cow I ever seed." We use her butter and buttermilk here.

I saw a very poor mountain cabin the other evening . . . The people had a field of sorghum, and for a scarecrow, on top of a thin pole, they had hung a wire coat hanger with several little bright copper-colored snuffboxes (the women all use snuff) fastened on each end. It looked and sounded like a very superior Calder mobile.

I hope you are well, Marianne. I felt rather bad when I first came here. Red analyzed the symptoms according to his First Aid books as "heat exhaustion," but the last few days I am quite recovered.

[P.S.] I tried the snuff, a variety called "Tuberose," but although it is a pretty substance the effects are not.

October 23, 1941

What Are Years came two days ago. Thank you so much—thanks are quite inadequate and conceited for the poems, but I *can* thank you for the inscription at least. It has cheered me up very much and made me think I am a person again after all. I think the cover is very nice, and everything in general, but I'll never forgive Macmillan for the "bell-boy" mistake [in "Four Quartz Crystal Clocks"]—*my* line. It is so wonderful to have all the poems right here. I tried reading "The Pangolin" out loud last night to the friend with me but I'm afraid I always make everything sound like "The Raven." And I like "Four Quartz Crystal Clocks" more and more and more, and the ostrich one, and I have always adored "See in the midst of fair leaves." Well, it is a beautiful, beautiful book and what I like best of all is the wonderful *alone* quality of it all—like the piano alone in the middle of the concerto.

Holly House closes November 15, but I hate to think of leaving here. Last week has been the most beautiful autumn weather. For three days the woods were blazing and we just wandered around admiring this leaf and that. But yesterday there was a windstorm and they all blew off. The cornfields, where the corn is drying for seed, are very bleached and tattered and they rustle all night long. Betty, the cow, ate too many apples and "foundered" and a man had to come and hold her head while she was given a bicarbonate of soda—so the butter this week is very strange . . .

623 Margaret Street
Key West, Florida
December 28, 1941

. . . I am rather depressed about Key West—and my house—just now [three weeks after the Pearl Harbor attack]. The town is terribly overcrowded and noisy (at least on White Street) and not a bit like itself. It is one of those things one can't resent, of course, because it's all necessary, but I really feel that this is no place to be unless one is of some use. They are talking of evacuating the civilians. I don't believe they will, but still, what I want to do is to rent the house again and go somewhere. I haven't given up the idea of South America. I'm not a bit sure of the ethics of it all—what do *you* think? If the government stops issuing passports, I guess I'll stay here with Marjorie at Margaret Street where it is quieter, probably. The house [on White Street] was in a FRIGHTFUL condition—indescribable—and it is impossible to get any kind of help. Mrs. Almyda is working part-time in the cigar factory, but she isn't at all well. We've exchanged visits and presents and she is the most wonderful person in the world, but I can't afford her by myself, even if she were well enough to do the work. But my friends here have all been so nice—Marjorie, Charlotte, and Red, who are all here. Red (the canoe man, who is giving an Instructor Course in First Aid here, working for the Red Cross) has almost repaired my [former] tenants' damage—painting and carpentering, etc. We've scrubbed the floors and waxed the furniture and even done our laundry, and now things are fairly normal again. But of course I haven't been able to think of poetry for a minute, and won't be able to until I get the house rented and get settled somewhere. Tell me how on earth you ever manage to do all you do?

The clavichord was sent to Mr. Kirkpatrick to be rented while I'm away. Now if I don't get "away," of course I'm going to want it back badly. Oh dear! . . . I should love to see the Defoe book. I think that *The Plague Year* and [*Adam*] *Bede* are my two favorite books.

For Christmas Red gave me *A Field Guide to Birds* by R. T. Peterson. Have you ever seen it? I think it is marvelous and very different to most bird books: the pictures give the birds as they look at a distance and in all stages of age and molting, etc. If you haven't seen it, will you please let me get you a copy?—the descriptive writing is quite good and different, too.

We have a new addition to the "family." I answered an ad in the paper that read, "Nice clean painter wants work"—and a very little, delicate, middle-aged man arrived and has been here ever since. He has tiny bright blue eyes and a pointed face and a red nose, I'm afraid, and I think he cuts his own hair—a curly fringe straight across the back. He wears his pants, pale blue, tucked into his socks. One day I was whistling "Loch Lomond" and he said, "I'll bet you've never seen that place," and then he said he was "born on its banks." I paid him two days before Christmas and of course he just vanished, with the work half done. At first I thought I'd put another ad in the paper: "Nice clean painter, come home, all is forgiven." (We still don't know his name—he's very reticent about it.) Then I went and found him in his "cabin," he calls it—a little shack about five feet square in a vacant lot almost hidden in bushes and weeds. He put his little head out the door and said, "Merry Christmas," and I said I thought he'd overdone *that*, and so now he's back at work again, looking a little self-conscious . . .

I've been watching every week for the piece [about MM] in *Time;* I wonder why he doesn't hurry up, or have I missed it? I am vaguely upset because [anthologist] Oscar Williams didn't ask me to contribute again. I was "mentioned favorably" and all that. Oh I do hope I can get to work soon . . .

To Charlotte Russell

623 Margaret Street
Key West, Florida
April 2, 1942

All my underwear is full of little bits of straw. I also sprinkle it in my hair and shoes—awfully prickly, but I smell like the rose, and everyone compliments me on it. I don't know where to reach you at all, so I guess it will have to be Alexandria again. I've been bad about writing, but so frightfully busy here. I hope you and Red are still in the Deep South and really enjoying yourselves. It sounds wonderful—particularly the part south of New Orleans. Have you read any of Lafcadio Hearn's books?—about New Orleans, etc. They're not wonderful, but it seems to me he has a book of stories about that section of the country that is very good.

Marjorie [Stevens] and I are leaving for Mexico on the fifteenth. We're flying to Mérida [Yucatán], where we'll stay a while. Then we're going up to Mexico City and then find a cool place—on a lake—to stay for the summer—in fact maybe for the "duration," I don't know. It is impossible to live here any longer. The Navy takes over and tears down and eats up one or two blocks of beautiful little houses for dinner every day. Probably the house on White Street will go, too. At present it's rented by a *divine* housekeeper—even if she does take boarders (I know) and has two men sleeping in every bed, and a row of blue, yellow and red *tin* chairs along the front porch. One poor old man committed suicide two days ago because he heard they were going to take his house. And the point is that it is *unnecessary*—you have all these vast tracts of land in other parts of the island. They are just tearing down all the good work the government has been doing here in the last ten years, and when the war is finally over, Key West will be more ruined than ever—nothing but a naval base and a bunch of bars and cheap apartments. Pauline [Hemingway] and I are now conducting a campaign to get everyone to wire [Senator] Pepper about it, but I'm afraid it won't do much good. Some people have received only a day's warning to get out, and there are Negroes sleeping in cars and vacant lots all over town. Well, it is all very gloomy. I don't want to be unpatriotic about it either, but it *is* unnecessary, I'm sure.

My latest idea is for you to join us in Mexico. If you're going to be around New Orleans for a while, it could be a *cinch*. We'll be coming to

Mexico City about the middle of May and probably will be there about two weeks. You could join us there . . .

Spring is coming, interwoven with the constant sound of airplanes, here. Gloria is about to have kittens, and looks like a little fur ball, with head, tail, and legs sticking out, a little . . . Marjorie's husband has just left after quite a long visit. I don't think you've ever met him—he's really very nice and very cute, in an over-Bostonian way.

Sunday we went out on the Keys with Jane [Dewey] and her father. It would have done Red good to hear Jane argue with Kip—i.e., Mr. Stevens—on every occasion. She was even more severe with him than she was with Red. We went to dig up plants and had a very good time. Dr. Dewey did all the work of course, wielded the pickaxe, and carried everyone's coat.

. . . It would be *marvelous* if you could meet us in Mexico. With much love to you, and Reddy-pie too. (Poem.)

To Marianne Moore

7 Calle de Paris
Mexico City, Mexico
May 14, 1942

I just put my address there for effect (I received your letter safely at the American Express office yesterday, *with joy*) because in this section of town all the streets seem to be named for cities, and further up the boulevard, or whatever it is, for rivers. It *is* rather like a lovely section of Paris, however not as much as it thinks it is, though. We (yes, Mrs. Stevens, Marjorie is with me) came to this place through the Chilean poet [Pablo] Neruda, and like it very much. This house is a sort of pension and was (I think—my Spanish leads to so many misunderstandings) the home of the painter [David Alfaro] Siqueiros. Anyway the house is full of his paintings and others of a similar nature, mostly people demanding BREAD, etc.—all very gloomy, but then I'm afraid I loathe Mexican painting.

It is always such bad taste to gloat over a favorable exchange, don't you think? but it is extremely inexpensive and we've settled down to stay at least a month and get lots and lots of poetry written. In fact my feelings about Mexican art, and painting in particular, are so strong I haven't even looked at a mural yet, except one Orozco that is unavoidable, being, as it is, incorporated in the entrance to the Ladies' Room in the building next to the American Express office.

This letter, which is my second start, is getting even more jumbled than the first one. I'm sorry, Marianne, it may be the altitude, but I really think it is just that the concentration it requires for me to write without lines to go by [on the notepaper] leaves me so little over for the sense. I'll make myself rules for next time.

You have no idea how glad I was to hear from you. I'm afraid, from your letter, I must have given you a very glamorized sketch of my travels in Mérida. We *have* had extraordinarily good fortune so far, but I am not so transfigured and upraised that I didn't almost weep when your letter was handed to me. We had just been through a rather bad stretch, and any big modern city is depressing just at first, I think, particularly when it is a mixture of all the others together as this one is. Thank you for telling me about the circus and the Rousseau show, and for altogether giving me that feeling that I should be back in New York, where I belong—that uneasy heightening of sensation that I think is really essential to travel! You not mentioning the cold means that it is all over, I hope, and that you are rested and STRONG. And I do hope Mrs. Moore is well, and tell her to *stop* ironing; you must wear things rough-dried. I should like to read The Psychology of the Christian Personality very much. Did I ever show you the book I had by Dr. Karen Horney (the one I went to) called, I think, *The Neurotic Personality of Our Time*? I admit that it sounds awful, but it isn't really. But horrors, I just remember that in *The N.Y. Times Book Review* this week it announces a new book by her on how to psychoanalyze oneself, which sounds very overpopularized. But one can't tell—she is foreign and may have just been browbeaten into the title by her publisher. I had infinitely rather approach such things from the Christian viewpoint myself—but the trouble is I've never been able to find the books, except Herbert.

At the moment I don't know anything about the house [in Key West] and I am rather worried. But I left it in the hands of the other agent—a nice, old-fashioned one whom I have and who is very slow but extremely dependable and understanding of what kind of tenant I want. He transacts his business by calls, long ones, in the morning, and he wears a striped shirt, white collar and stickpin, and dislikes modern business methods, and he even went to my house himself to count over the sheets, so you see I really shouldn't be worried too much. I am getting $90.00 a month ($81 less his commission) for it, so you see it is worth all the trouble.

I wonder if I can write on the other side of this. I am collecting *seeds* as I go (I haven't seen anything else I want) and already have two strange herbs and the seeds of some tiny wild tomatoes, about as big as raspberries, I found growing on the side of a pyramid at Cozumel. I'll bring you some to plant in a pot. (I'm so glad this writing seems to be working—now I can go on and on.)

We haven't found a Spanish teacher here yet, but hope to soon. I bought Pablo Neruda's poetry (he and his wife have been very nice to us) and I am reading it, with the dictionary, but I'm afraid it is not the kind I—nor you—like, very very loose, surrealist imagery, etc. I may be misjudging it; it is so hard to tell about foreign poetry, but I feel I recognize the type only too well. His chief interest in life (or did I tell you all this?) besides Communism seems to be shells, and he has a beautiful collection, most of them laid in the top of a sort of large, heavy, specially built coffee table, with glass over them. That is how I happened to try to recite and explain to him what I could remember of "A Glass-Ribbed Nest." I want very much to get him a copy of your works. I must see if they have it here. He is the Chilean consul here.

Just before we left Mérida the younger Mrs. Camara, our special friend—a perfectly beautiful girl with the most beautiful tragic eyes you have ever seen, about to have a second baby, and so *dumb*—invited us to spend the day with her at the beach at her aunt's villa in Progreso. I had always thought of Progreso as a bustling, hot, unhealthy port, not at all the kind of place one would want to spend a day at the beach at, but we were very curious and packed our bathing suits and went. In Mérida they go to Progreso to get away from the heat; there is a fairly cool east wind most of the time, so constantly, too constantly. We left at 6:45 a.m. on a little wooden train that rushed straight through the henequen fields and got there in an hour, and were met by Gloria [Camara], our friend. Then we went marketing for our dinner, and bought all kinds of strange things, also a watermelon, mameyes, and plums and bunches of flowers. Then we got on the tiniest trolley car I have ever seen, smaller than the Toonerville, and went round and round the town, so close to all the little buildings you could touch them. The trolley car had a small engine inside that kept boiling over, and the wind blew, and the waves (the same color as Key West) splashed, and the band played in the park, and the church bells rang—it is really very nice. We made the trolley trip twice, then went to—or rather stepped into, from the trolley which almost deposited us in the living room—the aunt's house, which was also very small, like all of them, and made of stone, and right on a beautiful beach. But all the houses are very close together and there are too many buzzards sitting on them (they rather worried me when we went swimming). Then we had a glass of some extremely sweet wine the Mexican ladies adore, and an enormous dinner. The house had three small rooms and a kitchen (with them, besides their two children, our hostesses had five Indian servants, women, and one of the women's husband! But they conserve space, very sensibly I think, by all sleeping in hammocks). After lunch we were each stowed away in one, our first such experience, and we both slept two and a half hours. I think it is a pity they have never been adopted in Key West—they are beautiful to look at, and all the women looked extremely graceful lying in them, and they are cool and clean, and don't take up any space in the daytime, and are very comfortable.

Well, Teacher—our Spanish teacher—was at the beach, too, with her mother, so when we woke up we went and drank coconut milk with her large and handsome family and then went back on the train with her father, who told us all about the time he lived in South Boston. In Mérida the people were so nice to us, and yet I have never met people so completely insulated and self-absorbed. Mr. Camara (or did I tell you?) used to take us driving in his car that he bought by winning in the lottery. We have bought tickets regularly since, but no luck.

I'm afraid I made rather too much of our outing, and that again I've presented myself as the grasshopper-type girl, but you know I have a *serious nature*, really, Marianne. I can't help letting these details, however inappropriate, distract and entertain me. But I'm working every day now. I read "Precision" over every day too. I love what you said about the elephants. No, Mérida is *not* wholesome—I *feel* the corruption.

May 23, 1942

This is just to say that I received your note of April 14th last night and I'm so glad you liked the eggs. Margaret [Miller], to whom I sent some, too, also seems to marvel at them, and I feel almost like the man who made the glass flowers in Boston. I always thought it was something anyone could do. But I'm afraid yours, except for the transfers, were plain. My marbleized ones are much the best. (There is a woman staying at our pension here who confided in me that she came to Mexico on the $450 she earned "marbleizing") . . .

I sent J. Laughlin "The [Imaginary] Iceberg," "[The] Weed," and "Roosters." How strange that you should quote the Herbert poem to me, when it was just the one I needed and wished I had along! I'd copied out a piece of another one, but yours was the one I wanted. We went to this place on the back [picture of "Piramides de San Juan Teotihuacan" on envelope] the other day—the pyramid, that is. The foreground was entirely thought up by the Post Office Department, I'm sure. What is my "automobile"? EAT THE CAKE (I'm afraid this will resemble a bitten-into confection by the time you get it). I should have put EAT ME on it.

c/o The American Consulate
Insurgentes 105, Mexico, D.F.
September 28, 1942

Thank you for sending back my ms. [of poem ("Cootchie"?)] so quickly and for all the useful suggestions. I am so sorry that it upset you and I'm afraid I'll find your reasons quite unanswerable—for not liking it. I have another one, about Key West, to send you but I think I'll wait until I can present it in person and perhaps help to dissipate some of *its* gloom.

Yes, Margaret sent me a copy of her article on Géricault—isn't it good?

A *tejón* [coati] is about the size of a small-sized raccoon, and a little like one, but it has a long pointed nose that turns up abruptly at the tip, and its tail isn't bushy. They are very quaint-looking; they sit up and look very smart and are very affectionate.

I wish I'd known, years ago, that you liked hooked rugs. I could have got you all you wanted, beautiful ones, so easily. My grandmother's house and my aunt's house, in Great Village, were covered with them, of course, and all the women there hooked. I used to be able to do it myself. I went to several hooking parties with my grandmother, and one quilting party. I like the formal designs, with scrolls and Maple Leaves, etc., don't you? In the Primer Class there we used to have to sing "O Maple Leaf, Our Emblem Dear" every morning, as well as "Rule Britannia."

The house in Key West is still a nuisance, but *not* the garden. Charles has been so good all summer and writes regularly about everything. In his last letter he says: "The pears on the trees are growing fine. (Alligator.) The vine has a lot of Grapes one of the Coconut trees in front has started to shoot and everything is beginning to look fine since we had a little rain and no dogs to disturb nothing."

Oaxaca is very nice—I like it next best to Mérida, I think. We came from Puebla by *narrow-gauge Pullman*, the tiniest train I have ever seen. It ran all day through a narrow mountain gorge filled with cactus, beside a raging torrent of mud, and it kept coming off the tracks and bumping along on the ties. Then the engineer and the conductor would hop off and somehow boost it back on again—and set up a miniature broadcasting station beside the track to let the day train behind us know where we were so they wouldn't bump into us. We were ten hours late, but apparently that wasn't bad—sometimes it gets stuck for days, and the company seriously suggests that you bring some groceries along.

They have been celebrating the birthday of The Little Flower here for the last three days. Last night from my window I saw an amazing *float* going by. It was built on a truck, made of purple-blue iris on fleur-de-lys about six to eight feet high, and tall green bullrushes, all paper, carefully glued on bamboo frames. Over the lilies hung six enormous white paper doves, wingspread at least three feet, tumbling and swaying on wires, and a man rode on the hood armed with a forked bamboo pole to push the telephone overhead wires out of the way. In the float stood six little girls dressed in nightgowns of pale blue satin, and blue crowns, all laughing and having a wonderful time drinking Orange Crush out of bottles. There was a brass band fore and aft.

The prettiest things in the celebration, though, have been the set pieces of flowers made by the Indians. They had them lined up all along one side of the plaza, under those magnificent laurel trees, and everyone walked around carrying little tissue-paper lanterns, to look at them. There were harps, for example, all made of solid small carnations or roses, outlined with mignonette or Queen Anne's lace, with the strings wrapped in tinfoil, or crescent moons, or *flowers* of flowers. The fireworks were very disappointing, however—they make a great deal of hissing and sputtering and a long *whoosh* and trail of smoke, and then a very mild report and no light at all.

We're leaving day after tomorrow to take the toy train back to Puebla, and then on North, and so back to New York, I guess . . .

To Lloyd Frankenberg

Poet Lloyd Frankenberg (1907–74) and his wife, the painter Loren MacIver, were close friends of EB, who introduced them to Key West. His book of poems, The Red Kite, *appeared in 1939. This letter was mailed to their home at 61 Perry Street in Greenwich Village, where EB often stayed. As a conscientious objector during the war, Lloyd went to a CPS camp in Maryland, and the "document" was apparently a statement of his wartime views.*

Saturday
[June 29, 1943
Key West, Florida]

Thank you for sending me the document. You didn't say anything about returning it, so I'm keeping it for the time being. I think it's a little unfair to try to judge it now, in 1943. In general you prophesied awfully well, though. There are several points I'd like to ask you about—and I've just re-read all of [poet Wilfred] Owen this morning and there are several points there I'd like to ask you about. I think the first part (of your answers) is particularly good and not "stuffy" at all—and I'm sure, considering the audience it was written for, it is all extremely well-planned and skillful. I only wish poetry hadn't had to be brought in at all—but then I suppose there's no use in trying to protect it, either. The whole piece affected me like an 18th-century "character"—I mean the impression is so concentrated—and I'd love to know how it affected *them*.

I do hope the [CPS] camp won't be too bad, and if you ever happen to feel like writing letters, I'd like to hear about it. Maybe Loren will keep me informed. I am so worried about her without you and do hope she gets along all right. She owes me a letter, but I imagine you must both be frightfully busy and upset right now. Thank her for me for sending the Museum of Modern Art catalogue—and I do hope you get the novel sold before you have to leave . . .

To Marianne Moore

623 Margaret Street
Key West, Florida
July 15, 1943

. . . Somehow all this difficult time I've been finding it easier to write business letters than real ones. A neighbor here had that tea and I liked it as well as any I've ever had (except Mrs. Crane's Mr. Morgan's Private Brand) and immediately wanted you to have some, too—so you see I am not altogether as hardened and indifferent as I've appeared. Please don't be put off by the label that implies it "tastes like tarred rope and is for company only"—it's very mild and quotidian.

Lester [Littlefield, friend of the Moores] may have told you how I called him up the other day (I'm afraid you won't forgive me that). He said that you are both well, which was a great relief to me. Then some time ago in one of the advertisements from the Gotham Book Mart it said that you had once given them one of those "favorite book" lists, so I wrote Miss Steele and she very kindly sent me a copy of it. I was particularly pleased to see the Book of Job. I've been reading Job off and on for ten years and always trying to "do something" with it—from a story to an opera libretto. I sent for that Modern Reader's edition that you mentioned and I think it is marvelous.

Then Lester sent me [MM's new war poem] "In Distrust of Merits," which overawed me into another two months' silence, I guess. Oh Marianne, all my congratulations. It seems to me so intricately impressive, with a kind of grinding caterpillar tread that is almost too upsetting. I admire the repetitions, I admire the "O's," I admire Job again—and "The world's an orphans' home." The only other comment that has produced anything of the same effect was the remark an old colored woman who worked for me a week made. She was very religious and very good but much too old for the work. She was ironing and she said to me in between solemn thumps, "We'll have *wars* as long as people's *hearts* is so *hard.*"

Mrs. Almyda is working in the furniture store here. I think she is enjoying being an "office girl." She comes to call quite often. I am still at Marjorie Stevens's house. She is working as a bookkeeper and is away all day long and it is very quiet and lonely here—although the town has now reached something like 50,000 inhabitants. I'll send you a picture that will give you an idea of what we have had to contend with—only of course for the "old" they picked about the worst house in town. My house troubles continue and are much too tedious to go into. I had a wonderful garden, really wonderful, for a while. I didn't know I was capable of such farming—now it is getting too hot, but I still have tomatoes, zucchini, and some endive, herbs, etc. I'm planning to come North about the first of September for several months—maybe for good.

I keep dragging on with about six bedraggled old poems and a couple of stories. I find it awfully hard to work properly. Everything seems to lead to everything else, if you know what I mean. That is another thing that seems to me so remarkable about your poem—that sense of the present terrible *generalizing* of every emotion.

I am afraid it has been awfully hot in New York—even hotter than here. Have you ever tried salt pills in the hot weather? I really think they help. I'm also taking a vitamin medicine called "Abbott's Elixir" and am feeling extremely healthy and energetic. I do hope you and your mother are both very well and that you are getting lots done. Now that I've got this much written to you maybe I'll be able to go on and be more entertaining soon. I have thought of you and your mother so much all this time.

P.S. Have you seen Kierkegaard's *Journals*? I've been reading it off and on for several months—there are wonderful things in it and it's the first of his books I've been able to understand. And did you like the *Four Quartets*?

September 1, 1943

I've just come back from a very depressing shopping trip to Miami, the vulgarest, hottest place in the U.S.A., I think, and while there my pleasantest moment was when I went to Hickson's and sent you and your mother a box of unnecessary and probably unwholesome foodstuffs. I always lose my head in those places. I found myself about to send a jar of horrible ground-up coconut-glucose-powdered milk-imitation flavor, etc., and I forgot to enclose the card which I wrote to tell you that the mango will not turn color when it gets ripe. It stays green and just gets a little soft and *smells* ripe, and that the papaya stuff is really quite good with ice cubes and soda water, or plain water if you prefer. I've always wanted to send you a Hodon mango, they are so beautiful to look at, but I seem to miss the season every year. This is a Brooks. In the summer all the Key Westers drink what they call "*cool*-drinks" (all one word, accent on the "cool") all day long and some of them are very good, like tamarind water, etc. And the only nice thing about Miami is the innumerable fruit-juice stands all decorated with palm leaves and pyramids of fruit. PLEASE don't write to thank me, Marianne, will you?—as I said, it really was the only nice time I had in my three days there. I hate shopping and of course it's extra difficult now. I shall come to New York in rags and bare feet, I guess.

In Cuba and Mexico they have special two-pronged forks for mangoes, but you can use a kitchen fork. You stick it in the stem end and if you do it right the fork will go into the soft end of the seed and hold the mango firm. Then you peel it down from the top and eat it off the fork like a lollipop, being very careful not to get the juice on your clothes because it stains badly.

It was awfully nice to get your letter before I left and I took it with me as a sort of amulet or password. I've been to Holyoke and as I remember it is very pretty there. Have you seen this article about the *entretiens* [talks] in *Time*? Did you talk "for an hour"? I am hoping you will tell me your "points" when I see you again, or even let me see your notes. Miss White was head of the French department at Vassar when I was there. I just knew her by sight because I stupidly never took any French, but I think Margaret had some courses with her.

Well, I got the "job" in the Optical Shop and went to work as a "helper-trainee," taking binoculars apart and putting them together again. I'm afraid I misrepresented it to you, but then I wasn't quite sure myself what the work was when I began. I only lasted five days, I'm sorry to say. The eyestrain made me seasick, and the acids used for cleaning started to bring back eczema, so I had to give it up—and I must admit I was only too glad to because the work was so finicky and tedious that it was getting to be a torture to me and I was doing it all night long in my sleep, and getting up cranky. But I'm glad I tried it. It was the only way of ever finding out what *is* going on in Key West now, seeing the inside of the Navy Yard and all the ships, and learning lots of things I had no idea about before. It took three whole days of red tape to get in, before I could wear a large tin button with my photograph on it and "Industrial Worker" printed underneath, and it is taking me at least two weeks to get my "honorable discharge." I got $5.04 a day, to begin with. The "shop" was very nice, open across one end and right on the edge of the water, where hundreds of ships, submarines and all kinds, are coming and going, being repaired and painted, all day long. The water is jade green, the gray ships looked bright blue against it, and of course I could spend a lot of time—had to—watching everything through magnificent optical instruments of every kind, including periscopes. Then the people were so nice, all of them, just as polite and kind and helpful as could be. I don't believe I could bear office workers, in whose ranks the labor board was very eager to place me. They seem to comb their hair and file their nails most of the time. The men I worked with were all sailors. They worked in their undershirts and were all, every single one, heavily tattooed. I've never seen so much tattooing, some very interesting Oriental varieties, too. The foreman was a great big Scot—a sort of Spencer Tracy type—who was endlessly patient in teaching me, and called me "kiddo" and "sis." Then there were a few older civilian workers, a Frenchman and two Swiss watchmakers who talked to me in French. The atmosphere was very nice. There was a store and the sailors brewed very strong Navy coffee all day long, and passed it around, and they took turns "treating" everybody to ice cream or Coca-Cola in the afternoon. Once the Frenchman even made an avocado salad in lunch hour. He challenged everybody to a game of checkers at lunch hour, too. There were two kittens who climbed all over us and got into everything. My introduction to the place was hearing the "boss" shout, "Who put Spam in this kitten's bowl? You know they don't like it!" But in spite of all the gaiety they really worked awfully hard and I never saw anyone idling and I was infinitely impressed with the patience of those men *fiddling* day after day with those delicate, maddening little instruments. I don't think I could do it, even if it hadn't made me sick. And their lack of imagination would get more and more depressing—not one of them had any idea of the *theory* of the thing, *why* the prisms go this way or that way, or what "collimate" and "optical center" really mean, etc.—and of course I kept fussing and fuming because I was so sure certain things could be done better in some other way, or that some very simple change would make it all easier. The foreman, who was perfectly happy spending *five* days adjusting one lens, or *four* hours on one screw the size of a pin, would look at me very mildly and say, "Don't let it get you, kiddo."

Some of the things we worked with were beautiful, of course—the lenses and prisms, and the balsam for gluing them. Eventually I would have worked on sextants and periscopes and all kinds of wonderful-looking things I don't know the names of. However, the seasickness I experienced was not unique—a good many people can't do it at all, it seems, and while I was there every once in a while a sailor would get sick and have to go outside and rest a while. So it hasn't proved I couldn't work, I trust.

Next week Marjorie [Stevens] is going up to Asheville to spend her vacation with her husband, who's stationed there. My original plan was to go along with her, stay there a few days, and go on to New York, but now I've decided to stay on here while she is away. The housing shortage is so bad that if the house were left vacant for any time the landlady would probably put her out and put in someone else, and then of course—almost worse—she [Marjorie] would be bound to lose the intellectual Flossie. So I'm going to stay and hang on to the house and Flossie for her until she gets back, then go to New York. This week there has been a great deal of discussion over the purchasing and financing of Flossie's new glasses. I have an idea that glasses are replacing gold teeth as personal decorations with the smarter Negroes here. We had to help decide what *tint* the lenses should be—the last were green. Now she is happy, and very effective, with pale pink with amber frames.

You speak of being "handicapped by solitude," but to me you seem the very height of society. It is terribly lonely here and I felt myself growing stupider and stupider and more like a hermit every day. I'm going to try to stay in New York all winter. Thank you for returning the grade C-minus poem [unidentified]. Does that mean I should send yours back? I've always held on to them like—a barnacle. I want so badly to get something good done to show you. I don't know what the obstacles are or why I don't really take up lens grinding.

I wish you could have seen the beautiful sight I saw from the bus going to Miami—nine tall white herons in a group, each on one leg, standing in shallow water where mangroves are just beginning to spring up—just an arch here and there with a few leaves on it. The bus was stopped for almost ten minutes—only one heron moved all that time, took one slow step, and looked from the bus down into the water.

This is too long, but I want to *talk*. I hope it is getting cooler and that you and your mother are both feeling well.

I've had quite a bit of news of you from various sources the last few days, but the most important was that you were, or had been, sick—and I think Loren [MacIver] said *bursitis* but I'm not sure. I'm terribly sorry to hear this, and I do hope you're better now. If it's what I think it is I know it's very unpleasant—but please tell me. She also said that in spite of it you gave a talk at the Library, which she and Margaret [Miller] and [E. E.] Cummings enjoyed very much. (This is all from a very hurried, three-cornered telephone conversation Sunday—Lester was the third party.) Anyway it sounded like heroism to me and I do hope you're well and taking care of yourself.

Then Margaret wrote me about seeing you at the Calder show opening—described a beautiful pale blue dress, taking pictures, etc., and asked me if I had seen a poem about "Elephants" in *The Nation*. I *must* see it, also the one in the Oscar Williams anthology, but I guess I can wait until I get to New York, eager though I am. Please don't dream of bothering to satisfy my curiosity now, will you? What Margaret said about the pictures reminded me again, though, that I wish I could have one, too, sometime. Please, won't you be a pin-up girl?

I hope you got *The Expression of Personality* safely. The book about tropical plants is called *Tropical Gardening and Planting, with Special Reference to Ceylon*, by H. F. Macmillan—4th edition. Mr. Macmillan seems to have been the head gardener of some famous botanical gardens there. He's slightly snobbish, I'm afraid, and frequently diverges to describe the special arbor he built for the visit of Her Highness Princess Maude in 1886, etc., but still it is the best book of the sort I've seen. I'll bring it to New York. It's rather pointless, I suppose—I mean, there's the flower in the yard, and then you go and look it up and there it is in the book—but it's a peculiar sort of satisfaction. So many things are misnamed in Key West, too, and no one knows where anything comes from. Have you ever heard of growing "Trap-Crops" of insect-eating plants, on purpose to keep the insects down? I also discovered I had papyrus growing in the front yard and didn't know it.

Marjorie has been away for about three weeks and I've been living in almost complete solitude. I don't really mind so much. There have been several more fringes of hurricanes for excitement. I was sure I had described waterspouts to you long ago—maybe I'll develop it a little, since I hadn't. They move across the surface of the water very rapidly and the water in the base of one looks white and foaming. (This is about one half a mile away, the closest to one I've been.) They are translucent and you can see the water or mist or whatever it is going up inside in puffs and clouds, very fast, just like smoke up a chimney—and the top of the chimney is lost in a storm cloud. They look particularly awesome on a calm bright day, of course.

I've discovered a place in an alley here where they raise rabbits—also dogs, puppies, cats, hens, roosters, chickens, bantams, etc.—all loose together in a large shady yard. I went to get a rabbit to *eat*, but changed my mind. They had a litter of gray angora ones, with their eyes just opened. I've never seen anything cuter. They sat up and scratched their ears, which seemed to be just as long as their bodies, with first one hind leg, then the other, and arranged the fur on their chests with their tongues, just like kittens.

The other night I went to hear the "Independent Quartette" of Atlanta, which had been making a sensation at Lillian's (the present maid's) church (colored). They were really a sextet and extremely good—the best thing of the sort I've ever heard down here. They wore zoot suits of narrow black and gray stripes, enormously padded shoulders, coats to the knees, and yellow shoes with knobs on the toes, very high collars, tie pins, black ties, white handkerchiefs arranged in four points, enormous white carnations, and around their necks on cords hung crosses three or four inches long that glittered like emeralds and rubies. In spite of all this and their rather lurid presentations—they prefaced their hymns with "Give us a hand, dear Christian friends"—they sang marvelously, and acted out some of the songs in a very queer dreamlike way, walking around the church and making very large, slow gestures. At one point they ran what they called a "contest." Each one put a handsome white silk muffler around his throat and took up a collection, individually—apparently 10¢ was a "point," and the littlest one, the bass, wrote the results down in a large account book. I didn't catch on at all and just handed my quarter to the first one that came by. The tenor won the "contest" and then showed off a little, humming a very high note until the audience nearly burst and then going off into a long falsetto yell. I almost thought I should wire Louise [Crane] about them—I don't think secularization would hurt them much!

. . . I feel I *must* do something about my Life & Works very soon—this wastefulness is a sin—but I just can't figure out what. I wish it were 1934 all over again. I'd do everything quite differently. Ringling Brothers is going to be in Miami next week—I hope to combine it with a trip to the dentist.

Isn't *bursitis* a bump on the elbow or something like that? I do hope you'll let me know how you are, and how your mother is.

I've started to take typing at the Convent now. I thought it was about time I learned to do it the right way. Sister Catherine (who teaches Spanish—also chemistry, Latin, etc. etc.) teaches individually. She is a little black dynamo of energy, high spirits, and devoutness. I go every other day for an hour and a half. Maybe I'd better just settle down and go to high school all over again with Sister Catherine!

It is cool and so beautiful here. Tomorrow is some big Cuban celebration—the Cuban army band is coming over, there is to be a parade, etc.

[P.S.] I can wash quite well. We do it outdoors here—heat the water in an iron kettle on a little fire (only Marjorie has a heater now)—and have done it several times, but I *can't* iron. The present incumbent has me starched so stiffly today I can scarcely sit down. I also got her some pine oil to use and she likes it so much the house is just like the heart of a forest. I think you and your mother are wonderful to do all the things you do.

December 29, 1943

I am so upset to hear of your mother's fall. It is *dreadful* and I can imagine how many miserable days you spent afterwards. I am so glad to hear that she is getting over it so well. Are the sidewalks icy now? My grandmother used to wear little spikes on straps on her shoes in the ice and snow of Nova Scotia, but probably one can't get them any more. Please give your mother my fondest regards and *make* her get better fast. I'm glad you got the oranges safely. I didn't mean them exactly as a "Christmas Gift," feeling about the way you do about Christmas, I guess, but it just seemed like a good time of year for extra orange juice . . .

46 King Street
New York
October 9, 1944
Sunday morning

At last, on this perfectly beautiful quiet *Sabbath* morning, I have time to write you again and tell you some more about how I like *Nevertheless* [MM's new book of poems]. But first I want to say that I do hope you managed to throw off the cold and that your mother didn't catch it. I was just going out to call you, to tell you not to come because I was sure it was going to rain, when your note came—and then I was so glad you didn't because it drizzled all afternoon and was very cold and disagreeable. But the last two days have been so beautiful. I hope you've felt much better for them.

Well, you don't bear any resemblance to my "current product," to *me*—I was just thinking as I re-read the poems in bed this morning before getting up. If I'd never seen anything by M. Moore at all, and noticed "The Mind Is an Enchanting Thing" in a magazine, I would immediately start off all over again and look up everything I could find in the library [by this writer]. General compliments don't mean very much, I guess, so in "Elephants" I like *particularly*:

> *sleeping with the calm of youth*

and

> asleep like a lifeless six-foot
> frog, so feather light, etc.

—it sounds so completely relaxed, and "magic hairs!" and of course "he /

> is not here to worship and he is too wise
> to mourn

it just couldn't be better, and of course the last two lines ["Who rides on a tiger can never dismount; / asleep on an elephant, that is repose"], but I like all of it. Is it Buddha who *is* able to shoot through the four plantain leaves?

Where is "A Carriage from Sweden"? I should like to see it. I was so glad to see the word "Brooklyn" and I like "freckled / integrity" for it, too.

"Compromise archipelago / of rocks" is wonderful, and sounds wonderful, and the part about the spruce tree "from a green trunk, green shelf / on shelf fanning out by itself" takes me straight back to Nova Scotia. I like the last stanza with all the S's, too—it sounds so nice and solid.

The balancing, suspended-in-air quality of "The Mind Is an Enchanting Thing" fascinates me. Did you do it to a tune? I like best the lines from "the mind" in line 4 of the second stanza, to "strong enchantment." And the next to the last stanza, particularly "it takes apart / dejection." It is my own stupidity that makes me fail to understand things. I'm not quite sure just which "mind" you mean—just brain as opposed to heart? or no, I guess you mean something more idealistic, the part of the mind we think of as constructing, or "striving" as Charles says?

Well, I love "The Wood-Weasel," as I said before. I can hear your mother saying the last sentence ["Only / Wood-weasels shall associate with me"] . . .

The doctor gave me a couple of kinds of new medicine to try, and took various tests, etc. I'm to go back in two weeks. I'm still having trouble, but really not very bad. I am sure he'll be able to do something for me eventually, anyway.

Your mentioning Ceylon at the end of "Elephants" reminds me that I must show you my book [by H. F. Macmillan], and also tell you sometime about when I met a Saigonese princess last winter. It is so warm I hope you and your mother are on your rooftop . . .

To Edmund Wilson

December 7, 1944

I hear that you and Mary [McCarthy] are in town again but since I'm not sure of the address I'm sending this in care of *The New Yorker*.

I have a literary problem just now that I wondered if possibly I could ask you about—sometime when it would be quite convenient for you. I can't get a telephone [in wartime], so I'll have to trouble you to write me a note.

I hope that you and Mary and Reuel [their son] are all well and I look forward to seeing you.

To Marianne Moore

December 8, 1944

This is a fresh start. I am looking at "Propriety" [MM's new poem] again and I think I'm beginning to "catch on," although I'm awfully slow. I liked the various things in it from the first reading, and the form of it, but something bothered me—now I think I GET it, and the effect of the dialogue at the end I particularly like. It suddenly doubles it. I think I hear a maternal note there, but that may just be my imagination. I like the woodpecker very much (and, as a matter of fact, Anna B. Lindsey quoted that part to me before I'd seen the poem, although she pretends to scorn "poetry"). I am mad, though, because I have tried to use "fish spines" about palm trees a few times, but I guess it's really better about the fir pines ["The fish-spine / on firs"]. And I admire the repetitions at the end highly, and "born that way" [poem's conclusion].

You went to such trouble to write me that nice letter while I was at the Lindseys'. I'm sorry my wailings were heard all the way to Brooklyn, Marianne. I won't even attempt to thank you, or anyone—everyone was so extremely kind and considerate, including Dr. Baldwin, whom I put to endless trouble and telephone calls. But I'm feeling much, much better and everything looks brighter and I hope to prove myself almost human quite soon now.

Here is Mr. Rodriguez y Feo's letter. You see, he is under a considerable misapprehension as to [Gregorio] Valdes's work—the number of pictures, that is—and certainly their quality. I have only five, and the only three that were any good were reproduced in *Partisan Review*. Louise took the pictures, which came out *fairly* well. As far as I remember, *P.R.* never returned them, so I've written to ask them about it. In any case, since my piece appeared there first, I suppose I should write them [for permission to reprint], shouldn't I? Edwin Denby had a lot [of Valdes's paintings], but most of them were destroyed when his apartment burned up. The best one of all was owned by Orson Welles and I believe it was in the fire too, but there might be a picture of it. Then there's one in a bar in Key West, and I suppose Marjorie could somehow get me a picture of that. It would be a good choice, since it is of a famous plaza in Havana. I'm not sure whose esthetic judgment should rule the matter!—since it *is* my article, I almost feel mine should. So I guess I'll write Mr. Janis for the one good picture he had, and Edwin Denby, and in the meantime write to Mr. R. y Feo and tell him I'm gathering pictures for him . . .

I am enclosing the letter from Houghton Mifflin Company. Since I have no idea who Jean Pedrick is, and he or she may have thought of writing all by him or herself, I suppose it is rather meaningless—and will be to you anyway, I'm afraid, because of the writer's taste! I've written the terms on the back, instead of sending the form to you, first, because I've been trying to compose some answers, and, second, because I think I'm going to see Edmund Wilson next week sometime and I thought I'd ask him what *he* thought about it. He might be able to tell me what I should do about Harcourt Brace and Company since they are his publishers, etc. At any rate, Marianne, please don't let me bother you with it because I am not taking any of it very seriously and you see there is plenty of time anyway. I'm writing to thank Jean Pedrick—and I'm preparing a lovely brand-new set of mss., just in case . . .

There's a man going by with a little furnace on wheels selling baked yams. Loren brought some in the other morning and they were delicious—we ate them with cider. It is almost two o'clock, so I'm hoping you'll arrive just in time.

To Edmund Wilson

December 26, 1944

After seeing you the other night I received another letter from Houghton Mifflin Company sending me an application blank [for their fellowship]. Until then I hadn't realized that it was necessary to have two or more "sponsors." Besides the sample of work and a "description of the project," it asks for "letters from at least two responsible persons." These letters may be sent directly to Houghton Mifflin Company or may be enclosed with the application. They may refer either to the applicant's "character, or literary qualifications, or both."

Marianne Moore has kindly offered to be one sponsor for me. I dislike bothering you very much. Please feel that you can refuse without hurting my feelings at all—but would you be willing to be the other one? I shouldn't think the letter would have to be very long. It has to be in before March 1st.

I don't know how many of my poems you have seen. I have thirty-odd on hand now, and my "project" will just be to write some more and some better ones. If you'd like to have a look at the work so far all together, I'll be glad to send you the manuscript. But please don't feel obligated in any way.

I hope your cold is better. Please give my best to Mary and thank her for me for a very nice dinner and evening.

[P.S.] This thing is called "The Houghton Mifflin Literary Fellowship Award in Poetry."

To Marianne Moore

January 5, 1945

. . . I know you aren't well enough—besides being too occupied—to bother with writing to me, Marianne, much less to Houghton Mifflin, etc. (Possibly that should be the other way around. There are several constructions like that that I think I must get your mother to explain to me sometime.) Since the letter doesn't have to be there until *March 1st*, please just don't think of it for a while, and don't *dream* of writing to them about any "delay." I haven't sent the manuscript yet, and won't until you say you're "ready." Mr. Wilson sent me a very flattering "recommendation," so I'll send it along with the manuscript, I guess, or at the same time. You please do everything exactly as you think best. There is something so embarrassing about this going around *fishing* and I think the whole idea is very stupid. People like you and Mr. Wilson shouldn't be annoyed, and what on earth are their judges for, anyway? Well—

Sometime I should very much like to hear what you thought of the Gide dialogue, and Malcolm Cowley's piece at the end. I thought I learned quite a lot from that—things I should have known before. [Louis] Aragon's *Crève-Coeur* has some quite interesting experiments in rhyme—for the French, that is—and also an essay on the French system that I find very helpful.

I'm writing in bed, Marianne. I have had a touch of "flu" myself—it is very slight. I've stayed in bed two days and will get up tomorrow. In the meantime I am enjoying myself very much and have actually started writing again. Blanche is here this morning. (I don't believe I have mentioned Blanche—this is the fifth Friday she has come and washed and ironed, and I feel almost as if I had an old retainer. She is going to mail this for me.)

You don't mention the [Harriet] Monroe [Poetry] Award, but I don't believe you could *mind* it, and I was so pleased to hear of it . . . Please don't overdo, Marianne. Please don't relapse. They say that is the greatest danger of the disease. It was "flu" you had, too, wasn't it?—and it must have been ten times worse than this of mine. My only trouble just now is a strange wavering when I stand up. Did you—do you—have that? It's a beautiful day today and fairly warm. I hope it is doing you both good . . .

January 8, 1945

I was just sitting down to write to you this morning to thank you for the "reference," when a letter came from you (postmarked *January 8th, 2 a.m.*—isn't it amazing?). You shouldn't have bothered to write or to send back those scraps. My Hermes is so light I can type in bed —not well, but almost as well as usual. And—oh *dear*—you haven't been a drag in the slightest degree. I don't see that there is any hurry at all. I've got everything together now, except that I expect to hear from Dr. Dewey today or tomorrow, and I'll mail it all as soon as I do, and I hope that you won't give it another thought even, unless I let you know I've received $1,000! (And in that case don't you think a "commission" would be only fair, Marianne?) I'm sure the writing was beautifully legible, and vice versa, and I can't thank you enough. I think so little of the whole idea and have so little confidence in it that I'm being quite perfectly honest when I say that if it comes to nothing, I'll be much sorrier for having put you to such trouble and wasted your time, than for myself!

. . . I'm going up to Dr. Baldwin's this afternoon and I shall certainly ask him about Afaxin. He seems to think that if you eat properly and drink milk you don't need any such things. If you don't drink milk, you should take vitamin B—which I do faithfully—but the whole idea is still questionable, isn't it? But don't let my skepticism bother you. It's just that I hate to think that the human race can't get proper nourishment from all the beautiful things—meat, fish, fowl and fruits—that there are to eat in the world.

Yesterday the snowstorm was so beautiful, particularly from about 8 to 9 in the morning as it grew lighter and the snow got icier and more glistening. Did you see it? It is almost a novelty to me again now and I'm enjoying it.

You are right, of course, about the construction of the first sentence of my "project." I wrote that off very carelessly. I've changed it now to read: "to finish 6 or 7 poems of what I hope may be a serious nature and in a more appropriate and intense form than those enclosed," etc. I think that's a little better, don't you? (rhetorical question, Marianne, I'll be mad if you reply).

Don't tell me that *Nevertheless* has earned only $13.31 the past year! Or is that an average?—it must be. Something should be done about it all, and I wonder what. I think Mr. Wilson ought to get to work on it— he is a good fighter, I'm sure. And I do hope the Monroe Award will cover the doctors all around and lap over some.

It seems to be thawing. The tree and my porch railings are dripping and the sparrows are acting very pleased about something . . . What you say about "small things that must be done" is what I *curse* all the time. But to have you feel the same way, apparently, cheers me up.

To the Houghton Mifflin Literary Fellowship Award

January 16, 1945

Yesterday I mailed to you a manuscript of thirty-two or -three poems, to be entered in your Poetry Fellowship contest. With the manuscript I enclosed letters from two "sponsors": Miss Marianne Moore and Mr. Edmund Wilson. I have a third sponsor, Dr. John Dewey, but I am not sure whether he is sending his letter directly to you, or to me to send to you. In any case, if you have not already received it, you will in a few days.

To Ferris Greenslet

Author, editor, and publisher Ferris Greenslet (1875–1959) wrote books about Pater and James Russell Lowell, edited The Atlantic Monthly, *and served as literary advisor to Houghton Mifflin from 1907. In 1933 he became general manager of their trade book department. He accepted EB's first book of poems for publication in January 1945, before the judges (including himself) awarded her the Poetry Fellowship for* North & South *the following June.*

January 22, 1945

I was very glad to have your letter awaiting me when I arrived Saturday night, and to learn that you approve of what new poems there are at present, at least. I have often wondered where the "King" in King St. [her New York address] came from, too—it certainly isn't either very kingly or gentlemanly now, I'm afraid.

Yes, there is a type that I especially like for poetry—Baskerville. I think that Baskerville monotype, 169 E, makes the best looking poetry pages I've seen printed. I particularly dislike those light type faces some publishers seem to think appropriate for poetry. It seems to me that the Baskerville monotype 169 E, eleven-point, would be perfect—but eleven-point might be too big—it might make too many run-over lines—maybe they could try and see. It would all depend on the size of the page.

I have one more request. Don't you think the title would look well as *North & South*, using the "&" sign? It seems more forceful that way to me. Maybe after a while they could send me a title page to brood over. As you see, I guess, I am very much interested in typography.

I have another idea that I think you will agree with. The fact that none of these poems deal directly with the war, at a time when so much war poetry is being published, will, I am afraid, leave me open to reproach. The chief reason is simply that I work very slowly. But I think it would help some if a note to the effect that most of the poems had been written, or begun at least, before 1941, could be inserted at the beginning, say just after the acknowledgments. I'll enclose a sheet with the acknowledgments and such a note, to see what you think.

The sudden change in temperature from Key West to here has been very stimulating so far. As a Christmas present, I went out fishing the day before I left, but we didn't have very good luck. I had a sailfish on and lost it, to the captain's disgust—but did catch a *wahoo*. We had a beautiful day in the Gulf, though . . .

June 3, 1945

Thank you very, very much for your telegram and for your kind letter containing the check. Of course I am extremely happy to receive the award and the money could not have come at a more acceptable time. The feeling of not being rushed about the book is most agreeable to me, too.

The quotations you sent were highly pleasing to my vanity—in fact, thank you for your very thoughtful letter. I have only told my immediate circle of friends, all of whom are close-mouthed to extremes.

I haven't any photograph of myself on hand but I have already made arrangements to have one taken and I should be able to send you the results toward the end of next week—I hope that will be all right.

As you say the title *North & South* might be improved upon—and of course it will depend somewhat on what poems I can finish to add to the collection. I am working on several now that I feel may turn out better than anything so far—and if so I could eliminate some of the weaker ones from the book you have. Anyway, the award has made me feel like trying very hard.

Thank you again—and I hope you have a nice vacation and catch many fish. I have been planning a short trip to Boston sometime this summer and I am looking forward to meeting you then or in New York. I don't know whether I should write to the other judges or not. I hope they will accept my thanks and best wishes.

To Marianne Moore

June 6, 1945

Here are Mr. Greenslet's telegram [announcing that EB had won the fellowship] and the letter that came a few days later—I thought you might like to see them. I wonder if you'd send them back at your convenience? I think the letter shows a great deal of thought and consideration, don't you?—but of course he is quite right about the "collocation." I wrote him a kind of thank-you note for the GRAND [$1,000 prize] to say how it would come in very handy. I wonder if I should write the judges, too—or does that smack of *post hoc, ergo propter hoc* bribery?

I am so worried about you and wish I could be of some use to you and your mother. I do hope you got over the insomnia period safely and that you are both feeling well. But you don't sound right—and I wish I could do something about it. Maybe soon you will come over some sunny morning and sit in my "garden" with me—come to breakfast. It's all planted, in boxes and pots, and although not quite a bower yet, it will be, I hope, in a few weeks. There is sun on it—now that we seem to be going to have some again—from 8 till 3 sharp, when it sets behind a factory. *Please* come—it would be so nice.

I hope the poem about the dogs came back and howled at the door and was let in this time. Could I see it?

P.S. I had my picture taken by a Mr. Breitenbach Tuesday—haven't seen them yet, of course. He has done some nice ones of Maillol, Dewey, Bemelmans, etc. He is a German refugee. I'll show you the results. He wanted to see the poems first, but I forgot to take them so I sent him some afterwards. He is very SERIOUS.

To Ferris Greenslet

> 623 Margaret Street
> Key West, Florida
> September 10, 1945

I wonder if you could let me know about when you are thinking of publishing my book? I have just sold three poems—new ones—two to *The New Yorker* and one to *Partisan Review*—and they would like to know the publication date so that they can print them in the magazines first. I have two or three more about ready to send off and it seems to me that with them the book will be about large enough. Naturally I should like to publish as many of the poems as I can in magazines first because of the additional money to be earned; I also hope to have two or three previously unprinted ones in the book. I should think I should be as ready as can be by the end of October.

Could you let me know about this quite soon, as the magazines are waiting to hear? I'm sorry to trouble you and thank you very much. The above will be my address for the next six weeks at least.

> November 20, 1945

Your letter was forwarded to me here where I think now I shall be until shortly after Christmas.

I have just been looking over the carbon of the manuscript I originally sent you and have found several mistakes and omissions. I wonder if you would be kind enough to send that manuscript back to me here? Then I can make a perfect copy, adding to it the new poems I have, and send it all back to you—*promptly*.

I think at present there are five new ones. I wish there were more, but two more Key West ones may be done in time yet.

It will be possible for me, won't it, to have some choice about the "physical embodiment" of the book that you mention? My ideas are not eccentric nor grandiose but I should very much like to have some preference about color, shape, etc. I imagine we shall agree about it.

I think you said something about never having fished here, didn't you? Well, of course it has been almost impossible to go out the last few years because of gasoline rationing, but I am hoping to get out one day before I go back to New York. I was taken out last year and caught several dolphin—a fish I'd never caught before. One of the poems I'm working on is about a dying dolphin, one of the most beautiful sights I have ever seen. But I'm not a real sportswoman—most of my fishing is done off docks and the bridges of the Overseas Highway. Another [unfinished] poem is "The Life of the Hurricane" (the one you inquired about), but since it went right around us and hit Miami instead I'm afraid that one will have to wait. Delighted the Key West Chamber of Commerce, though.

To Marianne Moore

46 King Street
New York City
Christmas, 1945

I can't *bear* to think of you being so sick and wretched and my not being able to do anything at all for you. I know you will not like what I am doing, but it will make me feel a little better, and won't you please look at the whole thing that way? It would be good for me and make me very happy if you'd let me come over and be a cook, maid, nurse, "sitter"—anything you can think of. You will promise to let me know (by way of Loren's is quickest and easiest) if there is anything I can do, won't you? That in itself would be a comfort. Please have the doctor come to call—I'm sure you haven't.

I saw Mr. [Edmund] Wilson last night and he was very kind about my work and feels that Houghton Mifflin (this is, at any rate, regardless of my plans) is a much better house than Harcourt Brace. He almost seemed to want to fight Harcourt Brace physically because of their peculiar behavior about me. He had a terrible cold too, and I felt he was just staying up to be polite and I appreciated it.

Everyone, it seems to me, has been sick or sad or both, and I do wish we could all get over it soon. I am so distressed about you, Marianne— you *mustn't*. Mr. Wilson spoke about all your recent poems in the most complimentary way. He thinks the "war" poem ["In Distrust of Merits"] "magnificent." I want to write some more but I guess I had better get this off to you. I am sorry it is so badly written. I am much better now than when we talked . . .

I saw Margaret [Miller] at the Museum and she was so sorry to hear you weren't feeling well. If I go on now I shall just start repeating myself, so I'll stop. But remember I am ready—just like the Fire Department.

THREE

1946-1951

North & South, MAINE, HAITI, YADDO

WASHINGTON

At the Bard College Poetry Conference, October 1948, from left: Louise Bogan, William Carlos Williams, Jean Garrigue, Lloyd Frankenberg, Elizabeth Bishop, Joseph Summers, Richard Wilbur, Richard Eberhart and Kenneth Rexroth (both in shadow), Robert Lowell

To Ferris Greenslet

623 Margaret Street
Key West, Florida
January 11, 1946

I shall send the manuscript back to you today or Monday. I hope it will be all right and that from now on I'll be able to work more rapidly and prolifically. I really feel, although there isn't too much to show for it, that I have learned a great deal in the past six months. But I have been worried for fear my output may have been a disappointment; the only excuse I can offer is that I have been "enjoying poor health" all the past year.

All I had in mind about format was this: I dislike the modern unglazed linen bindings so very much that I wondered if I could have a glazed one? And could it be a dark gray? I think that quite a dark gray with a gilt *North & South* down the back would look nice, don't you?—and if gilt is not possible maybe a dark blue lettering? Looking over the ms. as a whole it seems to me a slightly squarer than usual book would suit it —but I don't know how large you intend to make it and it would all depend on that. Is there any possibility that I can have something to say about the type?

I'll be back in New York the 19th, at 46 King Street. I wonder if you could set me an absolute deadline in case I decide to include some more new poems? . . .

46 King Street
New York, New York
February 22, 1946

In going over our correspondence I find that with this last postponement it will be almost a year that Houghton Mifflin has put off bringing out my book. As I said in my last letter, and as of course you must understand, this is getting to be very awkward for me.

I have a second book planned and under way. It is hard to know where to place things and when they should appear—in fact, hard to work properly under the circumstances.

You speak of "build up," "advance propaganda," etc., and it seems to me that the Award itself had a great deal of publicity value which by now, I'm afraid, is lost.

There are at least two New York publishing houses who would publish the book as you have it now, and would have several months ago.

I realize that this is probably not your fault. However I do feel that in view of all the postponements I should be released from the option clause of my agreement with you and left free to sell the next book to a house more interested in getting my poetry on the market. Don't you agree with me?

February 27, 1946

I wonder if by now I might not be able to ask you for the definite publication date of my book? Not having heard from you makes me feel that there have been further postponements. It is really getting to be embarrassingly difficult for me—not only because of inquiries, but because I have the next book of poems quite well mapped out and I don't know what to include in this one, what to work on next, etc. I sold some more things to *The New Yorker* and they want to know the publication date so they'll know when to print them, etc. Could I please hear from you about it?

P.S. I wonder if you could also tell me, for the benefit of the Internal Revenue Dept., whether the Poetry Fellowship Award is taxable or not?

April 19, 1946

I am terribly sorry to hear that you have been so sick and I do hope you are feeling better and making a very quick recovery. I hadn't realized how ill you had been until a week or so ago when someone here spoke of it.

I have been sick myself the past two weeks, but very slightly, but that is the reason I've been slow about answering your letter.

The type and the shape of the page please me very much—just what I wanted. At first I thought I didn't like the lines at the top but after some consideration I've decided that I do after all. The only detail I'd find fault with on the two sample pages you sent me—and I guess it can be remedied easily enough—is that the page numbers are too close to the last line of type. You say in your letter that the type is imposed a little lower than it should be, which when corrected would make the numbers look even worse. And I much prefer them without the brackets, don't you?

There are a few other things I'd like to ask you about:

I notice that both on the proof and in the publicity announcement the book is referred to as *North and South*. I think that quite a while ago you agreed with me that *North & South* would be more effective and I should think it would be better to make use of the "&" sign, not only on the cover but all the time.

I have done some work on the [catalogue] description and am enclosing it. I hope it will meet with your approval. "Torrid south" sounded rather lurid, I thought; also it didn't strike me as very good advertising even to hint that all "poetry lovers" wouldn't be crazy about the book! I have really just corrected what you sent—if you'd like me to try to write some more, I will.

You may remember my sending you a sort of little foreword some time ago? I still think it is very important. Miss Anderson wrote me that it was mislaid while you were away. I can't remember the exact wording of the first one, which I think pleased me more than the one I'm enclosing, but if it doesn't turn up would you please use this? It should come just after the list of acknowledgments.

Another thing is when and how would you like me to arrange the order?

And although this may be a little premature I should like to ask about the paper dust jacket. If you are going to be able to give me a gray cover, it seems to me that a pale blue dust jacket would be very nice—maybe with dark gray lettering. But of course I know that booksellers often object to light dust jackets. I like the type used for the titles and should think that in a larger size it would look quite handsome on the cover and jacket.

I don't know whether this is at all likely or not but it occurred to me that you might be using some of my original "sponsors'" remarks for publicity purposes. In the letter that Miss Marianne Moore wrote for me she commented on some likeness to the painter Max Ernst. Although many years ago I once admired one of Ernst's albums, I believe that Miss Moore is mistaken about his ever having been an influence, and since I have disliked all of his painting intensely and am not a surrealist, I think it would be misleading to mention my name in connection with his. There was probably no danger of this in the first place and I do know what Miss Moore had in mind—however I thought it would be a good idea to mention it, just in case.

Just as I started to write this letter, the galley proof came and I shall get to work on it right away. The approximate date of publication is now September, isn't it?—which I believe is supposed to be a good time? You may be interested to know, although it sounds like boasting, that I have been receiving many requests for poems lately and am beginning to feel very optimistic about the book.

Again I hope you are feeling better, and if I should be writing to anyone else about these things instead of you, please let me know.

April 26, 1946

I have just looked through the various books of poetry in my bookcase and find that with one exception the page numbers are all *without* brackets. I don't know quite what to make of this, except that it obviously can be done. Even more important from the point of view of appearance was the lack of space between the numbers and the last lines—they looked very cramped, at least in those two sample pages you sent me.

I am doing the proof and settling the order now and will get it back to you the first of the week.

April 29, 1946

I am returning the proof today. I have arranged the order but cannot really decide on it for good, until I know for sure whether each poem is to begin on a separate page or not—but of course I imagine it will. Could you let me know about this?

I have left out one poem that seemed to be too slight when put with the others and it will also mean leaving out the acknowledgment to *Harper's Bazaar* in the list of acknowledgments.

Could you also tell me if I shall receive page proofs? . . .

May 30, 1946

I haven't heard from you since I returned the proofs of the front pages about two weeks ago. At that time I thought you had written me that the cover was on its way and I believe that the book was to appear in June? Someone just told me that they had seen a copy of the *Publishers Weekly* in which it was announced for August. Could you let me know? I am going away for a while in about ten days and want to be sure everything gets sent to the right address, etc., and also would like to know the date.

June 6, 1946

. . . It has just occurred to me that possibly you would like to have another picture of me for advertising purposes. I think the only one you have is that profile. I have a portrait of myself just painted—not quite finished—by Loren MacIver, that everyone seems to think is a very good picture. If you'd be interested in using it I could get it photographed here and sent to you inside a few days, I think. I should have thought of it sooner of course.

I am going away to New Hampshire in about ten days—I am not sure of the address yet. I should like before I go to subscribe to a clipping service and had thought of Romeike's. Have you any suggestions to make as to this?

To Houghton Mifflin

The Nova Scotian Hotel
Halifax, Nova Scotia
July 8, 1946

I don't know whether you are the person whom I should address or not but since my last communication [from Houghton Mifflin] was from you, I shall write to you and you can hand the letter on to the proper people.

Since I understand the book is being postponed now until September, I feel that the bad misprint that occurs in one of the poems should *certainly* be corrected. Mr. Greenslet said it was to be in the first place and it was just recently that someone else wrote me saying it couldn't be done. Now that there is extra time I see no reason for it. The misprint is in "The Imaginary Iceberg," in stanza 1, line 7: "ships'," as it is now printed, should be "ship's."

Mr. Greenslet also told me to begin with that I would receive page proofs. Later this was changed but again I don't see any reason why I shouldn't, now that there is more time. I also was to receive a *sample* dust jacket, and cover. I haven't received any cover at all and the dust jacket was recently sent to me already printed and is a great disappointment. I suppose nothing further can be done about that but I don't understand why things are done in this manner.

The most important thing of all however is that I should like to be given an opportunity to see what you are going to print in the way of blurbs on the jacket before they are irrevocable. Quite a while ago Mr. Greenslet sent me some such material and I partially re-wrote it at his suggestion. It was so full of mistakes and wrong emphasis that it makes me very nervous to think what may appear on the dust jacket. Will you please let me know about this?

I think you are perfectly right about not using the reproduction of the portrait. This address will reach me until further notice.

To Ferris Greenslet

Ragged Islands Inn
Allendale (Sherburne County)
Nova Scotia
July 24, 1946

I'm afraid all my recent changes of address have been rather confusing. The one above will be right until further notice, probably for three weeks more.

Of course I am eager to see the book as soon as it is ready and I think from your letter of the 12th, that was supposed to be the 16th? I am afraid you may possibly have sent a copy to the Nova Scotian Hotel in Halifax, which in spite of my instructions hasn't forwarded some other books which were sent me.

My being in another country just now is a little awkward. I have just sent the publicity department a list of people & publications I think should be sent review copies, including the other judges besides yourself. I also mentioned sending a copy to Pablo Neruda, the Chilean poet, who has been very kind about my work and when I was in Mexico talked of publishing some translations of it in Spanish. He is now, I believe, in Chile, and I think a little South American publicity would be very interesting, don't you? I was very pleased to hear that Mr. Eliot was interested in my book.

About my "12 free copies" and those others I should like to purchase—I believe they had better wait until I return, don't you?

July 26, 1946

Our last letters crossed in the mail, I see. I hope the list I sent of places I think the book should be sent to be reviewed, possibly, is all right—there may be more. Since I am away and the mails seem to be rather uncertain here and I also am not sure when I shall get back to New York, I think it would probably be much better if you can send out my other copies for me. I am enclosing a list of names and addresses. Perhaps the other judges would have received copies anyway? As you see I have more than my eleven "free" copies here. I believe I am entitled to purchase extra copies at a 40% discount and I wonder if these extra copies could be sent for me and you can send me a bill for them, etc.—since I don't know what the book is selling for, I can't send you a check. I want to give some copies to my Canadian friends and relations so I am asking for five to be sent to me here for that purpose.

Perhaps a reviewer's copy to the English magazine *Horizon* (Cyril Connolly, editor) would be a good idea, too. And I believe you said you were sending one to Mr. T. S. Eliot?

As I said I should very much like to get a copy to Pablo Neruda somehow, and I have also listed a very good young Spanish refugee writer in Mexico who also wanted to do some translations of my work.

No copies have reached me as yet, but I imagine they will eventually.

July 30, 1946

The book reached me here last night and I thought I would let you know how pleased I am with the general appearance of it. I like the cover very much; in fact I like almost everything about it except the jacket. And I am sorry there aren't more poems.

I am trying to remedy that at present, though. The next book of poems is to be called (I hope) *Faustina & Other Poems*.

To John Malcolm Brinnin

Poet, critic, and biographer John Malcolm Brinnin wrote EB from Yaddo asking her for some new poems for his anthology.

Halifax, Nova Scotia
[August 15?, 1946]

You see I am in your native city. I wrote Houghton Mifflin and asked them to send you a copy of my book. I'm afraid there isn't much in it that you haven't seen. I may be publishing some things in the fall or winter you might like better [for the anthology]—if your selection doesn't have to be made until spring.

To Marianne Moore

46 King Street
New York, New York
August 29, 1946

. . . I wish so much I could be of some help in the troubles that you and your mother are going through. Please, if there is anything I can do for you—from errands to scrubbing floors—call on me right away, won't you?

I thought you might be interested in hearing a little about some of my farm experiences. I stayed first for a month at a little inn on the south shore among the "Ragged Islands," then I visited in Halifax off and on for a while, and then I went back to Great Village, where my mother came from and where I lived when I was little. My aunt lives on an enormous (for that part of the country) farm about three miles from the Village. It is always described as the most beautiful farm on the Bay of Fundy, and I think it must be. You know about the Bay of Fundy and its tides, I imagine, that go out for a hundred miles or so and then come in with a rise of 80 feet. The soil is all dark terra-cotta color, and the bay, when it's *in*, on a bright day, is a real pink; then the fields are very pale lime greens and yellows and in back of them the fir trees start, dark blue-green. It's the richest, saddest, simplest landscape in the world. I hadn't been there for so long I'd forgotten how beautiful it all is—and the magnificent elm trees. One of the hugest right behind my grandmother's old house in the Village is known as "the Landmark Elm."

On the farm they raise pigs, potatoes, strawberries, supply the local dairy with most of its milk and cream, etc., and they used to raise race horses but they only have two now—the sulky racing variety. But I wanted to tell you about Pansy, the children's pony. She's a Sable Island pony, a breed that's supposed to have developed all by itself from a shipload of horses that was wrecked long ago on Sable Island (where my great-grandfather was wrecked, too). They're not much bigger than a Shetland, but better shaped, more like real horses, and beautiful velvety thick hair. They think that Pansy is over thirty years old. Aunt Grace and I went out to the pasture to see her and when she came over to the fence Aunt Grace lifted up her mane and it is all gray underneath—like a woman's hair combed not to show. She used to have lots of tricks: she'd walk right in the kitchen and put her front hoofs up on the back of a chair to beg for a doughnut. And my aunt said, "And she knew where the cookie jar was, too, and she'd follow me right in the pantry after cookies." The children even took her upstairs one day to see another aunt of mine who was sick in bed. They used to drive her to school every day in the winters in a little sleigh and sometimes when it was terribly cold they'd bring her in in the mornings and harness her beside the kitchen stove. All the schoolchildren used to take their lunches out and eat them with her in the minister's barn, where she stayed, and my cousin said, "She'd eat anything but oranges."

I've always loved those big farm collies, haven't you?—the present generation wait along the side of the roads for the buses to stop and their owners to get off. There are two now at my aunt's, an old one named Jock, and his son, whom he's trying to teach to herd cows, etc., and getting quite disgusted with because he will bark and run around too much. Jock is supposed to be such a wonderful cow herder that other farmers come and borrow him when they lose their cows in the woods. One day while I was there a man drove in in an old sedan and said a few words to my Uncle Will, who just said "Jock!" and opened the car door. Jock, apparently knowing exactly what was wanted of him, got in the back seat and sat up looking very pleased. He went thirty miles down the bay and found seven cows and was driven home that night looking very tired and complacent.

I went to call on a family in the Village, the MacLaughlins, and as I came up Mr. Mac was coming out of the barn with another farm collie—a very old one, his face was all white. He came up to me wagging his tail but barking in a very loud rather hollow-sounding way and Mr. Mac said to him, "Stop it, Jackie!" and then to me, in a sort of polite aside behind his hand, "He's stone deaf." We went in the house and as soon as I sat down Jackie promptly brought in a very old small bone and dropped it at my feet. Mrs. Mac shouted at him, "That's very hospitable of you, Jackie, but take it away!" and then said to me in the same polite aside, in a lowered voice, "He's stone deaf." I asked how old he was and they said about fifteen. "Yes," said Mrs. Mac. "Last winter they said we'd never keep him through the winter. But he had a very good winter, yes, a very good winter, didn't he, Don? He went to the woods with Don every day, and he only had rheumatism in one leg." And they both sat back and looked at him admiringly. Meanwhile we were all sitting on straight kitchen chairs, while a beautiful big gray cat lay sleeping in the nice padded rocking chair . . .

But of course being kind to animals is a very minor part of the farm life there. It is such hard work, I don't see how my aunt stands it at all —she is really one of the best and nicest people I know. There are so many people around all the time, coming and going, something is always happening, the cows get in the corn or the milking machines break down, distant relatives arrive unexpectedly for dinner, etc.—but she keeps going somehow and is always cheerful and funny. Fortunately all the sons, stepsons, hired men, etc., seem to adore her.

My plan was to take a room at a nearby farm so that I could have a little peace and privacy to work in, and stay on a few weeks. But the deed to the Key West house had to be signed right away, and in the U.S., for some legal reason, so I had to leave. I came back by bus—a dreadful trip, but it seemed most convenient at the time—we hailed it with a flashlight and a lantern as it went by the farm late at night. Early the next morning, just as it was getting light, the driver had to stop suddenly for a big cow moose who was wandering down the road. She walked away very slowly into the woods, looking at us over her shoulder. The driver said that one foggy night he had to stop while a huge bull moose came right up and smelled the engine. "Very curious beasts," he said.

Your letter, Marianne, has been such a comfort to me. The book seems so thin and says so very little, actually. Well, next time I hope to do better.

Margaret sent me the article from, was it *Harper's Bazaar?*—she'd cut it out—the Marguerite Young one. I thought that Miss Young had tried awfully hard and was certainly sincere and doing her very best— but oh, she really said so very little, don't you think? It made me think of lots of things I'd like to say myself and I'm trying to right now. I'll send you the results when I have done but I'm afraid they will strike you as pretty simpleminded. Well, they are sincere too—that's about all I can say for them . . .

To Ferris Greenslet

September 8, 1946

I had to come back from Nova Scotia two weeks earlier than I had planned, I am sorry to say, and I don't believe I have let you know yet about my change in address.

It was too bad that Edward Weeks [of *The Atlantic Monthly*] didn't like *North & South* better but I really feel he was slightly unfair. There is to be a "good" review in this week's *Saturday Review*, and a "better" one in the coming *Partisan Review* as well. I was very much impressed with the advertisement in the last *Saturday Review*. I have another advertising idea that may or may not be worthwhile. The Gotham Book Mart (to whose customers I should think I might "appeal") often encloses little cards for advertising and ordering some of the books of poems they have for sale. I presume these are got up by the publishers, but I don't know what you would think of it. I shall also get in touch with Miss Green here in New York about the radio interview.

Almost everyone who has spoken to me of it admires the format of the book very much.

October 1, 1946

I have enjoyed reading the many good reviews of your book about the [James Russell] Lowells very much and am looking forward to reading it—tonight, I hope.

I have an idea for *North & South* that I suppose I should send to the advertising department only I am never sure whom to address there. If you think it is good maybe you would be kind enough to pass it along? I am enclosing the two rather embarrassingly good reviews by Randall Jarrell [in *Partisan Review*] and Miss Moore [in *The Nation*]. It seems to me that just about now would be a good time for another large advertisement possibly quoting them? What do you think?

Also I have been thinking over plans for a book of prose I should like to write during the next six months. I don't know whether you have ever seen any of my stories or not. The book I have in mind is not stories, but maybe you would like to see them in order to have some idea of whether I can write prose or not. I should like very much to discuss this book with you or someone at Houghton Mifflin sometime soon. Possibly I can get to Boston sometime in the next two or three weeks. Could you tell me if any special time would be good, or if you might be interested? And thank you.

November 28, 1946

I still hope to get to Boston soon to discuss some writing plans with you or whoever would be the proper person, but in the meantime something else has come up that I believe I should probably mention to you before definitely accepting. *The New Yorker* has offered me what I believe they call a "first reading" agreement. You probably are familiar with the details—anyway they would want to see anything I should write during the coming year, verse or prose, first, and if they accept it they would pay me 25% above their [usual] payment price for it. I understand from Mrs. [E. B.] Katharine White that they have had this arrangement with several of your authors so I do not imagine that there would be any objections, however, I thought I should mention it to you first.

I doubt that they would actually be interested in any of the more serious poetry I have in mind for the coming year. The prose that I had in mind was in the nature of a book of travel essays about certain parts of South America, animals, buildings, etc. I wanted to see if you would be interested in giving me an advance for such a book. What prose I have that might give you an idea as to my qualifications for such writing is out at the moment, but I shall send it on to you in a few days. There is one story ["In Prison"] in the recently published *Partisan Reader*, however. I am also working on a couple of Mexican stories that would probably fit in, that I shall send to you when they are finished. I have several ideas that I really think might interest you.

I shall go ahead with *The New Yorker* business as soon as I hear from you.

I wonder if they will advertise *North & South* again before Christmas, using some of the good criticisms? I should think it would be a good idea.

December 18, 1946

I was very glad to receive the check for royalties. I have been told by several friends that they have been trying to get the book for Christmas presents at Brentano's and other bookstores and were unable to—but possibly that is a good sign. However I have been rather disappointed not to see any Christmas advertising whatever, since people do often give poetry for Christmas gifts, I believe.

What I am really writing about is to explain and apologize for a liberty I took quite recently. Someone suggested to me that I might try for a Guggenheim Fellowship, as a way of possibly coping with inflation. The idea had not occurred to me and it was already past the deadline but they were willing to accept my application if I "acted promptly." So I went ahead and used your name as a "sponsor" and only trust that it may be all right with you. I am sure you are probably greatly bothered with such requests—but I was so late that you may very well not hear from them at all. Anyway I do hope it will be all right and not a nuisance to you.

I am sending you some prose works in a few days with the hopes that you may still consider some sort of travel book by me . . .

To Arthur Mizener

Biographer of Scott Fitzgerald and Ford Madox Ford, teacher and critic, Arthur Mizener (1907–88) sent a copy of his review of North & South *to EB before its publication in* Furioso *(Spring 1947). He seems to have made one change she suggested; his printed text attributes the first quote she questioned to W. H. Auden.*

46 King Street
New York City
January 14, 1947

It was very thoughtful of you to send me the copy of your review of my book.* In fact you are the only reviewer who thought of doing it, although I shall eventually receive a copy of it after it appears from a clipping bureau. Although your name is of course familiar to me, I don't seem to remember the discussion in the [Vassar] *Miscellany News* at all, but I do think I remember your wife, a very pretty girl a year or two after me, wasn't she?

I think your review is very flattering and I am very pleased. You don't say when it is to appear and it may be too late for any alterations but, if you don't object, I am going to suggest two. The first isn't really a change. In the first paragraph you quote someone to the effect that "love which does not 'leave the North in place / With a good grace' " etc. As it stands surrounded by quotations from me, this looks as if it were by me, and I think it might be a good idea to give the name of the author, don't you, to avoid giving a false impression or possibly getting into difficulties with him, whoever he may be?

The second change I should like to see made is in the use of the quotation "It would be hard to say what brought them there, / commerce or contemplation." I think I know what you had in mind, but I am very much afraid that gives the impression that I may write for "commercial reasons"—in which case I am certainly a decided failure.

Thank you again and if it is too late to make these changes please don't worry about them.

To Dr. Anny Baumann

Born in Berlin, which she decided to leave after reading Mein Kampf, *Dr. Anny Baumann (1905–82) was a general practitioner on the staff of Lenox Hill Hospital in New York. She had many writers and other creative people among her patients.*

Briton Cove, Cape Breton
Nova Scotia
July 11, 1947

I am afraid it's impossible to practice medicine at long distance and I am hoping that by the time you get this my troubles will be over, but I

* The conclusion of Mr. Mizener's review: "We have waited a long time for these thirty poems, seeing that Miss Bishop was writing good verse when she was a senior at Vassar (at least one of these poems was written then). It is easy to say they are well worth having waited for; they are. It is not so easy to say why, to say how honestly they use, without abusing, the rhetorical resources of verse, how perfectly they balance devotion to fact and to memory and desire, how beautifully they combine toughness and elegance of mind."

thought I'd write and tell you about them anyway and see if you had any suggestions as to what I might do. As you may remember, I had been having asthma steadily for several weeks before I left. I was taking about 2 cc of adrenaline every night. I guess the two nights on the train didn't help much, and it's been getting worse ever since—I have to take about 2 cc during the course of the day and 3 or 4 during the night. I stayed in bed yesterday, thinking if I didn't move it might help, but last night was as bad as ever. There is absolutely nothing here that I can think of that might cause it—the boardinghouse is very clean, it's on the ocean, the animals aren't near, etc. Along with the asthma a rash has come out on my wrist and arm where the poison ivy started. It itches like poison ivy but looks more like eczema to me, I'm afraid—but I sometimes get that when I have a lot of asthma.

Maybe this will just wear off after a while. The only thing I can think of is that maybe you could suggest a change of medicine or something drastic to break it up. There isn't any doctor for 40 miles or so, but I can order things sent from a drugstore in Sydney. I think a prescription from the U.S. isn't any good here, but I suppose if one were necessary you could send it and maybe I could get a copy from a Sydney doctor. Mrs. MacLeod thinks her doctor would do it for me by mail. Of course there may be nothing I can do but just keep on taking adrenaline.

This is one of the most beautiful places I have ever seen—much nicer than Lockeport. We want to take a lot of trips and long walks, etc., that's what makes the asthma so discouraging. But as I said, it may just stop and then I shall have put you to the trouble of writing for nothing.

I haven't had anything to drink . . .

July 22, 1947

Thank you very much for your letter and I wish I could report some improvement but I'm afraid I can't. It is maddening. After I wrote you we had to get *the* Cape Breton doctor to drive over the mountains one night. He left me a supply of adrenaline and ephedrine and ephedrine capsules. At first the capsules seemed to do some good, but now I think they make me nauseated & dizzy—at least something does. I am still having to take injections two or three times a day & three or four times in the night.

I have sent your prescriptions to the druggist in Sydney. I guess I never happened to mention it but I have used those nebulizers from time to time for years, and they never seemed to do any good after the asthma really gets going. Also didn't I take Tedral last winter? It seems to me I did and that that didn't work very well, either. However, I'm only too glad to try them both again. I really don't know what to do. There would be no point in returning to New York and the conditions here seem ideal. I am just hoping it will decide to go away soon. There is so much I want to do here & I can scarcely get up & down stairs. However, I am getting some work done so I guess it isn't so bad . . .

My record is still perfect—do you suppose my system is wheezing away for alcohol? Horrors . . .

To Robert Lowell

This is EB's first letter to Robert Lowell (1917–77), whom she had met through Randall Jarrell in January 1947. Their friendship was to become increasingly important in her life and work (and in his). In this letter, a response to his review of North & South, *she is unaware that his nickname was "Cal."*

[Cape Breton, Nova Scotia]
August 14, 1947

Dear Robert, (I've never been able to catch that name they call you, but Mr. Lowell doesn't sound right, either.) I had meant to write to you quite a while ago, to answer the note you sent me in New York, and I certainly meant to do it before your review of my book appeared in the *Sewanee Review*—but someone sent me the magazine so it is too late now. However, I loaned it to some other boarders here and they made off with it so I shall have to rely on my memory which saves me some self-consciousness about it, anyway. I agreed with your review of Dylan Thomas completely—his poems are almost always spoiled for me by two or three lines that sound like padding or remain completely unintelligible. I think that last stanza of "Fern Hill" is wonderful—although I don't know what he means by "the shadow of his hand"—I haven't got the poem or the review to go by. I haven't read *Paterson* but your review is the first one that has made me feel I must.

The part about me I was quite overwhelmed by. It is the first review* I've had that attempted to find any general drift or consistency in the individual poems, and I was beginning to feel there probably wasn't any at all. It is the only review that goes at things in what *I* think is the right way. I also liked what you said about Miss Moore. I wish I had it here now to tell you the many other things I liked in it, too. I suppose for pride's sake I should take some sort of stand about the adverse criticisms, but I agreed with some of them only too well. I suppose no critic is ever really as harsh as oneself. It seems to me you spoke out my worst fears as well as some of my ambitions.

---

* "The splendor and minuteness of her descriptions soon seem wonderful," Lowell wrote. "Later one realizes that her large, controlled and elaborate common sense is always or almost always absorbed in its subjects, and she is one of the best craftsmen alive . . . Bishop's poems are so carefully fitted together, her descriptions give such body to her reflections, and her reflections so heighten her descriptions that it is hard to indicate her stature and solidity by quotation . . . *North & South* can be read straight through with excitement" (*Sewanee Review* LV, Summer 1947, pp. 493–503).

The clipping bureau sent me the first page from the July 20 *Chicago Sun Book Week*, the one with that silly piece by——

Heavens, it is an hour later—I was called out to see a calf being born in the pasture beside the house. In five minutes after several falls on its nose, it was standing up shaking its head & tail & trying to nurse. They took it away from its mother almost immediately & carried it struggling in a wheelbarrow to the barn—we've just been watching it trying to lie down. Once up, it didn't know how to get down again & finally fell in a heap. Now it seems to be trying *not* to go to sleep. It is dark brown and white with a sort of cap of white curly hair quite long. The boarders & the children of the household are all pleading with Mr. MacLeod, the landlord, to keep it—such excitement.

Well, as I was saying—by George Dillon. On the back of it I saw your poem "The Fat Man in the Mirror." I am not sure but what my interpretation of it may be too literal, but whether I have it all wrong or not, I admire its sense of horror and panic extremely.

When I was in Boston, shortly after you were there, I guess, I met Jack Sweeney, who asked me to make some records [at Harvard]. In the course of making them he played me yours and I liked "The Quaker Graveyard" even more than I had before—didn't you think it came off very well? V & VII I admired particularly. I thought making the recordings was rather fun—like a fish being angled for with that microphone—but my results were dreadful.

This is a very nice place—just a few houses and fishhouses scattered about in the fields, beautiful mountainous scenery and the ocean. I like the people particularly, they are all Scotch and still speak Gaelic, or English, with a strange rather cross-sounding accent. Offshore are two "bird islands" with high red cliffs. We are going out with a fisherman to see them tomorrow. They are sanctuaries where there are auks and the only puffins left on the continent, or so they tell us. There are real ravens on the beach, too, something I never saw before—enormous, with sort of rough black beards under their beaks.

I think I heard before I left New York that you had received the Library of Congress post for next year, although I don't believe it mentioned it in the notes in the *Sewanee Review*. If it is true, congratulations and I hope it is an interesting job. Thank you again for your review and I hope I shall see you in New York sometime in the fall, or perhaps even in Washington. I am in the New York telephone book & I do hope you will get in touch with me. Maybe, if you are in correspondence with the Jarrells, you could tell them the same thing—I don't know where they are.

The calf's mother has started to moo, and the cow in the next pasture is mooing even louder, possibly in sympathy. It seems that if they take the calf away immediately, then they don't have the trouble of weaning it. It will drink out of a dish, says Mr. MacLeod; he has promised to call me when they try it the first time.

I hope you're liking Yaddo and I should like to hear about it some-time. I almost went there once, but changed my mind.

To Joseph Holmes Summers

Joseph Summers and his wife, U.T., became close friends of EB. An authority on EB's "favorite poet," Professor Summers is the author of George Herbert, His Religion and Art *(1954) and has also written on the poetry of Donne, Jonson, Marvell, and Milton. A visiting Fellow of All Souls, he has since 1985 been professor emeritus at the University of Rochester.*

Halifax, Nova Scotia
August 24, 1947

I came here last night from Cape Breton and I was awfully glad to get your letter, forwarded from New York. I've been up there since the first of July. I guess Loren didn't mention it. I haven't heard from her since before they went to Boston, but I think they're on the Cape. You know when you offered me (at least I hope you offered me & that I didn't just demand) a bibliography of Herbert, I somehow had the idea that you probably had one all typed out, with mimeographed copies maybe, and that it wouldn't be any trouble at all. I never dreamed of your sitting down and writing all that for me. Thank you ever so much; I'm delighted to have it and I think a good week's reading in the Public Library is just the thing to get me off to a good start when I go back in the fall. I think the only things I'm familiar with are the *Story Books of Little Gidding*, which I seem to remember I found rather dull, and Helen C. White's book. Maybe the Counterpoint one—at least some article somewhere that had quite a lot to say about his meters and also the picture poems. How can we *both* get the Hutchinson edition?—I suppose you've got requests for it placed around, or would it be a good idea for me to write some places?

I was extremely interested in the Latin poems. I've only worked over a few of them a long time ago, and of course my Latin is just a small melting snowdrift here & there by now. I wouldn't dare say anything about your translations—or shouldn't dare, because I'll now proceed to without a dictionary even to help. But this isn't criticism, just conversation. I think it's odd the way the translations sound like Rilke—or rather like translations of Rilke—don't you? But that must be partly your phrasing since the poems themselves, the ideas in them, are so typically Herbert. Why is *Patria* called that? I wonder. I find the connection between *flam-mae* & *scintillae* hard to get.—And the change as you say, from outer to inner, is again *just like* Herbert, to me—the last line makes me think of "He that is weary, let him sit," etc. Are you doing the translations with an idea of publishing them or using the translations in your thesis? I think you must be—if so, I do hope you won't think I'm butting in, but they *do* sound like those translations of Rilke, to me. As you say, I guess translation is almost impossible. It seems to me possibly one should stick to Herbert's own English vocabulary (but then again, why?)—what he would have had in mind in English that he put into Latin. That's why "The Angels" (which is beautiful, isn't it?) bothers me more than the first one. "Images" seems to me to be used with our modern meaning for it. I don't believe it was used that way in Herbert's time, was it? I think I'd object to the word "knowing" for the same reason. Probably this is all based on my dislike for a lot of Spender's poetry and nothing more. They are beautiful poems and I'm glad you sent them to me, particularly with translations. Do you ever write poetry yourself? I'm sure that you must. And how is the thesis coming? . . .

Give my love to U.T. and I hope she is well and that everything is going pleasantly at Houghton Mifflin. Remember me to Gertie & Ellen if you see them again. And thank you again for the information about Herbert. When I've read all that maybe we can talk about him together sometime! I'm glad you liked "At the Fishhouses"—I haven't been able to get a copy yet. At the last minute, after I'd had a chance to do a little research in Cape Breton, I found I'd said codfish scales once when it should have been herring scales. I hope they corrected it all right. The records I made for [Jack] Sweeney sounded pretty dreary—but if you get a chance, do listen to Robert Lowell's—they aren't at all professional, but they are extremely good in parts.

To Selden Rodman

Poet, art critic, and Haitianophile Selden Rodman reviewed EB's North & South *favorably on publication in* The New York Times Book Review.

907 Whitehead Street
Key West, Florida
November 25, 1947

. . . I've just re-read your book [*The Amazing Year: A Diary in Verse*] & there are a lot of things in it I'd like to ask you about; most of my thoughts about it are more suited to conversation than writing, I guess. I think the diverse, casual tone is right for that kind of thing, also its being so personal. In fact I could wish it were more personal, I think, since that seems to be the only possible way now of producing an impact with such large & terrible material as you are using. I guess of the "news" ones I like #2 best except for the title (& I think I saw the same remark in some review). That is May 2nd. On page 22 is the image I like best in the whole book—the gull's cry following the boat "like a soundtrack"—I don't know if soundtrack should sound correctly *sad*, but it does. I like August too— the first two lines extremely except for the word "spoke." In fact all of that one has a wonderful tone, to me, except the last four lines, which seem to me not so good. (You see I'm hopelessly critical but I don't think you'll mind.) I also like October 19th very much. I like the last part of January 14th, too, but wish it weren't called "the Poet"—"page of sky" would be so much finer, it seems to me, if it weren't. I like stanza 2 of January 20th—the smoke is nice. I think it's interesting, that February 7th, the one about the picture by Pippin, about the same picture that so took my eye when I saw the book at your house & I think you have described exactly the first thoughts I had in Feb. 19th—are you an Aquarian? Some of the more personal ones seem to me the best ones, to have a little the tone of D. H. Lawrence's love poems. I like and agree with the idea of Dec. 29th so much that I wish it were more elaborated and *finished*. The Haiti section is of course fascinating because of its strangeness and makes me want to go there more. Thank you very much for giving me the book. I have learned a lot from it & I hope you won't think me too overcritical. As I said, in conversation it would all sound much better, I'm sure (& I think you must be quite proud of your accomplishment) . . .

Mrs. [Pauline] Hemingway is coming back sometime around the first of December. Then I shall have to get out of my "tropical atmosphere," I guess. I'm thinking of just taking a room on here for a while, through January. *If* I get enough work done before then, or by then, and earn a little money, I am seriously considering Haiti, if only for a month. I shall not come unless I get certain things done here first, but I am hoping to. I am extremely curious and eager to go there. How much do you suppose one could get a room, apt., small house, etc., for? Those photographs you showed me were wonderful—they reminded me quite a bit of some of the West, but of course Key West is very diluted and getting more American-Miami-ized, rather, every day. A beautiful little colored boy, age 7, with sort of dark reddish hair and eyes and really bronzish skin has brought me five tissue-paper kites he made me, with fringes that are supposed to "whistle," cut-out hearts, etc. I've seen neater work but they are very nice. I'm having them made for Loren, who painted all of them once here but it was unsuccessful and she wants to try some more.

The only Haitian poet I know anything of is Emile Roumer, and only a few poems. What do you think of him and can one get a book of his? I hope your book is coming along well, the art one, also the other, though both may well be done by now (you seem to get a great deal done). I hope it won't be too much trouble to let me hear from you sometime, and thank you again for your interest.

To Dr. Anny Baumann

December 2, 1947

Thank you for your letter. I am still having some asthma, although not so much as at first. I can't account for it at all. When I first got here

I had it very badly for about two weeks, just like during the summer. I also had bad eczema, or something, on both hands, and some around my ankles—hundreds of little blisters. I took Benadryl, which worked, I guess; anyway it cleared up.

Except for the asthma everything is fine. My record hasn't been quite spotless but almost so. My weight is now about 134—I'm working for 120. And I feel well and extremely energetic and I'm getting some work done, although I never get as much done as I feel I should, I'm afraid. The asthma is mysterious—I won't have any trouble at all for three or four nights and then I have to take two or three shots of adrenaline in one night. I am trying the adrenaline in oil some more . . .

I hope you're well and that you'll like the soup—some people find it too sticky.

To Robert Lowell

This letter, in which EB first addressed Lowell as "Dear Cal," was her response to an early draft of his poem "Falling Asleep over the Aeneid." Her queries caused Lowell to change "mass" to "morning service," to spell "turms" (squadrons of horsemen) correctly, to delete "Johnny Comes Marching Home Again," to revise "Mass is over" to "church is over," and to make other minor improvements.

December 3, 1947

I am terribly impressed with the dream poem and I gather from it that when you dream you dream in colors all right—(a psychiatrist friend of mine is writing an article on color in dreams and I've heard quite a lot about it). It is a really *stirring* poem; I don't think I've enjoyed a poem in that particular way since reading Macaulay when I was little—no, I guess some plays by Dryden affected me a little like that. There are a few spots that I am not sure I'm getting right—I guess I'll ask you about them. I hope you don't mind—I'm not being "critical," you know, just curious or dumb. At first I thought I'd like the first three lines [the epigraph] better in prose, but now I don't know. But the combination of [the old man's] forgetting *mass* in *Concord* while reading *Virgil*—I do find it a little gratuitous. Why Concord?—the "colored volunteers" marching through Concord are nice—but I wonder if they aren't too much of a piece with the "Abnaki partisans"?—or is it a deliberate motif that I'm not getting very clearly?

The first word that bothers me is "filings"—which so immediately suggests something else. Maybe "file" is a good word for dream imagery particularly—then I see you use it again about the Italians "who must file"—but "filings" does bother me. "It asks, a boy's face, though its arrow-eye" puzzles me. *It* must be the "sword"—is the sword Pallas, or what? (Maybe if I knew the story I'd be better off.) I think the part "the design / Has not yet left it," etc., is very beautiful. I'm not sure why the feet "turn"—they must be the feet of men marching by, rather than those of the corpse, but "turn" doesn't seem to fit either, exactly. I guess I can't see "stately tears" lathering—although the first time I read it I liked it. I think the sentence beginning "At the end of time" is—well, ravishing —even if I don't know what a "term" of horses is.

The transition of "Farewell / Forever. Mass is over . . ." is just *right*, I think. (I had wondered every line how you would ever manage it.) "Johnny Comes Marching Home Again" strikes me too suddenly after it, I think—the three lines before it seem perfectly acceptable to a half-awake state, and so does "Virgil must keep the Sabbath." I'm not sure what "Shadows by," etc., means—just casts a shadow by? Why does the great-great-aunt laugh, I wonder. The last is plain marvelous, particularly the dust business—and of course the last line. Maybe I'm wrong, maybe he isn't half awake at the end, but "It all comes back" would indicate it, I should think—his eyes are deliberately shut at the end, surely. I don't know why I have to reveal my naïvetés like this, except that I find it such a fine poem that I don't want to miss any detail.

Everything goes very well here. I have been working some on another poem called "Faustina" but it is hard to choose among the various versions she gives of her life. I am also doing a couple of Cape Breton ones started this summer, and am beginning to worry lest I have only two poetic spigots, marked *H & C*. We had a small tornado last week—I was upstairs in my room here where I have quite a good view on all sides over the low roofs—palm branches and coconuts went hurtling through the air, and I watched the ground heaving up and down around several trees in the yard and thought they were going down. Nothing of any consequence did, though. An enormous blue & white plastic ball blew out of the swimming pool and up into a tree, where it stuck. The sun came out in an hour or so & a friend drove me around to see the damage and the ships still crashing around in the bights. The streets of colored town were full of people all out walking around as if it were a holiday, and everything had a chilly bleached look—but a dreadful mess at the same time. The big excitements have been the tornado and [President] Truman. I just came in from watching him drive by the corner. A slight clapping from the people, but not much, as he sat up on the back of a car & waved his hat. I wonder why his hats, besides being so awful, always look brand new.

I hope you're over the cold, and give my kindest regards to the Jarrells if they are still there. Thank you again for the poem—it has so much richness and almost gaiety in spite of the subject. I should think you'd be pretty pleased. I hope to see the other one sometime.

630 Dey Street
Key West, Florida
January 1, 1948

Happy New Year.

Thank you so much for sending me *The Compleat Angler*. I had a copy and read it once but lost it long ago and I am delighted to have it again. It is wonderfully soothing reading & wonderfully "precious" reading here in the land of big game fish and Hemingway. I sent you something that I thought reminded me of your Bathsheba poems a little, or maybe even of just your "poems," though I could only say why in the vaguest way—something masculine, emphatic and regular but sort of toughly so, and slightly somber, etc.

[Continued fourteen days later] January 15

Well, your letter just came and I'm sorry not to have written before; the new year has gone like a dream so far. I was very pleased to find how close I'd come to your changes in the wonderful Virgil poem. In the copy you sent me the first three lines of explanation all began with capitals so of course I managed to make them scan. It reminds me of the story about the Harvard professor whose pupil brought him a paper in blank verse and the professor said he must remind him that in writing prose it wasn't customary to begin each line with a capital . . . I really understood everything except the "arrow-eye," which I mistook for something like "eagle eye" or "gimlet eye." I am trying to make "lather" incorporate itself, but it still sticks out, to me, like an elbow. When is the poem to appear in *The Kenyon Review*? And are the earlier two appearing any place soon? Or Jarrell's poem about the colored child?

I am beginning to get that feeling of missing things here. I received an ad for *The Hudson Review*, and I think your name was on it but I can't find it—what is it? I also just received the first two numbers of *The Tiger's Eye*—like a couple of simply-mad-my-dear little gas balloons, I'd say—& they must cost fortunes to get out. I wanted to see the bits of Miss Moore's notebooks in the first but somehow the editors have managed to ruin them too as much as possible. I don't think she should have let them use them like that. I cannot *abide* this adulation of "work in progress" stuff, and that photograph of the "little worn old books" etc. seems to me a real tearjerker that should not have been allowed until after Marianne's death . . .

Pauline Hemingway came back at New Year's and I moved to the above address. Some dear old friends of mine—the wife is a daughter of John Dewey—come here for two or three months every winter and usually they keep the upstairs apartment for guests, but this time they kindly offered it to me—it seems to be my lucky-in-real-estate year. It isn't as de luxe as my other quarters were but better to work in in a way—the kind of meager hideousness you can look at once and forget completely—and it has a beautiful view over the harbor, the fishmarket, etc. (When somebody says "beautiful" about Key West you should really take it with a grain of salt until you've seen it for yourself. In general it is really *awful* & the "beauty" is just the light, or something equally perverse.)

I like it very much but I am in a quandary. I take your remarks about writing a lot *now* very much to heart & I'd like to look forward to a long stretch of nothing but work. I've been sick most of the last month—asthma—it doesn't completely incapacitate one but is a nuisance. Well —I was asked to speak at Wellesley, too, on March 22, and at the time I accepted. Now I am wondering if it is really worth it to go all the way back North at that time of year when (1) I don't think I have much to say. (2) The English teacher who wrote me is an old boarding-school teacher of mine, a Miss Prentiss. She was very nice to me in those days but she is a very sentimental creature who doesn't really like anything she considers "modern." And I gather the audience would be mostly like her. (3) This is in confidence—I'm sort of scared. But I remember the little you told me about your speaking experiences in Washington cheered me up tremendously, and I suppose I should or must begin sometime.

Selden Rodman has written and wants me to come to Haiti. I could board, it seems, with Margaret Sanger! He has a jeep and knows all the little villages where the painters and poets live and I know it would be beautiful, but—you can imagine why I hesitate. I suppose it is too good an opportunity to pass up, and maybe, if I can get a friend here to go with me, I may go. I seem to be talking to you like Dorothy Dix but that is because you apparently are able to do the right thing for yourself and your work and don't seem to be tempted by the distractions of traveling —that rarely offers much at all in respect to work. I guess I have liked to travel as much as I have because I have always felt isolated and have known so few of my "contemporaries" and nothing of "intellectual" life in New York or anywhere. Actually it may be all to the good.

I didn't think much of Jarrell's poem in the last *Partisan Review*, did you? I re-read a little Browning & if that is the kind of poem he wants to do I think he should, too. How do you feel about Browning and why don't the critics ever mention him in connection with you?—although give me you any time. I just finished "Trial of a Poet"—& didn't think much of that—the tone seems to me so often false—the "Recapitulations," cheap as they are, sound sincere and spontaneous anyway.

The water looks like blue gas—the harbor is always a mess, here, junky little boats all piled up, some hung with sponges and always a few half sunk or splintered up from the most recent hurricane. It reminds me a little of my desk.

I don't believe I have written to you since the recordings came, have I? I played them on a friend's machine, which may have been a little slow—we couldn't adjust it and they all sounded much too slow to me.

And of course so sad and dreary. I think the "Colored Singer" ones came off the best, and "Faustina" next best and the others were good in spots once in a long while. "Fishhouses" was sheer torture to listen to. But I am very glad I made them, except for all the wasted time it cost you, because now I think I know what to work for to improve them. Is there anything to pay for them? . . .

As soon as I can make up my mind—I hope maybe with a kind word or two of help from you—about the two possibilities in the paragraphs above—well, I'll know what I'm going to be doing and I hope I can manage to stay in Washington again on my way back North and see many more pictures this time. I am working on the fishing trip too and have one wonderful idea, I think. I shall let you know.

The local bookshop is run by an Englishman and his wife, who is about twenty years older than he, very cute really, with dyed bright pink hair. They play chess in the corner and very much dislike being interrupted by a customer. The other day a man I knew went in to buy a book and asked for it timidly. Hugh, the Englishman, said, "Good Heavens, man! Can't you see I'm about to make a move?" When I first went in this year the wife asked me in her jolliest way what I was doing now—writing or what? I said writing and she replied, "Ha, ha—always *something*!"

But Good Heavens, I am impressed with the long poem—was that the one in fifty-line sections? I should like very much to see it and I wonder when on earth you work, what with the problems presented by Harvard. Hope you're not freezing as well and I shall try to profit by your stern example.

To Selden Rodman

March 1, 1948

Heavens, what horrible troubles you've been having. I think something is wrong with the stars just now, everyone I know has been sick or something unpleasant has happened to them. I do hope you're all recovered.

Well—now I'll proceed to add to your problems. Esther Andrews Chambers, her nephew Tom Wanning [one of EB's closest friends], brother of the Andrews Wanning who teaches at Harvard & I are all planning to come to Haiti, arriving either March 8th or 9th—that is, if there is any possibility of our finding rooms. They wouldn't necessarily have to be together, I suppose. We'd want to stay until the 19th; possibly Tom & I might stay on after that awhile. We've all been sick—in fact I guess I'm the healthiest of the lot—and Esther *has* to get away somewhere for a while. So if Haiti is impossible she'll probably go some other place & I'd visit Haiti again when I'd have some time, as I'd prefer to do anyway.

So please don't be distressed if you have to discourage this emigration from Key West. But if you think places to stay are out of the question, would you wire me here—COLLECT. Tom & I are not at all particular —Esther rather more so.

I am sorry to do things in such a precipitous & troublesome way. But as I say I think it is something in the stars. Having made up our minds, we are all getting very eager & excited & I do hope it is feasible. We can fly very easily—here to Haiti & from there on. I do hope it works out.

I'm very pleased about your [anthology] *100 American Poems* [which included EB] and, if I get there, shall have lots to ask you about.

[Mid-March]
Monday morning

God knows what you must think of me by this time—anyway, you have been most helpful and patient. I decided last night not to go because of the continued asthma & various allergy troubles. I won't go into *that* anymore because I feel my correspondence with you is beginning to sound very much like Proust's. The Miami doctor advised against it & your note this morning corroborated what he said. Esther & Tom are off, though, and I am giving them this note to you to apologize for all my indecisions & requests, etc. The accommodations sound ideal. I am hoping to come next year, when I can stay longer, anyway. I wonder how your book is coming & if you are writing poetry. I am just beginning to get some work finished now.

It is already getting hot & I think I shall be going back North about April 1st. I am sorry not to meet you and to meet your wife. And thank you again for all the trouble you've gone to, Selden.

To Carley Dawson

Mrs. Dawson, believing herself "engaged" to Robert Lowell, who was serving as the Poetry Consultant at the Library of Congress, invited EB (at his suggestion) to stay with her in Washington. Mrs. Dawson had met Lowell in February 1948 at a party honoring her lover, the French poet St.-John Perse.

April 5, 1948

It is extremely kind of you to ask me to stay with you in Washington, sight unseen. Of course I had planned to go to a hotel—and still shall if anything has happened to change your plans—but your letter is so very convincing that I feel it is quite all right for me to accept, with pleasure. I'll be getting there sometime either the 16th or 17th. I shall let you know as soon as I hear about my reservations from Miami . . . I am eager to get to see the paintings from Berlin [at the National Gallery] before they are sent back.

There is one thing I must ask, although I dislike to—do you have any dogs or cats? I am extremely allergic to dogs, cats a little, not much. A cat wouldn't bother me unless it was a family of cats, and on all the furniture, but I'm terribly afraid that if you have a dog I won't be able to accept. I am very fond of dogs, too, but even so I hope you haven't one!

As soon as I hear from Miami I'll let you know the day and time of my arrival, because it might be when your maid is not there, in which case maybe I'd better go to a hotel for the first night anyway? I am really looking forward to Washington very much, and it was awfully nice of both you and Cal to think of it, and you to write to me . . . After all these months in Key West I feel very low-class and un-Sublime and am afraid I'll not be in your and Cal's exalted frames of mind when I get there.

April 21, 1948

Thank you for being so patient with all my vagaries. I don't know why, but Key West has always been a very hard place to get away from at a definite date. The friend I was planning to drive with has now decided to take her French poodle along, so that is out too—but I have another train reservation now . . . and shall *really* leave Miami the 30th, getting to Washington around noon [May] the 1st. If this is not perfectly and completely all right with you, I'll go to a hotel of course. I'll call you when I reach Washington, and if you are away or even then too provoked to see me, I shall understand it quite well.

I plan to return to New York on Wednesday, the 5th, possibly staying over a day in Baltimore. I can't bear to put you to any more inconveniences of letter writing—and now I hope Cal will be there too. I am looking forward to hearing your account of the symposium. I feel like an unlettered "cracker" by now, of course.

To Loren MacIver

[POSTCARD]

Wiscasset, Maine
June 22, 1948

A very pleasant trip here, once aboard in an ancient parlor car, with a handful of ancient ladies who all ordered themselves Manhattans at five o'clock, while I had tea. Willy [the canary] shrieked at Providence and Worcester. It is unbelievably peaceful here and everyone has been awfully kind helping me move in. Hope all goes smoothly—love.

To Carley Dawson

Wiscasset, Maine
June 30, 1948

It was very nice to have a letter from you when I got here even if it did seem a little remote by the time I received it. Marianne [Moore] came up two days ahead of me. We considered taking a drawing room together, but probably it is just as well it didn't work out. She insisted on bringing "our food," in the old-fashioned way, and I had a canary with me & I'm afraid we'd have both been nervous wrecks by the time we got to Portland . . . When I saw her in New York she showed me quite a bit of the La Fontaine translation she's been working on for several years now. It is really peculiar, I'm not sure how good, but it will be a great literary curiosity, I should think. For example, this is what she quotes to me in a letter today:

THE SWALLOW AND THE LITTLE BIRDS
There is but one resource not to be feared;
Hide in a well where no mortar was smeared.

Which I must say baffles me considerably. I think her own sense of rhythm is so peculiar to her, so much a part of her respiration, heartbeats, etc., that even when she thinks she's writing something in a regular tum-tum-tum style she isn't at all . . .

I had a note here from Cal, too, when I arrived, in which he referred to your little boy [from a previous marriage] as being "quite angelic"—so he must be an archangel with three sets of wings, I guess.

I have been so concerned about our conversations in New York and do hope you'll write me how everything is, what you finally did, etc. I think I know pretty much how you were feeling that day. I've been through something of the same sort several times recently, and one very bad one in Key West. I just wish I could have been of more practical help . . . I do hope to goodness that everything is all right—that you feel it is, that is.

I don't know, though. It seems to me that Cal isn't nearly as much alone as most of the artists I know, and that all artists have to go through long stretches of it, at least. Maybe I'm just saying that because this is certainly one for me; I am beginning to feel like Admiral Byrd. Wiscasset is perfectly beautiful, a museum town, and sound, sound asleep. One takes walks, once in a while one talks with the fatuous librarian, but it is good for working—up to a point. I hope the point is soon reached.

Cal said he thought he'd like to visit here the 14th of August. I'm not sure for how long it would be. I have beds for three . . . This is all just leading up to my saying that I do hope you may come to visit sometime, and of course it would be very nice if it were while Cal was here, too. I'm afraid you would die of boredom. It is pretty, and maybe you will need a rest after Cummington, where Marianne used to hold her classes in the graveyard. I wonder if you'll be doing some writing? I suppose if I could just get any visitors to Wiscasset writing hard, the boredom problem would be solved.

The house isn't bad at all, now that I have taken up all the rugs and got in a few screens. Maine people never open windows in the summertime, it seems. There's a hideous new fireplace with fire screens that pull with brass tassels—looks exactly like the end of a hearse. I don't know when you go to Cummington, so I shall address this to Washington . . .

To Robert Lowell

June 30, 1948

I talked to Carley on the phone the day before I left—you were attending a wedding or something, I think. I read your Williams review [of *Paterson, Book Two*] on the train with great interest but not absolute agreement, having just worked over the book again a day or two before. At least, I agree all right with what you do say and think you've done an awfully good job in the first part, of presenting the poem. But really when I re-read it all (the poem) I still felt he shouldn't have used the letters from that woman. To me it seems mean & they're much too overpowering emotionally for the rest of it so that the whole poem suffers. I noticed in [Richard] Eberhart's review in the *Times* he said the prose parts were made up, but I don't think they are, are they? However, it has wonderful sections, and I think Williams has always had a streak of insensitivity. I wish I'd brought it along, now.

And then maybe I've felt a little too much the way the woman did at certain more hysterical moments—people who haven't experienced absolute loneliness for long stretches of time can never sympathize with it at all. You say something about working in "boring solitude" at Yaddo—and I had just been thinking that probably I should have tried to go to Yaddo instead of this, because at least it wouldn't be quite such completely boring solitude. That is if they would take me. Could you tell me how one applies? I don't want to sound as if I were tagging along, but I had already thought I might try to go there in October, or possibly earlier if this proves to be too lonely. The house is very nice, and of course Wiscasset is amazing—so beautiful and dead as a doornail. I think its heart beats twice a day when the train goes through. I like a moderate amount of solitude and dullness to work in, but this is almost drugging.

Well, I certainly shouldn't complain to you and things will undoubtedly improve.

I went to dinner with Marianne one night before I left, and then we had a confused day or two when we thought we might travel to Maine together—it is probably just as well that didn't work out. She showed me quite a lot of the La Fontaine—I just don't know what to think. It all has a sort of awkwardness & quaintness that's quite nice—& sounds very much like her, of course; I'm not sure how much like La Fontaine. And Macmillan has treated her very badly about the whole thing and after three years' work has turned her down. But I think Viking is now interested.

She asked me to say grace and I had a minute's dreadful blackout, then something out of the remote Baptist past mercifully came to me in perfect condition. The only trouble was that Marianne liked it very much and made me repeat it until she knew it, too. She is up near Ellsworth [Maine] now. I had a letter yesterday—apparently she is having difficulties with her hostesses because they refuse to let her mow the lawn. My best friend in N.Y. thought my poem about her ["Invitation to Miss Marianne Moore"] was "mean," which I found rather upsetting because it wasn't meant to be & it is too late to do anything about it now, I'm afraid. Well, of the readings I liked yours & hers best. I think [Allen] Tate does it a little too well.

The 14th would be fine, of August—and how long can you stay— two weeks? I asked Carley to consider a visit when I talked to her, and it would be awfully nice, I think . . . I have beds for three. However, if my house is full there are several nice places I could get a room at, I think, so it would all work out all right. The only thing I'm nervous about now is that any guest of mine, unless he or she is absorbed in writing a novel, or sleeps twenty-two hours a day, is just going to die of boredom. I can't seem to discover a single thing to do except possibly go swimming. Of course if Carley had her elegant new car that would improve everything a lot . . .

I have an idea for a new book—only being halfway through a second [book of poems] yet—all about Tobias and the Angel. Don't you like that story? There are wonderful birds here—three nests in my two apple trees. Is it hot in Washington? Tell me if and when & where you are having any reviews or poems printed, won't you. We might be able to take a trip to call on Marianne, even though she feels that we are continents apart. Well, I guess I must wander down to that dream-town and pick up the mail.

P.S. I really feel you should *struggle* against your feeling about children, but I suppose it's better than drooling over them like Swinburne. But I've always loved the stories about Shelley going around Oxford peering into baby carriages, and how he once said to a woman carrying a baby, "Madame, can your baby tell us anything of pre-existence?"

It's very hot today, for here, and I guess I must hike down to that so-called beach and get into that icy water for a while, although I guess there's going to be a thunderstorm after a while, the robins are shrieking with that particular note they use for storms. Having just digested all *The New York Times* and some pretty awful clam chowder I made for myself, I don't feel the slightest bit literary, just stupid. Or maybe it's just too much solitude.

Thank you for your nice long letter, which did me a great deal of good. The 6th or 7th would be fine—but would you let me know as soon as you can? I'm having trouble getting the right people at the right time, with so far no one except a few rather odd New Englandish callers who mostly tell me about the state of their "nerves." I had a letter from Carley in which she said she thought she'd like to come in July, or later in September, so I have just asked her tentatively for the 26th.

I have no car, you know, and I am afraid any guest will be bored to death—better bring your knitting. I am working my way gradually through all the Hardy novels in the local library and find they are just the thing. Edwin Arlington Robinson is also dutifully recommended to me as a local character but I really can't get very excited about him, although I try. On the 9th I insulted several people, I guess, by not wanting to go to hear Mr. R.P.T. Coffin at Bowdoin. Someone asked my landlord here if he didn't have an "author" living in his house, and he replied, "No, not an author, a writer."

Well, things must improve, I'm sure, and the place is beautiful, there's no getting round that. I am working on Tobias and the Prodigal Son and I just started a story called "Homesickness"—all very cheerful. I think almost the last straw here though is the hairdresser, a nice big hearty Maine girl who asks me questions I don't even know the answers to. She told me (1) that my hair "don't feel like hair at all," (2) I was turning gray practically "under her eyes." And when I'd said yes, I was an orphan, she said, "Kind of awful, ain't it, plowing through life alone." So now I can't walk downstairs in the morning or upstairs at night without feeling I'm plowing. There's no place like New England . . .

I've just read a marvelous life of Juan Gris, the best book I've read in a long time, I think. Now to return to the "Trumpet-Major."

Sunday evening
[July 18, 1948]

I hope I didn't sound just too grumpy and churlish in my last letter, so that you've abandoned the idea of coming to Wiscasset. Things have improved quite a bit and I don't feel quite so ungrateful about the place. I can see why this part of Maine would have a fascination for you. One of the Sortwells was telling me a long tale about the Kavanaughs of

Damariscotta the other day, but I didn't really prick up my ears & connect it with your poem at all until it was too late to ask any more questions. And last night I was shown through one of the biggest houses from cellar to attic, even to the dolls in bed in the attic, paintings of all the family's ships, etc.—and today, my dear, I've just returned from a church service at Head Tide. I guess you probably know all about it & its church, etc. —but I did leave before the sermon. I guess maybe what I don't like about this place is that its local atmosphere is so thick as to be distracting, like a fog—and of course after the rather high meat of Key West, the society is like breast of chicken.

I found a place yesterday where you can rent a small sailboat, very cheap—that might be fun when you came. At least I think you sail, don't you? I haven't for ten years and have probably forgotten how.

I hope you aren't suffering very much from the heat in Washington—it's been pretty hot here a few days but I go & submerge myself in that ice water once in a while, and then in the evenings it suddenly gets cool, as it's just done, and the fireflies appear.

I found [Eudora Welty's] *Curtain of Green* in the local library and I liked it very much. I'd read "Why I Live at the P.O." & "Clytie" in anthologies but the others were all new to me, and I think that last one, "A Worn Path," about the old colored woman, is really marvelous. I should think she could write a long, long, really good novel if anyone could, if she wanted to. She can do all that wonderful personification the colored people go in for so well—and then when I think how [*letter discontinued*]

Next Saturday morning
[July 24, 1948]

I don't know whatever happened to this letter—I thought I'd finished and mailed it. I've had a guest the past few days—asleep upstairs at the moment, so I won't type—and have let everything slide.

Can you go abroad? I've been considering a long trip of some sort this fall, and I have a wonderful catalogue of trips one can take by freighter—I'll show it to you. But the world is in such a state I don't know whether it's a good idea to go to Europe or not. I've always promised myself I'm going to spend my declining years just taking walks in Rome—nothing could be more profitable, I think, for the last twenty years of one's life.

Just as you come into Wiscasset, Route 27 branches off to the left of Route 1. I'm about the fourth house along it on the left, known as "Mr. Grove's Cottage"—you can't miss it; it is the only small house around, with a lot of tattered rosebushes and two apple trees in front. It is DULL but pleasant, particularly when the sun shines. Yesterday we were reduced to walking in the graveyard. Carley is coming Tuesday, to stay just a week, I think. I think you should incorporate the whole Sortwell family in an epic—wait till I give you the details.

[Stonington, Maine
July 26, 1948]

Came up here yesterday for a day & night & I like it so much better than Wiscasset I'm hoping to be able to break my lease there & move up here, so please hold everything & I'll let you know. Could & would you get up this far if I do? I'm afraid this is much more my style & I am beginning to find Wiscasset *deadly*. Poor Carley—I hate to inflict it on her.

[July 30, 1948]

Carley and I arrived an hour or so ago and it is at least twenty degrees cooler than at Wiscasset and very nice. Why consider Yaddo when you can come here? Tonight we are going to see *The Mating of Millie*.

[August 2, 1948]

Either it's very dry here, or the fog gets into our bones. We wonder if when you come you'd bring something to quench the thirst or keep out the fog.

To Dr. Anny Baumann

August 5, 1948

Wiscasset proved to be a great mistake & I like this place so much better (it is a little like Lockeport, Nova Scotia) that I am moving here for the rest of the summer. The people are nice, I have friends in the neighborhood, etc. I have been working quite steadily, particularly since coming here, and with the exception of two days, or rather evenings, at the first of my stay in Wiscasset, the drinking has been nonexistent, or else a minimum with friends, so I feel very encouraged about that. In fact everything is fine & I really have no right to take up your time— except that I am getting awfully tired of constantly having asthma.

I ran out of theoglycinate & the order seems to be very slow in coming so I have had to use adrenaline for about two weeks now, which may be why I feel more than usually annoyed by the whole business. I am taking about 3 cc. in the course of every evening & night, and I am constantly coughing, choking, etc. The only time I've been relatively free of asthma was that last stay in New York—which I find rather depressing, since I dislike New York. But for the last eight or nine years I have had asthma almost every day and night. I've never been able to lie down in bed, etc., and I'm getting very tired of it.

It seems to me that every magazine or paper I pick up has an article proving that asthma is psychosomatic, everyone now thinks it is almost entirely, if not entirely, mental, etc. I had hoped that going to Dr. Foster might help, but it didn't seem to—at least not yet, at any rate—I suppose it might eventually. I hope that sometime, when you have the time, you will tell me exactly what you think—if you have any ideas about anything further I could do about it, or if you think there is any possibility of my ever getting over it completely. I feel so well in every other way that I can't understand why this persists so—but maybe I expect too much!

Please do not feel this has to be answered except at your convenience. You may be away on vacation now. I suppose it is damp here—frequent fogs—but I've lived by the sea, with and without asthma, most of my life.

To Carley Dawson

In Stonington the previous weekend the Carley Dawson–Robert Lowell affair was abruptly terminated. Mrs. Dawson: "I realized something was very wrong with Robert. And so in the morning I went in as soon as I dared and woke up Elizabeth and told her I thought Robert and I were finished. And she arranged to have a friend of hers [Tom Wanning] drive me to the station . . . And that was it. I never saw Robert again." EB's muted allusions to this drama are in the second and third paragraphs and in the final phrase. While sympathetic to Mrs. Dawson, EB was determined not to lose Lowell's friendship.

Wiscasset, Maine
Monday morning
[August 16, 1948]

Just a note before I attack the really frightening list of things to be done before I can start back to Stonington. I thought you might sort of like to know how things went. The landlord has just been to call and to my surprise, without any urging from me, offered to "let me off" the September rent—that's $100 saved anyway. But he's sold the house, so probably I'm just being idealistic in attributing any generosity to him about it.

Cal and I hiked off to Burnt Cove in the fog. It was very beautiful but I was almost beyond sensation at that point, as you probably were, too. Almost his only comment was that he was sorry to have dragged me into it all, and I said nothing. I really don't know whether I should have or not. Maybe someday I'll feel able to.

I hope you and Tom got to Bangor safe and sound and that all went well in Boston. I hope I'll have a letter from you when I get back to Stonington.

We went to the Eberharts' Saturday morning. We thought we were to get off the bus at Bucksport but didn't know where, and were just riding dreamily along when fortunately Dick caught sight of us at South Brooksville and dragged us off the bus to the giggling of all the passengers. His or his in-laws' camp was nice & wild. You have to go to it in an outboard motorboat. We went to another island to fly kites, and that part of it I think I really would have enjoyed very much but a storm came up after we had flown them only about half an hour. So we had to go home in the motorboat. We also had to read two new poems by Mr. E., etc. Yesterday morning we started very early and they drove me back here. I think they were planning to stop at Frank Parker's in Ipswich.

Wiscasset seems frightfully hot & I'm afraid Boston will be. I hope you really did enjoy some of your stay in Stonington, because I did, and honestly I feel your painting improved enormously and that other things are a remarkable and wonderful escape.

[Stonington, Maine]
Saturday morning
[August 21, 1948]

Mrs. Gross just found your painting. You will be delighted to hear that Wally admired it & had apparently taken it upstairs to bed with him. I'll send it to you shortly. I finally made it back here Thursday evening, although for a while I thought I never could. I broke down and hired that car again, but by good luck when I got back I found I had another of those mysterious little checks from *The New Yorker* that just covered it, so I felt I had done the right thing after all . . .

Yesterday I called on *that* Miss Moore, who proves to be really very nice. Her father is a retired Latin professor from Columbia, who has been at work peacefully, all during the war, on a volume of Livy for the Loeb Classical Library. He also writes Latin poetry for amusement. Too bad we didn't cultivate him while Cal was here. At least they will be pleasant to see if I get too lonely. Tommy [Wanning] is coming over this afternoon & tonight we are going to see Mickey Rooney—so you see the mad whirl continues.

No, Cal's only direct references were his apology & something about its all being a "mistake"—that was all. We were both somewhat embarrassed, and I suppose wanted to avoid discussion, for different reasons. I was afraid I might get mad & say things that were none of my business & might spoil the somewhat precarious balance of our friendship, such as it is. I like to talk about poetry to him & he is one of the very few other poets I know. At present I have commissioned him to find me a rich husband in Washington. I think a nice comfy Oriental would do—one with lots of diamonds & absolutely no interest in the arts . . .

It is *beautiful* here—the moon has been full, shining all over the harbor through a slight fog. A wonderful effect that, seen *through* the lace curtains, is overpowering. Mrs. Gross & I are going flounder fishing together. She is really so nice, isn't she? I do hope you'll get to feeling better soon, Carley, and I hope Cummington will be good & distracting. It has all been very tough & I'd like to know what a good psychiatrist would make of it—but I can't help a feeling of great relief when I think of you.

To Robert Lowell

Sunday afternoon
[August 22, 1948]

I think you've done an enormous amount of groundwork already &
I can see I picked the right person to solve my problems about my future
for me. I must say I like the sound of the uncle best so far, but I don't
like the idea of any unnecessary publicity. Don't forget the Oriental
angle—in fact I'd settle for some form of dignified concubinage as long
as it was guaranteed.

Carley's room is occupied by a very cheerful lady—a watercolorist
who transports a Yoghurt-making machine around with her, and also the
works of Mary Baker Eddy. I suppose I'm going to find out how she
reconciles them, although I don't want to. Another watercolorist called
on her & remembered having traveled on the boat from Halifax with me
last summer. They talked and giggled until midnight, & I suppose made
Yoghurt . . .

I had a wonderful letter here from *Poetry* magazine when I got back
Thursday night. It requests a contribution & congratulates me on my
poetry's having "perceptivity" & "sureness," etc., that "seem often lacking
in the output of the *run-down sensibility of the forties.*" I think we should
make a modest fortune by working out a prescription for run-down sen-
sibilities . . .

Now I do wish we'd get to see Marianne [Moore] too. I think Tom
and I are going to drive over Tuesday or Wednesday & it would have
been so much better with you along, too. I do hope you had a good time
here in spite of your troubles, because I did. I just hope I didn't get too
teasing and opinionated, which I guess I'm apt to do with any encouragement at all. Last night . . . I lay awake composing sentences of a review
of your next book—I really hope I'll be up to it when the book appears . . .

Mrs. Gross is blossoming like a rose—asked if I'd mind a few personal
questions this morning & sat down on a stove to inquire as to inspiration,
imagination, etc., while I ate breakfast.

I am alternately thinking of Yaddo & studying my freight-trip
booklets.

To Carley Dawson

August 30, 1948

Ye gods, Carley!—I went to the P.O. this morning to send your picture
to you at last (I sent it to New Lebanon, where I'll send this letter, I guess,
and trust it will be correct) & found *three* hair-raising communications
from you . . .

As I was saying last night—those hair-raising communications. I had felt I wouldn't be surprised by anything in Cal's future, so I don't very well see how I can be by anything in the past—but it is all so awful . . . My one feeling just now about our better intellectuals is—*stay away*. It may be some comfort to you to know that I had a letter from Cal in the same mail & he has already begun to be "mean" to me, trying to get "rises," etc.—it began even before he left, of course. He just can't help himself, I guess. I had thought that maybe I was "good for him"—maybe I am, but I think sooner or later I couldn't take any more of that ego-maniacy, or whatever it is—it is too bad, I do want to remain friends, but I think it is going to require great care & fortitude & a rhinoceros skin into the bargain. [*In margin*] And one can't remain completely objective always, you know. One of his recent letters concluded: "Be a good girl & come to Yaddo." And that is all the poor dear knows about how to get along with people!

. . . Mrs. Eberhart was going to take [the canary] Willy for me & keep him in Cambridge until I went to Boston, but it was Sunday when we drove to Wiscasset & the house was locked up—we could see Willy through the window but couldn't get him. I planned to bring him back here then, and would have, I guess, but at the very last minute I gave him away to that female taxi driver. She was delighted—wanted to buy one; her husband is very old and an invalid & it seemed like just the thing for him, so she carted him off, already talking her variety of baby talk to him, rather rough-and-tough. And I think it will be a very good home for him. I felt awful about it, but I guess I have no business having a pet, and my plans are so uncertain now, anyway . . .

Cal wrote that he had heard through a friend by way of S.'s sister (remember her?) that we had "wild Bohemian parties" here & "drank *absinthe*." Of course it is ridiculous to let it upset me because I have known all along just how twisted S. and her family are—but you can see how I feel somewhat misunderstood & abused at the moment (& that was so typical of Cal, too, to hand it all on). Although every meeting of any sort except the very last was always S.'s own idea (I was very careful about that because I could feel something like this building up) & al-though I don't think anyone ever got drunk at all, except Cal, that last night—there it is—my "reputation" is gone & I imagine that by now I *drove* S. out of her perfect working quarters with my wild goings-on! It is a little like your troubles with Miss A.K., I guess, and it is what we get for trying to be nice to too many people at the same time.

Because of this, I'm not sure whether S. ever got your present or not. Tom told me about it & I think she went by Blue Hill once, but I've forgotten. However, I did get mine & simply forgot to thank you the last time I wrote. I do thank you now. I was very surprised, and Tom & I have had several pleasant sessions, and I am still provided for. It was very nice of you to think of it. He and I & maybe Andy [his brother] are going to see Marianne tomorrow. She liked my poem about her, thank goodness—and refers to the article as "those fearless pages." Please, Carley, for heaven's sake don't send me anything else—you have done enough, and I wasn't even your hostess, as it turned out . . .

It is awfully kind of you to ask me to stay over in Washington—and it sounds very nice too. I've just written to find out about a place to stay in Key West—but I'm not at all sure of anything just now & may still go on a freighter trip somewhere. I was tempted by the idea of Yaddo just for a day or so because, after all, it is free, but soon I realized that if I wanted to remain friends with Cal at all, I'd better not see him for some time. I'll be here until Oct. 15th or 16th. It is boring, but I like it.

I don't think I'll say anything about the poem [Carley's sonnet] in this letter—it would be easier to say what I think in conversation. It is odd—well, I don't think I'll go into it at all except to say that I think to be able to write poetry about a situation already shows that one is interested in other things, so it may be a very good sign.

Will you please destroy this letter right away, Carley, as I just have yours? It is full of rather foolish things, however it is a slight relief to tell them to someone who knows the facts, and you are the only person who does.

I find I should send this to Canada. I hope you get your painting safely & have a nice time in the wilds of Canada in spite of all.

[P.S.] Tommy had Cal's number pretty well. I said something about how he seemed so confused & unhappy, and T. said, "And how he loves it!"

To Robert Lowell

August 30, 1948

You sounded very tired & hot & cranky. It has even been frightful here for four days, so I hope you haven't died of it in Washington. But today is beautiful, cold & clear. I'm quite looking forward to September, unless it gets too lonesome . . . I had a letter from Marianne, and thank goodness I guess my thoughts on her were all right. She starts off, "Words fail me, Elizabeth." Her postscript is: "I hope R.L. is able to go on with things he wants to do & is not too trammeled by government and academic plans." Tom & maybe Andy & I are going to see her Wednesday & it already promises to be quite an expedition.

Did you get a copy of Eberhart's endless *ubi sunt* poem, too? I thought it started off pretty well, for him—but really, he uses up words so fast it's a wonder he has any left by this time. Or that they'll come when he calls—like the Red or White Queen's remarks on Time in *Through the*

Looking-Glass. It's probably a sign of a generous disposition even if it doesn't make very good poetry—and I imagine he is very generous.

The ex-Latin professor read me a long ode to one of his daughters on her birthday, in Medieval Latin, and is going to give me some Macaronics, too. He is very cute. I am reading the *Nonnes Preestes Tale*, which I'd never read before, and of course I was much taken with:

> *His comb was redder than the fyn coral*
> *and battailed as it were a castel-wall.*
> *His bill was blak, & as the jeet it shoon;*
> *like azur were his legges, & his toon:*
> *His nayles whyter than the lilie flour*
> *and lyk the burnèd gold was his colour.*

& "his sustres & his paramours" & "For Goddes love, as tak som laxatyf."

I've just found the word for Mr. Tate, only for Goddes love don't tell him: hypsidolichocephaly, or -ic.

I'll read *Adolphe* sometime with the greatest interest. Please don't worry any more about *that*.

To Carley Dawson

September 3, 1948

Your two packages came yesterday. Tom & I were on our way to have a sort of picnic—just beyond that tree you painted out on the rocks there—so we took the packages along & opened them there. I don't know why you should feel apologetic about the bottle. We both are crazy about it, and I showed it to Janet Moore & her father & they were too. It is awfully pretty, I think, and looks very well on the windowsill against the fog we're having again this morning. (I'd thought it was all over—in fact the weather has been heavenly, much nicer than when you were here.) I wonder what came in the bottle originally—probably good old "Winter & Summer Gin." The boxes are very impressive & handsome, and *what* shall I put in them? One had had coffee in it, I think. I have a feeling that Loren MacIver will like them so much she'll try to get them away from me. The colors are just right for her—and you'll probably see them in one of her paintings sooner or later. All in all, I'm delighted to have presents sent me, even if you shouldn't have done it, and they have cheered me up a great deal. I've been a little upset by the S. business although it's pretty silly to let it bother me, I guess. Thank you ever so much, Carley.

Although Andy couldn't go, the trip to call on Marianne was very successful. Her two hostesses were very sweet & pretty—older than M., I think, and she was so eager to show them off to us. One of them had made a very elaborate *torte*, meringue & almonds & mustard, and a fancy tea with homemade bread & wild honey, etc. We were shown every inch of the house, one of the ladies' original home, including the bathroom cupboards. (M. ordered Tom, who was hanging back, "Come in, Mr. Wanning! This is part of the exhibition!") The woodshed where the skunk *used* to live, the new electric iron with a marble tip for ruffles, etc. M. keeps wintergreen leaves in her room to chew & *okra* tablets. I said, "Are they green?" "No, Elizabeth. They are fawn color." That was that.

It was, however, as I said, "a long day," and yesterday we were both exhausted, and even today at 11 a.m. Tom is still asleep. Guess I'll take him a cup of coffee—as Mrs. Gross says, "Men love to be waited on." How is Canada? and thank you again.

To Robert Lowell

September 8, 1948

I think you said a while ago that I'd "laugh you to scorn" over some conversation you & J. had had about how to protect yourself against solitude & ennui—but indeed I wouldn't. That's just the kind of "suffering" I'm most at home with & helpless about, I'm afraid, and what with two days of fog and alarmingly low tides, I've really got it bad & think I'll write you a note before I go out & eat some mackerel. The boats bringing the men back from the quarries look like convict ships & I've just been indulging myself in a nightmare of finding a gasping mermaid under one of these exposed docks—you know, trying to tear the mussels off the piles for something to eat—horrors. Also there is a small lobster pound with four posts at the corners that reminds me strongly of your sunken bedstead-grave [in the last stanza of "The Mills of the Kavanaughs"]. But I can't think of any more that would be practical for the next month, so—

Sometimes I wish I could have a more sensible conversation about this suffering business, anyway. I imagine we actually agree fairly well. It is just that I think it is so inevitable there's no use talking about it, and that in itself it has no value, anyway—as I think Jarrell says at the end of "90 North" or somewhere. I've just been reading through that new collection of Eliot criticism (some books arrived, thank goodness) and he is one of the few poets now, I think, who can really write about suffering convincingly—and then I don't even like him when he gets that oh-so-resigned tone.

What I really object to in Auden's "Musée des Beaux Arts" isn't the attitude about suffering—you're probably right about that—it's that I think it's just plain inaccurate in the last part. The ploughman & the people on the boat will rush to see the falling boy any minute, they always do, though maybe not to help. But then he's describing a painting so I guess it's all right to use it that way. Oh well—I want to see what you'll think of my [new poem] "Prodigal Son."

I like this story from *The N.Y. Times*—a composition by a child in the third grade: "I told my little brother that when you die you cannot breathe and he did not say a word. He just kept on playing."

I have just read a strange essay by Goethe on *granite*—it seemed so appropriate—and have you ever read *The Sorrows of [Young] Werther?*— which Napoleon said he read seven times and carried around with him? It makes very cheering reading these days.

Write me a note when you have the time.

Tuesday
[September 1948]

I guess I'd better return these letters. Really Eberhart (after what I said to you the other day about his use of words, I keep calling him Expendable Eberhart to myself) is extraordinary. "Thought bullet"— what *does* he mean? and "locking tremblers"—I suspect he means *temblors*, don't you? But I guess he is really fond of you & it is mean to read it as meaning anything much else than that. I'd also like to know, though, what he had in mind by the word "truth."

I like the first part of Mr. Flint's letter very much & am so glad you let me see it—the part about the two motions of thought, etc. But doesn't it amaze you a little when people hand you back, like an obligation, flat statements of what *you "meant"*? [*In margin*] It seems to be a sort of convention when writing to an author.

I've been to Quebec, although I didn't see much of it, but when I visited my aunt in Montreal I remember—it's a long time ago—I was very much surprised to look out her window & watch the nuns & priests playing tennis. Also have you ever been to the Church of the Perpetual Adoration in N.Y. on 28th St.? You see those beautiful habits there. I think the "insistent rhyming" at the end [of Lowell's new poem, "Mother Marie Therese"] is wonderful, too—but I don't think "coda" is correct as applied to it, is it? (Since you told me the story behind the remark "Nothing is so dead as a dead sister" I keep wishing that more of it were stated somehow in the poem—at least I had missed the significance of it & was rather baffled—& so was Tom, my only literary acquaintance at the moment, here.)

You don't say anything about the rest of the letter, so I won't either. Except that you know his not being ready yet to "sort out" the [Thomas] Merton poems & "grade them" is pretty funny. Maybe he's extremely young—or what do you know about him? It's such a mixture of good interpretation & conceit.

Oh, dear Mr. E. "The spiritual is the fascinating." Let's publish an anthology of haunting lines, with a supplement on how to exorcize them.

I don't seem to remember the line about the tamales so the blackness of your tongue was wasted on me, I'm afraid. And one more amplification or correction: I don't think Harcourt Brace ever turned me down—they were going to publish me when I had a few more poems, etc., but were very slow about it & the Houghton Mifflin thing seemed like a good thing to try for, so I wrote to HB & got what mss. I had back from them—with their blessing, naturally. But anyway, that's the way it was.

I must see you in the rotogravure in sepia—is it for a Washington paper, or where?

Have you ever read Erich Fromm's books? I find him rather disappointing now, but still I think his summary of the Reformation in *Escape from Freedom* might interest you—at least I'd like to see how it strikes you. And if you can place what I'm talking about, could you tell me once more the name of the American reporter-historian you have recommended to me several times?

It is COLD here today—we have the duo-therm going, so I hope you are at least just a natural 98.8 in Washington.

To Carley Dawson

October 1, 1948

. . . September was an absolutely beautiful month—bright & clear —but today has started with the first thick fog in a long time, dead white and very wet. I just went downstairs for a moment and found poor Mrs. Gross in tears. It seemed so suitable that I hardly noticed at first, then she said she was "blue" and dissolved even further. Oh dear, I'm afraid I retreated rather quickly. Last night, thinking Tom and I were leaving today, she insisted on giving us dinner—at five sharp—on a card table with everything under the sun. We ate and ate manfully & then went out for a long walk to try to wear off the worst effects. Poor woman—she leads a hard life with her awful children—and I guess it's just as well I'm leaving before I get more wicked. She's just too "easy" & so is Papa Gross.

Jarrell's poetry seems to be getting more & more diffuse. Mr. Graham, whoever he is, makes some good points, I think, although what he says about "incidentals" is surely wrong. But I do wish Jarrell hadn't adopted Corbière's system of hysterical punctuation. I'm afraid Corbière has been a bad influence on him, bringing out more & more of his rather maudlin, morbid streak. Maybe it's a combination of Corbière & trying to write NOT like Cal. I can't remember the poems *Rondels pour après* well enough to know how closely he's stuck to the originals. To me they don't sound anything like Cal, but of course you & Jarrell both know him better than I do & the words "hearse" and "penitentiary" are certainly reminiscent. The originals—what a child—may have reminded him of Cal. If you haven't read Corbière, do, by all means. He is really a marvelous poet & these "adaptations" only give the poorest idea of what he's like.

I haven't heard from Cal since before he left for Yaddo.

I forgot to tell you if you really wanted another copy of *North & South*, Brentano's had some, I think, but the Gotham Book Mart didn't.

I think Jarrell at his best has a remarkable dark, creepy Grimm-Wagnerian quality, but I just wish he'd pull it all together more & not be so afraid of being neat, or solid, or whatever it is.

My Key West friends, Pauline Hemingway & Marjorie Stevens, are in New York doing their buying, etc., and I'm looking forward to seeing them. Also my friend Margaret [Miller]'s collage show is on at the Museum of Modern Art & I'm dying to see it at last; she's been working on it a long time. I have to go to Wellesley the 18th & I shall probably stay in Boston around then, and I hope to be going to Key West sometime in November . . .

I've managed to get a lot of work done, I think—I'll know better when I get back to a typewriter . . .

46 King Street
New York, New York
November 10, 1948

I have so much to tell you I wish I could see you—but maybe it's just as well because I'm afraid most of it is on a rather low level of gossip. After being so social in Boston once the "reading" was over, and then here, and then the weekend at Bard & then yesterday a reception—or something—for the Sitwells, I don't feel like myself at all. I'm exhausted all over but particularly the face, which I suppose comes from wearing a horrible fixed grin for so long. I've just put some Arden lotion in the icebox and am looking forward to lying down and putting a nice cold washcloth full of it on my poor hypocritical features . . .

The Bard weekend was very successful on the whole, I think. Dr. [William Carlos] Williams read Friday night—talked, rather, in a completely scatterbrained but charming way. Afterwards there was a big & sort of awful party at which they served (I suppose they'd been counting on cold weather) a kind of hot punch called GLUG full of raisins and almonds & things and terrible. The room was so hot I felt faint & one enthusiastic undergraduate spilled a cup of Glug all over me, to begin with. Finally Cal & I just ran away and found the college cafeteria, where we drank some nice cold milk and cooled off. He shared somebody's quarters with Eberhart.

I went up with my friends Loren MacIver & Lloyd Frankenberg and we all stayed with Joe and U.T. (remember the girl named University of

Texas?) Summers. The next morning Miss [Louise] Bogan gave a talk—it seemed to be a sort of attempt to refute Dr. Williams, but it was pretty dull and academic and I feel that that sort of thing should be left to someone like Eliot, who really knows what he's doing. And after that there was a "panel" in which ALL THE POETS were dragged up front around a table and you know *made points* and dragged in dynamos and for some reason the rhythm of milking a cow seemed to figure quite a lot, too—amounting in all to no more than each one's elucidating his own style, but all very well received & everyone kept saying it was the best thing that had ever happened at Bard.

Those present were Richard Wilbur, Eberhart, Cal, Lloyd, Jean Garrigue, Dr. Williams & Miss B., me, and a wild man from California in a bright red shirt and yellow braces named [Kenneth] Rexroth, who did his best to start a fight with everyone and considered us all effete and snobbish Easterners. He never quite succeeded and finally had to prove his mettle or his reality or something by taking three of the prettiest undergraduates off for an evening in the cemetery. "Reading" had not been part of the bargain, but somehow it was brought about and everyone got through a poem except Miss Garrigue & me. I said I was too tired, so Cal read for me, "The Fish." Saturday night was worst—a really drunken party, I'm afraid, with everyone behaving very much the way poets are supposed to. But Sunday was nice. The Summerses, Loren & Lloyd & I & Cal took a long walk by the Hudson, very peaceful and pleasant.

Then we came back and had a long peaceful luncheon that went on—with several bottles of wine—until it got dark. Cal is apparently working very hard at Yaddo—said he had 1,000 lines done, which is extraordinary, I'd say. Hopes to have the book done by June and then (& this is what I like about him—his sensible attitude about working) revise it all *next* winter. It sounds awfully dull at Yaddo and I don't think it would suit me at all, although I have thought of going there for a month or so. No ladies in his life—at least that I know of.

Yesterday was rather like a party in a subway train—at the Gotham Book Mart with *Life* magazine somehow horning in on it. Miss Steloff rushing about in an Indian print dress, Miss Sitwell wearing a gold turban that looked like a tiara from the front, Marianne in one of her large black numbers (& me in what M. referred to as a *nominal* hat), hordes of people, everyone, my dear, including Auden and Spender, whom I'd never seen before. Miss Sitwell was very nice—much nicer than I'd thought from the poetry. It was there that my grin really began to hurt. Jarrell was there—and Jean Stafford came up & introduced herself to me—quite different to the way I'd thought of her, and very pleasant. (How I've disliked her last stories, too.) I'm having tea this afternoon with her & Jarrell. After the "party" Marianne & I made our escape in a cab and met Tom, with whom I'd had a movie date but we were (oh, dry up) [letter discontinued]

All the above total recall was done with two plumbers in the same room with me, in a mess of tubes and pipes & pumping machines. The gas stove had broken again. The worst feature, though, was that they kept fighting with each other all the time. I finally managed to get dressed (found a third man crouching in the closet behind my clothes—apparently the gas pipe goes through there, so everything is perfumed with gas now) and out to meet Randall. Jean had to go to her psychiatrist & couldn't come. Randall was very nice—and now I'll stop this literary gabbling—except for one thing. Eliot is speaking at the Congressional Library November 19th and I thought I might go . . .

Would it be all right then for me to stay at your house, probably only Thursday night, or at the most Thursday and Friday? It would be wonderful and make the whole thing so much more enjoyable. I think Cal, Tate, etc., are all going, but a day or two earlier for Library business, and I'm going alone or maybe take Tom (who would go to a hotel) or have Jane Dewey come down from Aberdeen just for the lecture. If this isn't all right, be sure to tell me . . . I can perfectly well go to a hotel, of course—but it would be nice to see your nice house again . . .

My insides are all fine again thanks to my doctor . . . It isn't so bad but leaves one so tired and shaky. I'm seeing the doctor today and shall ask her about Enterol (not that I don't take your word for it, but I'm taking something she gave me which may be Enterol for all I know). I do hope you're liking San Francisco—just don't join the Henry Miller cult and all will be well.

To U.T. and Joseph Summers

[November 10, 1948]

What a really nice time you did provide for everyone. I'm afraid you must both be absolutely exhausted by it and I can't think of any other people I know who would have dared to undertake so much, and having undertaken it seen it through with such skill. I've heard that sometimes women in U.T.'s state do take on odd things, like shingling the roof, etc.—but U.T. seemed to be quite in her right mind and this was much much more difficult. Anyway, as Marianne once said to me, I am quite disabled thinking of it. Lloyd slept peacefully all the way back on the train but Loren and I couldn't stop gossiping for a second. I wonder if Cal ever did get off. I wouldn't be surprised if he were still with you right this minute, drinking Milk and talking Milton. He was obviously having a marvelous time.

I think I liked yesterday, the walk and the lunch, best of all. I also like to think of U.T. sitting in that bright green bathrobe. She looked so exactly like a nice healthy little plant in a field or maybe a—if you don't mind my saying so—kind of well-shaped gourd. I've never seen a more becoming pregnancy. It seemed to be a help rather than a hindrance—but I'm afraid Joe was worn out when we finally got off. I'm glad the Weisses showed up. I haven't had time yet to think back to the beginning of it & Dr. Williams. I suppose he really deserves a lot of credit for setting the right tone somehow.

I had a letter from Marianne this morning in which she describes a small dinner given for the Sitwells Friday night—they are " *'perfect'*; they are so very peaceful and yet alive, and 'literary,' " etc. etc.—it's very funny.

You can see I'm still sort of wound up but hope I'll run down gradually today. I keep thinking of Joe interviewing those students. I'll dry up now & go to the dentist's.—It really was a great success, I think, and thank you for all you did and I just hope I was a credit to you, more or less.

To Carley Dawson

[Washington, D.C.]
November 26, 1948

I don't know how to begin this letter or what to say or how to say it—but I guess the only thing to do is to take the plunge & get it over with. Not to alarm you unduly, I'll tell you the worst at once—& maybe it isn't so bad as it seems to me right now. I got to feeling sorry for myself (why, I haven't the slightest idea) at your house on Saturday (this spell had been coming on for two or three weeks, I think) & drank up all your liquor & made myself good & sick & finally got myself (under my own steam) off on Monday to a weird kind of convalescent home here.

Florence [the maid] could not have been kinder or sweeter & I don't believe there was any "mess," etc. I have talked to her on the phone & written her a note since. She is a wonderful woman. A Mrs. Easton was coming in Tuesday morning, I think, but F. assured me that everything was fine for her. And of course I'll replace your liquor.

There is no point in wailing & gnashing my teeth over my depravity, I know, and I'll try to spare you that. I'll only say that I believe you must have realized I had this trouble occasionally all along, &—poor Carley—must feel by now you not only attract neurotic lovers but friends as well. Also will you please believe me when I say that in spite of this episode the *graph* has been uphill now for a long time, that something that's an exaggeration like this—I mean *this* bad—has only happened to me once before, and that for the last two years I've felt like quite a different person. Apologies are pretty feeble, too, but I do hate to think of *adding* to your troubles. My chief hope right now is that you will remain a friend in spite of it.

I think I had just been doing too much, seeing too many people, etc. I get along better on boredom & adversity than on gaiety and, relatively speaking, success. That's enough about it . . . It's just I feel I can't be hypocritical with you any longer. Now I won't say any more about it, ever, or this crazy place—the Kalorama Convalescent Home, either—unless sometime you want me to.

CHAPTER TWO

Maybe you'd like to hear a little about the Eliot lecture. Pauline Hemingway & I came down on the train together & spent the afternoon at the National Gallery. She slept in the room I had slept in before & I slept in yours. She had to leave about 8 the next morning. She was much taken with your house & most appreciative & we had a lovely time & I hope it was all right. Apparently I'd been supposed to meet Cal & Allen [Tate] for dinner but of course all the wires got crossed & we dined alone at Rectors. The auditorium was packed, queues of hundreds, literally, outside. We found ourselves sitting separately in back of & beside Dr. Williams and his wife & it seems Pauline had known them, etc., and it was all very nice. Eliot looked white & hot & exhausted & although he was quite funny once in a while, I was a little disappointed in what he had to say about Poe. I spotted all the POETS in the reserved section, an impressive array, & most, I should say (although I shouldn't), quite tight.

As we were leaving with the Williamses, Cal suddenly appeared—it was pouring rain all the time—and we were all taken off to a rather strange, I thought, party at Mrs. Bliss's—the POETS mostly drinking in one room while Mrs. Bliss urged scrambled eggs on the non-poets in another—wearing a glove on her right hand only. Pauline found several old friends & had a wonderful time. I met [Karl] Shapiro, who was very sweet. In fact it was all very pleasant & it wasn't until the next day & I'd seen Pauline off & was supposed to go to have lunch with Cal and Auden (who looks nice but scares me) that my troubles began.

Carley, I want this to get in the mail. I should have just thanked you days ago. It was so nice of you to let me stay there, everything looked so nice but a little forlorn the way shut-up houses do . . . The nurse says this has to go.

I am feeling much improved & going back to New York Saturday or Sunday. Meanwhile, as I said, my chief hope is that you will remain my friend, because I want you to & because I KNOW things are going to be better . . .

[New York City
December 1, 1948]

Thank you so much for the kind letter that just came. I've just been *holding on* here, trying not to think about you at all. However, I realize now that of course I was exaggerating the whole thing terribly . . . It is just so alien to everything I really want to do. I didn't even have so very much to drink (fortunately there wasn't much there). I think that when something like that happens I'm so overcome with remorse, before I even

1 9 4 8 [*177*

get drunk, that that's why I get to feeling so damned sick—and it's much more the mental aftermath than the physical. But I wasn't feeling depressed or anything like that to begin with, and that is what proves it really *is* a disease. I'd been having a marvelous time in New York and that one evening in Washington as well—but I just can't take very much excitement or very many people. I get to going faster and faster . . .

To go way back, in Washington two nights before the lecture Lloyd Frankenberg and Loren MacIver (my painter friend & her husband) and Cal and I had dinner and spent the evening with the Tates. I believe I was the only sober person present (I'd been on the wagon for a long time) and didn't enjoy myself too much because it was all pretty wild and noisy. But everyone was having a good time—Caroline [Gordon, wife of Allen Tate] and Cal predominating, both pouring out literary opinions & gossip at a great rate. Yes, I think we probably feel exactly the same way about the Tates. I think it was the next day Cal came here and had lunch with me and a very nice quiet conversation—but that's the last time I've seen him alone. He must get very dull at Yaddo and obviously has such a wonderful time making up for it when he gets away and is very over-excited, drinks too much, etc.—but there is something so childlike about his enjoying himself that I can't seem to mind, although I wished he'd looked a little better at the Washington affair. He wanted me to go up to visit him at Yaddo and I think now that I have an extra week I may possibly do it, just for a day, to look the place over and see if I think I could stand it for a stay sometime. At the Tates' my friend Pauline Hemingway was mentioned and Caroline said, "It's funny. Ah nevah really laked Pauline . . ." etc. Allen had, I gathered—greeting her in Washington with a most tender kiss.

Two nights ago a friend & next-door neighbor of mine who for a year has been playing understudy to Jessica Tandy in *A Streetcar Named Desire* was suddenly "on"—Jessica had a cold. Tom and I went and managed to get seats. No dinner, because we only knew at the last minute, so we ate Hershey bars from time to time. It was very exciting—I'd never seen her act before although I have known her for years & she was much better than I'd ever dreamed she would be.

Tom—or have I told you?—is living in what he calls "the oubliette" at a hotel over on Washington Sq.—the same dream-life as ever. I want him to stay here and go to my various doctors (even dentist). He says that's "incestuous"—and I suppose that after I go sometime or other he will vaguely get himself back to Key West, but I wish he wouldn't. Pauline said something very good about him, though—that probably if he changed and got "busy," etc., he'd lose a great many of the qualities that make him nice—he is so completely disinterested now . . .

New York is awful now with the Christmas crowds and gray dirty weather. I am investing in a new bicycle and a new typewriter and wish I were in Key West in that wonderful sunlight . . . Carley, I'm sorry you had to be in on this little stretch of my life. I think I learned more in those five days than I have in the last fifteen years . . .

December 11, 1948

. . . NO—I don't think these cartoons are a bit like you & I'm almost tempted to tear them up just so you won't think such ridiculous thoughts. As far as Cal goes, Carley, you know we confine our conversation to books and literary gossip; it is almost never personal & I like it best that way. He has never said anything about you since that one day in Stonington & I think that is probably right. And I imagine I'd understand that side of him as little as you do.

I do wish you'd stop feeling badly or questioning yourself about it all—but I suppose it takes time. Anyway, I'd very much doubt, from what I *do* know of him, that "gossip" would play any part in it all. To be very trite—love is cruel & that is all there is to it, and it's never any reflection on one's character, really.

To Loren MacIver and Lloyd Frankenberg

[POSTCARD]

611 Frances Street
Key West, Florida
December 21, 1948

Had the good luck to find a huge, wonderful apartment with my former landlady, Mrs. Pindar—upstairs, with the biggest Poinciana tree in Key West shading the screened porch. Don't know what I did to deserve it. Hope you're both getting as much work done as I hope to start getting done tomorrow. Jane [Dewey] and I went to the museums in Baltimore, and to Poe's grave in the pouring rain. Love.

To Dr. Anny Baumann

December 30, 1948

I had been meaning to write to you, although I haven't very much to say—and then yesterday your letter came, by way of Wiscasset, with the good news about Tommy Wanning. His aunt is so happy about it and so, of course, am I. I am just afraid that if Dr. Foster can't take him he won't be willing to go to anyone else, he discourages so easily—also that in one interview with him she might not realize how extremely intelligent and worthwhile he is—really one of the smartest people I know. But maybe I am underestimating Dr. Foster, who is pretty smart herself, after all. Mrs. Chambers is very grateful to you and so relieved that something is being done at last.

It makes me rather angry to have to say that I have been having asthma again here. I had comparatively little in New York, but as soon as I get to the place I like best of all it starts again. I can't think of anything in particular that would cause it. I had the good luck to find a wonderful large upstairs apartment, ugly, but I like it very much and everything seems ideal for a winter of good hard work. I am NOT drinking, anything at all. But I have asthma every night more or less and even with the theoglycinate pills I have to take one or two shots of adrenaline in the course of the night. I don't believe it's quite as bad as last year, though. At least in the daytime I seem to have enough wind for bicycling and swimming. But I am awfully sick of it. Otherwise everything is fine . . .

P.S. We all wish you'd come to Key West. I could guarantee you a large and fascinating practice.

To Robert Lowell

EB was finally persuaded by Lowell to serve as the Consultant in Poetry at the Library of Congress for 1949–50, following Allen Tate, Robert Penn Warren, Louise Bogan, Karl Shapiro, Lowell, and Léonie Adams, starting in September 1949. At Yaddo that summer she suffered from anxiety attacks as a result of having taken on the Washington job.

January 21, 1949

I've always felt that I've written poetry more by *not* writing it than writing it, and now this Library business makes me really feel like the "poet by default." At first I felt a little overcome and inclined to wire you a frantic "no," but after having thought about it for a day or two I've concluded that it is something I *could* do (there isn't much, heaven knows) and that even if I feel I haven't written nearly enough poetry to warrant it, that maybe it will be all right—particularly if I work hard from now until then. Another thing, I think I was pretty cheered up by the Wellesley business, which really went off quite well. But I haven't heard anything from Washington, so of course I suspect that everyone has changed his mind & I am not breathing any of this to anyone and if they have changed their minds I hope you're not going to be embarrassed, etc. A letter just did come from D.C., but it proved to be an invitation to a reading by Léonie Adams. I'm kind of glad I'm so far away, I'm afraid. I suppose by the "meeting" you mean when they all get together at the start of the year? The people that I already know I like and am not afraid of, and with your kind offer of help—well, I won't say any more about it until the thing is certain one way or another, except that your letter was extremely thoughtful and nice.

Things have been rather pleasant here, if dull, and not at all comparable to your intellectual carousings with Burgundy. The only intellectual life here, I gather, is taking place below stairs at the Casa Marina (that's the $40-a-day hotel—where Selden stayed, and where the tennis stars are). The little Polish tennis assistant, who seemed to be Selden's *amie* of the moment, came to see me, bringing me S.'s poems and riding on a huge boy's bicycle all headlights and horns & flags, etc. She said it belonged to the head dishwasher there (who also has a *horse*) and that he is avidly reading Selden's poems and wants to get hold of mine—all the dishwashers do. (When Selden came to my party he brought along the tennis champs and the elevator boy and the newspaper concession girl—all modern poetry addicts, I gathered.) Maybe I should move out to the Casa Marina as a scullery maid. The Polish girl of course writes poetry, too—I think she said "one every night" . . .

I have also just had a call from Faustina. Since I'm putting her in a book I feel rather mean the way I often try to get rid of her—but, as Pauline says, she's too much of a lady ever to admit anyone's being rude to her, so she just settles down to her "cognac" and her cigar—I have to keep some on hand for her . . .

Of course I still wish you'd come here sometime—say when you get a bad cold in March & have to take a rest. The new beach is nice and the fishing is marvelous and we could take a trip to Havana—35 minutes away—you don't have to have a passport for that so I should think you could go.

I think I'll write to Mrs. Ames [director of Yaddo] right now and ask about July. I think that would work out all right—I might even stay on here until then if I manage to keep working. I'm glad to hear your poem is coming along. Oh, I now have a small marbleized French notebook that Loren gave me devoted exclusively to Lowell notes, with that review in mind—so far I've only covered two pages but they're awfully profound I'm sure. A wonderful tropical downpour—I have to rush around and close all the windows so the paper curtains won't dissolve.

If I get the Washington job—I don't *have* necessarily to give a lot of "readings," do I?

I just read Meyer Schapiro in the last *Partisan Review* about a French painter & critic I don't believe I'd ever heard of—but I do think he writes wonderfully; it makes one want to get to work immediately.

[P.S.] I really wish Marianne had accepted [the Washington chair for poetry]. I should think she would whenever she finishes the La Fontaine, don't you?

I'm anxious to know what you consider me being "moral."

January 31, 1949

. . . I still haven't heard from Washington—but then for all I know I may not be supposed to until sometime in September—but I did hear from Mrs. Ames and am hastening to fill out the forms. She says graciously that she thinks I need not send any manuscript. It doesn't say how many sponsors and I'm so sick of pestering people. I think this time I'll just ask Marianne and *you* and then you could do it orally possibly. I'm saying the "July–August" period. I have read the booklet from cover to cover . . .

I'll stay on here until I go to Yaddo almost, I guess. I think it would be so much fun if you came here—although June would be pretty hot of course. We could go bonefishing, which I've never done but think I'm going to do next week—the gamest fish there is, very small—10 lbs. is an enormous one. You have to pole through the mangrove keys silently and not even speak, etc. Also in June the tarpon come—that's moonlight-night fishing and ravishing, but hard to catch. Bonefishing is fairly cheap—$20 a day, I think—because of the poling, they don't use much gasoline.

Oh yes I've been being the female Hemingway again, I guess. The Polish girl and a boy from the hotel—dishwasher or elevator boy, I don't know which, but an expert—are teaching me pool, and Sunday I am going to the cockfights. Pool will be such a useful thing to know. There's always a pool parlor wherever one goes [*In margin:* think I'll use this line in a poem] if one gets bored. There was even one in Stonington but Tommy was too conservative to take me.

I decided I was being too much of a hermit so I've spent the last four days just loving everybody I meet and swimming, etc., but today I am back at work. I sold *The New Yorker* a medium-length bit of plain description, but have three more serious things just about ready to mail. Good lord, there's a fifteen-year-old girl next door whose voice & general personality is just about as restful as a stuck automobile horn. I love the [poet Alexis] Léger [St.-John Perse] story—Pauline is now dreading his visit, of course.

I'm glad you like "In Prison." I had only read *The Castle* of Kafka when I wrote it, and that long before, so I don't know where it came from. But the à la Turgenev story I wrote this summer, if I can ever revise it, is really better, I think—no posing. I'll save money in Washington and then let's go to Italy together, if your friend [Santayana] lasts that long.

[P.S.] Pauline's sister is here, who lives in Rome & is chiefly interested in making movies of colored people—very nice.

Grand Hotel Oloffson
Port-au-Prince, Haiti
February 21, 1949

I was sort of hoping to hear from you before I suddenly left Key West for a *petit changement*—in fact I meant to write you again but didn't. I was afraid that (1) You are sick. (2) You are MAD. (3) Well, various wild fancies. After my 38th birthday [on February 8] I fell into a slough for a few days & then decided to come with Pauline's sister, Virginia Pfeiffer, to Haiti for about ten days & see if I could get out of it. It was a very good idea & has worked perfectly—nothing could be more of a change than this unlikely country & I think it is much more interesting than I'd ever dreamed any of the West Indies, etc., could be. I'm having one batch of mail forwarded here. I think we're going back next Saturday—and hope to get a note from you in that, to quiet my uneasy imagination.

Selden, of course, is here & two nights ago gave a talk (in French) on "Primitivism in Modern Poetry." I understood every word but still don't know what he meant by "Primitivism"—although I missed the first five minutes of it & so maybe the definition. It was a grand tour in his anthology—introduction style, bringing in every name since 1900. I was in the front row (between the Lewis Gannetts) but kept turning around to see what the effect of all this was on his mostly black audience. A great many slept. Mr. & Mrs. G. got the fidgets & embarrassed me considerably by tearing open envelopes rather noisily & then writing each other notes on them which they handed back & forth across my knees . . .

Today we are going spearfishing, out to islands in the harbor where you can see coral gardens, etc. You spearfish wearing goggles, using an oxygen tube & carrying an 8-foot spear that works by powerful springs, under your arms, so you swim only with your legs. If Ginny doesn't spear *me*, I'll have to write you an account of it.

The racial situation is the most interesting thing about Haiti, I guess—always thorough mixtures everywhere, at everything, & yet with it all a caste system that's supposed to be worse than India's.

We have a little black man who sleeps outside our door to protect us from burglars—clutching a knife two feet long in one hand & a large rock in the other. Mass starts at 4 a.m. in the churches so that the very poor (90%) who haven't any decent clothes can come in the dark. We went to ten o'clock mass in the cathedral—for the "elite," and then saw a lot of elite black babies baptized. The godparents holding them shook them up and down just like cocktail shakers & it was a rather riotous baptism, with lots of howls.

I haven't tried to write at all, but yesterday morning I woke up at 4 —the poorly clad were trooping by my balcony in the dark on their way to church—and wrote a lot of stuff.

Ginny just took this picture of me with the new Polaroid camera that develops instantaneously. I really don't look quite so fat nor so much like a French postcard. The other picture is like one of Selden's primitives, only better. I'll be in Key West by next week . . .

To Dr. Anny Baumann

611 Frances Street
Key West, Florida
March 22, 1949

Perhaps it is too soon for me to write you any kind of "report," but I want to thank you for being so kind . . . The prescriptions came yesterday and I had them filled. I had felt pretty good up in Miami but Facing Things back here was bad; but after I talked to you Saturday, everything seemed to start clearing up and I have been progressively less nervous & melancholy, etc., ever since.

Things had been neither too good nor too bad all winter, but about the 1st of February they took a decided turn for the worse, I don't know why. I—or my friends—decided a "change" might help, so I went to Haiti and everything was fine there and I had a wonderful time, but a day or so after I got back everything just seemed to blow up. It was all aggravated by worrying about this "job [in Washington]" (still uncertain) and a couple of other problems that I really can't do anything about at all.

The asthma, strange to say, has been gradually going away, I think. I had none at all in Haiti and have less & less here. I am hoping it is a good sign and that this last sad business I put my friends and myself through may mark the beginning of some sort of metamorphosis.

Everyone has been unbelievably kind. You know I'm sorry so I won't say that. I'm taking the pills and at least feel sane again and thank you once more for your help . . .

P.S. I think I'll enclose a poem about Key West that was in *The New Yorker* a few weeks ago. I wrote it last year but I still think if I can just keep the last line in mind, everything may still turn out all right. [Apparently "The Bight," which ends: "All the untidy activity continues, / awful but cheerful."]

To Lloyd Frankenberg and Loren MacIver

Tuesday morning
[Key West, Florida
April 1949]

Dear Lloyd, I hate to deal you this blow below the belt, but on re-reading your two last letters I've been forced to come to the reluctant conclusion that your correspondence with publishers must be affecting your style. Because what I *think* you're still saying is what I thought you were saying the first time—that there's a pretty good chance of one album of eight records, but I'm not to be in it. Which, as you should know, is absolute music to my ears. Anyway, I do hope it is all working out satisfactorily and that you don't have a nervous breakdown before it's published.

I got sick when I got back from Haiti—had too good a time, I suspect, and just couldn't get back to work here. Anyway after my experiences with Key West doctors & hospitals I went to Miami for about a week, and just got back. Completely recovered, but feeling at least five years behind history, socially, financially, artistically and morally.

Dear Loren, I'll call up Dr. Thompson at the hotel tomorrow & ask her to dinner, I think. David was just here with a poem—I hadn't seen him in ages—and I'm very pleased to say I thought it was very nice—much the best of his I've ever seen. He wants to see Dr. T. & Marjorie is eager to meet her, too, so I guess I can arrange something.

I was surprised that Ginny actually got those pipes to you, since I smashed a few just on the way home from the store in Haiti. She is a really wonderful traveling companion—terribly funny. I've just been wading through a long biography of G. B. Shaw and find them quite similar, at least in his younger days, so I'm forced to admit there may be something to this Irish business after all, and Wit and Wilde and Shaw & Ginny, etc.—only it's all based on contrariness, I'm sure.

Tell Lloyd (the person addressed above) that I saw his review of Patrick's book and liked it. I've had the book ordered for some time but it hasn't come yet . . . I had a wonderful letter from Tommy, partly about seeing some galleries with you. I have never felt quite so out of things in my life but I am hoping it is merely a mood rather than a real situation.

Pauline & I are about to go to a small circus—the first in Key West since 1912. I think it may be nice, and less exhausting than Madison Sq. Garden. Have you any summer plans and if so what? I'd love to see the Fratellini picture—what else have you been working on? I seem to remember that I once used to rhyme a mean rhyme, but it all seems awfully long ago; that Black Republic did something to me, possibly I am a zombie now.

To Lloyd Frankenberg

Written at an unnamed hospital (Blythewood?), where EB was "isolated," this undated letter reveals her growing uneasiness, apparently induced by the poetry consultantship looming in Washington and her inability to write. The emotional isolation she felt at Yaddo, the writers' colony where she went in July, brought on a serious anxiety attack, recorded in the next letters.

Wednesday 5:30 p.m.
[May/June? 1949]

I don't seem to let you or Loren out of earshot a moment these days. I sent her a card this morning and am glad to report to you now that the *mumps* (if that's what they were) have much improved. I can almost open my mouth and say "ah" now and am feeling much better in general. How long they'll continue to "isolate" me in this dreary splendor I don't know. I find it's dangerous to get out of the swim here for 24 hrs.—you just don't want to get back in again at all. I felt awfully mortified at being such a bad guest (almost said "camper") but the doctor and the one boy who is allowed to come to call & bring me meals both assure me that it had been such a dull & well-behaved season that everyone has been grateful for the short 24 hrs. excitement I've given them.

Thank you for the Rexroth thing. Heavens what "spring" did he mean? I wonder. (I'm getting in training for Washington all right. Did you see that wonderful *New Yorker* blurb about the Congressional Library two weeks ago?—about my "boss" too.) But heavens, all that typing. Why can't they pick them out of books? I'm still trying to get out of writing [John] Ciardi a 5,000-word essay on my innermost thoughts, too, but he at least just requests titles.

I think the Italian thing would be nice. You don't say anything about whether it has to be new material or not—I shouldn't think so. I don't have any new stories done, but it seems to me that maybe "The Farmer's Children" might be slightly improved by being put into Italian, and I'd be glad to send that if you think it would do. I haven't a copy here, though—I can get it when I *get things* at your house or send him the book with it in.

I'll be in N.Y. for a week at least. With love to you both.

To Loren MacIver

Sunday afternoon
[Yaddo, Saratoga Springs
July 3, 1949]

I've written a couple of letters to you & then torn them up. There really isn't very much to say, I guess, except I do want to thank you for your many kindnesses in New York and since. The only thing to do now is to stay on the wagon and "try not to worry"—but if the first is hard, the second is impossible.

I have never felt so nervous and like a fish out of water—and *dizzy* all the time—although I have had nothing to drink since last Wednesday & won't either. I'm beginning to think there may be something the matter with my "middle ear." Anyway I'm going to see the doctor tomorrow morning, but since she seems to be a dear friend of Mrs. Ames I don't want to tell her much of anything, so— You got me to feeling pretty good for a day there in New York, and how I wish you were here to do it again.

There's not much point in describing this place. It would take forever and was obviously all the dream of a mad millionairess with high ideals, etc. The room I have was hers. I'm trying to paint a picture of it for Margaret [Miller], to see if that will cheer me up some. For you maybe I'll paint a picture of the neighboring racetrack, which is very nice, when I've bought some paper. I forgot it all in that box of my stuff I gave you.

I'd like to go to the races at night to see the lights but don't feel like going alone and for some reason, although everyone is really kind and pleasant, I can't seem to "mix" any more here than I could at Blythewood—where I was mixed about like a drop of oil in water. I don't know what can be the matter any more, but Blythewood and its attendant evils seem to have destroyed whatever social gifts I had ever acquired forever and I just tremble and stutter, etc. My chief worry seems to be that Dr. Baumann will "give me up." Also that Harriet, Mary, Marjorie, Margaret, you, Tom, Cal, as well as the pf [Pfeiffer] sisters have all come to dislike me. I really think those damned doctors have undermined me thoroughly and for good & all.

The people are mostly rather young and ebullient & I never was any good at horseplay, even when I was as young as they are. A couple of the youngest boys I like quite well but god, are they intense and a new poem appears about every hour. Lucy, the Haitian girl, is really quite nice but I feel that she is in a very lost position, too. I haven't been to see her paintings yet, but have seen two other women's, both very sad and poor—& one man named Shooker, I think. Last night there was a huge bat in my room (it is all very Charles Addamsish, I'm afraid) and Mr. S. gallantly got it out for me though I suspect he was more afraid of it than I was. Wallace Fowlie came last night—very polite anyway, but I don't know anything about him. Pearl [Kazin] is coming tomorrow. Am I in a nest of Communists or not, I don't know, and I'm scared of writing to Cal about where I am, etc. Everyone says he is about to marry E. Hardwick—maybe already has. Ye gods! It really is all too intense here for me and I'm at a complete loss what to do or say any of the time. That feeling grows & grows on me more and more & was certainly not helped much either by Carley's saying she'd got me a rather small stuffy room and she doubted I could receive gentlemen, etc. Maybe I should try to take an apartment, I don't know. In fact I JUST DON'T KNOW anything except that I'd like to die quite quickly.

Read *The Barbarian in Asia*—it has some wonderful things in it— parts about fish & birds you'd like, I think.

Had another card from Tom, but I have no idea what address to write to him at. I just saw a very nice poem by Lloyd in *Harper's*, tell him. It rained all night and today is much cooler—I like it best when it rains. This is much much worse than one's first week at boarding school and I feel like such a fool for minding it as well. John Brinnin is here looking just like a sign of the zodiac—only he's gone off with Howie [Moss] for the weekend as have quite a few. I like Saratoga, except for its horrible climate, very much and feel one could have a great deal of fun here if one had friends—or a friend who stuck to any plans & promises. We (not you) had all sorts. I suppose one can endure anything for a month but I've been feeling that way for so long now I don't know. And the letters from Léonie make me feel more and more appalled at my trying to take on "desk work," etc. [at the Library].

What about Marianne? WHAT SHOULD I DO? And for god's sake

don't tell Lloyd any of the stuff I told you in N.Y. This is the letter I've already torn up twice more or less, so I guess I might as well send it, disgraceful or not. I am so frantic about—I DON'T KNOW WHAT TO DO and I've GOT to do something. Maybe it was entirely my fault, I don't know. I did know more or less what to expect, I suppose, I didn't think it would be so thorough, and I wildly overestimated my own strength, I guess. Do you really think Dr. Baumann has given me up as a bad job? I don't want to be this kind of person at all, but I'm afraid I'm really disintegrating, just like Hart Crane, only without his gifts to make it all plausible . . .

You don't need to bother to answer all this self-pity. Just tell me some news about grown-up people and if possible that you love me & if you do please tear this up right away.

Tuesday a.m.
[July 5, 1949]

Did you notice Tommy's card of Venice? I wonder how your picture of it is progressing. Are you having a show in October? No, Katherine Anne Porter didn't come after all. I wish she had. I am absolutely miserable and so sick of being miserable, and can't work and don't know what to do and so on & so on.

Later

Well I talked to you, which helped for an hour or so there, but I really don't know what to do any more. If it weren't so bloody hot. Now I'm dreading everything, everything and particularly those few days I have to spend in N.Y. at a hotel alone. The last six months have been a total loss and I don't feel as if I could ever write anything again and I don't want to go on living. I can't work on any of the old things any more and I'm so bloody lonely I think I'll die just of that.

The people really *aren't* very interesting. I'm sorry but it's just plain true—it could all be so much gayer. I think Mrs. Ames has given up, too—she's been in bed and no one's seen her for days now. Well I'm going to get my hair done and then this evening I'm going to the yearling auctions with one of the very young poets—Bill Burford—that may be nice. Brinnin has left. Let's see—Wallace Fowlie is here, very polite and cherubic, and [J. F.] Powers. They told me last night how beautifully Léonie Adams reads and now I'm scared all over again about *that* and wish I could give up the whole thing and feel so sure I'm no good & am dreading the year in Washington so.

Forgive my writing this to you. I simply have to say it to someone and maybe you can think of something vaguely reassuring about my situation because I certainly can't. All my affairs are still in chaos, clothes, papers, belongings, work—and I CAN'T GET OUT OF IT and I'm scared scared scared scared scared. And I'm scared of seeing Anny B.—terrified.

How on earth can I ever explain to her anything and I'm afraid she'll just suggest some place like Blythewood again and that I'll never do, no matter what. Margaret heard from Jonny Putnam, who is staying in Dr. B.'s apartment taking care of her Siamese cat—I never even knew she had one. Oh Loren, can you help me—

WHILE SOMEONE TELEPHONES

Wasted, wasted, minutes that couldn't be worse,
minutes of our barbaric condescension.
—Stare out the bathroom window at the fir trees,
at their dark needles, accretions to no purpose
woodenly crystallized, and where the fireflies
are only lost.
Hear nothing but a train that goes by, like tension,
nothing. And wait:
maybe even now these minutes' host
emerges, some relaxed uncondescending stranger,
a soul's release.
And while the fireflies
are failing to illuminate these nightmare trees
might they not mean his green gay eyes.

This version is a little better, I think—but I guess they're all (three now) unpublishable. [This poem *was* published, with revisions, as one of the "Four Love Poems" series in *A Cold Spring* (1955).]

Thank you so much for your kind letter. I doubt you'll ever know how much it has helped. It's silly to be miserable, I know, & maybe it's partly HEAT. My God, but it's hot here. May P. wants me to come back to Westhampton & I am certainly tempted by those waves—but I guess I haven't the courage to leave, either—& one does work, a little, somehow.

Charles Shooker [the painter] seemed very proud of having a watercolor hung next to yours at the Brooklyn Museum. He described yours to me very carefully & I was so mad—I'd never even seen it. He's nice—they're all "nice"—it's just me that's wrong, as always. He raves about your picture of [the clown] Emmett Kelly. Have you finished [E. E.] Cummings? The only painter here I'm really interested in is a very young boy who "works here"—very sweet. He studied with Mark Tobey for five years. He's going to show me his pictures tomorrow.

Well, if I were a painter none of this would ever have happened, or so I keep telling myself. Much love, Loren.

[July 19, 1949]

You must be utterly sick of me & my troubles by now, but I still feel I have to give you a blow-by-blow account. After having tortured you that way from the phone booth, I went out and wandered around and got drunk—not very, just dismally. Then I finally called up J. and I'm glad I did—she sounded glad to hear from me and was very nice, so that made me feel so much better that I retired to my room and cried my pretty eyes out for a few hours with the result that I couldn't go to dinner at all and shall undoubtedly soon be kicked out of Yaddo. I guess not, though. Mrs. Ames was very nice this morning & the place is so vast I don't imagine anyone could hear me howling and carrying on. I also decided NEVER to attempt to write a review, make a recording, or do another reading, and NOT to take that job.

This morning, however, for some strange reason I feel fine & relatively cheerful, although I was scared to death to go to breakfast, I was so afraid everyone *knew*, but all seemed to go well. And I am going to take the job, although maybe the other decisions still stand, I'll see. If there is anything one gains from psychiatry at all it's the simple thing you kept saying yesterday and said for nothing, too—that one must be oneself.

Anyway, I am feeling much better, your pains weren't wasted, and I don't think I'll drink again. The pressure really seems to have gone and I don't give a damn any more and I think J. and I are friends which is something. However, I wish I didn't feel so bloody unpopular. I was the most snooty and unpopular person at Blythewood and I guess I'm being it here, too. Such a blow to one's vanity, but so silly. Or do you suppose I picked up some unfortunate habits at B. that I'm unaware of? Notice any? But I do wish someone would ask me to go to the races with him or her—I'm dying to. I had a very nice letter from Carley, too—& probably you were quite right about her just being worried when I talked to her. She is really a very good sensible friend to have in Washington, I know, in lots of ways, and also she told me more about the boardinghouse and I don't think I'm going to mind it so much, maybe—sounds kind of cute. I bought myself a huge bottle of soap-bubble stuff and now I can sit on my balcony & blow bubbles, at least, when I get too bored.

I love you and you have been most good and kind and patient and I honestly think the worst is over for good and all. I just don't know why I have to go at these things so violently and awkwardly. I do hope you are feeling better. This is not the right place for me at all but I guess it will do for a month. I can't seem to "get my bearings"—or that's the way I felt until this morning. I am still afraid everyone *knows*, but then what of that even, I suppose. Almost bought you a miniature hot-dog wagon, umbrella and all—glass cases, etc.—but you can see one in Woolworth's too, and it really wasn't quite worthy of you and made of plastic, too. Will you do one more thing for me, Loren darling? Finish that little picture of the lights so I can take it to Washington with me? I'm even beginning to think maybe it might be a good idea to have photographs of one's friends about, although I never did before. Maybe I could get a copy of that one of you and Lloyd that I saw at *Harper's Bazaar*—I think I like that the best. I suppose you're right too in that people here may be a little scared of me, although that always baffles me—because I'm older than a lot of them and maybe, by their standards, famouser, I don't know. Now I'm even worried for fear Pearl won't be glad to see me when she comes . . . God save us.

Well, I suppose nobody's heart is really good for much until it has been smashed to little bits. But no more doctors. I'm going to get my repair work done at the doll hospital from now on.

How do you like "Yr. eyes two darkened theatres"? It's going into the third of this unfortunate sequence [in progress]—or is it too clumsy? [It does not appear in "Four Poems."]

> Your eyes two darkened theatres
> in which I thought I saw you—saw you!
> but only played most miserably my doubled self.

And I don't know what this poem means—Anon, before 1600—but isn't it nice and it goes on like that:

> And can the physician make sick men well?
> And can the magician a fortune divine?
> Without lily, germander, and sops-in-wine,
> With sweet-briar
> And bon-fire
> And strawberry wire
> And columbine.

Much love, Loren, I really feel all right and myself again—for good. *Pray for me*—and tear this up, too.

Friday a.m.
[July 31, 1949]

Thank you again for your letter—it has helped so much and I really think maybe I'm on the right track at last—at least we'll hope so. I got drunk again (I might as well tell you all) but am all over it and feel very cheerful, thank god, and then several nice things have happened, too.— A letter from J. which puts things on just about as good a plane as they could ever be, I think, which cheered me up enormously. I spent last evening talking to Pearl—very nice. Then letters from Harriet and Marjorie both very nice and affectionate so maybe I can stop worrying a bit about all these silly things.

Oh—and a mysterious letter from Cal. But I was glad to hear from him, having not dared to write to him at all—you know he married

E. Hardwick last week. He said he was glad I was at Yaddo, so that's a relief. However I really feel Mrs. Ames will never get over his attack on her, and he shows absolutely no remorse about that. They are living in Fred Dupee's house near Bard and want me to "visit" them on my way back . . .

The auction of the yearlings was fun and very beautiful—particularly the chestnuts under the bright lights and against the bright green grass. Strange racing types of all classes, including Bernard Baruch. Did I tell you that the Haitian girl's paintings are really pretty good?—very Picassoesque—but surprising and very Haitian at the same time. I have got Ginny interested in buying one now, my one good deed, I guess. She's terribly hard up—and I thought maybe if you had the time, you might let her come to call on you in N.Y.—I'm sure you could tell her lots. She's a little savage, a real Haitian. It rained a lot last night and has been much more bearable today, thank god. Everyone, I think, has been drinking too much and feeling low. Oh god help me never to again. It has all been *all right*, however, I'm pretty sure. I've just made myself wretched to no purpose and I won't again.

Margie says (I wrote her some of my worries) that P. is a "scrapper"—"A fighting cock condemned to spend his days in a poultry yard"—I think that's rather apt, don't you? She also expresses great sympathy for you getting a show ready in the heat in N.Y. I have almost resigned myself not to doing anything here (something wrong with that) except catch up with my correspondence and do my accounts—but that would be a great step in the right direction, heaven knows. But I really feel more sure of myself today than I have in ages, so maybe things ARE going to be all right and thank you for being so sweet & patient with me, Loren. It has been a tough stretch but the agony has abated, as Macaulay said at the age of nine when he burned his finger & someone asked him how it was.

I took a long walk in the woods with the young colored poet—very nice boy—we were both scared by another BAT and in the daytime, too. That will give you an idea of the really slightly sinister and oppressive nature of the place. This morning it was quite beautiful, though—everything dripping. I walked in the kitchen gardens—huge—& never saw such handsome red cabbages and broccoli. The trees are the best thing, though. In fact, the only thing I guess I really like—huge—one fir you can get right under and it's like a good-sized room—almost the size of your studio.

One of the men guests got terribly drunk two nights ago and was put in jail. Mrs. Ames went and bailed him out. This is all a very good example for me and let's hope I profit by it. I worked on "The Prodigal Son" all morning and shall give up this other sequence for a while. I've had enough of it & drinking and all forms of trouble and I think it is mostly due to you that I have pulled myself together again. If I can just stay together

—but things do seem MUCH better and I find myself looking forward to Washington. I want to get in such good shape that I can go see Dr. Anny without a tremor. Well, I've just been out blowing bubbles on my balcony, my chief diversion. Now I'll give you a rest, Loren dear . . .

To Robert Lowell

Yaddo, Friday p.m.
[July 31, 1949]

I was so glad to hear from you this morning. I had been trying & trying to write to you but didn't know where to reach you and just couldn't seem to, anyway. I wish you great happiness in your marriage and I do hope your troubles are over now for good. You have had too many lately for one person. I've been having quite a few of my own, but things seem to have straightened out pretty much now. I was quite at loose ends for this month so finally decided to come here, with some qualms—and I must say that nothing you or anyone else ever said about the place prepared me for it in the slightest.

I have that huge room with 34 windows—bloody hot—but very grand. I haven't been able to "work" at all so spend most of my time very pleasantly sitting on my balcony blowing bubbles. There is something a little sinister about the place, though, don't you think? I keep getting bats in my room and even met one in the woods in broad daylight—and then all those awful scummy ponds. But I think what is really the source of the trouble is the *smell*—old lunch boxes, I guess. Your friend Jim Powers is here and is very nice and Wallace Fowlie. Most of the others I never heard of. One former "proletarian" novelist got put in jail for drunkenness and had to be bailed out this morning.

I remember hearing what a nice house Fred Dupee had [where the Lowells spent their honeymoon]. And are my friends the Summerses there? They have a very pretty baby now.

A friend of mine may come up for the end of the racing season and to drive me back to N.Y.—around August 31st—maybe we could stop off to call on you? . . . Give my kindest regards to Elizabeth.

[*In margin*] I am so glad you're better—take it easy. I still haven't got your present from Haiti to you, but shall.

To Pearl Kazin

Pearl Kazin (Mrs. Daniel Bell) was literary editor at Harper's Bazaar, *and later was an editor at* The New Yorker. *Her memoir of EB, "Dona Elizabetchy," appeared in the Winter 1991 issue of* Partisan Review.

[September 16, 1949]
1312 30th Street N.W.
Washington, D.C.
Sunday a.m.

. . . After Yaddo I'm used to a certain amount of grandeur so I am not too overawed by my surroundings, but tomorrow I begin on my own, without Miss [Léonie] Adams to speak for me. I've been playing dumb, but the secretary [Phyllis Armstrong] handles us very gently and just suggests one little chore at a time, and serves sherry to callers, etc. You *must* call—it is quite pleasant in some ways.

Washington doesn't seem quite real. All those piles of granite and marble, like an inflated copy of *another* capital city someplace else (the Forum?). Even the Lincoln Memorial, which I went to see, affected me that way . . .

Boardinghouse life will never do, I'm afraid. I wish it would, though, because I don't mind the room, the food is almost too good, but the people—ladies all, with one exception—oh well, I've got someone looking for an apartment for me, and an ad in the paper. The landlady wears a black velvet band around her neck; the place is stuffed with antiques— even things under bell glasses—and for some reason there's no sink in the bathroom so it seems to be a question of either taking a complete bath or going dirty . . .

If you ever run across any poems that strike you as particularly good, I wish you'd let me know since I seem to be in the business now. With love, Pearl, and I'd like to hear from you—or better, see you here.

To Loren MacIver

Monday a.m.
[September 1949]

Will this count? I've just been over to the House of Representatives to buy a new pen at 10% discount—as a politician, I guess. I still like the old one better, though, and I wonder if by any chance Mr. Matisse found it—black with a gold band & a white spot, answers to the name of "Schaefer." I must have dropped it on the floor when I took down G.'s number. I'm sorry I was so silly the other morning, though I wasn't too bad. It was a mixture of anxiety & relief which still goes on. You were a darling . . .

I am a little worried about Tommy, too. He seemed so well that first night but not after that & I am so fond of him. Your show [of paintings] was so lovely & do tell me if you sell any more. If I were rich, I'd buy the crocus one, I think—oh, several. The first impression is one of such beautiful colored *atmosphere*—air, breeze, mist, etc.

To Dr. Anny Baumann

September 30, 1949

. . . I have been taking an occasional drink before lunch or dinner, in company—quite wrong, I know—but I haven't had any interest at all in any more drinking, and again I can't imagine why, but it is a nice change & very pleasant.

Having been such a loafer all my life, I find I am getting very tired working steadily, but maybe I'll get used to it after a while & be able to do some of my own work in the evenings. At least I never need any sleeping pills.

The boardinghouse is all right, but maybe I'll be able to get something better later on. Washington is all right too, I guess, but sometimes I wish I were in New York & suffering from a very slight ailment that necessitates occasional trips to the doctor, nevertheless.

To John Malcolm Brinnin

[official letterhead]
THE LIBRARY OF CONGRESS
Washington 25, D.C.
October 14, 1949

Thank you for the lovely ball. My temptation is to drop it from the heights of my balcony here to see how well it can bounce. (I noticed it was put in a drawer when I had a caller from the Library.)

. . . I notice that you advertise Dylan Thomas as one of your readers at the Y.M.H.A. [Poetry Center] and I hear he is coming to this country sometime this winter. Of course the Library would very much like to engage him to give a reading here, too. I wonder if you could let me know how to get in touch with him? Thank you very much.

I'll probably see you in New York sometime before April 6th—is it?

To Loren MacIver

December 21, 1949

Since I'm going away Friday I was very bad by your Christmas standards, I'm afraid, and I did open the big box. I was delighted—Jane [Dewey] and I were going to a concert that night, afternoon rather (a Stravinsky mass and wonderful, but I don't think the boys of Washington Cathedral were quite up to it), and afterwards we took the records out to her apt. to play. We found that mice had been nibbling at the wires and we couldn't hear a thing. So yesterday I brought them in here and my machine isn't too good—however I could hear enough to know they're marvelous and brilliant . . .

I really see vast improvements, I think. My presents for you and Lloyd may be a little late—*through no fault of mine.* I was in Schwarz's buying a lovely lion for Mary Eliott Summers yesterday when Mrs. Longworth, whom I've met a few times and like very much, came up and said, "I bought one, too."

Oh heavens—the page boys are raising their changing voices in carols. Had a nice chat with Jane—she's going to Key West right after Christmas . . . Aunt F. has got us tickets to see Grace George, Walter Hampden and I've forgotten who else in something or other—all in wheelchairs, I understand. Well, Boston never says die, I guess.

There is rather a good review of the Library records and records in general in the last *Accent*. Emma Swan's book just came—my, she's intellectualized or something. Have you seen or heard anything from Tommy? Or did he die? . . .

The holly trees in Georgetown are really beautiful. In my yard we have Papa, Mama, and Baby—a Holy Family effect, that is if it's males that have the berries—otherwise Papa, Mama, and Infant Daughter. Where are you going to spend Christmas Day? I hope you and Lloyd can get down after Christmas sometime. I think we might have fun—or "fun," as Miss Moore puts it. You know, that rumored-of, dangerous article?

To Robert Lowell

[*official letterhead*]
THE LIBRARY OF CONGRESS
December 22, 1949

I don't know whether you're going to Boston for Christmas or not. Anyway, I am, and if you're to be there I hope to see you and Elizabeth . . . I'll be at the old Vendome from Sat. a.m. until Tuesday night—maybe a day or two longer if the money holds out.

Everything has suddenly become very hectic and unpleasant here, with holly ground into the linoleum and the page boys behaving worse than usual. Also it's so DAMP. Washington winter weather is rather like Paris, I find, without the compensations. I had a nice letter from Jarrell with a long long poem about Austria, etc., that I am still working over without too much success. I seem to be losing my grip on poetry completely. Overtrained, I guess. I'm about to go to see Pound and take him some eau de cologne. So far my presents have not met with much success, but maybe this will. He's reading Mirabeau's memoirs at a great rate. Mrs. Pound now has a telephone and calls me up. I think she holds out very well.

I am dying to see you and tell you about the strange tea party for

Frost, at which Carl Sandburg suddenly turned up to everyone's horror —everyone who had any sense, that is. It was very funny. With love and best wishes for everything appropriate right now.

Saturday
[January 1950]

I like it in here over the weekends, so nice and silent, even the view looks improved somehow. It's the only time I can think about my own WORK, too.

Thank you thank you for the lovely book—I had wanted to buy it for myself and thought I was being extravagant . . . I have just finished Fromentin's *Dominique*, too, and recommend it highly if you haven't read that. In your book I notice they attribute several pictures to London, etc., that are right here now in the National Gallery . . .

Boston except for the actual duration of Christmas dinner wasn't so bad . . . I went and spent two days at Frank Parker [artist friend of Lowell]'s and had an awfully nice time. I had only just met Frank that time and I am so glad to find someone I like so much . . . He & I went for a wonderful walk along the shore.

I saw the Eberharts in Cambridge, and the Wilburs—oh, Red Warren was there and said he'd seen you. I liked him very much—in fact I just seem to love everyone these days and must stop it at once. However I won't draw the line before the end of this letter, and also wish you and Elizabeth a Happy New Year. I wrote a note to Gregory Hemingway, who is at St. John's, to go to hear you if he's there—he's a nice boy—I wish I could get there myself but I'll hope to see you Saturday anyway . . . Oh, I forgot, business—[Rudolf] Serkin and a violinist are giving two concerts at the Library the nights of the 19th and 20th and I'm supposed to ask the Fellahs if they care to go and which night so as to reserve tickets. It ought to be pretty good, I think. So will you tell me if you want one, or two?

[January 1950]

Miss [Phyllis] Armstrong has hidden my typewriter because all those people are coming & I guess it isn't presentable enough, but I still do my best to write LEGIBLY. Catafalques or no catafalques, you were an ANGEL & I can't thank you enough. You can come and be an angel on mine at any time, and today I really feel that is just about where I belong. A sort of numbness has set in now that everything's over.

Marcella's party got rather drunken, but was very pleasant. Allen [Tate] presented the flowers & the memento and little Léonie just sat there clutching it in complete silence. I really thought we might have to pour cold water over her. I think she really liked it, but insists that she wants "Bollingen Forever!" added to the inscription. Mrs. Biddle's party was extremely nice—we played charades & something called "Adverbs" & everyone was quite hilarious. "Huntington Cairns" proved to be a great favorite for a word to act out, & my favorite moment of the party was when Huntington, acting out "Hun," put an enormous brass wood kettle on his head & chased Léonie with a long iron lamp base—being Attila, I think. Unfortunately the kettle fell off & onto Léonie so it all got almost too realistic. Then they acted "avuncular," & somehow or other Miss Bogan was being Ophelia with her hair down her back.

Then they acted out the adverb "intimately," for the benefit of Mrs. Biddle, and Mr. Biddle was very funny, saying, "Come here, little girl, and let me whisper to you." All good clean fun, as you see, and no hard feelings, I believe. My only worry now is that it all seemed to go *too* fast & that there are probably lots of loose ends left hanging over.

I went back to the Vienna pictures yesterday, along with 45,800 other people [at the National Gallery]—infants in arms were being lifted up to look at the Cellini salt cellar & all kinds of improbable people were there looking mystified.

Well, I wish they'd hurry up & arrive & get this tour of inspection over so we can relax. I do hope your moving wasn't too difficult & that your new place [at the University of Iowa] is satisfactory. It *was* nice of you to come under the circumstances—and I thank you again. Some parts of this job don't bother me at all but I must say I'm hopeless at the public appearance part & hope I never, never have to make one again. Miss A[rmstrong] sends her regards & I send mine to Elizabeth.

[P.S.] When you have time, do send me a note about your new job & how you like it. I do hope Randall accepts—he'd be so good.

To Dr. Anny Baumann

January 9, 1950

I saw Mrs. Dawson last night, who spoke with pleasure of her visits to you & said your office was as busy as "Grand Central." So it seems wrong to take up any more of your time. However—for about a week I've been feeling very depressed and having a terrible fight to keep from drinking. I did drink for two awful days—no damage done, but I scared myself half to death. Up until now I haven't had too much trouble, just an occasional evening, but I feel some sort of cycle settling in & I want to stop it. A very important meeting is coming up the 20th of January— that may have something to do with it, also I may be getting bored with my job, also I can't seem to work at my own work. I am nervous about the meeting, which involves a good many people, etc., and I think maybe some of those Bellargel(?) pills might help, or some sort of soothing syrup to take for a while until I manage to get back to feeling cheerful again.

I'm sorry to trouble you with all these imaginary ailments, but maybe you'll be able to think of something this side of going to a psychiatrist, which I never want to do again.

P.S. I forgot to say that I am having asthma constantly, usually clearing up in the morning & then beginning again around four o'clock . . . I know it's pretty bad because one night I ran out of the [sulfate] cartridges & had to take four shots of adrenaline.

To John Malcolm Brinnin

[*official letterhead*]
THE LIBRARY OF CONGRESS
February 2, 1950

Thank you so much for offering your help in getting Mr. [Dylan] Thomas to record for us. As I believe I said, the second series of recordings is now made up, so he would not be in that, and at present his records would be for the "archives." However, they will probably publish more albums from time to time, in which case he would undoubtedly be included . . . It seems to me it would be a very good idea for him to have these records in reserve in this country, for future use.

Mrs. Ames writes asking me for recommendations for Yaddo; have you any suggestions? It will be nice to see you in Washington. Please come to call, or maybe you'll be with Mr. Thomas at the recording?

February 15, 1950

After an awful stretch of indecision I am writing to tell you that I don't feel I'd better try to do that reading on April 6th [at the Y.M.H.A. Poetry Center in New York]. I feel like a heel. I hope this will be the last time I'll ever let you down in this respect—but I am not much good at it & suffer too much, and I don't think people enjoy seeing someone miserable. The reading I did at Wellesley seemed to go over well—it was informal & a very sympathetic audience—but here at the Institute I was a terrible flop, and since then my records have only proved to me—they & a teacher I tried to go to, who gave me up as a bad job—how hopeless it is. I think "experience" is the only way—but scarcely see how to get it! People who teach, or have taught, are best, I notice—maybe I'll improve with age, or some teaching experience. I was asked to read at the Museum of Modern Art & felt I'd better refuse, too. I read in the paper that "500 to 800" were showing up for your series—that is really very impressive & encouraging, but depressing for me personally. I am awfully sorry— I'm sure there are others who enjoy doing it, or Randall (who does) might do it alone. He does enjoy doing it & the contrast [with EB, who was to join him in a reading] would probably be fearful.

Thank you for being so extremely nice about my shortcomings. Maybe in time I'll learn how. I just had a very good account of the [Dylan] Thomas readings—you are really making a great success of those poetry readings, aren't you?

It seems that besides the recording I'd like to have Mr. Thomas make, *they* would also like to have him make a short transcribed radio program. They give them from the Library in the intermissions of their concerts, usually 10 or 15 minutes of reading, or question-&-answer, or both— you know the kind of thing. One with Tate & R. P. Warren will be given this Friday evening . . .

I'm looking forward to seeing you & hearing Mr. Thomas—do you suppose he'd record "Fern Hill" for us? I'd like extremely to have it— and thank you again, John, for being so kind.

To Loren MacIver and Lloyd Frankenberg

[*official letterhead*]
THE LIBRARY OF CONGRESS
April 19, 1950

. . . I finally up and left Miss Looker's [boardinghouse]—not very wisely, I'm afraid, because I picked a time when the tourists were all arriving & 6,000 DAR ladies. However I think I'm getting a one-room apartment at a hotel at the end of this month. In the meanwhile I'm staying at a place named delightfully & simply "*Slaughter's*." However, when you come to visit I can still get that room for you across from Miss L.'s, or maybe you could stay at Slaughter's too—though it *is* gloomy & I'm afraid might give Loren the horrors. Let me know as soon as you can & I'll do my best. The town is lovely now & we can just stay outdoors. I'm making arrangements for Loren to do a broadcast on the 28th. I want you [Lloyd] to record, too, but I'm not sure whether Mr. Gooch wants any more done just now or not—I'm working on it.

At the hairdresser's yesterday, to coin a phrase, I saw the poem & picture [of both Loren and Lloyd] in *Harper's Bazaar*. They looked *lovely*, I thought. I knew something like that was up because Pearl [Kazin] had wired me to return the photograph of you-all, which I had here a little while ago.

I was rather pleased about Wallace Stevens [getting the Pulitzer Prize], weren't you? even though I had cast my vote for Cummings. How was the Frost reading, and give Dylan my kindest regards—except I'm quite sure he's forgotten me by now. I told Mr. Biddle the story of the shirts & he was very amused.

I think I'm going to Jane's—Jane Dewey's [at Havre de Grace, Maryland] this weekend. Maybe we could all go spend Sunday with her on your way back, or something. It is really worth the trip it is so beautiful.

To Randall Jarrell

Randall Jarrell (1914–65), a leading poet of his generation, was also a novelist (Pictures from an Institution), *an author of children's stories, and a brilliant critic* (Poetry and the Age). *He had hoped to succeed EB at the Library of Congress as Poetry Consultant; his wish was fulfilled in 1956. Conrad Aiken followed EB. Jarrell also sought EB's help in finding a new publisher; he was unhappy at Harcourt Brace because he felt Lowell was getting much more attention than he.*

[*official letterhead*]
THE LIBRARY OF CONGRESS
April 26, 1950
After hrs.

I have to write you such disagreeable letters—I'm awfully sorry. Not a word from Mr. Aiken yet, and what ails him?—I've tried all approaches here, aerial & subterranean, in case the Library knows and isn't telling, but I can't find out a thing. And this morning I heard from the girl I know at Houghton Mifflin, to this effect:

About publishing Randall Jarrell: after a long discussion the editors decided that, much as they respect Jarrell's poetry, because of the limited amount of energy (and advertising money) they have to contribute to the cause of poetry, they would rather save it for a poet who is not already well established with a good publisher. They feel they would like to take on a new, or less well-known poet who is in greater need of being heard.

Personally, although I admire Mr. Jarrell very much, I don't see why he should want to leave Harcourt. If he has had "bad treatment"—what does poetry ever get, really, but bad treatment publicity-wise, compared to second-rate novels and "soul-saving" books by glamorous priests? . . .

I love that "energy" & a poet "in greater need of being heard"—but that's what they probably said to her because as I remember her—a conversation about two years ago—she knows perfectly well the true state of affairs & as far as I know anything about it I agree with her. However, I've only one book, so probably my really bitter experiences are yet to come.

Your story of the Y.M.H.A. reading did make me feel awfully glad I wasn't there, but I admire your fortitude & wish I might have been in the audience. I hear the series at the Museum of Modern Art ended with a bang with Dylan Thomas. I want very much to get a record of his into this series here but I can't seem to. But after having spent all of this beautiful spring day listening to MacLeish, in an air-conditioned closet, and trying to make a "selection"—I am so sick of Poetry as Big Business I don't know what to do. What on earth is the happy medium—readers, certainly, but all this recording & reading & anthologizing is getting me. Actually I suppose it's the people who like to run such things rather than the dear consumer.

The funny thing about that letter from Houghton Mifflin—she winds up by asking me, I think, to board with her at her house in the Cape this summer, an address just down the road from Mr. Aiken's! I am going to the zoo here this weekend to see two new baby elephants & the baby leopard, who chases his tail constantly, they say.

April 27, 1950

This place! this pile of masonry! I don't know what to say & it's so hopeless I can't even get mad. We have just found out, by behaving like a couple of horseflies, that Mr. Aiken accepted the consultantship on the 27th of March. The letter got here April 1st, was presumably read by *someone* & stuck in a "file." It has never been answered by anyone, or even *seen* by anyone except some lady in the reference or other department. I am to have a "conference" about what to do about it as soon as somebody gets back from lunch, and then I suppose I'll compose the usual gobbledygook letter for someone else to sign about how glad they are to have him & how they do hope he'll go on with his own "creative work" while he's here. Dear Randall, I am terribly sorry about this, as you can imagine. (As a matter of fact in my own case they kept me waiting, not knowing what to do, turning down a job, etc., for about five months because a letter got "lost.") You may feel you're well rid of it all. On the other hand a lot of it's extremely pleasant—on the third hand Mr. Aiken, I gather, is apt to change his mind about things, get sick, etc., and his letter of acceptance even doesn't sound wildly enthusiastic. So that's where we are. I guess I *have* got MAD once I started to write & I think I'll be a sensation at the "conference."

To Robert Lowell

May 6, 1950

. . . Mr. Aiken has *accepted;* at least we're pretty sure he has—and I'm afraid someone (not me) had told Randall the opposite & Randall had started to make plans—we had even discussed switching jobs next year. It's too bad. However, I wouldn't be at all surprised if Aiken changed his mind again.

When Dylan Thomas was here he was very curious as to how everyone makes a living, etc., and he asked me what I was going to do after next September: "Go back on the parish?" So I guess that's what I shall be doing—or going back on Yaddo, possibly, for a while. My vague plans for a Fulbright fell through, as I thought they might.

As you may know, Ransom is now a Fellow [of the Library] & so are Thornton Wilder & Samuel [Eliot] Morison. Frost is still making up his mind.

[*continuation of letter*]   May 8th

. . . Spring is exceptionally nice here. I've been to New York two or three weekends—saw *The Cocktail Party*, which I guess I didn't like as much as you did; in fact I thought it was a MESS. I saw *A Member of the Wedding* too & liked it very much. I had a nice time with Randall when he was here—he's in love with his new pale green convertible. [Dylan] Thomas's visit was the high point of my incumbency, though, and he made absolutely beautiful records—when they'll ever be used I don't know. I've been to see the baby elephants Nehru presented to the zoo— Shantih & Asoka—Asoka being so infantile that he sucks his trunk as if it were his thumb. The "Institute" staggers along—the latest faux pas was their announcing a reading by Juan Ramón Jiménez as by José Jiménez (an inferior Brazilian) so Mr. J. called it off at the last minute. It's really about as bad as calling T. S. Eliot *George* Eliot, but they all seemed unaware of the enormity of it all. I finally went to see Mt. Vernon, which was very nice, even with 1,000 standing in line to get in, eating ice cream cones.

I just had a note from Aiken inquiring about where he's to live—a problem I haven't solved satisfactorily for myself yet, so I guess he's coming. Well, I must get to work . . . Have you settled on a place to teach yet? If you hear of any extra ones around let me know. Karl told me he'd seen a couple of your students & they were very enthusiastic about you. He also said Roethke was en route here but I haven't seen him, have you? Dr. Williams says, in print, that Peter Viereck's poetry "rises like a lovely bird from a cow pasture." You see where that leaves the rest of us.

I hope you & Elizabeth are enjoying yourselves—I'd love to see you.

June 27, 1950

I think you must be at Kenyon by now, but I'm not sure. I am wondering how you are and what your plans are for next year—if you are really going abroad, etc. (that is, if anyone can, by next fall). I'm going up to Yaddo when I get through here, for three or four months, I think —so long as I can stand it & work, that is, because I want to get a new book off to Houghton Mifflin as soon as possible. Then in January or February I think I'll be going abroad, too, and if you're there, seeing you there. I haven't been able to do any work here at all—I don't know how you ever did—but I have made a few starts & if I can finish about five poems I guess there'll be a book, I don't know.

Randall stopped over one night on his way to the Cape. He'd been painting pictures. They have asked me to visit them on my vacation, but I'm really rather dubious about taking one, since I've just got over six weeks of bronchitis & asthma & have been out a great deal—besides which I should go to Nova Scotia if I go anywhere. The evening he was here—at the Starrs'—I had a new asthma machine & he said I looked exactly like the caterpillar smoking a hookah on a toadstool in *Alice in Wonderland*. I can get away weekends quite easily to Jane Dewey's, anyway—the most beautiful place. I just came back from there. We attended a large party for [John] Dos Passos, his new wife & brand-new baby (unseen). He seemed nice—or at least in the mob of strangers he was someone I could manage to talk to—but what surprised me about him was that you & he have a great many of the same mannerisms. I couldn't think who it was, at first.

Washington is hotter than Key West—someone said hotter than Dakar. The Scotch tape *flows* onto the photostats. I shall be very glad to leave. Marcella did paint the picture—three awful days—and I come out looking exactly like those old cartoons of char-ladies in *Punch*. Did I tell you I am now living at a hotel—sort of—called "Slaughter's"?—run entirely by colored people for Eurasians, strange gray people, poets, etc. I like it much better than the boardinghouse. Mrs. Aiken arrived yesterday to find a place to live—found one—she wasn't at all what I'd expected.

I spent most of the weekend reading Samuel Greenberg—have you? I got so mad at the introductions, particularly Tate's—and if you haven't read the poems I recommend them highly. He was certainly one of the finest poetic *characters* I know anything about, and phrases are magnificent—and no critic has ever apparently appreciated either at their real value.

I went canoeing on the Potomac—one of the few nice things to do now. I guess I'd better get back to work. I'd love to hear from you sometime & hear about what these conferences are like. Please give my kindest regards to Elizabeth—have you been able to get much writing done? Pound is mad at me because I put off getting something microfilmed for him—he thought there wasn't a moment to waste because once Luther (who'll be hung, anyway) finds out what inflammable material it is, etc. etc.

July 18, 1950

I've just had a letter from Margarita Caetani, or Princess di Bassiano, or whatever one prefers to call her, from *Botteghe Oscure* saying how she'd like to have your address & how eager she is to have a poem of yours, etc. etc. You know, she's Mrs. Biddle's sister & has always sounded awfully nice. Probably she'd be nice to call on when you get to Rome—if you *can* get to Rome considering the way things look right now. The number is 32 Botteghe Oscure, Rome.

Just had a visit from the Dutchman who works here & writes poetry incessantly. I hope he wasn't one of your problems, too. One poem this time about his soul fermenting in a barrel of sauerkraut. He is so grateful to God for sending him such marvelous ideas, but personally I'm afraid God is playing tricks on him. I hope you & Elizabeth are doing well in spite of all the bad news now.

August 23, 1950

I sent the flowers—some rather nice white chrysanthemums with petals curled up so they look like porcupine quills. I spoke to your cousin Miss Mary Winslow on the phone, to get the address, and she said, "How nice of Bobby!"

I must write to Marianne immediately to get her version of the Harvard Conference & to hear how she enjoyed "Pakistan's Leading Poet" (so he said, and I guess it was true), whom I sent on to her in despair. He wanted to meet "poets"—while here he called on Pound but seemed to retain a very confused impression of his visit, since Pound talked about nothing but Confucius & Mr. Jasimudahun knew no Chinese (he confessed) & not much English. Sometime I must tell you about our luncheon party.

Yesterday I had lunch with John Edwards [Lowell's pupil], his wife and nine-month-old baby. They were taking *him* to spend the afternoon with Pound & I'm sorry I couldn't see that interview. Did you see MacLeish's *Poetry & Opinion?*—his usual mellifluous & meaningless periods. I am just reading Yeats's *A Vision*, or trying to. Have you? Sometimes it's very Jungian. The picture of Yeats going "Woof! woof!" in a lower berth, in the dark, in California, in order to wake up his wife, who was dreaming she was a cat, is very pleasing, I think.

From here I am going (the 15th, I hope) to visit Jane Dewey for about ten days, then a week at the New Weston in New York, then to Yaddo October 1st. I'm going to try to get passage—probably to France —around the end of January. (I think I've told you about Jane Dewey, the physicist daughter of [Dr.] John Dewey? At present she is in charge of "Terminal Ballistics" at the Aberdeen [Maryland] proving ground, and when I stay at her farm on weekdays the rural scene shakes slightly once in a while as Jane practices her art about 15 miles away, and then there is a faint "boom." It seems there are three kinds of ballistics: Internal, External & Terminal.)

"Fernhill" is a nice name & I hope you have a nice trip—do you go straight to Italy? Did you see Eleanor Clark's endless piece about Hadrian's Villa in *Kenyon Review*? That is a *lovely* trip, to the Villa d'Este, then to the Villa. I walked it & had a beautiful time although in complete ignorance of most of what Miss C. knows. You must do it—but of course you will—and I like the Catacombs enormously.

To Marianne Moore

Yaddo
Saratoga Springs, New York
October 22, 1950

. . . I've been wanting to write & tell you what a lovely luncheon party you gave me that day. I had a wonderful time and you're a very good cook as well—as well as—I'm not quite sure what I have in mind. I had a card from Robert Lowell from Tangiers—so excited. I imagine he's talking to Santayana [in Rome] right this minute.

I am sending you—or the Gotham Book Mart will, I trust—a little book of poems called *The Forever Young* by a girl here named Pauline Hanson. I don't like the title and there are a lot of dead lines in it—but it's the first book of poetry I've read in ages that I really and truly admire. There are some things in it beautiful enough to break your heart. It's a long sort of *In Memoriam* thing, in the meter of all things of *The Rubaiyat*—and you may not see what I do at all or it may have just hit me at the right moment. She has had one poem in *Poetry*, a great improvement over the book, too, and I have seen one more poem—always the same theme. She is excessively modest. I don't think she'd ever publish anything at all, but Wallace Fowlie is her cousin and he did all the work, and wrote a very silly blurb. I wish I could write reviews—maybe I will. It's funny—I find it a very consoling poem, and there are some lines that beat *In Memoriam* all hollow. It was such a pleasant surprise to me, after reading a solid year of drivel at the Library. She works here as Mrs. Ames's secretary.

I was a little nervous about who the other guests were going to be but it is really all turning out awfully well. There's another girl who writes poetry, May Swenson—not bad, either; a Negro painter; an archaeologist whose books about South America I've been reading for years; and Alfred Kazin, who is an old friend. I do hope you don't think my sending you this book is an imposition. I'm sure Polly—that's what she's called—would be very upset if I told her I was. She's very Bostonian—the poem is, too.

It may have hit me at the right moment because of Dr. Foster's death—did I tell you? It was so sad—she was so nice—I wish you had met her, or maybe you did. Louise [Crane] was going to her, and Tommy Wanning. I had lunch with Louise just before I came up here and she was very upset about it. Dr. Foster was so good and kind, and certainly helped me more than anyone in the world.

I have my clavichord with me & it is a great pleasure to have it again at last, although I play wretchedly. It is perfectly beautiful here now—much nicer than in the summer—and there are so many birds and chipmunks. Also I take a walk every day to a sort of "Pub" down the road where they have a half-grown colt and a half-grown [illegible] both very affectionate and charming. Oh—I've at last got out of Polly that she has some copies of her book, so I'll mail you one myself, I guess.

I am taking cat & dog shots twice a week. I haven't much hope of them, but wouldn't it be wonderful if they did work and if my friend who raises poodles gave me one. I hope you are well. Alfred Kazin said how much *somebody* he knows at Viking likes the La Fontaine.

To Loren MacIver

[October 1950]
Before breakfast
There is an apple tree here—a very small one that looks exactly like a child's drawing of an apple tree—and not too much unlike mine [*drawing in margin*]. It's absolutely beautiful here now—I think you'd like it. There are lots of chipmunks, right on my porch, and they feed the birds. They say in the winter the chickadees get so spoiled they won't eat crumbs unless they're from *buttered* bread. Very bad for them, of course. I just finished a lovely book, which I recommend for bedside reading to both you & Lloyd—*Kilvert's Journals*, edited by Alex Comfort—a little like Hopkins's Journals only more everyday.

After breakfast
I had a wonderful letter from Jane Dewey—all about her calves' new diseases. Things are getting quite exciting here with a full-fledged explorer & archaeologist—whose books about South America I've been gobbling up for years, only unfortunately I didn't connect him with them until I'd made a bad faux pas. The clavichord is a great pleasure to have again. I wish I were better at tuning it, though I'm improving, and practice three simple pieces every day.

Loren—here it comes—will you do something for me? I feel I simply cannot live much longer unless I have a wool jacket in *Black Watch* plaid. There was one at Abercrombie's I almost bought, then thought I was being extravagant, also I didn't think the plaid was authentic. But they're all over the place now, and since one of the first things I remember about you is that little book bound in plaid you had on the Cape, I feel you're the natural victim for this commission. Will you? I want just a regular sack coat, I guess you call it, or blazer—like a boy's, or a boy's would do if there aren't any girl's right. I like dark buttons better than brass but it doesn't matter—I can change them . . . I have charges at Best's, Saks, Bonwit, but since that's involved maybe they'd send it C.O.D. In fact I think the best place would be Brooks Brothers—you know me, nothing but the best . . .

I am writing so fast I expect to be rich before long. The story about Nova Scotia is coming along fine—the one with the dog in it—I think I told you? That's one, if I can sell it, and sell it to an illustrated magazine,

I'd give anything to have you do some pictures for—much better than that old one. There are rocks with lichen on them & the wagon wheels go by them & the little boy trails the buggy whip—I should think you'd do that *beautifully*. A large hound dog is a very important character—can you draw a hound?

Well, I must get back to it. I never realized I'd be so happy to get here. I guess Washington made me appreciate work and solitude, at any rate. I had a lovely letter from Phyllis [Armstrong], very sweet about how the photographers seemed to upset Mr. Aiken.

Ask Lloyd if he has ever noticed any poems by Pauline Hanson. I never had—a little book called *The Forever Young* came out in 1948, I think, and one poem in *Poetry* in November (?) 1949, much better. I am honestly impressed for the first time in years. She is extremely modest. I do wish Lloyd would look into it. The one in *Poetry* is spoiled by archaisms at the end, but the beginning is something. I can't believe it—you get so sick of all this bloody stuff written for effect.

I had very bad news from Joe [Frank] in Paris. He got sick and wound up in the American Hospital for ten days . . . The rest of the letter was fascinating gossip about Paris. [John Malcolm] Brinnin had been there but, said Joe, "had eyes for no one except Alice B. Toklas." Pearl & Dylan the talk of the town, etc. Dupont on the Boul' Mich is just like the San Remo only worse, everyone keeps telling each other—except there are always a few respectable families with baby carriages—to take the curse off. The Existentialists have left the St.-Germain Quarter and the Deux Magots has become as stuffy as it used to be when I was there, I gather—but maybe this is all old stuff to you.

To Edmund Wilson

November 13, 1950

I hope you will forgive me for descending on you again, like an Egyptian plague—I think I must be almost up to the seventh by now, too—to ask you a great favor, and I hope you will feel perfectly free to refuse it. I shall understand if you do, and really not mind.

About a month ago Mrs. E. B. White wrote to me, suggesting that I apply for a fellowship at Bryn Mawr for the next academic year—something you may know about, called the Lucy Martin Donnelly Fellowship, for $2,500 for "creative writing" or research. At first I didn't mean to apply for it, but then I began to try to plan ahead and realized that I'll have to make some money somehow and that if by any chance I could get this fellowship it would mean I wouldn't have to get another job for another year. I gather that one wouldn't have to be there all the time, just some of it—at least, if, again, by any chance I could get it, that's certainly the way I'd prefer it. However I don't think I'd mind being there for a stretch, with a library to work in, etc.

I didn't get a Fulbright. I think Allen Tate received the one I wanted, so you see the competition was too much. Also I think I may have filled out the forms all wrong, or applied in the wrong category, and done it in too much of a hurry at the last minute . . .

I *hate* asking people if I may use their names, but I wonder if once more I may ask you for yours? In the meantime all kinds of things may have happened. You may hate poetry, particularly mine, you may be sick, or much too busy—as I said to begin with, I'll really understand if you refuse.

I'd just want to go on writing another book of poems (a third, since I've one almost done here now), possibly some stories, and, of all things, a play I have thought up here, to my great surprise. I didn't do anything at all while I had that odd Library job, but since I've been here, about a month now, I've been doing quite a lot, stories as well as poems—the more serious ones I hope you'll like.

The form doesn't have to be returned until January 15th. It's very simple, just says: "the names of three or more people who can give information about your work"—so maybe it wouldn't take up too much of your time.

I hope you're well and wonder when we can expect a new book.

To Loren MacIver

Sunday morning
[November 1950]

I'm sorry if I sounded rather goofy last night—terribly sorry. So many things seem to have been happening all at once to me and my friends— and on top of it I simply can't stop writing. It's the strangest thing and I think I'm just worn out. I'd only had two drinks after dinner & you see what they'd done to me. However, after a couple of agonizing hours I did remember the name of the warehouse and this morning I sent them a note special delivery, so they should get it first thing tomorrow morning . . .

It's funny—I felt so sorry for Dr. Foster's patients who got left in the middle of things. But I had a very reassuring talk with Marjorie, who said that Dr. Baumann had told *her* that for some reason or other it's always the other way round, people who went to her earlier mind it much worse—very mysterious—and just before I left I had a very upsetting phone conversation with Robby, etc.—anyway, this is all by way of apology, you know. I feel *exhausted*—and you sounded it over the phone . . .

A long "literary" talk with a girl here named May Swenson who writes quite extraordinary poetry—some in *Tiger's Eye*, I think. She's awfully cute, lives on Perry St. too, and maybe at Christmas time if I get to N.Y. as I hope I could bring her to call on you. We're having a Halloween party tonight and Beaufort has made the lanterns and decorations. I can't imagine. Alfred Kazin works terribly hard and is, next to myself when I get like this, the most exhausting personality I've ever known. How on earth does he ever keep it up? After all, I have long dull stretches in between. But I like him—in fact I like everyone including the poor dear archaeologist who is going to wind up the evening's gaiety by showing us his "slides" of Peru. He has hundreds, it seems. We had our pick of about seventeen different countries but finally all agreed on Peru.

I sent Lloyd the little book of Polly [Hanson's] poems. Now it may all just be *me*, or the time they hit me or something, plus the fact that I like her so much—but I swear there's something awfully good *almost* there. Maybe you'd better not read them for a while, I'm afraid they'd make you cry. But it's all very restrained & Boston at the same time.

I had a card from Elizabeth Lowell—very nice—they've taken an apartment in Florence for the winter. And I guess that's all my news—I told Polly about my agonies over the name of the warehouse & she said that was nothing—a boy here during the summer came to her one day quite frantic to have her tell him his landlady's name—with whom he'd lived for five years.

Well I guess I'll wind up this spiel by sending you a little number I turned out the other day ["View of the Capitol from the Library of Congress"]. If I could *only* get on with those wretched sonnets.

To Dr. Anny Baumann

Yaddo, Saratoga, New York
The day after the hurricane

I'm going to write you a letter that I'll probably not send but maybe I'll re-read it every day as a reminder to myself. I've been having a sort of brainstorm ever since I got here, just can't stop writing, can't sleep, and although at the time I wrote before I had managed not to drink for a stretch, I've certainly made up for it since & made a damn fool of myself & got into a peck of troubles—& made a very good friend of mine here very unhappy.

Well, last night as the trees came crashing down all around me and I felt like death, it seemed a sort of natural phenomenon equal to the brainstorms and I suddenly made up my mind. I will *not* drink. I've been stalling along now for years & it's absolutely absurd. Dr. Foster once said: "Well, go ahead, then—ruin your life"—and I almost have. I also know I'll go insane if I keep it up. I *cannot* drink and I know it.

The doctor here has been very nice—but I don't think she has any idea how bad it really has been . . .

You know, two of the people I like best in the world never touch a drop—and Father had to stop, and his father, and three uncles. It can be done. And I'd like not only to do it, but be cheerful about it—and shut up about it. It would be so nice if I never had to have one of those painful conversations with you again. Well, somehow the hurricane seems to have cleared my head. Yaddo is a complete mess though, and one of my *walls* actually fell off—maybe did me good too—all that fresh air—and water.

I've got to, and I know it, with all the horrible clarity of the morning after. I'm afraid this doesn't sound very convincing and I can type, more or less, but I shake so I can't sign my name.

[P.S.] You might like to know that I think I have a job for next year. You're quite right about steady work being a help.

To Alfred Kazin

With his book On Native Grounds *(1942), Alfred Kazin came to prominence as a leading critic of American literature. His major critical work,* An American Procession, *appeared in 1984. Authors whose writings he has edited include Emerson, Hawthorne, Melville, Dreiser, F. Scott Fitzgerald, and William Blake.*

November 29, 1950

It was very kind of you to send me the Blake book. I read through your introduction again last night and I really think it is one of your very best things—at least of all the things I've seen. And it must have been fiendish-difficult to write, too, but you cover a great many almost-inexpressibles.

Yaddo has been getting better and better in some ways since you left—even more sympathetic people—the Barkers, a very nice couple, and a boy named Calvin Kentfield. We've held the fort, along with you-know-whom, until yesterday John Cheever, who also seems very pleasant, arrived. Elizabeth [Ames] was away for about two weeks—just got back. You can imagine what the storm did here: the road was blocked, the plaster all fell off one end of my house, a gigantic pine fell right across the roof of Pinetree, only fortunately the people were out at the moment—and it didn't do much damage, anyway, though no one knows why. It looked—still does, only now everything is buried in snow—a shambles, but actually the only real loss were some of the enormous & beautiful Christmas fir trees, all lying on their sides. They're to be given away to various orphanages, etc., for Christmas trees. Elizabeth was in N.Y. for the storm & of course it was so much worse there that I believe she was relieved more than anything else when she saw Yaddo.

You-know-who gets worse & worse, I swear—you'd have fits if you could see him in his Tyrolean hat. Well, everyone suffers from him equally & I've promised myself not to say another word about him because I almost believe he belongs in quite a different sort of institution. He's scared of Mrs. A[mes], though, which makes mealtimes a little more bearable.

This is the first snowstorm I've seen, the first real one, in twelve years or so, and it certainly is beautiful & brightens up Yaddo a great deal.

I hope you're well and getting lots done. My run of work continues, thank goodness, and by now it seems to have outstripped its former undesirable companions. I am myself again & very *calm*. Thank you for being so nice when you were here—and thank you again for the Blake.

To Robert Lowell

December 5 or 6 [1950]
You must be thinking I'm not very polite to let all this time go by without commenting on ["The Mills of the] Kavanaughs." Well, the answer is quite simple—as soon as I got here I started to write some poems, too, rather to my surprise, and as I think I once told you before I find your poetry so strongly influential that if I start reading it when I'm working on something of my own, I'm lost. So I haven't re-read the "Kavanaughs" since the first two times way back in October. However, my own fit seems to be letting up, and this evening I'm determined to write you something about your poem.

It is absolutely beautiful here today—I just walked to town & back for my Dog & Cat shots. The people are very nice, too—a painter named Kit Barker (younger brother of George) and his wife, a German refugee, quite a good writer, and another young novelist named Calvin Kentfield—actually named for Calvin Coolidge, who was President when he was born. John Cheever was here for about a week, very pleasant. I don't know what we have in store for us now. Did you ever get over to Glens Falls when you were here to see the Hyde Collection of paintings? The Barkers met the curator someplace, and we all took a little jaunt over there last week—really marvelous things. You may even remember the famous Rembrandt Christ that was in the World's Fair. There's one of everyone you can think of, all good—and all right there in Glens Falls. But heavens I forget I am talking to someone in Florence. Well, tomorrow night the big thrill is to be that we're all going to see *King Solomon's Mines*.

You may have heard about the Hurricane. It wasn't as bad here as in N.Y. City, but it certainly was bad enough and dozens & dozens of those great old trees came crashing down. At one point—I was sitting up in bed trying to read and forget the racket—all the stucco came off the end of East House, right behind my head, with a loud report, leaving me—still—exposed to the elements except for some lathes & a thin coating of plaster. All the chimneys came down, all the birds disappeared for several days, but then came back again mysteriously, and all the squirrels and chipmunks went completely berserk trying to get their supplies reorganized. They'd run right into you on the paths, carrying apples, cobs of corn, etc.

Well, I must make myself a dish of tea.

Later

I'm sorry I forgot to send this note to you the first time I wrote. It was sent me by Miss Armstrong—I think—anyway, without benefit of envelope, like this.

Well, I've gone through the "Kavanaughs" twice more and really it is one of the most harrowing things I've ever read. All the things I remember admiring in one of the earlier versions I recognized with pleasure again, and I'm sure the total effect is magnificent, horrible, what you wanted, etc.—I find it hard to tell. There is no earthly reason why I should attempt to *criticize* certainly, and so I shan't. I think "Green the clairvoyance of her deity" beautiful as some of Mallarmé and rather like him. The stanza beginning "The world hushed," etc., I also find very beautiful. The stone "bedstead"—although I know exactly what you mean—still bothers me, or rather I think it might bother some readers. And the stanza that begins "He is St. Patrick" bothers me—is Harry St. Patrick? I thought that drink was *glüg* in Sweden, but maybe in Norway it's gluck—etc. Nothing that really amounts to a pin, as you see. Also I'm bothered by the mussels being "white underneath." There are two lines I don't like. One, which I don't mind as much as the other, "I am just a girl"—which suddenly seems to weaken the tone. But it's at the end, where she says "a girl can bear just about anything" that I feel a real recoil. You may think this has all just to do with gender, but I don't honestly think so— it sounds to me as if the next line should almost go "if she has a good big diamond ring." Please forgive me.

This is the next day—the maid has arrived to sweep me out so I guess I'd better *get* out first. Are you working now?—do tell me your news. I think I'll be staying on until March, then I have hopes definitely for Europe. Had a wire from Léonie last night wanting me to read with *Cummings* at the New School—on April Fool's Day, a singularly appropriate day for me to make a public appearance with Mr. Cummings, I thought. Of course I won't, but I was kind of flattered. I've just been doing a lot of short things and some stories. Hope to get down to some real work now. Do let me hear from you & I hope you're both well—love to both.

To Loren MacIver

Tuesday morning
[December 1950]

I've just written you a postcard—and people are going to start getting awfully sick of my letters—but really, this is so strange I have to tell you about it before I forget it. Last night I had two weird dreams. The first was funny, but almost a nightmare (this has nothing to do with my real story but I'll put it in anyway). I had written a book review, and I was looking at it in the Sunday supplement of *The N.Y. Times*. All I could see was the title, and two captions, rather like a newspaper item—and the whole thing seemed to be taking place back about 1910—although no dates were visible. It said:

> "THE (word missing here)" BY MRS. ALDENAY
> Charming Book!
> Mrs. Aldenay does it again!

And I was naturally appalled to think I'd written *that*. Well, as the night wore on I dreamed up a poem—this was just about sunrise. I can't remember it very well, but it was about a couple, a man & wife, and the man was "owless"—owl-less—that was the end of line b. It was a simple a b a b affair. I was frantic trying to find a rhyme for owl-less, and so finally I had the wife be cow-less. Then at breakfast I got your letter. Now please don't tell me you're cow-less. But what is all this about owls? It's beginning to get me. Of course they hoot a great deal in the night here, which may have had something to do with my dream—there seems to be a particularly frustrated one quite near me.

My darling Aunt Grace has gone to live with her daughter, son-in-law, etc., in a place called Wawa, Ontario, on Lake Wawa. I can't resist telling you this. It's a brand-new mining town. They have to fly in, landing on the lake "if it's frozen over"—otherwise she doesn't say how they get there. And she's going to start a Bakery. Isn't she amazing? Even her most ardent admirer, like me, could never say she was a good cook. However, they're probably all so ravenous up in Wawa they won't notice the difference.

I'll enclose the card so you can see how sorry I am about the owl. I just don't see any way of getting it unless somebody feels up to tackling Thomas Ward again.

I'll send you an announcement when he gets them—there's a show opening the day after Christmas—or have I told you this already?—by an extremely nice young Englishman here—Kit Barker (brother to George, I'm afraid). I've only seen a couple of things and have no idea what he really paints like and I like him and his wife, Ilse (a German refugee) so much I'm probably prejudiced. However, if you're up to gallery going, and feel like it, I know it would cheer him up tremendously if you went in. They have had very bad luck. He is a great admirer of yours. He & Ilse will be in N.Y. at the gallery the first three days after Christmas, then back here. I'm pretty sure you'd like them, the least pushy kind of people in the world, and they have been very nice to me. Pray for me— I am desperately trying to stay on the wagon & it's harder than I thought. Much love.

[P.S.] This scarcely counts, as poetry, but I thought you might like it. Sonnets next time.

THE OWL'S JOURNEY

Somewhere the owl rode on the rabbit's back
down a long slope, over the long, dried grasses,
through a half-moonlight igniting everything
with specks of faintest green and blue.
They made no sound, no shriek, no Whoo!
—off on a long-forgotten journey.
—The adventure's miniature and ancient:
collaboration thought up by a child.
But they obliged, and off they went together,
the owl's claws locked deep in the rabbit's fur,
not hurting him, and the owl seated
a little sideways, his mind on something else;
the rabbit's ears laid back, his eyes intent.
—But the dream has never got any further.

To May Swenson

Poet May Swenson (1919–89), a native of Utah, published nine books of verse, including Another Animal *(1954) and* New and Selected Things Taking Place *(1978). She was awarded the Bollingen Prize in Poetry in 1981 and received a MacArthur Fellowship in 1987.*

December 12, 1950

I'm sorry to be so slow about answering your letter—exactly a month—only you know how one loses track of time here. Another thing that interfered some was my uncertainty about my plans for Christmas & when I did write I wanted to say something about your kind invitation. At present it looks as though I were going to stay right here—and in some ways I'm very glad because I'm afraid it's a choice between that and Boston. If I say I'm staying here to work—the truth—it may be all right, but if I dashed off to New York to have a good time I'd probably be in trouble. It promises to be quite pleasant here, though. They've already lit up one huge tree and heaven knows how many more we're to have, plus eggnogs, mince pies—everything I associate with the awful day except stockings, and maybe Mrs. Ames goes around and fills them for us too,

I don't know. But thank you very much for asking me. I'll be coming down February 7th—so at any rate I'll be seeing you then . . .

What is your "long prose thing"—a story? I have continued to do quite a lot, until a fever for making Christmas cards came over me last week. We have a lot of music now. Kit Barker, the English painter, sings very beautifully when it gets late enough—English songs—and the novelist Calvin Kentfield also sings very beautifully—American songs—and then he and I sing, not beautifully at all but to our own satisfaction, a great many awful duets. Tonight we're having a small musicale here. We intend to work out a number for those mysterious African instruments in the West House living room, plus voice, and clavichord—and we have to do it now because a real composer is coming soon and then we wouldn't dare. Polly is off on her vacation for two weeks and we all miss her very much. I think it grows increasingly pretty here as it grows colder—less gloomy. Alfred is on his way to Key West, to finish a book, I think. And I guess that's all . . .

To Dr. Anny Baumann

January 17, 1951

I am very glad I decided to call you yesterday; I feel as if I had got my bearings again—maybe. I was not drunk when I called you, just terribly upset, in fact the last few times this has happened I haven't actually drunk so much—it seems to be more emotional than anything else & I get myself into a fine state of discouragement and panic, sleeplessness, nightmares, etc.—and why, I really don't know, except that I know the other guests here know about it, and the woman who directs the place does, too. They have all been extremely nice to me, heaven knows why, and I suppose that makes me feel worse, if anything.

After I wrote to you the first time I drank like a fish for about three weeks, I think, stopped for a little while, then began again. After making myself good and sick at New Year's I made more resolutions—and almost immediately it happened all over again. When I went to the hospital for five days I had not been drinking so much, but I was afraid I was going to, also I wanted to get away where I didn't know anyone for a while. I was all right for about ten days, then three days ago I got very drunk one night. It does seem to be more an emotional upset of some sort than anything else, and I really don't know quite what it's all about. I have kept on working quite steadily in spite of it all. I have a couple of pretty insoluable problems—but actually not nearly as many as most people I know—which again makes me feel even worse. It is extremely lonely here and one has a great deal of time to oneself, probably too much for me, and perhaps some of it is all due to a letdown after Washington. What has me so very upset is knowing that everyone knows and that I am "no good," etc. etc. . . .

Although this will probably sound crazy to you, I am going to France for a while—I have several friends there now. The job I may get wouldn't begin until next fall. If the world situation makes this out of the question, I shall go job hunting in New York. I have a hotel reservation for the night of February 7th in New York . . . If you'd prefer, however, I can come a day earlier or stay a day longer—whatever you think would be best.

I am sorry this is such a stupid letter. I simply can't seem to think very straight about this, except I know I want to stop. I am exactly the age now at which my father died, which also might have something to do with it. Whatever it may be, I have a feeling I must be approaching the end of it. Thank you for all your help.

To Katherine E. McBride

On learning from a newspaper report that she had won the Bryn Mawr fellowship, EB wrote to the president of the college.

[Vassar Club
c/o Hotel Winslow, New York]
March 15, 1951

I should have written to you much sooner to thank you for your kindness in granting me the Lucy Martin Donnelly Fellowship for 1951–52 but, like almost everyone else in New York, I have been in bed with the "flu." I am very pleased and grateful about the Fellowship. I have never been to Bryn Mawr but everyone tells me that it is very pretty. I have several friends who are graduates of Bryn Mawr, or who have taught there—one of whom, I believe, was a friend of Miss Donnelly—and as soon as I am out and around again they have promised to give me all their information. I am looking forward to working there and I hope I shall be able to accomplish some things that will please you.

March 19, 1951

I am afraid the letter I wrote you a few days ago may have struck you as rather odd—if it did, it was because all my mail had been forwarded to the Hotel Windsor instead of this one and I didn't receive your letter of March 7th until yesterday, so that the first note I wrote you wasn't in reply to anything at all.

Your letter is extremely kind and certainly nothing could be more generous than your terms for the Fellowship. My plans, aside from finishing a book I have almost done, and getting on with the next one, which is started, are very indefinite. If you feel that an occasional visit to Bryn Mawr will be sufficient, I may try to find an apartment here in New York. I believe that Bryn Mawr is only about two hours away by train, so that I could come easily whenever you wanted me to. Possibly I could work some in the Bryn Mawr library.

I should be very pleased to meet some of the faculty and students and to help, if I could, with any verse-writing projects they might have.

To Robert Lowell

Hotel Grosvenor
35 Fifth Avenue, New York
March 31, 1951

I can't believe I am answering a letter of yours dated Jan. 24th. There *must* have been some exchange in between—but I'm afraid not. It's been a very confused stretch and even now I think I'm just beginning to see the clearing through the woods. I had a freighter reservation [for France] for the 16th of this month. Then Houghton Mifflin wrote that they really, apparently, want a book for this fall and it seems very important to me to get it all off to them, etc., before I do anything else. Also I found myself in a tax tangle so that I probably would have been arrested on the dock.

Also, I was waiting to hear from a Bryn Mawr Fellowship I'd applied for, but I didn't hear until just as I left Yaddo, and then had to find out whether I should really accept it or not. It's a literary thing, a new "resident writer" Fellowship, for $2,500 but I didn't want to live there. Well, I got it and I don't have to live there—just make a few visits—really very generous. Also I've got an [American] Academy [of Arts and Letters] award—maybe I told you that—but not till May 23rd, so I am hoping to get abroad as soon as I can get the book off, sell a story, etc. This is just a temporary address—but will reach me. I've got to find something else, see my way to earning a little money, etc.—however I think I'll make a couple of reservations just on general principles.

Joe Frank wrote me from Paris a while ago that even if I wasn't around he wondered if he could see you in Florence, so I sent him your address finally—but you may have met long before now. He's awfully nice and I think you'd like him. He wanted to go to Ischia this summer, too, I gathered. I want to go to Venice. I didn't get there on my brief Italian trip. Last night I saw a travel movie of it and feel that I must go there immediately.

Harcourt Brace sent your book [*The Mills of the Kavanaughs*] a couple of days ago—thank you very much. I haven't had a chance to compare texts yet but I've read the book through a couple of times and it seems to me you have improved K's a *lot*—but this is something I'm going to study Sunday—i.e. tomorrow. I like Frank [Parker]'s frontispiece much better than the first one—except for the little tree to the left which seems rather weak somehow. But it's a nice-looking book & I am eager to see what the reviews will say—out of idle curiosity rather than concern, you understand . . .

[Theodore] Roethke was here this past week to read at the Y.M.H.A. and see his publishers. I went to my first reading there—his records are much better. But I kind of liked him. We downed a great deal of champagne together our first meeting. I saw him off yesterday in a terrible rainstorm—we couldn't get a cab & he almost missed his train to Seattle. He is a very sad man, I think—not melancholy, but he makes *me* feel sad.

"Mother Marie Therese" strikes me as even better now than it did at first. In fact there are lots of magnificent things I'll expatiate on, when I have finished with my story and my last ordeal with the Public Accountant . . . I'm sorry about not writing for so long & still hope to see you both. Much love.

To Joseph and U. T. Summers

c/o Jane Dewey
Havre de Grace, Maryland
April 30, 1951

I am down here visiting an old friend for a few days—she goes to work for the Army at 7:30 every morning and I am left in imaginary possession of a huge estate, thirty-some steers, a housekeeper, a flower garden, etc.—and the entire spring, which is perfectly beautiful. I am trying to work but find it's always nice to start off putting it off a little by writing some letters. Pearl [Kazin] gave me an account of her visit to you, the babies, etc. I hadn't seen her for a couple of weeks before I left, but the doctor, now our mutual doctor, told me the morning I left that Pearl had been in to see her for a nasty cut on her head received from the door of a kitchen cabinet.

You probably already know this: just before I left New York Brentano's at last delivered the Oxford edition of [F. E. Hutchinson's] *George Herbert*—one volume now. Didn't it used to be two? Anyway, I remembered Joe used to want one, too—it's wonderful.

The Bryn Mawr Fellowship is very nice. I was hoping to get something to do part-time along with it, too—being very mercenary and extravagant—but I have just heard from them that I can't take on anything else—after I'd turned up something minor that sounded like fun at N.Y.U., too—so I guess I'll just have to write whether I want to or not. I've got a sublet until the fall, moving in the end of this week. It has lots of little rooms—railroad, five flights up—and if either of you ever want to stay in New York I'd be delighted to have you. The address: 233 East 69th Street, Regent 4–1920.

It is too beautiful to stay indoors. I must go see what everything is doing. You know how brooks are called "branches" here, and Jane has three of them to mix with her bourbon. I wonder how your garden is doing—here of course we are very "advanced." I saw a calf born on the neighboring hillside the other day—and in ten minutes it was on its feet, and in an hour taking little jumps, up and down. I bet Hazel can't do that yet. I would so much like to see both babies, and see *you* both too, but more in affection than curiosity.

To May Swenson

[April 1951]

I took my letter up to the R.F.D. box by the church this morning & found I'd missed the postman—so there it sits until tomorrow—but I got yours. I don't know very much about the Guggenheim Fellowship things but I think I'll go right ahead if you don't mind and tell you what I think. Now I hope you really don't mind (if you've already sent it all in) because it probably doesn't make much difference one way or another. I've been told that the shorter the better. In my own case that seemed to work . . .

PLEASE don't use the word "Creative." I think one of the worst things I know about modern education is this "Creative Writing" business. WHY? Of course even worse was the little job I almost got at N.Y.U. called the "Writing Clinic."

Oh dear, I guess I just wish there were somebody here [at Jane Dewey's farm] to talk to, namely you at the moment. This morning one of the heifers is in heat and carrying on like crazy and the whole atmosphere is a little unsettling until *she* gets "settled."

They ask these idiotic questions and some people are idiotic enough to answer them in full, but I really don't think one needs to. If you quote Wilde and de Rougemont, I don't think either of them will do you much good right now, either. Also, although you mention "scientists," May, I happen to know a few and I'm visiting one now. There's a gap that is quite insurpassable—it isn't socially—but it isn't at all the way you put it in your piece. The indifference to or active hostility toward every other field of activity—in spite of all the recent interest in poetry readings in New York, etc.—is enough to take the wind out of one's sails.

So—I don't think you need to send them your plans for work at all —but if you already have, don't let my casual thoughts bother you. It's just that I'm sure they get so many, and you would do better just to impress them with your actual work.

I guess you weren't [at Yaddo] while Margaret Marshall was there, were you? She was writing her autobiography—her mother was a Mormon, her father an exiled Virginian—a very fascinating story. I hadn't realized your family was Mormon. And have you read the Book of Mormon? You probably have, but I'd never seen it until I stayed this summer in a boardinghouse in Maine where they had it—sometime we must discuss it. I didn't read much but I hadn't realized before that they supposedly went to South America. Several of the places I hope to get to—they were there, carrying those gold plates along in a basket. But I'd like to know about the spread of Mormonism in Sweden.

Please don't think I'm being mean, May—maybe I'm sorry not to have seen more poems—but I do think you don't need to go into much detail. I'm sending back the biographical note and even being so bold as to put a couple of marks on it.

To Robert Lowell

c/o Brooks
233 East 69 Street, New York
July 11, 1951

. . . Just got back from a prolonged 4th of July visit in Maryland again. In the meantime I've done quite a lot of work, attended that dreadful Academy ordeal—Randall was there—a few parties, seen a few people, and that's about all. This place belongs to Kappo (that name embarrasses me) Phelan & Kenyon Brooks—a sort of railroad place up four flights—but very cheap and I have it until October. I'm looking for a permanent apartment but so far have had no luck—they are so dreadfully expensive as well as scarce. I'm going to Nova Scotia for the first two weeks or so of August—mostly to try to write an article and earn some money. I'm trying to get out to Sable Island—cheerfully known as "the graveyard of the Atlantic" (my great-grandfather & his schooner and all hands were lost there, amongst hundreds of others) and if I am not fulfilling my destiny and get wrecked, too, I think I can turn it into an article and maybe a poem or two. Then I'm going to visit Randall for a week—at least that was the plan, but I haven't heard from him for quite a while & possibly he has changed his mind. He and a Starr girl, Fred Dupee & his wife, Margaret Marshall and a couple of others & I all had dinner together after the Academy tea, then came here—Randall very excited and voluble. I hadn't seen Fred for a long time. I've always liked him very much—I've been to his house since. Just before I went to visit Jane Dewey in Maryland I had dinner with Nathalie Swan and Philip [Rahv], who is off to the U. of Indiana.

Your proposed trip has me very ugly and envious. However, if *The New Yorker* takes my article—they're interested—and I earn all I hope to, there's a chance I may still get abroad in the fall—after finding a place to live here, and paying my respects to Bryn Mawr—all that's expected of me, I gather. My book is about 85% at Houghton Mifflin but I must confess it doesn't jell at all yet—maybe the other 15% will prove to be pure pectin. I am going to call it—so far—and I hope you'll approve—*Concordance*—starting off with a poem called "Over 2,000 Illustrations and a Complete Concordance." On reading over what I've got on hand I find I'm really a minor female Wordsworth—at least, I don't know anyone else who seems to be such a Nature Lover. *The New Yorker*, I'm delighted to say, is quibbling with me over an indelicacy in a poem.

My views from this tenement are very Neapolitan. I was very depressed by Naples on my short visit there, but you may like it—and of course you'll go to Paestum, which is one of the most beautiful things I've ever seen, though coming after Greece it might not be, I don't know. Margaret Miller went to Paris for six weeks two weeks ago—maybe you'll run into her. Or Joseph Frank, or a Mary Meigs—I gave her your address, I think—a painter.

What is Elizabeth's novel about? Give her my regards. Send me your "short poem." I really need something to give my standards a jerk, I think—but it is nice to feel awfully well (which I do) and like working. And please, if you ever have the time, write me a travel letter. I should so much like to see you.

Penobscot Hotel
Bangor, Maine
August 19, 1951

I got off the train from Nova Scotia at four this morning & a taxi driver brought me to this old but rather pleasant dump. I thought I'd get to Stonington this afternoon, but of course the bus doesn't run on Sunday. I don't like to call the two people I know there—who would probably come & get me if I did—so here I sit for 36 hours although I suppose I should go out & see the sights of Bangor . . .

I wonder where you are now—Paris perhaps . . . I think you went to Greece, too, didn't you? I can't quite believe you'll settle in Naples for a winter, though, but maybe you will. The three or four days I spent there I found very depressing, as a lot of people do. (I've noticed it's only my nearsighted or half-blind friends who profess to like it.) But the time of year & the weather have a lot to do with it—and certainly the gallery there is worth a long stay.

I've just been in Nova Scotia for two weeks. I went down—well, I'll tell you from the beginning. One day when I was visiting Jane Dewey I was sitting outdoors with her Audubon bird book trying to identify some sort of sparrow & I ran into a reference to the "Ipswich Sparrow," which does not live in Ipswich at all but only on Sable Island . . . where there are wild ponies, besides the sparrows. My aunt had, has—Pansy the pony is about 40 now—one of them. I've always felt a personal interest in the place. So I thought I'd go and try to write a piece about it, which . . . is just getting under way. It was quite an interesting outing; I had to get permission from Ottawa to get taken out on a lighthouse tender, etc. The actual place is nothing much except sand dunes like Cape Cod, but its history is spectacular, just the kind of thing I feel you might like.

Anyway I'm hoping to sell a travel piece about it and make some money. If I do I may take a trip of some sort, probably a long freighter one . . . This summer at Kappo Phelan Brooks', she was writing poetry, I think, in the back room, and Jean [Stafford] was writing a novel in the front room, when I took over . . . I have done some work but am way behind schedule on the book of poems. H.M. wants it all in by Sept. 1st but I'm afraid I'll never make it . . . I had my doubts [about *Concordance* for the title] but yesterday morning, just as I was leaving the hotel in Halifax, I picked up the Gideon Bible and thought I'd make one of those test samplings, you know. My finger came right down on the concordance column, so I felt immensely cheered.

I'll be in Stonington about a week, then I'm going to visit Randall at Dennis for about a week. I haven't seen him since I did quite unexpectedly & with great relief at the Academy award affair. He's been in Colorado on one of those conferences, I think . . . Marianne has a selected poems coming out in the fall and I'm attempting to review it for the *Times*—I don't know why I said I would. I'm hoping to be able to turn it [the review] into a sort of poem.

Have you been able to finish any work? I'd love to see a poem. How is Elizabeth's novel progressing? I guess it is really too nice a day to sit here in this running-water, large-saggy-bed room & I'd better go out. It would be nice if you were both coming along for one of my famous little Stonington absinthe parties . . .

One news item from today's *Boston Advertiser:* "Storm Sweeps on Mexico Gulf." After describing the 125-mile winds, the damage done in Jamaica, the ships lost, etc., it says: "Linda Darnell of the movies was on the island, but a mountain range protected her from the worst of the blow." Would that we all had such useful Hollywood connections.

To Katherine E. McBride

c/o [Jane] Dewey
Havre de Grace, Maryland
October 8, 1951

. . . I shall be returning to New York on the 19th and I should be very pleased to stop off at Bryn Mawr whenever would be a convenient time for you on that day—or if Friday is a bad day, I think I could arrange to return on the 18th instead. Or if some other time is better, possibly I could go up from here & return here. Then, as you suggest, we could arrange about another visit later on.

Thank you also for the information about the Fellowship. My sailing date is at present for October 26th, but I am afraid I shall have to finish paying for my ticket by the 15th and I shall be in need of some money. I hate to sound so greedy but the ticket is a sort of investment, and I am hoping to get a great deal of work done on the long, slow trip.

I can't "read" or "lecture" but I should certainly be glad to meet some students informally and to talk to some individually, if you think I could be of any help to them. Thank you again for your letter. I realized I wrote to you at the busiest time of the college year—and I am looking forward to meeting you.

October 22, 1951

I want to thank you for the very nice lunch & pleasant visit with you on Friday. I hope that when I see Bryn Mawr again in the spring, I'll be feeling better than I was that day & shall be able to be of some help to somebody. Due to the longshoremen's strike the sailing of my freighter has been postponed a few days, but thanks to the Fellowship & the resultant traveler's checks I feel very optimistic & like working hard. I reported on the Indian swing to Marianne [Moore], who was very gratified.

To Robert Lowell

Merchant Ship *Bowplate*
November 26, 1951
Somewhere off the coast of Brazil

I sent you a postcard just as I was leaving N.Y. but I had to put so many stamps on it I probably completely covered up my message . . . It wasn't until I had decided on this crazy trip and went down to see the Rahvs one evening before sailing (as I then thought—I was held up a couple of weeks by the dock strikes) that I knew where you were. Philip said you intended spending the winter in Amsterdam, which somehow surprised me, but maybe no more than my decision to go through the Straits of Magellan will surprise you. At least I think that's where I'm bound for. At present we're approaching Santos—a couple of days late because of storms—and first I'm going to visit in Rio for a while . . . Oh dear—there is so much to talk about. I wish you & Elizabeth could join me in this dining-room-saloon-etc., for a Scotch & soda right now before lunch. This is a very small freighter—smaller than yours, I think—it sailed from the dock next to the Fern line. It's Norwegian, and hired by the Du Ponts—to take an enormous cargo of jeeps, combines, etc.

There are nine passengers; that includes a sad young missionary—

"Assemblies of God"—and wife and three little boys. The rest of us are an Uruguayan consul from N.Y.; a refined but seasick lady; and another lady whom fortunately I like very much, otherwise these 17 days would have been a little too much—a 6 ft. ex-policewoman who has retired after being head of the Women's Jail in Detroit for 26 years. She's about 70; very gentle and polite—tells how she accidentally solved such and such a murder, in an apologetic way—and confessed she was written up in *True Detective Stories*. She also has daydreams of going down through the Straits & up the west coast. Has also invited me to inspect a few jails with her en route.

It is funny but I almost went to Amsterdam too—before I knew you were there—but I couldn't seem to get a cheap passage. How is it? And how is it in the winter? Lots & lots of paintings?—& what about the language?

With me on the boat I brought your review of Randall and Randall's review of you & I've been brooding over them both. I wrote a (I hope) withering one of a book called *The Riddle of Emily Dickinson* for *The New Republic* the other day. Now I'm working on Miss Moore for the *Times* but find it very difficult since I left my original bright ideas behind in N.Y. I don't remember whether I wrote you . . . about visiting Randall and Mackie in September. It was all rather distressing because I like them both. I can understand what you mean about missing him—you wrote in the spring—his reviews infuriate me and yet that activity and that minute-to-minute *devotion* to criticism is really wonderful. I think he admires Richard Wilbur too much, though. (This is trusting you've seen the last *Partisan Review*.) I thought the Leavis piece on Pound was excellent, but probably you won't.

The missionary is dictating a letter to his wife at the next table. They are so sad—and the worst aspect of the trip has been the two Sundays we've spent at sea on which he held a "small interdenominational service." There are so few of us we all had to attend and sing "Nearer My God to Thee" (after he told the story of how the people on the *Titanic* sang it as they went down). The three tiny boys sang "Jesus loves me this I know" in Spanish and a song, with gestures, about how the house built on the sand went *splash*. I'd always wondered how it did go but I had never thought of it as splash somehow.

I've been completely without news since getting aboard. There is a Norwegian news report over the wireless but the officers although very nice are the silent Viking type—you probably ran into that, too—and don't translate. Please write to me. Send me a poem (that seems unbelievable at the moment but I can think of no Christmas present I'd like better). I hope to get around to the west coast—maybe write an article about Punta Arenas or something on the way—and stay in Peru and Ecuador until April or May, then come back in time to put in an appearance at Bryn Mawr. Pearl Kazin went down to Rio not long ago and got married to Victor Kraft. I expect to see her. I saw Alfred just before leaving & he raved, absolutely, about "Mother Marie Therese." I must stop—obviously having no literary information that could be of the slightest interest to you—and fill out my baggage declaration. *Please* write me about Amsterdam, how you both are, what you are each writing, etc.

To Alfred Kazin

Samambaia, Petrópolis
December 10th or 11th or 12th [1951]

I shall try to put my hand on a few impressions I must have lying around somewhere. After my 17-day voyage I spent two days in São Paulo (Pearl likes it much better than Rio & I think I know why—it's much more *city*-like), and then came up to Rio by train (an apparently undreamed-of procedure, although I enjoyed it very much. The "roomette" was just like those I've been trapped in before, except that all the instructions were in Portuguese which made it even more dream-like). Mary Morse and Pearl met me at the station. You probably have heard of Lota de Macedo Soares and her friend Mary. I knew them in N.Y. and they are extremely nice. And extremely hospitable—they have just turned over their apartment in Rio to me, maid and all, and I sit surrounded by Calders, Copacabana, Cariocans, Coffee, etc.—& of course a dysentery drug, which also begins with C. I am up spending a few days with them at their country place now, but I'm going back to Rio soon to try to work, do some sightseeing with Pearl, and stay until the second freighter from now goes south, about Jan. 26th. It is all very luxurious, and I never felt like Rilke before.

Pearl has been awfully kind to me. The cast is off her ankle but it was still pretty swollen when I arrived. She must have had a hell of a time for a while, though, with Victor away, and she felt very sick and the Embassy sent a stupid doctor—but then she got a good one later. I thought she looked rather badly at first, too, but the last time I've seen her—just two days ago, she seemed much better. We went to the Botanical Garden together and are planning some more sightseeing. She is job hunting quite hard, I think. I think she is particularly wonderful the way she markets and cooks. I went marketing with her and had dinner with her & Victor a few nights ago, and she really does awfully well, I think, knows her way around—shunted me on & off four or five different types of public conveyance—but of course all that kind of thing is very exhausting and I don't think she likes Rio much.

I don't think I do, either, but it's hard to say—it's such a *mess*— Mexico City and Miami combined is about the closest I can come to it; and men in bathing trunks kicking footballs all over the place. They begin on the beach at 7 every morning—and keep it up apparently at their places of business all over town, all day long. It is enervating, completely relaxed (in spite of the terrific coffee), corrupt—for about three days I felt horribly depressed, but then recovered—mostly thanks to Pearl. I think they hope to stay just a while, then see more of S.A. before returning to New York. We are planning a trip to Ouro Prêto together—one place I want very much to see—if they think they can afford it. Victor has been very charming to me—but I must confess it *is* mysterious. I don't know how much work he gets, actually. Their apartment isn't bad at all—my standards here are confused because of the way *I* am living—but the bed is uncomfortable, the gas as slow as everything else here, and it must tax Pearl's patience pretty badly—Enough for now. I must get to work. I'd love to hear from you—any LIT news?

1 9 5 2 - 1 9 6 7

BRAZIL, *A Cold Spring*, SEATTLE

Questions of Travel, NEW YORK

Elizabeth and Lota in their home, Samambaia (near Petrópolis), in 1954.
Photo © by Rollie McKenna

To Dr. Anny Baumann

Alcobaça [Farm]
Petrópolis [Brazil]
January 8, 1952

Happy New Year . . . I have a long tale of woe to tell you—about three weeks ago I suddenly started having a fantastic allergic reaction to something or other. The doctor thought it was to the fruit of the cashew, since it was the only thing I had eaten that I had never eaten before, and some people are allergic to it. But I only ate two bites of one, two very sour bites. That night my eyes started stinging, and the next day I started to swell—and swell and swell; I didn't know one *could* swell so much. I couldn't *see* anything for over a week. I started taking Pyribenzamine and adrenaline, and then my friends got their doctor to come all the way from Rio. He was very nice, had been in Memorial Hospital in N.Y. for five years, etc., but nothing he did seemed to do any good. (It was just the face that swelled & later the hands.) He gave me a lot of pills supposed to be the same as Pyribenzamine only better, and I took shots of some anti-allergic stuff, and went to a hospital here every day for 10 or 15 ccs. of calcium in the vein. I was having asthma all the time too—still am— and although I explained to him that I was having to take 7 or 8 ccs. of adrenaline a day, I never could seem to make him understand that part of it because he presented me with a ½ cc. ampule to take "in case of emergency." They also removed 15 ccs. of blood from one end of me and put it in another every day or so.

After about a week eczema appeared, very bad, the worst on my ears and hands—just the way I had it as a child but I've never had it since. I finally got sick of being stuck with so many things like St. Sebastian and just stopped everything completely—and now I'm all right, except for a few patches of eczema, not bad, and the asthma that continues although now I only have to take 3 or 4 ccs. of adrenaline in the course of every night. I haven't been able to write or type because of my hands.

Yesterday I felt so much better I started to wash my hair and fainted. My poor hostess [Lota] got so alarmed that *she* started to faint—surely the perfect hostess. It was very funny. Fortunately everyone has been extremely kind. All the friends and relatives come with suggestions and their own bottles of pills, etc., and I had a hard time dissuading my hostess from telephoning you at the worst of it. It probably would be useless to give you the ingredients of the anti-allergy drugs here, in Portuguese— but I thought that possibly since you are so familiar with my *System*, you might be able to suggest something to take along in case I get another attack, and then the doctor could translate it into Portuguese for me. Before this started I had noticed my mouth got sore from eating, I thought, too much pineapple, so I had eaten very little of it—and mangoes too— and I felt, without knowing anything about it at all, that the calcium was making the eczema worse. Would it have that effect? My ears were like large red-hot mushrooms and they're still very big and red. Oh dear. I am having such a nice time otherwise and there is so much work I want to do—but I am slightly nervous about starting off on the 26th of this month unless everything has cleared up. However, it is very interesting to be sick and take medicine in Portuguese & Brazilians certainly get enthusiastic about illness—I think it endeared me to them.

The Norisodrine sulphate doesn't seem to have much effect any more, I suppose because I had to use it so much. However I think I should order another supply of it . . . I think three of those boxes of twelve each, 25% strength, should do, and if they send them airmail they should get here within a week: c/o Lota de Macedo Soares, Rua Antonio Vieira 5, Leme, Rio de Janeiro, Apt. 1101 . . . In return I wish I could send you (1) some coffee, (2) a parrot, (3) one of the little wild monkeys that are in the mountains right in back of the house—they whistle. Probably you would only care for the first item. They even serve it on the first-class buses— a sort of kitchenette is built right beside the driver and while the bus is swooping down the mountainside a boy in a white coat is busy pouring out little cups of coffee & handing them around along with little boxes of cookies labeled "An Offering."

Aside from my swelled head and the asthma I feel fine & although it is tempting Providence to say so, I suppose, happier than I have felt in ten years . . .

To Loren MacIver

[Rio de Janeiro]
January 26, 1952

With luck this may reach you in time to wish you many happy returns of the day. The strange conglomeration of Aquarian birthdays seems to have hit Brazil, too—there is a plethora of them. The internal mails almost do not move at all (I sent Pearl [Kazin] a postcard from Petrópolis to Rio & it took 15 days—50 miles), but the exterior ones are all right, airmail, that is. It is nice & relaxing to be in a country where no one knows quite what season it is, quite what date or hour it is. It's safer to use people's *first* names because their last are so changeable—guests argue & argue about the common name of a common object like a teacup. I have a feeling it is very good for one & gives one what Lota calls a "good shake-up." (She was going to the doctor for one.) *Why* didn't you tell me about the Biennale in São Paulo? or should I have known, or didn't you know I'd have to go there from my boat? I was there 2½ days all alone and missed it completely—with Lota sending me wires that never reached me. Anyway I'm sorry I missed it. Your two paintings look very nice in the apartment here, in the dining room, on a sort of dark terra-cotta wall.

I have tried to explain all about them to several people, in assorted gibberishes.

I got quite sick around Christmas—fascinating, but since I left my typewriter in Petrópolis I can't go into details—but I am recovered now. Lota and Mary were so nice to me it was almost a pleasure. This Rio address will reach me until the end of February—then I'm starting off I'm not sure where.

Pearl came up to Petrópolis last Sunday for the day and read us your letter. I feel very concerned about her & wish she could leave Rio right away . . . It is very hot & rainy here right now. Pearl has got herself two or three jobs—very good about the whole thing. I'm just here for a couple of days to see the doctor, etc. If Lota & Mary knew I was writing they'd send their love . . . Love to you and Lloyd.

To Ilse and Kit Barker

EB met the English painter Kit Barker and his wife, Ilse, novelist, at Yaddo in December 1950. An intimate friendship developed which lasted till EB's death, with visits to the Barkers in England and later at Elizabeth's summer home in Maine.

Alcobaça [Farm]
Petrópolis
February 7, 1952

I'm not quite sure where to begin—& did I write you from my freighter?—I can't remember, and this trip is doing my memory no good at all so far because Brazilians can't remember a *thing*—not even what season it is right now, for example. My hostess, Lota de Macedo Soares, has one of those fancy watches that tell the day of the week, the month, the phase of the moon, etc., and almost every day we all consult with each other and think it all over & get out the latest *Time* (it comes airmail but often two or three numbers in reverse order) and then she fixes the astoundingly accurate piece of Swiss engineering with a pin. Also no one in Brazil knows where I'm going—they've never heard of the other places in S.A.—and Lota's knowledge of geography seems to consist of a little French poem learned in a convent here, about islands: "*Java, Sumatra, Borneo, les Philippines . . .*" However, I have liked it so much here, thanks entirely to my friends, that I've stayed on and on and now I'm planning to take off on my vague little freighter line around March 1st. (This is in hopes you'll write me a letter—it takes from four days to eight, and costs 10¢ airmail—most of my correspondents seem to think it costs 24¢.)

[Feb.] 9th

Heavens—yesterday was my birthday & I am fonder of Brazilians than ever. Friends of Lota's came bringing a large cake (we're straight up the side of a mountain and can only be reached by jeep, or as they say here, jeepy—an English "Land Rover" Kit will be pleased to hear). And then later on a neighbor whom I scarcely know—because we have no known language in common, for one thing—came bringing me my lifelong dream—a TOUCAN. Kit would be absolutely mad about him. The woman who gave him & her husband are Polish refugees and ran the zoo in Warsaw, I think it was. He does a huge animal business here with zoos all over the world and I'd been to admire his birds and animals but I never dreamed they'd give me a toucan—they're quite valuable. He has brilliant, electric-blue eyes, gray-blue legs and feet. Most of him is black, except the base of the enormous bill is green and yellow and he has a bright gold bib and bunches of red feathers on his stomach and under his tail. He eats six bananas a day. I must say they seem to go right through him & come out practically as good as new—meat, grapes—to see him swallowing grapes is rather like playing a pinball machine. And something I'd never known—they sleep with their tails straight up over their heads, and their heads under a wing, so the silhouette is just like an inverted comma. I am calling him Uncle Sam, or Sammy. He steals everything, particularly something bright, but so far the favorite toy is a champagne bottle cork, also from the birthday. I hadn't meant to go on so, but you are the first persons to tell about this and, as you see, I'm still too excited to type properly. Anyway, as soon as I get him cleaned up a little, I'll send you some snapshots & I expect Kit to do a painting immediately.

Petrópolis is the mountain resort town about 40–50 miles from Rio, where the emperor used to spend the summers (so-called—it's supposed to be summer now but I'd never know it) and lots of people from Rio have country places. Lota has lots of land here & is in the middle of building herself a large and elegant modern house on the side of a black granite cliff beside a waterfall—the scenery is unbelievably impractical. We are sort of camping in a third of it, using oil lamps, etc.—another American friend, a Polish boy, etc. I was very sick from Christmas on for about five weeks with a dreadful allergy—something my N.Y. doctor writes me is a "Quincke Edema." Anyway, my head swelled like a pumpkin and I was completely blind. It also affected my hands so I couldn't write. However it wasn't too bad because Brazilians seem to adore illness, and all took such an interest, brought their own medicines, crowded into the room saying "The poor one" and calling on the Virgin, etc., every time I had an injection. That was before we moved up the mountainside . . .

I distinctly remember a letter from you-all but whether I have it in the apartment in Rio or not I'm not sure. I was there for two days last week and just as we were leaving the *book* came—it had been to several places first. I thought it looked very handsome, type, jacket & all. I looked at it for a few minutes but decided to leave it there since there's no place for books here yet. The type on the jacket made me think—appropriately maybe—of boomerangs. I do hope you get some decent reviews and when exactly did it come out? I see *Time*, *The New Yorker*, and the airmail *N.Y. Times*—but that only gives summaries of the lead reviews which, as you know, are always of books like *Republicanism—a Triumphant Conflict*, or something by John Steinbeck . . .

I have done very little sightseeing; I'm waiting to go to the famous baroque town—Ouro Prêto—until the worst of the rains have stopped. Would you like a book of it? I missed the Biennale in São Paulo when I arrived there because I didn't know it was still on. There are some things in Rio but not too much. Lota worked with Portinari years ago on that famous Education building, which is very handsome, and we have a few of his paintings around. She has some good things but mostly in Rio— two beautiful Calders, one of a bug, right here with me. (I put the toucan in the kitchen because he distracts me so.) I must go make tea—wish you were here to make it for me. We have tried and tried but it never tastes quite right. The best they sell is "Rogers" do you know that? No, it's Queen Victoria's own blend but I think they blended it for her once & for all and are still using her supply. When are you coming East? I'll be in N.Y. in May, I imagine, and I'd love to see you. Is everybody working?—more than I am, I hope, but I have been so happy that it takes a great deal of getting used to. My troubles, or trouble, seems to have disappeared completely since leaving N.Y. Alcobaça is the name of a farm.

To Marianne Moore

> c/o de Macedo Soares
> Rua Antonio Vieira 5, Leme
> Rio de Janeiro, Brazil
> February 14, 1952

When I came down to Rio yesterday for two days to see about extending my Brazilian visa, I found these clippings [about MM's *Selected Poems* winning the National Book Award] in a letter from my aunt and I'll fly them right back to you just in case you didn't see them. The "Felicitous Response" is awfully nice and I'm so glad my aunt was smart enough to send it to me. I don't know whether or not I told you that before I left I had to give up being [a judge] on their poetry committee because I was going so far away—but since I had no doubt whatever about who the selection was to be, I didn't mind too much. An English friend of mine here (an admirer of yours) told me she'd seen it in *Newsweek* a week ago—then just as I was fixing my mouth to write to you (as my grandmother always said), I got my aunt's letter.

I'm afraid you must think I'm hopeless about the review, completely—but I know you will be sympathetic when you hear what happened. I have it just about done—I undertook something really too much for me, I'm afraid—and then before Christmas I had an attack of a fearful and wonderful allergy—Dr. Baumann writes me it was a "Quincke Edema," whatever that is—anyway, I swelled and SWELLED . . . I looked extraordinary and it shows how nice Brazilian people can be that it seemed to endear me to them rather than otherwise . . . Now I have started to work again at last. I wrote *The New York Times* at the worst of it to try to explain, and I think I'll be able to mail them my review at the end of this week. I am frightfully sorry to be so late, as you can imagine—but it honestly couldn't be helped. I wired them to get someone else, but they didn't.

There are so many things here you would like; I have written you so many imaginary letters and bored you to death with descriptive conversation many times. I have been staying mostly at my friend Lota's country place in Petrópolis, about 40 miles from Rio, and it is a sort of dream-combination of plant & animal life. I really can't believe it at all. Not only are there highly impractical mountains all around with clouds floating in & out of one's bedroom, but waterfalls, orchids, all the Key West flowers I know & Northern apples and pears as well. Lota has sold one of her places to a famous Polish zoo man and you just have to drive down the mountainside for two minutes to see a black jaguar, a camel, all the most beautiful birds in the world. I think of you every minute there. The zoo man—I can't believe this yet myself, and we have no common language even—gave me a TOUCAN for my birthday, the other day. He, or she (the toucan), is very tame and mischievous—throws coins around the room —flies off with the toast from my breakfast tray. He is black, to begin with, but with electric-blue eyes, a blue-and-yellow marked beak, blue feet, and red feathers here & there—a bunch under his tail like a sunset when he goes to sleep . . . Anyway, I've never had a nicer present and his name is Uncle Sam.

I do hope you're well—I gather from *Time, Newsweek, The New Yorker* and the airmail edition of the *Times*—all very late and in the wrong order—that it has been awfully cold and stormy. I hope you will forgive me for not writing sooner and, much worse, the late review, but I think you will understand how that happened. Now that I have written once I'll write again and stop this imaginary-letter business. It is not very satisfactory after all. I'll send some photographs of Sammy. I can't imagine anything nicer than to have you in Brazil, too. I'm afraid I'm a real "literalist"—I have to have a real toucan, and then I can't even do him justice.

Samambaia, Petrópolis
March 3, 1952

So *that's* where my stamps went to. I looked and looked for them, not that it really made much difference anyway because, as you may have noticed, they come almost without glue on them. The mailboxes are never collected so one has to go to the Post Office; and there are glue machines which are frequently incapacitated by their own glue, so that one gives up and goes to the woman who runs a stamping machine, even if the stamps are much nicer. I don't believe I've made that at all clear, but you'll be able to gather that mailing a letter here is quite an undertaking and actually what I do most of the time is hand my letters over once a week here to a friend going to Rio to mail for me. The mail from Petrópolis to Rio—30 or 40 miles—often takes two weeks. I used the above address because I think it is so pretty—it means "Fern"—but it is not really usable. The same friend brings my mail up from Rio every weekend. I don't mean to complain about the mails—they are part of the really lofty vagueness of Brazil . . . where a cloud is coming in my bedroom window right this minute.

You say you kept one stamp—it is a memorial to Santos-Dumont, "Conquista a Dirigibilidade Aérea"—and I had such a funny time when I went to the museum in São Paulo. I spent two rather awful days there, in terrible rains, and afraid of the traffic, which is worse than Washington, and naturally unable to say a word. The museum was closed but in one of those fits of aggressiveness that come over one in foreign countries, I got in somehow and a young man, whether janitor or head curator I have no idea, showed me around. There was wonderful Indian stuff but apparently he didn't think much of it, and every time I relaxed my attention to him a second I found myself back in the rooms dedicated to the memory of Santos-Dumont, and staring at his personal parachute, his little tiny Panama hat, or his little yellow boots. Since the museum was closed all this took place in a deep twilight, and I was half-hysterical as to whether I should tip the unknown young man or not.

You have no idea what a relief it is to me that you are so nice about my failure as a reviewer and how much happier I am about it now. I am really glad it has worked out this way. The "poem" I'm working on is turning out to be quite long and now that it isn't a review any more I have hopes of its really turning into something better; I also have hopes of getting it done soon enough to go into the book. And now I can just leave out all the necessary mechanical parts, explanations, etc., that would have had to have gone into a review. I hope you'll like it. A friend wrote me about how nice it was about your receiving "all those awards" and I am curious to know what other ones there were besides the National Book Award. I'm so sorry to hear you've been sick; and of course I wish you'd make use of Dr. Baumann's gifts personally instead of just sending others to her. During most of the daytime now I don't believe I've felt better in years, but I am still having asthma at nights so I have to get up and take two or three shots every night. It shows how tough I am that I feel no ill effects from this except that I sleep more than usual. The intimacy with clouds may not be too good, either, but I like it so much I don't want to move.

Sammy, the toucan, is fine. A neighbor built him a very large cage in which he seems quite happy, and I give him baths with the garden hose. Someone also brought him a big pair of gold earrings from the Petrópolis "Lojas Americanas" (5 & 10) and he loves them. He has two noises—one a sort of low rattle in his throat, quite gentle, if he is pleased with you, or cranky, if he isn't, and the other, I'm afraid, a *shriek*. He also has the shortest intestinal tract ever known, I think, and has to eat constantly and is far from neat. Just a few minutes ago I found a hummingbird in the pantry—quite a big one, yellow and black. I got it out with an umbrella. There are such varieties of them—and now the butterflies have come for the summer—some enormous, pale blue iridescent ones, in pairs. I gave Loren one in a box once, maybe you've seen it at her house. And I've never seen such moths. I wish I had my *equipment* with me & I'm going to try to get some in Rio. The house is all unfinished and we're using oil lamps so of course we get thousands, and mice, and large black crabs like patent leather, and the biggest walking-stick bugs I've ever seen. Well, it is all wonderful to me and my ideas of "travel" recede pleasantly every day.

I do feel awfully out of touch, though—even if someone sent me Selden Rodman's review of you!

Thank you for keeping the things for me. I expect I'll get back sometime in late April. Lota de Macedo Soares may come back with me for a trip, but I'm not sure. Did I tell you in my other letter that she likes your poetry very much and that when I first was here I spent several evenings reading it to her—something I should never dare to do on the other side of the Equator, I know, but here it seemed easier to. I do hope you're feeling better and trust it wasn't that fearful pleurisy again. I hope Malcolm Cowley doesn't nag or anything . . .

To Katherine E. McBride

March 19, 1952

Your letter was brought to me from Rio this morning by a friend. I am still staying up in the wild mountains. I hope it will be all right for you if I take the later date—May 5th—that will work out perfectly. I hope the talk will be really "informal" because I am not much good at anything else, but I don't mind sitting down reading, or answering any questions I can, etc. And I don't mind talking with individuals about writing at all. I think the whole Fellowship has been so extremely generous that I wish I could do more. The last six or seven weeks have been very good ones for me and I am feeling very grateful.

My address will be the above for a month, then c/o Stevens, Box 668, Key West, Florida, until April 27th, and then, as far as I know now, the

Hotel Grosvenor, Fifth Avenue and 10th Street, New York—in case you should want to get in touch with me . . .

To Pearl Kazin

July 8, 1952

Mary [Morse] has to go to Rio this morning to the doctor, a fitting for a new suit, etc., and I am sitting up in bed writing this in a great hurry—I thought she was leaving this afternoon and meant to write to you more at my leisure. It is awfully cold—I keep having the funniest feeling that Christmas is coming—but dazzling and beautiful. The *matto* has all turned red and in the early morning it is covered with thick dew. Then every morning the valley is filled with mist just like a bowl of milk—that floats up gradually and it gets hot and absolutely cloudless—superb weather. You put on all your clothes to start with, peel off all morning, start putting on again about three, and go to bed with a hot water bottle and socks about nine, absolutely frozen. I hadn't meant to give you quite such an account of weather conditions, however. Lota and I are flourishing; Mary has gained about eight pounds and looks much better; we've had quite a lot of company and are going to hear Gieseking play—that's the extent of activity here. At the moment the Tomska, the zoo lady, has just returned the jeep from Rio—8 a.m.—where she drove it yesterday with a load of parrots. She had to ship off dozens somewhere or other—so picked all those who use the filthiest language, to get rid of them—turned the wrong switch in the midst of Rio traffic, thinking she was putting on the lights, and the jeep stopped dead and she was bawled out by a policeman in front and all the parrots in back. She also has a baby lion that just flew in from Pretoria the other day—four months old and absolutely adorable. He stands on the sofa on his hind legs watching for her out the window—sleeps with her and tears the sheets to shreds, of course—goes to the bathroom only under the refrigerator. You can imagine what the house smells like. And he lies at night gazing into the open fire like a baby King of the Jungle. (I guess I should write all this to Marianne.)

I was awfully sorry to hear your sad news about the job—which may be better by now, I hope—and about the story, which is bound to be better in time, I know. I don't see how he could read those things into it, honestly. It seems to me that you gave very much the impression of him that he so much likes to give of himself, but any kind of accuracy, even flattering, kind of scares people, I suppose. Oh well—think how Mary Mc[Carthy's] *real* victims react to her stories. I wrote a story about Nova Scotia—a sort of fantasy, couldn't have been more sentimental, and the one character by name had been dead for years—and my aunt hides the magazine to this day . . .

Lota wants you to do one more errand for her at Bonniers and I hope you won't mind. Mary will put the dollars for it in this letter. Did I tell you how coming down on the plane [returning from a visit to New York] we remembered everything like our gift orchids and quarts of milk—and left Lota's prize purchase, two trays, on the plane? We started in to trace them right away and they should have been picked up at Montevideo. We suspect that either the wife of the Mayor of Rio got them, or that nasty stewardess. But Lota, who is much too attached to material possessions, I feel—at least too much so to live in peace in a careless country like Brazil—wants to get them all over again . . . She would also like two more of the Swedish wooden birds, whittled, bright blue with gold spots, to hang up from the girders—they're about 75¢ or 80¢ each. [*EB sketches the trays and the wooden bluebird in detail in pen-and-ink drawings.*]

I've been reading about the heat in the newspapers—how Sugar Ray [Robinson] passed out or something for the first time in his ring career, but from heat, etc. I hope it has cooled off, and that your apartment isn't too bad. Take salt. —Also been reading about [Secretary Dean] Acheson and think I'll send you a small clipping if I can find it. He didn't look "strong" in the pictures—merely gigantically tall. Mrs. A. came to lunch Sunday at Lota's old home, we learned later, and were awfully sorry we couldn't have gone to gawk. They'd been working on the road—the *worst* road almost—for several weeks—to the house—and the rumor was that they were going to entertain a "rich American farmer" and we were all agog. Well, it was Mrs. A. they were fixing the road for (like those false-front peasant villages they used to set up when Catherine the Great went traveling), only they didn't finish it all so Mrs. Acheson still had to get a few jolts before she got there. I must stop—I didn't mean to go on so long.

Next Day

My prayers and my guilty conscience are speeding that awful gray envelope on its way. I swear if it doesn't get there I'll just give up, as my grandmother used to announce so mysteriously. And now I have still another request to make. I suppose I could make it direct to *The New Yorker* office but do you know how confused their subscription dept. is? —I've tried it before with varying results and usually no luck at all. Maybe you won't have to do it in person, but can let them know there, or something—but I'd like to have copies of *The New Yorker* with [EB's story] "Gwendolyn" in it sent to my two aunts in Canada . . . and I bet Aunt Mary has still got that doll—she's that type.

Next Sunday—19th

I'll get my requests off my chest and then I can relax and enjoy writing to you. I would like so much to see a copy of *Perspectives*. I saw the last one announced with a piece by Cal [Lowell] called "Santayana to His Nurses" or something like that and I asked Brentano's to send it to me. Well, they can't because I suppose it's supposed to be for sale here in

Portuguese, or something. It isn't—so I wonder if you could send me personally, sometime, a copy of that?

. . . I have another small idea that is probably rather silly but that would solve my Christmas present problems here for a year, certainly. If you could deliver about six boxes of ordinary paper-folder matches, the kind you buy at the grocery store, all mixed labels—you know, about 50 folders to a box? —They pounce on any folder of matches here with joy; you may remember the "Fiat Lux" company . . .

Here is the little poem ["The Shampoo"] Mrs. White couldn't understand. I have changed three words, though, since she returned it. I wonder if I am in honor bound to return it to them because of the three words before I send it someplace else? [published in *The New Republic*, July 1955] & do you remember those tin basins, all sizes, so much a part of life here?

It is very cold but my fireplace works very well. In two days now Lota & I are moving into the new wing—two new bedrooms and a bathroom and a small living room with a *stove* in it. We cut pictures out of magazines and had the iron worker make us what is really nothing but an ordinary sheet-iron stove, oval, rather like a cake of soap on legs, with stovepipe. But since they have never used anything like that here before, it is creating quite a sensation; he swears it will never work, and every inch of it has been a battleground, and he and Lota have screamed their heads off at each other—worse scenes than usual, because carried on in the shop with twenty men hammering iron and working buzz saws and blast furnaces, etc., all around us. First he had it made so that you might have been able to poke about three little sticks in it, and balance them on two or three little bars soldered up in it about 2″ from the top. I had to go personally and draw pictures and swear I had lived in Canada all my life and *knew* about stoves before he would change it. It looks like any old stove to me now, and I'm sure it will keep the room lovely and warm. I don't know whether it's admirable or not to have absolutely no sense of comfort like the Brazilians. Anyway, it does give the room a certain domestic charm, I think. The bathroom is enormous, and we have just decided—or rather it was an inspiration of Lota's—to paint one whole wall in big diamonds, all different colors, harlequin-tights style. It's going to be marvelous—a fresco—we're preparing the ground now, and when it's ready Lota's friend Rosinha—I don't know whether you ever met her or not, but she is extremely nice—who still works with Portinari, Burle-Marx, etc., occasionally, is coming up for the weekend, and we're all going to paint diamonds.

I do wish you weren't so far away—I wish you could come for a weekend too—it is much more finished and civilized now, and I think you'd like it. And there is so much I'd like to hear. Cal seems to be all wound up in teaching. Randall J. was married again, some time ago now—I haven't heard from him, but there's a dreadful poem called

"Woman" in the last *B. Oscure* by him. Also the beginning of a novel, I guess, by Carson Mc. that I think is awfully good—her simpler style again. Mr. Zabel is here now to give lectures—I've only met him once but Lota knew him when he was here before, so we're going to have him up for a day—maybe he will be "literary" enough to satisfy that side of me for a long time—I suspect so. Oh—I saw a digested review by you in *The N.Y. Times*—I'll get it full-length soon—stories by Jaffe(?) I think—so you are getting some work done on the side, I'm glad to see. Mary is taking my better story, called "In the Village," back to Rio to mail to *The New Yorker* [where it appeared in December 1953] along with this. I hope you get to see it, although they probably still won't like it.

Do you know how much *New World Writing* pays? (I haven't seen No. 3, but I'll be able to get it here eventually—and Miss [Arabel] Porter said she was going to send me one, anyway.) . . .

Carlos Lacerda is creating great upheaval here now—has just landed the editor of the government paper in jail (he's an old renegade friend of Lota's who apparently has been a Communist all these years—plus selling out to Vargas) but it is all too complicated to go into. However, much as I dislike Carlos some ways, he is certainly a very brilliant and brave young man . . . I must stop; Mary is about to leave. Here is Habakuk prophesying doom.

To Dr. Anny Baumann

July 28, 1952

. . . I have been torn between just writing a letter and writing an account of my ailments—although they've been very few. I think Atabrine must cure *everything*. But I'll start with the unpleasant part. I got a cold shortly after we arrived and it went away in two or three days but then for about ten days I had the worst asthma I'd had in years—a real old-fashioned "attack." The Norisodrine sulphate didn't do any good at all and after a few days adrenaline didn't seem to work very well—for a few days I was taking a cc. or a half every hour or so, and it seemed to have almost no effect. I was in the country so we didn't get a doctor, and finally it stopped. I was fine for a while and then I began having slight asthma again and am still having it—mostly due to bronchitis, I think, that I can't seem to get rid of. I tried to get this prescription filled and the pharmacist said it was a trade name; and that such products go under different names here—although he probably has it . . . Aside from this complaint I've never been better—but it is so maddening. I stopped using the Norisodrine sulphate for a while because it seemed to be more irritating than anything else—now I'm using it again, but have to get up in the middle of the night (it's freezing cold), light a lamp, light an alcohol lamp, etc. It is very picturesque and there is an owl who sits outside the window every night and watches the proceedings, but I'm awfully sick of it. I wonder if you could recommend something for the bronchitis that I could keep on hand, and also don't you think it would be a good idea to have an alternate to adrenaline in case of emergency?

. . . It has taken me a long time to get down to work, I am sorry to say—I guess I have lived without any working habits for too long. And then everything is so beautiful it is hard to stay indoors. It is very cold nights and mornings, but hot enough in the middle of the day to eat lunch outdoors, and brilliant, brilliant blue—a few clouds spill over the tops of the mountains exactly like waterfalls in slow motion. I wear long woolen underwear, several sweaters on top, which I take off one by one during the morning and put back during the afternoon. It seems to be mid-winter, and yet it is the time to plant things—but my Anglo-Saxon blood is gradually relinquishing its seasonal cycle and I'm quite content to live in complete confusion, about seasons, fruits, languages, geography, everything. There are hundreds of birds now, but nobody knows their names. There is one little black one who, with his mate, jumps up and down on a twig or even a piece of grass, about a foot in the air and down, by the hour, just like a little rubber ball. The toucan is flourishing and has at last decided to take baths. I discovered he liked deep water, as deep as his beak, i.e. about 6 inches. He plunges in and out very fast several times with great splashes, as if he hated to do it but knew he should, and when he got wet he proved to have blue skin underneath, just the color of blueberries—or as if he had blue jeans on under the feathers.

While we were away, the cook took up painting—proving that art only flourishes in leisure time, I guess—and has turned out to be a really wonderful primitive, so we shall probably soon start peddling her on 57th St. & making our fortunes. We found a large rock painting she had done—a bird—using a big lichen as part of his body. We are afraid to comment too much for fear she'll begin on the walls. Lota told her to please *clean* the garbage pail—she is half-savage and very dirty, although a fine cook—and ten minutes later we found it painted in violent reds and pinks and blacks. Lota has some pots that Portinari did for her and we have to admit that the cook's are much better. When there is company she makes the butter into anthropological messes that I wish we could save. But she was sick recently & we had a dreadful time with her—the only recognized organ to most Brazilians seems to be the liver; one gets awfully tired of the endless discussions of the state of everyone's *fígado*. The cook's was all over her, and although we got the doctor and I attempted to give her the prescribed shots, she much preferred to brew strange teas and sing incantations all night.

There are so many mice that I said I wanted to get a cat and the animal dealer who gave me the toucan immediately said, "Oh—would you like a pair of Siamese? I'm importing 200." So I guess I shall have them soon—wishes seem to come true here at such a rate one is almost afraid to make them any more.

I shall stop this now and please do not feel any answer is necessary except perhaps a prescription—but it is very pleasant to write you the "news." Lota is supervising an enormous garden and building a dam that will eventually give us a pool big enough to sit in, at least, and building a road of cut rock up the mountainside that I think is going to compete with the Appian Way and the Amalfi Drive when it is done. It is really a wonderful country in some ways. Where, when you arrive, the janitor and the porter and the cook all hug you tenderly and call you "madame, my daughter"—and where I looked out the window at seven this morning and saw my hostess in a bathrobe directing the blowing up of a huge boulder with dynamite. I am really working some, some stories and a long poem about Brazil and, except for the asthma, things just couldn't be better.

To Marianne Moore

Sunday
August 24, 1952

. . . I hope you're having nice weather up in Maine—strange to say it's been rather like Maine weather, or Nova Scotian, here, too—heavy dew in the mornings, deep blue skies, fogs—only they're clouds here— that disappear. I think it is getting warmer now, and that "winter" is over. However my grasp on the seasons is pretty tentative. We have beautiful flowers, and a beautiful vegetable garden. This is the month for one particular small orchid to bloom—"Ólhos di Boneca"—"Doll's Eyes"— very delicate, pale lavender, with dark round purple spots in the middle. My Portuguese is progressing slowly because I get so little chance to practice it, all the Brazilians I meet being so fluent in English. But I like it very much—packed with diminutives, augmentatives, endearments, etc. "Buttonholes" are "button-houses."—Lota calls the workmen "my flower," "my beauty," "my son," etc.—when she isn't calling them names equally preposterous in the other direction. Did I tell you that the janitor in Rio called me "Madame, my daughter"?

I still feel sure that English has the advantage as far as poetry goes —but what is it—accuracy, range, or what?—because it seems to me that every other language is *enjoyed* more by the people speaking it . . .

Sammy is fine & can play catch with rounds of banana—I am very mean and throw them too low so that he almost falls off his perch trying to catch them and being overtoppled by his beak. Our little maid plays with him by sticking the broom handle into his cage here & there—and he hops onto it—always making that sound you described as gourds being knocked together, meaning he's pleased. I think for a creature who has no face at all, just a pair of blue eyes and a beak, he has an enormous variety of expressions. We liked what you said about "every animal has hours of privacy" and since there are still no locks here we thought of putting them on the bathroom doors.

I am still having asthma but right now I feel it is useful, like sandbags in a balloon. I'm trying cortisone so something wonderful may still happen.

Please eat a lobster for me. Please say boo to Malcolm Cowley for me—but I don't mind the delay in La Fontaine so much if it should happen to mean some more poems. And please don't take any more cold boiled potatoes—wasn't it?—to bed with you.

[P.S.] I forgot two things: One, *The Irony of American History* has arrived & I am reading it. Thank you again. Two, I don't believe I ever told you this, did I?—Mrs. [E. B.] White asked me if possibly you would ever consider giving them some poems. Mr. Shawn [editor of *The New Yorker*], who seems to be very nice (on the telephone is the only way I know him), is really interested in trying to get good, better, best poems, for a change—and apparently they feel very badly about some old mistake or other and would give their eyeteeth to print a poem of yours. Lota has just come down from the vegetable garden, right over our heads, almost—& she would like to send her love.

To Dr. Anny Baumann

September 16, 1952

Thank you so much for writing me that long letter while you were on your vacation, and all by hand, too. I didn't recognize the writing, but strange to say, Lota did. I hope you had a wonderful trip and a rest. If all goes well here and I make a little money, we hope to go to Europe next spring for four or five months, take a car. We've already planned the itinerary and I am learning to drive, something I never in the wide world thought I'd do.

Before I received your letter the asthma had got so bad that we came down to Rio for a few days to do something about it. I went to the doctor who had treated the allergy before; he is very nice, worked for several years at Memorial Hospital in New York, and with Dr. Pack, etc., and speaks fairly good English. I have a rather unjust mistrust of every doctor but you, I'm afraid, and so I was doubly pleased when I received your letter to have you suggest just exactly what he had already started to do . . . But just the last week things have started to improve a great deal and I have got through two nights now without getting up and am only taking a half cc. of adrenaline four or five times a day. He seems to think the improvement will continue. I don't know whether it is due to the cortisone or not, but in between the asthma attacks I have never felt better in my life . . .

The drinking seems to have dwindled to about one evening once or twice a month, and I stop before it gets really bad, I think. Of course that's still once or twice too often, but what is best about it is that I don't seem to think about it any more at all, or go through all that remorse. I get to worrying about the past ten years or so and I wish I could stop doing that, but aside from that the drinking and the working both seem to have improved miraculously. Well no, it isn't miraculous really—it is almost entirely due to Lota's good sense and kindness. I still feel I must have died and gone to heaven without deserving to, but I am getting a little more used to it.

At last I am mailing you a picture. However, I am not very well pleased with it. I'm afraid, to use an elegant expression, I bit off more than I could chew. However, it's big enough so that if you like any section of it you can cut that part out; and I'm doing some more smaller ones and if any turn out well I'll send you another one. The one I'm sending is from Lota's road, looking down over the land belonging to a florist, just below us—a very nice neighbor to have. I also am going to send you, if it is possible, some of the results of my jam-making—a very exotic and beautiful fruit called *jabuticaba* that makes the best jam in the world, I think. Lota is planting the trees all over the place, to raise them commercially, eventually. They are very beautiful—the blossoms are yellow-green, fuzzy, very fragrant, and grow all over the branches—no twigs— and then the fruit pops out on the branches, right on the wood, like thousands of large black cherries.

I have two more birds, adorable little green and blue things, very tame. They love each other very much and live in a wonderful old home-made cage that resembles the dome of the Capitol in Washington. On second thought I realize now I should have sent you one of the cook's paintings instead of mine. Hers are getting better and better, and the rivalry between us is intense—if I paint a picture she paints a bigger and better one; if I cook something she immediately cooks the same thing, only using up *all* the eggs. I don't think she knows about the poetry yet, but probably that will come. We are really in Rio to give her a honeymoon with the gardener, whom she married a few days ago. The atmosphere got so highly charged we couldn't stand it any more, and when we got cinnamon on the steak one night instead of pepper we decided to give her a little vacation.

I do hope you are well, and that none of my friends are ailing. I shall give you a report on how the cortisone works out . . . Lota wants me to say although I think it sounds rather conceited that I seem to get along with the people here very well. Now that I've said that I might as well go further—to my complete astonishment yesterday I got a "fan" letter from the editor of a newspaper here whom I've always thought of as being a very difficult man, so I was awfully pleased. So I guess that's enough boasting for once.

To U. T. and Joseph Summers

September 17, 1952

I just received a postcard of Giotto's Baptistry and I immediately thought of you both and decided to write you a letter on this cold wet rainy afternoon in Rio—the rains seem to have started again. We're down here on business for a week, but primarily to let the cook enjoy a honeymoon with the gardener. We married them off on Saturday; had a large luncheon—divided into two classes, the cook's former employers—rather a strain—in the dining room, and the lower orders making very Breughel-like in the kitchen. But the atmosphere was getting so emotional and so little cooking was getting done, and they kept shutting themselves in the pantry, etc. . . . so we just decided to give everyone a little vacation. The humor got very frank, to a New Englander, too. Driving away from the judge's the blushing bride said she wasn't going to sleep with him until they'd been married in the church (a fairy tale), ha-ha-ha, and Lota said, "Lulú" (the gardener), "insist on your rights—insist on your rights in ten minutes"—much laughter all around . . .

I hope you had a nice trip and that Fiesole is proving to be wonderful—the apartment—I know the place will be. I remember it with the greatest pleasure. A gardener climbed a tree and gave me a gardenia—a very small tree. If all goes well here and I manage to earn a little money I am really coming abroad in the spring, with Lota. We are going to bring a car, or buy one there, and stay four or five months. We'll probably go to Italy first, and there you'll still be. I haven't been since just before the war and she hasn't been since her convent days and we already have road maps, etc. Now I hope it works out. Pearl has written several very nice letters and has certainly been working like a house afire since she got back. There are three book reviews by her right here now, and I guess her new job has begun too. I'm sure she'll like it better than *Harper's Bazaar.*

Against all the correct theories of escapism, exile, and the horrid facts about the condition of Brazil, I like living here more and more. Maybe it's just age, but it is so much easier to live exactly as one wants to here. I did sort of miss the [presidential] conventions—I even wanted to see some television then—but it really looks as if Stevenson would get in, don't you think? At least it might be interesting to have someone nice & neurotic in the White House for a change.

I have a couple of literary questions to ask you. I wonder if Joe has read R. Tuve's book about [George] Herbert? She was teaching at Vassar when I was there—I never had her but she was very young and serious.

Anyway, I've just ordered the book. Something else—I've decided to do a translation. There's a book here that has become a sort of Brazilian classic—the diary of a child, a girl aged 13–16—brought up in a big & very Brazilian family in a very backwards diamond-mining town about 60 years ago. It is really wonderful—completely authentic and terribly funny and giving a marvelous picture of the life of the time . . . Well, I don't know, but it seems to me with editing and some notes it would really make a successful book in the U.S. What I wanted to ask you was what publisher you'd suggest? Houghton Mifflin? Putnam's is more interested in Latin American things, aren't they? Should I send large samples or what? or the whole Portuguese book?

It seems to me I should be able to write here, too [on back of airmail stationery] but maybe it's illegal. I am at last taking cortisone for asthma—absolutely the last resort, I guess. It has come down in price by half since I started . . . However, it produces a "state of euphoria" in between attacks, and that is really wonderful. I'm so happy all the time, or think I am, at any rate, I'm getting to be an awful bore with it, and I never worked so much in my life. I think I'll just keep on taking it forever. There was a piece about Mr. Merck, who manufactures it, in *Time* and it said he was such an idealist, dear man, didn't believe in the "profit" motive in drugs—then it went on to describe his $100,000 greenhouse just for orchids. So I shoot myself full of his $15-a-bottle drug and go out and admire the free orchids on the trees.

We have a wonderful vegetable garden, but rather odd—Brussels sprouts, artichokes, the usual things, some Golden Bantam corn, a great rarity here—and I have beds of watercress and mint around a spring, doing very well. But no bourbon is available unless I cultivate a U.S. Army connection and I guess it isn't worth it. But supposedly there are to be no more imports of foreign seeds and I don't know what we'll do next—the best seeds are French and American ones.

I do hope you are all well and that housekeeping isn't presenting too many strange problems. I'm sure they'll seem hard just at first, though. What is Joe working at and where? I do hope somebody will have time soon to write me a letter about it all. Is Jim Merrill there? If so please remember me to him affectionately. I hope to have some things in *Botteghe Oscure* soon. With much love to everyone and do please let me hear from you.

To Kit and Ilse Barker

October 12, 1952

. . . One of the charms of this place is that it almost never feels like Sunday—maybe because it's a sort of lukewarm Catholic country—but today it does, and I'm all alone for the time being in the large half-finished chilly house—with an oil lamp lit at 3 p.m. to keep me warm. No it isn't hot now, but it is starting to get warm again. It was scorching in Rio when I was there last week, but here it's always much cooler. I'll quote from my geography book: "During the summer months the wealthier people (that's me) of Rio de Janeiro seek the lower temperature (9 degrees) and the more active social life of the community at Petrópolis, on the crest of the Great Escarpment." It calls up a vision of everyone doing a samba along the skyline, but the social life up here where I am is very limited—a few friends make it up the mountain over the weekends, and arrive with their cars spouting boiling water, but the rest of the time we go to bed to read at 9:30, surrounded by oil lamps, dogs, moths, mice, bloodsucking bats, etc. I like it so much that I keep thinking I have died and gone to heaven, completely undeservedly. My New England blood tells me that no, it isn't true. Escape does not work; if you really are happy you should just naturally go to pieces and never write a line—but apparently that—and most psychological theories on the subject, too—is all wrong. And that in itself is a great help.

I was delighted to hear about the paintings and sorry to hear the writing hadn't been going too well. I wish Kit were having a New York show, too. Will he have one in London when you get back? Just give me a hint of what *The Innermost Cage* is about . . . I loaned *Fire in the Sun* to a couple of English-reading Brazilian friends. One was baffled, but the other, the intelligent one, admired it very much. Have you done any more stories? And I'm glad you've got going again. I wish I could get Kit to provide me with some titles—maybe he'll send any leftovers he has along. I am stumped about two right now. A story was to be called "Clothes. Food. Animals.," which I still kind of like, but finally decided was a little chichi—so now it's simply "In the Village" . . . To my great surprise—I hadn't finished a story in ten years, I think—I suddenly started writing some and have done three—two more part done—and the Sable Island, which I am just now getting down to. They all have to be sent to *The New Yorker* first, but I doubt they'll take them. However, if I publish them anywhere I'll let you know because I'd like very much to see what you think. It is funny to come to Brazil to experience total recall about Nova Scotia—geography must be more mysterious than we realize, even. The book of poems, *A Cold Spring*, should really be out this spring now. But it is wonderful to be able to work, isn't it—I hadn't been, really, for so many years . . .

I'd love to have a drawing. I should think it could just be sent to me airmail without any trouble. I'll ask Lota when she comes back, but I think they can be. I get books all the time. And I get the London *Times Lit. Supplement*, you'll be pleased to hear, *The Listener, The New Statesman and Nation*, and well—at the moment I'm carrying on a fascinating correspondence with Foyles. So when you get back I'll be watching for news of you in all the magazines. (It's just as easy and cheaper than getting books from New York.) Maybe you'll let me know if there are any new English magazines I should subscribe to, etc? Or books I should read? A neighbor gets *Scrutiny*. It is really funny to have *Partisan Review* arrive on horseback sometimes—although I mustn't give a false impression; it's really not that remote or wild, and just a mile away the villas of Petrópolis set in.

The clavichord—and my "library," etc.—are all sitting on the dock in Rio right now and should get here next week. To my surprise I didn't have to pay duty on anything except a bunch of old Victrola records—probably unplayable—from my "jazz hot" days—and Lota's new dining-room chairs, etc. Her house is under construction again now and is really going to be beautiful. It is in an architecture magazine called *Habitat* and will be in the next *Aujourd'hui*—if you should happen to see them—although it's only about a third finished now.

If all goes well here and I make a little money we are planning to go abroad next spring, for four or five months, probably . . . It would be wonderful to be able to see you in Kent or wherever you are. I've seen almost nothing of England except London, you know, and I'd like to very much. And now you have seen so much more of the U.S.A. than I ever have. I don't imagine I'll get back now for two or three years—I want to do some traveling in South America first, after Europe, that is.

Please write me again—but be sure, if you can't do that right away, to give me your various addresses—or one that will reach you in England. I hate to keep losing people. I also have some photographs of Brazilian Baroque I want to send you for Christmas that I think you'll like. I only wish I could send you coffee, orchids, birds, and monkeys. And I wish you could send me tea—in fact I wish we could sit down to some right this minute because as you see I have a sort of talking jag on—we've tried all available varieties here and Twining's seems to be the best, but it is never quite right. The coffee is superb, however—and you can imagine how good it is for me to live in a country where one scarcely ever dreams of drinking anything else . . .

I have a recorder among my stuff, too, I think—in fact a friend of mine who had an alto one used to play things on it with the clavichord —we had some special music. Music is the one thing lacking here—but we have found out that the waterfall is powerful enough for a turbine, so in about two months now there will be electricity, a Victrola, etc., we hope . . .

[P.S.] I remember a serious conversation I once had with Kit when I seemed to be at dead low tide at Yaddo. He probably won't remember it at all, but I do, because what he said was so sensible and has proved to be completely true. I just thought he was being overoptimistic at the time, and all along he was just being smart! So I thank him properly now!

To Pearl Kazin

December 10, 1952

. . . I just read a Eudora Welty story "Mingo"—no, "Kin"—what do you think of them? At least I thought there was more to this than that first one that just baffled me completely. But oh for the gift of the gab like that! I'd like to send something to *New World Writing;* I have several things all going at once, about three done—but as you know better than I—it takes so long to arrange things with *The New Yorker*. I am having trouble with "functional references" to the point I'm really getting embarrassed about it; *have* I a scatological obsession? And I get to feeling very petulant and want to say, "But I don't understand So & So's story *at all;* mine's much clearer—and he talks about going to the bathroom and *worse*, all the time!"

The excitement here last week—you may see something about it in *Time* or something, I'm not sure how important these affairs are in N.Y.—was Carlos Lacerda's going to jail for two or three days for an editorial about police graft. He had been here the day before, and was here a day or so ago, worn out. He said he'd had 3,000 visitors and two hours sleep, and the circulation went up enormously and the law that arrested him has been repealed, and they're having a Thanksgiving mass for him in the Candelária, so the whole thing was a tremendous success. I think I said I didn't like him the first time I met him, but I should take it all back. He has been extremely nice to me and I admire him a lot—with a few serious reservations, that is. Stephen Spender was here to give two lectures—I didn't go to Rio for them and am glad now because he annoyed people (at least those I know) by talking "down" terribly. They want to have—somebody does—the next Cultural Conference here—like in Paris—and Carlos Lacerda had assured Spender it was just the place, such impartiality, freedom, objectivity, etc.—no interference from local goings-on. The next day Spender went to see him in jail and asked him if he still felt the same way.

It is beautiful now—hot even here, though, so I hate to think what Rio is like. The "studio" is about done and I am so overcome I dream about it every night . . . I'm sure I'll just sit in it weeping with joy for weeks and not write a line. But everyone is working very hard, the yard looks like a quarry. Also I'm cooking again, but that's too long to go into now . . . The worst about cooking here is I run out of ideas, so unless I can go into a well-stocked store and spot something—

Well, that grisly business of Best's and I do wish I'd never bothered you with it. Stella brought back my damned pants because I found I'd got "medium" when I should have said "large." Best's is now after me, although I paid for the pants. I apparently didn't pay another bill I had there which I really had never received. Department stores being as woolly as they are I don't dare complicate things by trying to explain to them

. . . This is a damned nuisance and Christmas is coming too. I won't bother you again, honestly.

I see that Delmore Schwartz likes "Testimonies" too. I read *The Old Man and the Sea* and liked most of it—all except about six of his really horrible lapses—enormously. Such a wonderful sense of the sea and space, etc.

This rather indelicate enclosure is not the kind of Christmas present I'd like to send at all, but it seems to be the only feasible one. I do hope you and Victor are well and working, etc. Please do let me hear from you. How is Mary Lou? How is the second *New [World] Writing*?—I haven't seen it. Just read Alfred [Kazin]'s review of Edmund Wilson—very good, I thought.

Lota joins me in much love and best wishes. Mary is in Rio handling vast emprises there, coming today or tomorrow.

To Dr. Anny Baumann

December 28, 1952

. . . I stopped taking cortisone for a while but since my last visit to Rio, I am taking it again in very small doses—four half pills a day just now, for a week. I am feeling absolutely wonderful. I take a whiff of the Norisodrine sulfate once every two or three days, I suppose. When I stopped the cortisone the asthma did start coming back slightly. But the doctor here seems to think he can keep adjusting everything around so that I'll have almost none. It is amazing how energetic it makes one feel, although also I'm afraid it has a tendency to make one get even fatter. However, we have no cook now so it is easier to have a regime. The cook was wonderful but it finally got to be a choice between Art and Peace, and tranquillity seemed more important than a masterpiece every afternoon. I have written a story about her [unpublished].

We were given a tremendous turkey for Christmas, alive. One of the workmen killed it for me—he wanted to know if I wanted to give it *cachaça* first (a very strong sugarcane vodka stuff). I thought it was given for humanitarian reasons but no, it seems it's supposed to relax the poor bird and make it tender. Well, I roasted it and it turned out very well.

It is very beautiful here now—quite hot in the middle of the days but cool at night. I have a "studio"—I can't believe it yet at all but I just go and sit in it and look around—it isn't quite finished yet. There is one large room with a fireplace. Lota found a rock somewhere that is gray-blue with mica in it, extremely pretty, and had them make it out of that—whitewashed walls and a herringbone brick floor. Then there is a small bathroom and kitchenette with a pump and a Primus stove for tea, etc. It [the studio] is way up in the air behind the house, overlooking the waterfall. I have all my books together for the first time in ten years; all my papers, etc. They are working on the rest of the house full blast now. Sometime I should like to see a modern house being built in the U.S., because the way they do things here is so "empirical," as Lota says. To begin with, they were completely baffled by the house—the aluminum roof, steel girders, etc., and it wasn't until she told them that it was going to look like a Carnival building that they'd go ahead—they liked that idea. The man who was blasting rocks miscalculated several times and once showered us all with granite boulders and half-knocked down the gardener's little house—and gave all the dogs hysterics. I guess that's enough about my affairs. As soon as we get a cook I'll get back to work, I hope; I have done quite a bit, though, even so . . .

Except for occasional morbid swelling of the conscience, I guess I never felt better, and thank you once more for all your help—and for encouraging me to start off for South America.

To Paul Brooks

Editor in chief at Houghton Mifflin from 1943 to 1969, and later editorial consultant to the publishing firm, Paul Brooks is the author of many books, including The Pursuit of Wilderness *and* The House of Life: Rachel Carson at Work.

January 2, 1953

Here are two poems, a table of contents (not in final order) and the acknowledgments, etc. I believe I sent you a group of additional poems about a year ago now, or a little longer. The list comes at present to twenty-four poems; however, since several of them will run three or four pages I make it come out about the same length as *North & South*, or perhaps a little longer. I also have two fairly long (two-page) poems that I'd like to have go with this group but they still need some work. I am afraid you will think it is a little short—however, I feel that it is a fairly coherent book, and that since I have moved to the other side of the Equator and have started a lot of quite different things, the work I am doing right now will be a new departure and will not go with these poems very well. If the book is not to appear until the fall, I shall certainly be able to send you the two and possibly others that might go all right. The last six months I've been working more than ever before in my life and I have many projects, including probably a book of pieces about Brazil.

As you may remember I wrote once, a long time ago now, that Loren MacIver was interested in doing a jacket for me. I don't know whether she still would be or not, but I think she would—and would undoubtedly do something nice. Would that be a possibility?

I am thinking hard about another title [instead of *A Cold Spring*], and I shall try to get the other two poems off to you before the end of the month.

To Katherine E. McBride

It was so kind of you to write to me about the Shelley Memorial Award [given by *Poetry* magazine]. I was taken quite by surprise by it & thought there must be some mistake—I felt I had published so little in the last year or so to warrant it. Anyway, it was extremely nice & I think these things do have a stimulating effect. As soon as you believe them you start planning . . .

I think a book of poems is coming out in the fall. When I have the proof I believe I should send you or the committee for the Fellowship the acknowledgments page to see if it is all right.

Yes, I like it so much here that I am staying on—& I am still amazed every time I think what changes the Lucy Martin Donnelly Fellowship made in my life . . .

To Pearl Kazin

February 10, 1953

. . . The story about *The New Yorker* is wonderful—they really are incredible, aren't they? When you wrote you were going to work there, I mentioned you in a letter to Katharine White. I thought I said just enough to intrigue and stimulate interest. Oh dear—those people make things so hard. I know, others have said the same things about Katharine, and yet she really couldn't be kinder or more sympathetic editorially—considering the position they're all in—than she has always been to me. I don't know what it is they're afraid of losing, but it must be awfully precarious. I wish you were here so I could show you my story ["In the Village"] and the correspondence it now trails behind it—it is fantastic. I think now it will go to *Botteghe Oscure*. However, I may try *The New Yorker* once more. They really do want it, but I refuse to put in enough "he saids" and "she saids" and "it was 4 p.m., a very hot summer, August 16, 1917, Great Village, Nova Scotia, and my father's name was William Thomas Bishop"s. But still some of their editorializing *is* good. The places they pick on to criticize are usually the right places, only they suggest the wrong changes. But when they find fault over and over with the story's being "mysterious"—while giving a perfectly lucid synopsis of it, so somebody around there must have understood it all right—and then publish those Eudora Welty stories that I honestly can't figure out—I feel a little put upon. The idea underneath it all seems to be that the *New Yorker* reader must never have to pause to think for a single second, but be informed and reinforced comfortably all the time, like newspaper writing a little—but then if one does attempt to publish there I guess one has no earthly right to complain. The one story they've actually bought ["Gwen-

dolyn"] isn't very good. There are a couple more I think they may take
—or one, certainly, and the Sable Island piece—but avoiding "functional
references" while trying to write a story about Brazil is impossible. I'm
sure Lota makes a functional reference every time she opens her mouth
and so do most of the people I know here . . .

I've been having a wonderful time reading Darwin's journal on the
Beagle—you'd enjoy it too. In 1832 he is saying, "Walked to Rio (he lived
in Botofogo); the whole day has been disagreeably frittered away in shopping." "Went to the city to purchase things. Nothing can be more disagreeable than shopping here. From the length of time the Brazilians
detain you," etc. etc. One wonderful bit about how a Brazilian complained
that he couldn't understand English Law—the rich and respectable had
absolutely no advantage over the poor! It reminds me of Lota's story about
a relative, a judge, who used to say, "For my friends, cake! For my
enemies, *Justice!*"

To Loren MacIver

March 21, 1953

Mary [Morse] brought up the catalogue [of the MacIver exhibit at
the Whitney Museum] from Rio last night, and thank you very much. I'd
had a sort of feeling it was on its way. We are awfully pleased with it . . .
The show must have been perfectly beautiful & you must be very happy.
I'm only distressed because there are several pictures I've never seen. I've
seen four or five reviews—all very good, or favorable even if silly, like *Time*
—and I heard from several friends who'd seen it. May Swenson (who lives
on Perry St.) wrote me *enraptured*. When I was answering her I said some
things that rather pleased me, and I guess I'll quote myself. I said I admired your "out-of-focus dream-detail" and your "divine myopia."
There! "Marvelous myopia" might be even better, although a bit vulgar.

It is the season of those pale blue butterflies like the one I gave you.
They are drifting along all over the place, sometimes in clusters of four
or five, and when they come close or come *in*, they are semi-transparent.
The "Lent" trees—*Quaresmas*, because they bloom in Lent—are purple
all over the mountains, mixed with pink and yellow acacias, and with
those butterflies flopping slowly in front of one's eyes, it is quite a sight.

Marianne wrote me about the show, Dr. Baumann, Mr. Strong,
etc.—it must have been a great occasion. I saw a picture in the *Times* of
people sitting outdoors at the zoo & I must say it made me quite homesick
for Northern spring—& even New York. I *do* feel that way once in a while,
you know, even though usually I'd prefer to admire it in your pictures.

Lota is in conference with the architect & a photographer & a drafts-
man . . . With love to you & Lloyd.

To Marianne Moore

April 11, 1953

. . . I was completely surprised by the Shelley Award of course, not having published any poetry to speak of for so long—I thought it must be a mistake. Yes, I thought Auden's poem—in parts—was much the best in that pretty feeble 40th Anniversary *Poetry*. It is odd, and I wonder if it is consciously done—and it's what I don't like about the poem—that air of artificiality, and why is what's on a shield realer than anything else, etc., as I used to ask myself when I had to translate those endless confusing descriptions when I studied the "classics." However, I *like* yours much better. Thank you for being nice about "The Mountain" because it really is just a "contribution."

I was so glad to hear about [Stravinsky's] *The Rake*. I'd been reading all the reviews in the various English periodicals we get—some pro, some very con. I think it went over much better in New York.

I am covering your letter from top to toe and now I'm at the toe, and I'm going to step on it. Excuse me. I ordered *Charlotte's Web* for Lota, because she liked some of E. B. White's other books, and because when I visited the Whites two summers ago I was exploring their barn and saw some beautiful big webs. Just then Mr. White came along & when I said something about them he told me about the book (he was writing it then) and later Katharine told me some very nice stories about how he had taken a spider back to New York with him. It lived on top of his bureau, and finally had an enormous family of little spiders on a hairbrush or clothesbrush. He wouldn't disturb it, and the maid was scared of it, etc.—So I ordered the book but, Marianne, it is so AWFUL . . .

Sammy is fine (the toucan) and now we have a cat as well. Did I tell you about Tobias? He's black with white feet and vest—perfect evening wear, only not so immobile. (I said he was dressed to go to the opera and L. said "Yes, he's going to hear *Die Fledermaus*.") L. was so impressed with your poem about the cat with the "prune-shaped head" that we named him Prune—or rather we had a Prune family, another little female, black too, named Dona Ameixa, and then Senhor Tobias Ameixa. (It's pronounced a-maysha.) But poor Miss Ameixa died.

I am liking living here more & more. Lota has been extremely busy for months now with building—the "east wing" is getting done. First they built the studio . . . I guess "study" is the name, but it sounds like James Russell Lowell . . . The front view is stupendous mountain scenery interspersed with clouds, and in the foreground the vegetable garden. The house and the weather have at last reached the point where we can go away for a week on a trip and tomorrow we're starting for Ouro Prêto. I am delighted—that was the one place in Brazil I really meant to see on my "South American trip." It is a national monument, etc.—almost solid 18th-century Portuguese Baroque. Everyone talks of it, but almost no one ever seems to get there . . . So we have cans of gasoline and extra automobile parts, and Lota is insisting on a revolver, etc. I'm hoping to be able to write a piece about it.

I've done some stories, and I think the book of poems is ready—but first I procrastinate & then Houghton Mifflin does. However, I guess it *is* done. I'm very pleased right now because I'm going to have some poems in English & Portuguese in a Literary Supplement here . . . Somebody wrote me a while ago about a poem of yours in *The Nation*. I wonder what date it was and if I've missed anything?

I've just finished Darwin's Diary on the *Beagle*—not the Journal, although I guess it's mostly the same—and I thought it was wonderful. I think I'll begin right away on all his other books. The pages about Rio de Janeiro are so true even today, and he's such a hardworking young man, and so *good*. (Do you know that story about him and one of his little boys?—much later, of course. He took the little boy to the London Zoo and the little boy looked into a cage where a huge rhinoceros was lying asleep, and said, "Papa, that bird is dead.") I'm also reading Simone Weil after staving it off for several years—the mysticism often repels— and then suddenly she says something so amazing & so simple you wonder why no one ever said it before. I get lots of magazines and so does Lota—it's wonderful to be staying with someone who likes to read as much as I do and begins at 6:30 a.m. usually . . . We get books from England, having discovered it was much cheaper, of course, but more efficient than Brentano's—and much pleasanter because instead of Bren- tano's monthly insults I receive old-fashioned notes in long hand in purple ink—about my "esteemed order."

To Kit and Ilse Barker

Good Friday, 1953

. . . The studio is mostly gray-blue—sample of upholstery on the two armchairs included; it's what they make workmen's pants out of—white- washed walls, old brick floor, gray ceiling. I have a couple of Chinese objects in white & blue—so you see the bright green [of Kit's painting] will really just make the colors right. I'll send you a snapshot of it in place. I think it is really *very* good and it makes me eager to see the oils or whatever the larger ones are. It seems very cheerful, too—cheerful isn't exactly the word—energetic, maybe. The smaller one I think we shall use probably in the new living room. The "east wing" contains two bedrooms, an enormous bath, a linen closet where the Victrola also goes, and it plays into a small sitting room, rather long and narrow, with a magnificent view out one side. I think it is going to be a nice quiet room. We are having a real, old-fashioned stove made for one end—but "modern"-looking at the same time. Near it goes a Calder now in Rio

—the only busy touch—the clavichord is on one wall, and a small early picture of Loren's I brought with me; also I bought Lota a Schwitters for her birthday. So you see your small picture will fit right in that intimate atmosphere, only I wish it were you instead.

I do wonder if Kit is having a show? I got the catalogue of Loren's & I. Rice Pereira's recently, and I am getting rather wistful about seeing paintings. We called on Portinari a while ago—saw all his UN sketches, etc., but I don't like what he has been doing *at all*. I now like some of his earlier paintings quite well—I didn't used to—but now I see he really did have exactly the feeling of the Brazilian landscape around these parts, and "feeling" as well—but no longer.

I've been thinking so much about writing you that I've collected a lot of related themes and odds & ends. It would be several years' work to relate them properly so I won't try: The mountains I live in are called the "Organ Mountains." There's a place called "Bingen" nearby—I used to see it on the buses and think of Ilse every time, but I was disappointed when we actually went there. There are several German place-names around of course, because of so many German settlers.

Lota is extremely pro-English & I've at last begun to understand it better. I hadn't realized how England really ran Brazil all through the 19th century. When I knew Lota in N.Y. even, I noticed how she constantly spoke of things being "well-made," "well-finished" or "beautifully tailored," etc.—and now after living here I see how everything is wretchedly made, unfinished, and that for so long only the rich with good taste could have anything better, and of course then it was always English. The same thing is true of looks. I think I take it for granted that my friends are handsome, their babies are pretty, etc.—but here there almost seems to be an obsession with looks—everyone describes children's eyes and noses and chins endlessly—and when I see them I'm often disappointed. But the general level of looks is rather low, I'm afraid—and the ugliness of the "poor people"—I don't know what to call them—is *appalling. Nobody* seems "well-made," except some of the Negroes.

The other day twelve little boys suddenly appeared in the vegetable garden, with a man—an English school here, some of them were camping on Lota's land. The headmaster is a doctor, and Oxford, I think he said too—very tall and blond and skinny—oh those knees!—blue-eyed and a stutter—he didn't seem real. Lota's nephew Flavio was in the group so we invited them all to take a swim and made them cocoa. It was really a wonderful sight—all the naked little boys scrambling around in the waterfalls. They are called by their last names and poor little Flavio is called "Nascimento," or "*Birth*"—which is apparently sad for him any way you look at it, since Lota's sister "married beneath her."

There is a thunderstorm and I have just lit my Aladdin lamp—we have a small generator in the house now, but it can't work this far—and made coffee. I have a Primus stove. I remember hearing you talk about cooking on one. It must take a very special kind of cookery. This is a very pretty Swedish affair, glittering brass, two burners—but I am still trying to light it so I won't smoke everything up. Sometimes I get it right off but not often. Lota came to have coffee and we were discussing the English—referring to Queen Mary—and *I* said (I have to tell somebody else right away) that Queen Elizabeth, in the newsreels, waves like someone unscrewing an electric light bulb.

I am thinking of trying to send you a story I am having trouble with *The New Yorker* about—they don't follow it or something. I'd like to see if you do—I have finished three now, almost five. I am still surprised at writing stories but think I have enough for about two years more now, and enough for a book already . . . In some ways *The New Yorker* is not a bad writing school—in other ways of course deadly but after looking at a couple of *Botteghe Oscure*s I think they could do with considerable *New Yorker* editorializing. And it certainly pays. The first story they took, before Christmas ["Gwendolyn"], I am not proud of—and it is very short—and with one thing and another I've already been paid about $1,200 for it. It's quite crazy.

Saturday morning

To return to Kit's picture—obviously it did come safely, and I should also thank you for the mailing tube, which I am saving and which you will receive those pictures in I think I mentioned, eventually—mailing tubes don't seem to exist here. I *do* have some pictures of Brazilian Baroque, but on our rare trips to town we haven't been able to get hold of the photographer who takes them—we want to see his collection. Also, next week we are really going to Ouro Prêto . . . It is a famous place and everyone talks of it, but it is really quite an expedition. We are going in the Land Rover, with an American friend, taking extra gasoline, spare parts, flashlights, a revolver, etc. Lota is making endless lists, a favorite occupation of hers, starting off with "bottle opener," etc.

Oh—a title, please, for a book of stories.

You said you were going to put an ad in *The New Statesman* for a cottage & I've been reading them every week to see if I could spot you. I wonder if you have found something by now—you probably have. How is the novel coming, have you been able to get back to it? I chiefly envy you spring right now—here it is autumn, or as far in that direction as it is willing to go. I have never seen anything of England at all, just Ireland. I drove from Liverpool to London at a great rate and remember nothing but power lines and lunch.

My sad news is that I don't think we'll be able to get to Europe this summer at all—probably not until next year. Lota has so much building still going on and not only that but of course it takes all her available cash. I think I'd like to save up some more money from *The New Yorker*. We do want to have a car and be able to stay at least six or eight months—and Lota likes luxury. I shouldn't say that since I just lap it up myself, but I think that one of the reasons I'm dreading going abroad a little is because the years I spent there just before the war I lived so cheaply, always sat up all night on trains, traveled third, etc.—and I know everything will seem so changed and sad and fearfully expensive to me. (I went from Barcelona to Paris to New York once for $90, for example.) And I do wish now I'd been a little smarter and seen more of England then—it always seemed to be there, you know, and it was so much more like what I knew already that one felt one could put it off. I wonder often how you are finding it.

We have now switched to *Pickwick* tea. Lota has a cousin staying nearby—a rather awful Spanish society lady, cousin by marriage—who has a house on the Isle of Jersey—it sounds beautiful. We're about to get two Jersey cows, if we can take them to the bull in the Land Rover, and other such problems. Then we can make butter, we hope. The milk is dreadful—even if we pay more for ours "because it has very little water in it," says the little boy who brings it.

One night a while ago we were driving up from Rio in a fog and I suddenly realized that I had been distracting myself from my nervousness by indulging in a very childish, wonderful daydream for about an hour. I was frightfully rich and I sent you the money—several thousands—to come and visit me for six months or a year. Kit could paint in one of the new storage rooms, an excellent studio. You arrived. I met the boat. You were wearing—I was wearing—You said this and that about Rio. I replied—pithily—We drove (*I* drove) to Petrópolis. Kit completely bowled over by tropical vegetation, etc. Ilse taking it coolly. Well, I had a lovely time, and ended with Kit having a show at the Museum of Modern Art in São Paulo, winning the Biennale there, Ilse and I finishing a book each—all swimming in the pool with mint juleps sitting on the brink—and perhaps a side trip to Ecuador & Peru.

I have just re-read my story and I guess I won't send it after all. I've let it rest for two months now and I see a lot of little changes, but I will send it soon. I'd like to see if you can "follow" it all right. The book will be in the fall, I guess. The publisher is slow, but I really think it is all set now. I'm trying to sell him a book of stories and another book as well—a translation from Portuguese of a very charming journal written by a young girl here about 50 years ago—authentic, and terribly funny. It has become a Brazilian classic. The woman who wrote [it] is a rich old lady here now—has lots of good old photographs to illustrate it with. I am hoping, if I can interest a publisher, that Lota and I can do it together. It's now called *My Life As a Young Girl*, which is bad in English (so give me another title, please) . . .

To Pearl Kazin

April 25, 1953

. . . Lota and I left a week ago Tuesday for Ouro Prêto. I really never thought I'd get her to go, but the weather was good—fortunately perfect, all the time—and the house had reached the point where she really didn't have to be here. We had a wonderful time, although Lota thinks it has just confirmed all her suspicions about traveling in her native land. We started by jeep but at the last minute heard, directly from the wife of the director of the Património Artístico, or whatever it's called, *who had just been there*, that there was a brand-new road, etc. We went in the rather elderly Jaguar. Of course there was no new road at all, after 10 kilometers on it, and the old one was so incredibly bad that we drove 58 kilometers in 6 hours. The last hour it got dark and something scraped underneath (the trouble was not so much the road as the lowness of the Jaguar) and we were both pretty scared, but we made it, and the scraping was only the exhaust pipe. The garageman said only one other Jaguar has ever been to Ouro Prêto and it broke its gasoline tank, so we were quite a sensation in the town.

There *is* a new road and we were told it was to be opened in five days, so we thought we might as well settle down and wait for the grand opening. The governor of Minas and about thirty people had reservations at the hotel. But when we made inquiries, it all grew vaguer and vaguer. In the Prefect's office they were writing invitations to the opening, but no one knew the date. After a day or two it dawned on me that, if the new road was ready, *where* did it come into town? That thought stunned everybody—nobody had seen a sign of it. So we went back the way we came, all right, and by that time there had been rain. The 10 kilometers of the new road—very broad & straight—were a deep river of red mud.

And two hours from home, the next morning, we had a flat tire & Lota changed the wheel *in a jiffy*. I was admiring her performance & stepped around behind her. She had on a wrap-around skirt which had fallen open as she bent over & there was a little white behind, dressed in really old-fashioned long white drawers, exposed to the oncoming truck drivers. The wife of the Património Artístico, we discovered, had come and gone by train. We had our revenge, though. In a little grocery shop we found three huge old soapstone jars, really enormous beautiful ones, and bought them immediately. After we'd got them all packed in, in dusty hay, the man told us of course he'd *promised* to keep them for the wife of the P.A.—etc., so off we went. They will look very handsome on the "terrace."

We spent a night at Congonhas, three or four in Ouro Prêto, and one on the way back at Juiz de Fora—only three hours from home—but we were just too exhausted to go on. The hotels are pretty awful—the Ouro Prêto one not so bad, of course, because it's that fancy Niemeyer one. The rooms have a downstairs sitting room with a terrace and most of the room taken up by a very chic spiral staircase that goes up to the bedroom. It was almost deserted. The town is really worth the trip. I haven't been sightseeing for so long that maybe I overrate it, but all those churches and chapels—white with the soapstone trimmings, sort of greenish-gray—are very fine, I think. I'm hoping to write some sort of piece about it, but the information is poor, or just technical, and I'm afraid it doesn't make much of a "story." The prophets are really impressive— almost spooky, they look so real at a distance. We arrived just at sunset and were determined to see the front of the church before dark. Lota started rushing up a wall-like stone street, calling out the window, "The Prophets! The Prophets!" One old lady, sitting on her stoop, yelled that the road was too *aguda*—apparently a very strange archaism—and it certainly was . . . There were the prophets, brooding and prophesying doom and destruction, against the stars—really quite a sight above that funny, completely dead little town. Our pictures are being developed in Rio now—I'll send you some if they're any good.

Mrs. White sent me a sheet from *Vogue*—me, Randall and Peter Viereck. Oh dear I hate that picture of myself, and that insistence on my "coldness and precision," etc. I think that's just some sort of cliché always used of women poets, at least I don't *feel* as if I wrote that way . . . Somebody sent me a magazine with a poem of Lloyd's about Chestnut Lodge in it—a magazine called *City Lights*. I'm afraid I find the poem entirely too "cute" for comfort or for the theme of insanity . . .

I guess I really have to go down to the house—my fire is hissing out and it is getting dark and I forgot to bring my kerosene can up [to her studio]. This place is *wonderful*, Pearl. I just spend too much time in looking at it and not working enough. I only hope you don't have to get to be forty-two before you feel so at home.

To Arthur Gold and Robert Fizdale

The noted duo-piano and writing team of Arthur Gold and Robert Fizdale first met EB through Lota, who had earlier been instrumental in arranging for their musical concerts in Rio. The joint letter that follows was handwritten by Lota (italics) and typed by EB (roman).

Samambaia
5 de Maio de 1953

The world [drawing of globe] *being such a small place, a friend of mine just arrive from Paris and is a friend of a Madame Je-ne-sais-pas-quoi, qui est your impresario in Paris and she said that you and Robert are the most wonderful thing that Paris saw last year etc etc! and Elizabeth received a letter from Miss Moore just mad about you to the point of writing*

all the program in wich she heard you and commenting about! It was
wonderful! I would like to write more, but Gramática is not my strong
virtue, and I talk a lot with you both composing lots of imaginary letters
that I never come to the point of writing.

Lota is getting depressed about her English prose style—but I think
it is very good and only notice one "h" missing in "which" and only wish
I could write half as well in *any* other language. We were awfully pleased
to hear from you—a letter from Marianne Moore in the same batch about
the concert [at MoMA] too. She seemed particularly taken with the [Sam-
uel] Barber number ["Souvenirs"].

Didn't you like Robert Penn Warren—in spite of the accent? I've
always been very enamored of that red hair and that blue glass eye,
although I can't stand those novels with round-breasted heroines and
wicked heroes—just like *Gone with the Wind* with metaphysical footnotes.
I have the clavichord here, but aside from the fact that it's probably the
only one in Brazil I'm afraid I don't get much pleasure out of it, I play
so badly. It is wonderful for prestige, though, and Lota almost ordered
one caller out of the house for suggesting we have it electrified, like an
electric guitar. The house is growing and growing—it looks enormously
long. The roof is very shiny—rippled aluminum where it isn't thatched
yet—and we flatter ourselves that airplanes sometimes circle around to
see what it is. Someone said they probably thought it was a wrecked
plane, so I suggested we write BRANDY in big letters on the roof.

We had a plumber for a while who came up the mountainside—I
don't know how—on a bicycle with a very frail sidecar attached—pale
blue with "God Guide Thee" in red letters on the back—and in it was
his little black apprentice. Right now we are bewitched with the idea of
two telephones in every room, a two-way radio ($79.95 in *House & Gar-
den*) between the house and the studio, etc. And the bathroom is to have
a sunken tub—since it rests on the ground anyway, it is really not so
much conspicuous waste as it could be. Mary [Morse] is alternately extremely extravagant in her ideas—all the telephones are hers—and Bos-
tonially modest. I think I'll let Lota take over, since she had been relaxing
and thinking away easily in Portuguese all this time. Portuguese is a
dreadfully hard language; I'm hopeless at it but I can say *Adeusinho!* and
love to you and Bobby—yes, let us meet in Lisbon. When's your concert
so we can plan?

the 7th

Had to take a night rest after that effort! Yes, we are planning to go
to Paris and Rome next year, and if by any chance we really go, we would
write to you before, to see if we can meet somewhere. It was good to see
you again—the only thing that I miss in New York was not to hear you
both play. My love to you all. My kisses to you and Bobby and also to little
Arthur.

I meant to ask you about Ned Rorem, who wrote me a very nice letter mentioning you, asking for songs [settings for EB's poems]. I have never heard any of his music and I wonder what it's like.

Elizabeth is the slowest personne in the world. She is very thinking about to send something to that boy, but she is going to take some time. You should see the mail she gets asking, begging, etc. and nope, she is cooking a cake! Like now! En tout cas, she is getting used to be happy and sleeping well, and less scared—ETC. Morsie is coming from Rio today, she send her love too.

To Kit and Ilse Barker

Rio, Sunday a.m.
May 24, 1953

I came down [to Rio] just two weeks ago because I again got *cashew poisoning*. I don't know whether I told you about the horrible time I had when I first came here, after eating two bites of one of the damned fruits. Well, naturally I never ate it again, but this time Lota did, at the table, and apparently I am so susceptible to it that just the smell, or the oil from the skin floating in the air, or something—anyway, the next day I resembled a balloonlike Chinaman, and my ears were like large red terra-cotta classical casts of ears—so we rushed to Rio and the doctor. I was only sick a week this time because I didn't eat it, I suppose, and am now recovered except for many scabs. It is a sinister-looking fruit, you know, and nothing should combine fruit and nut in that indecent way—but to think I had to come to Brazil to find out. Oh well, there is probably a weed in Siberia or a leaf in India that could kill us all. And the nuts are so extraordinarily large and good that I am thinking of sending you a can. This was Lota's idea, after reading your last letter—I am ashamed to say it never occurred to me. Tomorrow I'm going to one of those package export places in town and see what I can send you . . .

Then you can tell me what you could really use there—sweets are unrationed now, I know—but do you like coffee, guava jelly, tongues, nuts, Brazil nuts & cashews, honey—or what? I really don't know exactly how things are now, in spite of all my English periodicals. Tinned butter?—we use it, too—figs?—they have excellent tinned ones here. Chocolate?—candy is bad, but the cooking kind good. Please tell me. The coffee of course is marvelous and if you had a mill I could send you the beans and you could astound your friends with the best in the world—but it is true that many people don't like it . . .

But oh dear the European trip looks rather far away. If Lota's land starts selling soon now, and I sell, say, five stories and articles, we'll have enough. The house is taking up every penny of Lota's of course and soon she is going to have to stop again, we're afraid. I will send you pictures —although it's hard to tell much now—the guest "wing" that we're still living in has already been in *Domus* and a couple of other architectural magazines. The architect is quite a young Brazilian, a good friend of ours, but actually this is his only house that I think is really good and *it* is good because of Lota's taste and her fighting him every inch of the way more than anything else. He is all for cantilevers, flying buttresses, brise-soleils that look like factories, etc. Lota wants to go first to England and buy a new car there. We are both hopelessly smitten with—don't disown me— the new Jaguar two-seater with a hard top. I *hate* cars on general principles, but this one I want, I have to *have*—and if I were rich I'd buy it like a shot, although as L. says it would be the *comble* of idiocy.

. . . It is hot in Rio, and heavy, and the beach is covered with bathers and umbrellas, etc. Last night I looked out and saw, just at the water's edge where the sand was wet, what looked like a large glowing coal or the remains of a small fire. The breakers came right up to it, almost around it, and it throbbed and glowed. Finally I thought it must be some kind of red-phosphorescent jellyfish. I could stand it no longer and went down—11 floors—in the elevator and crossed the street and waded down to the water in the sand. Someone had dug a little pit, about 18 inches deep, and at the bottom of it there was a lighted candle. We don't know whether it was just a trick for someone to watch from an apartment, like me, to see how high the tide came or something—or maybe it was some kind of *macumba*, voodoo. (We see them around in the outskirts of town quite often, but usually there is a bottle of wine and a dead chicken, and bits of red wool, etc.) The nicest thing I saw on a drive yesterday was a man trying to sell papayas by the side of the road. He had them hung up by strings, like a little clothesline, and was seated beside them on the ground and as each car approached he raised an old bugle to his mouth, blew a *bugle call* and pointed majestically at the line of big sagging yellow fruits. I think they all are slightly crazy sometimes (the cliché remark about Brazilians). We stopped to buy oranges on our trip, about 8 a.m., and while we bought, the man put on a Victrola record on an old wind-up Victrola standing in the ditch.

I am dying to get back to the country and the studio, and the cooler air. "Alcobaça" is just the correct name of Lota's place—or rather "Al-cobacinha," little Alcobaça. It's named for a mountain place in Portugal famous for wine, meaning "High place" or something or other—sometimes we get wine with that label. But Rio is the only address that will reach me. My Anglo-Saxonism is *really* shocked by the mails . . . Well, while you read *Lorna Doone* I've been here in bed reading Dickens. I really never had, very much, and I have polished off *Martin Chuzzlewit, Great Expectations, Oliver Twist*, his U.S. travels (guaranteed to raise my fever). How *can* Orwell say he was just being fair?—but then Orwell was never in the U.S., and Edmund Wilson says he asked if it wasn't true that English had deteriorated so much there that we had no separate words for insects but called them all "bugs"—and now am in *A Tale of Two Cities*. It's the energy, the amount he just threw away.

Well. *You* didn't think all U.S. people were Barbarians, did you? That cheers me up sometimes after listening to them here. I think the clichés about the U.S. are about 50 years dated, that's all. And poor Rio, "culturally." Ah well . . .

Well goodbye, good stalwart girl—didn't she characterize Kit in some equally easy and graceful phrase? Oh, *Glass Organs* is back here from the framers and looks highly distinguished; all visitors very impressed. You will be in the next São Paulo Biennale I'm sure, if you'd care to. With much love to everyone and tell me how your work is going, etc.— and the gardening . . . We have a new maid here named "Zhew-deetchy"—Judith—and keep wanting to ask her to bring in the head, please.

Samambaia
July 13, 1953

. . . I had my library, or what was left of it after having it handed around for ten years, shipped here, as I may have told you, and between us I suppose we have about 3,000 books now. One just has to, really, since there isn't much in the way of libraries here. I do get books all the time, though, from the British Council—did I tell you? They got rid of all their fiction a year ago when they almost eliminated it here—but I am working my way through their travel section and Lota has exhausted all the works on *compost*. We have started a correspondence even with a madwoman in England who believes in "radiations"—I must tell you more about her later. Anyway, Faber & Faber seem to be great publishers of books on anti-chemical fertilizers. They also have several books on cat raising I am going through (because of Tobias) and we are now reading Burton's travels here, which are absolutely *marvelous*. I hadn't realized he'd been here, too, as well as Arabia. The book was published in 1869 and the pages had never been cut. His knowledge of languages is fantastic. Lota says she hasn't found one mistake yet in his Brazilian Portuguese, Negro dialects, slang, place-names, Indian names, etc.—and they are almost impossibly difficult—and he has explained a great many words to her that she never knew about before. On the same trip that we took— to Ouro Prêto—he explains all the place-names, etc.—things we had tried and tried to find out about and failed. Of course he hates the Baroque and admires above all a good straight wide main street. He says of Ouro Prêto —"What they will do when they come to put in gas and water mains?" (everything's so crooked). Lota said "Ha-ha, Mr. B., they knew perfectly well they never *were* going to put in gas & water mains." But in general it is an extraordinary & fair book to have been written 85 years ago.

I have a story in the June 27th *New Yorker*, but it is the slightest and poorest of the group I've been doing. I did it one rainy day, the first thing I ever wrote right off on the typewriter, and I'm grateful to it because it started me off on what I think are the better ones. It's called "Gwendolyn" and I've already spent the huge sum it brought in—$1,000 altogether, I think—so you see you really must sell them something sometime . . .

This morning I found myself typing a story called "True Confession" and putting in Yaddo—I never thought I could. I found myself saying this about Polly (maybe it's mean, although it isn't meant to be): "As a child, just about at the point where she was able to read Dickens—say, *Little Dorrit*—she and her doll had decided it would be better all around for them to change places. I don't know where the doll had gone—off being an unfaithful wife somewhere, probably—but the doll's looks were very becoming in an unnatural way, so that one looked twice at that tiny chin and those dimples, and the little laugh, opening to have crumbs poked in by birds, perhaps." (But a character out of Dickens has its drawbacks, these days.) Well, of course I couldn't put it in, but I do think it's rather like Polly, don't you? . . .

What exactly are "fairy lights"? How stupid of me—I've just looked it up in the OED and now I know.

15th

Mary [Morse], our American friend, came up for lunch bringing cans and cans of the cement necessary to lay the floor, etc.—and another letter from you-all. (You have no idea what it is to build a house here. This is Lota's third, I think, maybe fourth, so she's pretty good at it, but so many things have to be imported, everything has to be improvised as you go along, and everything keeps giving out. This is the first floor to be laid. We've been living on cement all this time, as I may have told you—full of dog and cat tracks—and a few of our own—so we are very excited and couldn't bear to stop and Mary very kindly arrived with the black goo— no more in Petrópolis.) I left Lota having a terrific argument with José, the head workman, who looks exactly like a young Fernandel. Our individual cesspool is being installed—for L.'s and my new super-bathroom. L. thinks a 15-degree drop in the pipes isn't enough and was screaming away, "José, you know perfectly well it's enough for just peepee, but for peepee and *cocô, too*—" etc. That is actually the way Portuguese and Brazilians talk and I am getting quite accustomed to it. I find that all this frankness makes it much easier to get along with people than it used to be in New England, say—or am I just getting old and tolerant?

Yes, I liked *Rashomon* enormously. It was so *beautiful*, first of all, and then to tell something so subtle for the movies in such a direct way was amazing—and then the contrast (at least as I thought) between traditional Japanese acting and extreme naturalism. And of course the Coronation picture is superb. I just wish one could have had more of a sense of the crowd, and the various personalities, etc.—And of course I lost Christopher Fry completely, the version here being in Portuguese, although even I could spot a bit of translated Fry-ese occasionally—and if I weren't living in Brazil so happily I think I'd head straight for Tonga.

I've only read a couple of Angus Wilson's stories in *Partisan Review* some time ago and I thought they were brilliant, but enough for me for a while. I think what you say about him and Mary McCarthy hits the nail on the head—hits poor Mary on hers, exactly.

I'm really writing this, I must say, ungraciously, because I'm so sick of re-typing my best story. I gave up after long correspondence with *The New Yorker* last January. Now I've re-done a little, but will concede not another comma for clarity's sake, and although I know they *really* want it. If they don't accept immediately I'm going to send it to *Botteghe Oscure* . . . One tires of typing even a masterpiece, I find. [You wrote] 20,000 words! Why this here masterpiece I'm typing is, I suppose, 7 or 8,000 and it is killing me.

I find Mary is going back to Rio after tea—I thought she was spending the night—so I guess I'll send this along. Yes, film is fearfully expensive here, too. I *do* have pictures for you, though— . . . some portraits of Tobias being developed . . . He's about 10 months old now, handsome, and a brilliant cat intellectually, of course. So we now have four birds, two dogs, and a cat, having at last got rid of the last of six mongrel puppies—or so we thought. It was just like the woodcutter and the baby to be abandoned. Paulo, the gardener, swore he had found homes for them all and in the middle of the night one fat helpless thing wandered up to the house and howled under our windows. Paulo wants to keep it for himself although Lota had forbidden any more animals, particularly mongrels. We thought we should raise the *tone*, somehow. One young lady guest was horrified at the two dogs—one supposed to be a cocker but more like a setter and one who just dropped in. Then Lota horrified her by saying whoever *bought* a dog anyway, you accepted them like children. You have no idea how nice it is to get your letters here. Love.

To Paul Brooks

July 28, 1953

I wrote to you some time ago now, five or six months, I think, to ask you about the possibility of publishing *A Cold Spring* sometime soon. Somebody else answered—I'm sorry; I don't have the letter here now—saying they were waiting for more poems, etc. However, according to my count and the tentative index I sent then, I did have enough. I am enclosing another index again for you to see. Also another poem, soon to appear in *Poetry*. These poems will make a book a little longer than *North & South*, I think. Because of the title & title poem, I thought it probably should be a spring book or late winter, and that is why I have waited, expecting to hear from you again. I think the poems form a fairly unified book as they are now . . . There *is* one, however, a sort of farewell to Key West, that I should like to add to this one, and trust I can in a few weeks.

Now I should like to know if you really are interested in bringing *A*

Cold Spring out come next spring, or if you have lost interest in it. I think it is really time for another book to appear. As you know, I received that Shelley Award last year; the poem "The Prodigal" in this collection was in *Best Magazine Poems of 1952* (or was it '51?), etc., and I am eager to get it over with and get on with the next one. Can you give me a definite answer so I can make my plans?—since it is a little hard to make them at such long distance as this. There are enough, I feel sure.

Also I *know* there is a possibility of an English edition, about which I think I've asked you before. English friends keep writing me about when one is to appear and I noticed a while ago I was on the London *Times Literary Supplement* list for recommended reading in American poetry. From what I have heard from the English poets I know, I feel sure there is an opportunity for this—or possibly some sort of combined edition?

In my other letter I also asked about two other things. The first is about the possibility of a volume of stories. I know that they are as unwanted as volumes of poems, nevertheless it seems to me that if *A Cold Spring* came out in the spring, and was at all well received, the fall might be the right time to follow it up with some stories. I have about a dozen now, written over a long period of time, but they have been well received—two in *Best Stories of something-or-other*, one in *Partisan Reader*, one read over the radio in Boston, etc. There was one, a rather slight one, in the June 27th *New Yorker* and Robert Lowell wrote me: "You are one of the best, you know, and you *must* get out a book." (I loathe blowing my own horn quite so brazenly, but I don't know how else to tell you that this is not just an idle fancy.) If you like, I can send you the manuscripts of the stories on hand at present. I also have a first attempt at a Brazilian one that is turning into something very long—90 pages or so—but I had better leave that until later.

The other thing I asked you about was a book I am translating from the Portuguese, and in case you do not have my letter I shall describe it again. It is, I am certain, a real literary "find," and a "gem," etc. (and I'm rather critical) and should be known outside Brazil. It is the authentic diary of a young Brazilian girl in the 1890's, in the diamond-mining region, living in a large family, very poor, very religious, and extremely lively. She wrote really beautifully; the characters, the Negro servants, the old grandmother, etc., are really well presented, and it is *funny*. (I have seen a dignified lawyer here laughing his head off, reading it.) It isn't a Daisy Ashford kind of book—she's about 14 or 15, and toward the end the man she later married appears. It is not "cute," but it gives a beautiful little picture of a way of life that has vanished, etc. The woman who wrote it is now a rich old dowager in Rio; the man she married became head of the Bank of Brazil, I believe . . . I am going to be taken to see her the next time I am in Rio (I live in the country most of the time) by *the* elderly Brazilian poet Manuel Bandeira, who knows her well

. . . I suppose the only way to interest you, really, is to send some sample pages, which I shall do. In Portuguese it is called *My Life As a Young Girl* . . . The woman's name is Helena Morley. I wrote telling U. T. Summers about it, I was so excited when I first started translating it, and she said it sounded like "a publisher's dream."

I hope I shall hear from you soon. I shall send the final Key West poem as soon as possible; but what you have is *really* a book already, I think. I shall also try to send some pages from Mrs. Morley's diary soon; and if you are interested in the stories at all will you let me know? I am finding this an excellent place to work. I hope you are well and that Boston is not the way it usually is in the summertime. Here we are in the middle of "winter."

September 10, 1953

I mailed a letter to Miss Minahan yesterday, enclosing the poem "A Cold Spring," and then in the afternoon I received your letter of September 4th. I am in town [Rio] for two or three days—without a typewriter —so I thought I would answer it and mail it before I go back to the country—the resort town of Petrópolis, 40 miles or so from Rio.

I'll probably be able to mail you "After the Rain" by next weekend (my mail goes by friends from Petrópolis to Rio). It will be three or four pages in a book. I *measured* the poems & I thought they would come out just about as long as *North & South*—but I may have been mistaken. Would you consider spacing the four poems of the "Love Poems" [published as "Four Poems"] on separate pages? I also believe I shall have another pair of sonnets—maybe more—companions to the "Prodigal Son" pair.

I didn't mean, in my letter to Miss Minahan, to imply that I was considering, or wanted to leave Houghton Mifflin, certainly. It is just that I feel there *is* a book there, even if small—although you may not want a small one—and I am very eager to feel free of it. I have been working mostly on stories for about a year now. I think I have eight good short ones & one fairly long one. Miss May Swenson, who is typing them for me in N.Y., will send the short ones fairly soon. I'm afraid you can't possibly read this [handwriting], but I shall send the last (I hope) poem of the book in ten days—and a more *legible* letter.

To Kit and Ilse Barker

August 29, 1953

. . . We'd be awfully pleased to see Mr. Gross—or Dr. Gross, as I suppose he is. (Almost every man one meets here, of the meetable class, is a doctor. I think I'm even a *doutora* because of a simple B.A.) Also almost everyone one meets speaks English, and as you say I don't know how they do it sometimes. Lota says they just have to be good at languages, like Russians, because no one ever speaks Portuguese. It would be a great pleasure to see him—we don't see very many people, really. Lota has "retired," as she says, from "society," and just sees her old friends & I don't know a single American here . . . We can see him in Petrópolis on a weekend—or in Samambaia, which is 6 or 7 miles out of Petrópolis. Now that Lota has finished her road, almost anyone can drive up from the highway. At first we could only make it in the Land Rover. But now we have about a mile of cut stone that I feel rivals the Amalfi Drive.

31st

I am leading up to a joke. A friend of ours has just started working as secretary for the Minister of Foreign Affairs here and the other night she went to an enormous ball given by the Chilean Embassy. Her boss's wife, a very simple soul, was sitting beside President Vargas at dinner. The ices were in the shape of ballet dancers, with sherbet inside, and she said to Vargas (or Getúlio, as we say here): "The *best* part is under the skirt!" (He laughed.)

I move only in very anti-Vargas circles. Things are looking very bad for him now, though. But there is another awful man who is determined to be the next President and probably will be, just through publicity. Lota says if he gets in she'll leave Brazil for good. Until Vargas, her father was always in politics. He was exiled several times; they have the straw hat with a bullet hole through the brim he was wearing one day when shot at. Lota says at the convent for a few years the girls whose fathers were in prison—hers was—didn't speak to the socially inferior girls whose fathers were out, all in the best South American tradition. Now there is going to be a tremendous banquet and Freedom of the Press Day in honor of her father. He's a newspaper editor. The papers are full of it. Unfortunately she hasn't spoken to him for years. But it is very strange to me to live in a country where the ruling class and the intellectual class are so very small and all know each other and are all usually related. It's certainly bad for the "arts" too—it's entirely too easy to get a reputation and never do anything else, and never have to compete. Well, it's all because of NO MIDDLE CLASS.

Lota just told me that a little boy who is helping Paulo has a "very good old Portuguese name." It turns out to be *Magellan*. It's funny how in this undeveloped-yet-decadent country one feels so much closer to the past than one ever could in the U.S.A.

My last *Botteghe Oscure* finally arrived and yes, I thought George Barker's poem was about the best thing in it. Also Carson McCullers's story, or beginning of a book, I guess it is. Did I also tell you, I can't remember, that *The New Yorker* finally took a very long story, "In the Village"? I am feeling very rich. I asked Pearl to have them send you the one with "Gwendolyn" in it, but it really is *not* much of anything.

The other one is much better. I am really getting interested in what I now think is the Art of story writing. I just wrote off some prose-poetry from time to time before. I'm afraid "In the Village" is pretty much that, too —but now I am taking it more seriously and thinking about *people*, balancing this with that, time, etc.—and I'm hoping whatever I write will be a little less precious and "sensitive," etc., in the future. Which mostly means that I appreciate what you are trying to do more.

I read a lot of reviews of the book about [General] Gordon. Mrs. Carlyle's letters are wonderful—I read them long ago and am now thinking of acquiring them for myself. I have just finished two volumes of letters—Hart Crane's and Edna St. Vincent Millay's and I don't know which is more depressing. I suppose his is, it was all over quicker—but she isn't quite so narcissistic and has some sense of humor, at least. But it isn't really fair to judge by letters—modern letters. People seem to write to complain, mostly (present company excepted of course)—and chiefly write to their families, and to families one always has to boast in order to make oneself clear, etc. I boast terribly to my aunts, just so they'll have some notion that I do *something*. I am also reading at bedtime all of Dickens, volume by volume, with the strange ambition of writing, or rather finishing, one sonnet about him.

[September] 5th

I've been interrupted in this many times and also I have been very lazy lately. Now it is another weekend and someone will take this to Rio to mail, so I'd better finish it. The pool is full and looks very well—but now Lota is on the point of tearing it apart and making it twice as big. Tobias is fascinated and watches himself like Narcissus and climbs around on the rocks to play with the stream falling from the bamboo pipe. In fact even the workmen seem to enjoy it, everyone likes playing with water so much. And here we have so much running, rushing water. It is just piped down off the mountain into the house. The way it is arranged is my favorite thing here, I think—the men just dug a narrow gutter across a rock with chisels from the top of the cascade, and it flows straight into the pipes, cold of course, and delicious. (Meanwhile the guests at the Copacabana Palace, the fanciest hotel in Rio, are shaving with bottled water.) Here the pressure is so great that when we first used the toilet, it came right up and over—refreshing but surprising.

I am glad you and Kit (or is it Ilse I'm addressing?) believe in "tending to enjoy yourselves." So do *I* now, after about forty years of tending very much the other way & I really think we are all extremely fortunate right now.

We have an old old friend of Lota's staying with us for a week or so—he's extremely nice and no trouble—reads all day long—only at night he & Lota *will* fight about religion. He's "converted" in the Brazilian sense, meaning they've all—a great many people we know—just rediscovered the Catholic Church. The awful Spanish cousin-in-law was here for tea, too, and I somehow let myself be drawn into an argument, in Portuguese, French and English about *annulment.* She comes from a long line of Spanish Inquisitors—and in the heat of it she rose and shook her finger under my nose and screamed at me in English, which deteriorated rapidly until she was shrieking: "ANNULMENTATION! My dear girl, I *know* about ANNULMENTATION! Annulation!—The Protestations don't know a thing about Annullation!"

It is a beautiful clear day—we just drove to a nursery where I couldn't resist buying a beautiful tree about ten feet high already—a *Menaca,* I think—big, separate flowers of white, purple and pale lavender—each one of those colors, not mixed, all over it, like a big bouquet . . . I hope Kit is all better now and painting again . . . With much love to you both. I am sorry for people who can't write letters. But I suspect also that you and I, Ilse, love to write them because it's kind of like working without really doing it.

October 8, 1953

You should see our "yard" now—three English cars, all the finest, sitting in it, and why the workmen on the house don't murder us all as dirty capitalists I don't know. I read an ad for an MG for sale in the Sunday paper; a friend who "knows about cars" investigated for me and in doing so turned up a couple more MGs. Finally in my excitement Lota and I rushed to Rio and I *bought* one. It is 1952, driven very little, black with red leather—a two-seater. The 1953 one I thought of first cost several hundred dollars more and when it appeared turned out to be painted with metallic paint—they had called it "beige" but it was pure vulgar gold, and I wouldn't have set foot in it anyway. My sensations of ownership are just beginning to sink in now. I guess I'm getting so old that I don't feel rapidly any more, or something—but really, it is a wonderful little car. Lota drove it up from Rio and was very enthusiastic about the way it goes up our mountain roads. It steers so quickly that it seems rather like my old bicycle (a Raleigh) to me. I had my first lesson yesterday, and *then* I began to feel it was MINE, and wiped the radiator cap with Kleenex, etc. My long story in *The New Yorker* will just about cover it.

It is silly to have three cars here—but Lota wants to sell the Land Rover as soon as the house is almost finished. She couldn't have built it without it, though—a friend was trying to meet us in a café in Petrópolis and the waiter said, "Oh yes, I know Dona Lotinha—she's always driving loads of cement." The Jaguar is rather elderly (Lota's daydream is that we're going to buy another car in England at the beginning of our Grand Tour, whenever it will be)—and I think it will be very good for me to stop being the passenger-type I've been all my life, like a baby in a baby carriage. And Lota *loathes* going to Petrópolis to market and I don't mind a bit, so it will save emotional wear & tear here. But, Kit—I know *you* drive—isn't it fun! —Have you driven one of these little MGs? I wanted one for purely esthetic reasons to begin with, but now I think it was a good choice for here, anyway. It feels just like a big car and just zooms up our steep road to the house. They are not as beautiful as they were three years ago, I'm afraid. Apparently those narrow rims and wire spokes and small tires that gave them their real elegance proved to be very uncomfortable, so now the wheel is spoiled, and heavier—and they've changed the mudguard line a little, too, I don't know why—but I think it is still beautiful—and plenty of leg room, too, surprisingly. Lota, who is very very short, had to stop and buy two rubber pillows so she could reach the pedals. I don't know how she's ever going to get another Jaguar, either, now that they have ruined *them* and made them like big squashy American cars—they're much too big for her. Well, I have taken the bit in my teeth with this subject long enough, I guess, but it is my first car after all. I am memorizing the handbook as bedside reading. One can use an open car in comfort here the year round—except for the very rainiest part of the rainy season.

Have you sent anything to *New World Writing*, Ilse? You probably see them in England, don't you? There are three out now, no four . . . The editor is Arabel J. Porter—they have visiting editors, too. You could use my name if you want to . . . I imagine they pay fairly well . . . *The Dead Seagull* seems odd to me here, a neighbor had it—but I really liked the sentence about "My brother was drawing a picture of two horses killing each other." The Biennale sounds bigger and bigger—something like *8,000* items, now. We'll go down to São Paulo for three or four days, probably, and I hope to get in a trip to a big coffee *fazenda* while I'm there . . .

Our "Coronation" sweet peas are in full bloom—a friend brought the seeds last winter-summer, and we planted them a little late. I don't know what subtleties I was expecting, but I was rather disappointed in the red-white-&-blue—although they are beauties, enormous. We also have pots & pots of white pansies, phlox all over the place, and one water lily in the pool . . .

Our other excitement, besides my joining the car-driving class, is that Lota and I together have bought a dog for our friend Mary, who lives here a part of the time. I think maybe I should ask you to look into his family for me. The headmaster of the English school in Petrópolis raises cockers. This one is six weeks old now; his mother, "Betty," came over from England pregnant; the father, according to the schoolmaster, and I guess it must be true—he's got all kinds of cups all over the place, and photographs—was Champion of England, *Treetops* something-or-other —black. Betty is gold. This one is gold, too—and with my *dollars* he is much cheaper than one would be able to get such a dog any other place. He's a Christmas present. Mary adores them and is delighted. To be English, we have named him Philip. Now he's "Dom Philipe." We'll be bringing him home pretty soon now, I suppose. They're not my very favorite dog, being a little on the silly side, I think, but these are lovely ones, and if we can make Mary be *firm* with him. What I want for myself some time is a Highland terrier.

I must tell you something rather nice, I think. I wrote my Nova Scotian aunt that I had a pair of "bishop's socks." Lota got me some of the magenta ones they wear in a clerical store here. And such is the Protestantism and Gaelicism of Nova Scotia that my aunt wrote me and said she was *sure* "Bishop" was an *English* name and that there was no Bishop clan and she'd looked it up in the plaid book and couldn't find it, and what kind of socks could they be?

Lota's uncle, the one who went as Ambassador to Holland, died just a few days ago, and was buried in The Hague. Lota is not unsympathetic, but she is also sad because she was going to get some magnificent enameled ironware dishes from Holland. There were seven brothers or so.

This page is for Ilse

I do hope you've been able to get to work again. I have been in a dreadful slump for over a month now and I know how awful it is. I keep starting poems and working like mad for one day and then the next I think, my god! how could I have ever thought of anything so *corny*—or else it still is a good idea but there just isn't any form for it. I've decided that possibly it gets harder rather than easier as one gets older—discouraging thought—because when you first start off you don't stop to think so much—you're delighted to have the idea at all. When you're older you realize the possibilities too much—the different treatments, the different tones, the different levels, etc. Don't you think so?

But what I wanted to say was that I do hope you are feeling more hopeful about your life in general, and that it was just a mood that's gone away now. I just can't believe that people don't like you! . . . I know so many people in the U.S.A., at any rate, that do like you and it can't be so awfully different there. But I think I can probably really understand that mood pretty well now, after having lived in a foreign country for exactly two years. I used to feel the strain very much at first, in Rio particularly. Lota was naturally so eager to have her friends like and admire me, and I felt she probably was giving me too much of a build-up ahead of time and that everyone was naturally somewhat let down, and I couldn't—still can't—speak the language, so it was hard for them to speak English or French a whole evening, etc.—I have had some rather bleak stretches in which I wonder, my god, what am I doing *here?—who* am I, anyway?—did I *ever* have a personality? etc. And then two or three who were supposed to like me best, being "literary" or something, were naturally pointedly uninterested, or attacked the poor old "culture" of my great big country, or were obviously jealous. But things have gradually improved; they are accepting me more and more (Lota being so loved by her friends made them usually a little jealous that way, too). Anyway, I am caring less and less and understanding them better. But compared to being a painter, the career part of writing is a cinch, I think, and I do sympathize with you with all my heart. It *is* necessary to push more—pushing rarely does pay off, thank goodness, in writing—to "sell" and it must be very hard if one isn't naturally made that way . . . I liked you and Kit right off because you didn't show any signs of "pushing." It is one reason why I am content to leave New York for good. Everybody is so intent on using everybody else that there is no room or time for friendship any more.

As you say, work's the thing. When I'm busy I don't give a damn what anyone thinks except the very few people I really care for. But painting *is* hard that way. I am sure you don't need to reproach yourself. I was pleased that you spoke of it & maybe we can give each other a few helpful hints.

To Pearl Kazin

November 16, 1953

Lota just came back from marketing in Petrópolis & when we sat down to lunch she opened *Time* . . . and there was the notice about [the death of] Dylan Thomas. Just a few lines, saying "of undisclosed causes," "in Manhattan." It must have happened just before they went to press, or surely there would have been more in the "news" section. Good lord—I suppose it must be true, but I can't begin to believe it yet. My imagination keeps rushing from horror to horror because of the way that awful *Time* put it. Oh Pearl, it is so tragic. I hope you are not too upset by it, by whatever *did* happen to him—if anyone knows—and I hope you will be able to write and tell me what did. I want to know and I don't know anyone else I can ask.

The first time I met Dylan, when he spent a day with me doing those recordings in Washington, he and Joe Frank and I had lunch together, and even after knowing him for three or four hours, I felt frightened for him and depressed. Yet I found him so tremendously sympathetic at the same time. I said to Joe later something trite about "Why he'll kill himself if he goes on like this," and Joe said promptly, "Don't be silly. Can't you see a man like that doesn't *want* to live? I give him another two or three years." And I suppose everyone felt that way, but I don't know enough about him really to understand *why*. *Why* do some poets manage to get by and live to be malicious old bores like Frost or—probably—pompous old ones like Yeats, or crazy old ones like Pound—and some just don't!

But his poetry has that desperate win-or-lose-all quality, of course —and of course it too eliminates everything from life except something almost beyond human supportability after a while. But why oh why did he have to go & die now? Was he unhappy about those readings? I wonder.

Or recent work? I think there's a new book with some poems in it I haven't seen yet. Poets should have self-doubts left out of their systems completely—as one can see most of the surviving ones seem to have. But look at poor Cal—and Marianne, who hangs on just by the skin of her teeth and the most elaborate paranoia I've ever heard of. And of course it isn't just poets. We're all wretched and half the time or three-quarters I think it is a thoroughly disgusting world—and then the horror vanishes for a while, mercifully. But in my own minor way I know enough about drink & destruction. Please, Pearl, tell me what happened to the poor man, if you know—and can bear to.

Lota & I have been excited all week by the thought of going to Italy—and not next year, but in January. (That had something to do with my dream of you & the deck chairs.) If I sell two more stories; if she gets some expected money, we may—although I think I'd rather wait until April or May. We'd be going, idiotic as it sounds, to save money. Food has gone up about three hundred percent since I've been living here— there is talk of a revolution—again—and I don't know how the POOR are managing to keep alive. Here, feeding three or four servants—and they make the most of the privilege, poor things—besides ourselves, is costing Lota a fortune. She could rent this house while it is still bare enough and unfinished enough to rent without anyone's doing much damage, and rent the Rio apt. . . . Some ways it's a good idea, some ways not—and L. and I could live in *pensions* for six months or so and when we returned the roads would be finished here; the legal situation clarified—great messes now—and we'd both have some money. It's hard to decide and actually I don't care much—I'll travel anywhere at all or just stay here— and I don't give a damn, being such a compliant sobersides these days, more or less . . .

I have been thinking about you a lot—even dreaming, you see, and I was worried about how you were . . . And now this sad awful news. I have no way of knowing how you felt about it recently or what your feelings about Dylan were. I think I had really expected to hear news like that at any time, but even so it is a bad shock . . . But please write and tell me everything if you can. I have met few people in my life I felt such an instantaneous sympathy and pity for, and although there must have been many things wrong, disastrously wrong, Dylan made most of our contemporaries seem small and disgustingly self-seeking and cautious and hypocritical and cold . . .

To Ilse and Kit Barker

November 23, 1953
. . . We're really coming, but now it is definitely the first part of March. We plan to stay from nine months to a year, probably mostly in

Italy, Spain and Portugal, but with trips first to France and England—and of course I hope to pay at least one visit to you during this time. I have gradually learned that Lota's greatest trouble is she hates to *decide* anything—wavers back and forth for days and gets really sick about things—whereas although I have plenty of other quirks of my own, that isn't one of them. So now I just save us both a lot of trouble by saying, "All right, let's make it the 2nd of March 1954," and everything is settled. (I can do it because I think that most human decisions don't mean two pins one way or the other; it's just like throwing dice, and doesn't seem to bother me at all.) We'll probably fly, although I'd really rather go by boat—but at that season it's apt to be terribly rough and I guess I can stand 24 hours' fear to save Lota 15 days' acute boredom. Besides, it's even cheaper to fly now . . .

Oh!—*Moulin Rouge.* Yes, I saw it, and although I agree with you and all the critics about the marvelous use of color for the first time—at least the first time I've seen it that good—on the whole I didn't like it. It was untrue to Lautrec's life and personality—just a bunch of sentimental lies. I found it so infuriating I almost walked out! Have you read any of the lives of Lautrec? —There's a good study in French, I can't remember who wrote it now—and then the Gerstle Mack one. The story was completely idiotic in the movies; the family was nothing like that. His father was completely indifferent to him—didn't even go to his funeral. (His father also kept bees in his house in Paris and had a favorite mare he *milked* outside his Paris house.) And Lautrec wasn't any self-pitying poker face like that. He had many friends and was a wit, a critic & notorious for his sexual exploits—the prostitutes adored him, etc. It's impossible to imagine him mooning around because of romantic love for one of them. Drink certainly got him—but that incredible "pure" model! Well, maybe I'm being too severe, but I thought it could have made a really good movie if they'd only half-tried to tell the truth. I did like seeing all the blown-up paintings, though. What you said about the inexplicable appeal of Zsa Zsa Gabor to the gentlemen was so funny—exactly the same thing happened here. An old friend of Lota's, a very worldly gentleman, about 35, what they call here a *gran fino*, came to tell us we *must* go to see it. "Ah! That Zsa Zsa Gabor!" he kept saying, snapping his fingers, "She's *uma uva*!"—a *grape*. All that redundant squirming didn't even strike me as being voluptuous, but I guess I just don't know—he is still talking about that "little grape"!

"Mary" is an American girl a few years younger than I am who's been living in Brazil for 10 or 12 years and is an old friend of Lota's, a very nice tall bony Boston type. She was here this past weekend with the spaniel, Philip, again—now just about three months old and getting really pretty—but heavens, the flower beds went like snow. I got her a good book—even if it sounds silly—*How to Live Your Dog's Life*—something like that—an American trainer and breeder, full of helpful hints—but

I'm afraid Mary will never learn to say NO the way the book says. *It* says NO isn't guttural enough for most dogs, and you should say ACH! instead—you should be able to manage that, Ilse . . .

I shouldn't have picked the rainy season here to start learning to drive. I haven't had a lesson in over a week. The last time Lota and I came up from Rio it started pouring about halfway up. The MG did beautifully until we came to one stretch of our dirt road that had just been fixed and was covered with just a little loose dirt and we stuck and couldn't get it up. By that time it was dark and of course we had no flashlight. I timidly poked rocks under the rear wheels and Lota tried and tried and we got wetter & wetter and finally we had to give up and walk up the rest of the way. It was so dark that we kept walking off the road, and skidding ourselves. We held hands across the middle and tried to keep in the ruts but even so got off into the woods or over the bank— all I could see of Lota was a small pair of *white* shoes. It was about a mile up the mountain. When we finally made it, Lota and Paulo, the gardener, went back in the Land Rover to collect our bags because I was being very boring about two new sweaters I had just received from New York that I didn't want stolen, etc. It wasn't until the next morning Lota remembered that she had left the week's pay for all the workmen on the land here in the glove compartment—but it was there, strange to say. (I've already had two hubcaps stolen in Rio.)

. . . In *Time*—two weeks ago now—I saw a mysterious little announcement of the death of Dylan Thomas. It must be true, but I still can't believe it—even if I felt during the brief time I knew him that he was headed that way. I just can't believe it and dread what might have happened to him—in New York . . . Thomas's poetry is so narrow—just a straight conduit between birth & death, I suppose—with not much space for living along the way.

To Marianne Moore

December 8, 1953

. . . In a frantic attempt to catch up with you, I've asked Brentano's to send you a little book for Christmas, but you may well have seen it already—Huizinga's *Erasmus*. It is very slow at first, but around Chapter 5 it starts getting better. I like Huizinga very much . . . Another one of his that I have just read in French, and admired—I don't believe it's been translated yet—*Homo Ludens*. Much better than the *Erasmus*, really. Also sometime in a month or so, if they have it in stock, you will get a book from London called *A Naturalist in Brazil*. I found a copy here quite by accident and I like it so much—the only book that really tells the things one wants to know—that I decided you should have it too, if possible . . . It's just a very good, old-fashioned account of the flora and fauna and the man who wrote it sounds nice—although he was a dreadful photographer, you'll see. He's particularly good about insects, I think, and forestry. (One of Lota's great interests. We have a neighbor who is determined to be the President-after-next—he might even make it—and who says he'll appoint her head of the Dept. of Forestry if he is!) The fireflies *are* extraordinary, in case I didn't tell you before, large and green and much steadier than ours, and they keep right on even in the heaviest tropical rains. Also there is another variety, quite a large insect, we see once in a while, that floats steadily toward you with a really big milky blue light—it can be quite frightening, like a burglar, or a distant train even.

Trains—there is a funny one below us, called the *Leopoldina*, for some Portuguese princess. It is narrow gauge, with a really 1860-looking engine, a funnel-shaped smokestack, lots of brass, and little flags on either side. When L. was small it was very chic. An English company ran it and it was built in England, beautiful paneling, hanging gas lamps, wicker seats, etc. She used to come up from her convent in Rio and her house had its own little station beside the track. Now since the highway has been built and the country took it away from England, it has deteriorated very much, but it still looks pretty and toy-like, and goes very slowly. In the summer now we occasionally go to a neighbor's house to see movies, and the track runs right below the garden. At one point in the entertainment *Leopoldina* whistles coming around the curve below, and there on the screen is the shadow of her cloud of smoke. Everyone says that its station in Rio is exactly like a miniature Paddington.

I am still liking living here very much, more and more in fact, and in spite of occasional cycles of asthma-bronchitis, etc., I am feeling better than I have in twenty years, I think. I have also got very thin. I believe it is the wonderful coffee, and the *maté*, which is really a good drink—not as delicate as tea, but supposed to be full of salts and minerals, etc. The gauchos in the south live on it and beef, supposedly. I've been working quite a lot recently but I haven't too much to show for it yet. I think the book of poems will appear in the spring, although I've been very unreliable with Houghton Mifflin, I know. It is my fault now, not theirs. I also think I'll have a book of stories out in another year. (There is to be one, I think, in the December 19th *New Yorker* ["In the Village"]. I wish you would read it and tell me, please, exactly what you think. At first I thought it was my best, so far—now I have doubts . . .)

Did I tell you—I don't think I did—how Manuel Bandeira, *the* poet here now, a very nice man about 65 or so—took me to see his apartment one night? Although not nearly as big as yours, it reminded me so much of yours I felt quite homesick. He had put up some shelves too—his kitchen was just as neat—although he says he can cook nothing except coffee and an awful sweet much in favor here made of boiled milk and sugar. He had all his pots and pans on another very Brazilian arrangement—like a small Christmas tree. But his books and pictures and sofa and desk were so much like yours. He is extremely interested in your poetry, too, and I imagine he can really appreciate it because the translations of his I've seen are excellent—although he refuses to speak a word of English. We left him about 1 a.m. and went downstairs in the elevator. They have a system of locking the outside apartment-house doors at night, and . . . for some reason or other we couldn't get out. And there was no porter. Finally Lota started back to get the poet—and neither of us could remember the floor or the number of his apartment. However, after two or three tries, she found him and the poor man came down in green striped pajamas and a bright red dressing gown and flapping slippers, to let us out.

Poets—even when they're bad, as they mostly are—are much more highly thought of here than in the U.S., a nice old-fashioned romantic idea of the *Poet*. Bandeira was annoyed by the view from his window: a dismal courtyard which had never been paved and was full of mud and garbage, etc. So he wrote a complaint to the city in the form of a poem. Someone, no one knows who, wrote a beautiful poem right back, and the courtyard was promptly fixed! (I doubt the Dept. of Sanitation in Brooklyn would do that—but maybe they would now for *you*, after what you have said about Brooklyn.)

I have been very saddened, as I suppose so many people have, by Dylan Thomas's death. His visit to the Library [of Congress] was one of the few nice spots of my dismal year in Washington. (And I wonder what on earth the Library has done with all the records he made for me.) I don't think I ever discussed his poetry with you—but I think he had an amazing gift for a kind of naked communication that makes a lot of poetry look like translation.

. . . Sammy is flourishing. The cat, Tobias, is a beauty, and so good and hardworking—we couldn't keep house without him. One night recently it started to pour—this is the rainy season—and I had forgotten to put the cover on Sammy's cage. I rushed out and he was standing stretched straight up, like a stick, with his beak pointing to heaven and his eyes shut tight, the water pouring down him. I didn't know he could make himself so long. I suppose it was a protective trick, but he looked exactly like Brancusi's *Bird in Flight* . . .

I am sorry about this strange paper. Lota has gone to Rio for two days—to finish renting the apartment there—and she is getting me some more. Also I realize my typing is very bad, but please forgive me. I wanted to write to you badly, and for a long time, and I was afraid if I started slowly I'd stop all over again. Here are some seeds I've been saving for you since the tree bloomed last month—an enormous tall thin tree with a bright green trunk (like some of Rousseau's trees that have green trunks as well as leaves) with feathery plumes at the top and bright yellow flowers—a *Saboteira*—supposedly because the French made sabots from the wood. Lota's sister, who has a house below us, has a beautiful wild garden that goes on and on, exactly like old travel engravings, with grottos, waterfalls, rustic seats, etc. For a week or two the whole garden was littered with these seeds and the air full of them . . . We built a little pool outside the dining room, with a bamboo pipe coming out of the rocks, like a spring, and the water falling into an old soapstone bowl—and over. It is quite pretty—brick pavements all around—we fancy somewhat like Siena. The pool has an overflow pipe that is flush with the edge (a drain is called here a *ladrão*, or "thief") and Tobias sits for hours beside it, thrusting his front paws, first one then the other, down the pipe and then pulling them quickly out again . . .

To Joseph and U. T. Summers

December 9, 1953

. . . I can't find your last letter, and realized if I conducted a thorough search I'd probably put off writing to you again. And what is Joe teaching, and did you get any work done on your trip—Italian or English? Weren't you going to see [George] Herbert's church? . . . I finally got Miss Tuve's book and although I admire what she is trying to do—attack other Herbert criticism, or Empson—I must say I find her rather hard reading. And my beautiful new Herbert was one of the books that got lost coming here. I have promised myself to buy the next one in England.

Paul Brooks is good and annoyed with me and I can't blame him a bit. I've stalled and stalled about two or three last poems for a year almost—but still I hope he'll put me on that spring list. The [*Diary*] translation I think I told you about is coming along slowly—very slowly —but I really think that Houghton Mifflin or some other house will take it; it seems a safe thing to me. However, now I guess I'll stop working on it while I'm away—& I'll probably be away just long enough to forget what Portuguese I have so painfully acquired. (It is a difficult language —much more so than Spanish—and here I don't get much chance to speak it—except kitchen Portuguese. I can recite recipes, that's about all, and tell how to baste, fry, marinate ["let sleep"], etc.) Lota will probably speak fluent Italian in no time—fluent and incorrect. She can read it now, but apparently all the Latins can understand each other all right and never learn the other's language well.

I like living here more and more all the time, I think—but it isn't because it's Brazil, particularly, or even a foreign country—or at all a foreign country, I should say. It is just that where I am living and what I am doing seem to suit me perfectly for the first time in ages—and surely at this stage of history and airplanes *and the wireless* we don't have to brood too much about expatriation. I wish it weren't quite so expensive to get to New York but I really don't want to go back just yet anyway.

Probably winter after next I'll try to get there for three or four months. Pearl has been such a helpful friend and a good correspondent, too. She has sent us curtains and blue jeans, and—illegally—paper matches and Major Grey Chutney. (I finally came to the conclusion that *was* a little too effete, and got some mangoes and ginger and made my own—a fair imitation—by following the label on Major Grey.) . . . I also read all of Dickens, Trollope, Freud (Lota has a large psychological library), all the memoirs of and travels in Brazil that the British Council has, innumerable works on compost and orchards and beekeeping (another of L.'s good sections in her library). I found her reading the *Nut-Grower's Manual* the other day—we haven't any, though, though some date pits have sprouted into small palms. Are your gardening activities big enough to consider compost? If so I'm going to give you a list of fantastic books—English— in which compost has been elevated to a sort of religious cult. Here there is a question as to whether it's of any use at all—everything rots so fast anyway. But we have ants that have been making compost for millions of years—you see them carrying large leaves. I think we have them in the U.S. too—but I'd never realized before that in the compost they breed a kind of worm to eat that is only bred by the ants—never appears in a natural state . . .

To Randall Jarrell

December 12, 1953

Bill Cole of Alfred Knopf, whom I've just barely met, was very nice and sent me *Poetry and the Age* when it came out and I've been meaning to write you about it just about every day ever since. I think I'd seen everything in it—but read right straight through; the *wallop* is ten times better, I think, and I really think you deserve a medal—not an arts & letters one, but a real one. You are the only person I know who can speak *naturally* about poetry—it doesn't seem as if it should be so hard, but apparently it is—and who doesn't seem to be apologizing to the reader all the time for bringing up the rather awkward and embarrassing subject. Or going out of his way to *show off*—which is what they all do more or less. Your showing off is nice and the right kind—it just comes from someone getting excited and enthusiastic and "carried away" and funnier and funnier. I don't always agree with you about particular poems— there's something still *unturned* about Frost—something slightly unpleasant under that lichen-covered stone—but I lack the clarity and drive to see what it is. Anyway—it's a breath of fresh air, to coin a phrase (Viereck's one being so very obnoxious)—I think it was very well received, too, wasn't it?—I see *Hudson, Kenyon, Partisan Review, Poetry*—some reviews. And it is all so much fun, too—and you have really superb comparisons, like turning a 100-watt bulb on & off. It's the kind of thing I say to myself, or think I do, in my best moments, or dream just before waking up, and lose—or at least that's the effect of *positive* insight it gives me—why of course; it's true, it's almost a law of nature.

I am a little embarrassed, I don't know why, about my small share in it and I think considering the stature of the others you're discussing it was most gentlemanly of you to keep me in. And thank you very much —that review of yours is the one I hold on to in dark stretches and in a foreign country!

Someone is waiting to take my mail to Rio and of course I only started this letter, the most important, at the last minute. I wish you'd write me a letter and tell me what you are doing. I know you have married again—Margaret Marshall wrote me and then I had a kind of dismal visit—so it seemed to me—from Zabel, who emitted cool bits of news from time to time, as if anyone younger than 50 were, of course, mad— I don't know why. He got going on Cal and I put a stop to that by saying I liked him *very much*. Mr. Zabel said, "Oh yes—you would!" I have been rather depressed about Dylan Thomas, as I suppose everyone has —I don't believe I ever talked with you about his poetry—which some-times moves me to tears and sometimes infuriates me. I've been holding up H. Mifflin for months with two or three last poems—but I think it's really a sure thing this spring now, and I'm rather scared. Aren't you having a new book of poems soon or have I just missed one by any chance?

I like it here better and better—not because it's Brazil at all, but just a good place to live. I even bought a car, an MG—two-seater—black and red upholstery—very adolescent taste but I am crazy about it and zoom up the mountains—rather slowly, to tell the truth—with the cut-out open. It is fun driving; I'd never driven before. I am going abroad in February—mostly Italy. Is there any chance of your being in Italy to *see*? Lota is going to buy a car there first thing. I think you have daughters, too—& you & they must both like that! With love . . .

To Ilse and Kit Barker

February 5, 1954

. . . The cruzeiro here took a sudden and awful plunge, a real inflation, and Lota of course just doesn't know what to do. For example, prices in Paris for her would now be exactly twice as much as they were for a friend of ours who came back just before Christmas. Things remain the same for me, and here, of course, I've been getting richer and richer; but for about a month Lota gave up all ideas of travel completely. Now things look slightly better—they are supposed to get back to normal in two months, although no one believes that, really—and we're beginning to plan again. But Brazil has never been in a worse state, apparently—food prices are incredible and I just don't know how the poor *poor* people are keeping alive. So from week to week we were waiting to see what was going to happen to the currency. Then besides, Lota was in a state of indecision about the car. The currency doesn't matter too much as far as that goes, because the worse it gets here, the more she can sell the Land Rover and her old Jaguar for, and from the sale of those she's planning to buy the new car. (I'll be doing the buying, officially. There are new laws, too, that will make it impossible for her to bring one back, but a spoiled American still can.) We have gone through Mercedes-Benzes, Alfa Romeos, Ferraris, etc. etc., and now I think we are back again at the Jaguar. The Italian cars are much the most beautiful, but highly impractical for here. L.'s architect bought one and it heats up so on short drives that every time he starts out he has to go all the way to São Paulo, the only long, straight, good road in the country—which is playing havoc with his work, it seems. L. doesn't like the new Jaguars—they are so puffed up and Americanized—but now I guess it really will be one after all, since the best repair shop is for them; she knows them, etc.

Oh this incredible country! (I have to say that sometimes and since I can't aloud, may I please say it to you, who won't repeat it, I'm sure?) We have received some wonderful pamphlets from the Jaguar people, also the Sunbeam Alpine. I am writing the Jaguars today, too. They seem to think we don't know about importing laws—that's the only aspect we *do* know about, of course—but well, anyway (I don't know why I always write you such particularly confused letters and I'm sorry—I have too much to say) I *think* we're planning to come still, if the cruzeiro doesn't get sicker, but it will probably be about a month later—in April . . .

I don't know whether you'll care for it ["In the Village"] or not, but at least it *is* better than "Gwendolyn," which never was very good. There are one or two spots that *The New Yorker* changed—I am mad, but it was my own fault because I let it go without the final proof. But please make allowances! I'm not really a story writer, you know—never meant to be at all. Writing stories is just much better for one, when one can't write poems, than dissipation, say.

The Biennale was thoroughly exhausting, but we had a nice time, even so. As I said, in my note that you may never get, I was quite reconciled to Henry Moore by the two *beautiful* things he had there—*King & Queen* and a reclining woman, in a good old Mayan pose. (I can't say I understand why he brings in Mexico so much in those things for the *Time & Life* building, can you? Except that they're some form of Calendar stones, but that seems both obvious and farfetched.) The English painters I thought were pretty disappointing—one—Scott—makes one feel, "My god! what rationing has done!" I think I almost liked Patrick Heron and his snarls of twine best of them all. There were many too many paintings from most countries. A couple of ravishing Marinis. Fortunately we got there rather late and almost everything good had been sold to rich São Paulo coffee planters—otherwise I don't think Lota—who adores to buy things—

would ever be able to leave Brazil for the rest of her life. She could only get two Kokoschka lithographs; and I bought a drawing by a young American I know and like. But she is determined to get a classic figure, about six feet high, twisted bronze, draped in a toga, by Mascherini—know him?—to put on the corner of the terrace here. Even if I find the *feet* a little *chichi* I don't blame her a bit. It is lovely, really—a young Paulista had reserved it, but he may well change his mind. I'm afraid if he does that you will not see me or Lota for a couple more years.

But in spite of inflation Lota is feeling very set up these days. Her house won the first prize in the architecture exhibit for an architect under 40, or something like that. Gropius was a judge, and naturally Lota is busting with pride because she knows, and I know, and a few other friends, that all the good ideas were hers and not the architect's at all, charming man as he is. So not only does she want to adorn the terrace with a bronze statue but she'd like very much to finish the house, and is torn between that and going abroad. Now I think I can get some photographs from the show to send you, at last. The photographer shut himself in the *sala* and turned the chairs all catty-cornered and turned the sofa pillows diamondwise on the sofa. Otherwise they're pretty good.

I think it is very nice the way you write me about an *old* house, and I write you about a *new* house, all the time. But after all, they are the only two kinds good to live in.

It has been so long since I've written that I haven't yet told you that your Christmas card was much admired and was by far the prettiest I received . . . I am eager to see "The Age of Discretion"—and shall undoubtedly be seeing it in *Botteghe Oscure*. I hope *The New Yorker* takes your story, too—if only for the money—it would pay for your new wall, and more besides. You know Lota has sub-rented the apartment in Rio. I think I wrote you when that was going on. Everything we had there is of course stored here now and every day of my life my package to you stares me in the face. It has been an unusually hot summer and I haven't been near Rio in months . . .

An American couple finally took the apartment—a very sad, stupid couple—he is some kind of specialist for the government—lost, and loathing Brazil, of course, but glad to get a nice cool apartment at last. The woman's first name happens to be Elizabeth, too . . . It led to the utmost confusion. Apparently she had got it through her head that they use only first names here, so when anyone called she always said, "This is Elizabeth," then gave up. Several friends called day after day and screamed and yelled and asked me what was the matter with me, where was Lota, etc., and the poor woman kept on saying it was Elizabeth, over and over.

Christmas here was very nice—we had a couple of guests—I stuffed the turkey—I received the Phaidon *Vermeer*, among other nice things— It was a hot day with intermittent thunderstorms, and late at night we made a few calls on our elderly neighbors—much kissing and hugging, hand-kissing, and little glasses of *caocaça*, while the rain poured down and an enormous frog called the "Blacksmith" lived up to his name just beyond the porch in the garden. There is also a bird that makes an even louder metallic noise—like Arthur Rank's gong, only right in your ear. People even keep them in their apartments in Rio. —Oh, I have seen one good movie, *Jeux Interdits*, did you see it? The last night we were in São Paulo, and too tired to think any more, Lota and I were lured into *Quo Vadis* because the sign said it was "refrigerated," as they call it here—and I had yet to see anything outsize. But don't—even as a joke —don't go. It is too disgusting.

For two weeks we have had Lota's adopted son's wife and baby here—did I ever tell you about Kylso, the adopted son? Well, the wife is very young, somewhat dumb, and terrified of Lota and me, although we are naturally kind and gentle, it seems to me. The baby is just a year old, a little girl, Maria Helena, the nickname is "Nené"—very cute and good. They have just gone. Brazilians take having babies around so much more for granted than Americans do—even I am improving with them, I think—and I certainly could not resist Nené, who held up her arms and showed all her teeth and called me *Auntie*! She calls Lota *Vové*, or *Grandma*, which disconcerts L. a bit—being my age. But it was our chief entertainment to watch her playing with the cat and the cocker—all in a heap—occasional shrieks, but usually the puppy seemed to get the worst of it. But the visit was somewhat of a strain. Now Kylso wants Lota to adopt the little girl, too, but I don't believe she will. Children need both parents if possible—and younger parents, too.

I am very interested in the possibility of Kit's studio—after having one of my own now I don't see how anyone ever gets along without one. You can get really handsome "pre-fab" things now, too. Heavens, *let's* see you in Rome! Wouldn't that be fun. I am dying to discuss art, literature, and lesser things with you both and I'm just afraid I'll talk too much. I've been somewhat pent for so long now. Please forgive me for stalling about writing—it is hard to make a letter about complete uncertainty—all I can say now is things look more hopeful. L. seems to have gone back to a Jaguar—and we thank you very much for your help in the matter . . . Are you both well? Did I tell you I'd got very skinny, for me?

Feb. 7

Heavens, I'd like to see that Flemish show I keep reading about. Have you been able to get to see it?

This is Sunday p.m.—a friend here for the weekend—called here Osh-*car*—is about to go down to Rio and will take my mail. This is a dreadful letter and please don't think I am getting mentally confused in Brazil. I'm really much more clear-headed than when I used to be seeing you. The situation looks very grim today—the cruzeiro took another slump. I think it's up to me to earn a lot of $$$$$$ somehow. We saw an old friend of Lota's in São Paulo—a beautiful girl and a particularly beautiful one here, since she has blue eyes—who owns over a million coffee trees. I hadn't been talking to the really rich for so long I'd forgotten how incredible they can be, even if nice, like this one. It was a ghastly hot day and at luncheon I remarked something about salt tablets, and she said, oh yes, they sold them now in São Paulo. So I said had she ever tried them, and she said with the most innocent astonishment, "Oh *no*! They're just for people who *perspire*!" . . .

To Paul Brooks

[CABLE]

February 12, 1954

TERRIBLY SORRY DELAY. AFRAID I CANNOT PROMISE ANYTHING IMMEDIATELY ALTHOUGH WORK PROGRESSES. HOPE YOU WILL CONSIDER PUBLISHING BOOK AS IT IS NOW. WRITING.

To Pearl Kazin

February 22, 1954

Lota and I were going to Italy next month, but now I think it's all off because of the dangerously feeble state of the cruzeiro . . . I really don't mind much, having lots of work to get done, and I'd like to have more money saved up before I start off, anyway. But it's made me suddenly realize I must take Brazil more seriously and really learn the damned language. I'd stopped all efforts when I thought we were going away for a year. I must decide what I'm going to think about it if I live here for good and all. As a country I feel it's *hopeless*—not in the horrible way Mexico is, but just plain lethargic, self-seeking, half-smug, half-crazy, hopeless. The U.S. may be in a fearful moral mess right now, but I feel what made it great was not geography (as the Brazilians say) but the enormous moral *push* behind it to begin with. There has never been one here, as far as I know—and there has never been a revolution, which every country needs, I should think—successful or unsuccessful. The few honest & intelligent men one hears about—like Ruy Barbosa—seem to have been like comets—but so very few of them. I sometimes feel if I could only meet *one* man here who seemed really concerned and honest—I suppose Carlos Lacerda is honest all right, but I think he's got too much ego and will probably end up in about ten years as a cynical politician. (We see a great deal of him, and I must say he's much the most interesting and entertaining person to talk to I've met so far.) . . . I wish there were somebody I could talk to about it! Lota is, after all, a

Brazilian, and no matter how fair everyone wants to be, nationality always gets in the way sooner or later . . .

Manuel Bandeira sent me a hammock for Christmas—and since then I've seen pictures of him writing in one, so I guess that's the Brazilian spirit in literature. His elderly Dutch mistress, whom I've never met and who has the unbelievable name of Madame Blank, was so overcome with "In the Village" that she sent me a large Dutch gingerbread. It is rather curious, because Cal had written me that the story reminded him of a Dutch landscape. All I can think of is that just the idea of a cow is Dutch to some people. I had some awfully nice fan letters—one from the president of the Ball Bearing Rolling Pin Company with a picture of one at the top. It wasn't to me, but to *The New Yorker*—very cranky—saying at last they had shown the *sense*, etc. He didn't sound at all like the kind of man who'd like that story and I was rather surprised at Katharine's sending the letter to me—but I liked it the best of all, naturally. I had a good spell of work and then a long bad one, but now I think I'm taking up poetry again at last.

And I'm getting off a blurb—my first—for *Pictures from an Institution*. Bill Cole asked me for one and I felt I couldn't refuse, although it has been a dreadful chore . . . I'm trying to say something true enough—he [Randall Jarrell] *is* funny, but this book affects me like an overlong visit. It's too incessant and hysterical, and then when he isn't being mean about Mary [McCarthy], he gets sentimental about Germans, etc. Well, maybe one shouldn't say "mean." I haven't seen much of Mary for years and years, but it's *her*. She's still saying some of the same things she said at college, apparently. Oh poor girl, really. You know, I think she's never felt very real, and that's been her trouble. She's always pretending to be something-or-other and never quite convincing herself or other people. When I knew her well I was always torn between being furious with her and being very touched by her—because in those days her pretensions were so romantic and sad. Now that they're so grandiose, I suppose it's much harder to take. And I still feel mean about writing a blurb for a book about her—she was so pretty at 17! Well, I imagine I'll get over that. Did you see her last effort in *PR*? The note said it was a chapter from a book called *The Group* and I already recognize the characters, more or less. "The Group" is the—or was the—Vassar rooming system, and a rather cruel one. I never belonged to one, thank goodness, and Mary was a year ahead of me, anyway—but I've seen her reduce members of her "group" to tears many times, and I have an awful feeling I'll probably appear in the book, and with all of Mary's second thoughts, heaven help me. It's fantastic writing—good, but without one shred of imagination, something that seems almost impossible—but Mary does it.

Saturday two carloads of people arrived—including the architect and L.'s adopted son, Kylso—a very heavy American boy—and three little girls dressed to kill and badly made up—"models." Since the house got ιe prize we've had quite a few such visitors to see it. The American ιrned out to be a photographer for *Reader's Digest*, taking pictures for the *cover*. I said I didn't know they used them, and he replied, "Oh of course in the U.S. they use *watercolors*." If you can follow that. He decided the house wasn't finished enough to take. Apparently the idea was that Lota and I should conceal ourselves, while the three sad little models posed in the house—later to have the table of contents superimposed on them, I suppose. It was very queer. It is beginning to remind me of my stay in Hemingway's house, where I had to chase tourists out of the front yard all the time . . .

To Ilse and Kit Barker

February 25th or 6th [1954]
Friday, anyway

Fridays always seem to be the days when everything goes wrong— with the hired help, at least. We seem to have to have a weekly blow-up equivalent to that last volcano in Mexico to keep things going, and Lota has just retired to her room, rather pale and tired, to recuperate from blowing up everybody—four people—consecutively, and I've just had a trying session in the bottom of the little swimming pool with Julinho, the little gardener, so called, trying to get him to clean it right. (He did it beautifully the first time, but this time did nothing at all, and that is one of the chief troubles—no one *ever* learns *anything*, and a "habit" is unheard of.) I pointed out to him one of the beautiful little wine-color and yellow crabs that live in it, and *wham* went his shovel and that was the end of that crab. Sometimes one gets awfully tired of primitive people, I must confess. And now I've made us sound like a couple of disagreeable old maids when actually we get along better with our help and put up a better *show*—at a luncheon, or something—than any other people I know here, except one wonderful lady in Rio. It's a sad country, and it hasn't gone through yet—and I suppose never will—a period of having *good* servants, as England used to have, and then emerging into another period. There is a really pleasant intimacy with the people who work for you and Brazil is by far the most "democratic" place I've ever seen, in some ways—but nobody knows how to do *anything* well, and nobody has the slightest sense of "style," I suppose is what it amounts to. So having underlined enough words for three letters, I'll sit back and relax and write you a note right off the bat, because I was so pleased to get your letter last night. I'll answer *it* too, and not just wander off on my own any more.

Well, I'm glad you agreed with me about the English part of the Biennale because that's what I thought, too . . . I think Herbert Read is an esthetic glutton—he just has to understand and feel the "significance" of everything, regardless, and mentally he is an enormous fat man eating away indiscriminately. Ivon Hitchens I have certainly heard of but I can't seem to recall any particular pictures. I'll have to look through Lota's collection of art books, I guess. I received the new book about Klee for my birthday but the woman is awfully silly—though the pictures are worth it. I also got a huge, fairly new, Cézanne book—this one is best for Meyer Schapiro's text, chiefly. The Biennale just whetted my appetite for some more pictures. It's too bad Lota's uncle in Holland, that ambassador, died, because we were planning to stay with him on our trip and see paintings. *Did* you see that Flemish show?—I've read good and bad reviews. (I get so many more English magazines than any others that I know more what is going on there than in N.Y.—and perhaps the English magazines have a higher average of criticism—in fact, they do.)

I'm going to order the *London Review* today—I had just read about it—and *Encounter*, too, I suppose. And I never can spell *Botegghe Oscure* right, either.

. . . I'm nervous about your seeing it ["In the Village"]. I know I'm not a story writer, really—this is just poetic prose. And completely autobiographical (although not in the usual *New Yorker* manner). I've just stuck a few years together. Fortunately the aunt most involved in it all— my only nice relative—likes it very much and even corrected some names, and reminded me of this and that. We have equally literal imaginations . . . A poet here sent me a hammock for Christmas—bright purple and green fiber underneath, like a large soft brush. I was surprised, but very pleased and it looks well outside the studio, against one slate-blue wall —and it is very comfortable, too. I notice that literary people here often seem to have their pictures taken in them, and whether that's what's wrong with Brazilian writing or not—perhaps I'll find out.

Your parties sound so nice they make me feel slightly blue. We've just had two weeks of one of Lota's oldest friends, Alfredo—a very sweet, literary fellow, but in a terrible state of neurosis or something or other, and certainly not much fun to have around. Now it is the beginning of Carnival and we're going to have a couple more friends for four or five days, ladies this time, one of whom I like very much—she has a little more *esprit*, possibly—and I probably like her because she thinks I'm *terribly* funny. Rosinha Leão—or Rosie Lion, which I think is very cute. There's a Rio politician now called So-&-So Panta Leão, and all over the billboards people have changed it to *E*spanta Leão, which means "He frightens the lion."

We've been hearing the *sambas* for this year's Carnival. They make a new batch every year, all the samba clubs, and sometimes they are terribly clever. Their political wit and love-affair wit here is better than ours, I think, but the Latin approach to LIFE in general is much more serious—less self-conscious, I suppose. Your saying you sang *Carmen* made me think of it. Sometimes Lota and her friends go through the best sambas of the last twenty years. One friend, very tiny, is famous because one year she never stopped sambaing for 48 hours (or maybe it was 72), and Lota & various partners, now rich businessmen or elderly playboys, won many *cups*. We're always running into baldish gentlemen in Petrópolis, and after the hugs Lota introduces them and says, "We won a cup for a samba in 1935." That is, for dancing them, not composing them.

I made a birthday cake for Mary Morse—February 14. My dears, it was a triumph—four layers, chocolate, full of chocolate cream, with pink peppermint icing and her name in silver dragées. Then Maria, the cook, decided to make a surprise and produced another cake in three tiers, slightly crooked, rather like a romantic false ruin. *Heavy*—you could almost hear it thud in your stomach—and for days we gave pieces to the dogs on the sly. Yesterday she made a *pudim* (that must be "taken from the English") of *Aipím*, a manioc root that is pure undiluted starch—and *côco* or coconut. *Côco* with that accent, means coconut, but with the accent slightly different it means *merde*, so you can see the infinite possibilities for humor. "Sheets" and "handkerchiefs" also sound almost alike to the beginner in Portuguese and are good for a laugh anytime.

Lota *approves* of you, and always reads your letters with great satisfaction. She thinks that some of my correspondence depresses me—probably true—but that you always cheer me up. This morning at coffee she had a lovely daydream about you. She is planning to build a little house up on the next hillside for Kylso, the adopted son, to spend his vacations in with his wife and baby. But he'd only be using it, probably, two weeks out of the year. So Lota thinks it would be wonderful if sometime you & Kit would take a year off from England, perhaps rent your house for a fabulous sum—to that American—and come here and work. The only expense would be a freighter passage or whatever way you wanted to get here. I think it is a wonderful idea for the future, to think of, and hope you will think of it, too—that is if you feel the slightest interest in South America. Our life up here is very very quiet, and we don't see many people—just Lota's old friends, mostly—but heavens, it *is* beautiful, and strange. Maybe if Kit sometime decides on a new "period," or if you do (although place doesn't matter so much to writers, I think. I'm in the midst of a long poem about the Third Avenue El at the moment) you'd consider it. I think it would work well.

The architect, Sergio, arrived the other evening in his new Ferrari. We had to go down to the highway to see it, he thought it was too low to get up here. Lota was enraptured and wants one—but realizes it's foolish—she just loves cars. It was a pretty sight—gray, sleek, quite small, a plastic windshield with no rims anywhere (and no way of covering the—well, cockpit—at all), wire wheels, a small fish-mouth radiator grille in front. The leather is black and pebbly—exactly like a dog's nose, only a little coarser. But they're really only for racing. It heats up too much in traffic; it has five forward gears—the *first* goes to 90 kilometers (I think that's 54 miles per hour), so you see—but I'd just as leave have my *MG* any day. Lota took a cute little old lady neighbor to market in it the other day—she's about 80; she tied her head up in a scarf and was dying to go. She's about 4′ 4″ high, I'd say—like a doll—and she got in and said happily, "Why it's really quite big—there's plenty of room for my legs!" And by the way—do you know what MG stands for? I can't find out, even in my book of instructions.

Lunch and a swim in the now full, clean pool—*delicious*. The water is a pale green, straight down off the top of the mountain, with a few yellow leaves floating on it, and many blue dragonflies and gorgeous, or tea-tray, butterflies. Oh, I've continued Lota's daydream about your sometime visiting here. It would resemble Yaddo, only much more cheerful, I think. You could have absolute privacy, make your own breakfast, lunch if you wanted to, too. I must get back to that poem & I've said my say. I hope everybody's well & the daffodils are a foot high. *Sammy* is fine. I just left him taking a bath.

To Austin Olney, Houghton Mifflin

April 25, 1954

I am very glad to hear that you are really going ahead with *A Cold Spring* now, and I am also genuinely sorry that I have been such a slow worker the past two years. I think I can honestly say that the "block," or whatever it was, seems to be disappearing and I believe I'm going to be much more prolific, for a stretch now, at least.

I am also glad to hear about Chatto & Windus [who had contracted to publish EB in England]. It seems to me that a combined volume— *North & South*, or the best of *North & South*, and *A Cold Spring*—would be an excellent idea for the English edition. It is what I had in mind myself. However, I have turned against the title *Concordance* completely, and I am trying to think of something better to cover the two volumes together. I'll send you another title as soon as I can.

However, after three days' thought, it seems to me a combined volume would *not* be a good idea for the U.S. appearance of *A Cold Spring*, nice as it would be to get some of *N & S* back into print again. I have no one here to consult and perhaps I am wrong, of course. It seems to me that it is so difficult for most people to buy poetry, anyway, that no prospective customer who already had *N & S* would bother to buy it over again. Also, I should imagine that in general my "buying public" would be people who are already familiar with *N & S*, and possibly own it. I mean I don't think the audience for poetry changes much—although perhaps it is enlarging. But I really do not know. Would there be any possibility of doing *both*?—first, say, a small edition of *A Cold Spring*, and then a little later an edition of both—even a cheap paper-cover one? Have you considered any publications like that? I make *A Cold Spring* to be about 40-some pages. I've just measured it and found it a little longer, for example, than Howard Moss's recent *The Toy Fair*, Scribners.

I'm afraid that coming from me this statement will have absolutely no value but I have here at least seven poems, three of them long ones —three or more pages—and all seem on the brink of being finished. Two or three certainly belong in *A Cold Spring*. I feel certain—although I cannot blame you for not feeling the same way, naturally—that I'm going to get them along to you within another month now. I have been working steadily on poetry, after a long lapse, for some time now. I have a Key West one, two New York ones, and a General Travel one, no two—that all would go in *A Cold Spring*.

I won't say any more about this now and perhaps at my next week-end's mailing time (I really am not in Rio although that is my mailing address, and I can send mail from the country only at weekends), I'll be able to enclose at least one. I have also some new photographs to send you as soon as I get the glossies made—in about two weeks, I think. I shall write again next Sunday.

You say in your postscript that you received *two* stories—I don't understand that exactly, because May Swenson, who was typing for me in New York, wrote me that she had mailed seven to you. Possibly she sent some separately, although I don't know why. I hope you have received all seven, at any rate. One or two should probably be omitted but I think that with the two more long ones I am finishing now, and possibly one or two short ones, it would make a book. Several people have also suggested to me that I bring out a small book solely of the Nova Scotian stories. There are three in those you should have, and there will be at least three more eventually. I would be interested to hear what you think about that.

I am not going abroad this year after all and I have again taken up my translation of the Brazilian book I thought might interest you. As soon as I get a few poems out of the way I'll send you some sample chapters . . .

In the meantime I think I feel fairly strongly that a double book would *not* be a good idea in the U.S. But I am open to conviction. What would the price be?

P.S. I hope that you can keep the same shape and size of page as the *first* printing of *N & S*. And the same type. Loren MacIver wanted to do the jacket—still wants to, that is—but I don't know if you have made any arrangements with her.

May 9, 1954

I have been sick in bed for ten days with an attack of asthma and I didn't write when I said I would. However, I have been thinking a great deal about the joint book idea, and now it strikes me more favorably than

it did at first. It seems to me it would be all a matter of editing *North &
South* very carefully, and then finding a good covering title, with the other
two as subtitles, and I have a few ideas in mind. However, if you would
consider *A Cold Spring* as a separate book I think I'd still prefer it. But
I am willing to do it the other way if you want to. I have a chance to get
a note off to Rio now so I am taking it, but in a few days I shall send you
my ideas for joint titles and possibly a poem or two.

To Joseph Summers

July 10, 1954
I think when I wrote you before to say I had received *George Herbert,
His Religion and Art* I was just on my way to Rio and the book had just
arrived. (That is, if you got that letter—it was written about the first of
June. I've been having a lot of mail trouble lately.) Well, this afternoon
I'm on my way to Rio again. The last trip I ended by spending two weeks
in the Strangers' Hospital, trying to throw off a spell of asthma that had
been going on for two months or so. In spite of the gloomy name of the
hospital it is a good one and I am much better, but I've been kept coming
and going to Rio ever since for various "tests," and I think I owe everyone
I know a letter now. This test tomorrow morning should be the last for
some time and I'll write you a real letter when I get back. I took *George
Herbert* to the hospital with me, and although I was too sick at first to
think about it very hard, I finally was able to, and I think it is a first-class
scholarly performance and I have learned an enormous amount from it.
I suppose they will send you this review, but I was so pleased to see it I
thought I'd send it along to you just in case . . .
This is absolutely all I have time to write; I am catching a bus down
to Rio. Oh, I didn't notice my name in front at first and when I did I was
almost reduced to tears and I do think your fine honest scholarship breaks
down a bit there. I don't think I've ever offered you a single original
thought on the subject. But thank you, anyway. Did you know—you
probably do—that Simone Weil in one of her "Farewell Letters" tells
how she *"found Christ,"* I think—while reciting "Love bade me welcome
yet my soul drew back"? I'd like to see her translation of it.
Give my love to U.T. and the children and please forgive this ungracious and piecemeal way of getting around to your book. I have promised it to two people here when I have finished with it—to loan, I mean.
Some of your Italian information I handed on to a young Polish friend
of mine here, Maya Osser, who left last week. *Anyone* you can think of
who might like to meet her I wish you'd let me know—she'll be all over
Italy for the next three months. She is about 30, I think, speaks all the
better-known languages, the way Polish people do, has beautiful man-

ners, is tall, blond, good-looking in a chic way, and as for brains she has her own architect's office here, and is Henri Bergson's niece.

To Paul Brooks

August 2, 1954

I was somewhat surprised to receive a letter forwarded by May Swenson to me, that you had written to her, July 9, about my stories. I received it just a few days ago. I think she must have written to find out if you had received them, that is all—because she was just doing the typing for me and I don't believe I ever gave any indication that she was acting as an "agent" for me . . .

I have been really sick here for three months with asthma and almost completely good for nothing . . . However, before all this began, I *did* write to Mr. Olney, twice . . . the first, somewhat objecting to your plan of putting the two books of poems together; the second, shortly after that, saying that I had thought it over and had decided it was a very good plan after all . . . His last letter to me was May 14 and he said that "all the stories" were in then; but I haven't had another word about them until Miss Swenson forwarded your letter . . . I had much rather be told personally what you think about the stories, naturally.

I think the best thing to do with them would be to send them back to Miss Pearl Kazin, *The New Yorker* magazine, to keep for me . . .

I do not know what to say about my poems . . . If you still want to go ahead in the spring, it is all right with me. I just wish someone had let me know . . . I *know* it is very irritating to want to publish someone who just can't "produce"—and then to make no money on it as well— so if you want to send the poems on to Miss Kazin, too, please do so, and let me know. I cannot resist saying, I'm afraid, that I have had a good many offers for both the poems and a book of stories as well . . .

To Marianne Moore

August 17, 1954

The beautiful red TOME came last Friday, and this is the first opportunity I have had to write you about it, although I wanted to sit down and do so immediately, of course. When I came down to Rio last week there was an announcement from the customs here that I had a package waiting for me, "2nd notice"—although I hadn't received the first. I suspected it might be the book, so I went to the customs, only to have my notice stamped "Return on the 13th," and even though I was sure I could immediately spot the package from Viking among those on the shelves (they're supposed to be *40,000* packages in arrears) that was the best I could do. So I went in again the 13th and received it, from an enormous pleasant Negro wearing a long white "duster." He opened it, took it out of the slipcover, smiled, and said, "Oh—*La Fontaine!*" (Tell that to Wallace!) and he showed it to two or three other customs clerks who all had a nice leisurely look at it before I even got my hands on it. The sheer weight was the first surprise; so I put it on his scales, and now I've forgotten the exact number of kilos and kilograms, but I'll have to do it again . . . Then I took it along to the dentist, where it was handled and admired by the dentist and his secretary. Then I went on to a lecture at the Ministry of Education by Agnes Mongan of the Fogg Museum, and showed it to her and my friends among the audience. I think the weight and the solidity of the binding and the clarity of the photograph make the biggest immediate impression here—Brazilian books as a rule being paperbound and printed very badly on very bad paper, with wretched reproductions—that is, aside from the amount of WORK, which although it is rather an ungracious and cliché thing to say, I can't imagine any Rio de Janeiran contemplating. (That may be mean—I know there are scholars who do a great deal of work; but in general the books are slight and rather carelessly done.) So you certainly made a sensation here last Friday the 13th . . .

I wouldn't have missed the black man in the white coat handing it over for anything. It is certainly a handsome book. I hope you are pleased with the way it looks. It seems to me if I were you I'd just sit down & hold it on my knees in a rocking chair and rock gently to & fro and admire it the rest of my days. I was really dumbfounded, Marianne, to see my own name in your Foreword, because you know perfectly well I never made one single little comment of the slightest use to you, or made any "comparison of rarities—possible" that I can think of!—just that bad old valueless edition I have, maybe, that's all I can remember. But of course I was touched almost to tears, and I went & woke Lota up to show her. I was in bed, cutting all the pages, before I went to sleep that night. My pride was such, as a matter of fact, that I had explained away to the men in the customs office all about how it was a translation by an *amiga*—in my idiotic Portuguese, while they smiled at the crazy *Americana de Norte* with all her rush and excitement and, probably, face to match the cover.

Last week we came down to re-rent this apartment . . . and also to see or hear Robert Frost—a "literary conference" has been going on in São Paulo. I didn't want to go to it but I thought I'd like to call on Frost. (He made records when I was at the Library.) He gave a reading at the Embassy—the first function I've ever attended there—the first time I'd ever been there, even. He is amazing for a man eighty years old, and the audience—mostly Brazilian—liked it very much. But I was so appalled at our ambassador here and his behavior (he sat with a large unlit cigar in his mouth, between Frost and Frost's daughter) that I haven't got over it yet. I had heard, but I'd never quite believed it all—Miss Mongan's treatment was equally bad. I had been trying from time to time to defend my country, etc., as far as "culture" goes. Now I feel no matter what Pritchett, etc., may have said they couldn't put it too strongly. Our State Dept. is—well—I just don't know what to say, really, they behave so STUPIDLY and rudely and (the ambassador) pro-McCarthy-y—it is incredible. I have one extremely nice friend here—an old friend of Lota's, that is—who has a beautiful old house & garden, and she gave a luncheon for us for Frost and was so nice—attended the reading although her English is not too quick. I said to her, "I don't think I can try to defend my country any more," and she said immediately and gracefully, I thought, "Now you are in exactly the position we Brazilians have been in for some time!" Lota says Lincoln Kirstein had an even worse time when he was here, too—they decided his ballet were "Reds." Almost the only remark Mr. Kemper (the ambassador) made to Miss Mongan was to ask if the new president of Harvard wasn't a "Red." She replied, "Well, he reads a chapter from the Bible beautifully every single day in chapel, if that is being a Red."

I shouldn't bother you with this—everyone knows it, I suppose—I just hadn't been exposed to it before.

It is too bad to rent this apartment, but Lota has so much to do in the country and ordinarily we get down so rarely—and I have so much work to do (about 20 years') too in the country, that it is silly to let it stand empty for months on end. But today the sea is so blue and the breakers so perfect, with pinkish rainbows showing over them diagonally here & there. Very few people on the beach, because it is "winter."— One man has a kite up, transparent bluish-gray with a white tail—it must be cellophane. It looks like something up out of the water itself. Here is Lota & I must fix us some lunch. She sends you her regards.

Houghton Mifflin is putting me off again until spring, I think—but it is my own fault, or due to some misunderstanding or other—and I just *haven't* enough poems, of course—but now I shall never never promise anything again—now that it's too late and they're good and mad, that is.

I have a beautiful new *inlay*, of red Brazilian gold. I do hope you are well, Marianne, and I'll write about the contents of the handsome new book when I return to Samambaia.

To Austin Olney

Sunday, August [?], 1954

I received your letter only a few days ago in Rio—the last mail received, as a matter of fact, before the political crisis you will undoubtedly have read of. There was no way of mailing anything to you sooner and I am hoping you receive this. Will you let me know if you do? There has been a wave of anti-American feeling and there are the usual rumors to the effect that the mail to the U.S. is being destroyed, etc. . . .

I am going to Rio on September 6th and by that time surely things will be settled enough for me to find out. The city is quiet now but it is impossible to get anything *done* anywhere—and I shall let you know at once. I was in Rio really desperately ill when the political upheaval took place. Carlos Lacerda, of whom you have probably read now, just happens to be one of my best friends and a neighbor here. The friend I am staying with is also involved politically, so there has been little time to think of "work," as I'm sure you can imagine. I am in my studio in the country now, and incredible as it seems to me, with a .22 at my side. (Please do *not* repeat this. Brazil has been very good to me.)

I am all for the combined volume now. I think the joint title should be merely *Poems*—maybe with the dates—with the two titles only appearing on the inside, to avoid awkwardness on the cover . . . *Poems* just seems like the safest bet as well as sounding important! Yes, I approve of this order & have checked it. There is some doubt in my mind as to whether "Insomnia" is worth re-publishing. Will you tell me what you think, or what anybody else around might think, too? I just can't tell any more. Thank you for sending the stories to Pearl Kazin . . . I still feel I should have been given some sort of personal reply about my stories . . .

[P.S.] I put in the remark about the gun just for its shock value but please do not repeat it . . . Brazil and my Brazilian friends have been very good to me. They are so good, as a matter of fact, that they concealed from me *for two days* the fact that there had been anti–U.S. riots, etc., for fear of hurting my feelings! And I have yet to be able to get a copy from any of them of Vargas's suicide note in which, I finally gathered, he tries to put some of the blame on the U.S. The regime had been so rotten something just had to happen.

To Marianne Moore

October 30, 1954
—A wild & stormy night
at the *estudio*

I received a batch of mail yesterday including the letter from Allen Tate that I think you must have been kind enough to put ten extra cents on and forward to me. Thank you so much—he wanted some poems for an anthology, as he probably did from you as well. I cannot repay the ten cents, I'm afraid—in *kind*, maybe, somehow sometime.

I've been receiving clippings from various friends about the Dr. Williams business at the Library.* I had wondered off and on what was going on, suspecting something, but had been told a few times by the secretary there that he'd been sick, etc. She is extremely discreet—and I am appalled to learn what is the truth—or at least the *New York Times* version of it. Also a few remarks, I don't know how accurate, in *The New Statesman and Nation*. I feel I should probably have resigned long ago but now don't know exactly whom to write—well, I've been asking around, and may know more soon. I'd like very much, if it isn't too much trouble, if you'd tell me what you feel about it. If anyone can feel anything more about these stupidities, that is. And if you can put it in a few sentences and not waste any of your valuable time on it.

The summer rains have begun and we have a big storm between five and eight regularly every night. Last night the heavens opened just after dark. The toucan was caught in the rain again and I threw on my raincoat and grabbed up his cage—it is enormous, but one person can do it in an emergency—to get him under the kitchen eaves. When I got it in the light I found I had the cage but no toucan—there is no bottom in it. There were a few awful moments while Maria the cook, Paulo, her husband, and I, all being soaked to the skin and afflicted with contagious giggles, looked for him—but he was sitting on a little tree above the garbage can, too drenched to fly, poor bird, and quite willing to be picked up and given a piece of meat and dried off with a cup towel. He really must be tough. The cat teases him all the time—takes naps on top of his cage and dangles a paw over him—and Sammy just cocks his blue eyes up at him first on one side then the other, and goes on swallowing his endless bananas and when he gets a good chance taking a terrific peck at the cat's nose . . .

Please tell me if you do not receive the [George] Herbert book in about a week more now. I shall write again—I am reading a lot of the La Fontaine with the French now, you have got me so fascinated—many of them I had never read before.

To Joseph Summers

December 19, 1954

This letter from Marianne [about his *George Herbert*] is in such a different style from her usual letters, and typed as well—she usually writes—that I think she must have meant it expressly to be shown to you. Anyway, I'll send it along, and some time or other could I trouble you to send it back to me? I had another note from her Friday in which she

---

* Appointed Consultant in Poetry in 1952, William Carlos Williams did not serve because of false accusations of his being a "Communist" (this was in the Senator McCarthy era). The post remained vacant until 1956.

again refers to you and says: "The precious Herbert. What a solace to me it is. *One* book which is sane, factual and also exciting." (That's better than the first letter, I think, but Marianne's combination of understatement and hyperbole is always a little confusing! To me she says "*brave* E—*gallant* E [?], I fear you are not well," etc.—"having a struggle," etc.—and I've been racking my brains to think whatever gave her *that* idea *now*, and Lota, who inadvertently read the letter, thinks I must have been *complaining*, etc.)

I am up to my neck—or at any rate exceedingly sticky and steamy —with plum puddings, and must get back to the Primus stove I'm using to save our bottled gas. Nothing comes prepared here and I never realized how long it takes to *seed* raisins—but I suppose it must be an immemorial female chore.

I'm having more and worse troubles with Houghton Mifflin and wish to goodness I could talk to U.T. and you about them. I really just don't know what to do next. They want to put off the book until fall again, because they say in a brief note they have "three other poets in the spring who would compete" with me—there have been so many "delays," etc. In spite of my slowness—six years—I think *these* delays must be their own, since they've had the book as it's to be since last spring now, really—and I've been getting more and more uneasy as I heard never a word about proof, jacket—Loren never heard, etc. Olney says, "Let me know immediately if you are unwilling to postpone until the fall—" or words to that effect, so I *guess* I'm about to cable him "Unwilling"—and then if they insist take the whole damned thing away from them—which may be what they are trying to get me to do, I don't know—but I don't quite know why. I have been disagreeable, I admit—and there's certainly not much future in me for them—but that business about the stories still strikes me as unforgivable. They now have 50 sample pages of my translation too, the photographs, etc.—want to see more. Can I just take it back? I'm really at an awful loss what to do and need advice badly. I thought, "Oh anything to get the book out and over with, then I can feel more like getting on with the next one, maybe." Also, as I may have said, it's a reprint of *North & South*—same plates, etc.—which I thought might not be a bad idea.

If I take it away from them, it will mean more poems to make a new book with someone else, and the whole thing will probably take me another year or two. And I just can't get over the way Paul handled those stories—things were amicable enough then, I thought. One cannot of course take a publishing house personally but *hell*—N & S did all right, as far as poetry goes, and I think maybe one of the other three poets should be put on to the fall—or at least there might be some faint expression of politeness—or am I being temperamental and vain? I didn't mean to write you this at all. It's had me upset for two days now—but I think you know a great deal more about these things than I do, naturally, from both sides—and I seem to have reached a sort of crisis in which I'd better hurry up and take my "career" a little more seriously—at least if I'm going to conduct it from Brazil.

I have—or had—several other houses interested. Random House would be the one I'd try again first, I suppose, but heavens—I forget what New York is like sometimes and maybe now I wouldn't have a chance. (I am not fishing—I'm just trying to use my head, but it's not working very well, I'm afraid.) Anyway, any advice from you or U.T. would be most welcome and most seriously considered.

I wish I could see you, and am dying to see the little girls—maybe you'll have another card of them this year. Our cook is due to have her baby in a month. Hope it holds off till after Christmas at least. I know it's bound to be adorable and I like black ones better than white, even if we are letting the cook do our living for us.

To James Merrill

James Merrill, who became one of EB's closest friends, was awarded the Bollingen Prize in Poetry. He twice won the National Book Award, for Nights and Days *(1967) and* Mirabell: Books of Number *(1978); the Pulitzer Prize for* Divine Comedies *(1976); and the National Book Critics Circle Award for* Souvenirs *(1984).*

Samambaia
March 1, 1955

I've just read through your *Short Stories* again, by the swimming pool, before going for a dip—it is still summer here—and now I think at last I'll try to write you a note about them. Although unless one is really a critic or a reviewer probably one should just sit back and enjoy things and not say anything much except "Thank you." But I think you might like me to elaborate on my thank-you a little, which is really all I have in mind—it would be rather fatuous of me to say you write "awfully well" when you've obviously polished these poems so carefully and lovingly.

I'd seen "The Greenhouse" and "A Narrow Escape" in magazines —and wondered a little what you were up to. Now I am somewhat enlightened but still wondering a little, too. The *Stories* together strike me as a laboriously [*in margin:* I mean selected with *care*, nothing derogatory] and personally and dearly purchased *present*, a delightful present to be able to give and receive; but the reader who isn't the exactly right recipient just has to look on and admire. The poems kept reminding me of *The Golden Bowl* (without cracks) and then just now I thought they also reminded me of some of James's short stories—only boiled down, or distilled, so that the impression I got reading them was a sort of *liqueur de James*. Or maybe I should leave James out and say it's a *liqueur du voyage*, with a great many evocative but unplaceable flavors—"The formula has been handed down for generations." Your imagery, however, frequently does remind me of the imagery of the later Henry James, only with a paragraph or a page or two compressed into one or two lines.

I think I like "The Cruise" best—maybe because I feel I understand it best, in my literal-minded way, but I also like the beginning of "The Wintering Weeds," although I'm not sure I understand the end of it, and I suspect "About the Phoenix" is best of all, isn't it, although again I confess I get lost here and there. I like "those frail poles charred with age. / They mark a village of bird-worshippers" very much, although I'm not quite sure whether you're speaking of the Lake Dwellers or not!— also, "A battered egg-cup and a boat with feet"— In fact I find lots of lovely and valuable lines "to take home," and I have the impression that that is exactly what you have done on your travels.

You say you imagine me in a "Rousseau jungle"—well, it is as beautiful as one, I think, but a lot sparser and rougher, and where I live, 50 miles or so from Rio, much more perpendicular. Like the Sugar Loaf in Rio harbor, only a great many of them, much bigger, inland a ways— with clouds spilling over the tops sometimes, or waterfalls coming and going according to the weather (there's an awful lot of weather here). Things are very much out of scale, too, like a Rousseau—or out of our scale, that is. The "Samambaia" mentioned at the top of the page is a giant fern, big as a tree, and there are toads as big as your hat and snails as big as bread & butter plates, and during this month butterflies the color of this page and sometimes almost as big flopping about— Combined with the "Quaresma," or Lent, trees, a mournful purple, the color scheme is wonderful—maybe a little Dorothy-Draperish in March. But scenery aside, I like living here very much and have a very nice place to live and nice friends.

I hope maybe to get in a short trip to New York soon but it depends on earning some money first. Houghton Mifflin now says my book is coming out in July. Will the 28 West 10th St. address reach you so I can have them send you a copy?

I wonder if Copland is coming to Rio this spring—your spring—I must watch out in the papers, I'd hate to miss him. That is one thing I've been missing here very much, good music—where I live we can't have a Victrola yet because we don't have electricity, just a small generator that everyone says wouldn't give good results with a record-player. If Mr. Copland is coming here and you are in touch with him, please tell him please to play a "highbrow" program—I've almost given up going to the concerts that do come along because the artists play down so to the Rio audience, as a rule. (And they resent it very much. Stephen Spender also made the mistake of talking down to them—and handing out a Portuguese translation of his speech when he spoke at a gathering where probably everyone understood him perfectly, or so I was told.)

The Rio address is my permanent mailing address. I hope you've been having a nice winter in New York and writing a lot—and thank you for *Short Stories* and your nice encouraging note—

[P.S.] How is the novel coming? You'll have to provide me with a special *clef*, I'm afraid, I'm so out of things!

To Loren MacIver

April 27, 1955

I found a letter from you in Rio when Lota and I came down yesterday afternoon for a couple of days of diversified business and pleasure. I am awfully pleased with the jacket. I think it's pretty as pretty can be, *chic*, and will stand out on any counter of books—which I suppose is one requirement. Now I just hope Houghton Mifflin will let you do it exactly as you want to. Lota likes it very much, too. I think your idea of carrying it all the way around—back as well as front—is excellent, and I've just written a note to Mr. Olney saying so . . . That would mean that any "printed matter" would have to be confined to the inside flaps, which is exactly what I'd prefer. We have a group of "blurbs"—I *loathe* "blurbs" and wish the custom would die out quickly, but since they do use them I suppose one has to, more or less . . . And also any danger of their using a photograph on the back would be—would be—obviated? "Blurbs" and the photograph have been mentioned—and then no further answers, you know the way. But now with your jacket and what you say to them and what I say to them, I'll feel quite safe. I do think it will be extremely good-looking.

It's funny—I was also just sending them a picture of Mr. Blumenthal's title page for Edward Taylor's *Poems*—just to give them some idea of how well a title page can look. It is all in Baskerville, which is what *N & S* was to begin with and which I begged them for two years just to keep on using, with its own caps and italics and nothing *else*. But no—they had to change everything . . . Now I'm praying they've got rid of the hand lettering or whatever it was—much worse than *N & S* originally, which was pretty bad—COLD looked exactly like COLA in COCA-COLA—or did you see it?

Lota sends her regards to you & Lloyd. With love to you both.

To Marianne Moore

July 1, 1955

I had no intention of Houghton Mifflin's sending you the proofs of that misbegotten book of poems. It came about, I'm afraid, through my own slowness in making up my mind about "blurbs," etc., and the difficulty of arranging the details of a book at such a distance. I do hope you didn't take too much time and trouble over it, but I'm afraid you did. I *still* am not sure whether they are using "blurbs" or not—I've never received a definite answer. I hate blurbs but since they seem to be the American custom I didn't quite have the strength of mind to say no, and I thought they should be as good as possible, at least. What I finally wrote them, if they *are* using them, is a short quotation from your review of *North & South* in *The Nation*, long ago—the first two or three sentences. But I haven't heard nor seen anything yet . . .

I'm so sorry you missed the Smith Art Gallery—they have some really wonderful things, including one of my favorite cubist Picassos—also one of Loren's, I think. I'm glad you agree with me about Loren's nomination for the Institute—I'm afraid what I meant was that you should nominate her! I guess I had a picture of its being done by someone just standing up at the dinner table and saying loudly, "I nominate So-&-So" and then the two seconds popping up to confirm it. But I see now it's rather different and will have to wait until next year. It says in the letters they send me that anyone can nominate anyone—from another "art," that is—but then the two seconds both have to practice the same art. So maybe I could begin writing letters after a while and be prepared to do it by mail when the next opportunity comes around. That is, if I'm a legitimate nominator—I don't know.

The parrot, a *papagaio*, is from our matches. The favorite variety for pets is a medium-sized green and yellow and blue one—because those are the national colors. We have a *gang* of wild ones near the house— thirty or so—they fly in a band from tree to tree, talking away, particularly in the early mornings—in Portuguese, I'm sure. Also a few small, almost-black monkeys, but they're so shy we rarely see them . . . Lota is building the living-room wing of the house now. It looks enormous and we can't think how we'll ever furnish it unless I sell enough stories to buy a grand piano. There is a little library at one end where she can have her *estudio* and we've decided to build in three "stacks" just like a wing of a small public library. The other day the architect was here for lunch and I happened to say that I was about to buy the Encyclopaedia Britannica on the installment plan. He said oh, he'd give me his. I said but didn't he want it and he replied calmly, "Oh, I've read it." So now we have it, all except the last volume, which is still at his house in Rio and which I suppose he is still reading.

You ask what I'm doing and the answer is nothing, except living here very happily in the country and working on the translation and some poems and some stories—and managing the kitchen part of the house-keeping. I hope to get the translation all to New York by September or October. I imagine Noonday Press is the best place to try, since they publish Machado de Assis, the *other* Brazilian writer besides my child-writer, and seem to be interested in Latin American translations. I am very much impressed with all your trips (and degrees). It is so hard to go anywhere here, unless it's a real trip, a long plane one. But this month we do go to São Paulo for a week to see the Biennale, and in September we're going to fly to Diamantina for a week, for me to try to write an introduction to the translation. *Porgy and Bess* is coming to Rio soon and since Lota's never seen it I think we'll have to make an effort to get to that—but intellectual pleasures are very few and slight, on the whole.

The [cook's] baby is marvelous. Her mother dresses her, now that it's cold, in bright rose or yellow flannel garments, with bright green or yellow socks—the father helps crochet them. They are so proud of her that we have to fight every Sunday to keep them from taking her on grueling long bus trips to show her to all their relatives. It's all due to the fact that we supervise the feeding, bathing, etc. There's never been such a fat, good baby in the neighborhood, and the men working on the house keep coming to look at her and ask about her diet. One of them said he thought she laughed too much.

Please let me say again that I didn't have any idea Houghton Mifflin had sent you that proof and I'm awfully sorry—it is really my fault, I suppose, but I think they should have let me know, at least.

To Loren MacIver

July 18, 1955

. . . I received a copy of the book [*Poems: North & South—A Cold Spring*, published on July 14] airmail and I think the jacket is very successful, don't you? I even think the rest of it looks fairly well—much better than I'd expected—and the blue is very nice, thanks to you. It's too soon to get many reactions by mail here—but Joe Summers, who seemed to receive a copy before anyone else, has written that he thinks it's one of your "best jackets" . . .

We got a big batch of mail and books and magazines by a friend late last night and stayed up till all hours reading. It's rather fun getting mail like that, almost like Christmas.

To U. T. and Joseph Summers

July 18, 1955

I think you got a copy of my book before anyone else, or else you just wrote right away. It was a lovely send-off, anyway, and I have read it several times and this morning at coffee remarked to Lota that I was going to take one *more* compliment to start me off for the day, so picked it up again. She approved of the letter, too—in fact she has thought Joe must be wonderful ever since she exchanged a few words with him over the telephone and he said he was washing dishes. (A Brazilian husband that would stoop to that would be a saint, I imagine.) She also thinks that he "speaks well"—not that he doesn't, but I suspect the accent had something to do with it. Well, the letter cheered me enormously, made me very happy, in fact, and I am so surprised that the "View of the Capitol" means something. I was really quite unaware of it, until you pointed it out to me! Now I see it does. Please don't tell anyone this! I made the change about the hymn because "A Mighty Fortress" isn't sung by Baptists. (By the way, the present President of Brazil is a Baptist and no one has any idea what this means—we suspect it's something like a Freemason.) I liked everything you said, just lapped it up, and now feel a little better about Houghton Mifflin's having talked me into doing it that way. I think probably "At the Fishhouses" & "Faustina" are the best. Something wrong with the middle of "Over 2,000 Illustrations," and I really shouldn't have used that title if I wanted to drag in the old books we had with the Seven Wonders of the World in them, too. Well, I hope I do better next time, which will probably be in ten years or so.

We immediately put into action all the information you sent about [the cook's] baby—and then just the other day Lota's [Dr.] Spock turned up . . . I'm going to give it to the father who reads English, and see if he won't improve the nutrition in that family . . . Lota has been considering translating it for a long time. I think if she has a spark of patriotism in her bosom she certainly should—it could be cut quite a bit, I think—and I'm urging her on with it. The diet here is unbelievable, for the rich as well as the poor, usually. It's always been that way. I read that at the heyday of the sugar production in Bahia, when they had their slaves dressed with gold and silver ornaments, there was scarcely any meat to be had, or it would be rotten—it's always scrawny—and the richest families would be suffering from scurvy, etc. (There's a rather startling book about Brazil that really gives one some idea what it's like, translated as *The Masters and the Slaves* by Gilberto Freyre—fascinating and depressing.)

Well, the baby took to spinach like a duck, wanted more & more . . . She's absolutely beautiful and healthy and good now, and graduating to something new every day. She is five months and a week old and rattles a rattle and can play with her toes, so I guess she's all right—even tries to pat a dog . . . It's all rather sad, though, because servants here being the way they are are apt to spoil it all at any minute, or up and leave us—but at least she's getting a good start and Maria, the mother, *may* have learned something. She shows her off to everyone so the neighborhood may benefit. The men working on the house come and ask us what she's fed, etc. The state of infants here just doesn't bear thinking about. I think the Catholic Church has a lot to answer for—as well as the schools . . . Since I am not judged suitable to be this baby's spiritual mentor (I told you, didn't I, I couldn't be the godmother, not being Catholic), in real American style I must put her material welfare first.

The Eucharistic Congress is under way—a million pilgrims, I think. The papers have been running warnings about watching out for pickpockets while you pray (with illustrations) and items like "Half a Ton of Host Required" and "Cocquetail before Cinema for Eucharist" that surprise my protestant eyes. The best "modern" architect designed the altar right against that magnificent bay in Rio—it's really awfully well done. But as an added attraction for the pilgrims the Paris Waxworks museum has been imported and set up in a luxury hotel here . . . This mixture of good taste and atrocious taste seems to be *very* Brazilian . . .

I had an apartment right off Varick Street (lower Seventh Avenue) and there were printing presses across the street that kept going nights sometimes, using those pale blue daylight lights. Also Schrafft's factory was on one side and the Antiphlogistine place on the other, so in summer the odors became very strange. After one uncomfortable night I woke up reciting the refrain of that poem, "Varick Street," and it seemed somehow applicable to the commercial outlook and my pessimistic outlook on life in New York and in general at that time. It is a dream poem—the refrain was in time with the presses which were going full blast, and all of it, except a few fixed-up words toward the end, was in my head. So if you can't understand it—maybe I shouldn't make use of dreams quite so directly. I'm pleased that I have that gift but it's not very reliable. Quite a few lines of "At the Fishhouses" came to me in a dream, and the scene—which was real enough, I'd recently been there—but the old man and the conversation, etc., were all in a later dream. The "Four Poems" are certainly fragmentary & probably too much so, but I thought that together they made a sort of emotional sequence (maybe not) à la *Maude*, with the story left out . . .

Virgil Thomson is in Rio giving some lectures and conducting (poor man) the Symphony Orchestra. We're having him up for lunch tomorrow, and after reading his contributions to *The Alice B. Toklas Cook Book* that someone sent me for Christmas, I am getting more nervous every minute and go and feel those chickens we're proposing to fry and pray that the strawberries will have reached the right point of ripeness, etc.

We may have electricity here now and still can't quite believe it, after having managed so long with a kerosene refrigerator and a generator that sometimes works and sometimes doesn't, so that we have to keep oil lamps around all the time. Now we're talking of a Victrola. My jazz collection of the thirties is here—what's survived of it—waiting. I have also—to Lota's disgust—made negotiations for a Steinway three-quarter grand, secondhand. The new living room when finished will be enormous and I think I might as well put a piano in it. It's supposed to be a good one, very cheap, but I haven't seen it and it may prove to be in Louis XVI style or something—just the thing for modern architecture and Saarinen and Aalto furniture, etc.

To John Malcolm Brinnin

November 9, 1955

I don't believe I've ever done this before, and I apologize since I realize it means more work for you—but I have changed three or four words in my poem, "Exchanging Hats," and I think it is improved enough to risk asking you to make the changes for me. Or may I just wait and make them on the proof? I wasn't satisfied with those aunts—now I think they will do, and since I am being precious I feel I might as well be good and precious while I'm at it.

Here is the improved version and I believe the punctuation is correct—but people have different ideas about punctuating dashes at the beginning of lines, and whatever the rule at *New World Writing* may be, it won't matter to me if they change this a bit.

The changes are: the first word of stanza 3 is "Anandrous" instead of "Pajama'd."

Last stanza: the first two lines now read, "Aunt exemplary and slim / with avernal eyes," etc.

To Loren MacIver

November 20, 1955

I'm writing on my knees in bed, having a slight cold and deciding to take a day off and really get over it, since the rainy season is with us . . . I don't imagine you follow South American politics much in the papers—aside from Perón maybe—but perhaps you did see some notices of the quiet revolution we had last week? It was an anti-revolution revolution. The one *for the better*, that we were expecting, was staved off, and that means that the man who was instigating it, fighting for it in his newspaper, etc., was immediately in great danger and had to get out. He fled first on a battleship, then back to the Cuban Embassy here, and now he's flown to New York, today, where he'll be until things take a turn for the better for him. His wife and children are joining him later.

His name is Carlos Lacerda. He's 41, a brilliant man, completely honest, wants to be "democratic," certainly; somewhat Catholic; but in the way politicians and journalists often are here, unlike the U.S.A., also interested in culture in general, painting, architecture (his little country house is right near us, built by the same architect as Lota's), gardening, cooking, drinking, etc. He got the Mary Cabot Award for journalism from Columbia University a couple of years ago, and has his own newspaper here, and has been shot at, etc., I don't know how many times, being of course violently anti-dictatorship.

If, after that somewhat effulgent account, you think you & Lloyd would like to meet him, I'm sure you'll find him very interesting and entertaining. He speaks English (with a beautiful voice, I must say) and of course he has seen some of your paintings here. I've written him, offering Dr. Baumann and mentioning you and Lloyd. I think Lloyd would find him particularly interesting, and I think Carlos would like very much to see a real American painter too. He'll be doing some broadcasting and articles and I think you would be doing a valuable patriotic service by giving a practical demonstration that all Americans don't live surrounded by washing machines and automobiles, etc. I see I've neglected to say that he's one of Lota's & my best friends . . .

Revolutions notwithstanding, everything is peaceful and hardworking here. My translation [of the "Helena Morley" diary] is on the last lap now. Lota is installing bookcases in her library this week—awfully nice, I think, three "stacks," and she'll sit at her desk and look just like the librarian of a small public library.

You may have seen something in the papers about Carlos Lacerda —but never go by what they say about things here. I saw the *New York Times* account of this last business and it had everything almost completely the wrong way around—"reactionary" for "liberal" and so on. I think our reporters just believe whatever the man in power at the moment tells them . . .

To Marianne Moore

December 1, 1955

You finally received my book—and Miss Ford finally *came across* with your wonderful and generous remarks for them. I am angry that they couldn't be used, and yet in some way feel they are too good to be used. Anyway, although lost to the public for the time being, they were far from lost on me and have cheered me up enormously, and I'm thinking of requesting that they be engraved on my tombstone. I think that kind of thing is so difficult to produce—at least it is for me—and I am so sorry you had to do it and then they didn't use it. But thank you very much, Marianne, and please think how much it meant to me personally and how much good it is doing that way—I hope. I am really so sorry Houghton Mifflin got confused or careless, or whatever it was.

And day before yesterday Brentano's finally got *Predilections* to me. We still cling to Brentano's, but I wonder why. They are far worse than Houghton Mifflin, and every order has something missing. I wrote for *Predilections* as soon as I read about it in *The New York Times* and when they surely must have had it right on that front table—but they wrote back they were "ordering" it! . . . I've read it with great pleasure and it is so nice to have at least that many prose pieces together. I'd seen all of it except the Bryn Mawr pieces and "Anna Pavlova," but I think I notice some little changes here and there in the pieces I do know, don't I? I'll have to see what I can find in my papers here and compare them. (I miss something I liked from Cocteau, I think.) I like the pieces on Eliot and Auden tremendously—they are both full of wonderful remarks—and useful remarks, as well. I'll have to read it through again and much more carefully. I started a "supervised reading" with Lota this morning and just because I have to explain quite a lot to her, naturally, I keep finding more and more profundities, and meanings enjambed. It is amazing to me how consistent the tone is over such a long period of time—and of course I like that tone so much—a sort of reluctant(?) sincerity and dryness. But I should leave comments to the critics and just stick to being an admirer.

I have a chance to send this to the mail now and think I should take it.

P.S. I forgot to say that if you should happen to meet a friend of Lota's and mine in New York sometime this winter—a Carlos Lacerda —I do hope you will talk to him, because I know he knows who you are and would very much like to meet you, and I think you would find him interesting. He's a newspaper editor, a Representative, a very brilliant young man and certainly the most interesting Brazilian I've met. He is in political difficulties now and is in exile until things simmer down a bit here and it is safe for him to come back . . . He asked us for letters to friends in New York and we wrote to everyone we could think of. I didn't write you, since poetry is not exactly his line, nor politics yours!—but Lota did write to Monroe Wheeler and Louise [Crane] and I think perhaps you might meet him somewhere. He is interested in everything under the sun and speaks good English.

To Randall Jarrell

Caixa Postal 279
Petrópolis
Estado do Rio de Janeiro
December 26, 1955

It's the day after Christmas and all through the house not a creature is stirring, not even a mouse—and I wish I weren't, but I'm doing a hideous rush job of translation, about modern Brazilian architecture [Henrique Mindlin, *Modern Architecture in Brazil*], and have to keep going while everyone else takes naps. —Have to do it to help out a friend and because I live in one of the examples of it, so feel somehow involved, but since my knowledge of architecture is probably a little less than my knowledge of Portuguese, if that's possible, it is rather hard going.

Houghton Mifflin and my small-town (or so it seems, I don't know anything about it) clipping bureau sent me what you said about me in *Harper's*—I must have had it over a month now. It has made me so happy that I really can't put off writing you a note about it any longer. Particularly living so far away now, and having only three or four friends here who read English poetry at all, to show anything to—and they are all prejudiced so much in my favor, having read nobody else alive, to speak of! Sometimes I have the odd sensation that I am writing solely for you—which, after this piece, I don't mind a bit but shall try to relax and enjoy. I couldn't believe it at first, honestly—had a ridiculous fancy that it must be a misprint prolonged—shed a few tears—(they come from taking cortisone, partly—one gets highly emotional)—but I would have felt like shedding them even without the cortisone. I still, from the bottom of my heart, honestly think I do NOT deserve it—but it has been one of my dreams that someday someone would think of Vermeer, without my saying it first, so now I think I can die in a fairly peaceful frame of mind, any old time, having struck the best critic of poetry going that way . . . Something else rather funny, too—I've been working on a long poem about an aunt of mine, and when I don't write on the poem I've been trying to use all the same material for either a long story or a short play—and in both of them Vuillard was the person I had in mind for the exact effect I wanted to produce. In fact, in the beginning of the play version I'd already written (in the stage directions) that it was to *look* like a Vuillard, before I received your clippings. —Well, communication is an undependable but sometimes marvelous thing.

Someone wrote me—I can't find the letter—that there was also something in the October *Yale Review*—I don't take it, but I'll see it eventually. But I am quite happy with what I've got, as children say about Christmas, thank you very much. —One thing I did *get* was a big book of Bonnard lithographs—they are lovely ones—

Wherever you are I hope you are doing lots of writing. I liked what you said about the E. Dickinson edition very much—in fact I always agree with you in matters of taste. I have been morbidly afraid for a long time now that I'd hurt your feelings in some way or other—I know I do say fatuous or smart-aleck things sometimes, although I can't remember anything particular at all. Cal wrote me during the past summer about seeing you and how you had a beard, with a dash of white in it, I think—I'd love to see that. I liked the poem, long ago now, about the Pekinese, very much. —Your girl in the library means more and more, I think, as time goes on. I could and should and would like to go on, but my cantilevers and reinforced concrete are hanging over my head and I'd better get back to them.

Exile seems to work for me—I have almost a new book of poems, I think, and only hope and pray you'll like them, too.

With best wishes for 1956—love.

P.S. Did I ever tell you that I have an MG too?—had it two years now—black and red. We have a friend who has a small Ferrari, perfectly beautiful—dark gray with black leather just like a dog's nose— But I still only like to drive very *slowly*. Somewhere, maybe from Cal, too, I remember hearing that you were getting a Mercedes-Benz—I have my eye on a small one for my next, when I feel I should get slightly more dignified—they are so beautifully made. They all cost about the same here—all an awful lot, that is—so nationality doesn't make much difference, but probably the MG will be my one & only. Surely there must be a reaction setting in against those U.S. fantasies of tin and cardboard?

To Pearl Kazin

January 26, 1956

I was relieved to hear you had received the ms. [*Diary of "Helena Morley"*] safely and that you seem to go on liking it. No, *thank you* for telling me there are too many *coitados* ["poor dears"]. Take out every other one, if you want to. I'd be extremely grateful for *any* criticism about anything, honestly, so say exactly what you think. It is awfully hard to judge something one has worked over so much, as you probably know. I've tried to make it sound "natural," too, and probably sometimes I haven't. For example, I've usually put "doesn't," "isn't," etc.; "he's"— or "she's going to," etc.—and also to work in the English continuing present or whatever it's called—"she keeps doing so & so"—whenever I thought it was the right translation. But as you may dimly recall, Portuguese is much purer, heavier, and more formal than English, and I am getting so used to it that sometimes I'm sure I've overlooked little things like that. I'd be only too glad for any suggestions or if you want to make any changes yourself—anything as long as it sticks to the meaning, which I do think I've got pretty accurately now, with Lota's help—I'd be pleased and grateful. Of course I'll be going over it again and again, anyway, here, and will probably make little changes up till the last gasp . . . There will probably have to be endless small changes for the English edition too. I hate the way English reviews endlessly carp about "Americanisms," and I'd like to avoid all I can.

I am also grateful for your suggesting the agent . . . She [Bernice Baumgarten] sounds just right. What should I do about the English edition? Will she send it to Day-Lewis, too, for me? Chatto & Windus have actually taken an option, you know. Houghton Mifflin's contract with me says they have an option on my "next two books"— Well, I suppose this last little fiasco counts as one, and I should think turning down my stories would count as the second one. And maybe a translation wouldn't figure at all— That's just why I need an agent, I suppose . . . When I send the last part to you, will you just give it to Miss Baumgarten or what? Tell me when or if I should write to her, etc. I think it is a very good idea for me to have one, anyway, if I continue living in Brazil. What do *New Yorker* writers do in general? Since I've always done everything through Mrs.

White I never felt the need of one there, or for poetry in general, but if I'm to be an expatriate maybe it would be a good idea all around? I'm not a bit proud of it, but I know my business capacity is pretty meager & it would be well worth the 10% or whatever it is.

I hope Katharine [White]'s feelings get more enthusiastic. "Anti-Catholic"—I can't figure out where she got that. Helena seems to enjoy all the parades and dressing-up part of the church but isn't very religious, except in a superstitious, nagging-conscience way, wouldn't you say? And I may have further troubles with the family, who still don't want pictures (they're ashamed of having been poor, apparently—and don't seem to realize that anyone's going to gather it from the text!). One of the daughters talks to Lota *for hours* on the telephone about it. (This is one reason why I feel *I* should get a little money out of it!)

I am hard at work now and you won't be hearing from me again until the last part is done—about a week's work for me . . . Although she can't read English, the old lady is delighted so far, apparently. Two other people started in, and never finished, you know, and *she* tells Lota on the phone that she never thought she'd live to see the day, etc.

You have been an angel, Pearl, or a pearl—I'm sure I never would have gone through with it without your help and encouragement. Lota and I both thank you once more—and wish, as I said last time, we could put you up here to do some writing, or *something* to express our thanks a little more.

Please don't look at the Winter *Partisan Review*. Philip Rahv wrote me a very nice letter saying that their reviewer [Edwin Honig] attacks me. It certainly was kind of Philip to say what he said, and I am steeling myself, but feeling pretty low about my own work at the moment. I've never minded criticism a bit, strange to say—but what if this reviewer (I haven't seen it yet) says the TRUTH?—does point out all the awful faults I know are there all right? Well, I've been just too lucky and spoiled, I know, so I must grit my teeth and write another poem, that's all . . .

To May Swenson

January 27, 1956

Do you remember, some time ago now, you said that in the October *Yale Review* Randall Jarrell mentioned me and said he was going to write something more in the next one? . . . I asked Houghton Mifflin and of course *their* reply was that I wasn't mentioned in the October one (that gives you an idea of how kind and helpful they are). I do have a clipping bureau, but it seems to be breaking down completely and sending me chiefly copies of my own poems out of *The New Yorker*, just what one wants, of course . . . *If* Randall did write anything, would you buy and send me a copy airmail? This is sheer self-indulgence on my part, but

I've just heard from *Partisan* that their reviewer is attacking me "heavily" in their winter number and am foolish enough to hope I can find something around somewhere to cheer myself up a little!

. . . At the rate things seem to be going in N.Y., I often wonder how you do manage on your money. I can, here, but only because our exchange keeps pace pretty much with the Brazilian inflation, and food is very cheap, comparatively, and I wear nothing but blue jeans! But it is getting tougher on Lota all the time. The price of bread *doubles* today—for example— and we have a "staff" of four or five—who get very little pay but eat about a loaf each a day. We also have a nursery now; that's rather fun. I think I once told you Lota has an adopted son, didn't I? Well, his wife has just had their third, a boy, in four years of marriage, and we have been keeping the oldest, a little girl just three, for about a month. Fortunately she is an adorable child and good as gold and we love having her—but the cook's Betty is now learning to walk and sometimes our days seem to go by with rescuing first Helena and then Betty from the ornamental pool, or out of the jaws of a dog, or the claws of a cat or a toucan, or stuffing vegetables into little mouths. Lota is called "Granny" and I am "Aunty." The little girl has gained three pounds and now goes to bed at the right time every night, without a bit of fuss, and we feel quite proud of ourselves.

The New Yorker took a long, long poem ["Manuelzinho"]—to my great surprise, it was such an impracticable shape for them. It's supposed to be Lota talking, and I do hope you will like it.

February 5, 1956

Imagine your reading me too at the "Y"! If it weren't such a beautiful morning and I didn't feel so cheerful, I think I could shed a tear or two over that. It was awfully nice of you, really . . . and you have no idea how admiring I am. I backed down from reading at the "Y" once and all others ever since. I suffer so and come off so poorly I decided it just wasn't worth it. I suppose everyone improves with practice, though—at least I know Miss Moore has, enormously, since the first time I heard her in Brooklyn in 1936, I think. She may not actually read much better, but her stage personality is superb now. What is the matter with Delmore, do you know? . . .

The last two weeks or so, I am ashamed to say, I did work up a sort of state of nerves—imagining all the awful things Mr. Honig could say if he wanted to. I'm relieved that I don't mind him a bit! I even agree with his general thesis, I think—but he didn't quote the disastrous things he could have, easily, to prove it. He really should have kept that thought at the end to himself—that maybe some people do like poetry like that.

I rather like the [photo in] *Voice*, though—maybe the original is better? You look like a nice young Russian Nihilist of 1890. And please send me the poems when they appear there. Is it a paper like the old

Villager, or what? I loved appearing against my rocks (they're part of the garden here—or rather, we squeeze in a bit of garden here and there among the rocks) in an old shirt . . . But "wise," May! I'm forty-five Wednesday and never felt foolisher.

Lota and I both wish you were here this morning to go for a swim right now and slide in the waterfall with us and have ripe figs and prosciutto for lunch (she said so herself). The figs are wonderful now—a wooden box, about two dozen big purple ones, for $1.00—but of course they used to be 25¢ a box so it seems exorbitant to Lota . . . It's going to be a hot day and since it's the "season," Sundays are entirely too sociable. Last Sunday we had over 30 callers—a lot come just out of curiosity to see the house, though. We've put up a big sign half a mile down the road but it doesn't seem to stop them. A bunch of Franciscan monks, among others, and an aggressive German lady we'd met once, for a second, who took off her clothes and spent the morning in the pool (this was a weekday) and every time she saw me at the window up here called to me to come on in, the water was fine, etc.! She came twice like that, but after we'd refused to see her both times, and sent the maid out with very stiff messages . . . she hasn't appeared again . . .

I think maybe I'll stick to *Black Beans and Diamonds* [as a title for the *Diary*]. At least I'll see what the publishers think. I'm acquiring an agent, finally . . . "Helena Morley" and her family are from Minas, here, the mining state—and real "miners." They say here that the *mineros* eat out of drawers, so if anyone comes in they can shut the drawer quickly and won't have to offer anything, so you get the idea . . .

February 18, 1956

This is pure vanity, I guess—no, maybe not vanity—but "Roosters" was not "inspired," as they say, by a Picasso rooster at all . . . It's all so long ago I can't remember, except that it was a mess by the time I got through, and went on for four or five years. But I started it and wrote all the beginning, and bits here and there, much more directly at 4 or 5 a.m. in the back yard in Key West, with the roosters carrying on just as I said. I vaguely remember the Picasso (that was his Rooster Period) and sticking one onto the page somewhere a year or so later in N.Y.

. . . No, Lota hasn't any "new property." We've been living in the same house, still under construction, since a few weeks after I arrived here and unexpectedly stayed for good. But I do think and can say—since it isn't mine—that it is the best "modern" house in Brazil, finished or unfinished, and Henry-Russell Hitchcock said so too, although maybe he was being polite—when he visited us, and he was sorry not to be able to put it in the show that's at the Museum of Modern Art now, because it wasn't finished. Lota's thanked in his dedication, though. We think it was because we gave him some cold pills and a lot of detective stories!

She owns a big tract of land, i.e., Samambaia, left her by her mother, and the ancient *Fazenda* of Samambaia (a "national monument" now), down below us, was her home when she was little. The land down below, near the highway, is being "developed," which is her source of income, but she's kept a couple of square miles here at the top where we live, so it will always be protected from neighbors.

To Dr. Anny Baumann

May 10, 1956

We had a very funny day, day before yesterday, when I received the news about the [Pulitzer] Prize from a Rio reporter. Fortunately we had no time to brood about what was happening to us. The reporters and photographers descended—ascended, rather—much too fast, and before we knew it, Lota, my beautiful Negro namesake, another American friend, the cat, and I were all sitting like bumps on a log having our pictures taken for the Brazilian newsreel. We'll probably all look horrible, except for the cat—he *likes* photographers—all those trailing wires and black boxes, etc., and always makes up to them. I was really very much surprised—I somehow had the idea that prize had already been awarded this year and I'd missed the announcement—and I'm sure it's never been given for such a miserable quantity of work before. But I hope to goodness I'm a "slow starter" and will have another book done this year, or next at the latest.

While I am on this subject I'd like to tell you that I had another award, a fellowship, a while ago—I don't think it's been announced yet. *Partisan Review* gave me $2,700—from the Ford Foundation—which was extremely nice of them, since I haven't had anything printed there for several years. So I feel loaded with undeserved honors. The Pulitzer one was particularly nice for here, though, because it is so well known, and now Lota doesn't have to prove to her friends personally that I do write poetry! We think we'll take some of the extra money and buy a good Victrola right away—something we need badly. I'm buying two new tires for my MG today, too . . .

The translation is really finished. The authoress's husband [Brant], aged 82, I think, is "going over it," though, word by word by word. A lot of his corrections are completely wrong, poor dear, but it is his right, and every so often he does turn up something local, or old-fashioned slang, etc., that I couldn't have got right without him. I went to Diamantina a few weeks ago for five or six days and had a wonderful time and have now finished the introduction. It's the highest town in Brazil, about 5,000 feet, very tiny, almost a ghost town, but still concentrating ferociously on finding gold, and diamonds, in every little brook.

To Pearl Kazin

. . . I'm sure you know how embarrassed I feel about that Pulitzer, fun though it has been getting it. Never has so little work dragged in so many prizes, I'm afraid, and I catechize myself minutely, worrying about *why*. And WHY not Randall? he seems the obvious choice to me . . . It was a surprise when a man from *O Globo* called me up here to tell me the news. And we have had a lot of fun ever since and are still keeping *Cruzeiro* (you remember the dreadful weekly full of sex, crime, etc.?) at bay. Manuel Bandeira wrote a little piece titled *Parabéns, Elizabeth* and relating, all wrong, the story of the *caju* poisoning. Even the Embassy, our Embassy, rose to the occasion—all the way up the mountain, in a huge black station wagon—and now they're going to invite us to some movies, we hope.

The nicest story is about how Lota went to buy vegetables in the market and our vegetable man asked if it wasn't my picture he'd seen in the papers. She said yes, and then he said it was amazing what good luck his customers had. Just the week before another lady had bought a lottery ticket in the *Qui Bom* lottery and had won a bicycle. Then my elderly Aunt Florence gave an interview to the Worcester newspaper, and with true family ambivalence announced that I would have made a great piano player (I don't believe she ever heard me play the piano once) and that "lots & lots of people don't like her poetry, of course," and that she was my "closest living relative," thereby insulting two perfectly good live aunts on the other side of the family . . .

Last night Mr. Brant got back the first two sections [of the *Diary*] to me with more pages & pages of corrections in his tiny pencil script. Now he'll tackle the last one. My introduction is done but I keep fussing over it . . . I do think it is a good idea to show it to Miss Baumgarten, even before the last part arrives, probably—strike while the iron is hot, or slightly warm, at least, don't you think? (I scarcely think it would hiss if I spat, but anyway.) Houghton Mifflin is now all eager-sounding—but I don't know if they'd ever be persuaded to get out the kind of luxurious job I'd like . . . I think you may like my introduction although it's pretty simple and of course I had to be very careful and tactful. But this Prize has helped enormously, even with the Brant family!

To Robert Lowell

I don't know why I've been so slow about writing to you, since I think of you every day of my life, I'm sure. But now I really must, because a week ago Saturday—to my great astonishment and joy—your Christmas present arrived. Not even tarnished. Nothing to pay—they didn't even open it. I think you were very foolhardy to trust it to these mails, but I am delighted with it and we have used it for milk for tea every afternoon since. It's an awfully pretty little pitcher and where on earth did you get it? Yes, it is very much like here except for the elephants, and I don't think we have *hooded* cobras (but maybe we do), we certainly have enough of them, called *cobras*, too, and all sizes. The inscription makes me very proud and self-conscious—always hoping that some observant guest will ask me all about it; and if they don't, I'll tell them anyway.

You probably know all about the Pulitzer business . . . I was really surprised, having thought all along that it had already been given out . . . It was very funny here—a reporter from *O Globo* shouting at me over the telephone and I kept replying in a cool New Englandy way, "Thank you very much," and he shouted again, "But, Dona Elizabetchy, don't you understand? O Prémio Pulítzer!" I honestly feel from the bottom of my heart that it should have gone to Randall, for some of his war poems, and I don't know why it didn't. I really do seem on the frivolous side compared to him, and there's so little of it. Well, one never knows about these things, or how one *should* feel about them. As I'll never forget Caroline [Gordon] saying to you [about Lowell's Pulitzer], I'll try to "live it down."

We had lots of fun here for a while with reporters and photographers and their amazing fantasies. There was a snapshot of Portinari on the wall doing his last UN mural and the reporters asked if we knew him (he's an old friend of Lota's). *That* appeared in the papers as their asking her how we carried on a conversation, since he speaks no English, and then "Oh—Art is the universal language," replied the lively and intelligent Dona Lotinha . . . (The reporters also said I lived "an austere life, without a radio.") If you happen to see Harvey Breit in the *Times*, don't believe it. It's all wrong, both times, except of course that I *am* terribly handsome.

I just read yesterday Elizabeth's story about the man who lived in a hotel room for fifteen years, did nothing, etc. It reminded me uncomfortably of my friend Tom Wanning—remember him?—except that he is much richer and lives in a much worse hotel. The whole thing is so like him that I even wondered if E. knew him. I think it's very well done, and the magazine editor scenes are awfully good . . . I thought E.'s review of the Dylan Thomas book by [John Malcolm] Brinnin was superb, really—it came the same day that MacNeice's review did, and that was so poor, and mean!—heavens, the English can be mean. He accuses Brinnin of being handicapped by his faulty American sense of humor so that he couldn't appreciate D.T. "as a clown"—which strikes me as speaking rather well for the U.S. sense of humor. I thought the book suffers chiefly from a helpless romanticism about alcoholism—confusing it with philosophy or something—but actually I think he did have to write it, good or bad.

You mentioned—months ago—Lord Acton (I'd been reading him

too) and history writing. Did you know that Southey wrote a very good history of Brazil, without ever having seen it, of course? Lionel Trilling . . . did an awfully good piece about Santayana's letters—did you see that? At least it put for me exactly how I feel about Santayana myself— although I haven't read the letters. I saw a piece about you by somebody named Jumper in the *Hudson Review*. He starts out implying he's really going to tell us ALL, and then after telling nothing at all, and repeating the obvious, I thought, petered out and wound up by saying you should be more cheerful! I haven't read Mary's last [*The Group*] and probably shan't. She somehow keeps chopping away at her own feet until there is nothing left at all. I read *The Quiet American* expecting to be made mad, but it's just rather silly, or else poor Hemingway. I am pleased you said you liked my "Manuelzinho." Somehow when he appeared just now, in *The New Yorker*, he seems more frivolous than I'd thought, but maybe that's just the slick, rich surroundings. Please do forgive me for being so slow about writing; thank you for the really lovely pitcher, and I hope you and Elizabeth are both well and flourishing on Marlborough St.

To Aunt Grace

Mrs. Grace Bulmer Bowers (d. 1978) was EB's favorite aunt, to whom she dedicated her poem "The Moose." Aunt Grace, the second-oldest sister of EB's mother, Gertrude Bulmer Bishop, remained a lifelong resident of Great Village, Nova Scotia.

July 5, 1956

Your dinner party with Aunt Florence sounds rather grim! . . . You can see why I had my doubts about your having Aunt F. as a guest or anything else. She is really absolutely impossible, poor thing, and always manages to get under one's skin and say *the* most unkind thing of all, whatever it may be, sooner or later—though she doesn't want to; you can almost see her trying to be nice, and then out it comes, some horrible, mean remark! (One of her favorite cracks to me is that being a writer makes a woman coarse, or masculine.)

I don't think you got the funny clippings about the Pulitzer P. that I sent you from here, did you? I sent both you and Aunt F. the same set (no favorites!) and she never mentioned them either. I have an awful feeling that whole batch of mail got lost, about eight letters. The pictures of me were far from flattering, but Lota's library came out pretty well, etc., and I thought they'd amuse you. Also I want you to see what a sylph I am, I guess—118 lbs. 115 is my goal, though.

I wonder how your trip was and I really envy you being in Nova Scotia now. My old friend Frani, whose name you may remember, wrote me that she and her husband and three children are going there for a trip but I'm not sure when or where, or if they'll go through Great Village.

She's half Scotch so wants to go to the "Mod" at St. Anne's, Cape Breton.

I have an absolutely ravishing photograph of Betty & I'm getting some copies made. She's almost 18 months old now, has 10, almost 12 teeth, and is "into everything." But she doesn't talk—just because her mother and young aunts are too stupid to talk *to* her, I think. She doesn't even say "mama"—just "yes" and "shoe" and "good." Now I know why poor children cry more than rich ones. It isn't that they don't have enough to eat or anything like that; it's just because their parents are so dumb the way they treat them. We can't seem to get Maria to understand that she has to put things *away*, keep doors shut, or just *let* her play with anything she wants to that doesn't do any harm—instead of saying "No, no" all day long and keeping the poor baby confused all the time. Then if she does cry they're apt to give her a slap (if we aren't in sight) to make her stop—and then she *howls*, naturally. I really think that stupid or ignorant people *like* to be mean to babies unnecessarily—her father & mother are crazy about her and proud of her, and they should be, she's so beautiful—but they say NO all day long, when it's so much easier to put the carving knife where it belongs or something! She's so good, naturally, and good-natured, and we hate to see them, but there's not much we can do after a certain point, after all, and she does have to grow up with them. (Of course we're awfully tempted to keep her but I'm afraid it isn't a good idea really.) You should see her when I bought her some new shoes, looking at them & immediately holding up first one foot then the other. And the other day she found a piece of material and was holding it around her and looking down at it just like a woman trying on a skirt. She copies her mother and dusts and polishes shoes and "cooks." I think one could teach her to do anything at this point. We have a small square hole cut in the bottom of the brick wall that divides the back yard from the front yard, for the dogs to go through, so they wouldn't try to dash through the kitchen all the time, and now Betty has discovered it and crawls through it, too, with the greatest glee . . . Well, all this about babies isn't exactly news to you, I'm afraid . . .

The poem you saw must have been "Manuelzinho"—about L.'s kind-of-a-gardener—wasn't it? It's all completely true—how he hired the bus to go to his father's funeral, etc.

I'm investing some money here—borrowed it from my U.S. bank and invested here, where interests are fantastically high; and I can pay them back and still make quite a bit. Since I'm no businesswoman a friend of mine who's supposed to be a great moneymaker is doing it for me. I don't see why it shouldn't work and eventually I'll have enough to live on here in Brazilian money, and send more $$$ back to the U.S. I never thought of doing anything like that before. I think it must be the "Bishop side," as Aunt F. would say—the Grandpa B. side! Anything *artistic*, I feel positive, *couldn't* come from there, even if my father did do well in high school or whatever it was she always tells me! Oh well, we should just thank our stars we're not miserable the way she is.

August 28, 1956

. . . I've been to Rio for two or three days each week to go to the dentist, the allergy doctor, and the dressmaker. I have a wonderful allergy doctor, the best here, and a very nice young man, too—and he won't take a cent. I don't know why. Said it was "an honor"! so I gave him a copy of my book, and now I'm trying to get someone in New York to buy me some sort of very elegant briefcase for him. One can't get good things like that here and I think he'd like it and use it. He has been giving me tests and serums for a couple of years now, and I hate to think what I would have paid a doctor in N.Y. for it all. And he actually seems to have hit on the infection or whatever it was. I've had almost no asthma for months, for the first time in 15 years or so. I'm having a suit and two dresses made at the dressmaker's—I hadn't had any new clothes for four years! So I *have* to stay at 118 lbs. If I gain an ounce I won't be able to get into them; they're like the paper on the wall. It's a good way to make oneself stay thin, I guess.

I went down last week and spent a horrible day making a recording of poems. They have a recording studio at the U.S. Embassy and they let me use it. It had to be a 50-minute record (for a commercial company in N.Y.)—and 50 minutes is a *hell* of a long time, I find—uses up almost my life work! And I had to do it, and do it—from 10 to 5 with lunch out. Lota couldn't get away, so my friend Rosinha went with me and held my hand, figuratively speaking. I record abominably, but sort of felt I had to. They do make a little money, too, although I just can't imagine anyone buying them, really. By 5 p.m. we were all exhausted—Rosinha and I and the sound engineer . . .

To Robert Lowell

September 24, 1956

Your fan letter has been greatly appreciated—shall I look her up for you?—she lives near the apartment in Rio. Every word is literally from the Portuguese. That's the best I've ever seen, I think. I had a strange one from a boy who loves "all the arts," his paintings and drawings are in Canada or he'd send them to me, so instead he appends a long list of all their titles *The Death of Marat, The Bohemian, The Musselmen,* etc.—& on the back of the envelope (the letter's in Portuguese) he wrote: "U R 2 GOOD 2 B 4 GOT 10." But nothing can approach your Miss M.

I don't believe I've congratulated you yet about the baby—and I hope you are both keeping well and strong and cheerful. I'm very pro-baby these days. "Maria Elizabeth" is 18 months old now and beautiful as an Abyssinian Princess and learning to talk . . . Couldn't you arrange to have the christening coincide with Marianne's 70th birthday? I'm really hoping to get back to the U.S.A. for that.

She wrote me about her Boston visit: "Then Harvard's little magazine conference at which I *throve* (useless as I was professionally), cool pleasant weather and such companionable people R. & E. Lowell. I do like them—heartfelt, generous, genial, initiate; and so prepossessing! Philip Rahv gave a stern A-One talk on values in use as over against mildewed dictatorial culture. The L.'s invited me to a tea that was notable: flowers in a stone dish, a Boston-in-its-glory pair of drawing rooms, large window embrasures, and millions of books ascending the walls. William Alfred [playwright and teacher at Harvard] was an ornament of the conference, so punctual, so learned, so cheerful."

I saw a picture of Randall in *Time* and think the beard is extremely becoming. I wonder if he got his Mercedes-Benz. My dream car has now switched to a Giulietta convertible; the MG is really getting rather old. I am writing *New Yorker* stories, too, with this in mind—a Giulietta with "*spider springs.*" Somebody wrote me, I can't remember who, that Catharine Carver [New York and London editor] said your autobiographical piece is "wonderful," and Philip wrote something stern and A-one masculinely equivalent, so I wish it would hurry up and appear. I loved Mary McC.'s saying you were "brassy." Well, I like trumpet music very much, if that's what she meant.

We've had a house guest for over a month now, one of a pair of famous sisters, Rio "beauties," old school friends of Lota's. She really is beautiful, too—tall, grizzled blond, magnificent teeth and one blue eye and one brown eye. But she is an extreme hypochondriac and it's a little like having Proust to visit—no, I'm sure she's much nicer. But "resting" and making up her face and taking endless baths occupies most of her day. One interesting thing about her is that she's still, at 45 or so, completely dominated by her old Scotch governess, who died 15 years ago, but was with them for thirty years. She has her picture in her prayer book, looking just like a Scotch Highlander. I know of several of these Scotch governesses—their charges, no matter how "delicate" they are, all still take a "walk" every day and start off every morning with a dish of oatmeal (it's almost all the nourishment our guest will take) and speak perfect English with slight Scotch accents. Maria Cecilia (the guest) says: "My, you gave me a turn, as Miss Killough would say." Miss Killough bossed the mother around completely and every so often they had big fights and she'd pack her steamer trunks to start back to Aberdeen. But when she died, she left them all the money she'd saved, out of the salary they paid her, and just before the end became a Catholic. (The second case of that I know)—said her own church seemed "cold" to her. But I bet it was because of being snubbed by the English colony here, over the years, as a "governess." Well, Maria Cecilia is a fiend for "altering" clothes, darning and mending, and she's got my wardrobe in better shape than it's been in years. There's a nice Portuguese word meaning to make the most of or take advantage—*aproveitar*—and we've been *aproveitar*-ing shamelessly.

There's another nice humane verb that English needs—when you want to get out of an engagement, or dis-invite yourself—*desmarcar*. Something else I've found out about the language. Portugal was such a remote part of the Roman Empire that Portuguese changed more slowly than any other Latin language—they still have some Roman *Republic* forms, dropped under the Empire—and the open and close *e* & *o* correspond to differences of length in Classical Latin. Also the days of the week—"2nd Day," "3rd Day" are early Christian, when they couldn't use the names of the pagan gods. After a while the other nations went back to *lundi, mardi*, and so on. However, I'm still hopeless at *speaking* languages and really only talk freely to the cook.

I've been reading a superb book—but you probably know it—Marchand's *Memoirs of Napoleon*? If not, do read it immediately; I'm sure you'd like it, too. I wrote a kind of a poem—not much—for Mr. Rizzardi's number on Pound. Do you know him?—from Bologna. He writes very nice letters.

P.S. No new poems to see?

To Randall Jarrell

October 7, 1956

Those two volumes of Coleridge's *Letters* arrived last night, and I read until two and woke up at six to start in again—and only the pleasant and relieving prospect of writing you can tear me away from that adorable man. As Alice J. says of Henry James: "His intestines are *my* intestines; his tooth-aches are *my* tooth-aches." I'd never realized how wonderful the letters could be in bulk like that, and how contemporary he sounds. Have you read them?

It's funny, but true, that just the day before your letter arrived I'd been giving your collected works a thorough re-reading. You know, I was pleased about the Pulitzer business, and particularly here, where it was lots of fun—but I really cannot for the life of me understand why they didn't give it to you. Some of the war poems are surely the best ever written on the subject, honestly—and as far as "our" wars go, the only ones. But re-reading them I began to think that perhaps that's just why; that's why they settled on someone innocuous like me. The war is out of style now and they want to forget it? And of course I don't know who "they" were, anyway—it all depends on that, I suppose. Perhaps I'm just as happy not knowing, so don't tell me, if you know, who the committee was! I saw a very good photograph of you in *Time* recently, too—much better than the snapshot you sent in which you look *slightly* like Bébé Bérard! (It must be a party look.) The beard is vastly becoming. I think I recognize Mr. Starr, don't I? Your wife looks extremely pretty, and so do the girls. And so does the dashboard of the Mercedes. Lota, my Brazilian friend here, wants to know if you'd mind telling us the price, in the U.S.A. We're dreaming of one, too. The MG is getting rather old and tired—I just brought back several new pieces on my lap in the bus from Rio Friday. I am also dreaming of a Giulietta—have you seen them?—I only have in one *Sports Cars Illustrated*—but I'm dying for one—with "spider springs." It will take several stories of the length of "In the Village" (with which I bought the MG) to buy anything now, I'm afraid, but I am working on some and have hopes. We also have an elderly English Land Rover but the road & the house are almost at the point where we can get rid of that one.

I hope you like the Library [of Congress] better than I did, although I don't think I'd mind it quite so much now, being in a much better frame of mind, and in good health. I can't imagine what goes on there now. Phyllis [Armstrong] is an awfully nice girl—we were too shy of each other for months ever to get really acquainted, but she *is* nice, and really interesting, with her horse racing and shooting, etc., and very kind-hearted. We nursed a baby rabbit through one awful day or two in the office, I remember. I used to go to the zoo quite a lot, too—but it seems to me they had rather a plethora of pigmy hippopotami when I was there—but some fine giraffes and a wonderful young chimpanzee—possibly grown up by now. Another place I like very much and wish I just owned is the Dumbarton Oaks museum—just the right size. And if you're ever in the National Gallery take a look at the Delacroix of a little Algerian girl for me—it's one of their best paintings, I think. I tried and tried to write a poem about it but never succeeded. Also a beautiful Gauguin landscape of Brittany, spring-like—oh there are lots of things, of course. Well, I really hope to make a trip back next year.

This [*Partisan Review*] fellowship has helped a lot financially. (And I think they gave it to me because they felt so sorry for me after an "attack" they printed on me! Did you see it?—it didn't seem to bother me much; distance makes the heart grow tougher.) And now I have at last finished and mailed my Brazilian translation (over two years on it) and can work on some stories. Next year will be Marianne's 70th birthday and I'd like very much to see her, and it is time to see New York again and hear some music and see some plays—and it would be fun to get to Washington again while you're still there, if possible.

I think I may have told you about the translation—endless finicky work for very easy-sounding results. It's a real diary—a young girl in the '90s in a little diamond-mining town here, and in its way I think it's superb—no Anne Frank, but happily very different. Chatto & Windus has an option in England; I don't know who'll take it in the U.S. Oh, I recently saw your extremely good-looking Faber & Faber collection, with a slight feeling of envy, I'm afraid—it looked so nice, and purple linen has always been my goal. C & W is bringing out a small *plaquette* of me soon, though, so I should be properly grateful!

I'm terribly sorry about having given, I think, a lopsided emphasis to my remarks on *Pictures from an Institution*. That was just a part of it, of course—and the part that recedes quickly. I think the book really is a "minor classic"—I've been expecting to see it reprinted in the paper-bounds any time—or maybe it has been and I've missed it. I know it is that kind of a book because of the way whole bits, scenes, sentences, etc., have stuck with me ever since I read it and keep popping into my mind at the right moments—just the kind of thing that should happen with a book that eventually every literate person *should* know. But it *is* terribly funny, Randall—you can't get around that. I saw one or two good English reviews—more objective than the idiotic American ones, at least. And as a piece of prose I think it is brilliant and no reviewer I read ever said anything about that aspect of it at all. *Poetry and the Age* is everywhere, in Rio, even newsstands.

Peter Taylor's long story about his & Cal's trip to N.Y. and their girls was marvelous—at least to me. I don't know how it would strike a reader who didn't know the people, or some of them. I didn't dare mention it to Cal, of course! But Peter Taylor sounds like a very sympathetic man —I wish I'd see more things by him. I finally wrote Cal about the baby. Oh dear, I'm afraid I feel exactly the way you do about the poor little thing, but maybe E. will make a good mother. And almost all babies seem better off now than they used to be, at least—maybe it's better feeding!—I have really gone one better than you in the matter of children, though—I am a grandmother before my time, or at least a great-aunt. Lota has an adopted son who has six small children (Lota is my age) and we have the older two here for long visits. I also have a Negro namesake, "Maria Elizabeth," aged 19 months now (the cook's), and with Helena age 3, and Paulinha age 2, it is like a nursery school. The littlest one is almost too much to look at—she used to look exactly, except that her eyes are *dark* brown, like the youthful Dylan Thomas. This trip she has a little less mouth, but even more eyes, large and tragic, just too romantic—the older one is beautiful in a classic Latin way, and together they look like two Picasso periods.

[P.S.] I haven't read Giraudoux's *Electra* but I think Lota has it, and I shall. I'm sorry to hear of Kitten's death—but he had a lovely life, and a very long one. I have a handsome, ordinary cat—Tobias—full-dress suit, black & white, and my toucan, Uncle Sam. I'd love to meet you for a nice damning-all-round conversation! It is Sunday night and I must go down and heat up the lasagna. Lots of love and all my best to your pretty family.

To Dr. Anny Baumann

October 13, 1956

Thank you so much for your letter, written on the eve of your taking off for Scotland. I think you must be home again now, and I hope you & your husband had a good trip and a good rest and that it was all as beautiful as it's supposed to be.

I'd been meaning . . . to tell you, really, that everything goes well here. But today I've just seen Carlos Lacerda for a few moments and he talked so much about you that I feel I want to write to you right away. He arrived back from Portugal two nights ago. The plane was a day late, first, and then didn't get there till 2 a.m. in the pouring rain, but there were 2,000 automobiles full of people waiting at the airport to greet him. I wasn't there, but heard a firsthand account and it must have been a very emotional affair—Carlos making a speech and crying at the same time, a parade through town in the rain in the middle of the night, etc. We hope that all will go well and that he's really safe here now. The day he came back two of the men who attempted to assassinate him before he left were sentenced to 25 & 33 years—but of course they were just the hired gangsters, not the brains behind the plot.

He and Laetitia were having lunch at a neighbor's and we dropped in just to see him. They both look fine and years younger than when they left, and I think a great deal of it must be due to your efforts—perhaps a little to my dentist's, too! Carlos spoke of you with the greatest admiration . . .

I've been very well and working hard, for me, and maybe gradually making up for some of my misspent youth-and-early-middle-age . . . I finally got my translation all done and off and am now working on corrections. Pearl found me a fine agent, I think, just before she left. My one worry is that I am completely deluded about it and that no one besides myself will find it interesting—well, Pearl did, and a few other people have. I'm now at work on some stories that I hope will earn enough money to take a trip to N.Y. on sometime next year. I've about half a new book of poems done—with luck I might have another book next year; certainly the year after, I think. I have also planned out a small book of travel sketches about Brazil—I don't know how they'll work out, but it will be fun to do and perhaps I can print some of them in *The New Yorker* as I go along. So you see we're very busy . . .

The allergist friend found I had a slight streptococcus infection and has been giving me a vaccine for it and asthma combined—it seems to be working somewhat, too, I think—I now take one, or just a half, a Metacorten every day, and sometimes can even stop for stretches. Whether his vaccine worked or simply being more cheerful in general, I don't know. I'm sorry to have gone on so about myself, but I think perhaps you like to get reports on your patients once in a while.

We hope very much to get to N.Y. next year, maybe for some months in the fall and winter. It will be Miss Moore's 70th birthday . . . Lota sends her best regards. The house will really be done inside another 8 or 10 months, we think—and she has just planted the hillsides with 440 baby pine trees, plus a lot of flowering trees . . .

To Aunt Grace

October 19, 1956

. . . If you really enjoy having TV like that, why not get one? I've seen so little television that I really don't know anything about it, although my friends all say the sports things are the best. My friend the poet, Miss Moore, lives in Brooklyn and is a great Dodger Fan—age 69—wrote me all about the last games and has even written a song for them!—I can't quite imagine its being sung, but anyway. They do have television in Rio but I've never even seen it, and they say the programs are dreadful here. A very few people have sets in Petrópolis and I think if they have big enough ones, or big enough aerials, they get Rio on them. Lota has been trying to get a neighbor of ours to get one for himself and his elderly sister—four elderly people living together, and he has plenty of money —but he can't get used to the idea, so far. Then *we* could go to see things on it that we wanted to see! But where we live, up against enormous steep high stone mountains, they say we'll probably never be able to get it, even when Rio gets more powerful stations. (It's just in its infancy here, of course.)

I haven't heard from Aunt Florence for about a month, or more, either—I've been writing, too. I hope she's all right. I had a letter from F. a few days ago—the first I've ever had—about a piece of land I own but have never even seen. He works for the J. W. Bishop Co., you know. I was very surprised—he can scarcely *write*, poor boy. Maybe he never has to and is out of practice, but I was rather shocked . . .

It's pouring rain. The rains seem to have begun early—in fact there was scarcely any dry season. But the garden is looking really nice, for the first time. We have huge blue or white lilies agapanthus—know them? —all up the hillside—three or four ft. high; azaleas just past blooming here; alyssum, phlox, sweet William & iris, all over the place. And now we are starting to keep bees! I've always wanted to. A man is coming this week with four hives of Italian bees. He will install them and care for them when you need him. Some friends of ours got about fifty pounds of honey this year. The only thing here is that the ants will move right in and take over unless you build the hives specially. The ants here would eat us, I think, if we didn't watch out! Write again—how is the job?— tell me your building plans. Now I can daydream about your house—I adore planning houses!—and I do want to help when I can . . .

To Rollie McKenna

Rollie McKenna, the distinguished photographer well known for her superb photos of authors, knew that EB was never happy about being photographed, or happy with the results. Her book, A Life in Photography *(1991), contains three excellent photos of EB, including one taken when McKenna was a guest at Petrópolis.*

Sunday, November 19 (?), 1956

. . . The house is almost DONE; we can't believe it. Just the front door missing, and the *brise-soleil*—and six more squares in the terrace that will be done in two weeks at the rate they're going now. In fact, all we need for perfect happiness is about $100,000 tax free to finish everything plus the garage, equip it all with large padlocks and a reliable watchman—the Angel Gabriel maybe—and then we'd fly off to N.Y.

We don't need the porcelain stove any longer, thank you! Lota finally built a large, freestanding fireplace. She sat in a safari chair and *produced* it, with Negro boys streaming past her, each with a rock from the mountainside on his head, just like Cecil B. deMille directing *The Ten Commandments*, or the building of the pyramids . . . We almost lived beside the fireplace last "winter" and have ordered a new popcorn popper made, so you see it's successful . . .

Now I just have to say something I'm dreading and that I hope you'll understand and not mind—won't just think I'm abnormally vain and abnormally selfish. Perhaps I am vain to the point of thinking you might be going to put me in that book of poets, when you hadn't had any such thought. But because of that prize, on the other hand, you might be. If you are, would you *please* not use the pictures you took of me here or in New York? The N.Y. one makes me look—or rather, I did look—like an unhappy, fifth-rate lady-Dylan Thomas–type, so you probably wouldn't use it anyway. In fact, couldn't we wipe it out of existence? The ones you took here I do realize are awfully good pictures—animated, *like*—all the qualities that make good pictures. But I hate them. I was a lot thinner then than in N.Y., certainly, but my face *was* swollen from cortisone (the medical term is actually "dish-face," it seems), and even Lota says that although they're good they do make me look twice as fat and old as I am, or almost. In the past few years I've lost 30 pounds; I'm back to "normal," weigh 115, which is what I used to, and look *happy*—and I really can't bear the thought of perpetuating the way I looked and felt during one bad stretch of my life. Maybe one has no right to one's own life or looks—but I hope you'll be one of the few photographers who doesn't think so!—but it would make me miserable, really. Jim Merrill wrote me he saw one in a bookshop somewhere and that bothered me. Perhaps the book isn't coming out so soon after all—and maybe of course you don't want me, anyway—and I promise you that when we get to N.Y. you can take me standing on my head or cutting my toenails if you want to. This is not the slightest reflection on your work, which I really admire. It's just vanity, VANITY.

I've been to Stonington, too, in the dim past, and remember enjoying sailing there in a small boat. How's the poodle? One problem about leaving here is what to do with my cat—should I bring him? He has the seasons the wrong way around, too, of course—and would freeze in N.Y. in his summer coat in December . . .

We have been reading the Sunday papers out on the new terrace— a strange contrast to a beautiful crystal-clear day here, everything blooming and all the birds building nests or feeding their babies. Mary has owls nesting down at her house—she complained that she could hear them "breathing heavily" in the night. Last night we went down to see them and decided that what she thought was asthma was really just the young crying for food when the parents fly back to the nest—a loud hoarse gasp. It's wonderful—they swoop down out of the darkness (or the full moonlight last night) from those cliffs, give us a dirty look *en passant*, and drop things in the nest—I hate to think what. Quite big birds. Me with my black cat and she with her owls—we can set up as witches pretty soon.

I do hope you'll understand my feelings about pictures. *Why* didn't I look like Duse, pray?

To May Swenson

November 25, 1956

See our new [note]paper that turned out to cost so much that I don't think we'll ever use it except for crowned heads. The stationer is French, a famous one here, with a dark jumbled office approached through shoe-shine boys & up a flight of dirty stone steps, off an alley. (One charm of "shopping" in Rio is that things always turn out to be in such unexpected places.) On the walls hang medals in glass cases, from all the crowned heads of Europe, to him and his ancestors. But I was overawed, I suppose, and he talked so fast, and is such a crook, to boot, that of course I spent a fortune in two minutes flat & we both have enough calling cards now to go dropping them from an airplane, if we wanted to . . .

I'm glad you've heard from Katharine White. I never happened to mention her, I think, but she is a very good friend of mine and has been wonderful to me, editorially as well. She's the one who stood up for my [story] "In the Village," [the poem] "Manuelzinho," etc.—and I've found her criticism of stories very good. She doesn't try to cut everything to the *New Yorker* last, and is somewhat more adventurous, I think, than the others. Also she'll work over prose for a long time if she likes it at all . . .

Lota refuses to fold up the legs of jeans. Also she refuses to accept the U.S. idea that they are more beautiful when faded. She's classical, and also likes her temples and statues painted in bright colors, I suppose, the way they should be! . . . Lota just sent up a note by the cook; it's rather funny so I'll quote it: "Rosinha is coming 5:30. Wrote that letter to Pinto (about my hi-fi). Sending the maids to the *festa* with Julinho comme chevalier servante. Maria (their older sister, the cook) is scared of gossip from her husband. Aren't they funny?"

Explication, as the highbrows say: A friend is arriving for the weekend at 5:30. Our bricklayer's baby is being baptized today. The poor infant's name is going to be Jaime Jorge (Jymy Georgy, it's pronounced) and the father spent most of yesterday not working, gathering up the necessary chickens, suckling pigs, and *cachaça* for the *festa* to be held afterwards. Maria's two younger sisters, now here as maids (she has four sisters, and we get them in rotation, like a chorus), are dying to go, but being well-behaved young Negro virgins can't go and come back at night up our long mountain road unescorted. So Lota has ordered our kind-of-a-handy-boy, Julinho, to go and come with them. This means Maria's husband, a mean little character, isn't going to approve and will scold and grumble. Also I think the two girls (they're awfully pretty girls; one's ravishing and one's engaged to a bus driver, so they're rather superior) look down on poor Julinho—who is *very* black, has two extra teeth that stick out in front, and never wore shoes until we bought him some last year—and Lota has created a slight social disturbance. However, she's democratic and tries constantly to bring up these ex-slaves to be less snobbish! It's a small sample of life here.

The house is looking beautiful, really—almost done—and I must send you pictures, somehow. Now it seems a sin to leave it, but I think if we can manage to scrape up the money we're coming to N.Y. for six months next year—early next fall, probably . . .

Lunch

Well, lunch was pretty lively today. The argument about whether Virginia and Antoninha should be permitted to go to the *festa* went on and on. At this moment someone shrieked that a snake was eating baby birds up in a tree and everyone ran! Sure enough, right beside the house, a really big snake, five feet long, was up in a tree and had just dragged out a baby bird from a João do Barro's nest—a big clay oven-like house. It was starting to come down again, with the bird's legs still feebly waving out of its jaws, and the parents shrieking up in the air. Lota got out her .22 and *said* she got the snake with her first shot—probably she did; she's pretty good. Lots of bright scarlet blood, lighter-colored than human, but that baby was dead. There may be another one still in the nest. So we returned to lunch, or rather didn't care to go on with it after that, and the fate of the girls' evening was never decided, as far as I can remember. (Next day, they went and *danced*.)

. . . Thank you for the New Directions books that came yesterday, two batches of them. I was very glad to have [Scott Fitzgerald's] *The*

Crack-Up and [Henry James's] *Stories of Writers & Artists.* I used to own them both in hardcover and they were among those that got lost. *In the American Grain* [by William Carlos Williams] is going to make a perfect Christmas present for someone here. I'd never seen those Dylan Thomas stories—just three in that book, and read them all last night . . . Another lost book is good old *Nightwood* [by Djuna Barnes] and I'd like the three Lorca plays. *Nightwood* would also be good for someone here who likes purple prose; and the plays for when I get lazy about Spanish and can refer to them. You were an angel to send them . . .

To Pearl Kazin

November 30, 1956

Just a note to convey this somehow ungracious Christmas gift to you—but I can't think of any other way of showing you my general gratitude & affection that will be bound to reach you & also be of use! I'm not sure whether you'll still be in Málaga or not, not having heard. We've had a terrific four-day storm here and there wasn't a scrap of airmail at the P.O.—perhaps the planes have been held up. Lota was away in Rio and I was all alone with the servants and the toucan (who has a sore foot) & the cat (who was being wormed) and the *roaring* waterfall. I feel as if I'd undergone a sort of Robinson Crusoe experience. Also I kept reading Coleridge's letters—just couldn't stop—and *his* weather got worse and worse & his health more and more excruciating, until when he had "flying irregular gout," had got drenched one more time, and his finances were beyond hope, I could scarcely believe that I was dry, had no symptoms of anything at all, and was at least solvent enough to send you this very small memento. I feel as if I could scarcely be said to exist, beside C. You must read him, though . . .

I heard last week that Houghton Mifflin have turned down *The Diary of "Helena Morley."* I'm relieved, in most ways, but even so it is slightly discouraging, of course. But I'm still very optimistic about it even so. Miss Baumgarten is waiting on me now, for the corrections, before trying again.

Everything is fine here except that we do need a new car and both Lota and I suddenly have begun to crave N.Y. We allow ourselves to daydream over coffee every morning. With any luck, and a little hard work, I think we'll make it next year all right.

To Robert Lowell

December 2, 1956

Last night and this morning I've read your piece ["91 Revere Street"] in *Partisan Review*, that just arrived. It is *very* good; I feel as if I'd sat through one of those Sunday dinners. And being thrown out of the Garden, just like Adam, is marvelous. I hadn't realized before how closely connected with the Navy you were. In fact it is all fascinating and I hope I see more soon—is *PR* going to publish more, and when will the book of it appear, and how far along do you go? No, really—it's excellent. And what's more, you *keep it up*—and can keep it up, I should think, your life being more all of a piece than—well, mine, for example. Or perhaps other people's lives always appear to be.

I'm glad it came along now, because for several weeks I've been completely absorbed in Coleridge's *Letters*—that new edition. (Maybe I was when I wrote you last; I can't remember how long it's been going on now.) . . . I want very much to write some sort of piece, mostly about Coleridge, but bringing in Fitzgerald's *The Crack-Up*, Dylan Thomas, Hart Crane, etc.—but don't know whether I know enough, or have enough material at hand. Well, your chapter was a decided change in tone.

Marianne is wonderful, that's all. If I don't mention my health she writes implying that she knows I'm concealing my dying throes from her. If I say I've never felt better in my life (God's truth), she writes *"Brave Elizabeth!"* (Lota says it's a form of aggression.) Marianne used to send one rather stolid, timid friend of ours on Errands of Mercy, to people he'd never met. She told him that *"poor* Peter Monro Jack" was in desperate straits, sick, lonely, heaven knows what all, and the friend went to call, probably taking a bag of groceries or a bunch of flowers, and found a large gay party going on, with everyone in evening dress. Also Marsden Hartley—dying and all alone in a miserable garret—*he* was found to be in a friend's most luxurious apartment, with a Steinway grand and a cook and a maid waiting on his every wish!

Yes, I saw that extravagant remark in the *New Statesman and Nation*. (The writer is probably aged 19 and known to be slightly feeble-minded by his intimates.) Did I really make snide remarks about Emily Dickinson? I like, or at least admire, her a great deal more now—probably because of that good new edition, really. I spent another stretch absorbed in that, and think (along with Randall) that she's about the best we have. However—she does set one's teeth on edge a lot of the time, don't you think? "Woman" poet—no, what I like to be called now is *poetress*. I was at a friend's house here the other day and he introduced me to a Brazilian lady—he murmured to her in Portuguese that this was the American poet, etc., and the lady, determined to show off her English, shook my hand enthusiastically and said, "You are the famous American poetress?" So I allowed I was. I think it's a nice mixture of poet and mistress. The lady actually turned out to be quite interesting. She & her husband, a team of lawyers, and she's writing a book about the U.S. Supreme Court—. . . all most unusual for a "woman" here!

I had a wonderful letter from Randall, after a long silence—full of news and excitement and snapshots. I was awfully pleased.

Summer is here, which means lots of visitors—this past week too many. One a tall, elegant São Paulo *gran fina* arrived without any warning—telephoned from the foot of the mountain—with her BOOK (600 pages) for me to translate. She had taken a bus and even started to walk—her five-inch heels dipped in red mud—all completely unheard of here, and we were so taken with her that we kept her all afternoon. A diamond in each ear, and two on one finger . . .

To Aunt Grace

December 2, 1956

. . . I've written a long poem ["The Moose"] about Nova Scotia. It's dedicated to you. When it's published, I'll send you a copy. All my best Christmas wishes, Aunt Grace. Hope to see you in '57.

To Marianne Moore

January 19, 1957

Lota brought back your book [*Like a Bulwark*] from the Post Office last night and I was so relieved to see it. I'd been afraid it was lost or that I had really been too cruel to Eisenhower! First of all I think it looks lovely—the first of your books published, in the U.S.A., at least, to do you justice as far as looks go. The inside cover is so pretty and I do like that large type. I think it is only used for poetry now as the seal of SUCCESS, but I wish it were always used. It seems to make the meaning clear immediately—even to be saying the poems, in a clear, simple, cultivated voice! And printing the titles in the same type, only heavier, is right, too—don't you think? The only thing I'd object to—I can't help being critical—is those little lines at the top of the page, and I know that publishers are all mad about them, I don't know why.

I hadn't seen "Apparition of Splendor" and "Logic and 'The Magic Flute' " before, and I think they are both wonderful. "Spines rooted in the sooty moss," "when the lightning shines / on thistlefine spears," "needle-debris," "lets the primed quill fall," "insister, you have found a resister"—it's really *superb*, and so marvelously true. The first two lines of "Logic and . . ." are superb, too—"in what theater lost." I'm grateful for the word *wentletrap* and shall do my best to see that it passes into common usage (not that I can while living here, of course). But the beginning is so good and so Mozartian, too—that light, direct attack. I do admire it! "Peculiar catacomb, / abalonean gloom" is also perfectly Mozartian, too—his glooms would be abalonean, I should think. Without ever saying red or blue, it *is* colored.

I'd seen "The Sycamore" reprinted in *The N.Y. Times* recently and admired it almost to excess—doing my best to describe the sycamore to Lota. Ah Marianne! How *do* you do it. I like that one as much as Hopkins's "dappled things"—and it is so much better without that emotional *rushing* effect he produces. Perhaps it is the uncanny meter.

Well, I think I've exclaimed enough and repeated enough already about the others. I do think it's a wonderful little book & you must be very happy having presented these things as they are, and as they should be—not exaggerated nor flattened out, nor blown up—just with 20/20 vision. Thank you so much for sending me the book and I am sorry you apparently had to go to the trouble of doing it yourself.

I was surprised to learn of T. S. Eliot's marriage in the paper last night—perhaps he hadn't "banish'd sloth" [phrase in "Logic and 'The Magic Flute,' " for which MM gives her source as Ovid's "Banish sloth; you have defeated Cupid's bow"]. Are you going to do it, too? [*In margin:* But you *have* "banish'd sloth."] Lota sends her kindest regards and we also both send love & best wishes for 1957. I hope you've been well & recovered completely from the sickness you mentioned before.

To Howard Moss

Howard Moss (1922–87) was poetry editor of The New Yorker *from 1948 until his death. His* Selected Poems *(1971) received the National Book Award; his critical works include* The Magic Lantern of Marcel Proust *(1962) and* Writing Against Time *(1969); and he edited the poems of Keats and an anthology,* The Poet's Story *(1973).*

January 25, 1957

This is a personal note, so I'll send it to your home address. My friend Lota de Macedo Soares & I are planning to come to New York around the first week or two of April—I don't know the exact date yet. We're going to be staying six months (have to stay six months to bring back a car with us, for one reason) and we want to sublet a furnished apartment, if possible. I know it's an awkward stretch of time, etc., but I thought I'd write to you because I know you have a vast circle of friends and might possibly know of someone going abroad then. We'd like two bedrooms, or three rooms, anyway—or two big ones with a kitchen—and could pay from $200 to $250 a month, the less the better, naturally. We'd rather not be *in* the Village (around where you live is all right, though), nor *way* uptown (Riverside Drive, etc.)—but I know we can't be too fussy.

I'm an excellent housekeeper. We have to buy quite a lot of linen, dishes, etc., anyway, so we'd be using mostly our own shortly after we got there . . . I like to be up high—& I'd probably also be buying an air-conditioning unit to bring back here, too.

I've had four fan letters about *your* poem. I hope to get a couple of

my own off to you soon. I hope you're all over the gall bladder trouble
—my 83-year-old aunt writes of hers as her "Gaul bladder."

[P.S.] If we couldn't move in right away—or had to move out a little
early—it would still be all right. And I see I haven't said that it's going
to be awfully nice to see you again.

To May Swenson

February 10, 1957

I should have thanked you long before now for your fine reporting
of the Y.M.H.A. shindig. Some other friends went, too, but they don't
write nearly as good letters as you do! I also had a very nice note from
Louise Bogan *saying*, at any rate, that she hadn't found it a burden (as
Miss M. would put it). I do hope your reading went off well and wasn't
too tiring. Thank you also for the clippings—I was very much interested
in the Billie Holiday review and thought it was pretty good, didn't you?
I've ordered an album but it hasn't arrived yet, if it ever will. I have quite
a few old records of hers but they're getting pretty worn out now. Last
week I did get a copy of Robert Fitzgerald's book—with a card from
Laughlin . . . I liked Fitzgerald very much the one evening I spent with
him, and I admire his poetry in some ways—and he is a fine, careful,
scholarly type. But it never seems to ignite, or rarely—one or two of the
slighter ones strike me as best, still; and the rest often like very superior
translations from the Latin. What do you think?

. . . We're really coming to New York. Around April 1st, and staying
probably about six months. The length of time depends on whether I can
bring back a car IF I stay away six months, or not. I don't know where
we'll be yet—Howard is very kindly helping me find a sublet. I can't really
believe we'll make it—so much to do about passports, mothballs, traveling
outfits, *praying* that the servants won't all walk out on us at the very last
minute, taking the cat to a friend in Rio, boarding the toucan with an
animal-dealer neighbor up here (banding his leg so I'll get the same dear
Sammy when I get back!).

Day before yesterday was my birthday and I spent most of the evening
sitting outdoors in the half moonlight informing two Brazilian intellectuals why they really should read Edmund Wilson, say, instead of Henry
Miller, to get an adequate idea of U.S. letters. The French influence is
so strong here, and H. Miller is mentioned by some French mystical
writers, and so they've all got the idea that he's the new American Blake,
I think. It's funny—one can't get furreners to read the GOOD things! I
had another horrible evening arguing that we really didn't ignore Dreiser
completely (as they think), but that Henry James IS better! It finally
dawned on me that Dreiser, Anderson, some of Miller, etc., correspond
better to the mental picture they have of the U.S.A. and they just can't

bear to have it spoiled by any first-rate writers. And they don't know our critics at all, just pick up the notions of a bunch of anti–U.S., Catholic Frenchmen, who also don't know very much about the U.S. and its writers—in any quantity, that is. But my Portuguese is scarcely equal to enlightening them. Heavens, it will be nice to carry on an all-English conversation again!

We hope to hear a lot of music and possibly see whatever plays worth seeing are still lingering on . . . A dreadful picture of T. S. Eliot's bride in *Time*. Lota said, "Why she's a real English *pudim*" (Portuguese for pudding). I have about twenty notes to get off before going to Rio tomorrow to see about papers, clothes, etc., so I'd better stop.

[P.S.] Farrar, Straus has taken the translation [*The Diary of "Helena Morley"*].

To Isabella Gardner

Isabella Stewart Gardner (1915–81) of Boston, who became Mrs. Allen Tate in 1959, was an editor of Poetry *magazine in the 1950s. Among her books of poetry are* The Looking Glass *(1961)*, West of Childhood *(1965), and the posthumous* Collected Poems *(1990).*

115 East 67 Street (1E)
New York, New York
May Day, 1957

Thank you for your letter—and for the beautiful white azalea (which we say aza-lay-a). It must be a very superior plant because it's the only one we've had here so far that has lasted at all, and it looks as fresh as ever and is still putting out new blooms. It was awfully nice of you to send it. We did have a lovely breakfast party with you; Lota enjoyed meeting you so much, and I am horrified when I think how condescendingly I asked the inhabitant of a Mies van der Rohe house if she was at all interested in modern architecture! But I'm afraid I've bored so many people with those pictures, who couldn't tell a barn from a barracks and didn't care, either, that I usually preface showing them now. I'm also glad you did feel "at ease" with us. I have been so shy all my life that of course I think that other people *never* are. However, I didn't feel shy with you —partly because the more natural manners in Brazil have helped a lot, I think; partly maybe equinal!—but mostly, I think, because I did feel at home with you immediately and just burbled on, I'm afraid. Even acutely, or problem, shy people like myself occasionally don't feel shy at all with someone—and it's always a good sign, I've found! Anyway, we thank you for a nice lunch, a nice party, and the beautiful plant that I am watering and grooming several times a day.

I am awfully sorry about those poems being returned. I certainly wouldn't worry about Mr. [Rolfe] Humphries's rejections, though—his taste seems to be very strange, and he's sent back most of mine, too— and I think probably will send back the rest soon now. They can only be 25 lines long, NOT from *The New Yorker*, and so many other restrictions that I don't see how anything or anyone can get in. (Or almost not from *The New Yorker*—he'd prefer them not to be, he said.)

We are doing our best these days at conniving and plotting somehow to get a car back to Brazil with us. If we can arrange it we'll buy one immediately. If we have a car we shall undoubtedly be taking a couple of trips this summer—to the Cape, Maine maybe, even perhaps to Nova Scotia. But I really don't know whether we can do it yet or not—and if we can't take it back it would be foolish to buy one. However, we may be able to borrow or rent one. Or even car-less we might get to the Cape, I suppose. But won't you be getting to New York again before October 1st, surely?

Loren [MacIver] is also sorry to have missed meeting you. I don't believe you took the catalogue along, so I'm sending one. I called up the gallery yesterday just to find out for myself how much things cost. There's one small fairly old one that I want very much if I can possibly afford it, to take back with me. While I was at it I asked the prices of the recent ones I'd liked particularly, so I've jotted them down here just to give you an idea. The *Rue Mouffetard* painting is a beauty—long and narrow, in a slightly earlier style—thick paint and wonderful bright little details, fragments of letters, etc. (I don't like the collage of the same street so much.) Also the *Hellenic Landscape* I liked very much—all gray-blues, and those tiny buildings also have letterings on them, fragments of advertisements, in Greek of course. It has much more depth and feeling than that bad reproduction gives any idea of. The big one, not shown, called *Acropolis*—pillars that cross the canvas completely, at one side, and mysterious fragments at the other—I've been told by those who know much better than I do, is one of her finest. I think I still prefer the smaller one, but I'm no kind of judge, and have no idea what you'd like, or what you have in mind, or whether they strike you as too expensive, etc. etc. (I'm not telling you about the little one I want for myself!) Anyway, sometime perhaps you can see what she has on hand here; we'll take a trip down to her studio, if I'm still in N.Y., or if not you must go anyway the next time you are here. (Her husband is Lloyd Frankenberg—but I guess you know that.)

Lota's name is—part of it—Maria Carlota de Macedo Soares.

I am so pleased that you liked the Pound poem ["Visits to St. Elizabeths"]. I really couldn't tell much myself whether it conveyed my rather mixed emotions or not. It came out in Italian, I think, first—that Mr. Rizzardi translated it—and sounded rather well in Italian, I thought!

We spent a wonderful afternoon and early dinnertime with Marianne day before yesterday and she was marvelous—telling us how two years ago she got her driver's license. It was $5.00 a lesson; she took 37 lessons (this was in the summer, in Boston); toward the last she was taking three lessons a day. I asked her how fast she drives. "Oh, not fast, Elizabeth. About 50."

Please don't worry about having been indiscreet at all. Of course I had heard the fact of O.'s having a son before, and yours were by far the kindest and most sympathetic words and interpretation of it I had heard. I don't like gossip, either—although hypocritically I'm afraid I sometimes like to listen to it, particularly after having been away for five years . . .

I also hope I see some poems by you appearing soon. Lota's gone on an outing to Vassar with a photographer friend, for the day—otherwise I know she'd join me in sending love and best wishes.

To Robert Lowell

Thursday
August 15, 1957
[New York, New York]

I'd mailed my letter to you when yours of the 9th came. We really covered somewhat the same subjects, I think—but yours made me feel both awfully sad and extremely optimistic. You weren't "inconsiderate," Cal! You were a wonderful host, and we had such a nice time with you, really. Even if Lota does think all fir trees are deliberately planted, she liked Maine very much, and you were so good about driving us all over the coastline.

As I'm sure she's told you, Elizabeth & I had only about three minutes' conversation, in which I told her that I was worried about your coming down to Brazil alone. I just spoke about Brazil, not New York nor Boston nor anything. (Except that I think I said I thought Boston alone in the summer didn't sound very promising, either.) What both Lota and I felt, feel, about Brazil is that much as we'd really love to have you visit us there, show you a few of the colonial towns, etc.—it's really *not* a place to spend any time in alone. Rio is absolutely beautiful, the most beautiful harbor in the world, and parts of the city are enchanting—but once you've seen it there is really very little to do there. Up in the country with us is also beautiful and peaceful and we have lots of books and hope to have the hi-fi going—but I'm afraid you'd really feel restless after a stretch of it, and even a trip to Ouro Prêto (THE Baroque town) only takes three or four days.

Our idea was that it would be better if you all could come some-time—we could find you an apartment in Rio, find Elizabeth a maid and a *baba* (nanny) (such things do exist there) and then you might stay for two or three months and I think find it more interesting. [*In margin:* Suggest this to E. I think she might really be able to work there, too.] If you got bored in Rio you could come up and visit us (1½ hours by excellent bus service, every half hour). If you got bored up there you could go back to Rio. And we really have plenty of room for you and family, too.

When we started thinking about various friends you might stay with in Rio was really when this all grew on us—we just knew how strange, difficult, and *boring* it might get for you. It really is much more "foreign" than Europe, you know, in some ways, and the language is difficult and there aren't cafés, simple restaurants, places to go sightseeing, etc. etc.

Please don't worry about anything connected with me, Cal—don't worry at all, if that's possible. I saw Giroux the other day about this awful proof [of "*Helena Morley*"] and he talked & talked about how much he liked the autobiographical piece in *Partisan Review* ["91 Revere Street"]. I'm not going to give those readings, so we think maybe we can go back to Brazil sometime the first week of October now. Lota's Dr. Moulton (her old doctor—former! she's young and beautiful!) is out of town but she's written her, and any information about Boston doctors I'll send on to you immediately.

Maybe I should add to the inscription in the Herbert [book], "E.B. the 1st" (?) (but I shan't, of course). I do hope and pray you are feeling better and please write me whenever you feel like it. I got the German anthology right away and have found some wonderful things. Did you notice Morgenstern?—Klee-like and Stevens-like? . . . I plan to go to Key West for one week, starting August 31st, back [to New York] the 6th. I do hope to see you again before we leave. Lota sends her love and all best wishes and so do I, as I'm sure you know.

To Aunt Grace

115 East 67 Street
New York, New York
September 16, 1957

I'd *love* to have that portrait of my mother—I've wanted it, as you know, for years. Do you suppose you could possibly have it sent to me here? Would it come parcel post?—and insured for $100, say? I don't know about Customs, but I think that works of art, antiques, etc., can come in free. At any rate I don't think there'd be any duty, or not much, and I'd gladly pay it, of course. Thank Aunt Mabel for me. It seems a shame to break the pair of portraits—and tell her I do appreciate it. Our freighter is now sailing on October 8th—about a week earlier than we thought it would.

I took your letter down to Key West with me and then never did get a chance to answer it, and while I was away your postcard came . . . I felt I couldn't leave the U.S.A. without seeing Marjorie [Stevens], so while our Brazilian friend was here to keep Lota company, I went off for about a week (also this place is pretty crowded with three, and all three shopping like crazy). It was fearfully hot in K.W. but I'm awfully glad I went. I saw several old friends and Marjorie was dying to show me her new little house, etc. She works so hard and hasn't been off the island for several years, I'm afraid, but her health is much better and she looks quite well—she asked all about you. She was keeping two Siamese cats for a friend, "Blue Points"—pale gray with silver-gray markings and blue eyes, beautiful animals. I let them sleep with me—fine, but hot, and they also talk a great deal! I came back to find New York hotter than ever—an unusual heat wave for September—and a new batch of *proof* awaiting me. This means I'll get it all done before I go, but it's another week or ten days' work.

This, plus the earlier sailing date—plus the fact that I'm completely BROKE, of course—means that I don't see how I can possibly get to Nova Scotia, although I've been hoping against hope all the past month that I'd somehow find the time and the money. I *thought* I was getting a refund on my income tax that would have paid for the ticket, but it seems the accountant applied it on next year's instead—fine, but no good to me right now. Unless something unexpected comes along, I just don't see how I can make it. I'm going off with lots of unpaid bills and unseen friends, as it is—I am so terribly sorry, really—that glimpse of you wasn't enough—and I promise I'll come, by plane, if I can see my way to, at all, in the next two weeks.

If it's any consolation, Aunt Florence tells me my Worcester relatives are mad at not seeing me again! (She got Lota on the telephone while I was away—called her "LOLA" and told her how smart I am, but how it was only natural because the Bishops are all so smart! Lota thought it was awfully funny.) Then I talked to her yesterday. She wants some pink pajamas, "pretty ones, dearie" (as if left to my own devices I'd buy ugly ones), and she also says you're getting married. Is this true, and if so I wonder who is the lucky man? Or is it some of Aunt F.'s fancies? I think it is *a fine idea* but I'm surprised you'd confide in Aunt Florence first! I spent the morning at the dentist's and read the September *National Geographic*—a very silly piece about the Bay of Fundy, but I think I'll buy it just for the photographs. Some of them made me feel homesick, and I do wish I could get there now to see the colors of the maple trees. Something may turn up—I hope so.

To Joseph and U. T. Summers

Petrópolis, Brazil
November 26, 1957

I was awfully glad to get U.T.'s letter just before we left New York and Joe's just after we, finally, got home. That last month or two in New

York was just too rushed to write any letters, but I did want to tell you how badly I felt about having left N.Y. and gone to Florida just at the time you sailed for England. I had the date written down and everything but what happened was that I postponed my Florida trip several times and finally got all dates confused. At least I heard from Pearl, through Katy Carver, that you did get off all right, but I did want to see you doing it for myself. The English house & housekeeping amaze me—and your previous tenants—but they sound more English than American, surely. Well, I can sympathize somewhat about moving in, packing, unpacking, etc.—and maybe the easier time we have of it because of no children and more "servants" is compensated for by the Brazilian Customs—a prolonged nightmare—and the fact that the servants went off sort of like Sleeping Beauty. We got to the house, but it is taking ages to get them awake again. The Customs!—well, about half our stuff is still there, although we've been in Rio seeing to it almost ever since we arrived (three weeks, but I can't believe it). We have to make one more trip to retrieve the rest and *pay*. Poor Lota and all her lovely cans of tuna fish, dozens of napkins, dishes, etc. All the laws were changed just before we arrived, of course—"household effects" don't seem to mean what they say any more—just one sample will give you the idea of the Kafka-*puro* we've been through: They *weighed* our Victrola records, pasteboards & all!

However, the house is standing and as beautiful as ever, the animals all alive and nicely and unresentfully demonstrative (I have a Kissing Kat, surely a rarity), "Betty" looking healthy & beautiful—her only defect is that her front teeth stick out just slightly, in a little arch. I wish I could say it came from using a "comforter" to excess, but I suppose it didn't. (She still carries a supply of the things with her, but hides them when she sees L. or me.) There's also a new and so far very unloved one, 2 months—named, poor baby, "Alisette Mara." Where her mother got that we can't imagine. She looks *exactly* like the handyman—not a bit like her violent little pa—but he seems to have accepted her all right. And her mother had an awful crush on the handyman for months, too. Well, as Fats Waller says, "One never knows, do one."

I've asked the publishers to send you a copy of the translation, out Dec. 3rd. If you don't get it *tell* me . . . If it hadn't been for Pearl's help I think I would have abandoned the whole thing. I did swear for a week never to publish anything again in my lifetime. Please don't expect much. It's a mess, "physically," and there are loads of corrections we just couldn't afford to make, finally. I also think now that my introduction is long-winded. However, if you "get into it" I think you'll enjoy "Helena" . . . I almost feel I shouldn't tell you the latest about "Helena" but then I think from her early diary you can see she was no idealist. Yesterday Lota called her up to tell her I'd got my copy—and after screaming to make her understand it was really *out*, "Helena" 's one comment was, "Is it giving any results?" meaning money, of course. (And she's a billionaire now.) If ever I translate again, I'll choose someone good & dead.

As you say, "drabness" is what characterizes all countries except the rich, gleaming, deodorized U.S.A.—and I think that that bright cleanness is what I always miss most at first. Even here where Nature is so bright & fresh and the weather so brilliant, etc., and the buildings pink & white and the sidewalks black & white mosaic—all the crowds, buses, trolleys, shops, *kitchens*, look so dingy and dark and grease-stained. But one gets used to it quickly. I was incredulous of your story about the moment's silence for the dog in the satellite—until I read the same story in that organ of truth and accuracy *Time* . . .

The national bird of Brazil (I'm going through Joe's letter and these paragraphs relate to it, not each other), I'm sure, is a cousin of our robin. It's called the *Sabiá*, and all the poets write about it. It looks very robin-like, only not so deep a red breast, but the song was what made me think it *was* a robin at first. You know those very liquid loud notes robins make after spring rains—but here I finally realized it was much too loud, and terribly insistent. But Brazilian birds are a subject I've barely approached. There are too damn many species, of everything.

Our trip lasted 18 or 19 days, and the boat was very bad. As they say, don't go American. Maybe it's democracy, but it's really too much I think when the captain keeps telling the steward to please go & put his teeth in—and everyone grumbles, grumbles all the time, and the boat is a mess. I like the sea so I didn't mind too much, and we stopped at Savannah, Charleston, and Aruba—but Lota nearly went crazy with boredom and *noise*. They did all the things that should have been done in drydock en route. Also the capt., the radio man, and the chief engineer all had tape-recorders and seemed to have recorded mostly Kostelanetz mooing Tchaikovsky, etc., to which they'd treat us in the afternoons. I fell in love with the radio man's parakeet, though, and I do think you should have a pair when you get home. It said, "Kiss me, cutie," admired itself in a mirror, and paraded around the wireless panels as if it knew what it was doing, pulling a wire here or a switch there.

Well—I'll do better when I get settled. Don't forget that "screw" means one's wages in England, etc.

To Isabella Gardner

December 9, 1957

(I think "Bella" is the form of your name I'll choose. Do you know the old song that goes: "She'll be full of surprises / In the morning when she rises / When she hears I'm in the toon. / I am the fella / That's going to marry Bella / Bella, the belle of Muldoon." Or some town that rhymes with "toon." I was very fond of this when my grandfather used to sing it to me, an old Harry Lauder song, I imagine.)

. . . Our freighter took forever, and since arriving, just five weeks ago, we've spent most of our time trying to wrest our belongings away from the Customs. Half our things are still there, and the latest is that they've lost the papers, including our passports of course. Lota has driven down to Rio in a howling storm this morning to cope with this, poor dear, while I stay here in my *estudio* with a nice fire. However—there seems to be no decent writing paper and the ceiling has mildewed in my absence—a slightly discouraging beginning . . .

I think "The Widow's Yard" [in *Poetry*] is very good—one of your best. The only word I'd object to, and you may be using it perfectly, I'm not sure, is "secrete." One *secretes* oneself in the closet, but one doesn't *secrete* the closet door, does one? "To place in concealment"—well, that may be all right. I find I hesitate over it every time I read the poem. I'm being finicky, but the rest of the poem is so accurate and logical I don't like to have to figure out that bit twice each time. I like the canned heat very much and "blue with bliss." Dear me! is it a French window? Anyway, I think it's very well written and just sinister enough. Congratulations.

You should hear Lota describing Roque Island to her Brazilian friends. She was very distressed by the *beaches* in Maine (at least your island has a beach!) and kept saying that *here* they have miles of fine white sand, etc., while I kept saying they weren't supposed to be beaches, they were "rugged coastlines." Also it seems that all fir trees look artificially planted to her, the way palms do to us, so altogether it is hard for me to see our Northern beauties through her eyes, and she's giving her friends a sort of 18th-century vision of the wild and "Gothic," I think. Our house is still standing, no plate glass broken (one of our worries), and don't forget if ever you plan to come to S.A. we are expecting you to visit us. There are snails here—but I think I told you—as large as bread & butter plates.

To EB from Robert Lowell

Lowell's letter to EB, part of which follows, is given here to provide a needed preface to her response. Before EB left New York for Brazil, Robert Lowell on August 15 had sent her an unusual letter (six single-spaced typewritten pages), written shortly after her and Lota's visit with the Lowells in Maine. After a five-page account of sailing with the Eberharts and Wannings, he breaks off and comes to the point: the revelation that nine years earlier he had wanted to propose marriage to EB but had never found "the right stage-setting." He also refers to it as a "Strachey and Virginia Woolf" relationship.

EB waited four months before replying in two letters on December 11 and 14, though she had cabled Lowell at her departure for Brazil in October. What she writes is remarkable: the letters show friendliness and admiration for his new book, and are filled with news, but she makes no direct reference whatsoever to his dramatic statement that "asking you is the might-have-been for me, the one towering change,

the other life that might have been had." There may be irony in her statement that,
in looking back, "the real marvel of my summer" was "the whole phenomenon of
your quick recovery."

Castine, Maine
August 15, 1957

Dearest Elizabeth B.: . . . After so much buffoonery, like Pat Wanning I want to make my little speech. Your advice about [my] going to a doctor and keeping up one's patience, sobriety, toughness and gaiety is dreadfully true, and I am sure that all is beginning to be well and that Elizabeth and I really profoundly love and are charmed by one another and we will be a safe happy place for little Harriet. All will come and one begins to see the ways.

Also I want you to know that you need never again fear my over-stepping myself and stirring up confusion with you. My frenzied behavior during your [recent] visit has a history and there is one fact that I want to disengage from all its harsh frenzy. There's one last bit of the past that I would like to get off my chest and then I think all will be easy with us.

Do you remember how at the end of that long swimming and sunning Stonington day [in 1948] after Carley [Dawson]'s removal . . . we were talking about this and that about ourselves, and I was feeling the infected hollowness of the Carley business draining out of my heart, and you said rather humorously yet it was truly meant, "When you write my epitaph, you must say I was the loneliest person who ever lived." Probably you forget, and anyway all that is mercifully changed and all has come right since you found Lota. But at the time everything, I guess (I don't want to overdramatize our relations), seemed to have reached a new place. I assumed that it would be just a matter of time before I proposed and I half believed you would accept. Yet I wanted it all to have the right build-up. Well, I didn't say anything then. And of course . . . [it] wasn't the right stage-setting, and then there was that poetry conference at Bard and I remember one evening presided over by Mary McCarthy and my Elizabeth was there, and going home to the Bard poets' dormitory, I was so drunk that my hands turned cold and I felt half-dying and held your hand. And nothing was said, and like a loon that needs sixty feet, I believe, to take off from the water, I wanted time and space, and went on assuming, and when I was to have joined you at Key West I was determined to ask you. Really for so callous (I fear) a man, I was fearfully shy and scared of spoiling things and distrustful of being steady enough to be the least good. Then of course the Yaddo explosion came and all was over. Yet there were a few months. I suppose we might almost claim something like apparently Strachey and Virginia Woolf. And of course there was always the other side, the fact that our friendship really wasn't a courting, was really disinterested (bad phrase), really led to no encroachments. So it is. Let me say this though and then leave the matter forever. I do think free will is sewn into everything we do: you can't cross a street, light a cigarette, drop saccharine in your coffee, without it. Yet the possible alternatives that life allows us are very few, often there must be none. I've never thought there was any choice for me about writing poetry. No doubt if I used my head better, ordered my life better, worked harder, etc., the poetry would be improved, and there must be many lost poems, innumerable accidents and ill-done actions. But asking you is *the* might-have-been for me, the one towering change, the other life that might have been had. It was that way for these nine years or so that intervened. It was deeply buried, and this spring and summer (really before your arrival) it boiled to the surface. Now it won't happen again, though of course I always feel a great blitheness and easiness with you. It won't happen, I'm really underneath utterly *in* love and sold on my Elizabeth and it's a great solace to me that you are with Lota, and I am sure it is the will of the heavens that all is as it is . . .

Love, CAL

P.S. The last part [meaning all the above] is too heatedly written with too many *ands* and so forth. I guess it doesn't much matter though . . .

To Robert Lowell

Petrópolis, Brazil

December 11, 1957

Dearest Cal: I don't know why I haven't been able to write to you sooner, really. I don't often get these letter-writing blocks & particularly about my favorite correspondents. All the way down on our freighter I composed endless letters to you, full of profound new ideas, but they just evaporated into the ocean air. Then when we finally got here (not until November 4th) so many complications arose immediately that I couldn't write any letters for two or three weeks, or not real letters. We were kept going back and forth to Rio to get things out of the Customs—in fact half our belongings are still there . . .

I did write some necessary letters to aunts and agents—but I think I felt that writing you would somehow make my exile just too final again. Well, I must face it!

Thank you so much for so many things that have accumulated by now. The photograph is a very nice one; I'm having it framed in Petrópolis. Lota's "grandchildren," the two older ones, that is, are here and they asked me who that "disarrayed" man was. They also want to know what everyone has died of—all portraits apparently strike them as being of dead people! The Christmas present—well, I kept it unopened for a week, thinking I'd keep it that way until Christmas. But finally that label "*lava cameo*" was too much for me and I opened it. Sydney Smith speaks somewhere of an Englishman dancing at court in Naples, wearing "volcanic silk with lava buttons," and I'd wondered what it meant—it sounded slightly Emily-Dickinson-ish for Mr. Smith. Now I think I know—perhaps "volcanic silk" was shot silk, or else just scarlet—but I think the buttons, like your cameo, must be straight from Vesuvius, don't you? It's really a marvelous, curious, quaint, and evocative piece of workmanship and I am crazy about it. It makes me think of the Brownings, *The Marble Faun*, *Roderick Hudson*, and my own strange stay in Naples. Did you notice the high point of the carving—that one romantic curl that you can see through? I also like the other cruder curls of the gold, which remind me strongly of sucked dandelion stems; but I'm getting altogether too Marianne-ish about this, I'm afraid. You can see I am very much taken with it. It is really pure 19th-century romanticism, late. Do you know anything about where it came from and if I am right?

I am so glad you liked the Purcell. I had intended to send you, for Christmas, Purcell's *Dido & Aeneas* but I wasn't sure whether you had it or not. There's a version I bought with Flagstad singing Dido. Do you have it? I also hesitated because although I bought it for myself, at the last minute, I haven't been able to hear it yet so I don't know how good it is. My idea is to wean you away from those French songs because I think the English ones are so much better and so much more appropriate to us! (However, I got the Boulanger recording of Monteverdi's songs— the same series as your French one—and it is ravishing. Do you have that one?) My hi-fi is all here and the local carpenter is making a case for us. Jane Dewey's parting gift to me was a magnificent transformer for it! Now if we can just get it installed before another year goes by . . .

Thank goodness you got that cable—one never knows. I am delighted with the reception your poems have been getting. In fact the whole phenomenon of your quick recovery and simultaneous productivity seems to me in looking back to be the real marvel of my summer. I'm not going to tackle them in this paragraph because I'm not sure I'll have time to do them justice before we go to town. I do want to get something in the mail to you today. I'll write again tonight, I promise, if I can't now. Our financier friend, Oscar, is here. He came up on the bus in a great rush last night to tell us of a new investment; and after lunch we have to take him back to catch the bus to Rio again. We sat up till two like a group of wicked old capitalists, conniving. At one point I mentioned you, and immediately Oscar was off again, scribbling away and figuring the fantastic interest on $30,000 in 2½ years. I went to bed seeing us all millionaires. This morning we don't seem quite so rich; maybe "comfortable"! Perhaps you'd like to try a small amount, say $5,000, just to see? I think I'd feel worried if you wanted to invest a lot here the first thing. What I'm doing will bring about 100% in 2½ years, however— something quite conservative for here, and quite safe. This is a dreadful paragraph—how did I skid from poetry to percents?

Your hammer has been much admired and we keep it in our bathroom now instead of with other tools, just so it will be safe. You should hear Lota describing Maine—it sounds like the 18th century's ideas of the "Gothic." We are going to visit friends for a week over Christmas, to the seashore, a famous place called Cabo Frio, "Cold Cape," where I've never been and where I'm supposed to see Lota's ideal ocean landscape—also go fishing for amberjack, etc. The friend is the champion fisherman here (strange the way one's life goes in little cycles). Since Brazilians are mad about anything chocolate (and get a special thrill from it because it's so bad for their "livers") I have been requested to bring along 4 dozen brownies (something I've introduced to Brazil) and a large chocolate cake. You see how innocent our lives are here—just making money and eating sweets.

I asked Farrar, Straus to send you the translation . . . I don't know whether you'll find it interesting at all or not. I think you just possibly might think "Helena" is funny. My introduction now strikes me as long-winded.

When you write again do tell me, if it isn't too far behind you, about your visit with [Edmund] Wilson. I wanted to see him again someday, but really had no reason to, I suppose, but he has always been very nice to me.

I am so pleased Randall liked the poems—also Philip [Rahv], but Randall's liking them really means infinitely more. I had him sent a copy of my translation, too, and I think it's the kind of thing he might like. However, our long and peculiar silence (which I really feel was my fault this time, probably) weighs on me, and I just don't know how to go about writing to him again. Lota also likes your poems very much and amazes me by the way she "gets" every detail—or else Maine really sank in much more profoundly than I realized! She likes "Skunk Hour" best and so do I, I think—and I'd be particularly charmed to have that one dedicated to me. The one poem I've done anything with since I've been back is a long one I started two years ago, to you and Marianne, called "Letter to Two Friends," or something like that. It began on a rainy day and since it has done nothing but rain since we've been back I took it up again and this time shall try to get it done. It is rather light, though. Oh heavens, when does one begin to write the *real* poems? I certainly feel as if I never had. But of course I don't feel that way about yours—they all seem real as real—and getting more so.

While I remember it—one small item that I may have mentioned before. If you ever do anything with the poem about me [an early version of "For Elizabeth Bishop 2. Castine, Maine"]—would you change the remark my mother was supposed to have made? ["All I want / To do is kill you!"] She never did make it; in fact I don't remember any direct threats, except the usual maternal ones. Her danger for me was just implied in the things I overheard the grown-ups say before and after her disappearance. Poor thing, I don't want to have it any worse than it was.

Just as I left N.Y. my Aunt Grace sent me two family portraits from Nova Scotia, and I brought them down, unopened, in an enormous crate. They are awfully nice; just as I'd remembered them, except that I'd had Uncle Arthur leaning on the red-plush-hung table and my mother leaning on the red-plush chair, instead of vice versa—I suppose because I like the chair so much. They are in huge gold frames, a little hard to reconcile with our modern architecture, but so charming we can't resist them. "Gertie," aged 8, wears little boots with one leg crossed over the other, and "Artie," aged 12, has *his* little boots crossed the other way. (He looks very much like me.) And how strange to see them in Brazil.

My buzzer is buzzing, meaning lunch. Now that I've got started I'll go on, and I have so much to say about the poems. Remember me to your lady, as Sam. Johnson says (& I'm afraid the rest of the quotation applies, too) and how's the lovely child? Lota sends her love.

Devotedly, Elizabeth

EB's comments in paragraphs 4 and 5 below are about poems Lowell had given her in typescript, not published until 1959, in Life Studies.

December 14, 1957

I dated my letter yesterday as of the 12th [the 11th, in fact]—then I found out it was really Friday the 13th. We had another deluge last night so I didn't get back up to the *estudio*—settled for a few games of back-gammon and then reading *War and Peace* in bed. I hadn't read it for many years & decided to go through it again and it certainly is *the* novel. Coming down on the boat I started reading Conrad—it wasn't a very good idea because the ship was very slipshod and all our officers were much worse than Lord Jim, I'm sure, and as for that "silence" Conrad says is the reason men go to sea—there was very little of it. They drilled fore and aft all day long and in the afternoons we were treated to music above and belowdecks . . . *Don't travel American*, as they say. The sailors wore large billowy shorts, black oxfords and socks, white linen sport caps, sunglasses. Few of them spoke English and many were very fat . . . It was all just too democratic and Lota nearly died of boredom. (I stood up much better since I like the sea, but the Latin races haven't really liked it since the 15th century, I think.) We actually did go through the Doldrums—a day of them. The water absolutely slick and flat and the flying fish making sprays of long scratches across it, exactly like fingernail scratches. Aruba is a little hell-like island, very strange. It rarely if ever rains there and there's nothing but cactus hedges and prickly trees and goats and one broken-off miniature dead volcano. It's set in miles of oil slicks and oil rainbows and black gouts of oil suspended in the water, crude oil—and Onassis's tankers on all sides, flying the flags of Switzerland, Panama, and Liberia. Oh, our tug was named *La Créole Firme* and one young engineer had a nice tattoo, simply MY MOTHER. I guess that will be enough about our trip.

But what I started to say was—I was reading Conrad when the toothless steward observed me and said that was one of his favorite authors; he used to hear him lecture at Chautauquas and always liked that speech called "Acres of Diamonds." Well, that was all right. The next day one lady passenger was reading Somerset Maugham and started telling me how he was her favorite author, and then all about his hunting in the green hills of Africa. I began to grow a little uncomfortable. And the third day another passenger was reading Thomas Mann's short stories (this was a dear old lady of 78) and *she* started telling me all about what wonderful things Thomas Mann had done for the U.S. educational system—and I began to wonder if it was me or them.

(I'm afraid Philip would disapprove of this letter so far and I must stop being anecdotal and be serious.)

I find I have here surely a whole new book of poems, don't I? I think all the family group—some of them I hadn't seen in Boston—are really superb, Cal. I don't know what order they'll come in, but they make a wonderful and impressive drama, and I think in them you've found the new rhythm you wanted, without any hitches. Could they have some sort of general title? I see now that Randall may not have commented on them all yet, and I'd like to see what he thinks of this group. Pound's remarks mystify me completely, too, and so do Philip's, slightly! (Except that his are meant to be complimentary, obviously, and I'm with him there.) "Commander Lowell," "Terminal Days at Beverly Farms," "My Last Afternoon with Uncle Devereux Winslow" (the one I like best, I think. I think I'd like the title better without the "my" maybe—to go with "Terminal Days" better?). "Sailing [Home] from Rapallo," which is almost too awful to read, but a fine poem. They all also have that sure feeling, as if you'd been in a stretch (I've felt that way for very short stretches once in a long while) when everything and anything suddenly seemed material for poetry—or not material, seemed to *be* poetry, and all the past was illuminated in long shafts here and there, like a long-waited-for sunrise. If only one could see everything that way all the time! It seems to me *it's* the whole purpose of art, to the artist (not to the audience)—that rare feeling of control, illumination—life *is* all right, for the time being. Anyway, when I read such an extended display of imagination as this, I feel it *for* you.

I still like the skunk poem enormously, although I suppose it's exercises compared to the other ones. I also like what you've done to the marriage sonnet one. Some things I like especially: "sky-blue tracks . . . like a double-barreled shotgun," "less side than an old dancing-pump," the last lines. Practically all of Uncle D. I'm a bit confused about why the maids should look like sunflowers or pumpkins. Fat, in yellow dresses? I love the face in the water, and the marvelous description of Uncle D., his cabin, his trousers, etc. etc. In "Commander Lowell" I think the name is Helene Deutsch, isn't it? (I'll look it up.) Yes, and have you ever read her? Unless your mother was very peculiar I don't think she could be "drugged to sleep" by Dr. Deutsch—she's fairly hair-raising. That's finicky, I know—but I do think that Deutsch stands in the popular mind (if for anything at all) as the ruthless exponent of female masochism—she's apt to arouse some opposition in the female reader.

I'm sorry I can't seem to say all the right things I'd like to. I really should learn to be more articulate, I know. Oh—your mother might read Harry Stack Sullivan—he's by far the most soporific, stylistically. But not so well known, maybe.

(I'm reading the last volume of Dr. [Ernest] Jones's life of Freud now. It is a really magnificent job; you should read it—beginning with Vol. I, though, in some ways the most interesting. I'm sure you'd be so fascinated by the time you got through that you'd rush straight to Dr. Kaves to find out some more.)

But "broken through to where you've always been" (me)—what on earth do you mean by that? I haven't got anywhere at all, I think—just to those first benches to sit down and rest on, in a side arbor at the beginning of the maze.

Reviewing your letters: Frank's ideas about [artist] Hyman [Bloom] and me are awfully funny. Who(m) else could I put on my list? I wonder if ever you see Hyman if you could find out if he did receive that book of poems I had sent him? I know he'll never write, but I'd like to know because Houghton Mifflin has made so many mistakes about mailing things. How are the Rahvs? I must confess that I got the notion when I was in Boston that perhaps they had said they couldn't bear to see *me* & you were both being tactful about it! But even if they did, it doesn't seem to matter much from here. Looking back on my slight *Partisan Review* connections I realize I always feel I should be brilliant, profound, take the floor, etc., so usually stay silent—then when I try to remember what *they* said it's not particularly impressive, after all! But as I said before, I wish I were more articulate and I suppose I'll never be now, living off in the mountains and meeting only Brazilian intellectuals who got stuck at Valéry, and with whom I really *am* silent, necessarily. And here I must confess (and I imagine most of our contemporaries would confess the same thing) that I am green with envy of your kind of assurance. I feel that I could write in as much detail about my Uncle Artie, say—but what would be the significance? Nothing at all. He became a drunkard, fought with his wife, and spent most of his time fishing—and was ignorant as sin. It is sad; slightly more interesting than having an uncle practicing law in Schenectady maybe, but that's all. Whereas all you have to do is put down the names! And the fact that it seems significant, illustrative, American, etc., gives you, I think, the confidence you display about tackling any idea or theme, *seriously*, in both writing and conversation. In some ways you are the luckiest poet I know!—in some ways not so lucky, either, of course. But it is hell to realize one has wasted half one's talent through timidity that probably could have been overcome if anyone in one's family had had a few grains of sense or education. Well, maybe it's not too late!

I'm not really complaining and of course am not really "jealous" in any deep sense at all. I've felt almost as wonderful a sense of relief since I first saw some of these poems in Boston as if I'd written them myself, and I've thought of them at odd times and places with the greatest pleasure every single day since, I swear.

I shouldn't complain about my Brazilian friends, either. Last night our weekend neighbors, an historian and his novelist wife, gave me a beautiful Nonesuch edition of Blake, with all the notes, etc., all inscribed in the Brazilian way—they'd just bought it for me in London.

The weekend before this one we took them to the circus—my first South American one, "Circo Garcia," "the greatest on the continent." It proved to be just what the circus should be: one ring, in a bright green tent with red and yellow poles. About a dozen performers did everything, appearing first with the wild animals (two very fat, elderly lions), then bicycle tricks, then juggling, a motorcycle act, high wire—the same two youthful couples, with unflagging energy—while Mr. & Mrs. Garcia supervised everything. When he wasn't performing he wore a blue silk dressing gown and she a red velvet evening dress with sequins on her eyelids—both very squat and strong, built exactly like tops. The clowns were very good, too—jokes straight from Aristophanes that would never get by on our continent. The lady novelist's face was a study when the tiniest clown made an exit breaking wind in huge puffs of blue smoke, with reports like a cannon—again, and again, and finally just once more from behind the red velvet curtain. One nice moment (Cocteau would have *adored* it) was when a huge moth, a local moth, lit on the shoulder of one of the young Negro roustabouts—it was really about 8 inches down one wing, with its wings folded, just like a fairy wing on the Negro's shoulder. It rested there for a long time and of course the boy kept grinning, not knowing what the audience was laughing at. At another moment the loudspeaker announced that it was Mrs. Garcia's birthday and the wretched four-piece band burst into "Happy Birthday to You" while everyone cheered. Lota and Octavio (the historian) told each other that was "very Brazilian," and I think they were right—the innocent feeling of *intimacy* the people in general seem to have. It is like what one reads of the Russians in the old days. They're confident we're all interested in the same things and in *them*.

I must get this off to you before Christmas. We go away Wednesday. I haven't been fishing for so long I'm afraid I don't have enough muscle to pull in an amberjack. (I once got a 65-pound one in Key West—that's really big.)

Tell me about your teaching, etc. . . . A. came to see me in N.Y. and I thought he was improved; I haven't seen her for six years. But I'll never forget their coming to my railroad apt. in N.Y. and her urging him to recite his Phi Beta Kappa poem to Tom [Wanning] and me. It was midnight; Tom finally got out: "Er—uh—I think it's a little late for poetry reading." But it couldn't stop him. In the kitchen Tom kept asking me, "Say, what's the matter with her buzzies?" (that was the awful word he used). "Take a look and tell me. Is it her brassiere?" I finally ordered him to stop staring. They're a sad couple (of people!) I think.

I've typed myself into a fine nostalgia. I miss you very much. Lots of love.

P.S. *Would* you like *Dido & Aeneas?*

To Marianne Moore

Petrópolis
January 13, 1958

I seem to be writing letters almost in inverse order to my duty and affection . . . I don't know why. We have certainly talked of you and thought of you every single day since we left New York, and we have your portraits in four (4) places in our house and studies—and yet I've written lots of letters I shouldn't have bothered about, paid bills, and all kinds of unnecessary things like that, and only two days ago did I write to Dr. Baumann, and now am writing you—almost my two most favorite people in the U.S.A. It's something perverse. Thank you so much for writing me again about the Introduction to *"Helena Morley"*—that cheered me up enormously; I'd about decided that it was much too long-winded and detailed. I hope by now you've had time to read Helena herself—she's much much better than any introduction, I think, although you won't approve of her wholeheartedly in some places. We have been very pleased so far with the reception the book's been getting—nothing very profound, but the newspaper reviewers seem to like her . . .

I do hope you are well and not getting pleurisy and that Dr. Laf Loofy is giving you lots of vitamins, etc.—maybe even tranquillizers during the coldest months. (I thought of her name always as Dr. Laugh Loofy, but I think Henrietta spelled it La Floofy, and we may both be wrong.) And don't forget, please, that if she ever fails you there's always Dr. Baumann, who'd love, I know, to fly across Brooklyn Bridge to see you in any emergency. I also think it might be a good idea to send Mrs. [McKnight] Kauffer to her—unless she has someone else as good. I've seen her do wonders with that kind of person. At any rate, please please don't try to do it ALL yourself.

We missed New York very much when we first got back and then began to feel at home again. The animals were all in good health and affectionate and forgiving—also "Betty" and a little new black one, named, poor thing, *Alisette Mara*. At present we have Lota's two older "grandchildren" here, and one of her nephews, a very bright gangling boy of 15, with big horn-rimmed glasses and asthma. Since both Lota and I had it, we are very good at advising him, spraying him, etc. There is a fourth "grandchild" now, about a month old, and this one was at last named "Lotinha."

Over Christmas we went away for a week to stay at Rosinha's brother's seaside house at a place called "Cabo Frio" (Cold Cape). There are wonderful dunes and countless little beaches; also they make salt there in lagoons, and it is very strange and pretty. When you come to visit us we'll take you there, of course. The most wonderful tiny tiny shrimp, local pineapples, lobsters—we had them all for Christmas dinner, then lolled in white string hammocks. I think you'd like it. Now we're back with all these children, but getting down to work at the same time. Lota has designed a very handsome cabinet for my hi-fi (eee-fee, as they say here) and the whole thing is almost ready to install. We are also reorganizing all our electricity, which is still on the eccentric side, and have just ac-quired our first (for here) electric refrigerator. Next comes a lot more plate glass and then I think we'll be all ready for you to come and stay —forever, if you want to . . .

It was wonderful seeing you there and I just wish we'd seen you oftener. I gather that the Western tour was a great success. We have heard several times from Loren and from Margaret [Miller]. We do miss you all very much and if we can't get back soon you really must come here, I think—do you think you'd mind such a long flight? They say in a year or two there will be jet planes that will fly between Rio and New York in nine hours. Lota is overjoyed with the idea—I still think I prefer our freighter, even if it wasn't a very good one. With all best wishes for a Happy New Year, Marianne, and please please take care of yourself— eat proteins, vitamins, carbohydrates, and everything else they discover, to *excess*, and please also write a poem; a nice long one.

To May Swenson

January 15, 1958

I am at last getting down to work after not doing a thing for nine months. It's taken almost two months just to learn how to concentrate again. I was so glad to hear you'd got the book ["*Helena Morley*"] and like the introduction—don't you honestly think it's a bit long? We've had awfully good reviews so far—favorable, that is, but they haven't been anything but résumés, really, and never quote the things *I*'d quote—but then maybe that shows there's something in it for one and all. I do think you'll enjoy the rest of it. It will take you back to your early family life with a bang. (Lunch.)

No, I never did manage to make Mr. Brant show me the original manuscript. I worried about it at first, but if you'd ever met the Brants you'd realize that they are incapable of *faking* anything, and probably the reasons he gave, like bad spelling and handwriting, for not showing it, were the real ones! There actually is a lot more, and now—particularly if they get a little money—I think he might even consent to make another book. We'll see. The stories she tells of her suitors and her courtship are as good as anything in the present diary. But the Brants haven't the slightest idea of why the book is good—it's like dealing with primitive painters. The only aspect of it that interests them at all is $$$$$. It's very interesting from the point of view of ART and its WHYS. I've kept all the old man's notes to me and think sometime I'll do an article called something profound like "Unconscious Anti-creative Impulses in the Self-made Man." Or "The Degeneration of Taste in One Generation." (One of her daughters actually remarked to me that she'd written some stories and was now going to be able to get them published, of course "under mother's name.")

Your Swedish Christmas sounds wonderful and I find I've been feeding the "grandchildren" and the nephew *risgrynsgrot* almost every day, or as I used to call it in my early days before I talked very well, "lice & laisins." (Family joke—please excuse it.) I have a large supply of cardamom seeds with me so perhaps you should send me a recipe for *Kaffebullar*, although it's probably one of those fancy coffee cakes, isn't it? And now that I think of it, I remember my grandmother's Swedish cook (not the Nova Scotian grandmother, the other one) making marvelous coffee rings and braiding them.

Right at the moment I don't want to think of food for a month. Last week Lota's oldest nephew got married and we had nine or ten people here for every meal for three days, plus five children, and I thought we'd never get enough supplies in. I made a wedding cake—frosted with white, and silver balls, and a hideous bride & groom on top, from the local bakery.

. . . We came back [from a holiday at Cabo Frio] burnt black and almost too relaxed, to face the wedding, the grandchildren's visit, etc. The nephew here is 15, a bookworm, very bright, rapidly going through our library in four languages. He likes to read English best. The first night I presented him with *Kim, Huckleberry Finn, Tom Sawyer,* some Hemingway, *Brave New World* and *Oliver Twist,* and he'd read them all. He also has asthma so we're all quite congenial. Lota drills him in pro-Americanism, the UN, and loving thy neighbor as thyself in general.

I wrote the Guggenheim [Fellowship people] just what I said before only with increasing warmth. Now I hope it helps. I saw your name coupled with Benson's in Frank Sullivan's Christmas poem—surely they can't ignore such fame! If you do get it I imagine you're thinking of travel, aren't you? We never did talk about anything very "serious," as I suppose we might have—I'm not very good at it . . . I do think it wouldn't do any harm to take a course at Berlitz, say, in French—or Spanish, if you're still considering Mexico . . . I know I wish to goodness I'd *made* myself learn to speak *something* well.

I don't think I like [the title] *A Cage of Spines* too well because of the backbone association—or is that the idea? Could you use Thorns? Or am I being obtuse? Anyway I'd certainly like to see the whole book and if you think I could be of any help with it let me know.

To Marianne Moore

February 23, 1958

. . . Lota has been having a rather hard time, because her sister was, and still is, very sick and has been operated on and Lota has had to go back and forth to Rio a great deal, stay at the hospital with her, etc. Meanwhile a fifteen-year-old son (who has asthma) has stayed with us, but school begins again next week. Also there has been no water in some sections of Rio off and on for months, so we have the "grandchildren" here as much as we can.

Carnival was last week and I was determined to see the samba schools—the wonderful Negro groups of dancers who parade and dance all night. We got press tickets to sit on the grandstand and went down rather late, armed with thermos bottles of iced coffee and Roquefort cheese sandwiches. (The sambas go on all night usually, and it's always very hot.) They were supposed to begin at seven, but actually started at ten, and instead of going on till three or four, it seems they wound up at 11:30 the next day. We'd abandoned our planks long before, of course, before even seeing any of the "good" schools this year. Indignation ran rather high. The best ones are superb—several hundred Negroes dressed in silks and satins—white wigs and the styles of Louis XV are much favored, or the early colonial period here—with wonderful bands. Electric lights in the costumes are popular now, too, and electric light buttons down the front. But we couldn't wait for the winning ones. The only good school we saw had taken for a theme the Brazilian Navy, and danced in bright blue and white satin replicas of uniforms, lots of tricorns, ostrich plumes, silver swords and medals, etc. One group of women had good-sized silver *cruisers* on their heads, with small light bulbs on the masts, of course. The crowd, and the outskirts of the crowd, are nice, too—exhausted people in all sorts of costumes sitting along the curbs or stretched out on the grass. One very young Negro couple we saw on the way back to our car had a tiny boy, about two years old, in a lovely gold satin clown costume, with a net ruff, spangles, etc. It was after two in the morning; the little boy was almost dead, of course, but when Lota told him he was "pretty" he smiled and then kissed our hands, in a very gallant way. I do hope Carnival goes on for ever—but I wish they'd get it to running a little more on schedule!

To Howard Moss

March 10, 1958

Thank you so much for sending me your review [of *The Diary of "Helena Morley"*]—it arrived on the day it was to appear in the U.S. I sympathize with you completely about that stupid practice of cutting reviews—it's happened to me, too, and it's one of the reasons why I hate to write reviews. But at least yours didn't turn out to be quite nonsensical or contradictory, the way the Sunday reviews often are. And I think you certainly said more than any of the other reviews, really. They've been very "favorable" but rather disappointing, I feel. You did attempt to give reasons why you enjoyed the book, and also you gave by far the best quotations. Thank you very much and I do hope it wasn't too onerous and maddening. No one else tried to explain its "charm" at all. Someone sent me another copy yesterday, and I must send it off to the old lady today.

I have several poems crowded on my one-burner stove and I hope I'll be able to send you a couple soon [for *The New Yorker*]. Lota joins me in love and good wishes.

To Marianne Moore

April 10, 1958

I was so afraid that "Helena" would go unappreciated that I had a hard time in the introduction not to keep saying, "See what she says on page **," and "Isn't that a wonderful remark on page **?" and "Didn't you, dear reader, feel exactly the same way when you were thirteen, as on page ***?" All the effects seemed so slight to me that I was afraid they'd be overlooked. But I've had so many nice letters noticing all the things I wanted noticed that I'm very cheered up about the book—and of course *you* noticed best of all. The things you quote are all my favorites too—and also didn't you like "Your father was always a good five years older than I was"? And the poor boy who thought he was a French citizen, and "The town's a regular asylum"? So many of those remarks took me right back to Nova Scotia; I'm sure I've heard most of them before.

I'm insatiable for praise for it, I'm afraid. The reviews were all awfully "favorable" but that doesn't necessarily mean sales, alas. You said you'd like to see Dona Alice (Al-iss-y). Well, here is a very bad photograph from an article on her in a picture magazine here. She's not very beautiful, of course, and many of her stories would have to be censored for your beautiful ears—but she is wonderfully animated and funny. One of the amazing things about that diary, I think, compared with other adolescent diaries, is that she sees *other* people so clearly. There's so little introspection—selfish but not egotistical, maybe? (Underneath the picture it says: "Grandma Alice, before becoming a famous writer"—oh dear!)

I, Lota and I, were so sorry to hear you'd been sick and I do hope there hasn't been any recurrence of it, with all those snowstorms. Loren wrote me of a party she gave that you did attend. And probably right now you are at Brandeis or Bryn Mawr. I liked the little bit of Brandeis I saw very much—a crazy jumble. I hope the Rahvs are well. Cal has been sick again, as you probably have heard—he's recovering rapidly this time, it seems, and I had a very nice letter from him about ten days ago, sounding quite like himself.

Lota's sister did have an awful time but is well now, and the boy [Flavio] is back in Rio. We got him going to my allergist here, who is a marvelous young doctor, I think—more like a detective than a doctor. And I gave Flavio shots all the time he was here—he refused to give them to himself, though. All Lota's "grandchildren" are here now—staying at a little house just down the road with their young mother. The baby, "Lotinha," is 4 months old and really such a remarkable pretty baby that even male guests, or former anti-baby guests, ask to dandle her. Of course Lota is very proud of them all.

Day before yesterday, Easter, I gave an egg-hunt party for them up here, the three older ones and our little black one. It turned out that they had never hunted for anything before in their lives and once they caught on they were all hysterical with excitement—I'd hidden almost a hundred little eggs in different-colored tinfoils all over the terrace, in the MG, and even stuck them on one big tree that has spines. Then we had pink lemonade, and then *Papai*, who was up from Rio for the day, flew kites he'd made. They were so innocent about games that they gave all their eggs to each other, so it was much pleasanter than children's parties are apt to be.

I told you, I think, about Lota's adopting Kylso, the son, who had had infantile paralysis when he was 12—he'd crawled about, washing cars in his father's garage. While he was here we stopped at the local garage and Kylso said to me: "See that boy? That would be me if Lota hadn't found me." Lota is running around with her measuring rod and our glass man, trying to find out how much it would cost to put in all the plate glass across the front of the gallery. She is rarely without a measuring stick, a trowel or a screwdriver . . .

I was just this morning reading a little book by Stravinsky and he says: "My freedom will be so much the greater and more meaningful the more narrowly I limit my field of action and the more I surround myself with obstacles. Whatever diminishes constraint diminishes strength." I immediately thought of you. I think you'd like the book, if you haven't seen it—there are lots of good things in it: *The Poetics of Music*, Vintage Books, 95¢.

We have several men working around the place now; one old gardener named Maximiliano, like a pixie. A little boy brings him his lunch every day, little tin pots in a cloth bag. The little boy hangs it on a tree —some of the other men do the same and I think it looks very pastoral somehow, Virgilian! They also dig out little arched niches in the hard earth at the sides of roads, or cut steps in it—dark red earth.

To Dr. Anny Baumann

May 22, 1958

I think Lota is writing you to thank you for sending her all the information. She got everything; took everything; and everything *worked*, I believe! At least she seems to be in very good form these days, bossing a crew of fourteen or fifteen "mens." We are starting the garage, which means first tearing down a hill and putting it into a valley—it looks rather like the start of the Panama Canal at the moment. But Lota is always very happy when there is some construction going on. We are also building the front approach to the house and installing plate glass. Eventually we'll be able to close it up, we hope, and even have a front door, with a doorbell. (And we hope so much you'll come and ring it sometime.)

The enclosed cartoon—in case you don't recognize him, because it really isn't very good—is of Carlos Lacerda, supposed to be dressed up for Carnival as Sherlock Holmes. There is also a rather nice joke current about him: At a wedding in Rio the service had reached the point at which the priest asks if anyone present knows any impediment to the marriage, etc. . . . and a voice pipes up from the audience, "Yes, I do." The bride whispers to the groom, "I *told* you not to invite Carlos Lacerda."—all going to show he has the reputation for knowing everything people, or the present government, don't want known . . .

As you may have read in the papers, they are building a brand-new capital city, called *Brasília*, way off in the interior. The best architects, tons of Carrara marble, an artificial lake, a complete set of government buildings, etc.—where there wasn't even a road to begin with. Friends of ours who have been there say that at present it looks exactly like old frontier towns in the U.S.A.—as shown in the movies, at least. Lota and her friends are violently opposed to the project—and it does seem pretty mad, when one considers that parts of Rio have been without water for months, the gas and electricity keep failing, etc. However, I think I'll take a short trip there fairly soon now—one can fly in—and see if I can write some sort of article about it. It's the only capital created from scratch, I think, except New Delhi, and I'd like to see it.

It is "winter" now, beautiful clear days, cold at night. The hi-fi is wonderful—one of the inventions of the age, surely. It has taken me forever to get back to work, but I do seem to be writing again now, although very tentatively. (My enormous black & white cat is trying to get into the typewriter right now.)

To May Swenson

July 3, 1958

Pearl is going with you on the trip, I gather. I envy you in a way, never having been West at all. If I ever get back to my native land I'm hoping to take a long trip in it. I am dying to see the desert. Yes—I think Isak Dinesen never wrote anything to compare with *Out of Africa*—all these last stories seem just too precious for words. I have a Danish friend here who knows her and tells rather disconcerting stories about her . . .

Saturday I am going to a literary dinner in Rio, just for fun—in honor of one of their best novelists, a woman who wrote one really wonderful little book when she was about 18. Since the intellectuals are mostly pretty anti-American and since I still can't carry on a decent conversation in Portuguese, I don't know quite why I'm going—but it will be fun to see everyone en masse like that and hear the speeches.

Yesterday we had fun listening to the return of the Brazilian football (soccer) team from Sweden—they finally won the world's championship and all Brazil is in ecstasies—even the banks closed. It's much more important to them than a Sputnik would be. It seems the team was presented to the King of Sweden and one of them lost his head and tried to hug him, in the Brazilian way. They are really pretty cute—small men, all shades of black and white, and they hug and kiss each other and weep with excitement when they make a goal, etc.—and terribly *fast*. Lota was coming back from Rio and it took her hours to get through the traffic— the airport was mobbed and the poor players couldn't be let out of the plane, even—sat locked up in it. Twelve jet planes accompanied them. Everyone seems to feel it means "better days for Brazil," God knows why or how—and that is a very good example of this foolish but appealing people. Our cook even arranged the stew with bunches of parsley and *bones*, I'm afraid, to represent her favorite player.

I was so relieved to receive your letter night before last. I had worried about mine and thought I'd been awfully mean, etc. Lota had said she didn't think so, so I finally sent it to you. It was a mess of a letter and just after I dropped it in the slot I had one of those horrible recollections that I had misspelled euphimism throughout! *euphemism*, I mean. I knew perfectly well what I thought I was saying—and writing, but I'm sure I used a strange version of it. This is an inherited characteristic, I think—my grandmother and an aunt did & do exactly the same thing! Grandma once wrote a long letter about a family wedding, using the word *ceremonial* for *ceremony*, dozens of times, consistently; and I seem to be starting to do the same trick.

You are very nice about everything I said. I'm still not at all sure that you understood my point about "physical" words, and it is hard to explain. After all, what could be more directly "physical" than some of Hopkins's poetry—"Harry Ploughman," say. It's a problem of placement, choice of word, abruptness or accuracy of the image—and does it help or detract? If it sticks out of the poem so that all the reader is going to remember is "That Miss Swenson is always talking about phalluses"—or is it phalli? —you have spoiled your effect, obviously, and given the Freudian-minded contemporary reader just a slight thrill of detection rather than an esthetic experience.

I think everyone feels that his or her best poems were lucky accidents—I know I do. But of course they really aren't at all—they are really the indication that you have worked hard on all the others, and felt deeply, and somehow managed to create the right atmosphere in your own brain for a good poem to emerge.

And as to experience—well, think how little some good poets have had, or how much some bad ones have. There's no way of telling what really is "experience" anyway, it seems to me. Look at what Miss Moore has done with what would seem to me like almost none, I imagine, and the more "experience" some poets have, the worse they write.

The New Yorker with your popular poem came—very nice—but I think they should have put it in front.

Speaking of mirrors—two men are putting up a big one in L.'s and my bathroom. I am supervising, more or less, that's why I'm down at the house typing on this wretched machine. The little kitten "Mimosa" is watching me—she is adorable, but I am worried about her—she's too timid, I think. Tobias was just the opposite and still is—climbs all over the most unfavorable guests. Mimosa is about to go into that long thin stage, too.

To Robert Lowell

August 28, 1958

I don't believe I have ever answered your last letter, have I? Although I have answered it, or at least written you many letters in my imagination, since—the letter in which you sent me another of the "family life" poems, the one about the nurse feeding the birds with bags of salt pork. Well, I like it very much; all together those poems will have a wonderful effect,

I think—family, paternity, marriage, painfully acute and real. (Penn Warren's on the subject seem so *voulu*, don't you think?)

We have been having quite a social and busy time here for a change, and everything seemed to happen all at once, too. There was one dreadful Sunday when [John] Dos Passos came for lunch. It would have been all right except that our political friend brought him, and brought a lot of other people along too, and the chicken gave out and the conversation bounced from Portuguese to English all day long—and the political friend went to sleep after lunch and snored, too. Then we discovered immediately that Dos Passos was here at the invitation of the State Department to see Brasília and write a piece about it for *Reader's Digest*. That should have been warning enough—and as our opinions on Brasília were violently opposed, that best subject of conversation had to be steered clear of. Do you know that Dos Passos is a very beautiful Portuguese name?—probably was Our Lord of the Steps, to begin with, or something religious like that. The change in the times is indicated by the way he sometimes translates it as "Johnnie Walker"!

Then for the last three or four weeks [Aldous] Huxley and his wife have been here—and that indicates the Brazilian ignorance of English literature, I suppose! To think that two writers as far apart as D.P. and Huxley would both be interested in seeing Brasília and—I suppose that's the idea—doing a little propaganda for it! Huxley's second wife happens to be someone I used to know, an Italian girl [Laura Archera], so we saw them quite a bit. I can't say he's exactly easy, though I think he'd like to be—even Lota was scared to death when they first came up here—but he is a remarkable man, don't you agree? He asked me about U.S. poets and when I spoke of you said he'd met you and you were a "nice fellow." They were sent on a trip to Brasília and then beyond, with the Air Force, to see some Indians—and I went along, the best trip I've made here so far. I don't know how you feel about Indians—I had expected to be depressed by them, the most primitive people alive except for the pygmies—but actually we had a wonderful cheerful time. It's only depressing to think about their future. They are quite naked, just a few beads; handsome, plump, behaving just like gentle children a little spoiled. They were very curious about Huxley. One who spoke a little Portuguese said he was "homely . . . homely." And then one, a widower, asked me to stay and marry him. This was a slightly dubious compliment; nevertheless the other ladies along were all quite jealous. But I am finishing up a long piece about it (and hope to goodness I can sell it and start building the garage) so I won't describe any more. Sometime I hope to go back there and spend a few days. We flew over the River of Souls, the River of the Dead (and presumably over Col. Fawcett's bones)—to the *Xingú*.

The group that went along was very odd—five nationalities. On these endless flights we kept changing partners for conversation like a dance

—and mostly whispering about Huxley. "Do you think he's interested in *literature* any more?" "Have you ever tried any of these new drugs?"— etc. I think it is one that you take that H. talks of a great deal—in fact medicine, mysticism, and God are his present themes.

Here your summer has gone by almost and I think you have been spending it mostly in Boston, haven't you? Have you had a dull time or how has it been and have you kept on with your doctor and do you like him? etc. etc.— Please write and tell me what you are doing and if you've written any more poems. I think I have done one—the first in 18 months—but I'm not sure yet and I have been very miserable and petty-feeling about it all, wishing I could start writing poetry all over again on another planet.

Marianne writes marvelous letters to Lota, beginning "Lota—dear thing." Now we think we'll work on the Brazilian State Dept. for her to come here and cast a bright eye on Brasília, too—why not? She's off to Vancouver now, I think. The Indians would be far too naked for her, I'm afraid.

How is Harriet? Elizabeth? Is Harriet writing articles by now? Whom do you see in Boston? Are you teaching? Have you heard from Randall? I'd like to write him but don't dare. Why don't you come here on a Fulbright?—they aren't like the usual Fulbrights at all. They want well-known people to come and give a talk, or talks, around in the larger cities, and they pay quite well, and the [rate of] exchange is really *too* good now. Wouldn't you consider it sometime?

I miss you very much and Lota is dying to get back to New York— but the exchange is too much for her to dream of it. Perhaps we shall meet here or in Europe.

To Howard Moss

October 29, 1958

I owe you two letters and I am very ashamed. We enjoyed your first longer one so much and then I meant to write you immediately when I got the second one a week or so ago—but I had, have, a poem just on the brink and I thought I'd be sending it along too. My brinkmanship doesn't seem to be so good and I think I had better write you a note anyway. The poem, or poems, will follow shortly, I trust—maybe even today, with luck . . .

Yes, I like Philip Larkin, too. Robert Lowell gave me the paper English edition last year. I haven't seen [Stanley] Kunitz's book but I like occasional poems of his very much. I have Cummings's new one. Well, I find him hard to judge, you know, he is such an institution—but I do like some of them as much as ever. You have to pretend you've never seen a Cummings poem before, and that's difficult.

I have never been West at all—do you think one *should*? I like San Francisco in detective stories and in the movies—and I'd like to see the desert, certainly. May Swenson wrote me a descriptive letter from Sausalito—and Calvin Kentfield lives there and likes it, too.

Marianne Moore wrote she had a poem in *The New Yorker*—so, I think, did I, but neither of those copies has arrived yet (they take over six weeks). I agree with you that things are "dullish" in that line. Robert Lowell has a whole new book, mostly autobiographical . . . Kimon Friar arrived just as we moved into the apartment—and it was really a wreck then—so if by any chance he tells you I live in a slum in Rio, don't believe him! The tenant had stolen furniture, seven windows were broken, and all the walls painted horrible rich *shiny* colors. We were there trying to get it cleaned and scraped when he appeared.

Here is a memento for you. I'm afraid this was almost the least attractive of the Indians. I went on a trip a while ago, when Aldous Huxley was here, to see the new capital and then farther west to see some Indians. I liked them very much—everyone does—I want to go back and stay a week sometime. The men are much better-looking, I'm afraid. They are short and almost plump, a nice color—very clean—they go swimming all the time—quite naked—a little red paint in the hair, and a necklace. One friend of mine was watching an Indian, a man, paint himself for a party—black and red lines all over his body. He admired the work, and the Indian, in his enthusiasm, grabbed him and hugged him, so that he had red and black paint all over his clothes.

Lota sends her love. We'd both love to see you. I must get to work, as you well know!

To Robert Lowell

October 30, 1958

I've read through the BOOK again and really, it is very fine. The older poems are good in the old way and the new poems are good in a new way, and altogether they are (the new ones) solid, real, intensely interesting, honest—and very interesting metrically. I think you should feel very proud of the whole effort—and at the same time all the new ones have a strangely modest tone that I like, too—because they are all about yourself and yet do not sound conceited! They really make almost everything I see look pretty dreary, or labored, or absolute silliness (like poor dear Eberhart). At first I didn't like the title [*Life Studies*] but Lota says I'm wrong—and she has a way of being right. I don't know what the real differences are—I suppose only the *critics* know them—but your poetry is as different from the rest of our contemporaries as say ice from slush.

I do know that much. However, I'm getting so I can't judge the poets we know so well any more at all. I was craving something new—and I suspect that the poetry audience is, too, and will like these new poems very much. I just got Cummings's latest, and a lot of it is very good Cummings. I've been reading Dr. Williams and a lot of it is awfully good Williams—but one does need a change. I have seen a couple of poems by Frank O'Connor I like pretty well. I like May Swenson in spots—and at least, I think it is all quite honest and real and she is enthusiastic. She really likes NATURE, too—almost no one seems to. I just read, for the first time, "The White Peacock" and you have no idea how refreshing and wonderful all that long-winded nature description seemed.

I've been asked to give a talk, or maybe two or three, to the teachers, I think, of something called the Instituto Brasil—Estados-Unidos. It's where everyone goes to learn English in Rio. I turned them down once before, but now I think I'll do it. Now I've accepted I find I'm reading American poetry with new ideas—in fact, I think I'm going to talk about *Democracy* . . . How Concord had a kind, like a Greek city a little; Whitman's steamy variety; Amherst's variety—Miss Moore and John Dewey the only two *real* democrats I've ever met, etc. And your interest in character will be stressed. After all, I can't think of any English poet who writes about *people* the way you do any more. Well, I may change my mind before the time comes. Frost—the Bad Gray Poet. I read some remarks of his about Pound—just what the public wants to hear, I'm afraid.

Here is a picture of me among the Uialapiti—not very good and, I think, somewhat censored. I want to get copies of some of the better ones. I was sitting at a table—the Indians are really very short. See the baby's foot?

When your letter came I *was* reading *Dr. Zhivago*—in French. I stopped partway through because the book's owner wanted it back and I think I'll finish it in English. I agree with you completely—I even liked the poems at the end, as much as one could tell about them. I also read some of Pasternak's autobiography and a long short story "Récit" in French. Lota kept telling me how bad the French was all the time and I thought even I could tell that it was—but I find him a very encouraging character, don't you? Since you wrote, all the business about the Nobel Prize has happened. However—I didn't find it "as good as" Turgenev— but intensely moving, and the first sign of real life, like the first leaves of spring, say. (At least—when I see Russian newsreels or photographs of Red Square I always find it hard to believe the sun is really shining there.) I wish I could take up Russian, although I know I never will. I'm sure from what little I know about it that it's as good, if not better, than English.

We spent two weeks and two days in Rio recently, getting back Lota's apartment on the Avenida Atlântica. It is such a wonderful apartment that we'll never rent it again, no matter what heights rents soar to, I think. Top floor, 11th, a terrace around two sides, overlooking all that famous bay and beach. Ships go by all the time, like targets in a shooting gallery, people walk their dogs—same dogs same time, same old man in blue trunks every morning with two Pekinese at 7 a.m.—and at night the lovers on the mosaic sidewalks cast enormous long shadows over the soiled sand. I think you'd like it. Now that we have the apartment we can really invite you and Elizabeth to visit. You could stay in it for a month, if you wanted—come up here for weekends. The new Moore-McCormick boats are very good and take only six days, I think. Please consider it sometime—I could devise a wonderful lecture tour for you! There are five rooms, a special passage to the beach for bathers. Food is very cheap, for *us*—the dollar is way up—you can get pasteurized milk now, very good—we could even get you a maid, probably (or a *baba* for Harriet). We both worked very hard while we were there and I didn't get swimming much, but next week I'm going down again and acquire a tan. At night there are occasional candles burning in the sand, near the waves—*macumba* (like voodoo), offerings to the Goddess of the Sea.

I am sorry to hear about the Rahvs. Lota, too, has lost about seventeen pounds—and looks very elegant. I have liked some Kunitz poems I've seen in magazines, but knew nothing about him. Adrienne Rich I've liked *fairly* well. Your life sounds very nice and well-peopled. Mine has been rather lonely and bookish but I don't really care much. I'm hoping we can get to Europe—Italy & Greece—next year, but I'm not sure. N.Y. looks hopeless because of the exchange for Lota—but maybe I'll somehow earn heaps of money. I made two friends on my Huxley tour—one of those terrifyingly bright young Englishman diplomats, but really nice and intelligent. The other a Brazilian newspaper editor, best Rio paper, a real darling, if only he didn't *write*, too. Piles of books arrive, all autographed in the Brazilian way. But he's a marvelous source of information. A man I'd heard of in N.Y.—Kimon Friar—arrived out of the blue, on his way back to the U.S. by way of Chile to see his Greek relatives there, with a 333,333-line translation of an epic by Kazantzakis—he took up where Homer left off. Odysseus goes to Africa and meets Hamlet and Napoleon, I think—anyway, dies adrift on an ice floe at the South Pole. All this has been paid for, hugely, in advance by Simon & Schuster.

Yesterday and today we've had terrific thunderstorms in the afternoons—the beginnings of "summer." The dogs and the cats all try to get on my lap at the same time, in terror, and it rains so hard I had two boys working away with squeegees yesterday, pushing back the water from under the doors as it came in, like a sinking ship. Then it stops suddenly and quite often there's a rainbow. There are wonderful birds now—one a blood-red, very quick, who perches on the very tops of trees and screams to his *two* mates—wife and mistress, I presume, again in the Brazilian manner. But oh dear—my aunt writes me long descriptions of the "fall colors" in Nova Scotia and I wonder if that's where I shouldn't be, after all. I have another marvelous Purcell—"Hail! Bright Cecilia" that I recommend highly. I've ordered another opera, *The Fairy Queen*, but now the Customs have made it impossible to get in *anything* except books. It has got so bad that it's bound to improve, if you know what I mean, but until it does it's an awful nuisance. A friend sent me two records for last Christmas—I got them this October, and had to pay about $7.00 duty.

I liked Spain best of all my travels, twenty years ago.(!) I don't think I could ever see a bullfight again (I saw quite a few, and *liked* them, then)—but the Prado is worth two weeks, at least—Granada, Ronda, Cádiz. I liked them all tremendously—Toledo, the bitter landscape. Well, I suppose it's more worthwhile than here—but I wish you'd come here.

[P.S.] How are you liking your doctor? Lota sends love—she now keeps the hammer in Rio . . .

To Arthur Gold and Robert Fizdale

When Lota wrote Gold and Fizdale, her "Dearest Boys," on November 29 she asked EB to add greetings, which the latter did a few days later in the letter that follows. The "boys" had reported the breakup of a nine-year affair between male lovers and Lota, saddened by love's impermanence and prophetic about her own separation from EB (which came late in 1965), wrote: "I was very sorry about Arthurzinho. We always have such a longing for a 'status quo'—and it is so difficult. Everything is always changing. I always thought a strange trait in the human nature—the desire for the permanent, when in realité we are always changing—does not make sense." EB's comment on the breakup comes in paragraph 2.

December 2, 1958

Lota has gone off in search of a new gardener, I think (this happens to us monthly this year) [in Lota's hand: *too exaggerated!*], requesting me to add a few thoughts of my own. I've read hers & it seems to me she sounds a bit *sad*. She isn't, really, but I think when she gets to brooding about the impossibility of ever getting to New York for years to come— plus your sad news this time—it makes her sound *subdued*. Why, just last night she treated us to a superb life sketch of Alice B. Toklas arriving to stay with us (small whiskers & all), and after that she did a lovely bear, wrapped in a rug, to the "Bear" Symphony—so you see the old Lota is still going strong, thank God. (Although my natural melancholia taxes her severely, I'm afraid.) And yesterday we entertained, *all day*, a young Austrian-German couple, just arrived in Brazil. The wife is a doctor of "Internal Diseases" (surely that leaves very few other diseases?) and the man some sort of fancy auditor. He made all the usual criticisms of the country (and every new arrival seems to think they're original ones), in a fast, low, vanishing kind of English, and the girl knew no English at all—just German. This kind of thing seems to happen to us about one

Sunday every month and we do our best, but I think we're getting too OLD. Mary [Morse] & I rushed them to the earliest polite bus, then rushed ourselves to take aspirin and mineral water in a café. Mary was so far gone that she told me the man had told *her* he wanted to find another wife, for his car. Even if he has been exposed to the U.S. for ten years, that seems a bit decadent . . .

I am awfully sorry, too, to hear about the A. trouble. Nine years is quite a long time. One can only say, tritely, that it "may be for the best." Most things are for the worst, I'm sure, but somehow in that department of life, they often do seem to improve with age.

I must write to Virgil Thomson and tactfully find out if he really wants to bump off Miss Alice B. Toklas, or what the big idea is. Loren said she was very old and shaky, and to send her off here to live in a hotel, on strange food, at 105° F. for three months, at 82, I'm sure is not *wise*. Now Lota will read this and say she can't read a word of it. (She thinks *her* writing is just like copperplate.) How much we miss you, really! Instead of you we keep getting these *heavy* visitors, like yesterday's— nice, good, intelligent, but quite unleavened. Can't you come anyway, and take it off your income taxes? It is beautiful here now; the house is at its zenith, and Lota's four grandchildren are all very sweet, particularly Lotinha, who waddles now. The last time I saw her she chewed up and spat out several balloons, trying to blow them up the way her older sisters did. The little boy is a darling too. "Oh look!" he said. "Grandma brought us clothes!" and he held a little dress up against himself, smoothing it down professionally. (He's just beginning to use sentences.)

Lota has lost *15 pounds*—and looks lovely. I'm afraid of being taken for her mother, or at least an aunt.

It has been unusually hot—and our swimming hole is marvelous— cold & clear & hung with ferns. A lovely frog panicked & leapt straight into my bosom the other day. There are also a few small garnet-colored crabs that cause the more effeminate guests to shriek.

We are going away for ten days at Christmas time to a nice fishing village place, miles of white dunes & really, hundreds of different little beaches, deserted, to swim at. It would be a second Cape Cod in the U.S. & covered with cement & ice cream cones—but here the spoliation has only taken in about one block, so far. The dunes really look like *snow*— you can see why Rosinha treated West Hampton coolly (we go to her brother's house). We feel we have to contribute something—I wish I knew how to make Bobby's Meat Loaf. Every day there they serve us heaps of very tiny shrimp—the best in the world. I calculated* I was eating at least $5.00 of shrimp every lunchtime.

This is enough. Ned Rorem is having a record made of the Ezra Pound song of mine he wrote (a soprano named Patricia Neway. Is she good?).

Até logo (see you soon, that is). Please write again. With lots of love.

*I'd never use that word *chez moi*. I'll be saying "Gol dern!" next, I suppose. Is it homesickness?

To Dr. Anny Baumann

December 4, 1958

. . . *The New Yorker* did not take my piece about Brasília. As I worked on it I felt fairly sure they wouldn't; the material just didn't go together, Huxley didn't say anything of interest—and I feel it was rather *dumb* of me to put in so much time on it. However, the chief loss is that we'd hoped to start the garage on the proceeds! Now I'll work on something more my natural bent . . .

To Aunt Grace

December 15, 1958

I hope they forward my card and Christmas gift to you from Great Village—wherever you are . . . The mails are getting worse and worse, obviously—I rarely lost anything until the past year. How I wish we had some more of that delicious venison you once sent us—and maple syrup, particularly—but it is out of the question now to send anything at all, in or out. We hope that in a few months the Customs service will be reorganized so we can begin again . . .

You ask me if it's warm at Christmas here. It has been the hottest November in 33 years—around 104° in Rio most of the time. (That is HOT.) Up here of course it never gets like that, but I never remember it being so hot, and we have been taking two dips in our pool every day, instead of the usual one, and making sherbets all the time. It's the season for wonderful pineapples, mangoes, etc.— We've had a lot of company, too—everyone trying to get away from the Rio heat. On the 22nd we are going away to Cabo Frio ("Cold Cape") for ten days . . . Friends of ours have a nice house there, on the beach. There is nothing to do but go swimming, and fishing a bit, but it is beautiful scenery and we like it and it gives the maids a rest from us and us from them. (I've been giving the smallest black baby her whooping-cough shots. I'd give them both Salk shots, too, if I could get the serum—it's hard to get here.)

When we stay home we do have a tree, of sorts—a tropical plant called *graveta*—that blooms on the rocks at this time of year. It's a huge thing, six or eight feet high, dark red, waxy, with yellow blossoms at the tips, and shaped like a Christmas tree, more or less. Anyway, with candles it is very striking, and we usually send a boy up the cliffs to cut us the biggest one he can find (we located one through binoculars one year!). But of course it isn't Christmasy at all. This year we are taking a ham with us as our contribution to our stay and will bake it and decorate it there, and I'm taking along a chocolate cake and tins of cookies! But we'll probably spend the day swimming and lying in hammocks. I don't like to think of you traipsing around in the freezing cold. Please take care of yourself.

To Robert Lowell

March 30, 1959

I went to Rio to have a tooth pulled & while there saw the assistant to the Cultural Attaché, who reproached me with "You didn't tell me that Mr. Lowell had taught at Salzburg!" So apparently they'd been doing a little research. Mr. Morris says that he's applying from his end but he seems a little uncertain as to his pull with the State Dept., and again said that the best and most certain way would be for you to make a direct application to the State Dept. It is called something like "Exchange of ——?" persons. I'm going down to Rio this afternoon and shall ask again. Lota says we will exchange you for a ton of coffee beans. But the sooner the better, I gather. And if Elizabeth got my long confused letter—I'd still like all the information whenever she can get around to it, to use here for publicity and also for the Brazilian Dept. of Foreign Affairs, where Lota still has considerable influence even if her uncle is *out*. They might well want you both for other lectures, etc.

I didn't know until about two weeks ago that Marianne had had what they think was a slight stroke. Incredible to relate, it affected her speech for a few days—but she was better the last I heard. I'd like very much to get back to see her, and Lota and I talk hopefully of next September— but the hope is rather faint.

You liked my "blurb" [for *Life Studies*] and I am glad and relieved. They are fearfully hard to write, don't you think—at least when you really mean them and are determined to say *something* in a few words.

Now I have got out your letter of March 5th and shall answer it. I'll make inquiries while in Rio, too, about the university—however, I don't believe you'd have difficulty giving lectures here. One good idea I think is to have the poems you intend to quote or read mimeographed, to hand out to the audience. They are amazing linguists, of course, but poetry is hard to get the first time. Just the poems—not the lecture itself. Spender made that mistake—gave them the whole lecture to read while he read it and the audience felt quite insulted. I suppose one should just speak a bit more slowly and clearly than usual. (Frost did marvelously, of course—the Brazilians got his every joke.) I know almost nothing about the university—there are two, anyway, the national one and Catholic University, considered the better for literature, I think. Of course the terms are all different—summer vacation has just ended and the college year begun here. But I'll find out what I can.

At the end of my letter to Elizabeth I suggested the apartment annex of the Copacabana Hotel as a better place to stay. I had just discovered that it was much cheaper than I'd thought. It would make everything much easier for you all—maid service, nurse service if wanted, English-speaking (more or less) switchboard, etc.—and kitchens, too. We're just about two blocks away. We could meet on the beach for early swims. However, if you really should be at the university for a term, or plan to stay in Rio for longer than a month, our apartment would still be the best plan, I think. Well, please do apply to the State Dept.! Clare Boothe Luce is about to come here as ambassador (heaven help us). I *heard* she was reading my translation, which I can't quite believe—but if I ever do get a chance to meet the lady I'll ask her about you directly, I think. These impossible interviews do have a way of taking place here, so I am not just talking through my hat.

I can't help but feel that Belle [Gardner] is making a great mistake —a fourth marriage at her age—but then, I'm afraid I've never understood Tate's appeal to my sex very well. I find him slightly creepy, if amusing. Yes, I like Baldwin's essays too—but he certainly writes some bad stories. There is one other poet I have found occasionally good—mostly bad in the surrealist way—but I think he's improving, and is very, very clever: Frank O'Hara. Why is Rahv "cowed"? I can't picture that. And is Nathalie practicing in Boston or what? I am delighted to hear that Elizabeth has been writing so much—although envious, too, I suppose. (See a grim little book by Melanie Klein, *Envy and Gratitude*—superb in its horrid way.)

I have no news of any importance—but then, I don't believe I ever have. We had a large dinner party for 20 on Lota's birthday and it was quite successful, I think—dozens of Japanese lanterns and lots of plants and orchids our florist neighbor happened to give us at just the right moment. We set up five card tables in the "gallery"—all different colors, reflected in the rippled aluminum ceiling—very gay, if modest; and I produced an iced chestnut soufflé with fancy work in whipped cream, etc. It looked almost professional, by lantern light at least.

We restored the children to their parents, after ten weeks—a bit too long for everyone concerned, but we hadn't the heart to send them back to their tiny Rio apartment in the fearful heat. And we have to have them back again for the month of May, probably—while the *fifth* is born. Lota behaves splendidly; I behave only fairly well, I'm afraid, alternating with fairly badly. The children think I have a speech defect . . .

During the ten weeks I read & read & read—the 3-volume life of Byron, Greville in 3 volumes, Lucan (didn't you say you were reading that, too?), etc. etc.—and now am finishing the new edition of Keats's letters—all to what purpose I'm not sure, but all fascinating. At the moment I find the Keats the best of the lot, though. Except for his unpleasant insistence on the *palate*, he strikes me as almost everything a poet should have been in his day. The class gulf between him and Byron is enormous. As Pascal says, if you can manage to be well-born it saves you thirty years. Now I am trying to finish a story called, so far, "Fancy, Come Faster."

Did you see Randall and how is he? I wish he weren't cross with me but it can't be helped, I suppose. Please let us not have falling-outs! When is the book to appear?

We have just been cleaning the living-room light fixtures—deep bowl shapes—because we had a short circuit last night and they all blew out. In each one we find about half a peck of baked assorted insects, moths, beetles, all sorts—completely dried up and the color of old manuscripts. Oh—and I was hit by a thunderbolt, I believe, our last big storm. It felt like a large rock falling on my feet, so that I looked up at the sky, like Henny Penny, to see where it had come from. Bang!—it almost knocked me over. I was standing beside an outside base plug. (Lota's fancy is to light up the outside scenery at night. I tell her it makes the house look like a concentration camp.)

To Dr. Anny Baumann

[Rio de Janeiro]
July 9, 1959

Lota and I came down to Rio over two weeks ago, meaning to stay three or four days, but we broke our car and have had to stay on and on while it's being repaired. We finally got L.'s son to send us down our accumulation of mail, by bus, and in it was your letter of June 18th and the report, and I want to let you know now, very hurriedly, that I did receive it and to thank you . . . I hope you really did like the coffee—lots of people don't, at first, anyway, and of course it wasn't as fresh as it should be. At home we grind it fresh each time and that's much better. I am afraid, too, that the butterflies smell like mothballs—to keep them from being attacked by ants here—but the smell should wear off shortly . . .

Miss Moore writes with all her usual fluency and I think she is much better. Louise [Crane] took her to a neurologist, I think—but of course she will live all alone, and go gadding about on the subways in all weathers!

We've just had two big saint's days—Saint John and Saint Peter. Saint John is the equinox—the longest day in the North, the shortest day here—and there were bonfires and fireworks all along that famous beach, right under our apartment terrace. On Saint Peter's there was a huge display of fireworks set off in a lagoon—we drove a group of friends almost to the top of one of the Rio mountains to see them from there—

far off, miniature, and almost *silent*. It was ravishing—with the sea and passing ships, etc., as a backdrop—but unfortunately that was the night we broke the car—and had to coast down the mountain back again, for miles—rather scary.

The New Yorker just cabled me that they were buying a long, *long* (nice for me) poem ["The Riverman"]. I don't know when they'll be using it yet, but you may be interested because it's about the Amazon. I've never seen the Amazon, but never mind! I've been doing a whole group of poems again at last, thank heavens. This Amazon one is the one I like the least, so I thought I'd send it off first—the others are better, I think, or hope, and all together should make enough for a new book sometime next year.

I've just found out that the reason why I was having asthma so badly for two weeks before coming to Rio was probably because the grass, the *matto*, was going to seed then. I don't know why it never occurred to me before. It all turns a brilliant rose-red and the mountains are wonderful then, particularly at sunrise or sunset—and I have asthma. As the doctor says, the Indians never do; the Brazilians rarely do; but "foreigners" quite often do.

Lota's fifth adoptive grandchild was finally born on June 17th, a girl, what they wanted, and all went very fast and easily. You may be interested to learn that right after the birth the mother sat up and drank a cup of —guess what—black coffee. Then "conversed," as they say here, gaily, for a long time. The baby is very pretty and I'm trying to write a poem on the X-ray taken of her shortly before birth—it is very beautiful.

We've been to dinner with Carlos Lacerda in his huge new double-duplex apartment. He was very entertaining and had cooked some of the dinner himself, but I am sorry to say he doesn't seem at all well, and politically things seem rather desperate here. It is such a pity—so much of his energy and intelligence goes to waste.

I wonder where you are going on your vacation this year, and maybe you have gone already. I hope you and your husband have a wonderful holiday. We should like so much to see you here, you know, when you get around to South America. And kindest regards from Lota (who is having an animated political discussion with our pedicurist, who is a bookie at the Jockey Club as well, so is very well-informed!).

To Howard Moss

September 8, 1959

Your one item of news that baffled me was "Jean & *Joe*" 's leaving for Europe—and that was cleared up at lunch here yesterday. I've never laid eyes on Mr. A. J. Liebling but it does seem an odd marriage—or doesn't it? But now Jean [Stafford] will surely never suffer from malnutrition again, as I remember she once did. I'm also surprised at your meeting with Huxley, somehow—he was always extremely pleasant when he was here, gentle, polite, etc., but not very communicative. Perhaps once or twice on that Brasília expedition I went on, he did insist a bit too much on the superior Inca culture of the West Coast and how altitude and *cold* air probably had a lot to do with it (very English, I thought), for a Brazilian audience, but in general he was very nice.

The weather has been perfectly awful lately, unseasonably hot and with a thick pink haze over our best feature, the view. Don might as well have been in Yonkers on a hot day. He took a lot of photographs of the disc of a sun showing through the haze and I'm sure they're going to look like advertisements for a North Cape cruise. Right beneath the sun were seven amazing mountain peaks, completely hidden for days now. He seemed a bit uncertain as to whether he should like Brazil or not, I thought!—but he has had awful weather and nothing is looking its best. The day before we had had the [Alexander] Calders here and that visit was more successful, I'm afraid. They've spent some time in Brazil before, and they love to *samba*. Calder went sambaing all over the terrace, wearing a bright orange shirt, just like a calendula swaying in the breeze. All our guests these days seem just to have seen *Orfeo of the Carnival* [*Black Orpheus*], that French-Brazilian movie that got the prize at Cannes this year. Have you seen it, too? It is not very good, being more French than Brazilian—at least that's one reason it isn't good—but there are some lovely shots of Rio (in clear weather) and I think you should see it & be tempted again to visit us. And the music is pretty good.

I am answering you promptly partly for business reasons—real estate reasons, again. You say you know some available sublets. Do you think you know of any that might be free from the middle of December until the end of March? It looks now as though Lota and I might get back to N.Y. for that stretch—more or less the time people go to Florida in. If you will be kind enough to pass on any information you have to our friend Mary Morse (I think you met her), who's in the U.S. now, she could go to look at them and perhaps engage one for us before she comes back to Brazil, the first part of October. She is on the Cape until the end of this month but you could send her a list.

Lota and I liked a poem of yours about *eyes* that we saw lately. I'd like to be more detailed but our recent *New Yorker*s are in Rio—and I have seen several more good ones by you. I liked Miss Moore's St. Jerome one very much. Thank you for your kind remarks about my Amazon poem—it's not a type I really approve of but maybe it will do—and I have a few more going I like better, I think. I do hope the plays are going well—maybe now we'll even be seeing them. Please don't go to Europe before we get there—maybe with some luck we all might go, in the spring. If I don't go traveling soon, *my* travel nerves will be beyond me, I'm afraid. What bothers me is not transportation but things like porters and anti-

Americanism. Perhaps traveling with a Brazilian will take the blight off me?

Your summer sounds awfully nice and I hope you're doing some more sea pieces. Thank you again for the letter, and I'll be very grateful if you'll let Mary know of any apartments you can think of.

To Pearl Kazin

September 9, 1959

Thank you so much for your nice long letter and please never apologize for them—you're one of the best letter writers I know. I answered it almost immediately and went on & on & on, and then my letter seemed high-flown in parts and mean in other parts, and I never sent it. Then we had to go to Rio again (we've been going back & forth steadily for six weeks or so now) and I seem to have your letter (*bem*) and my letter (*mal*) both there. (*Bem* means "nice," as you probably remember, or "genteel"—they speak of *gente bem*, "nice people." Well, outside Rio there's a big sort of half-outdoor terrace restaurant that is called simply BEM. There are also lots of miserable little shack-stands, where sometimes we go to eat a dinner standing up—kebabs, corn on the cob, etc. —and one of them put up a small sign calling itself simply MAL.)

. . . I HATED the Salinger story. It took me days to go through it, gingerly, a page at a time, and blushing with embarrassment for him every ridiculous sentence of the way. How can they let him do it? That horrible self-consciousness, every sentence comments on itself and comments on itself commenting on itself, and I think it was actually supposed to be *funny*. And if the poems were so good, why not just give us one or two and shut up, for God's sake? That Seymour figure doesn't impress me at all as anything extra—or is that the point and I've been missing it? GOD is in any slightly superior, sensitive, intelligent human being or something? or WHAT? and WHY? And is it true that *The New Yorker* can't change a word he writes? It seems to be the exact opposite of those fine old-fashioned standards of writing Andy White admires so, and yet it isn't "experimental" or original—it's just tedious. Now if I am running counter to all the opinions at present, tell me why, because I'd like to know how it can be defended . . . Perhaps Seymour isn't supposed to be anything out of the ordinary, nor his poems either, so that all that writhing and reeling is to show the average man trying to express his love for his brother, or brotherly love? Well, Henry James did it much better in one or two long sentences.

Now I see Mary [McCarthy]'s Italian pieces have started—we just got the first one and I haven't had time to read it yet. I am childishly envious of her ability to write that kind of thing. Oh, how I wish I could. I picked up a copy of *The Ginger Man* in Rio and like it very much, I'm not sure why. It's *awful* in many ways, but so funny in its squalor, and full of life in dead old Ireland. Have you read it? I keep going with [Lewis Mumford's] *The Condition of Man* and think it's wonderful, and now I'm reading [Hermann Broch's] *The Sleepwalkers*—fascinating, but he and Huxley both reek of vulgarity, why is it? And—oh well, we read and read and read, all the time, and the books pile up, and I remember a little here and there, and the magazines are snowing us under, and what good it all does drifting around in this aging brain I don't know! The only practical help seems to be that when we have "foreign" visitors, Lota and I seem to be awfully up-to-date.

The Calders were here Sunday (they are old friends of Lota's from their visit here eleven years ago) and we had a very nice day with them, one of the best Sundays in a long time. People who came to call from time to time were surprised or shocked or pleased by Calder and his costume and his incomprehensible conversation, according to their natures. He is very witty, though, a sort of dry New England turn of phrase. They neither of them eat much, just drink a lot, but are both very fat, and at the table Mrs. C. said to me, "Doesn't Sandy look wonderful?" The next day in Petrópolis I saw an elderly beauty-parlor man kissing his elderly and very homely wife goodbye—probably just until dinnertime—on the sidewalk in front of his establishment, and that kiss and Mrs. C.'s comment have cheered me on my way all week.

Thank you for your kind remark about "The Riverman," and I trust something much better will pass through your hands soon. I've really got a lot going, after two years, but worry too much, I think—maybe one worries poetry right out of existence, finally, and stops.

Marianne wrote a review of *The Diary of "Helena Morley"* for *Poetry*, the July number. It is very nice and it certainly was kind of her to do it, and she's picked quotations with her usual bright eye—but oh dear, she got a bit careless with quotation marks so you can't tell what's me and what's Helena, and at the end she definitely has *me* saying: "Happiness does not consist in worldly goods but in a peaceful home, in family affection—things that fortune cannot bring and often takes away." Well, I believe it but I'd never *say* it. I suspect that Mr. Brant wrote that for Helena, anyway, for the Preface.

October 24, 1959

. . . *"Helena Morley"* is going to appear in Japanese. They are using both Portuguese and English texts, so I'll get about $100 advance for that. Did I tell you that—even after the [V. S.] Pritchett review—the royalty check from England was *$4.90*? That's worse than poetry . . .

We went to São Paulo for the opening of the Biennale this year. They invited us and paid our hotel bills, so we really could relax and have a lovely time! Thousands of abstractions—horribly depressing after a few hours—but a few very good things—folk stuff from Bahia, a wonderful show, the Burle-Marx was good, and Francis Bacon and Mies van der Rohe. We stayed five days . . . Then we saw Meyer Schapiro for a day on our way back. I'd never met him, but got up my courage and accosted him in the hotel, and he couldn't have been nicer. It is rather nice the way things, or people, turn up—sometimes just as I think life is too isolated or provincial, we find ourselves with a whole bunch of celebrities on our hands. Just after Schapiro who should arrive at the house one day (I was in the shower!) with our architect but Neutra and his wife. He is very handsome but must be a bit gaga. He squeezed me tenderly to his side, upon introduction, peered into my eyes and asked me, "Do you know who I am? Have you ever heard of me?"

To May Swenson

November 10, 1959

You have FLOORED me . . . but of course I am perfectly delighted. It is the nicest and most overwhelming present I've received for years and years. While we waited for Mary [Morse] to get through Customs (actually for once she had no trouble at all—I'd gone with lots of money, expecting to have to pay 100% duty on the four records she was bringing me, and she didn't have to pay a cent)—all members of our welcoming party tried out the binoculars right away. I found I could read the titles on the pocket books at the other end of the airport, and after exhausting that pleasure I went outside and looked at Rio off in the distance. They seem *fearfully* powerful to me—but I've forgotten about binoculars, or put the science out of my mind since my wartime experiences with them.

We've been using them constantly ever since. Lota finds she can oversee all the trees she planted on the nearby hills without actually climbing up the mountain—the buds, the leaves, and even if they have ants on them. I have found out that I was missing a great many little *sitting* birds—the first thing I watched this morning out the bedroom window. By chance I spotted a little green female something-or-other just sitting, resting, after making the beds and washing the dishes no doubt —yawning from time to time, or examining a toenail. I watched her for a long time. The bigger, flashier birds are apt to be bolder and come close and we see them, but it was really a surprise to see the little ones like that. We are both so pleased and also so touched we almost wept. You shouldn't have spent the money—and it all goes to prove a theory (almost a law) of mine that only "poor" (or relatively so, if you don't mind my saying so) people have any idea of real generosity and real feeling about "presents." My "poor" aunt is the one who manages to ship me gallons of maple syrup, etc.—the "rich" members of the family never do anything at all! (Not that I'm so avid for gifts—but this was a wonderful surprise and Lota and I talked and talked about it last night.)

It is going to be wonderful in Rio, too—to watch the ships with. I like that red lining very much. The red with the orange-ish leather is so very Japanese. Now I realize how really very much we'd been needing binoculars, living in the mountains *and* on the ocean.

Well, we got home and Mary unpacked and then presented me with the records too. I haven't had time yet to play Odetta all through, but she certainly has an extremely beautiful voice. Of course I like Negro voices anyway—have most of Bessie Smith, Billie Holiday, etc. (as you may remember). I never heard of this girl before—please tell me what you know about her, if you've heard her in person, etc.

I was glad to see Lloyd Frankenberg among others reply to that silly review of Marianne Moore by Karl Shapiro. It seemed completely uncalled-for to me. To be able to produce something as good as her St. Jerome poem at the age of 72 should be enough, I think. Frost once said to me, "Karl's a nice boy, but he can't think," and I'm afraid it is true. How long are you at Yaddo for? Are you working on poems and have you had any published lately? *The New Yorker* now has three of mine, but the best I am still polishing up. The $ is zooming here, and it is too hideously expensive for Lota to go to the U.S. now. Maybe we'll all be seeing you in Europe instead. I've got to stop in order to send this to Petrópolis—it is really just to say thank you a thousand times for the present.

To Aunt Grace

November 15 or 16, 1959

I am so awfully sorry we aren't going to be able to make that trip, at least not when we thought we were going to—and I had better not say "in the spring" or anything like that. The dollar is *way* up—it is fine for me here (although prices have gone way up too), but it would be almost impossible for Lota in the U.S., the exchange is so bad—and also (I may have said this before, but anyway) she has just made a contract for her last big hunk of land—to be developed—and it is much better to stay on hand and see to it that things start off right, at least. It is very important for her, of course. I don't mind too much not getting to N.Y. now, except for seeing some friends, but Lota feels very badly . . .

The inflation here is so bad I don't really know what is going to happen next. For the first time there is a *meat* shortage—meat prices have gone up to about half of U.S. ones, which is fearfully high here, and since even poor people eat beef every day, with their black beans and rice—and there isn't anything *else*, no variety, such as we have—it is a great hardship. People are sleeping on the sidewalks all night to get in the meat lines early in the morning, and our Rio friends' cooks get up to start getting in line at 4 a.m. So far Petrópolis hasn't been affected too much—we even send meat down by bus to friends!—and I don't honestly care much, anyway—I can get along perfectly well without meat. But there have been bombs thrown, etc.

Maybe you even saw (it was on television in N.Y) how a *rhinoceros* got elected to be a city councilman? It's a famous rhinoceros in the zoo here and it started just as a joke, then people took it up and actually voted for him, just to show what they think of their crooked politicians. He got over 200,000 votes—then they stopped counting them. I think it is a very nice—and very Brazilian—gesture. Our friend Mary Morse (just back from N.Y.) went to a musical show and one of the jokes was "Well, I see that Macmillan got elected in England and a rhinoceros got elected in Brazil."

And now to cheer you up after the gloom of my letter of the other day, I'll enclose a new Christmas carol I just learned (I didn't choose the names; that's the way I was taught it)—to be sung to the tune of "Hark, the Herald Angels Sing";—and DON'T sing it to Aunt Mabel! (or any genteel friends):

> *Uncle George and Auntie Mabel*
> *Fainted at the breakfast table.*
> *This should be sufficient warning:*
> *Never do it in the morning.*
> *Ovaltine will set you right,*
> *You can do it ev'ry night.*
> *Uncle George is hoping soon*
> *To do it in the afternoon.*
> *O what joys Aunt Mabel's seen*
> *With the help of Ovaltine.*

Do you think the Great Village home would be a good place to retire to in my old age? Our friend Mary has been having an awful time with her aunt—86—and the aunt's friend who lives with her—83—and both semi-invalids. They forget everything all the time so that they are in danger of being robbed by their maid, doctor, or anyone who comes along (they're rich, or the aunt is). Mary has been with them for five months and had a terrible time. I don't think I could have stood it—48 hours of Aunt Florence were *more* than I could take. Mary tried to get them into various nursing homes, etc.—finally left them the way they are—but brought back a lot of "literature" on nursing homes near N.Y. and I've been reading it with morbid fascination. "Where you get *loving* care," etc., or "Have your own furniture"—and all so fearfully expensive. Sometimes I think of poor old Aunt Florence—and no one can *possibly* love the poor woman. Nancy does go in every day, I think (not that that would comfort me much!). But poor Aunt F.—she gets drunk once in a while and calls up her lawyer and tells him he's "ruined" her and she'll "expose" him, etc. (not a word of truth in it, of course!). I don't blame her for drinking, but I'm afraid of accidents. Well, heaven preserve us—or kill us off quick.

I must get to work. If only poetry made more money—alas. However, I am happy and that's the main thing—even if I don't deserve to be!

To Lloyd Frankenberg

March 22 (I think), 1960

I have been expecting to receive the new contract [for a poetry recording] but so far I haven't—it might come today. I haven't been to the P.O. for four days now. I am just as always amazed at your business acumen and really think somehow you should make vaster and more frequent use of it . . .

(I am an hour slower with this [letter] than I thought I'd be this morning, too. I just locked myself in my studio toilet. Shrieks & screams finally brought Sebastião, João, and Albertinho to my rescue. They have been handing all the screwdrivers in the house through a slit in the shutter to me and I have been taking the door off its hinges, very clumsily. Lota was off helping Mary build her new house—she arrived just as the door gave way at last. I was imprisoned exactly one hour and everyone had an awfully good time.)

I think it is wonderful the way that record has kept on selling, though. I keep getting little checks—and now maybe it will have a renaissance. At Christmas I received a huge recording of Kenneth Patchen—I wonder why—from him, I think—and you know how I feel about recordings. However, I am very grateful! DO I have a poem called "Early Sorrow"? I thought it was just called "Sestina," if it's the one I think it might be . . .

I left on the 17th of February to go to the Amazon—with our friend Rosinha and her 16-year-old nephew, Manoel. We were gone about three weeks and the trip was an enormous success and I am dying to go back and see the *upper* Amazon next time. We came down from Manaus to Belém by boat. It is much more beautiful than I'd ever imagined. (If only Lota didn't find boat life so painful!) . . . When we got back Carnival was over, but the Calders were still in Rio—in Lota's apartment—and Lota and Mary were still helping entertain, etc., and a very exhausting four or five days ensued . . . Then came Lota's birthday and a huge party in Rio. Then home at last, but to a brand-new cook and her husband. We still don't know—she was afraid to light the gas oven. When I lit it, she retreated all the way across the kitchen and hugged the wall. She also answers the telephone by saying HOY! However, maybe we can polish her. This is all to explain why today is the first day in over a month that I have sat down to write letters. Thank you for the lovely poems—I hope that vest *really* fits (my jacket doesn't). It is deerskin, and I indicated the size, more or less, on a snapshot of the shop owner's 13-year-old daughter . . .

Mary [Morse] started on her new house. The digging is done—she has a beautiful location down at the beginning of our road, overlooking a waterfall and huge rocks all around and mimosa trees. Lota is very busy with real estate at the moment, and I am hoping now to get a bit of work done after my travels. The cats are fine. Calder has left us the biggest pair of blue jeans I have ever seen and a red flannel shirt. We do like them (the Calders) so much. He composed a small poem one day after I had tactlessly suggested a *nap*—or maybe it was what I said:

> *If you've had too much booze,*
> *You can take a little snooze.*

I must write to some nuns—I seem to be rather popular with them at the moment; I'm sure it's a bad sign, oh dear. Give my love to Loren.

To Robert Lowell

April 22, 1960

This is TIRADENTES DAY—"Toothpuller Day"—a national holiday on which I think I wrote to you last year, too. He was a patriot who tried to get rid of the Portuguese, and he had been an itinerant dentist, and he was finally cut into eight, I think it was, pieces and the pieces sent around the country.

Yes, I saw the Orpheus movie—it opened here a year ago. It was an opera to begin with, written by a poet Lota knows—but we didn't attend that, and L. refused to see the movie, too. I liked bits of it, but the effect, I thought, was more French than Brazilian (you say "American"!—but that footsie game, etc., are pure French, surely). I liked the views of Rio at dawn—and they picked the best slum, of course, but had to build their own hovels—and Carnival isn't like that—it's much, much better. For one thing the samba schools are very proud and independent and they practice all year with professional teachers—and they *perform;* they'd never mix with the crowd like that—Carnival's one big glorious mess, but a more orderly and artistic mess, really. I was in Amazonas this year, but Lota went with the Calders, and it *rained.* The beautiful Louis XV costumes were all draggled, but they danced on until dawn. Calder stood up and watched for six hours—he is made of iron like one of his own creations, I think. Mrs. C. wore an Indian shawl over her dress, magenta, and she and Lota returned in the gray dawn both dyed all over from it.

It is something you really must see before it is quite ruined. Loudspeakers have almost ruined parts of it already. The *Orpheus* music is pretty fakey, too—only one true samba—and the words, being written by a *real* poet, are bad—they lack that surprise, the misused words, the big words, etc., that sambas always have. One of my favorites has a refrain: "Respect the ambient!" And one is about how Woman drags down Man—with all his "beauty and nobility." But Lota can sing them all night when she gets going. Oh—another is "The Cathedral of Love." I should really make a good collection, and translations, I think. I suspect they're some of the last folk poetry to be made in the world.

The New Yorker sent me the April 2nd number airmail and so I learned that you had received the Book Award, made a speech, etc. *Congratulations*, and please tell me about it. I was hoping Flannery [O'Connor] would get the novel one, but maybe her book appeared too late—if it had any chance . . . You don't have to like the "Riverman" poem. Lota hates it, and I don't approve of it myself, but once it was written I couldn't seem to get rid of it. Now I am doing an authentic, post-Amazon one that I trust will be better. I almost finished a story about the Amazon, too, but it is more or less a potboiler. Yes, the Flannery book is a bit disappointing, I'm afraid—one wishes she could get away from religious fanatics for a while. But just the writing is so damned good compared to almost anything else one reads—economical, clear, horrifying, *real*. I suspect that this repetition of the uncle-nephew, or father-son, situation, in all its awfulnesses, is telling something about her family life—seen sidewise, or in distorted shadows on the wall.

I wonder if you got my cards from the Amazon (also some snapshots mailed in Rio last week), and the ballad book? No—those are folk poetry all right too. The form goes back to Camões—and they sell thousands of them—displays in all the markets, like Marboro bookshops in N.Y., and people buying all the time. I know you can't read it properly—but sometimes they are quite good, and they are composed by people who can't read or write, and sung to guitars. Some stanzas go in for long lists of place-names, rhymed, or people's names—with very classical effect.

Well, speaking of opera—you'd like Manaus. Its most famous sight is the huge opera house built around 1905 at the height of the rubber boom. Rubber collapsed completely just after that and there the opera house stands, huge, magnificent, art-nouveau-ish, with the town dwindled to nothing around it, and the Rio Negro rolling magnificently below. It is quite lovely inside—rose damask and mirrors (the last governor stole a lot of mirrors and girandoles) and armchairs with cane seats, for coolness. The plasterwork is very delicate, all regional things, palms, coffee trees, alligators, etc., and huge paintings of *Guaraní*, sunrise on the river, etc. The ballroom is marble and tortoiseshell—but the pillars around the sides are *fake* marble, because that last shipload from Carrara was sunk. I've never heard *Guaraní* and suspect it's bad—but we had "Bifstek Carlos Gomez" on the menu every single day.

I think your Ford grant to study opera is amazing. When I got asked to *suggest* people for it, I vaguely thought of myself, since I need money badly, but couldn't think how I could get to enough operas—now I think I was rather stupid. Maybe we could have gone to Milan for a year! And I have dreamed of a libretto for years. Do you know Sam Barber? He wants one, I know—but then, I don't think much of his luscious music. However, I think a good libretto might be exactly your cup of tea. I think Auden's are too pastiche-ish—they don't have to be quite so simple, really. And as you say, there's no reason why they can't stand on their own without the music.

If you can think of anything *I* could apply for, please tell me. I sometimes think I have no right to, and then I realize other people who have small amounts of money do and I don't see why I shouldn't. Except that if I really worked— It's a problem, but I think that now in this Eisenhower splurge I might possibly get enough from Ford or Rockefeller to take a trip to Europe. I haven't been since before the war. I couldn't live on my money in the "States"—in fact I find by statistics in *The New Republic* that there I am actually in the "underprivileged" class. Rockefeller has long been interested in South America and I have an idea for getting money to see some more of it and finish up a book of stories about Brazil. But I don't know where to write, and any information would be welcome. Three people I recommended got Guggenheims this year and I am beginning to feel sorry for myself! . . .

. . . I want to go back to the Amazon. I dream dreams every night— I don't know quite why I found it so affecting. Did I tell you that I have been taking photographic slides? I always thought it was too bourgeois for words but they really are lovely and I have a small Amazon lecture and a small Cabo Frio lecture, etc. Lota does the machine part and so far we have to look at everything twice, I don't know why, but I'm hoping to solve this problem. (She wanted me to take all the house.) Who is ever going to look at these, and when, I can't imagine. I have some of passengers going ashore in a pouring rain and up a steep ladder—it is like the Israelites. Did I tell you (oh dear, I hope not) how we stopped at a place called "Liverpool" late one night—a narrow channel, nothing visible but a few white blurs of houses and candles, and one lantern. The ship waited and waited—then plop—plop—very gently, a canoe came out, a big one. Several men were in it, with two lanterns—one the old-fashioned burglar's kind of dark lantern—they were bringing out a dying man to be taken to the hospital in Belém. It was very hard to raise him up to the ship—in a sheet, I think, an old man with a nightcap on. The lantern light fell on his face, on the red, muddy water—it was quite incredible. They are very quiet people, and handsome—Portuguese and Indian mixed, "*caboclos*" and "*mamalucos*"—I must find out where that name comes from.

But I worry a great deal about what to do with all this accumulation of exotic or picturesque or charming detail, and I don't want to become a poet who can only write about South America. It is one of my greatest worries now—how to use everything and keep on living here, most of the time, probably—and yet be a New Englander herring-choker bluenoser at the same time.

Oh, I think your drunkenness poem is going to be superb! It started me off on mine again—mine is more personal and yet a bit more abstract, I think. Please send me your finished one and I hope eventually to send you mine . . . I saw your review of I. A. Richards—oh I do manage to see quite a few things but I do think we should get away this year if we can. Lota has had a very tough stretch. Two of our best friends here, a couple on whom she depended a lot for company over weekends, a historian and his wife, were killed in a stupid plane crash at Christmas time. (I had just got him nominated for the Academy, an honorary member, too.) And one of my oldest friends who was coming to visit me this month died just before Christmas. Then Lota's adopted son has been cutting up—so has her wacky sister—she has too many lawsuits on her hands and too much land and no cash, etc.—and I haven't earned anything to speak of. I think the best thing for her would be a trip to N.Y. or Europe—preferably Europe, but she prefers N.Y.

Next week I am going on another short trip—three or four days—down the coast to a place that one can only get to by boat—so no one ever goes, of course. It is supposed to be perfect 18th-century—tiny—and the tide comes up the streets every day and goes down again—no hotel. Lota refuses to have anything to do with anything Brazilian or "primitive," you know. She says she wants something more civilized rather than less when she goes traveling—so I am going with two neighbors. One is the father of a childhood friend of L.'s, he's almost 80—and the other is his boy-friend of over 40 years, who is about 65—a huge, Viking-like German, with the brain and soul of a small girl of 8. (Really Tennessee Williams should come here—but please don't suggest it.) They are amazing, however. Never a cross word in all these years, and they have ten times my energy, and are stupid as stupid—and we'll make a lovely trio.

Yes, I saw that Mary and Randall *got in* [the Academy]—and [Harry] Levin!—and Nabokov refused—and Calder's *in*, too. I think we might have some quite funny dinners in our old ages, don't you?

Yesterday morning at 6:30 a.m. we were awakened by a very noisy old truck full of twenty-two very noisy men, standing up—ten monks and the rest laity. Lota rushed out saying that this was private property and what was the idea, etc.—and then in the midst of her outrage she remembered she'd promised one Franciscan he could bring the gang here for a hike sometime, so she piped down quickly. You must imagine this in the full red light of late sunrise, the mountains hung with red wisps of cloud, the birds shrieking, and Lota in a pasha-like huge, paisley dressing gown, with red fringes, shrieking too, while the poor brown brothers cowered in their truck. So they started off—some of the monks carried *briefcases*, poor dears, and they waded off through the long wet grass holding their skirts up. They came back about six last night and I went out to talk to them. They had their hoods up and some actually had bottles of beer—it was like a bad painting. I hope you got the nuns I took at Cabo Frio—they were awfully nice, in wading. I wanted to take a picture of their boots and blue wool socks lying in the sand but I got shy.

But the Church here keeps giving me deep Protestant shudders. I borrowed a nightgown in an emergency one night in Rio. When I went to bed something scratched my bosom, over the heart, and I felt around and found something pinned to it. At first I thought it was a small powder puff—a new way of scenting one's self perhaps—but when I fished it out I found printed on it in almost invisible letters "Agnus Dei." This belonged to a woman whom I'd always thought of as Catholic but *intelligent*—one of the good kind.

You sound very well in your letter—and I am so glad. I'm in fine shape except for these worries about money and whether I'm going to turn into solid cuteness in my poetry if I don't watch out—or if I do watch out. Aside from that, everything is fine and I've been writing a lot again. Have you done any more poems? You know how happy all this success for the book makes me, I'm sure. We know how (can't think of the right word!) it is in some ways, and yet for once they've picked the right person and it is awfully gratifying and even makes one feel a bit better about all the world's horrors.

To Howard Moss

May 10, 1960

Your book finally arrived two days ago—I gather from my correspondence with Scribners that there had been some trouble about presentation copies. WHY is there, always? It is part of that general conspiracy. The book looks very impressive and I want to thank you for it right away and tell you how pleased I am to have it—even if others have had it for months now. I've already stated my simple thoughts and praise about many of the poems, but I do like some of the new ones very much—some I've seen, or am about to see, in *The New Yorker*, I think. I meant to write you when "Tourists" appeared how much I liked it—particularly the two couplets: about Copenhagen and Hostels—they are wonderful—your best manner. I am still awfully fond of poor Lennie. Both Lota and I were very much taken with "A Song Struck from the Records," particularly the first stanza. Maybe you hate to be told you should be funny oftener —I think I'd be—but you do do that kind of thing so well—and somehow "too old at the Hostel" hits me much harder these days than even the evanescence of perfect love, oh dear.

I'd like to say something brilliant, of course—but the truest and really most complimentary thing I can say is that your book makes me fearfully homesick for New York, all of it—all the excitement and confusion and fatigue and messiness and stylishness and horror and noise and romance and everything—and all the people. "The Feast" gives me the creeps. I hope I'm not the Hermit. "O miseries and appetites of the world"—but there are plenty, too many, of both, right here.

You look sweetly solemn on the jacket—don't you know that rubber tree is trying to get your attention?

Perhaps you have gone abroad already?—or are about to go? I do wish you'd write me a letter when you have time; in fact I'd like a long private conversation. Since I last wrote I have made a trip on the Amazon and now I am living to go back there again—it was much more beautiful than I'd imagined and I liked the people very much. I want to take a long and very tough trip *up*-river next time, into Ecuador and Peru—it can be done. I suppose I should be studying the stones of Florence, but geographic curiosity leads me on and on and I can't stop. Last night I dreamed there was a narrow road that began at Tierra del Fuego and went straight north, and I had started to walk it, quite cheerfully. A large primitive stone coffin was being carried on muleback alongside of me, ready for me when I gave out. The mule driver had a toothache (I can't understand that part).

To Robert Lowell

July 27 (I think), 1960
Friday, at any rate marketing day, and
the day someone is bound to arrive

Please never stop writing me letters—they always manage to make me feel like my higher self (I've been re-reading Emerson) for several days. Lots of things have been happening here, at least lots for me. But first, I don't think I've ever really commented much on "The Drinker." I find it even more horrendous in *Partisan Review*—although I hate to give up that soap dish. The most awful line for me is "even corroded metal," and the cops at the end are beautiful, of course—with a sense of release that only the poem, or another fifth of bourbon, could produce. As a cook I feel I should tell you that soured milk is NOT junket, but the picture is all too true. (I have a poem that has a galvanized bucket in it, too—it is one I started in Key West—and I think I even used the phrase "dead metal," oh dear—but it has nothing to do with my Drunkard one.) The sense of time is terrifying—have hours gone by, or one awful moment? How long have the cars been parked?

That Anne Sexton I think still has a bit too much romanticism and what I think of as the "our beautiful old silver" school of female writing, which is really boasting about how "nice" *we* were. V. Woolf, E. Bowen, R. West, etc.—they are all full of it. They have to make quite sure that the reader is not going to misplace them socially, first—and that nervousness interferes constantly with what they think they'd like to say. I wrote a story at Vassar that was too much admired by Miss Rose Peebles, my teacher, who was very proud of being an old-school Southern lady—and suddenly this fact about women's writing dawned on me, and has haunted me ever since.

I have re-arranged the Trollope poem ["From Trollope's Journal"], taking your advice, and I think it is improved. The whole thing should really be in quotation marks, I suppose; the reason it doesn't sound like me is because it sounds like Trollope. It probably should be quite a bit longer. Have you ever read his *North America*? I just copied out some of the Washington chapter. Well, I don't know whether it is a virtue or not, never to sound the same way more than once or twice! It sounds too much like facility, and yet I don't feel a bit facile, God knows.

Robie Macauley wrote me that I had been made a member of the P.E.N. by John Farrar, willy-nilly, and then Lota and I were invited to the Embassy luncheon given for the U.S. group—only Lota refused to go. So I went, and met Robie & his wife, and John Brooks of *The New Yorker* and his wife, and Elmer Rice, and May Sarton, none of whom I'd ever met before. I wished so much you had been there—all else aside, I would have loved to have introduced you to our Ambassador: "Mr. Cabot, Mr. Lowell." (When I told Robie about your having read to 3,000 people on the Common, he said, "A Lowell speaks to Boston.") I liked Robie very much and am only sorry I didn't have more of a chance to talk to him—he was very busy of course being a delegate. The next day, however, Lota and I did see more of them—we dragged the Americans, with the exception of Elmer Rice, all the way up here, by Volkswagen and bus, for dinner, and I think everyone had rather a good time. But I still didn't have much chance to talk to Robie because I was too busy being a hostess, and he is very quiet, or was here at any rate. He seems very very bookish and also, from time to time, extremely funny, and I liked him a lot . . .

I'm sure Anne Macauley would have had some wonderful things to say if she'd known me better. I remarked that I was afraid I'd had some sort of falling-out with Randall and she said "Good!" All wives seem to feel strongly about Randall! "Never lifts a finger," etc. Anyway, it was all very enjoyable: the weather not too good, nor the dinner. I only went to half a P.E.N. lecture, by Mario Praz, and found it sounded much better when read at home without the distractions of Graham Greene stomping out and Moravia scowling like a small Mussolini, etc. The advantage of that P.E.N. (a Brazilian finally told me what the letters stand for) seems to be that members get sent to expensive-to-get-to places, like Japan and South America. But the disadvantage is that they don't seem to have time to see the places when they get there and just have to submit to being excruciatingly bored—but maybe I underestimate what goes on, because I didn't see much of it, after all . . .

Robie told me you are going to Copenhagen—and that should be more interesting than this affair. Also that you have swapped houses with Eric Bentley for the winter in N.Y. I wish we could get there in the spring, but I don't know. I went to see a friend off to Europe last week—she was going third-class on a new English ship and it is dirt cheap, so I went to see what it is like and I think I could stand it for 13 days—to Lisbon and back for about $300. IF the Chapelbrook [award] comes through—however, I don't feel at all sure about that.

You ask if I have ever found "reading and writing curiously self-sufficient." Well, both Lota and I read from 7 a.m. intermittently until 1 a.m. every day, and all sorts of things, good and bad, and once in a while I think—what if I should run out of things to read, in English, by the time I'm sixty, and have to spend my old age reading French or Portuguese or even painfully taking up a new language? And then I've always had a daydream of being a lighthouse keeper, absolutely alone, with no one to interrupt my reading or just sitting—and although such dreams are sternly dismissed at 16 or so, they always haunt one a bit, I suppose. I now see a wonderful cold rocky shore in the Falklands, or a house in Nova Scotia on the bay, *exactly* like my grandmother's—idiotic as it is, and unbearable as the reality would be. But I think everyone should go, or should have gone, through a stretch of it—like your Third Avenue stretch, maybe—a *The Notebooks of Malte Laurids Brigge* stretch—and perhaps it is a recurrent need. But let us not say, to quote Miss S., "I've fallen in love with solitude."

What you say about meter—well, I have loads of thoughts on the subject and I think I'll have to write again tomorrow. I have a theory now that all the arts are growing more and more "literary"; that it is a late stage, perhaps a decadent stage—and that un-metrical verse is more "literary" and necessarily self-conscious than metrical. If I were Schapiro I'd write a book about it. (And have you read *Art & Illusion* by one Gombrich?—it is fascinating.) I find it is time to go to market. What kind of plan do you have for your opera, or is it an opera? Now you must teach Harriet to swim—or have you? It is just the age to learn. I believe in swimming, flying, and crawling, and burrowing.

To Aunt Grace

September 23, 1960

. . . It has suddenly grown HOT here, the past few days—much too early, so I hope it won't last. We got our little pool cleaned up and went for a swim yesterday, and then drank iced *maté*. Do you know about *maté*? It is the South American tea—they drink an awful lot of it, particularly in Argentina. It doesn't taste exactly like tea—a bit more like *hay*, I think—but one gets quite fond of it . . .

We went to explore a place we'd heard about, called *Paratí*—a small port that hasn't been changed a bit for about 200 years. It is right on the end of a long bay—in fact at high tide the water comes right up the ends of the streets; and at *very* high tide, in May, they put planks across the streets from sidewalk to sidewalk. A friend of ours went there in May and went out for a walk at night, carrying a *candle*, he said, and crossing the planks. They had had electricity for exactly one month when we got there—and everyone was still very excited about it. At night there were circles of children under every lamppost, just like moths. We were the only *car* in town, except for one broken one, and a few trucks. Everyone comes and goes by ferry, twice a week, and bus, twice a week. You can walk around the whole place in ten minutes, and every single house is perfectly beautiful—but so run-down and poor. You could buy a *huge* house, perfect 18th-century—three floors, beams two feet square, etc.— for about $2,000—huge garden and palm trees, too. I'd like to buy the whole town, just to preserve it. But unfortunately the bay is too shallow, no good swimming, and I'm afraid it would be hot, etc. Our "hotel" was something—one of the 18th-century mansions all divided up by wooden partitions, so you could hear everyone sneeze and snore—the traveling salesmen and us, that was. The traveling salesmen strolled through the dining room in their pajamas and brushed their teeth, etc., at a sink in the corner—and the *bathroom*! Words fail me. Lota put up a good fight, but we never could get it repaired. However the landlady, "Dona Zezé," finally did manage to give us a bucket of water a few times a day and *we'd* flush it. But everyone was perfectly charming! The fish was excellent (I ate nothing but fish and bananas for three days), the churches adorable, and everything ruined for us by the town's one loudspeaker—elections are approaching here, too. However, it was worth the effort—a long long drive, over dirt roads.

I think I told you I've been going in for bread-making—I am getting so good at it I can't believe it! I'd always thought it was much harder to make, but now I make oatmeal bread, raisin bread, wheat germ (wonderful for toast), etc. etc. We are starting our outdoor oven—and someone lent me an old copy of the famous "Mrs. Beeton" 's cookbook and I find that in 1897 she said that an oven exactly like the one we're building makes the *best* bread of all. It looks like this [*EB sketches the oven*]— bricks and mortar—ours is right on a flat rock that happens to be near the kitchen, so it doesn't need any floor, even—just waist-high. You can buy the oven doors all ready. You put in a stack of wood, let it burn up, then scrape the ashes out with a hoe and put the bread *in*. Very primitive, but it works, and saves our bottled gas. We have plenty of wood around—and we also have a man to do the cleaning out! It is going to be whitewashed and looks very quaint indeed.

This is what they call "the month of fires" here because it is always so dry and there are so many brushfires—I dread it. So far Lota hasn't lost any of her trees, etc., but they come awfully close and every night we can count five or six fires burning on the mountains around us. (I also always have asthma this month, from all the dust and smoke.) Today's the big marketing day—I have a list a mile long—last Sunday we had five people here, and five more came unexpectedly for tea. It was still cold then and we had a big beef and kidney pie—stewed tomatoes (we had too many to use up!)—and *caramelized pears*—do you know that dessert? It is so easy to make—with apples, pears, or peaches. You just cut them up in eighths and put them in a *very* hot oven with a lot of sugar on top, and a little butter. In about fifteen minutes they are beginning to burn and get caramel-*y*, then you throw on a cup of cream—or you can skip that—and that's all, and everyone thinks they are something fearfully difficult to do . . .

Lota has been gaining a bit and I am very *severe* with her—only salad for lunch, and beef and vegetables for dinner (& 1 piece of toast for breakfast) plus an orange or two. She complains, but then she complains worse if she finds she can't get into her city clothes!

To Dr. Anny Baumann

Petrópolis
Estado do Rio de Janeiro
October 5, 1960

. . . I'm mailing you today, just for fun, a batch of Carlos Lacerda's election posters. He is running for governor of the new State of Guanabara; in fact by the time you get this I hope he will have been safely elected. It looks very much as though he is going to win. When I told him, in Rio two weeks ago, that I'd like some of the posters to send you, he was enchanted with the idea and said no, he'd send them to you himself. But somehow I thought you'd be more apt to get them if I did it, since he was making ten or twelve speeches a day & speaking on television every night. (He seems to thrive on it and looks better, and thinner, but has lost his voice, naturally.)

When the capital [of the country] was moved to Brasília, a new state was made out of the old Federal State of Rio—called the State of Guanabara—with Rio de Janeiro as the state capital. *We* are still in the *state of* Rio de Janeiro, that is, Petrópolis is, but the city of Rio de Janeiro no longer is, if you can follow that. (So Lota can't vote for Carlos!) On his newspaper he has a very good young German woman cartoonist, "Hilde," and she has done most of his posters. I'm sorry I couldn't get the best one for you, a *garbage heap*—because part of his campaign is to clean up the sadly neglected city of Rio. He also is going to open up a new school a week, he says. In fact most of his platform is excellent and we just hope he can manage to get the money to put it all through. Monday was election day here, for the President too—and Lota drove all the neighbors to the polls. They don't have voting machines here, so the results will not be known for ten days or so. There is a horrible possibility of a particularly fatuous general being elected—but if he isn't it will mean a complete turnover for the first time in more than thirty years, and remains of the dictatorship will finally be out. If the general does get elected, I think Lota will leave Brazil!

Thank you for sending me the batch of entertaining papers. It was the first I heard about the "Shadowlight Theatre" and I wonder how it turned out. I have a strong aversion to poetry recited out loud, poetry recordings, etc. Lloyd Frankenberg and I have argued about it for years, but I realize I am probably wrong about it and that when it is well done it is a good idea.

I have been writing quite a bit of poetry; *The New Yorker* will soon print one about this house ["Song for the Rainy Season"]. I should be able to get out a new book next year, I think. I've also, thank heavens, been doing some non-*New Yorker* poems, and what I should prefer to do is just sell them an occasional story and publish poems in other magazines.

Yesterday I had some very good news—something called the Chapelbrook Foundation has given me a $7,000 fellowship for the next two years—starting now—to take a trip on and help finish the book. This is all thanks to Robert Lowell, I feel sure—he recommended me. I think I shall save it up for as long as I can and then, with luck, Lota and I will go to Europe early next spring for several months . . .

Day before yesterday an architect we know telephoned out of the blue and asked if he could bring a busload of German architects to see the house—in about half an hour! It was election day and we had given the servants the day off, so we scuttled around and put everything unsightly in the closets and locked the doors, made a gallon or so of *maté* to serve, and Lota went to meet them. There were about 25, I think—I lost track—three female architects and the rest male. Their bus refused to come up the mountain road and Lota made trip after trip, but a good many of them, to our great admiration, came up on foot—about a mile straight *up*, really—they arrived very hot, and loaded with cameras, and in amazingly good spirits. We asked in a German neighbor to help us with the conversation, and it was a polyglot affair; English, German, French, Portuguese, Spanish and some Italian were all being spoken. They took hundreds of photographs, including a great many of the cats, I noticed. I never did find out exactly who they all were, or why they were here—but it must have been some group going to see Brasília, etc. One young man with a beard I liked particularly; he said he wrote poetry too and that he wished his wife were along, because "She is very active in the German-American Women's Club of Heidelberg."

From your point of view (your professional point of view, I mean) we are both very well. I think the very worst is that we are both missing one tooth since I last wrote, and of course Lota is very cheered up by the work being done on her land and the probable imminent sales, and now I am very cheered up by all this lovely and undeserved money. We think we shall go to Portugal in March or April, probably, and pick up a car there and drive to Italy to stay for several months. Perhaps we shall run into Loren and Lloyd somewhere in the spring. With a lot more luck and some more money, we might make that famous "triangular trip" and come back by way of New York—but from what I hear of New York prices, it doesn't seem to me as if I could ever go back there again.

We have just heard from Rio that Quadros (the candidate for President that Lota wants elected) is ahead by a million votes so far. Carlos is ahead too, but not by as much as we had hoped . . .

To Marianne Moore

January 5, 1961

Everyone here is very cheered up by the way the Brazilian elections went—and the U.S. ones, too (although I'm afraid you're not) . . . Our friend Carlos Lacerda—who was in exile in New York for a year because of the last of the Vargas government—is *in* at last, as Governor of Guanabara. Lota and I had dinner with him when we were in Rio, and Lota's been to the "palace" several times now. He wants her to work for him, landscaping a whole long new stretch of boulevards along the bay, with cafés, restaurants, walks, perhaps an aquarium, etc.—and he wants Lota to take charge of doing it. It is just the kind of job she could do well. She has hundreds of good ideas about such things and she would be working with our architect and her friend the great gardener, Burle-Marx, etc. It may not work out, of course—there are so many complications in anything political—but I certainly hope it does. Carlos is a very good man—brilliant, hardworking and absolutely honest. He is trying to build schools, do something about the slums and the water supply—all the urgent problems that have gone neglected for years.

He is also an admirer of yours (see what a rare political type he is) and he wants to invite really good people here to give readings and meet Brazilian writers. The U.S. State Department usually sends very minor and dull novelists and professors. If you have the slightest desire to visit Rio and feel at all up to it, let us know. We could arrange the whole trip, paid for of course, and you would be very well treated. We could probably fly you all over the harbor (and Lota's new works) in the palace helicopter. And have you driven about in a car with two flags on the motor? They may even have a salute for you at the airport . . .

I received a grant—thanks to Robert Lowell's idea and Agnes Mongan's help, I believe—that makes an outing to Italy and Greece possible sometime in March, for four months or so . . .

To Pearl Kazin

February 27, 1961

. . . While we were in Ouro Prêto for Carnival I caught something —probably at the one good ball we went to— . . . and have had "conjunctivitis" for the first time in my life. My eyes felt so horrible and I couldn't read or type for a few days and I kept feeling if only I could cry I'd be all right. So finally I sat down and read *Little Women* for about two hours and wept a great deal, as I always do at sentimentality, and my eyes immediately felt much better. This is just to say that since then, yesterday, I have been in a golden haze of matrimony, "womanhood," death by—what on earth is it Beth dies of? *Little Women*, plus having a baby in the house, convinces me that probably matrimony, womanhood, babyhood, and all of it are Best. The baby particularly . . .

Lota—as I think I told you in my pre-Carnival letter—is working hard. We have spent all our time in Rio lately, for over a month now. This time I didn't go down with her and she called to ask *how* to use that Italian coffeepot—she'd made coffee upside down again, *coitada*. The job is enormous—I went "on location" with her and about a dozen engineers last week—and so far I think she's doing marvelously—just the right tone—but I don't trust these gentlemen, I'm afraid—they are all so jealous of each other, and of a woman, naturally. Lota is pretty skeptical, too, but oh dear, I do hope it works out for her. She has been so miserable the past year with the awful business of the adopted son, the lawsuits . . . and now the latest "developer" (a multimillionaire "playboy" type) is letting her down sadly, too, and we're getting out of that as fast as we can, without lawsuit this time, we hope. So all these innumerable meetings in the heat in Rio have been welcome to me, really. Even postponing our trip—if ONLY it works out. But I am pessimistic about anything Brazilian, I'm afraid. I've never known such a bunch of uncooperative, self-indulgent, spoiled—and yes, *corrupted*, even the nice ones—people. If Lota weren't as far away as Rio, I probably wouldn't even type this, but you know how true it is! Not that the friends she's working with are dishonest, corrupt in that way—but in other ways. It is just something in the air, maybe left over from thirty years of Vargas. However, most of the time here I feel as if I were living in the 19th century—it's hard to make it seem real or contemporary. Anyway Lota has been wonderful in action, what I've seen of it—and if only she could have started doing things like this years and years ago—as she would have in any more "advanced" country.

To Robert Lowell

EB was so worried about French mistakes in Imitations, *Lowell's book of trans-lations (which he had sent her in manuscript), that she attempted several versions of a four-page letter, never sent. The letter she mailed praises his rendering of* Phaedra *(published as a separate book) and limits her comments on* Imitations *to a single paragraph.*

March 1, 1961

—in like a lamb, if that

means anything here

I can't believe I *haven't* written to you all this time because I've been doing it so much of the time in my head. Then I did do justice, I thought, to the *Phaedra* and that one got lost. (I thought it had because one I mailed at the same time, in Rio, I knew did.) I have here my first version of it—dated New Year's! Lota read it first, and of course she knows Racine much better than I do, and she was amazed by the way you managed the famous lines and the famous meter—speaking of *"noblesse"* to me. Yet it seems amazingly natural at the same time, *pure*—but undated. Isn't real tragedy a relief for a change? I feel I've said all this to you before, of course. Anyway, it seems a *tour de force* to me, and I hope something is done with it. The nice letter I got from you three days ago mentions a movie! Couldn't we all just be in Greece when they make it—if they make it there? . . .

I envy you the [White House] dinner party, I think, and the [Kennedy] inauguration must have been fun, too. I see bits of it over and over in the newsreels. But I don't like that Roman Empire grandeur—the reviewing stand, for example, looks quite triumphal. Of course Mrs. Kennedy's hat looks Byzantine. I wish President Kennedy weren't so damned RICH . . .

I have almost decided that before my next trip to N.Y. I'm going to have my face lifted and my hair dyed pink. As it will probably be my *last* trip, I want to leave a dashing memory behind me. Please send snapshots of Harriet. She is at the clothes stage, I suppose—one of Lota's "grand-children" visited us, aged 5, and worried us for a few days because she did nothing but change her dresses all day—but she got over it quickly in a few months.

Pearl Kazin wrote me she'd met you and took to you enormously. She is a very nice girl and a wonderful friend—but she appears to much better advantage alone, or with one or two people. Some other friends of mine you probably know, or will, are Bobby Fizdale & Arthur Gold, the two-piano team. They are a little chichi but awfully nice and you ought to hear them play—they are the best going . . .

We are NOT going abroad now—in fact, I'm not sure when at all now. Carlos Lacerda has put Lota in charge of a huge new "fill" along the Rio Bay . . . I am very pessimistic about temperamental and spoiled

Brazilians ever cooperating for long on anything—or working under a woman. But Lota is even more skeptical than I am, so maybe she won't mind too much if she feels she has to resign after a few months. She is wonderful in action, though—just the right tone, firm but funny, the times I've seen her. We went "on location" last week—heat about 105°, I think—and stared at overpasses and underpasses (already smelling of urine, which is one reason why L. is trying to fight them!) and sewers and dumps and scows and steam shovels—accompanied by a dozen melting engineers, mostly in white linen. The oldest had a small black fan— a custom I love, but I'm afraid it's going out. But I have gone back and forth to Rio with Lota every week for almost two months now, and that is one reason why I haven't written to anyone—not just you, Cal!

My work (ha ha) has suffered badly, of course, but now we are getting a system worked out, have a cleaning boy in Rio, at least, and won't have to stay there quite so much. I do wish I could see you—perhaps if we can't get abroad for another year I might manage a quick trip to N.Y. I think I have a book of poems almost ready. How do you like *January River* as a title? (There's a poem of that name, or with that in it at least.) I saw the London *Times* piece on you—heavens—before Christmas, and the solemn exchange of letters about the misprints, too. Some of the piece was good, I thought—and to see it, the *whole page*, was very gratifying. Your star couldn't be higher—and looking as big and bright as Venus does here these evenings.

Then—somewhere along the line—I got the book of translations with the dedication that of course made me shed tears. I went through it very rapidly and concentrated mostly on the Montale—I've never read him, or barely, and I'd love to. Then I cabled you, I think. This last week I've been at home with some time at last and I've been reading them all carefully. The only ones I can judge at all, of course, are the French ones—and I know them all pretty well. I think Baudelaire is more sympathetic to you verbally (and probably emotionally) than Rimbaud—at least those early Rimbauds you've chosen. Sometimes you've done wonders with Baudelaire's language: "mansards," "chain-smoking," "purring," "narcotics." (Couldn't she look for *coco palms* instead of *coconuts*, though?) You say to let you know things I question. Well, here are one or two things that bother me because they *look* like mistakes, whether or no. And though you have left yourself "free," I don't want to think of your being attacked for mistakes. (Please forgive my sounding like French 2A.) In "The Swan" (one of my favorite Baudelaire poems), I think the line should read "—who drink tears / and suck Grief like a Wolf-Nurse." In "La Maline" ("The malicious girl"): "I listened to the clock, happy and calm. The kitchen (door) opened with a blast / And the" etc. In "At the Green Cabaret" (I did this once myself), the last line is: "with its foam gilded by a ray of *late* sun" (the adjective seems important for the atmosphere of fatigue and peace, etc.) Also *"tartines"* are the little pieces

of bread and butter given to French schoolchildren. And in "Ma Bo-
hème," he just holds his shoe *near* his heart—in the position of Apollo
playing the lyre, although what's elastic I've never been able to figure
out, exactly. Couldn't be elastic-*sided* boots—they must have used elastic
shoelaces! If you want me to, I'd be glad to give you more benefits of my
past experience in Rimbaud-translating. (I spent a month alone in Brittany
once doing nothing much but that.) Sometimes it seems to me you sort
of spoil his joke, or give his show away, by bringing in his horrors too
soon. (But of course not, if you don't want me to.) I just don't want you
to lay yourself open to stupid or jealous misunderstandings, like the "white
eye" in "The Sleeper in the Valley" when Rimbaud says nothing to show
he's not asleep until the very last phrase—or in [Baudelaire's] "La Cloche
Fêlée," too.

I lived in Paris one whole winter long ago, and most of another
one—and that "endless wall of fog" haunts me still. But isn't it strange
how those Rimbaud sonnets (early poems, that is) sound so gay and
healthy and normal beside Baudelaire? Do you have those Pléiade
editions?—they're awfully good.

And to continue being literary—will you please tell me what's a good
Pasternak to get for some idea of the poems? I have a little French one
here, and the English *Safe Conduct* with some poems—but I want to get
a lot more. Is any one better than the others? Now you have given me
courage to try Italian, I think. I can read quite a bit, because it is so close
to Portuguese and Spanish. Montale sounds very beautiful.

I have to go to market, I'm sorry. I have been worrying so about not-
writing, you have no idea. Lota keeps saying that, after all, most people
never write letters at all any more! Now I've started I find it is easy and
want to keep on, but the butcher, baker and candlestick maker call.
Abraços.

[P.S.] Do you read to Harriet? Does she like nursery rhymes?

To Pearl Kazin

April 23, 1961
Sunday p.m.

. . . We are leading such a strange life now. We go to Rio every
Monday or Tuesday and come back every Friday, and all week long Lota
talks on the telephone to brigadier generals, the heads of the Depts. of
Transportation, Parks & Gardens, etc. In the evenings she has conferences
with them until one or two; and in the mornings the phone starts again
at 7 a.m. But she is doing so well—I am not exaggerating; everyone is
terribly impressed with her skill. I couldn't believe it when I went to one
of these meetings, with eight or nine engineers, etc., and L. the only

woman (I didn't count, of course)—and she kept them laughing, won them over, etc. I have a feeling that last week she may have avoided a *student strike*, which as you know can be serious here. I am afraid that either she will soon find herself *in* politics, in the family tradition, or else she will get too fed up with the fearful jealousies, maneuverings, etc., and we'll find ourselves on the plane to Lisbon. However, so far very good, I'd say, and it is wonderful to have her doing something at last, using her brains and helping poor dirty dying Rio at the same time.

We were just getting it all more organized when (because of domestic dramas here—none of ours—the cook, the silly girl, was "carrying on" with another man—although crazy about the one she had)—we found ourselves completely servantless. We've made do with a tiny pretty little girl, aged *eleven*, for two weeks now (Manuelzinho's daughter, if you remember *him*—that family certainly is important in my life. I have just written my fourth poem about them). Mary Morse drives up twice a day to feed the cats and report to us in Rio, etc. It is awfully lonely for her, of course, but she has Monica so I don't think it has even occurred to her, she's so busy (and *well*—it's amazing how her health has improved with all the diaper washing, orange squeezing, etc.). Monica—well, I never saw a baby I really wanted to keep for myself before. Mary couldn't have been luckier. She is healthy, cunning, very bright, and *happy*. I've never seen such joy about nothing at all—or maybe she knows in her infant way that her life has taken an amazing turn, who knows? Her ears stick out like jug handles; she looks as if she had just come up for air, with her hair all in little points, the latest style, dark reddish-brown. She is a pixie or a nixie—*that-type-baby*—and even our most baby-hating men friends are enchanted with her. Mary just looks overcome and tries not to pay any attention to her in public. Well, you'll probably see her in N.Y.—Mary is probably going up to visit the end of June and refuses to stir without Monica, although we'd gladly keep her for her—no servants, jobs, and all. So you see what a really nice little baby she is—about six months old now, we think—can turn over, in fact she spends her time revolving happily, or sucking a toe—but not quite sitting up yet. (I really don't know how you feel on the subject of babies, but I am particularly fond of them up until about three—or until self-consciousness sets in.) . . .

I must get busy cooking a chicken. Do write me, Pearl. How do you like the political happenings? At least Kennedy's speeches—even in Portuguese, on the front page of the *Correio da Manhã*, are a great relief—they really make sense . . . Any literary news will be appreciated. I bought a *Harper's Bazaar* in Rio—first time in two years—to look at the styles, to start getting some clothes made, and my how it has gone downhill. Lota sends her love—so would Mary if she were on hand & so would Monica, who loves all the world and wants to eat it, or at least try eating it.

To Dr. Anny Baumann

Rio de Janeiro
May 2, 1961

Lota was put in charge of an enormous new "fill" along one of the Rio bays. Her title is "Chief Coordinatress"—really! There are several of the best architects working on it, and Burle-Marx, who is the best tropical gardener there is, I think; and because Rio is all one big family, intellectually at least, these people are all old friends. Also, unfortunately, there are Depts. of Parks & Gardens and Depts. of Transportation, and brigadier-generals, and many, many entrenched bureaucrats to deal with, and jealousies, politics, and the Position of Woman here! I think Lota is doing brilliantly. I am lost in admiration whenever I see her in action, or listen in on her telephone conversations with these difficult people. She is working at it very hard; we spend Monday to Friday here in Rio every week now, and she never seems to get to bed, and the number of "little coffees" drunk is staggering.

It was very clever of Carlos to make use of Lota's talents at last, I think—but she is refusing to take any pay (a good idea, maybe, to forestall some criticism). Anyway, what was going to be a mile or so of highways and uninteresting, shadeless, useless park is now going to have shade, playgrounds, two restaurants, outdoor cafés, dance floors, etc.—if all goes well. Lota is full of good, practical ideas.

Of course this is much more important than our travels, for the time being, so we have postponed them. Poor Lota has never had so many other worries, too—but I am sure in spite of them all she is much happier now that she is working at last. There will be a Sunday Supplement about the project soon, and if the pictures are any good I'll send you a copy.

My own work hasn't amounted to anything for months and months now, but I think I am beginning again at last—I hope so. This going back and forth has been upsetting, but we are getting it better organized gradually. Also we've had awful servant problems, but we *think* they are more or less resolved now . . .

Carlos is struggling bravely with the almost hopeless problems of the city of Rio, and of course getting criticized immediately by his ungrateful fellow men. He has some very good people working for him (some without pay, like Lota) and the hours they work and the direct measures they take are astounding the easygoing Rio de Janeirans. I think that's enough about Brazilian affairs. I can't believe I am so mixed up in them myself, and know so much about them, and of course the only thing to do is to write some short stories, I see that . . .

I wonder where you are going for your vacation this year. And I wish sometime it would lead you here.

To Aunt Grace

Rio de Janeiro
July 26, 1961

We are still in Rio—three weeks at this stretch—and yesterday a friend brought down some accumulated mail from Petrópolis . . . I am so terribly sorry to hear about that operation and I hope to goodness it is all over and everything is all right—do let me hear right away . . . What a nuisance the female (or male, as far as that goes!) body is. From what you say it doesn't sound too bad, but I hope you aren't just being brave! Please tell me all the reports—also how you are otherwise . . .

I think I told you, probably, that I got a grant for "foreign travel"— to be used this year and/or next—but because of Lota's job we decided to stay put this year, and I'm just hoarding it for the time being. Well, now I've taken on a job, too—and almost wish I hadn't, it's such a headache. *Life* magazine asked me to write the text of a small book on Brazil. They have a series of them—each a different country. Probably no one reads the text, anyway, just looks at the photographs, which are wonderful, usually—colored ones, and black & white. But that kind of writing is hard for me to do and I have to cover the whole country—history, economics, geography, arts, sports—*everything*, even if superficially. However, they will pay well, and also pay for three weeks in N.Y. to work on it with them—and the plane fare, of course—so I thought I might as well tackle it. I don't like the magazine and don't like *them* much—these high-pressure-salesmen types—but I am doing it for the money—and I do know a lot about Brazil by now, of course, willy-nilly. So I MAY get to N.Y. in October—and I MIGHT get to Nova Scotia, too . . .

Suzanne [the maid] is clever all right. This apartment *is* a mess—no doubt about it. When she left she thanked me politely for a book I'd given her and then said, "Goodbye, goodbye to you and your *funny* apartment"—looking very malicious.

To Pearl Kazin

Rio de Janeiro
Sunday, August 13, 1961

. . . Along with the rest of the mail was the contract with *Life* from my agent. Oh—oh—oh I don't know what to think or say—or do, except that I guess I've already done it—except that I'm having a *hideous* time writing the thing. But once I made the bargain I suppose the thing to do is just write as fast as possible and try not to think about it. No use the Flaubert stuff (although I CAN'T seem to compose any other way) since they will just put it through their own meat grinder, lawfully, and it will come out sounding like them no matter what I say. My agents did their best, but all that amounts to is that I at least have the right to *fight* with them. I only hope it's going to be worth the $9,000 I'll get out of it— doesn't look as if it were, to me, so far. And the worst is really that, like publishers, they keep paying lip service to "distinguished writing," "your own opinions," "your fine reputation," and blah blah blah—*lying* like RUGS . . . It is really a weird process—and now I KNOW, as others have before me. I'll be coming in October sometime—they'll pay $200 a week expenses for three weeks & first-class flight up. Lota says she won't come, but I do hope she'll change her mind. I'll need moral support all right!

I feel dreadful about the Hemingway [suicide]—he must really have been half out of his head for some time, don't you think?

I must tell you, the *Life* editor wrote me that "you'd be surprised how much help an *outline* is," also, "although it may seem like a burden" . . . (on and on) a *bibliography* of the books I'm using "would be a good idea." —Teach your grandmother to suck eggs, please. They are IN- CREDIBLE, that's all. It is really more like manufacturing synthetic whipped cream out of the by-products of a plastic factory than anything remotely connected with writing—even journalistic writing. I put on one display of temperament & the editor here came running around all flut- tering and consoling. The awful thing is I feel so *sorry* for him, with his "Great! Great!"s and "Thanks a million," etc. They also telexed from N.Y. to ask if I'd ever been a Communist! (Probably some infant editor saw a poem in *Partisan Review* and the name terrified them.) On the whole, they behave exactly the way the U.S. Embassy does here.

I am feeling horribly bitter and cynical for a beautiful Sunday morning—please excuse me.

I hope this new Ambassador Gordon is really good. Things look very grim here now—everyone talks of nothing but Communism and whether [President] Quadros is doing the right thing or not. I *think* he just wants more trade and money—but at the same time everyone feels Brazil is no country to let any more Communists into than can be helped—no FBI, no good police—no way of combating them at all. And the *favela* situ- ation's getting worse, apparently (and I sit and write drivel). However, I'm learning a lot about Brazil all right, and feel a whole lot of stories developing in spite of me.

Lota is working so hard and everything is going very well now. *Time* is supposed to have a piece about it next week—mostly about Burle-Marx and the garden part, of course, so far. A. Schlesinger, Jr., wrote me a note [from Washington]—thanks to Cal—asking for "cultural ideas." I was delighted—have written a rather violent letter on the subject back, and only hope now that the new Cultural Attaché will be faintly cultured and that perhaps I can really do a little. We couldn't be doing much worse here as things are now—and somehow managing to alienate all the people who like the U.S. *best*, too.

With these admonitory thoughts, I'll close.

To Aunt Grace

We came up for the weekend last night, Friday, and I found your letter of the 13th. I guess I didn't make it clear enough in my letter that I'm going to come to see you no matter where you are—either Montreal or Nova Scotia. Montreal is easier, I suppose—it's only about 1½ hours by plane from New York. Anyway I'll have to work hard in New York with that damned *Life* magazine for about three weeks, probably, and then as soon as I can get away I'll fly up to spend a few days with you wherever you may be.

Lota said she wouldn't come to the U.S. with me—the exchange is dreadful for her now—but I am hoping very much she'll change her mind. I am going to need her moral support while "revising" my little book with *Life*. Also Loren MacIver, an old friend of mine, has offered me her & her husband's studio apartment on Perry Street in Greenwich Village to stay in (they are in Europe). That will mean a big saving, and I get my trip paid for by *Life*, anyway, so I hope Lota will come with me. She'll go to visit some friends of hers near New York when I go to Canada, probably . . .

Yesterday there was a big political upheaval here. President Quadros *resigned*. God knows what is going to happen next—no doubt the Army will get in on it somehow. He was a wonderful economist, this President, but slightly crazy, I'm sure—and it wouldn't matter so much, but the Vice President is a real old crook from the dictator gang. Lota is terribly upset—everyone is—we just hover over the radio news. Now I must read the newspapers she's brought back. We might even leave Brazil—who knows? I haven't much more to say—the country is "remaining calm" but there may be a civil war. Don't ask me why—it's all too confused. However, things are never very bloody here, you know. There is no danger at all. I just feel dreadfully sorry for all my Brazilian friends and for the country.

Rio, September 4. I thought this had been mailed to you the other day, but apparently it got left behind. This is just to say that in spite of what you may be seeing in the papers, everything is pretty quiet in Rio. Just in one spot in town there is trouble, and we avoid that. The Vice President is coming back today, probably. We hate him, and dread what he'll do, but apparently civil war has been avoided at least.

We are fine and everything goes on as usual for me. Lota goes to the Governor's Palace to be with her pal, Carlos Lacerda, a lot, so we keep well-informed. I'll try to get to New York about October 15, I think.

To Loren MacIver and Lloyd Frankenberg

61 Perry Street
New York City
November 25, 1961

Everything fine here except that we'd like to have a letter from you in that mailbox. Plenty of heat—everything working. Lota did laundry in the machines nearby, came home with a big bag full, which we'll probably never get around to ironing. We're leaving December 11, so far.

My job at *Life* is a nightmare. I was prepared for it to be, but not quite this bad, really! They're incredible people!

We saw Marianne Moore again yesterday. She seems very frail to me. Speaking of *Mrs.* T. S. Eliot, her first comment was that "She is *unsordid*, Elizabeth." I haven't seen a galley proof yet, or much of anything except the so-called Life Building and its tiresome people.

We are in love with that pale-blue saucepan, rather thick, white inside. Where did you get it? I gave one drink of your gin to Nathalie Rahv & used one tablespoon of "Blackberry Cordial" in a fruit compote—delicious. Our only INROADS, I think. Much mystified by a bottle labeled "Cherry Blossoms." I'll be through the job in ten days, thank heavens. Are you both at work? Do please write. Wouldn't you like a good coffee mill? We bought a wonderful one & it looks so nice on your staircase we want to leave you one too.

December 5

I'm ashamed this hasn't got mailed yet and probably you won't be able to read the November 25 [handwritten] note anyway . . . It has been just too hectic. I don't think I could ever live in New York again—or at least not "live" and "work" at the same time. Yesterday I went to Boston and back, this weekend down to Jane Dewey's and back. We now plan to leave December 12. I haven't even seen the Guggenheim Museum yet. We may have to stay a week longer because it seems to me that odious *Life* book is still quite *un*-written. We had a nice tea party with the Meyer Schapiros. Everything going well at your house, only who is it that makes coffee at 5 a.m.? I wonder. The smell rises through the bedroom floor and we say, "Well, we might as well get up and make our own now." Someone named "Jo" has been very kind and taken in packages twice for us. I'll speak to the agent before I leave and have him send me the bills. You will find a very few souvenirs in the way of soap, light bulbs, a pot holder or two, etc., and we'll try to leave everything in order and clean, although it will naturally get dirty again, I'm afraid. We are so grateful. You have no idea how much nicer it has been— well, *it* has been *awful*, but staying *here* has been wonderful is what I mean.

To Aunt Grace

New York
December 12, 1961

. . . I was supposed to work for three weeks—well, it's four now and I am still working like mad and don't see much hope for ending it ever. I have never worked so hard in my life and never been so tired—and the book about Brazil is still going to be awful! It has been an interesting experience—but never again—not for *Time, Life,* etc. They are incredible people and what they know about Brazil would fit on the head of a pin —and yet the gall, the arrogance, the general condescension! However —I've saved some of the book, and it does tell the truth, more or less— and some of the pictures are pretty—but not nearly enough. You'll be getting a copy—I'm not sure when—March, maybe.

I have scarcely seen or done anything. I've seen friends in the evenings a few times—stayed up late and got up at six to start work (they give me chapters to bring home every night). Lota is with me . . .

Last Monday I went to Worcester—my only day off and not a very gay one, as you can imagine. I flew over in the a.m. and back that night in a snowstorm . . . We went to see Aunt Florence . . . The nursing home is NOT good—it has recently changed hands and gone downhill— However, lately . . . Aunt F. has been much better—at least she seems much happier, doesn't make scenes, talks to one or two other old ladies and watches TV with them, eats, etc. But she is terribly frail and seemed sadly changed to me. Also doesn't remember much—just in spots—but I'm sure you know all about it. She was really trying hard for my sake, poor old thing, asked about "politics" in Brazil, etc. Asked my age and when I said 50 she said, "Oh no, dear, you must be wrong. Auntie Florence is only 48 so you can't be 50." Then last Sunday I went to see my old friend Jane Dewey, who is sick . . . with an ulcer (probably cancer), a broken leg, *and* a broken arm. I felt I just had to see her, she's had such a tough time the past eight months. She is recovering but her right hand is paralyzed because of a crushed nerve—awful. I don't mean to tell you all this tale of woe.

What I want to say makes me feel *awful.* It breaks my heart, honestly—but I don't think I can get to see you . . . I called up my income tax man last week and it seems that as a foreign resident if I stay only 28 days I can keep all the money I earn on this job. If I overstay (they got me one week's extra because the job wasn't done), I have to pay a whopping tax on it—$1,500—which would make the whole six months' job scarcely worth having done. I'm afraid it is really a big enough hunk of money to mean a lot in my way of life next year—and apparently I have to leave the U.S. before next week. I'm dreadfully sorry—I wanted to see you so much. We changed our tickets once for the stayover, and now I'm supposed to leave the night of the 14th.

One nurse Aunt Florence does like calls her "honey" and Aunt F. asked her to call her "Florence"—always on the snobbish side! I thought it was nice she likes *someone*, at least. The nurse seemed the one civilized person around, I thought.

To Harold Leeds and Wheaton Galentine

Architect Harold Leeds and filmmaker Wheaton Galentine, who resided at 64 Perry Street in Greenwich Village, across from the MacIver-Frankenberg house, met EB through Louise Crane and became fast friends.

Rio de Janeiro
December 27, 1961

We are in full summer—in Rio, actually. It's very hot, even at 7:30 a.m., and the same familiar elderly people are out walking their familiar dogs on the beach. It is very beautiful but very sad, and poor old Rio looks shabbier and dirtier than ever after New York. We're going up to Petrópolis for the New Year's weekend but can't start until after four, when it starts to cool off again. However, our apartment here is wonderful—eleventh floor and gets all the breezes.

Lota is hard at work on her park—meeting after meeting, and bitter telephone fights about the dimensions of the trees, etc. And I, I'm sorry to say, am still at work for *Life*. We send each other increasingly nasty telexes every day or so. I thought everything was settled, but no indeed —they keep putting their favorite clichés right back in again and then send me the proofs for my approval.

We have described your house on Perry Street [almost directly opposite Loren's] in detail to all our best friends here. Since many of them have never seen a New York house of the 19th century, or anything resembling one, it is hard to know what impression they're getting. But we enjoy describing it, anyway. It really is one of the nicest town houses I've ever seen. Because of it, we have decided we simply have to redo this apartment, at last, starting the first of the year. We can't stand its state any longer. While we were away the water tank over our heads overflowed. Some walls are now blistered and streaked, on top of the coats of hideous dark blue or yellow shiny paint the last tenants gave them. We wish Harold was here to improve our plans for wall-shifting, kitchen-enlarging, etc., and changing the solid wall on the terrace for a terrifying fence, so you can lie in bed and see the sea—even if you're afraid to step out on the terrace any more.

You were both so kind and hospitable and we thank you very much. We loved seeing the movies; they are really superb. We hope you are feeling well, Harold. Don't overdo, as I'm sure Dr. Baumann keeps telling you all the time. It was wonderful seeing her looking so blue-eyed and balanced. I hope you received and now can destroy my scrawls from the airport. There wasn't any place to write properly, and I can't write very well at best. Best possible wishes for the new year and thank you again for all your kindness.

[P.S.] Have you used the *dendé* oil yet? Just a drop, with shrimp or fish. If you want more Brazilian coffee, ask for *straight Santos*, ground extra fine.

To Robert Lowell

Rio de Janeiro
April 4, 1962

Speaking of piles (wouldn't that be a good "opening phrase" to use for a Creative Writing course?), I must tell you a nice Brazil–American misunderstanding over that word when you get here. There are lots of lovely possibilities like that. Don't use the word *cocoa* the way we say it in English, it means *merde*. And the word "affair" in English still applies to "business." A Brazilian friend of ours, a man, remarked in Calder's presence, "During the war I was having an affair with an American Navy officer, and he—" and Calder began to burble and boil over the way he does, and had to be distracted immediately.

I am so glad Dr. Baumann is in attendance and I do hope you are better and gaining weight. Please don't go into a 19th-century decline! Dr. B. always made me feel that everything was possible if I only did my duty, and that my duty was plain and simple, too. Of course it isn't, but it's a good way to feel sometimes. I wrote Elizabeth a very boring letter about *clothes* (and incidentally got going on the awfulness of the *Brazil* book). Keith Botsford is coming to see me this afternoon and I may have more to tell then. As you say, he sounds "bright & shiny" on the telephone. Our preparations seem to be overlapping somewhat.

The *Brazil* book is awful; some sentences just don't make sense at all. And at least the pictures could have been good. Maybe, if you can read it at all, you will find a trace here & there of what I originally meant to say. However, as Lota keeps pointing out—most of the million "readers" won't read it; Brazil is very glad of any well-meant publicity at this point (the Governor has ordered dozens of copies to give away); and my name will mean nothing to most of the "readers" anyway. Headlines here every day about [Ambassador] Cabot's introduction, "spiritual values," and so on. I happen to have his original introduction with me; he didn't write a word of the one that appears . . .

Your dream is marvelous— And your evening with Roethke and his wife & Mary and Jim sounds hideous—but I wish I'd been there all the same. Poor Roethke! . . . Yes, *Time* is incredibly arrogant—but actually not as bad as I expected from them after my five weeks on the inside.

They love those false, let's-face-it, summing-up cracks. They have sneaked some into *Brazil*, too. "But to say they are the best is not to say much," etc. And they seem to quote the secondary of everybody—or poorer than that. So I'm "cool" and "eely"—that last word of course was unintelligible to my Brazilian friends and I found myself translating it for them with embarrassment all that week. But everyone is interested to learn that you are actually coming here. It's too bad all the poets mentioned don't have books out right now because I suppose they might sell a few hundred more.

Next morning

Keith Botsford arrived, we one-upmanshipped rapidly for an hour or so, and he never removed a large black pipe from his fairly handsome face. It seems he has three small children and is about to have a 4th baby. He also said he'd just celebrated his 13th wedding anniversary. He has a house, swimming pool, and an imported nurse, here in the city—and thinks it would be nice to have Harriet as a caller—although all the children are younger than she is—but they speak English, at least. He had plans for getting you a vacant apartment—but I think I convinced him the hotel-apartment would be much better for a month's stay. It's impossible to cope with foreign servants, etc., and no vacation at all for Elizabeth. We agreed pretty well about everything else. WHO pays for the Congress for Cultural Freedom, anyway? I really know nothing about it, except *Encounter* & Nicolas Nabokov. He wants more informal social life than lectures (which are usually badly attended here, anyway—but I think that's also usually due to poor advertising). My idea was to show you some of the country. Maybe I'll go to Bahia with you—I haven't been there yet.

To return to *Time*—"cubistic Browning"! "more vivid than sensitive"! a wonderful opposition. I think [Christopher] Logue is better than Larkin, from what I've seen. Well, as [Allen] Ginsberg put it so brilliantly: "Are you going to let your emotional life be run by *Time* magazine?"— it seems to me I have been, lately.

To return to your visit, the apartment is being torn down over my head almost. We have started remodeling and the place is full of piles of sand and bricks and bags of cement. It looks as though we were crazily building an air-raid shelter on the 11th floor. If I sound rather disjointed that's why. I have to keep getting out of the way of two black and one white bricklayer every other minute. If E. would like to lecture here, I think in spite of what I said about lectures being badly attended that the U.S. novel is a subject of some interest, and I'll do all the advertising I can—the personal approach works best, anyway.

I feel sorry for Mackie Jarrell—she ought to marry again and I gather she hasn't. It was a great loss to them both, I think, that they couldn't stay together . . . I have three poems about done—and a story called "Uncle Artie" [later entitled "Memories of Uncle Neddy"] . . .

Back to letter II. "Caixa" is pronounced *ky*-ish-a. *X*'s are like *sh*—and it's *box*, the French *caisse*. I like Texaco pronounced "Teshaco." (Also, here Buick rhymes with quick.) . . . I think a few hours in Brasília are plenty. They have messed up what I said about it pretty much in that book, but the general idea is still there. The point about its attracting the wrong sort was that no one wants to get into politics any more except for graft pure & simple, since it means having to live there some of the time, at least, and only the crudest political types can stand it for the sake of graft even. A representative gets, say, about $4,000 a year and will spend $25,000 on his election campaign—so you see. However, none of that could be put in, although I originally implied it fairly clearly. (All the gift copies I have to hand out here I am correcting, in green ink—a futile job, but I can't stop doing it.)

. . . I must re-read Henry Adams—I haven't read him for years and never really liked him very much, although I learned an enormous amount from him, as we all have. What I've been reading lately is several of those little paperbacks, the American Experience series. I started on them because one of my New England ancestors was imprisoned on that Jersey prison ship anchored in N.Y. Harbor during the Revolution. There's one little book about that—then went on to the others—some good, some indifferent. Lucy Larcom's *A New England Girlhood* I found fascinating, and so would you, I think. She was one of the Lowell factory literary girls (but probably you know all this already?) who spent her childhood in Beverly, etc.—some of that part is very good. Her moralizing is tedious, and it is depressing to think she was a well-known "poetess" in her day and I'm probably just about on a par with her—but the details, the influence of hymns, etc., are nice. Beverly in 1830 was very much like Great Village in 1920, I think. The Brook Farm volume has opened my eyes to the fact that you are really very much in line with the Concord people. I hadn't realized quite how purely the stream has run until I read it. Although I studied them at college, I'd forgotten—the conversions to Catholicism, then to Anglicanism; the skating parties. And now your piece in *Partisan Review*—the Cold War number—makes it seem even clearer. It is exactly what a poet should say, of course, and makes some of the rest sound like mental exercises—or a whole groaning orchestra with you as the clarinet soloist.

My aunt who still lives there has sent me an amateurish Great Village historical publication—but fascinating, and of great help to me with "Uncle Artie." The house she lives in, I find, is insulated with birch bark; the one I used to live in was an old wayside inn of "ill repute" that my grandfather had moved to the village—about 200 years old. The saddest thing is the Literary Society (my mother and aunts belonged) in the early 1900's: "The Society met fortnightly to read & discuss great literature. A winter each was spent on Keats, Ruskin, Mrs. Browning, Milton, Shakespeare, Dante, and two winters on Browning and Tennyson." I imagine no one in that village has opened a Milton or a Browning for years now, and TV aerials rise from the shingles. The dying out of local cultures seems to me one of the most tragic things in this century—and it's true everywhere, I suppose—in Brazil, at any rate. Small towns far inland on the rivers were real centers; they had teachers of music and dancing and languages—they made beautiful furniture and built beautiful churches. And now they're all dead as doornails, and broken-down trucks arrive bringing powdered milk and Japanese jewelry and *Time* magazine.

Our apartment is at the northern end of Copacabana Beach. We're only four blocks from where you'll be staying and we can meet on the beach on warm days for swims. I go in about 7:30 or 8 these days and it is lovely—blue, pure, cool. I only hope this June isn't too wintry; but one can usually go swimming most of the year. Would you like to see Rio by helicopter?—because Lota can arrange that for you. Then you wouldn't have to bother about the other views involving cable cars & cog railways & see it all at one swoop . . .

[Lowell had sent EB in typescript his new book of poems, *For the Union Dead*.] I don't know why I bother to write "Uncle Artie," really. I should just send you my first notes and you can turn him into a wonderful poem. He is even more your style than the "Village" story was. "The Scream" [a poem derived from EB's story, "In the Village"] really works well, doesn't it? The story is far enough behind me so I can see it as a poem now. In the first few stanzas I saw only my story—then the poem took over—and the last stanza is wonderful. It builds up beautifully, and everything of importance is there. But I was very surprised. "Water" I like very much—stanzas 4 & 5, the color ones, are marvelous—"iris, rotting," etc. Yes, I like "grain after grain" better, too. I have two minor questions but, as usual, they have to do with my George Washington handicap—I can't tell a lie even for art, apparently; it takes an awful effort or a sudden jolt to make me alter facts. Shouldn't it be a *lobster* town, and further on where the *bait, fish for bait* were trapped—(this is trivial, I know, and like Marianne, sometimes I think I'm telling the truth when I'm not). The houses struck *me* as looking like clam shells, because of the clapboarding—but I'll use that some other way. Oyster shells is right because of the way they stick in beds on the rocks, exactly—if not for their color. I can't read the word after "old" written in in pencil. I remember reciting that parody on Edna St. Vincent Millay to you: "I want to be drowned in the deep sea water, / I want my body to bump the pier. / Neptune is calling his wayward daughter: / 'Edna, come over here!' " I asked Dwight Macdonald why he hadn't put it in his parody book and I think he said it was "dated." "The sea drenched the rock" is so perfectly simple but so good.

Well, "David & Bathsheba" has always been one of my favorites the way it was, but I like this version, too. (I don't have *Lord Weary's Castle* here in Rio so I can't actually compare them.) I remember the leaves "thicken to a ball" but I don't seem to remember the wonderful lions *sucking their faucets* . . . and "Everything's aground." I like *that*, all right. The upside-down leaves, too. (You will notice a sad David & Bathsheba tale in my *Brazil* book—if you manage to get that far!) It is a very moving poem and very autumnal.

But "The Old Flame" reduces me to tears. I rather liked those imaginary bears—but maybe you're right to leave them out. The red ear of corn is fine—like the decorator's orange floats in the skunk poem. Is it *really* an antique shop? "simmering like wasps / in our tent of books"— I like that, too. And the ending is beautiful—particularly the way you have it altered. Alas, it is too real to me for me to judge it as a poem, I think. If I read it in *Encounter* under someone else's name, I wonder what I'd think?

"Jonathan Edwards" came just at the right moment . . . (All this nostalgia and homesickness and burrowing in the past running alongside trying to write articles about the Brazilian political situation—I can't— translating some Portuguese poems, etc. Are other writers as confused & "contradictory"? Or do they stick to one thing at a time?) "Booth" is a fine word there, reminding me of "Bartholomew's Fair." The italicized stanzas are lovely. Pompey, and the eleven children—the stanza with the stilts and the line from Herbert is wonderful. All the quoted stanzas at the end, as well.

(In Lucy Larcom—there were Indians who camped every year on the river that ran the Lowell mills—very degraded Indians, women wearing top hats, etc. They arrived in birch-bark canoes—this in 1840–50— but maybe you've read it?)

I feel I *must* write a lot of poems immediately—that is my test for "real poetry." Only they would come out, if at all, sounding like you. But (perhaps I've said this before) if after I read a poem, the world looks like that poem for 24 hours or so, I'm sure it's a good one—and the same goes for paintings. I studied a huge book on Bosch I have for several days—and the world looked like Bosches for a month afterwards—not that it really doesn't anyway, these days. Then recently here I saw a Jules Bissier show (do you know his paintings?—slight, maybe, but beautiful) and the world looked all like Bissiers for a long time, here, there, and everywhere. *Your* scenery comes and goes, half-real and half-language, all the time. The eye poem in *Partisan Review* gets better and better—I wipe my reading glasses, always covered with brick dust these last days here. I'll try to send you some things before long.

To Marianne Moore

Rio de Janeiro
June 7, 1962
. . . I think the Lowell family must be on their way, but I am not sure exactly when they will arrive. It has been awfully cold, the coldest

"winter" in years, and I told the poor dears to bring lots of bathing suits. However, it will probably warm up again; it usually does and in Rio, at least, I usually swim most of the year. We are painting the white roses red for them; at least my *estudio* was whitewashed and blue-washed, and all the books cleaned, and the Rio apartment is being re-painted, too. I have also just bought enough hot water bottles to put one in *each bed;* and Albertinho (I hope) is cutting a magnificent pile of wood for us, for the stove and the fireplace. But this is not the time of year to come here, really—nothing spectacular is blooming—just mimosa.

In spite of all Brazil's troubles the atmosphere has been very cheerful the last two days, because the Brazilian *futebol* (soccer) team is doing so well and will have a chance at the World's Championship again. Day before yesterday they beat Spain, a very close game. All the maids in this apartment house were listening to the radios with their heads hanging over the inside patio—ours was weeping for joy. This morning she asked me about the new pipes being laid along the beach, and I told her it was the new water system and *due to a loan from the U.S.* (trying to spread a little goodwill whenever I can!). She replied, "Well, I'm very sorry. I know the Senhora is American—but Amarildo is still better!"—Amarildo being the player who scored both goals and thus beat Spain. I think that *futebol* is something you'd like here—like baseball in the U.S.A. The players are incredibly fast and graceful.

Oh dear, we wish you were coming too. Lota would love to show you her park. Things are really appearing quite fast now, and they have a temporary shack-office to work in—not very shack-like; it has two bathrooms, and showers—in a huge slat-house for the hundreds of trees they're collecting. The world's second-biggest dredge is here, from the Panama Canal—named *Ester*—making artificial beaches. It has been very popular. When the beach was the size of two parked cars, there were swimmers and two beach umbrellas on it. Lota sends her love and we both hope you are keeping well and not overdoing. We . . . have re-polished your *Rio* frame—for the Lowells.

To Elizabeth Hardwick Lowell

Elizabeth Hardwick (Mrs. Robert Lowell) is well known as a literary critic (Bartleby in Manhattan *and* A View of My Own), *novelist* (The Simple Truth), *and editor* (Selected Letters of William James). *She is advisory editor of* The New York Review of Books.

Petrópolis
September 13, 1962

When you receive this you will already have talked with Nicolas [Nabokov] and will know of the events here and in Buenos Aires. Shocking as they are, I don't believe they will come as much of a surprise to you —since they really didn't to us, who know Cal so much less well. However, from all I have heard so far today, everything is now under control, and the Clínica Bethlehem (!), where Cal is, is supposed to be excellent.

I thought you might like to hear what I know about the affair—as briefly as I can put it—since Nicolas has heard it all through Keith Botsford, with later emendations from Lota & me—and none of us puts any confidence in K.B. of course, word or deed.

You left Saturday the 1st. Nicolas and Cal spent the next day out at Brocoió, that island, with Carlos, and Cal seemed very pleased with this outing. Monday he was here all the p.m. He seemed very overwrought and I tried to persuade him to give up the rest of his trip and go back to N.Y., but I made no impression on him. He, Nicolas, and Lota had dinner together and came back here afterwards and Cal struck us all as very nervous, etc. The next day, the 4th, he and Keith went to Buenos Aires. We saw Nicolas again that evening and he said he thought Cal wasn't "well at all"—but of course he hasn't seen a great deal of him before this and hasn't really as much to compare him with as we have. Cal and K.B. were supposedly returning on Sunday the 9th.

On Monday the 10th, I just *happened* to call Anne Botsford, about a money-changer. After some casual conversation I asked if she'd heard anything from the travelers and she said casually, "Oh—Keith came back Saturday night (the 8th). He's been having an awful time with Cal and he wants to talk to you." When I finally got Keith I asked him what the HELL he thought he was doing; didn't he know Cal's history? (he did); WHY hadn't he called me before; WHAT was he doing in Rio, anyway, and WHY had he left Cal alone and sick in B.A.? (Anne actually invited us to a party for the next night, and apparently K. was planning to go back to B.A. at his own sweet will. No one yet knows why he came back to Rio. He said "to consult" Nicolas and me—but he didn't; "to get money," and it seems Hunt had already wired money to B.A.; "to work"!—and "to get over a hangover"—it seems he took to drink, too. Of course none of this makes any sense.) K. had actually wired Nicolas, who was in Bahia, from B.A., saying that he needed help and would Nicolas (who was very sick again in Bahia) please come to B.A.—which he couldn't do.

K. turned meek at once when I started yelling at him, and got over here fast. Lota and I were terribly afraid that something might happen to Cal in B.A. He'd been talking politics, etc. Strangers, or the police, would naturally just think he was drunk; he doesn't speak Spanish—and he might get beaten up or thrown in jail, etc.—and you know the confused state of affairs in B.A. at present. We *ordered* K. to get busy immediately and get Niles Bond (the first minister, you may remember—a more experienced type than Gordon) to get in touch with the U.S. Embassy in Argentina, so in case anything did happen while Cal was on his own there (*four days*), they would take care of him. K. said he had asked his "friends" there to "see as much of Cal as possible"! The only provision he had made for Cal's safety.

K. then went to the Embassy. Bond was very nice and acted immediately. Then K. got the N.Y. telephone book there and found Cal's doctor's number (just by chance we did remember the name), and later that evening he called her up to get the name of Cal's medicines, dosages, etc.—Cal had thrown his pills away. K. kept reporting all evening—seemed quite surprised the doctor said the same thing we had, that Cal should be got back to N.Y. if possible, and into a hospital as soon as possible. Meanwhile I called the psychiatrist we know and have confidence in here (the Melanie Klein man) and he gave me the name and address of the psychiatrist he thinks the best in B.A. Then he (the Dr. here) called or wired B.A. so that if and when K. had to get hold of the Dr. there, that Dr. would know what it was all about. The man's name is Dr. Arnaldo Rosscofzky—although I probably have the spelling all wrong. He has worked in N.Y., speaks English, etc. At this point I don't know whether that is the doctor K. did get or not, but I imagine it was.

K. packed up the things Cal left in the hotel here and took them to his house. Anne has now sent them back to Nicolas.

K. was all for cabling you on board the ship. I pointed out that under the circumstances that would be simple sadism, and he said meekly that he would follow my advice. I hope he did. Nicolas and I now think it would be better to cable you shortly before you arrive home. I am seeing him tonight and maybe there will be more news from K. by then. We don't know how long Cal will have to stay in the clinic, how soon he can get to N.Y., etc. If this was going to happen, in a way it may be better it was out of the country, don't you think? Harriet can think Cal is still away lecturing and be spared a lot this time.

Nicolas is very depressed; we all are, naturally. K. kept asking us if we were "offended" with him!—when of course there is nothing left to be felt, as far as he's concerned. I felt I should give you this dry report of what went on, from this point of view, at least. Please remember that I did try to get him to go back. Looking at the sort of calendar I keep, I realize that I had felt this coming on for at least three weeks—but I didn't know how fast these things develop—or if it might be diverted . . .

September 14, 1962

[P.S.] Last night Mlle. Dubuis and I looked at the things Cal had left here and I took out three books of mine, threw away some used carbon paper, etc., & told her to throw out some dirty socks! Nicolas is taking all the rest with him. He hasn't heard any more from B.A. but hopes to before he leaves tonight. K. had told me Cal had taken nothing with him to B.A. but his *Phaedra*—but he must have been wrong. I know he got the anthology from me to take, and it wasn't with the things last night. When you have time, Lota and I hope you will let us know what goes on, how you all are, etc. We send our sympathy and all possible best wishes.

To Arthur Gold and Robert Fizdale

Rio de Janeiro
October 19, 1962

. . . The Schubert is lovely—I'd like to know if you did it on one piano or two, and are you going to do more Schubert? They both are absolutely perfect recordings—never a dull note. Monica dances to Stravinsky already . . .

We had quite a summer/winter here and are just recovering from it all—although Lota kept working regularly every day at her park. It is growing, too—full of slight but controversial hills, huge palm trees that we hope will all *catch*—and at the moment, hundreds of political billboards from the late elections, but they're supposed to be coming down. There is to be what they call a *tremzinho* [a toy train] to pull 60 little children through the park—also the original Brazilian locomotive, the *Baronesa*, absolutely adorable, with a hopper-shaped smokestack and lots of brass, etc.—which will be embedded firmly in cement, for children to climb on. Lota has lots of bright ideas and is a terrible *driver*—I mean in the sense of making her staff work hard, "realize their potentials," etc. In fact, a few weeks ago she was given a medal—two medals, one with grosgrain ribbon, for dress, and one in stickpin form, miniature, for every day.

[Nicolas] Nabokov was here—an ailing but very Russian bear, and full of bear hugs and bear kisses. The Lowells came for one month but stayed on two. As you probably know—other New Yorkers already seem to—he had another breakdown, sad to say—but it took place finally in Buenos Aires, and now he's back in the hospital in New York. If only it could be the last one. I think he had a pretty good time, though, until this started coming on. But there were so many inexplicable (to visitors) political crises. In fact I find Brazil itself rather big and exhausting . . . much, much more complicated than that *Life*-slicked book might lead you to believe. One very nice thing about having guests, however—one does get a lot of house cleaning and remodeling done. We look with satisfaction at our new corduroy upholstery, our newly painted walls, etc.—and why don't we have more guests right away, like you, say? I don't know how the music festival is going to take place next year, or if it will at all—the inflation is getting worse and worse. We have just decided to cut down from three to two newspapers a day, for example. I'll let Lota take over.

[*P.S. in Lota's hand*] Music is best for "rapprochement," n'est-ce pas? Likewise Bea Lillie. Dearest boys, it is a pity you are so far away, so many funny things to tell you that only you can enjoy. Mille baisers.

Lota

To Mrs. E. B. (Katharine) White

Katharine S. White (1893–1977), fiction editor of The New Yorker *from the magazine's beginning, greatly influenced its change to serious fiction over the years. Her book* Onward and Upward in the Garden *(1979) was published posthumously, edited by her husband, the noted writer E. B. White.*

Rio de Janeiro
January 15, 1963

. . . We went away to Cabo Frio to stay in a friend's empty beach house over Christmas (with servants, dog, and garden), and while we were there a friend arrived bringing Christmas mail from Petrópolis, including Andy's book. It was just the right thing to have to read there —I read it straight through under a beach umbrella on a lonely little beach without another soul on it—a beach that is almost like a segment of the Maine coast, except that the water is warm and the cacti were all in bloom—rocks, islands, a turtle swimming around and raising his head every once in a while, even a small waterfall. Thoreau—or Andy—would have felt quite at home and pleased that there *is* a great deal of the world still pretty much untouched, even if it is not in the U.S.A. Of course I was especially interested in the postscripts. I had missed the piece about Alaska, too—that number must have got lost—and I liked it very much —a wonderful bit of recollection! Then Lota read the book straight through, too—and since then it has been read by a good many Brazilian friends and always makes a deep impression. They always seem surprised by any kind of American "dissent," even such a graceful one. One of the few things I am of two minds about, however, after living here so long and seeing how deadly it is to have a spoken language *and* a written language, widely divided—is the problem of "correct" English. I'm all for it—nevertheless I have decided that one thing that keeps English poetry—and prose—alive and real is the fact that there has never been an "Academy" and that writers in English are free to choose their words wherever they want to. (I found I was backed up in this by Jespersen's *Growth and Structure of the English Language*—but you probably knew that wonderful little book long before I did.) Thank you so much for the book—I am delighted to have it, and mostly can only groan & agree. One day when I was sick an American friend brought me a huge batch of American magazines—the ladies' magazines, etc., the kind I never see —and after wading through them I suddenly felt extremely happy to be living in an "underdeveloped" country.

I have liked a lot of things in *The New Yorker* lately—the follow-up on jet planes, Dwight Macdonald's pieces, and although it's long ago now, for you, "Silent Spring"—I am sure Rachel Carson knows what she is talking about!

My friend Lota was one of the ten "Women of the Year" in the newspapers, for her work for Rio's huge new waterfront park. Three more years to go on it, if the Governor manages to stay in. She works without pay. I copy out huge sections of [Lewis] Mumford for the Governor, and terrifying books like *The Squeeze*, etc. He'd never have time to read the whole book—it is strange to be in such a role. He—Carlos Lacerda—has his faults, but he's much the most intelligent man in the country—according to Raymond Aron, too, not just my impression!

To Loren MacIver and Lloyd Frankenberg

February 1, 1963

Thank you for all your news. Please remember me to Alice B. Toklas—whom I know only by mail, but I did admire her writing paper and handwriting! Yes, Edmund Wilson gave Dawn Powell a wonderful review that should help her a lot, I think. He is a good friend. Yes, I saw Sylvia Beach's flat in Paris in (horrors) 1935–36. It was awful about her death. Yes, I knew about E. E. Cummings's death, and wrote to Marian C. right away. And yesterday or the day before, Frost died. (I do get the news, *mes enfants*! Newspapers, the radio, even shortwave. In fact, Cal thought we were much too *engagé*—or should it be *engagées*?)

Well, my life is very dull compared to yours. But Lota's is pretty lively and pretty harrowing and I am absolutely speechless with admiration for her. I think she is surprised at herself—managing these spoiled temperamental people, mostly men who ordinarily wouldn't dream of taking an order from a woman. The architects, etc., on one side, and then the entrenched and often hopelessly lazy bureaucrats on the other . . . The only trouble is that she has made such an impression on the bosses of Rio and the State that they are all after her to work for them when this job is over. However, Brazil being the way it is, and the situation being as chaotic as it is, she may be kicked out, or walk out, at any moment.

The other day she went off to a meeting for the "appropriations"—MONEY—and said as she left, "Well, if I get what I want, we'll stay here two years. If I don't, we'll go to Europe in March." My feelings are mixed, naturally. But so far, she's got what she wants. It is so wonderful for her that I try just to forget my dreams of travel and concentrate on work while this stretch lasts. I'm supposed to have a book of poems out this spring—*they* think—I think the fall looks more likely. I did tell you the title, didn't I? from one poem. I rather like it, and hope Lloyd will: *Questions of Travel* . . .

To Robert Lowell

Rio de Janeiro
August 26, 1963
Monday morning bright & early

I'll start a letter to you and heaven knows when I'll finish it. Virgil Thomson says, "One of the strange things about poets is the way they keep warm by writing to one another all over the world." I suppose you've read *The State of Music*? Very funny & frivolous—but I agree with him completely, when I don't occasionally think he's dead wrong: "All God's chillun got modern art." On psychoanalysis: "As venal a branch of science as that cannot be counted a bulwark of civilization." On poets: "Prehistoric monsters." But after an evening with some of the so-called critics and writers here, he does cheer me up with the spectacle of what an advanced society can produce. (Advanced, decadent, or what you will, it's better than Brazilian barbarism any old day.)

I felt very badly when I read about poor Ted Roethke—must have been a heart attack? Please, take care of your health! Being a poet is one of the unhealthier jobs—no regular hours, so many temptations! Mary McCarthy's in Paris, I gather. I think your one remark about Jim West [her new husband]—"He doesn't gossip"—is almost as good as Marianne's saying that Valerie Eliot was "unsordid." Jim must just listen . . . And I suppose I must order *The Group*. I loathed that pessary prose-poem in *Partisan Review*, and the one in *The New Yorker* I found dull, I'm afraid. As I said before, I think, I just can't get that interested in college days any more. However, she does recapture them awfully well. How does one know beforehand about "commercial successes"? Naïve of me? No doubt it's a campaign from way back. Mary has worked hard and deserves a lot of money right now—but the bitterness it entails is not what she deserves it for. Those *Group* pieces bring those days back only too well—me sleeping in a single cot, with Mary with her first husband in the other one. And how they worried about their *clothes*—endless discussions of new spring outfits & pathetic interior-decoration schemes.

Remember I told you Virgil T.'s remarks about the old-fashioned 19th-century parts of Rio? The yellow Frenchified villas, etc., being "very nice, just like Nice, when one gets away from that *ghastly* coastline"? (You say Nice was like Rio a bit.) . . . I went to an evening of quartets of "modern" music—wanted to hear Berg—took Flavio, who said it was "*way out*," and two of his sophisticated lady friends, Communists all. (And only Communists, I gather, like Beethoven and Shostakovich, really.) For an encore they played part of a late Beethoven quartet—and so badly that I began to think they probably hadn't done so well with Berg, etc., either . . .

Friday night was the fatal anniversary of Vargas's suicide. President Goulart staged a monster mass meeting here right in front of the opera house. Truckloads, trainloads, ferryloads, etc., of workers were poured into the city, a division of the Army—15,000 men—and tanks were all over the place—a horrible atmosphere. It was spite, pure & simple. The Army took over the city and Carlos Lacerda withdrew to his palace and kept the Rio police away somewhere. (Can you imagine President Kennedy moving in on his political rival with the U.S. Army and staging a monster rally in front of some State House? Well, that's what happened here.) All MAD. However, it was a great flop, to the relief of most people. Goulart is a coward and Brazilians do have a small sense of "fair play" and a big sense of the ridiculous. 15,000 soldiers surrounding about 9,000 imported workers were too much, even for the pro-government newspapers. We watched intermittently on TV because rumors of revolution were rife, of course. The best moment was when a farmer handed the President up a monster *mandioca* root—about 25 lbs., a huge phallic symbol. This was so Brazilian—giant vegetables are revered. I have a "pumpkin big as the baby," you may remember, in a poem. Just another proof of primitivism.

Oh, the dean wrote an encouraging letter and Flavio has applied to Harvard for next year. He has also passed his next-to-last set of exams for the diplomatic service . . . He got so excited studying the catalogue with me, he said he wanted to live in the U.S. and wants to take *your* course, naturally . . .

Yesterday was one of the weirder events of my life. To begin with, it was the inauguration of a big show at the Museum of Modern Art about Lota's park. Rather to our surprise, it was a huge success. Never so many people at any opening—and the wooden models, aerial photographs, model playgrounds, toy trains, etc., are all very attractive. I think Lota was very pleased, although she still isn't up to all the work and excitement and goes around looking like a ghost. And yesterday at 9 a.m. was the opening of the model-airplane fields—two of them, with surrounding benches, etc.—really pretty. *Aeromodelismo* is very popular, probably in the U.S. too, although I never gave it a thought, naturally. Even Carlos Lacerda, who "opened" the thing, said: "I didn't know how to pronounce this word until yesterday." Anyway, a huge success. Lota untied the ribbon & was dragged into the limelight & given sheaves of wilted roses. I sat on the tiny platform too and there were thousands of people. There is so little for the poor public in Rio; anything's a godsend. It was funny hearing the speeches praising Dona Maria Carlota Costellat de Macedo Soares to the skies as a lover of children & a benefactor of humanity. Meanwhile Lota was yelling at, and almost kicking at, little boys who were trying to climb up on the platform, cursing photographers, etc., with her most terrifying scowls and language. I kept saying, "Try to look *pleasant*! They're all looking at you!" But really, when Carlos was an editor and used to come for leisurely argumentative Sunday lunches with us, who would ever have thought he and Lota would sit on a shaky platform opening a show of *aeromodelismo*? What next? . . .

What "literary people" did you see in England besides Empson? Why is English bohemianism more sordid than other kinds? I wonder. It's always seemed so to me that the English are so much dirtier than Latins! Brazilians who send their boys to English schools are always horrified by the bathing facilities. You should hear about that school where poor Gerard Hopkins taught! And here it is true the only dirty *workers* you see on the street in after-work hours are recent immigrants from Europe, Northern countries. The most miserable painter or plumber we get always changes his clothes at work and takes a shower in the maid's bathroom and puts on his street clothes again before going out. They live in filth, unavoidably, but they're personally fastidious. And the English just aren't. Oxford graduates smell.

Had a card from Fizdale & Gold mysteriously saying that they and "the Lowells" are meeting in Portugal. And aren't Lota and I going to be there, too? Oh dear, I don't WANT to go back to Mexico! Unless to Yucatán or the southern parts, way off the beaten path. I imagine even Oaxaca is spoiled now, and it was so beautiful. It's a much sadder country than Brazil, and all those Indians are so awful, poor things, except the little Mayas in Yucatán. They're nice, gentler, cleaner, don't carry guns, big hooked noses, quiet and almost gay—like little parakeets. But I've had ten years of a backward, corrupt country, and like Lota, I yearn for civilization . . . Lota's secretary Fernanda is here & will take my mail, so I'll get off this installment now.

To May Swenson

Samambaia
October 3, 1963

I am glad you got the record safely . . . I shall expect you to be samba-ing next time I see you. That record *sounds* like Carnival—there are many more beautiful old sambas and *marchinhas*—but it's hard to get good recordings—they insist on jazzing them up, or making them pretty—and the words are the best part anyway.

Now our bird poem [Swenson's poem, "Dear Elizabeth," partly based on EB's letter]: oh dear I had the name partly wrong, I see—It's *Bico Lacre* [instead of Bica Lacqua]—I had the *lacre* wrong because I went by the way the man in the shop and our maid say it—and the "lower orders" often leave out "r"'s—sort of baby-talk. Also, I'm afraid they come from Africa. You can probably see them among the finches in that Radio City subway pet shop. Joanna swore they had them up in her northern state and described them most poetically, but a boy I know, a zoologist, was here yesterday and said they're either Australian or African. So you can go see them and check on my accuracy. There's no real "spot"—just a faintly deeper rose color on the belly. The egg is—well, I think I said "jelly bean" but maybe it's smaller: a *Boston* baked bean would be right—not a N.Y. one. I must put on my reading-glasses—not *tudo o mundo*. I'm just getting more & more far-sighted with age. There's no "stripe," just the male's black pencil-line moustache. I think you should have a pair too. Here I paid what—with inflation—came to 22 cents each for them. The brute of a woman in the pet shop said, "If you cut their claws they'll get tame"! If you cut their claws they'll die of heart attacks, more like it. The name might be different in English—but you should recognize them after writing a poem about them. I think the poem might work out rather well . . .

Actually a nice young American couple—he's here on a Fulbright, teaching Am. Lit.—the first really nice U.S. academic [David Weimer] I've met here . . . But it is fun to discuss Mark Twain again, or *Moby Dick* . . . Now I've just read *The Group*—felt I had to. Mary [McCarthy] was a year ahead of me so I was not in her "group" (thank heavens) although we were friends. My oldest friend [Frani], with whom I went to school, camp, *and* college, is "Helena"—if you read it. Mary lets her off lightly! but doesn't bring her to life. I recognize . . . Mary's first husband, and pieces of Mary herself, and Eunice [Clark] Jessup, and bits of the others—but it's too much like trying to remember a dream . . . I admire her *gall*. I dislike the age we live in that makes that kind of writing seem necessary, though. We're all brutes.

To Arthur Gold and Robert Fizdale

A brochure about Lota's unfinished park (later called Flamingo Park), which was enclosed with this letter, had Lota's note "Please come before it is too late." EB added: "??? What does she mean?"

Rio de Janeiro
October 10, 1963

We don't know whether you are in your château or back on Central Park West or shooting in Scotland. Anyway, Lota wants me to type to you, and she is sending these pictures of her "job." You can see how the park is progressing. No, I suppose you don't appreciate that, but it *has* progressed enormously, and you can see how big it is and how full of complicated engineering, horticultural, and architectural problems—all of which Lota deals with with the maximum efficiency and bravura. But Lota, poor dear, has had a bad time lately. I've lost track of the time, but first she had to have an operation, very sudden (intestinal occlusion) and was in the hospital a long time—very brave through it all. Then she went back to work much too soon and caught, of all things, typhoid fever. (It's the first thing that had made me realize we really live in the tropics.) Of course she had never been inoculated against it. Now everyone has, including Mary's *two* adopted daughters and Mary's cook's son. Lota came up to the country to recuperate—I think she'll be able to go back to work in another week or ten days—but it's been well over two months she's been sick, or asleep, and always, of course, *furious*, because she is never sick.

I gave up last week and went to a hospital that used to have a good reputation as a "rest home"—run by Seventh Day Adventists, way up on the peaks. Alas, the "unions" have also moved in there and—as I said to Lota—my visit was like a combined church picnic and a trip to Yugoslavia. I'm doing the writing because L. still cannot use her right hand—it's lame from all the hideous glucose stages. Her blood may be awfully blue, but her veins are too fine—perhaps a mark of ancient lineage, I don't know.

I just managed to get your Poulenc concert record—it is absolutely superb. (I first heard it played on the radio here one night.) Your playing is beyond criticism, as always—so I can throw in the comment that I think it's a perfectly produced record for once, too. Don't you have any more new ones? I miss music more than anything else here—even if I joined the Seventh Day Adventists in hymn singing from my balcony.

Lota's "Work Group" is so devoted to her that they threaten to resign if she doesn't come back soon—and one reason we had to get out of Rio was because each one telephoned several times every day, and if she happened to *see* one, all the others got jealous. She'll take over with her bandaged little paw. We do miss you both terribly.

[*P.S. in Lota's hand*] Miss you very much comme toujours. Hope to see you in '65 here. Tell you about later. We being have an orgy of hearing you in all your gramophone records. Affectueusement, Lota.

To Robert Lowell

Rio de Janeiro
October 11, 1963

Poor Lota went and caught, of all things, *typhoid fever*—because she went back to work too soon, I suppose, and was weak enough to pick it up anywhere. I forget it's endemic here and we should never neglect the shots. It isn't nearly as bad as it used to be, with the new drugs for it—but the fever goes up, and UP & UP—and it was quite frightening. When she got a bit better she went up to the country, with the maid, and *I* went to a hospital, just for a week's "rest cure" supposedly—a very funny experience. More later. Then I joined her up there and we spent two whole weeks doing nothing much, reading and loafing and listening to music. She seems almost like herself again, at last—and I wish she hadn't got quite so much "fighting spirit" back. There's too much going on for her to get into at present. I couldn't seem to make much sense when I tried to write letters—too much to catch up, too many things happening, etc. (I read a review of Fellini's *8½* in which it said it was about someone who was "*stuck* because he was feeling too many things at the same time"—and that's been my situation exactly, I see, for about two years.)

Two nights ago, about 9 p.m., we had a mysterious telephone call from the Governor. He was at *our* house—no names could be mentioned—we had to inform various people. Mary was very brave—saw a car race up and collected poor little Manuelzinho (in his underwear—he'd gone to bed) and went up. All lights on in our house and strange men on the terrace. Mary shouted at them, then who should appear but Carlos Lacerda—all were armed. She went and had whiskey with them (& he almost never drinks, so was obviously nervous). We think (but don't know) he started off for his own house and was probably followed—or found his house surrounded, or something. There was an attempt to kidnap him last week, too. Parachutists jumped down on a hospital he was visiting!—absolutely crazy, of course. I really don't care to have our house used as a "hideout"; it puts us in an awful spot. But I suppose he had to go *somewhere*. Well, you see how bad things are getting.

Dos Passos has a book about Brazil out—so shoddy I can't even read it, and so superficial. He sent it to Lota—mentions her various times, once as "a small woman in striped pants." L. is furious; says she has never had a pair of striped pants in her life. I read *The Group* at last. "Helena" is my oldest friend—we went to school, camp, and college together—but she was a year ahead, and in *The Group*—I wasn't. She and her mother and Mary's first husband and Eunice Clark Jessup are the only ones I really recognize—and Mary herself, split up into two or three. All the details of her first marriage and the '30s in N.Y. are remarkably real again. But I can't *attempt* to tell how good it is, really—it's like trying to remember a dream, to me. Some parts are awfully funny—the scene in the park, etc.—wonderful. I'm sure those set-fireworks-sex pieces will insure huge sales. I admire her for doing it, really.

Riots in the Senate about Carlos. One group wants to investigate the "attack on his life," most of the others don't want to, naturally—and they came to blows. What an unseemly mess. President Goulart would do almost anything to get rid of him, but at the same time doesn't want to make a martyr of him, of course, because then he'd get elected President. That clipping you sent from *The N.Y. Times* was so wrong—how can they get things so wrong? I wonder . . . I'd like to call up President Kennedy! It's almost too bad they *didn't* get martial law—that would have shown the rest of the world how bad things are, perhaps. Carlos would have been exiled to Amazonas, probably—if he hadn't escaped first.

Well, and now *Time* (I've just waded through that) is beating the drums for Goldwater. Save us. They wrote and asked me to do a small revision job on the Brazil book—not much work and a hunk of money, but in about ten days, of course—and it did me good to telex back NO.

We did enjoy the records up in the country. Joan Sutherland is awfully good, isn't she? I also had a marvelous blues record—Robert Johnson. I recommend it highly—he was murdered in 1938 at the age of 20 by one of his lady-friends. If you like blues, it's superb, the real thing. (Elizabeth would like him, I think.)

Flavio has written two really *good* poems. I think he should publish them here, and then send them to Harvard, too. I'm not exaggerating— they're influenced by João Cabral de Melo, but are really "felt." I am hoping so much this Harvard business works out . . . His qualifications are excellent and his English is getting better all the time. His French is also excellent. He got 100 in the Foreign Affairs English exam . . . I see Harvard even has a School of Diplomacy and maybe he could go to that . . . He's improving a lot, really. Even looks a *lot* better and is gradually changing his hairdo to something a bit less European-looking. (I've refrained from comment on this, of course, but am relieved.) . . .

Oh, I went to a small hospital way up near that [statue of] Christ. It used to be a wonderful clean, quiet place for just that kind of exhaustion—run by Seventh Day Adventists, vegetarian, hymn-singing, etc., but good. However, after I got there (& couldn't face moving) I discovered that, in order to make ends meet, in the past year they've had to go in with one of the "*syndicatos*," or unions—and the place has gone to pots, as L. says . . . The little garden has been ruined. I screamed from my balcony one day at a couple of young hoodlums calmly tearing the slats off a bench. Fat men in pajamas, and fat ladies, each with two or three shrieking children and a pocket radio, throng the place at all hours. No visiting hours kept any more, no quiet, nothing—cockroaches moving in, and black beans and meat on the menu once a day. It was a glimpse into the future, I'm afraid. When I asked the doctors or nurses about it, they just shrugged and said, "That's the way things are these days." And when I tried preaching my own gospel of brightening—or at least cleaning up—the corner where you are, etc., I think they thought I was really mad—a mad foreigner. However, I did begin to feel better and then minded the racket less, and the food is excellent—for Brazil. And the view superb—fantastic—particularly at night. I've almost done a short poem about it.

Life was so much pleasanter up in the country. I wish we could go back & stay. I do go up to my vacant apartment to work, mornings, here, and that's a help—but the city's unpleasant these days, and Lota works too hard and we both get too tired. I suppose it will take time to get back to feeling normal again.

To Frani Blough Muser

Rio de Janeiro
December 5, 1963

I did get your nice long letter and the pictures and I was so glad you seemed to be liking Belgium and your apartment and everything. I have also got two copies of a fascinating magazine, *Perspectives of New Music*—and I am really enjoying it. Yesterday I read aloud most of Elliot Carter's last piece to Lota's nephew, who looked suitably impressed with the situation of the American composer. (Flavio, the nephew, is a jazz addict.) I've been very much occupied recently in trying to get Flavio a scholarship to Harvard—as a transfer student. He's an extremely bright boy, the last brains in the family, after Lota's, I think—and we want so much to get him away from Brazil for a year or two, and somewhere where he'll really learn something. The university here is on strike most of the time, and when not on strike the professors seem to talk of nothing but politics. The students rarely go to classes at all as far as I can make out, and get all their education outside.

I wonder if you've seen Mary [McCarthy] in Paris? I had lunch with her and James West when I was in N.Y. in '61—she said she'd finished *The Group*—(this was in a taxi). I said severely, "I hope you've been nice to Frani, Mary." "Oh yes, I've been nice to Frani. Don't you think I am nice to Frani, Jim?" Jim: "Yes, dear." So I read it and I suppose she is nice to you, or that very small facet of your personality she presents. You and your mother come out as the only fairly human people. (But you've probably read it, too.) Poor Johnsrud [McCarthy's first husband] takes another fearful beating. Well, it is brilliant, parts of it, and I think she deserves this huge financial success. But Cal wrote me she was putting all the money into some peace foundation & also refused to be on the cover of *Time*—very admirable of her.

President Kennedy's death really overwhelmed Brazil. It was very moving—I think almost everyone I know here telephoned or came in person to present their "condolences"—and many in tears. Even now the taxi drivers, storekeepers, etc., when they spot my American accent, make me little speeches—and always conclude with "If only it had been *our* John instead of yours." (João Goulart, the President.) This country is so hopeless these days and I think they felt Kennedy at least was trying to help—rightly or wrongly . . . Do please let me hear from you. I am dying for the North, and if not for the North, for a Nordic letter.

To Loren MacIver

Rio de Janeiro
Saturday morning
January 25, 1964

On the front of this envelope is "Lota's Beach"—a part of her "park" and the most successful part so far, naturally, because everyone in Rio adores a beach and there aren't enough to go around. This was sort of a beach-by-mistake. A huge dredge, an old U.S. one from the Panama Canal, has worked her way down South America and arrived to dredge the bay. Shining new white sand comes up, tons of it an hour, very spectacular. A year ago it began—two days later we were driving by and there was a spot of white sand about ten feet square showing, and on it *already* were four people and a pink beach umbrella! Now, as you can see from the picture, it's a mile long and there are thousands of people on it.

Lota is getting so famous and powerful it is frightening. If our friend the Governor gets elected President (he's running, but a lot can happen here in the next few months), I'm afraid she'll be an ambassador or something—an awful prospect. But she's thriving on it and is too energetic, almost, for my taste—a combination of Lewis Mumford and Fiorello La Guardia.

We're here in Rio, having lent our house to a nice young Fulbright professor, David Weimer, the first *nice* academic from the U.S. I've met here, with three small children. So they're up there, probably fearful of snakes and thunderstorms, but at least he can get some work done. I can't seem to get much done *here*. It's one thing after another, to coin a phrase. The way one accumulates a "family" of dependents in Brazil is extraordinary. The sewing girl is blue and has to be cheered up; give her the radio and close the door. Then the maid cries, big hot tears, because the horrible TV we keep for her is malfunctioning and makes everyone look like dwarfs, with faces four feet long. Her second cousin, large and black, who works for Lota in the park but cut his hand badly, seems to be living with us these days and decides he'll "help" by washing the terrace with floods of water that come in the door of my study. His wife, from whom he's separated, arrives by mistake, has an attack of asthma, gets treated, then has mild hysterics and needs a sedative. Then I have to read them the plans for the Carnival from the afternoon papers because only the man, Leoncio, can read (but not too well).

Brazil was absolutely overwhelmed by Kennedy's death. It was awful, everyone crying in the streets. Even now taxi drivers, spotting me as an American, turn around—endangering our lives—and make me formal little speeches. I saw that Rosalyn Tureck played in New York—were you there then? What was her *last* record? I want to get it. Please tell us all what you've painted—we can enjoy the titles, at least . . .

To Dr. Anny Baumann

Rio de Janeiro
April 7, 1964

My letters, two of them, were mailed the day before our "revolution" started. President Goulart finally went too far. A few brave generals and the governors of the three most important states got together, and after a pretty bad forty-eight hours, all was over. Lota was very brave—or else extremely curious! The reactions have been really popular, thank goodness. The originally scheduled anti-Communist parade turned into a victory parade—more than a million people in the pouring rain. It was quite spontaneous and they couldn't *all* have been the rich reactionary right! Carlos Lacerda is happy, of course. Now comes the depressing part. Just don't believe what the U.S. papers say and certainly don't believe the news from France. De Gaulle is using Brazil at the moment as another anti-U.S. weapon. *Le Monde* says the whole thing was engineered by Standard Oil!

I'm going to England for a couple of months, where I can speak the language and where I won't have to talk about Brazil for a while. Lota and I may go to Italy first. We look forward to your visit here and we'll be eagerly awaiting you on August 28.

April 27, 1964

Lota and I are flying to Milan on May 13. She can take a month's vacation, then she'll come back here and I'll go on to England for about six weeks. Our dates roughly are: Milan, May 14–16; Florence, 20–28; Venice, June 1–8. After that Milan again until June 15. After that you can write me care of Mr. and Mrs. Kit Barker, Bexley Hill, Lodsworth, Petworth, Sussex. He is a painter friend I haven't seen for twelve years; she is a novelist. Lota, of course, will be back in Brazil, poor thing. I am sailing from England on August 1st on the *Argentine Star*, and shall be back here in plenty of time to welcome you . . .

Carlos Lacerda has gone off for two months—we've heard varying reports. He left last week with his wife and daughter after many dramatic scenes. A vice-governor has been elected and Carlos will be governor for a short time again, then resign to run for President. It is a good idea for him to leave the country now, strange as the system may sound to outsiders. He is such a fighter that Lota is afraid if he stayed he'd start fighting with the new President, Castelo Branco. Yet there's nothing left for him to fight, Communism having been more or less vanquished. He was exhausted, of course, but he exhausts his staff even more . . .

Hotel Pastoria
St. Martin's Street
London
June 19, 1964

. . . I left Milan on the 15th (already it seems weeks ago), and Lota left for Rio the same night. I did my best to persuade her to come with me for just a week, to *see* London at least, but I couldn't. She felt she couldn't leave the job any longer. I'll be in London until about July 5, then go to Scotland, and to the Barkers' again the last week of July.

Our Italian trip was a great success—the weather was almost perfect. Lota drove nobly and safely over mountains & through strange cities, and we saw just about everything we wanted to see, I think. Lota was leaving Milan carrying strawberries (*fraises de bois*), mushrooms, asparagus, cherries, etc. I hope she managed to get on the plane. I did want her to see a bit of England, too—but she was finally so depressed by the high state of agricultural cultivation in Italy, the advanced "civilization," the huge trees in the parks, etc.—as compared to Brazil—that perhaps it's just as well she didn't come. They're all even bigger and better here. (I really prefer something a bit harsher, I confess.)

I've decided to go to the theatre four nights in a row, to make up for all the years without any—before I have to start seeing a few people here. It is terribly cold—or else my blood is thinned by the tropics—and raining, naturally. Although I like tea very much, I am already beginning to feel hysterical when I see those *biscuits*.

The last I heard, Carlos had gone to Portugal. I am not sure where he is now, but his plan was to stay away three months—it must be about two now, I think. I'm waiting for a letter from Lota with all the news from Rio. The last reports—while in Milan—were good. I hope you and your husband have a "lovely holiday" and it will be wonderful to see you.

Rio de Janeiro
October 22, 1964

. . . Carlos is off campaigning all over the country now—elections not until 1966, but I think he is pulling his party together or something. We've had a visit from De Gaulle (Carlos refused to see him), who held out the enticing invitation for Brazil to be on his side in World War III. The park is looking better and better . . . by leaps & bounds. There was a long television program devoted to it Monday night. Lota refused to be in it, of course, but Dr. Peixoto (if you remember him) talked and talked and knew everything Lota had ever told him by heart, I think. Lota is getting so famous that shopkeepers, etc., all recognize her. She has just had a wonderful idea for children's reading rooms in both playgrounds —there is a dearth of them here. The Parque Lage affair is going well —although it meant that Carlos lost the support of the big evening paper in order to put it through (the paper's owner was one of the group who intended to put up skyscraper apartments there) . . . The road *around* Ouro Prêto has at last been started although, according to the papers, they only have enough money for part of it—but if they go around the town that's the main thing.

Lota has read this and approved so far, and now I can add that she comes home from work every evening looking so pale and exhausted that I get very worried about her. I wish I could get her out and exercising a bit more—but that's almost impossible! She falls asleep at 9 or 10, sometimes with her clothes on, etc. Do you think that vitamins help any? . . . But I don't see how she can keep going like this until next April, or whenever she'll consent to take another vacation. She does sleep better, though—I think—since you gave her your system. "Flamingo Park" is a wonderful project, but I don't want it to kill her.

I am trying to get my new book of poems in shape and just hope I won't change my mind again.

November 17, 1964

. . . I wish Lota and I weren't so involved in the politics of this hopeless country. I am beginning to feel almost fond of the present President—he keeps *calm*, never flies off the handle & seems to be doing better than anyone ever expected. If Carlos gets elected, I think I'll leave rather than live any longer in the hysterical atmosphere he creates around him.

I have had two or three offers of teaching jobs. I think I had had two when you were here, but the best one came later—the University of Washington (state)—not too much work, and I think I could do it, and what seems to me like a very high salary. I'd love to see that part of the U.S. (Seattle, etc.) and I wish Lota would go along with me for part of the time. The first phase of her job should be concluded in '66, but I wonder if I'll be able to persuade her to come. Anyway, I'm accepting tentatively for some of '66—and we'll see. I know you have many many other things on your mind now, so forgive me for bothering you with my vague schemes—but at the same time I hope you will approve of them!

. . . Lota is working harder all the time; I hope she'll take a week off at Christmas. I am probably going back to Ouro Prêto the first part of December for a week, with a rather nice Fulbright professor who's here this year. We can go to some of the interesting small towns and villages that you and I didn't have a chance to see. But alas, he won't be nearly as bright and energetic a traveling companion as you . . .

To Frani Blough Muser

November 11, 1964

. . . The award was a very nice surprise [$5,000 from the Academy of American Poets "for poetic achievement"]—a complete surprise, since I really haven't done much to deserve it. I have a sneaking suspicion that one reason why I did get it is that Mrs. Bullock, who runs it, wrote me last spring asking me to pick out the poems to run in their monthly magazine. All the world's best poems have been used long ago, so I settled for a group of my favorite hymns, or favorite stanzas from favorite hymns. This seemed to make a big hit with Mrs. B. She wrote me several times how much she liked them and how she had sung one of them Easter morning in church at Martha's Vineyard, etc. Maybe she has nothing to do with the fellowship elections—but if she has, I am sure that my fondness for hymns had something to do with it.

Well, *thank you.* I NEVER go to readings if I can help it, only when it is someone I know and like, so that I feel I should—and then, even, they reduce me to such a state of nerves and embarrassment that my eyes water, or I actually weep slightly, all the way through. I gave up *giving* them long ago, only did it two or three times. I did hear Randall Jarrell once at the Y.M.H.A., and I can't quite imagine my words on his lips. But they, the lips, aren't bearded any more, I hear. As someone here said, rather cattily, "He must have given the beard to John Berryman." He looks better without it—as Lota said, also rather cattily, "It looked homemade (*feita em casa*)."

It is a great relief to know where you are again—I think I have been wondering for over a year now . . . Now I am re-reading your letter. You say Randall seems to be suffering about turning fifty. Isn't it funny?— that makes three poets I know who are all busy commenting on this. I did attempt something about being forty-five once, and my eyebrows getting rather bald, but it didn't turn out well and thank heavens I've never wanted to try the subject of one's years again.

I don't know whether it was our side that won, exactly, but it was a great relief to get that really awful Hoffa-like crook out of the country— in spite of what the world press in general seems to think is a "reactionary" movement here. It doesn't seem that way to me, here . . . Carlos Lacerda has been a friend of Lota's for 30 years, and she is working because he asked her to, etc. He is brilliant and honest, but I dread his getting elected and so does she. Flying off the handle all the time, always "exposing" something, making two-hour speeches (his shortest). He'll probably want Lota to be Ambassador to Ghana, or Minister of Education—and that will really kill her—she is working much too hard now, as it is.

We had a wonderful trip, rented a car and drove around northern Italy only, not even going to Rome. Crossing the mountains from Arezzo to Urbino, on May 28, there was a bad storm and there were also small white drifts beside the road. I got out to make sure, and it really was snow! I heard about Mary [McCarthy]'s visit to London when she had such a big audience she had to give the same lecture on the novel, twice. *Il Gruppo* was on sale in Italy. I saw it in paperback here the other day, in English not Portuguese, and the blurb is amazing: "Eight wealthy Vassar girls," etc. . . .

I've been reading the Craft interviews with Stravinsky. They're coming out in paperback, two of the original books to a book. When I know who and what he's talking about, I find I always agree with him. Stravinsky was here last year. The only thing I wanted to hear was the mass, put on at the huge cathedral. I somehow thought they *couldn't* sell tickets to a mass, and when I woke up all seats had been sold—at prohibitive prices, for me . . .

I've been offered some teaching jobs in the U.S., one so good I think I should really take it for a few terms . . .

To Marianne Moore

December 12, 1964

Mr. Richard Kelley has been here for a week. He's the lighting expert who did the Seagram Building on Park Avenue and many other famous places and buildings. He was here to advise about the lighting of Lota's park—now called "Flamingo Park," which makes it easier—and I believe has gone on to do many more things in Rio, including the lighting of the Sugar Loaf mountain. He has kindly offered to take up this letter and a small birthday present for you. The pin is agate, in a crystalline form, and we of course wish it were two equal-sized diamonds, in pure diamond form . . .

We wish you weren't so far away and we think of you and talk of you often. Ashley Brown, a bright Fulbright professor here this year, is giving a series of lectures on American writers and one is to be devoted to you. I've promised to try to help him with details—but it seems to me he knows everything already.

We had a nice visit from my dear Dr. Baumann in September. She saw everything, tasted everything, investigated everything, and also went swimming every morning before breakfast . . .

To Dr. Anny Baumann

Petrópolis
February 8, 1965

I stayed away [at Ouro Prêto] over two weeks . . . and returned feeling 100% better, at least. Ashley Brown was an excellent traveler, and he stayed ten days. I had the whole downstairs apartment at Lilli [Correia de Araújo]'s house all to myself, worked mornings, and joined Ashley at lunch, then we went church-seeing, etc., in the afternoons—a very good arrangement, and I got quite a bit of work done, for me. The best part was our excursion to "Tiradentes" (Toothpuller). You have to stay overnight at São João del Rey, at an awful hotel (although I have stayed at worse, in Brazil) but it is worth it. By far the most beautiful church around, and a perfect little town, or village, really—one huge old fountain with many faces, about fifty feet long; a stream through the middle of the village; a little shop, The Most Holy Trinity, where they sell silver jewelry, by weight, really lovely things and about one-third the cost of silver in Rio. Everything looking nice, because that Património has just worked there for three years. And no one about at all—we were in the *only* car. There are big trees, too, and the whole place is just under one of those mountain waves of naked rock, very high—with waterfalls, and pools that looked as if they'd be delicious to swim in, at the base of it. I want very much to go back, perhaps next month, and try to write something about it . . .

We came up here Saturday for a weekend and Lota has decided to stay all week, I am awfully glad to say—but how long she can stick to it I don't know. The telephone is out of order, so perhaps we are safe for another day! It is beautiful and I wish you could have seen it this time of year. We have been in our pool, and the cascades are very big and white—the water icy.

Lota is more or less "on strike"—I don't know how it will turn out. She is fighting with Carlos. For some reason or other he will not sign the papers necessary—about five minutes' work—for the libraries for children, in the playgrounds—she's got the money, even—and the restaurant—that he did agree to, all along. I think he is making a bad mistake. The park is by far his most popular project and the one that will last longest, too—and yet he seems to enjoy making things complicated and never saying a nice word to anyone, just "Why is it taking so long?" This has always been his reputation—alas—Lota knew it, too, but never worked with him before. It is such a pity . . . Everything waiting for him, again just because someone doesn't put a check in the mail. It is *hopeless*. And yet perfect strangers passing us on the road lean out of their cars and shout, "Bravo for the new park, Dona Lota!" Really, it is very nice. With all the rains it is looking really lovely—the first Sunday of the "trains for children" there were over 3,500 passengers, and that first week 17,000. There is so little for the poor and the "middle class" to do in Rio. The man who owns that concession is building four more "trains."

Perhaps I should not bother you with these trials of Lota's. Of course we think about little else these days—and she *admires* Carlos, too. But he is a difficult man, all right.

Lota is in *Time* this week—under "Women"—supposedly about the blossoming out of the Latin American female in general, but a very bad piece of course. It may not even be in the U.S. edition. Joanna is thrilled that now both of her *patronas* have been in *Time-y*. It makes Lota sound like the engineer boss of a slave gang, but anyway— For one thing Lota does NOT wear "baggy blue jeans." She does wear slacks a lot because she does have to do a lot of climbing around, seeing things. Oh well— one can't expect much better from that awful magazine.

I am doing a piece about Rio for *The N.Y. Times* Sunday magazine. I wish now I had never accepted the job, I have such difficulties with prose, but it seemed easy at the time. I must get it in tonight, and must get to work. They may not even take it anyway.

I brought back a tuba from Ouro Prêto—a huge one. It looks big enough for any two Brazilian band players to march inside. It is from the old town band and it was a shame it was being sold, but since it was, I bought it. Alberto polished for two days straight—it was almost black. Now, gleaming and beautiful, it is hung on the wall and looks very nice against old bricks.

To Randall Jarrell

Petrópolis
February 25, 1965

Now I have at least two things to thank you for and I really must write you a letter. I was delighted to get one from you, naturally—a rare and wonderful event—and then last week I got a copy of *The Lost World* . . . I am getting out a book again at last, sometime this year, I'm not sure when. I'd be delighted to send you the ms. if only I had one. The agent in New York foolishly sent the whole collection—without having copies made, as I'd asked him to—to someone in England who's doing one of those Twayne books. He has finally got it back and Lota tells me by telephone (I'm up here for a week alone while she works in the heat in Rio, poor dear) that one copy has just come—and that they want me to put it in order and send it back . . . I think you've seen most of them, probably—the title is to be *Questions of Travel*, after one of the first descriptive Brazilian ones. I know I can't compete with you in the matter of good titles, but it seems all right to me—covers everything! I wonder if you saw the ballad ["The Burglar of Babylon"] I had in *The New Yorker* on November 21st, I think—an endless affair that will certainly make a bigger book, at least. I like it fairly well still. (Marianne thinks it my "best"—but I'm afraid that's because she approves of the moral.) I'm also thinking of putting in that story of mine called "In the Village"—the one Cal wrote a poem on. There are three or four poems that go with it, and it is more a prose-poem than a story, anyway. Well, we'll see. If you have any suggestions I'd be most grateful—or think the title awful—anything. And if I can I shall send you a ms., too.

It was kind of you to suggest Michael di Capua—and I gather that your next book will be with Pantheon because of him? But by the time I heard from you I had already had a rather long-standing agreement with Bob Giroux—and so far, so good . . . Yes, I too *hate* the idea of publishing. I really have to stir myself to consider it at all, and I think if left to my own devices, without friends urging me on, I'd never do it at all—just hand things around once in a while, in the good old way. Houghton Mifflin seems to be bringing out a paperback—they wrote other peo-

ple, not me—just cabled me mysteriously for corrections! . . . Also I think
Chatto & Windus is thinking of something, quite what I don't know. So
I seem to be being pushed slightly from several directions at once . . .

All kinds of very different people have written me they liked Cal's
Benito Cereno, too, and it is one thing I hate having missed. I thought—
didn't you?—that some of the poems in the last book, two or three of the
rather odd love poems, and the Copacabana one, etc.—were marvelous.
That water-tower one *gets me*. He has that weird gift—just when you
think a poem is falling apart it suddenly saves itself, and appears perfectly
clear and dazzling.

I'm sorry to hear you've been sick. I keep thinking I'm going to pieces
in the tropics, but then I find if I get away from Rio, up here, or into the
"interior" with a better altitude, and more exercise, I always feel fine
again. We've been living in Rio most of the last three years because of
Lota's job, and although we're right on the ocean with a superb view and
I can go swimming, or at least dip in the surf, whenever I feel like it, I
hate it, and find that poor shabby spoiled city very depressing. However,
it is worth it—Lota is in charge of building a new park—a huge affair—
and a huge success, now about three-quarters done. The trouble is she
has become so famous with it that I'm afraid there's no escape for her
forever, now . . .

And now let me get to the important part. I've read *The Lost World*
through, several times—read *The Bat-Poet* again, too—and I think, if you
will take it the way I mean it, that you are the real one and only successor
to Frost. Not the bad side of Frost, or the silly side, the wisdom-of-the-
ages side, etc.—but all the good. The beautiful writing, the sympathy,
the touching and real detail, etc. Also your psychology is, of course, much
in advance of Frost's! Not *his* kind of idealized "lost world" of the small
farmer at all—which may look as if it leaves me with nothing much of
him left, and yet it does, and if I were a more skillful critic I think I could
really write quite a piece on this. You're both very sorrowful, and yet not
the anguish-school that Cal seems innocently to have inspired—the self-
pitiers who write sometimes quite good imitations of Cal! It is more
human, less specialized, and yet deep. I had seen all except two or three.
I like very much those from *The Bat-Poet*. In fact almost my favorite, I
think, is "The Bird of Night"—and it strikes me that in every book of
yours I can remember you always have one ravishing small night-piece
poem that I always like almost the best! Next to that I think I like "A
Hunt in the Black Forest." You're awfully good in the art ones, too—I
like "A jar and a glass of flowers . . ." etc.—those next five lines, very
much. (I don't think Auden should mind this poem at all. I once wrote
a poem that starts, "I practically never think of those who were truly
great"—but I've never dared print it.)

I'm naturally fascinated by the autobiographical ones—I really have
to read them some more as poems, though. Right now I am so amazed

at how very different our lives were that that's what strikes me most of all. It is too bad, perhaps, that "The Player Piano" didn't get in this book, too. The ending of that is marvelous. Heavens, *I* remember the false Armistice—but, for some reason, not the real one. However, I don't seem to mind growing old at all, or rarely. I just get bored because any stories need longer explanations than they used to, because so many people are now younger. I suppose that means one should stop telling them. But not your kind—these are invaluable, and the *only* poems I know that do tell any of these things. You are truly "American," too—if again one can leave out all the unfortunate possible meanings of that word. You make me feel almost homesick and disloyal. I should go back and live it all over again, except that I always was an expatriate of sorts, from the beginning, and I suppose that's why your poems amaze me so with their realer U.S.A. than any that I ever knew . . .

My poor abandoned cats live here all the time with our "butler"— who does take good care of them, but they do like people, and have been so happy the last ten days because I am up here. There were three, but Mimosa (means "dainty" or "delicate"), who was always sickly, died of a heart attack and was buried where she died, under the orange tree. Suzuki is a Siamese—the people around here have never seen one, and a plumber who came one day was very startled and said "What's *that*?" when he saw a blue-eyed animal rushing around. When we explained he said, "Oh—a *beast of estimation*." That's the phrase for a pet, and I'm afraid it has a very Portuguese, commercial sense to it. Tobias is spending today in bed—basket, that is—even ate his breakfast leaning his head over the side. He claws at you to pat his head and then if you dare stop patting, he bites. However, he is almost thirteen and getting a bit demanding and eccentric. He is the cat who eats with his paw—sitting up quite straight and raising pieces of meat to his mouth. But I've since heard of other cats who do the same thing and I'm afraid it merely indicates he's a bit overfed.

Oh, I must say how much I like—pp. 36–37—"The moonlight streams up through the linden," etc.—another of your lovely, plain, true but exquisite night effects . . .

I haven't heard from Cal for an unusually long time, for him, and I hope and pray he is all right. Naturally he's awfully busy; I just hope he isn't sick. He's had a wonderful spell of writing, certainly.

I may get to Italy again this year—toward the end of April, for a month, and I might go on to England alone for two or three weeks more, the way I did last year. If you are planning to be in either of these places at these times, do let me know. I LOVE getting poems, also letters, but— well—I do know how some can and some can't!

P.S. I've opened this to say something more about the "Player Piano" poem. I like the last two stanzas so much—they remind me just a little bit of one I think is Roethke's best, "My Papa's Waltz"—but more, they suddenly brought back to me one of my very favorite of Hardy's—"The Self-Unseeing"—one of his most beautiful little poems, I think. (I've even been trying to write a poem *about* it.) But yours has a stranger and more contemporary—although still past—mystery to it—those *keys*. And the word "keys" itself seems to be so full of ambiguity.

Rio de Janeiro
March 20, 1965

I wanted to write you as soon as I could after receiving your book, but by now my letter to you seems a bit skimpy and I have read *The Lost World* a good many times and feel I should say lots more. I am NOT an articulate critic, as you know. I don't really try to be, since I read for my own pleasure and comfort and curiosity only—so I just get intuitions here & there, and love this and am repelled by that, and let it go.

Well then—Cal says he likes almost best the really violent ones, like "In Montecito" and "Three Bills"—and I see how awfully good they are although, for liking, I stick to my original choices. "A Well-to-Do Invalid" is terrific, too. The next-to-last stanza says it all so simply and well—one of those *awful* problems—put simply & accurately, like in the very best of Lawrence's poems about people.

The X-ray one—"My myelogram is negative. This elates me"—this line gives me the horrors, and must be *very* good. The "Mother Has Fainted" bit I like very much, too—on page 35—and the *moue* being a mouse, in the dream. That's just like my dreams, too.

Poetry aside, you make wonderful critical remarks, too—like "I feel like the first men who read Wordsworth. / It's so simple I can't understand it." That's a very profound remark, I'm sure, and I'd like to say it to a lot of people.

Here in Brazil I think people are more realistic about life, death, marriage, the sexes, etc.—although they go so rhetorical and sentimental about these things in their speechmaking and writing. Nevertheless, it is a country where one feels closer to real old-fashioned life, somehow. Tragedies still happen, people's lives have dramatic ups & downs and fairy-tale endings—or beginnings. You're buried, by law, within twenty-four hours after death. And children are really loved more than anyplace else—except perhaps in Italy. No sacrifice is too great for the children, and the most miserably poor boast about how many children they have —not that they should have them all—but the feeling is right. I think it is the kind of feeling you'd appreciate.

With all its awfulness and stupidities—some of the Lost World hasn't quite been lost here yet, I feel, on the days I still like living in this backward place. This is true particularly when one gets away from Rio, or the coast. The people in the small poor places are so absolutely natural and so elegantly polite. I'm not really off the subject of your poems—it is that I think the things you feel a sense of loss for aren't entirely lost to the world, yet. I gather up every bit of evidence with joy, and wish I could put it into my poems, too.

Cal seems recovered again, thank goodness—his last letter sounds fine. I hope you're well—remember me to Mary & pat the cat for me.

To Ashley Brown

With a letter of introduction from Flannery O'Connor, Ashley Brown first met EB in 1964 in Rio, when he was Fulbright Lecturer in American Literature at the Federal University. On the English faculty of the University of South Carolina since 1959, he is co-editor of The Achievement of Wallace Stevens *(1962). See his memoir, "Elizabeth Bishop in Brazil," in the* Southern Review *13 (October 1977), pp. 688–704.*

Ouro Prêto, Minas Gerais
September 2, 1965

How very nice to get a letter from you, by slow stages from New Orleans, to Petrópolis, to Rio, to Ouro Prêto. I am here again on a visit, and what's more, I've gone and bought a house. I never intended to. Lota and I have wanted to get an old one on the seashore somewhere, to restore, but had no luck, and when I found this house here was for sale—and might go to a rich man from the mines, and that Lilli was dreading having him as a neighbor, and the head of the Património didn't like him much, either—I decided to plunge in. You may not remember the house—it is down the road from Lilli's, just a bit nearer town, on the left—a long long sloping roof, like a dragon or an iguana. It perches on the bank, and has the same view as her house, a bit lower down. But what really won me over, I think, was that it has two large lots beside it that go with it, with very high stone walls around them—perfect for a garden. Also water running through one, a brook on the other side, palm trees, all kinds of fruit trees, etc.

Lota thinks I'm slightly mad, but is *interested*—and we've always wanted to have an old house as well as a modern one. The deal may not go through: Seu Olímpio, a gnome of 80 or so, who lives in it now, has ten children, and one of them doesn't like the idea, but will probably be won over. The others want their father to sell and get out, however— since he keeps climbing the avocado trees, which are very high, and they feel any day now he will fall out of one. He's living in the kitchen and one of the 12 rooms—in absolute squalor—ducks and hens and cats sitting on his bed, etc. I'm going to stay on until the deal is put through—then I hope we can both come back in December, when L. gets a vacation, supposedly—and plan.

Well—I wish you were here to see it! It is one of the oldest houses in town, and has all sorts of mysterious stone steps and platforms and cellars—where gold was washed. Also a legend of buried gold—but apparently before Seu Olímpio took to climbing trees, he had dug up the whole place pretty thoroughly. Oh dear, I am afraid Ouro Prêto in its tiny way will become the Cornwall or Provincetown of Brazil, and here I am getting into it—but it is a good "investment"; we can always sell it—and one doesn't feel normal in Brazil unless engaged in some sort of real estate deal.

Ouro Prêto is just the same—growing warmer, and I hear Rio is fearfully hot. The horrible "dry fog" prevented planes from flying for 5 hours yesterday, and Lota even urges me to stay here. Lots of French people—the hotel has been full constantly, although I don't go there very often—but I met Bidault coming out of the toilet the other day . . . We go to all possible movies and there was quite a run of fairly good ones— now they are all bad— Something incredible called *Women in Fury*, I think—French, and based—perhaps—on *Colomba* (didn't you have to read that in school?), laid in Corsica, everyone shooting or throwing knives at everyone else, and "French" at its worst—blondes—indistinguishable from each other—wearing nothing but the lower parts of their bikinis, rushing through the Corsican landscape. Then there was a wonderful pseudo-highbrow one—in Leopoldville—in French *and* Italian, with Portuguese subtitles. Ouro Prêto didn't make much out of that one. Well, it's a rather dull life here, but Rio was getting on my nerves badly, and I am getting some work done, or think I am.

I saw Mark Strand and his wife twice, I think. It seems her parents are old friends of my friend Loren MacIver, the painter—and he had various messages, books, etc., from her . . .

He did hand over Sylvia Plath's last book, and *About the House*. This one is rather disappointing to read altogether—a kind of determined coyness about the indignities and comforts of old age (a little early, I think)—but I still like the one to MacNeice, and some others. You've probably read it by now, though.

Another Rio caller was a fairly young Englishman who came to study with Roberto Burle-Marx—and then Roberto left him stranded alone in Rio for several months. He is rather a sad type—but was born in Assam and went to school in Darjeeling (and Cambridge) and so we had an interesting discussion about TEA, and I know why Brazilian tea is so bad now.

Lota is going through an awful stretch with her Fundação [Park Foundation] but things are beginning to look brighter, I gather. There was a big TV program about it—all the women's groups got interested —even Lota appeared for a moment on TV—and I wasn't there to see it. It will be voted on on October 5th—now if only the deputies don't go completely crazy. A band now plays every Sat. & Sun., and last week a samba school put on a special show on the dance floor for several hundred tourists here on a cruise . . .

Lilli and I have just had another wonderful linguistic misunderstanding. I said I'd like to have a Thonet rocking chair for my house—you know, that bentwood and cane kind, common here, but I've never had space for one. She thought I said "toenail rocking chair." I believe she thought at first it was some weird piece of American bedroom equipment! The reason I am here, really, is because she was driving back from Rio and offered to stop over at Tiradentes with me. We took three and a half days for the trip and saw everything seeable on the way. After half a day in Tiradentes I changed my mind about wanting a house there—it is too dead, even for me—but the church looked as ravishing as ever, and it is such a pity you didn't see the fountain—a marvelous huge high one, very baroque, water flowing abundantly from three big heads, and more grotesque heads on the back where women were doing their washing. We had a picnic lunch there. I took some photographs and, if they come out well, I'll send you one. But the hotels got worse and worse. Well, you remember the Espanhol—it was the second; the third was really awful —they seemed to take pleasure in how awful it was. In São João del Rey I was rather touched by having two or three boys come up to me and say directly, "Don't you remember me?"—and one asked where *you* were. That shows how much excitement they have in São João del Rey.

I must take a walk "downtown" and go to the Post Office and see about the possibilities of tonight's "show." Oh—the Incredible Geraldine—I've only seen her once—invited me to her *boite*, now open, but I haven't been. A male dancer she imported for the first week was asked by the priests to leave town, I hear. And that's all the gossip I know at present. I've just sent my mailing list to the publishers and asked to have you sent an "advance copy" [of *Questions of Travel*] if they have such things. I wonder how the U.S.A. is striking you, and please do let me know. They have paved the road at last, so Lilli's house—and perhaps mine—won't get dirty any more.

To Dr. Anny Baumann

Rio de Janeiro
November 9, 1965
. . . Please don't speak of Brazilian mails when you write me. Lota, who is so broad-minded in general, for some mysterious reason is a bit chauvinistic about the Brazilian P.O. And even when things obviously get lost, she doesn't like to admit it, or accuses me of being a complaining type! She was expecting me back two weeks before I finally made it— that's why she didn't forward your last letters to me there. I had to stay on one whole week because no planes left Belo Horizonte. Then there was a long weekend so she decided to come and get me personally. I got rather homesick, but it is a good place to work and I did get more writing

done than for the past two years in Rio, where I just can't seem to concentrate.

Perhaps this is because politics are very far away, up there, and the telephone rings once a day, and there is no TV. Also the climate is superior. It's about 4,000 feet, you know . . . Lota said when she read your letter she wanted very much to sit down and give you an account, but she never has time to do anything she wants these days. Carlos's Minister of Education . . . lost badly, and now he and Carlos are blaming each other for the big defeat. Lota thinks it was pretty much Carlos's fault—he got wilder and wilder toward the end, and is really a dreadful politician. After the sweeping anti-"revolution" victory, in eleven states, the present government has passed an act which will make presidential elections something done solely by the congress (this is a bad account, but roughly the idea). This means that Carlos is *out* as a candidate. He has taken it very very badly—seemed to lose his head completely—and "retires" from politics for good when his governorship is up on December 5th—and is going into "business." The atmosphere is very nerve-racking and the situation very gloomy—from Lota's point of view, that is—but probably from everyone's. Her "Foundation" was made an act—by Carlos—but now the big problem is getting *money* for it. Also she's been attacked awfully, indecently, by Roberto Burle-Marx and a couple of others. In England or the U.S. she'd win thousands for libel very possibly—but here there is no use attempting anything like that, so she has behaved with great dignity and good sense, I think . . .

Lota works about 18 hours a day and I don't know how she stands it—but then, she is a fighter, too, like Carlos, and these arguments don't bother her as much as they would me—or at least I hope so. The only thing I worry about is that I think now she's had a taste of public life she'll never be able to retire from it! The park is a tremendous success, really—but there have been times at which I thought it would kill us both.

By now I hope you have received a copy of my book [*Questions of Travel*]. I am very pleased with the way it looks, the type and everything. I just wish the contents were twice the length—it seems a bit thin . . .

I haven't received the Mistometers and wonder if you'd be good enough to check on them . . . I'm getting desperate. None of the Brazilian drugs seem to work at all and last week I had a really bad stretch. I often do when it gets very hot here, I don't know why—and have had to keep taking adrenaline. (But those disposable syringes have been a godsend.)

. . . I hope Lota will take a vacation. I was hoping for December 5th when the government (state) changes—but now she says no, MAYBE January. We can't afford to go abroad—the best vacation for her—but may go back to Ouro Prêto for a stretch. I bought a house there. (Please don't tell *anyone* this at present—it has to be kept a secret for a while.) But it's beautiful—about the oldest in town, about 1720—with a huge walled garden, and the most beautiful roof in Ouro Prêto . . .

To Robert Lowell

November 18, 1965

I have so much to write you about and so many things to thank you for I scarcely know where to begin. I have also put off writing to you too long. I stayed away in Ouro Prêto for over two months and when I came back—Lota came up and got me, finally, which touched me very much since it's a nine-hour drive—there was an awful lot to attend to, and I haven't been well—a bad stretch of asthma, don't know why—but I'm recovered now. When I did get back, your letter about Randall Jarrell was here, the one about my book came soon after. I've also got your book of plays [*The Old Glory*] and thank you for that, too.

I feel awful about Randall's death. We had just seemed to be getting in touch again, too, after a long silence. What do you suspect went wrong with him? Had he talked to you at all frankly lately, or since he was sick? I feel it must have been an accident of an unconscious-suicide kind, a sudden impulse when he was really quite out of his head—because surely it was most unlike him to make some innocent motorist responsible for his death. I feel sorry for whoever it was. When I heard about it, in Ouro Prêto—and then saw it in *Time* a day or so later—I tried and tried to write to Mary [Jarrell], but didn't. Now after what you wrote me I don't know whether to or not—perhaps I shall, just conventionally. Demerol is a *strong* drug, which would certainly make anyone "fuzzy," as you say. It is too sad, really. I hope he got the two letters I wrote him about *The Lost World* and that I managed to say something he wanted said . . .

You are awfully kind about my book, and your letter was a great comfort to me. I was wheezing away and full of adrenaline and feeling just too foolish, at this advanced age, to be in such a state—when it came. I love your expression "the bomb in it in a delicate way!" That was my idea exactly, I suppose. Well, "From Trollope's Journal" was actually an anti-Eisenhower poem, I think—although it's really almost all Trollope, phrase after phrase. You are too generous to go over the same old but so short list. I think the book itself is pretty, but the contents too slight. *Time* came again—same Mr. Denis. I wanted to use the old photos of you & me since they are better than he usually does, but they insisted so I finally gave in, and he was kind enough to let me see proof. He's a nice man, but a dreadful photographer. About 85% of them had me with my eyes shut, looking exactly like both my grandmothers put together. (He said that I blinked "unusually fast"—that's a new one.) I have a horrible feeling they're preparing to tear me limb from limb because of my quarrels with Time-Life Books.

I haven't heard anything from the Rockefeller Foundation and you seem to imply that perhaps they aren't giving any more fellowships. However, I think I'll write a note just to see if they ever got my application. Letters from Ouro Prêto seem more subject to loss than from here, even.

In the meantime I've made up my mind to go to Seattle a few days after Christmas to teach at the University of Washington. I don't want to one bit, but need the money, and probably it will be good for me! They are running a big risk, I think, since I've never taught before and all their forms and letters just confuse me more and more. I try to think seriously for a while every day, like Isherwood, on what poetry is all about, etc.— but my mind wanders. However, they do sound nice and friendly and I do want to see the Big Trees and Mt. Rainier—so it will probably be all right. If you do have any ideas on the subject of textbooks (they keep writing me about them), good anthologies, etc., I'd be extremely grateful. I'm not as dumb as I sound here, I'm sure, and I certainly see enough books—too many by far. I've re-read all of Saintsbury's book on prosody just for fun. It is a marvelous book, I think, all three volumes—so *funny*—and quite good until he meets Swinburne—or maybe we're wrong about *him*.

I'm hoping that Lota will come to Seattle for the last month and then we can do a bit of traveling and go to San Francisco, etc. She says no, she'll never be able to get away, but I hope she'll weaken. She hates having me go—very nice of her—but after a sad scene she is now resigned! And she is so awfully busy she really misses me only for about an hour at dinnertime or on long weekends. She is now president of the board to run the park—the "Foundation"—until 1968, and she takes office Monday. But it has been a hideous stretch. I am utterly sick of Brazilian politics, big and little. She is a fighter, after all, and in some ways enjoys all the bloodshed, I think. A while ago I was afraid it would really kill us both before the thing got finished. As Lota says, the people are *primary* . . .

I have been reading all about the blackout and wonder what happened to you and your family during it. We are so used to them here— sometimes they are even *scheduled*. It must have been weird and rather wonderful—and maybe a good idea in a way—to show everyone how helpless they are without *juice*. I like Ouro Prêto because everything there was made on the spot, by hand, of stone, iron, copper, wood. They had to invent a lot—and everything has lasted perfectly well for almost three hundred years now. I used to think this was just sentimental of me—now I'm beginning to take it more seriously. I am curious to see my native land again. I must say I hate it in *The New Yorker*. I did a couple of poems lately—one will be in that magazine next year ["Under the Window: Ouro Prêto"]. And I am dying to see you & talk to you.

To Frani Blough Muser

December 19 (no, 20), 1965

I just came down from the weekend in Petrópolis to find the temperature at 85° in my study—and I suppose about 95° in the city, where I stopped off to try on a nice thick new *tweed suit*. I don't think I told you, because I didn't make up my mind until the very last minute, but I am going to be one of those awful poets-in-residence for the two next terms (they have a three-term year) at the University of Washington, Seattle . . . I am not looking forward to this very much, but they pay awfully well—at least by my standards, which scarcely seem to be American any more!—and I thought I'd like to see the West & the big trees. I am even thinking of coming East in June by something called the Vista-Dome.

I hope Lota will be able to get away from her job and join me for May, at least. But at this very moment things are so awful for her that she may resign today and come with me on December 27th! Heavens, how I hate politics after the last four years—and I'm against the two-party system, and maybe even democracy, for all I know, after the latest events here. Anyway—it has been a nightmare stretch for her, and I don't like to abandon her this way, but I can't be of any help, and scarcely see her, so might as well go off and earn some money . . .

This is not the way to thank you for your nice letter that I found waiting for me here. You are very brave about the poetry—it gives me some courage about trying to teach the stuff! (But teaching anyone to write it is pure nonsense, I think . . .) I haven't had many reviews yet, but so far so good. I take Roethke's old job, and hope that someone sedate, sober, sane, and old-fashioned will have the appeal of novelty. One of the nice things about Brazil is that people (the "elite" that is) still all do read poetry and esteem poets very highly (too highly, probably). "Poet" is even a term of endearment among gentlemen . . .

Tell Cynthia [Frani's daughter, who designed it] I am quite pleased with the looks of *Questions of Travel*, if not so much with the contents. A book I liked a lot two years ago, and I think you might too, was Empson's last, *Milton's God*. I just re-read it, and liked it even more. He's an awfully niggling writer, but I like his style and agree with most of what he says. Oh dear, my "students" will probably know more about him than I do, though. I am going to make them MEMORIZE. I have a whole list of short poems—don't you think that's a good idea? Then a few lines should re-occur once in a while all the rest of their lives. If you know "The Emperor of Ice Cream," surely it should dignify every ice cream cone you eat in the future—or so I fondly imagine . . .

To Ashley Brown

December 21, 1965

This to you must positively be the last letter I write before I go—but I did want to thank you for your helpful information. I have been stalling along with the thought that perhaps something would happen so I wouldn't have to go at all—but it is creeping up on me—I leave the night of December 27th. (God knows when I get there, with stops in Lima,

Miami, Los Angeles, etc.). I have written David Wagoner about the books & we'll see. Anyway, I'll have at least five days there before I have to confront a student, so surely I can get things planned a bit. Lota keeps telling me how *"repenida"* I'm going to be. Also keeps giving hideous imitations of me with my beautiful new *pasta* for books & papers . . . Beatrice Roethke wrote and asked me to live with her! However—she's a thirty-minute drive away, and also has dogs, so I can't. I hope there is some such thing as an apartment within walking distance. (All I know about the city and the university I learned in a *National Geographic* for 1961 I found at Lilli's. Well, there seems to be a magnificent botanical garden, and that's something.) . . .

Some of your pedagogical (?) ideas are rather like my own. The writing course doesn't bother me at all—after all, they must want to take it or they wouldn't bother—and all is grist to that mill. Re-reading Hardy I was struck by his titles—just looking them over in the index—and thought what wonderful titles a lot of them would have made for Wallace Stevens, too—some even for Eliot—but with such differences in the poems. So I've been working out a sort of set of possible themes—and I think I'll try comparing poems when I can. "The Emperor of Ice Cream" is really very much like "Aunt Helen," for example. Hardy's "Her Apotheosis" is similar to that poem of Auden's about the matron having lunch at Schrafft's, etc. Thomas Hardy titles like "Voices from Things Growing in a Churchyard" or "On One Who Lived & Died Where He Was Born" could perfectly well be Wallace Stevens titles—and what would *he* have done with them? This is my one bright idea so far, and I find it rather fascinating. I suspect people make lots of difficulties about poetry just because they don't recognize the old themes quickly. I'm sending up a batch of my own books air freight this week, to have at hand, and shall immediately buy myself the new Fowler and a new dictionary (I presume they have a big bookshop)—also Klee's *Journals*, prohibitive here (about $15 there, I think) and wonderful . . .

When the weather was cooler last week, I made four fruit cakes and three plum puddings. I can't bear to think of them now . . . Mark Strand tells me that the worst feature now is that the young don't think they have to make sense—obscurity's the thing. I may not seem like a poet at all to them. At Seattle I may start calling you long distance for instant advice.

To Jean Garrigue

A native of Indiana, poet Jean Garrigue (1914–72) published The Ego and the Centaur *(1947),* The Monument Rose *(1953), and* Country Without Maps *(1964), as well as stories in* Kenyon Review. *She taught at Bard and Queens College.*

University of Washington
Seattle, Washington
January 7, 1966

I was sent *The New Leader* before I left Brazil, and brought along your very kind and generous appreciation of my new book, but I didn't bring the whole magazine. It was only yesterday I mastered the plan of the library here well enough to find *The New Leader* and get its address, so I can write and thank you in care of them, at least, since I have no other address for you. (Perhaps I could write c/o the Poetry Center, but I'm not sure of that one.) I was awfully touched and had never dreamed you would like what I have been doing that much. It was a great encouragement to me.

As you see, I am here—as one of those poets in residence. (No residence, however, almost the worst feature of the place so far.) It is too early for me to say anything about it. I know you have done this kind of work before now and I assure you that any advice would be extremely welcome. It would also be very nice if you happened to come here on one of those "circuits." Not now however—it has rained—or snowed—steadily for a week or more. This is a borrowed typewriter and I haven't mastered it yet, either. But please believe I am very grateful for everything you said. Several of my students have put you down among their "favorite poets." Of course Roethke comes first here, then Shakespeare—but they seem to have a fondness for female poets, too!

To Loren MacIver

[POSTCARD]

Seattle, Washington
February 10, 1966

This [photo of Parrington Hall at the University of Washington] is not an old high school, honey, but the second oldest (i.e., 60 years) building here, and where I pretend daily to be a teacher. I did not forget your birthday, but could not find the Western Union and had no telephone. Forgive me. I am just not used to *work*, you know, and find it takes a lot of time, effort, and character, etc.—things I don't have any of.

To Dr. Anny Baumann

4135 Brooklyn Avenue (Apt. 212)
Seattle, Washington
Washington's Birthday, 1966

. . . A few of my "students" found me this place, unfurnished, found a bed, chair, sofa, all kinds of things, and *moved* me—every last shoe and can of tea, etc., while I went downtown and peacefully had my hair done. It was one of the nicest things ever done for me, and I am much happier here, away from the incessant sound of traffic—even if I am still typing on my ironing board.

"Teaching"—I feel a complete fraud to call what I do that—takes up all my time and I have been very slow about writing to you or to anyone else. I suppose if one has done it before, one just repeats, but everything is brand new to me and I have to study a great deal to keep ahead of the two classes. However, it is probably "good for me" or something—and I know it is good for setting one's ideas in order and doing a lot of hard reading I'd probably never have done otherwise. My "students" are awfully nice, almost all of them—but I must say I am a bit concerned about American Youth. They are bright, almost all of them, but they don't seem to have much *fun*—so little *joie de vivre*, when I think how much amusement Brazilian youths seem to get out of a guitar, or a dance, or just a *cafézinho* and some conversation . . .

I think I am doing all right although I'll never take to classes, I know. Aside from that I am having a very nice time, and taking pills all the time. Lota doesn't believe this . . . I wish you'd write her a note and tell her you *know* I am, because it is true! She keeps scolding a bit, and this bothers me very much. I may get to N.Y. in March—if not then, probably later on—and then you will be able to see for yourself how healthy and sober I am keeping! This weekend is Carnival in Rio. I wished I had been there Sunday night to see the samba schools. Lota has bought herself, behind my back, a new blue sports car, and says the little boys run after her shouting "Grandma!" at her. The outlook in [Brazilian] politics looks pretty grim, if *Time* has it right. I do hope she will come here in May, but I'm afraid she won't . . .

To James Merrill

February 22, 1966

I received your letter of February 1st yesterday in an envelope of mail forwarded by Lota from Rio. You see where I am—well, I finally decided to spoil my record as the only American poet (except you, perhaps?) who doesn't teach, and took on Roethke's old job here—it is given to a different poet every year now, or even every "quarter." They have a strange 3/4 system, and I am here for the last two of them, that is until June. I tried to let my friends know my address but couldn't seem to write everyone before I left Rio; I'm sorry.

I did get your book [*Nights and Days*] shortly before I left and although I didn't write to you about it I sent a sort of "blurb" to Mr. Harry Ford and I had an answer from him saying he liked it and thought you would, too. I hope you did? It couldn't have been simpler, but I thought I'd leave the adjectives to others, and I said exactly what I meant . . . I thought there were some superb things in it. Some I think I had already commented on to you before, and I liked the whole book. And—well, I won't repeat my blurb, except to say that it is a rare and great pleasure when a friend keeps on writing better and better. I see you are up for the National Book Award, and I hope you get it.

Trying to teach verse-writing and something called "Types of Contemporary Poetry" (it gets called other things, too), when one has never faced a class in one's life, is rather staggering, and I found Seattle, the West in general, and all these academic people pretty staggering, too, at first, but I am enjoying myself more now. Henry Reed is teaching here, too, and I have always admired his poems and like him very much too, now that we've met . . . I keep running out of things to say to the writing class, and either they don't write at all, or the six or eight bright ones write so much I can't keep up with them. The problem all along has been iambic pentameter—and I think I have mastered that at last by way of the BLUES. I even sang them the last two lines of some of Shakespeare's sonnets. But tomorrow I'll see if their 10 lines of iambic pentameter scan at last.

Lota's park is finished, more or less, but now she is president of its "Foundation" for five years. This will mean a little less work, I hope, and much more time in Petrópolis, and perhaps we may even get away for a trip to Europe this year or next—I don't know. We both want to go to Greece badly. Oh dear, it is Carnival now in Rio. Sunday night was the "samba schools," the night I always attend, staying up all night and driving back to Petrópolis at dawn. Here I played a few samba *discos* I brought with me and samba-ed about all by myself.

To Dr. Anny Baumann

March 19, 1966

. . . The only reason I want to get to New York really is to see you for an evening if possible—but perhaps I can write to you sometime just as well. As you may have gathered, I have been rather upset by many problems in Brazil lately—well, not lately exactly, because they have all gone on since Lota took on the job. *Of course* I am going back, and of course I mean to live there, and with Lota, forever and ever. I couldn't possibly think of anything else—but I feel that lately I have not been managing my life there, and with her, as well as I should and I feel I need advice, quite badly perhaps. She has been wonderful about writing to me—I don't see how she does it. I called her last night but the connection was bad; I woke her up (I'd canceled the call, but they put it through anyway). However, I think I managed to convince her all was well with me and that I was quite sober, and that was the main thing.

She writes me that she wants to write you explaining the various things that went wrong . . .

I could *tell* you, more easily, and shall, if I do get to N.Y. But it is true that Lota has unfortunately fought with a good many people and made a good many enemies. In most of her battles I am completely on her side, but I think she often antagonizes people unnecessarily and has been getting more and more abrupt and rude with everyone. This is all only too natural—but I hate to have her lose some of her oldest friends (some of whom call me up and weep over the telephone) and she has also been increasingly hard to live with. I feel like a skunk saying this much—but I felt I had to get away for a while, and I think it has been a good idea.

Everyone here is so nice and *polite* to me, compared to my darling Lota, I can't get used to it, and I think I am getting a swelled head! None of them can compare with her in any way at all, naturally—but they do treat me better! I feel many of my Rio troubles are mostly my own fault. I am just not very good at handling bossy people, and Lota is bossy, of course—and I let her be for years & years, then suddenly find I can't stand it any more. Which isn't a very nice aspect of my character. But Lota is *like* Carlos. This is the universal complaint about both of them —not just mine—*no one can talk to them.* And it is very hard to live with someone you can't talk to about things. Really, it is too much when (I'll give one example only) Lota bangs on the wall to make me go to bed, when I am entertaining an American visitor! That's the kind of thing I mean, and I know she is protecting *me*, but I hate it; the visitors misunderstand—and I can't explain to Lota, because she won't listen. I think I must still be feverish to write you this, and I am afraid it will strike you as merely childish. However, I assure you it isn't at all. I would never have taken this job if I hadn't felt I HAD to get away.

To Arthur Gold and Robert Fizdale

April 23, 1966

. . . Last night, after having been taken on a long sightseeing picnic most of the day, I decided NOT to correct papers but to read *In the Courts of Memory* [by Lillian Moulton de Hegermann-Lindencrone]. I'd just barely begun it—and so I read & read and read, and it couldn't have been more unlike teaching verse-writing in Seattle, Washington, and this morning I woke up and finished the book by 9 a.m. I see what you mean about it, and won't you *please* send me Volume II if you ever run across it?—at least I think her other book, *The Sunny Side of the Diplomatic Life*, must go on from where this one leaves off. She hasn't even become Madame L. de Hegermann-Lindencrone yet. What an absolutely idiotic life and how fascinating it all is—her *clothes*, for example—and that song,

"Beware!" written by Longfellow and her husband, I think—although poor "Charles" certainly gets short shrift. I got so I knew when "Beware!" was about to be sung next. I MUST read Volume II. If you have never found it, perhaps we could get it through one of those finding services? I have given excerpts to Henry Reed over the telephone and he can hardly wait to read it now, too. He is an opera expert and so he'll probably enjoy it even more than I did . . .

I am so sorry I didn't get to your performance in L.A. Furious, in fact, and still paying hospital bills, and still feeling tired. I had "Asiatic Flu Type 1–A," they think—the worst. But why didn't those silly friends of mine go? I am not going to forgive them. Yes, Mrs. A. Huxley is the one who wrote that book. But Isherwood had been invited, too, and it all sounded very pleasant . . . Laura Huxley used to be a concert violinist herself. What's the matter with Hollywood people?

Sylvia Marlowe gave a harpsichord recital here two or three weeks ago, and gave me all the latest New York news. I am not sure whether I'll be getting to New York—it is such a long way home however I look at it. I want to go by boat so I can collect my thoughts and possibly do a bit of work of my own . . . I like some of my students very much, a few of the older ones and a few of the very wild ones, but feel I am off poetry for some time now. Lota and I may get to Europe in the fall . . . I hope to leave here around June 10 and make it back in a month or so, if I don't get waylaid in the Panama Canal.

To Marianne Moore

Rio de Janeiro
June 23, 1966

I am a disgrace to my family and profession, not having written to you for so long. It doesn't mean that Lota & I don't have a picture of you in each "residence" & study, or that we don't talk about you a lot, and explain these pictures to everyone who calls. And yesterday I cheered Lota up very much by telling her a story of yours I remembered from long ago, about how you and your mother went to see the famous elephant at Coney Island, when I believe *you* had been feeling depressed. I got back here and found Lota in a very bad state, from overwork on her park.

I had meant to come back by way of New York, mostly in order to see you and your new apartment (although of course I never wrote you this), and then I decided I had been away too long and that it would use up too much of my money. I've studied your floor plan and it looks like a very nice apartment. Isn't 9th Street one of those that still has trees on it, too? Well, I hope to get a trip to the U.S.A. sometime next year, with luck.

I had a small legacy from an aunt, and Lota has 45 days' leave of absence—so we are leaving this afternoon for a month or six weeks abroad, first a week or ten days in Holland, and the rest in England. We've never been to the Netherlands and Lota has never been to England & I think it is about time she saw London . . .

When I get back I am supposed to begin work immediately on a book of prose pieces—a sort of grab bag book—about Brazil, with which the Rockefeller Foundation is kindly helping me. It will mean taking some more trips, too. I hope to go down the Rio São Francisco (on a sternwheeler), and perhaps even the upper Amazon this time . . .

Oh how I wish I had three nieces to help me with my letters—not to you, but business letters. How does one manage? This is the result of being an only child.

Teaching—well, I'm afraid I haven't space nor strength to tell you about that—but I did like many of my students very much. I also liked the scenery round about, and especially Namu, the killer whale—maybe you read about him? I was opposed to *keeping* him, however. I went to see him a good many times and just before I left took a Canadian aunt and cousin to see him, too, and we were all upset because he did seem sick—then shortly after that the poor beast died. He was absolutely beautiful—dazzling white underneath—and would roll over when they scrubbed his back with a long squeegee—like an enormous marine Tobias. (Who still flourishes, age 15—but is awfully lonely up in the country. He does have a Siamese companion, though, and they sleep in the same basket.)

This is all for now but I'll go back to being a fairly good correspondent again.

To Dr. Anny Baumann

Rio de Janeiro
September 1, 1966

I am writing this in great sorrow. I really don't know what to do any more. I tried to tell you some of this by letter & on the telephone, and you said then that of course Lota was under "great stress"—which of course I've known only too well for over five years now, and I DO try to make allowances for. There are many many complications—half my fault, no doubt—but all I want to say at present is this:

While I was in Seattle there appeared an article about Antabuse . . . I found it so interesting I even went out and bought an extra copy and sent a clipping to Lota—but she didn't get it . . . Well, the gist of it was that Antabuse is regarded as a "punishment" remedy (heaven knows why—since anything of the sort would seem to be)—but the important point was it said that it produces "despondency" in the patient, and also that there is now a new drug on the market that does not have this effect.

This may all be a lot of nonsense; I really don't know. But I thought it was worth finding out about. You see, poor dear Lota has such an obsession about my drinking (which is of course entirely my fault and which I can't forgive myself for) that during some stretches she has even been almost physically forcing me (this was before I went away) to take one of the pills, a whole one, every day. I was already pretty "despondent." If this piece of journalism is true, no wonder I was getting even more so.

I ran out of Antabuse about 6 weeks before I left Seattle, and I didn't want to go to a doctor there, so I went without—and I had no trouble at all. As I think I told you, only three people there that I know of knew anything about my problems and they can all testify to this, if necessary. In fact I did not miss one single class because of drinking—and that's much better than anyone can say of any of the other poets who have had that job before me. Lota will simply not believe any of this. She has told me, and friends here, too, that I "spent 6 months drinking" in the U.S., and that I go away from her just to drink—when the opposite has almost become true. I have much less trouble when I am away from her, and it is the only time I ever can enjoy myself. She keeps saying (1,000s of times now): "It is just a harmless *salt*." Well, I know perfectly well that if I take one whole pill I can't take a drink even eight days later—I know because I've tried & got very sick. It is true that in the past I *have cheated*— particularly the last two or three years when things have been going rather badly and the strain and boredom of life in Rio got on my nerves. But I really do not LIE. I think the only times I lie about drinking are when I have already started. Lota wouldn't believe I really had "flu," etc., either, so I am glad I had you send those reports. She still seems very angry that I went away in the first place and won't let me mention Seattle, tell her anything about my work, etc. etc. A lot of this is my own fault, no doubt, and it is awful to think what I have done to her—but she really has things very much out of proportion, and I just don't know what to do about it. She doesn't seem to realize that I have perhaps grown up a lot (!—about time) in the past 15 years, and can really manage pretty well on my own, and stay sober about 98 percent of the time. I know I can, because I DID.

I know she wrote you about this before I came back—she told me she did, but I have no idea what she said, or if she has heard from you yet—I think not. I am sorry to write such a silly-sounding and dismal letter, but I am at my wits' end and can't enjoy life here at all. I was hoping things would be better when I came back—and after all, I came back because I *wanted* to. I had offers of other jobs, and could even go on a reading tour—6 weeks—for $12,000 (believe it or not)—and turned this all down because I wanted to come back to live with Lota. She won't believe anything I say—or what anyone else says, either, I gather from some of her friends—any longer.

She has had an awful time with the park and the new Governor— and it is even worse now. She did take about two weeks off—then had to come back to work instead of taking a month off as she had planned to do. I can't understand all the details—but I do know she has fought with many people, and is in dreadful shape, physically. I am terribly worried about her but *cannot talk to her*. No one can. She has dizzy spells all the time, even falls down—her medical doctor here (in whom I have no faith whatever) always talks about the liver or the gall bladder and keeps her eating macaroni and gelatin and recommends a certain kind of mineral water. I did suggest to him that perhaps the dizziness came from her ear trouble (she has really grown deafer, I'm sure) and he said no, it was all "emotional" and departed with a dirty look—so I don't know what she must have told him!

I AM TAKING THOSE PILLS—3 halves a week.

If you received her letter and haven't written her, or plan to write her—I wish you would not tell her I am writing this to you, but reassure her, if you can, that the small dosage *is* enough—or give her the name of the new drug for me to take, or something. I'll really do anything I can at this point, to try to help. What she needs—the doctor agreed with this much—is a vacation away from this mad country where she feels everyone has betrayed her in some way (and I agree with some of it—but I don't believe she has any idea of how violent her manner is, or how she really frightens me). I would like very much for us to go to Europe for 6 weeks or so in October. We could go to London, and visit in England, where I have several old friends. The only pleasant times we have had together since this job began were the four weeks we spent in Italy two years ago, when at last she stopped talking about the park and the people she has fought with. If you could just reassure her about me, a bit, *somehow*—and suggest a vacation—with me, if possible, or without—it might help some. I don't know. I know I can't endure the situation much longer and I am terribly worried about her health, even her sanity. I could even get signed papers from the university about my good conduct—idiotic as it sounds! In fact, the secretary of the dept., a very good friend now, who knew *all*, told me: "You are the soberest poet we've had here yet." This is God's truth.

[P.S.] I am sorry to write all this—perhaps you can make her *lay off* me a bit. (I know a lot of it is my fault, but I *have* changed.) You had better not answer this, please, because she opens my mail. I was six weeks *alone*, in England, two years ago—I had no trouble at all then, either.

Petrópolis
September 25, 1966

This will be rather messy, I'm afraid—I've lost the knack of this old machine I keep up here, and it isn't working very well, either. Lota told me a few days ago that she *had* heard from you, but I don't know when, or what you said, or whether it was before or after I wrote you a rather hysterical letter from Rio. I'm afraid I still feel the same way, although it is true she *has* let up a little bit on nagging me about the Antabuse. But she is really awfully sick, I think, and I don't have the faintest idea what to do for her, really. She has had one blow after another in that park—feels deceived, betrayed, disappointed, etc., all around—and I am on her side in most of it, as far as I can understand it—but she doesn't seem to realize that her increasing violence and rudeness have made things much worse for everyone. (I feel there's no point in concealing what I think is the simple truth.)

Of course at the moment she blames an awful lot on *me*, if not everything, and this makes it very tough. At the same time she does realize I just had to get away; I felt I was just deteriorating, and rapidly too, after those years in Rio. She suffers from vertigo—maybe I said this before—even falls down, staggers, etc. & says it's all "emotional." Well, we've seen the doctors we know—the medical one thinks only of the LIVER, etc.—the psychiatrist, the best (the one who studied with Melanie Klein), thinks *everything* is psychological—and I feel it's probably a bit of both. She won't eat; can't sleep; can't read; doesn't want to be left alone; but won't stop fighting with me when I stay with her, and so on.

I never felt so helpless and ignorant in my life, and unfitted to cope with my life or hers. You must surely know how a situation can get so that everything one does or says seems to be wrong, or is taken the wrong way. There isn't much point in writing you this, but I feel there is no one this side of the equator I can talk to or who understands me in the slightest if I try to. I wanted to get to New York just to see you, chiefly—but I was afraid that you, too, might not understand—and then I had hoped that things would be better when I got back, not much worse, as they are. The simple truth is that my darling Lota, whom I still love very much if she'd give me a chance to show it, has been simple hell to live with for five years now—and I am not exaggerating. Everyone has found her "difficult"—and no one else lives with her all the time the way I do. The work is a sort of obsession—and I seem to have got to be one, too—and I am not very good under these prolonged strains and don't know how much longer I can hold out, really (& some of it is my fault).

Well, the plan at the moment is to go away for a trip, just to the Netherlands and London (where she's never been) and visit some friends of mine I *think* she'd like, in Sussex, etc. She has 45 days of waiting to put in, because of politics, as usual, and I am a great believer in the old-fashioned idea of a "change." But I feel rather hopeless, really, and sometimes think the best thing I could do would be to leave Brazil forever. At least I know I can't face 15 or 20 years more of being made to feel guilty, etc. I'm determined to enjoy life a bit more, even if it *is* awful. Perhaps you could write me—no, she usually manages to get all my letters before I do, *coitada*; she is suffering & I'm *sorry* & I don't know what on earth to do, really.

[P.S.] I'm not much of an intriguer, but perhaps you could write me c/o the Leme Palace Hotel [in Rio]. We'd be going abroad, if we go, about October 10. I'm sorry to write such dreary letters.

Rio de Janeiro
October 3, 1966

I am feeling somewhat better now but Lota is in a very bad state, I'm afraid. I suppose it is what they used to call a "nervous break-down"—now I don't know what they call it. It has been a very bad stretch, however, and she feels betrayed and deceived by all the world. We finally went to an old friend of ours here—the analyst who studied with Melanie Klein—Rio's best, I suppose—and he has been able to do a lot of good, I think. At least every time L. sees him she seems much much better and calmer and nicer with me, at least, for 12 hours or so. I am not very good at holding up under prolonged strains, as you know, and this has gone on now ever since I came back, and some of it—the last straw or two—is undoubtedly my fault. However, I am feeling a bit tougher, I think—but it has been hell, that's all. I have great hopes that perhaps eventually and with this Dr.'s help things will get better—maybe better than before. I suppose a lot is my fault, because I crave peace and quiet so that I put up with things I don't like for years, and then finally start *resenting*—when it might be much better just to refuse, or fight in the first place. Anyway, L. is too intelligent not to see that some of the fault is hers, although this is the first time she has ever admitted it—and that's a big step for her. I wish I could see you—although I hate to be so dismal and foolish at this advanced age and with my supposed brains and talents—and that is one of L.'s big troubles, too. I think perhaps she never went through a lot of the disasters and betrayals that most of us get through somehow or other in our 20's or 30's, and that that is why she has taken everything so fearfully hard.

Two days ago, she did hear that the law about her "Foundation" will almost surely be passed—but even this didn't seem to change her mood very much, and of course I am afraid to mention any of these things to her. She won't *believe* in my interest or sympathy, and I always get everything all wrong, etc.—it is very difficult.

She has 45 days now in which nothing can be done at all, so she might as well take a leave of absence for a month, at least. We are now planning to go to Amsterdam (neither of us has been in Holland) the 9th, if we can get off . . . stay two weeks, then go to London for two or three weeks more. L. has never been there, and I have some nice friends we could visit in the country (Ilse Gross Barker is the wife—you may re-member my speaking of her, and your telling me her uncle had been a professor of yours). They are almost my dearest friends, I think, and both very soothing to be with, and I think that possibly a few weeks of Dutch stolidity (if they really are that way) and English stoicism will be good for Lota after all this Latin hysteria. WHY do they carry on so? I am so sick of it, and I think it exhausts L. without her realizing it, she is so accustomed to it. One of her best friends came last evening, supposedly to take her *out* a bit, etc.—instead of which he stayed until midnight, haranguing loudly. I could hear him through two closed doors. Poor L. can't sleep or eat & won't be left alone a minute—but all this does seem to be clearing up *a little*—and I do believe in a "change of scene"—it works for me, at least. I just wish I knew what to do—and had more confidence in myself to be able to do it. I seem always to do the wrong thing, alas. This doesn't need any answer—I very childishly feel the need of someone to talk to, I am so awfully isolated and helpless. Sometimes I think it would be better for me to leave Brazil—but I did come back because I wanted to, after all! Something else L. won't believe. Well—if we can get away, we'll see if things improve. I suppose we could be reached c/o Am. Express, Amsterdam, until the 28th, then the same, London— and I know L. would like to hear from you if you have the time.

To Ashley Brown

Rio de Janeiro
October 3, 1966

. . . Ouro Prêto was as wonderful as ever and my house—it is going to be a dream, I think, although it soaks up money like a sponge. I was finally invited to a tea party at the exclusive Domitíla's—if you remember her—and she did build a very nice small house and atelier *inside* the ruins of the Bishop's Palace—up behind the School of Mines. The yard provided by the ruins is huge—and she has twelve or so different views of the town through the ruined windows. It is a bit sad for my taste, although beautiful. I am hoping my house will be a bit more comfortable and cheerful.

Lota had her first automobile accident while we were there—not her fault; some crazy boys in a Volkswagen pushed her off the road, and she and Lilli (I wasn't along) turned over in her Interlagos (open car). They weren't hurt at all, thank goodness, but I feel that the shock of this has added to her general state of distress. The Interlagos is a very nice car, too—I like it, except we can't take any passengers along. Oh—very sad —Domício, our old driver—is dying, of cancer (he doesn't know it). I saw him and he asked about you. After my "flu" I took some injections at the local hospital and, before giving them to me, the nun *crossed herself*.

Today is election day and I suppose the senators are putting in Costa y Silva right now. There have been no "counter-revolutionary" disturbances here so far and I hope all will go off peacefully. I CAN'T understand the situation—no one can, as far as I know. Only everything seems worse, that's all . . .

To May Swenson

Rio de Janeiro
November 29, 1966

. . . The trip to Holland & England had to be cut short. Lota was just not up to it—in fact she has had a complete breakdown after the past six years of overwork, and is in bed in Rio, with a nurse, etc. We thought she was getting better and that getting away from Brazil would be the best idea, but it didn't work that way and we came back—the 12th, I think it was—meant to stay a lot longer. I talk to her on the phone twice a day and shall probably go back tomorrow or the next day. She sleeps most of the time, and the doctor—whom I like very much, thank heavens—thought I might as well get away and attend to business for a few days and get a bit of rest myself. The trip got to be pretty awful before I got us back here safely. (Please don't mention this if you write.)

. . . I love Amsterdam—a very cozy, completely bourgeois city. In fact, we both liked it a lot. In London I did manage to see a few friends (and [Cecil] Day-Lewis) and arrange for a book [*Questions of Travel*] to be published next September, I think. But what with that job [in Seattle], and Lota's being sick ever since I got back, I haven't done any work for a long long time. I read three back numbers of *Partisan Review* last night here. I didn't read, or write any letters, while in Seattle, or at least I read only what I had assigned. I saw a pretty good review of your work *en masse*, but not good enough. They haven't reviewed me at all and I'm dreading now that they might! (I believe they are *off* me.) . . .

Now of course I am very gloomy, and extremely worried about Lota. I do think she is all right, just exhausted. I really shouldn't write you this, I am not writing most friends about it—but feel sure of your sympathy, etc. Well, you must go to Holland if only to see the Rembrandts. And of course we'd be delighted to have you visit here—in all three of the "residences" we seem to have acquired. Don't work too hard!

To Ashley Brown

December 18, 1966

. . . We cut short our visit in England and came straight home again. Lota was getting weaker and sicker all the time. She has been in the hospital almost ever since, most of the time not able to have any visitors. It seemed the only way to *make* her take a rest. But tomorrow she is to be sprung at last and we are going up to Samambaia—for a good long stretch, I hope. I went up to Ouro Prêto for a while to see how the house was coming along—nicely, but oh so slowly.

I feel I should look up your friends again before I go, but I certainly shall get in touch with them as soon as Lota is feeling up to seeing anyone. As you can imagine, it has been a very tough stretch and I have not felt very sociable . . .

Yesterday I read your piece on Brazilian writing and thought you had covered it all *very well*—as far as I know anything about it! Of course I was very pleased to see my translations used that way. Vinícius de Moraes (gossip columns) has been in the hospital "reducing" for his next night-club round, but I'm afraid is already a bit out of style here, the public is so fickle (compared to the French, say). He had been for a long visit in Ouro Prêto, too—in fact tried to buy that house of Lilli's across the street—but was handicapped by not having any money to buy it with. He played and sang every evening at the hotel (they told me; I wasn't there)—but, sort of like Dylan Thomas, people sponge off him fearfully. Lilli is fond of him, said when he kissed her goodbye he asked her if she'd be his *next* wife (6th). Then he went to collect royalties in England—and apparently they did not materialize.

I have no news except that I am fearfully relieved that Lota is gradually getting better. At one point I thought we'd never make it back across all that ocean. She criticized London terribly (maybe it was her health) but even had *me* convinced that Trafalgar Square is ALL WRONG. But she enjoyed the Abbey, I think—as who wouldn't, it is just so awful—but wasn't well enough to do very much, really.

Now I must write to Mark Strand. I don't know how many letters from him have piled up while I was away and I feel guilty, but don't know why I should, really! I spent one nice day at Oxford—my old friend Joe Summers is one of the first few Americans at All Souls for a year. The first time he went to lunch *no one spoke to him.* Now he seems to have quite a few friends there, however—distinguished-looking old men, all unknown to me. He can go to meals whenever he wants, has a room, etc., but has only dined a few times. One of the Americans, however, dines there every night now, without his wife, who is threatening to divorce him.

This is a lovely letter of nice Christian gossip for you. If I don't make much sense, please just remember I've been frantic with worry for several months now—but I think everything is improving at last, and I am dying to get back to work.

To Lota de Macedo Soares

This is one of the few letters from EB to Lota known to have survived being delib-erately burned by EB's rivals. It survived only because, when Lota's library was being unpacked after her death, it fell out of a book. EB had addressed it to the hospital in Rio where Lota was having insulin shock treatments. The unidentified friends ("Sewanee" and "Adonis") apparently helped EB to cash checks and move belongings from Rio to Samambaia. Lota did not leave the hospital for good until February 1967.

[December 19, 1966]
Monday a.m.

Darling: I was scolded by everyone all around for having visited you [yesterday] and stayed too long, and I am awfully sorry if I overtired you. Joanna [the maid in Rio is] quite desperate about what to take you to EAT, so this p.m. I think I'll go out and try to round up a few more interesting items. It seems too hot to me for some of her heavier suggestions. Oscar [Simon] just called and said he was coming by to give me a *kiss!*

Sewanee's getting lots of money for me right now—will be back with it at two—then I'll call Adonis. But don't you think it would be better to have everything arrive *after* we get there? J[oanna] forgot to give me Mary [Morse]'s note about this until yesterday—otherwise I might have got it off on Saturday, I suppose. The next date M[ary] suggests is January 1st—oh well, I'll talk to Adonis shortly.

I must also go to the Embassy today and see about that contract.

I have not seen Décio [de Souza, Lota's physician] yet—hope to today or else tomorrow at three—but I CAN'T understand him over the telephone and we seem to talk at cross purposes. He doesn't seem to realize the boredom of hospital life for you, when you are not asleep, that is—but *I DO*, and think something should be done about it.

I wrote letters most of yesterday—done two already this a.m. Will I ever get caught up? I wonder. I even started a small poem called "Small Birds at an Airport." We'll see. I miss you dreadfully and hope you are feeling better. All my love.

To Dr. Anny Baumann

January 20, 1967

I'm afraid you thought I was drunk when I called you, but I really wasn't—just closer to hysteria or more hysterical than I have ever been in my life, and although I realized there wasn't much you could do or say all those thousands of miles away, it helped some just to hear you. I am afraid by now you are pretty bored with me and my neurotic friends, etc.—but I thought you liked and admired Lota when you were here and I sort of wanted you to know, maybe, that I wasn't entirely wrong in my complaints from Seattle. I felt at the time that you thought I was being disloyal and unsympathetic about her work, etc.—but as you can surely see now, it is all much worse than I thought, even.

I suppose the person closest is the last one to realize how terribly sick someone is—but things have been getting worse and worse for several years now, and that was one reason I decided to take the Seattle job—just to get away from the violence for a while—never realizing my going would have even more disastrous results—until I got back. The doctor—Décio de Souza—thinks this has been coming on for a good many years, probably. I was so used to Lota and saw her so constantly that it didn't hit me, really, I think, until we got to London—when I rushed her back as fast as I could. She had already been in a hospital here for a while, but did seem a lot better when we started out. She then went back to the hospital for insulin shock treatments—never receiving the full dose, I gather. She said something about "80 ccs"?—but of course she gets everything wrong now. The hospital was so awful, I thought it would kill her if nothing else did—so we tried Samambaia for Christmas, had to come right back, and now she is in the apartment with a nurse, Mary [Morse], the maid, sometimes another nurse, etc.—and I believe is kept asleep most of the time. I am not supposed to see her or get in touch with her in any way for at least six months—that's what Décio says. Like a fool I went to see the hospital psychiatrist, too, a most unsympathetic man, and *he* said "Two years"—if ever—or something equally hopeful. She has arteriosclerosis, which may account for some of the increasing bad temper over the past five years—or maybe I told you all this before, I don't know. She has had violent fights with all our friends except two —and it seems they all thought she was "mad" several years before I did. But of course I *got* it all the time and almost all the nights, poor dear. I *do* know my own faults, you know—but this is really not *because* of me, although now all her obsessions have fixed on me—first love; then hate, etc. I finally refused to stay alone with her nights any longer—she threatened to throw herself off the terrace, and so on. I am going to see Décio this p.m. for one more talk with him—but I suppose no one really knows. I still can't believe that this could happen to *Lota*, of all people. (And once in a while she speaks of it reasonably—but I haven't seen her for a month now.)

I tried a hotel for three days but finally gave up and came here—a supposed "rest home" (give me a boiler factory next time). I haven't a home any more—actually nothing but two suitcases and a box of old papers, all the wrong ones—and HOW to get the right ones out of the apt. is beyond me at the moment. I was going to start off on a trip on a river—for the Rockefeller book—but don't feel up to it yet. In fact I don't know what to do. I may ask for six months off the book and go back to the U.S. for a while. It is too lonely here now, and I can't write anyway, but might make some money by giving those damned *readings*.

I only wish to God I knew if they are doing the right thing. Her nurse comes here to see me once in a while and yesterday said she is staying awake more now, and eating more—but talks of me constantly, etc.

I have almost decided to try the U.S. thing—I don't know what is *right* really, and wish God would lean down and tell me—I hate to leave Lota like this, but it seems almost as if it were a question of saving my own life or sanity, too, now.

So that's the sad sad story, and I still can't believe any of it and think I've been in a mild state of shock myself for six months now.

I am not telling anyone in N.Y. I may come up. A few friends I've told that Lota was—is—very sick, and we met some in London, nice ones, fortunately, who told me very gently I'd better get her home *quick*, etc. I thought of putting her in hospital in England—but for once, she wanted to come back to Brazil.

And if she *does* get better—what then? I am terribly afraid the old Lota will come back—although Décio did wonders, at first. Well—we were very happy for ten years or so.

If you have *any* ideas—please tell me. The Leme address [in Rio] will reach me—the nurse will bring it over here.

[P.S.] Had a poem about Ouro Prêto in the Christmas *New Yorker*, I hear ["Under the Window: Ouro Prêto"]. I'll probably have to sell my beautiful old house, also.

February 26, 1967

It was wonderful to receive your most sympathetic letter of February 8th (my birthday, as it happened) . . . At last, at last, I think I have some good news to report, or certainly a greatly improved situation here. Lota stayed at that nightmarish clinic for two stretches, then went up to the country. Décio de Souza, the analyst, takes his vacation this month but will be back in two days now. After Lota, of course it was my turn. I'd held out pretty well against drinking for six or seven months, but finally caved in badly. I think the end of the trip did it, really. So then *I* went to the same clinic—I was away altogether about a month. They tried sono-therapy with me (Lota had a lot, and it seems, or something seems, to have worked miracles—I haven't seen her so much like her old self in years). But after three or four days of it, I developed the most spectacular case of asthma ever seen, haven't had one like that since I was a child—so they had to stop. However, it was useful in getting me LOTS of attention. I'm going to use the *clínica* as a chapter in my book—a chic touch these days, I think!

I hadn't known that Cal had been really sick again—although I had almost guessed, from his last few letters, that he was about to be.

Well, I came home two days ago—very wobbly, but all right other-wise. In fact there must be something in it. I have finished up two poems that had me stuck for years, and written a catalogue note for a painter friend from Seattle. (He'll be at the Willard Gallery sometime—Wesley Wehr—and I think you'd like his paintings.) One of Lota's worst symp-toms was a fearful jealousy of my "job"—so small, compared to hers, really—and all the mail I kept getting from students. Thank heavens, this all seems to have disappeared. I've never known her so reasonable, in the two times I saw her. She's coming back to see Décio the first—I'm here alone, with Joanna feeding me pills, orange juice, etc. It is fearfully hot, and Lota minds the heat much more than I do.

I am touched to think of poor dear Cal reading you my poem.

I like your address [in Jamaica] very much—Ochos Rios, Eight Rivers. There's a lovely expression in Portuguese for a spring: *ôlho d'água*, "eye of water." I've been trying to work it into one of these new poems. I wonder if you took that raft ride and I bet you did. I just received a magnificent new book from Cal [*Near the Ocean*]. Well, I hope to get out a big English edition next fall, and maybe a new small book of poems and translations in N.Y. Then the Rockefeller book, and now I've thought of a small children's book about Brazil, and have a wonderful illustrator—so if all keeps going well, I should be very busy.

I'd like very much to make a quick trip to N.Y. perhaps in April. I am having such complications with Houghton Mifflin threatening to "melt down the plates" [of her first two books]—that sounds very drastic. Will you be there then? I haven't mentioned this to Lota and shan't till things seem just right—but she does seem more reasonable, and also very much interested in this new "analysis." It would just be for two or three weeks. Well, we'll see.

I feel fine and more hopeful than in five years—but very wobbly. I keep thinking if I keep doing things I'll toughen up again. Tomorrow I shall try a swim, and make some mustard pickles or marmalade or something—our larder quite bare after this awful stretch.

Lota is very low first thing in the morning, they say—I only saw her afternoons—but gets better as the day goes on. She has certainly been through hell, the poor dear—and is so good about it, now it's over. But no one seems to have Cal's powers of recuperation—but his case is very different, I suppose—and hope.

My mother went to Jamaica on her honeymoon—I still have some little old "steamer trunks" with "Myrtle Bank Hotel" stickers on them. They also rented a yacht and went to funny places like Panama—but maybe the canal was a big new attraction then. I have a photograph of her at a cockfight!

I don't know whether Lota will work again at all . . . I'd prefer not at all, I think, but won't say anything. She is very much against Carlos Lacerda (& I'm afraid I'm with her there). He keeps writing her almost love letters, to get her back.

To Arthur Gold and Robert Fizdale

> Petrópolis
> March 18, 1967

. . . Our lives have been rather upset lately, but now we seem to be emerging from the woods at last. I also think Lota said she had had a letter from you—which probably she hasn't answered yet. Well, she was very very sick, two different stretches in a *clínica* here and is recovering now, but still rather slowly. I finally took to my bed, too, and went to the same *clínica*. Lota then got out and is convalescing up here at Mary's house—and then we stayed in Rio for a bit, but it is too HOT now, and now we've been up here for two weeks and I wish to goodness we could stay a good long time.

Lota had a real physical breakdown—nervous breakdown—from all those years of overwork and worry—and now I also wish I had not gone to Seattle, but it seemed like the best thing to do at the time. Her park —she did a magnificent job, but what's the use of working for any government, I wonder. After the last city elections the party in power has been doing everything they can to undo all she has done—not aimed at her personally (in fact, the new Governor offered her the same job *under him* and she refused it)—just politics. And damned shortsighted of them, since the park is extremely popular—two beaches crowded all the time —when it doesn't rain too hard—and bandstands, dance floors, *futebol* fields, a puppet-theatre—everything Rio needs. It's a city with nothing for the poor & what remains of the middle class now—nothing but movies, really.

Our big problem right now is what shall Lota do next? She's so used to being very important and working very hard that she is terribly lost without the full-time job, although she's on some committee or other. She is still very weak and depressed. Please don't mention all this when you write; her friends and I are all feeling desperate at the moment, but surely her brains and natural energy will get her through this bad stretch eventually. Everyone has been awfully nice to us.

Tomorrow we go down for two days to see the doctor and the dentist, and the tax people, then back up quickly, I hope. She has an open steel-blue Interlagos, THE sports car here—very pretty—and can drive again at last. She couldn't for a long time, nor write, even. She's also reading. I can get through anything as long as I can read, but poor Lota even lost that mercy for quite a while . . .

I loved the account of Marianne's & Auden's reading. I keep getting "pressurized" (as Lota says) to go on one of the reading "circuits." The idiots (it's the same agent Auden has) even call up long distance and say: "We can make you a nice piece of money, Miss B." but I still think I'd rather be poor. (Three poet acquaintances have ended their circuits in the hospital, that I know of.) When Sylvia Marlowe was in Seattle she said that was going to be the end of touring for her. I wonder if she'll stick to it.

Yesterday foggy and rainy, and no view to be seen. We entertained Alfred Knopf and a Brazilian friend for a rather unsuccessful lunch, I think. He wore a bright green tie for St. Patrick's Day, and he is going to get married here soon—the bride is 64, and he is 74. I told him the other famous marriage I knew of in Rio was Nijinsky's—did you know that? I read his wife's book when I was sick and there's a lot about Rio, when was it, 1918 or so—very funny now. Today we have a lawyer and wife to tea—to eat up L.'s old birthday *rocambole* I made (the 16th). She needs distraction and the weather has been so bad it is hard for people to come to the mountains. Brazilians hate rain like cats, you know . . .

Were you at that black & white [Truman Capote] ball? I wonder. I saw a very funny picture of Jerome Robbins doing the tango, apparently, with Miss [Lauren] Bacall, also Marianne with a white mask on. Please write Lota when you possibly can—she needs all the reassurance she can get these days. I feel of very little use to her, but she *is* getting better. I hope your tour was a great success. My, I'd like to hear & see some live music!

[*Addition by Lota in shaky hand*] Dearest boys: Just a billet-doux to tell you how much I liked your letter. Can not write more than that because still shaky and [out?] of the sanitorio 10 days. E.B. is undertaking a cure for all the nonsences and alcoholism she had this horrible year of '66. Affectueusement, Lota.

To Dr. Anny Baumann

Petrópolis
March 30, 1967

. . . I'd like very much to make a quick trip to N.Y. and Canada fairly soon. It would solve all my publishing complications in a few days, probably, too—but as yet I haven't dared mention this to Lota and probably won't be able to. She is still far from well, and something for her to DO is a constant problem, also her dreadful spells of melancholy, boredom, etc. She can't go back to the country life we used to lead and I can't seem to help her much. Now she has arranged to go to see the analyst one or two days a week, in Rio, then back here—but this cuts up our lives terribly and I hate to have her driving alone. It is an awful problem and I don't know what to do about it and just keep praying something will turn up.

I have so much work to do myself and have done almost nothing for 18 months or so now—just getting going again, because I am feeling almost myself again, thank goodness. I'm afraid my hospital letters sounded very strange. Well, it is over now, no more asthma, and the new drug, Flagyl, seems to be working beautifully. Also the analyst *is* helping L. a lot, I think. She isn't quite so obsessive about me and my medicines, behavior, etc. It was getting pretty impossible those last few years. Surely there is an important job for her to do here, but everything seems against her now & the park situation breaks her heart . . . Of course I'll go back to living in Rio again if necessary, although I loathe it. I am telling you all my troubles again—I have no one else to tell them to!—except once in a while I see the analyst, too—but he is not of much practical help to me, much as I like him.

It is absolutely beautiful up here now—the time of year I wish you could have seen. We are almost overgrown by jungle after years of neglect, but have a very good (so far) new couple. The woman even knows how to cook, somewhat, which is a great relief because I seem to have lost interest in teaching one more person the basic elements. The rains and floods have been awful.

Lota still can't concentrate—read or write for any length of time—but her temper has improved enormously and she is trying awfully hard, poor dear.

I had a nice letter from Cal in the same mail as yours—he sounds well for now. Yes, I have Marianne's last book and have written her about it. One thing I want to do is write up all my recollections of her over the years when I saw her a great deal—the 1930's & '40's—and when she was at her best. I have a lot of wonderful little anecdotes that I think I should write down for posterity, and hundreds of letters too.

. . . I hope you are well and that spring is coming there. Forgive all my personal woes—it has been the worst stretch of my life except maybe the first eight years of it. I almost did leave several times; there seemed no way out—but now I have hopes again.

Ouro Prêto
May 26, 1967

Lota is over at my old house, measuring the garden—I'll have a very large walled one. The house seems perfectly beautiful to me, although there is still so much work to be done and I seem to have run out of money, for the time being, at least. I must hurry up and earn some more and hope to be able to get some work done on this trip I am taking. Lota goes back to Rio, and I start off for the Rio São Francisco in two days. I think she is getting better gradually but still is far from being herself. She wakes up crying every morning, is very depressed by fits, and very bad-tempered, etc.—but still, I think I see a lot of improvement. I think this change has done her some good and at least the details of my house and garden have given her something else to think about.

I'm turning the garden over to her. But it is almost impossible for me to work in Rio at present. In fact both the doctors told me to come here *alone*, and take the trip alone—but since she really wanted to come here, I yielded that point. I am feeling so much better myself that I can take her troubles better than I could a while back. The weather here is wonderful now—cold and clear, and a full moon—also there are a few pleasant people who have nothing to do with her Rio problems, so that's all to the good.

The house was a rather foolish extravagance, I'm afraid—but at least the way the workmen are doing it, it will be good for another three hundred years! I have an old old man, sitting on the floor, weaving my ceilings out of fine split bamboo—like basketwork—then they'll be painted white—exactly like the original 18th-century ones. It is hard to find workmen skilled enough—but Lilli has done a wonderful job for me in general and I couldn't have undertaken it at all without her.

I'll be out of touch with civilization for a few weeks now—but I am looking forward to the sternwheeler and the river scenery—everyone says it is beautiful.

To May Swenson

Bahia
June 8, 1967

I am going back to Rio tomorrow and have to pack, etc., so this must be brief, but I did want to let you know I am still alive and your friend. I see news of you all over the place, it seems to me—readings here, readings there—maybe it is a good idea to get away from the college every once in a while . . .

We were both sick—L. much the sicker, of course—but now I really seem to see light ahead again. The long river trip I have just made seemed to act like a sort of eraser. I lost all track of time and distance—feel as if I'd had amnesia. I did it alone, thank goodness. Lota wouldn't have liked it a bit—in fact, after the first few days I think I'd have gone back except it was impossible to. Then it began getting a bit better—and now, in retrospect, and having spent three days here writing it all up, I am glad I did it. Oh (vaguer & vaguer) I went on a sternwheeler (made 70 years ago in the U.S.) down the São Francisco River—100s of miles of it, straight north down the middle of the country. I won't go into any more details since perhaps I'll be able to sell my account of it all to a magazine and then you can read it. It will make a longish chapter in my prose book, I hope. The Amazon is much, much more beautiful and grand. Though poor (as they all are) it seemed prosperous compared to the places I've just been in. I have never seen such human misery. I suppose India is much worse, but god keep me from ever going there . . . (Don't comment on any of these remarks, please! L. is very fond of your letters, and this kind of thing understandably makes Brazilians sad and angry, too. But I'll *have* to tell a lot of it in my "piece.") . . .

I found this picture I cut out for you ages ago, in one of my notebooks. The sternwheeler pictured is not the one I went on. Mine was considerably smaller—but you get the idea: wood, pigs, hens, a ram, a few hammock passengers (bring your own hammock) below—and a few, in my case only 15, cabin passengers above. We ate the animals as we went along —except that I stopped eating almost, and certainly didn't touch meat, after the slaughter of the big, gentle ram with curling horns. As for birds, the Amazon is a 1,000 times better—but still, a lot of white herons, an occasional huge gray-blue one, hawks, and tiny swallows, black and white—that popped into little round holes in the bank as we went by. And something like a cormorant. The gray-blue heron flew alongside, lit in the rushes, flew again, lit down again, etc., for quite a long way. I finally decided he or she was thinking we were after the nest and was trying to mislead the whole boat. The crew spent most of the time fishing over the sides—then we had fish for lunch. Everyone very polite and friendly—but such desolation.

The night I got here I went out to find something to read & strange to say found a copy of *Time* with Lowell on the cover. The *Time* man "interviewed" me twice in Rio—I didn't have much to say—but he didn't tell me it was to be about Cal. I gave him a list of names—yours included, naturally—and maybe I said what they said I said, but it doesn't sound quite right somehow.

To Harold Leeds

Rio de Janeiro
June 18, 1967

Thank you for forwarding Loren's note. In the meantime we'd exchanged another two, because I had thought I'd be getting to New York sooner than it seems I am going to—and even now I'm not sure when that will be. I'm working on a prose book about this country and always feel I must get one more section done, look up one more thing here, etc., before taking a trip away. Lota is much better, although it has been a long hard year—she is even starting a new job tomorrow, although she's not quite sure what it is all about yet. IF she likes it and gets going nicely, and IF I finish up a bit more work, I shall probably come north, to N.Y. for a while, anyway—even if it is summer . . . A Brazilian friend just came back from N.Y. and said she'd had perfect weather for a whole month—but people's, and races', ideas of weather differ a lot.

I wonder how our Margaret Miller is. You know, she wrote me several extremely nice and cheerful letters over several months last year—then suddenly stopped again. I have no idea why, of course. A little package came last Christmas and my spirits rose about her—only to drop again when I found it was a little French book I'd sent *her*, years ago. Oh dear, oh dear.

I hope your back garden does well. I recommend Nicotinea—or is it Nicotiana?—anyway, I had great luck with it in that sooty soil, and it smells nice at night, too . . .

[TELEGRAM]

June 28, 1967

DEAR HAROLD: ARRIVING MORNING JULY FOURTH. IF AWAY, PLEASE LEAVE KEYS WITH MAY SWENSON [23 PERRY STREET] OR SOMEONE AT 61 PERRY. GRATEFULLY, ELIZABETH BISHOP.

To Dr. Anny Baumann

Rio de Janeiro
July 3, 1967

I'm leaving for New York tonight. Hope to be able to stay at Loren's place on Perry Street. Wired Harold Leeds but haven't heard, but hope he got it . . . I am looking forward to seeing you so much, and hope you'll have time to see me soon.

However—this is because I am afraid of planes and realize I haven't made a proper will (something I shall do in New York right away). I have just made a holograph one that I think will hold up in the U.S.A.—if anything happens before I get the proper one made. I am going to ask you to do something for me and if possible keep it secret forever. I can't think of anyone else in the world I could either ask or trust. IF any of this comes about, you will find I have apparently left you $15,000. It is not really for you (there will be some other souvenir from me).

I want you to send it to a friend, X.Y. I am not sure what the address is now. She will need it *badly* and I feel a heavy obligation to her. Lota must NOT know of this. It would upset her horribly. I shall try to explain this when I get there—but if by any chance I don't—will you do this for me? Lota gets everything else, of course.

c/o Jane Dewey
Shadowstone Farm
Havre de Grace, Maryland
August 8, 1967

. . . This is really just to say thank you (once more) and to wish you a nice holiday. I am awfully sorry I have been such an extra-bad nuisance this last stretch. I do think things have improved a lot, however, and even dare hope that all may go well when I get back to Brazil. Lota's letters really sound better to me every day—even if she can't expect any action on the park for seven months more, and still hasn't started her new job —not her fault, however—she wants to. She did draw up a report for the Supreme Court—and that must have taken a lot of concentrated work.

Thank you for the prescriptions—probably they'll arrive today—but even if they never do I gather Jane can get anything she wants from the local druggist. He thinks she's a doctor, too, because she's called doctor—but it's for being an atomic physicist.

Yesterday I did say I might stay on until Labor Day, after one trip back to N.Y.—but I am afraid I really can't. There are several reasons why—but please don't jump to any of the wilder conclusions, will you— they are just sad and simple and I'll explain when I see you. It is too bad because I'd much rather be here where it is so beautiful, surrounded by all this green stuff and cattle (Jane raises Herefordshires along with being a physicist for the Army). I can work all day in peace and don't have to worry about food and house cleaning. However . . . I'll stay till the end of this week, or possibly another until her sister returns. It is all a great shame since she wants me to stay and I almost feel I should . . .

I am terribly sorry I have been so much trouble lately. Please don't think too harshly of me for it all.

I've done two whole poems, to my own surprise, and quite a bit on the book. I have to go back to do some work in the library, among other things . . .

It is wonderful how little the dog bothers me here. It is always better in summer, however—steam heat is what really brings out the dander. Also Jane now has an excellent maid who vacuums carpets all day long and that may have something to do with it, too! . . .

To Marianne Moore

61 Perry Street
New York City
August 18, 1967

Someone (could it have been Bob Giroux?) sent me "Crossing Brooklyn Bridge at Twilight," and I like it very much. I certainly didn't know that about Dr. Squibb before—nor many other fascinating details . . .

This rather battered postcard turned up in the papers I brought with me. The Brazilian soldier is a Naval Fusilier, always big and black and all dressed up. They have a good band, too—and sometimes blow big trumpets from the backs of white horses.

I'll pick up Loren's tray sometime. Meanwhile I'm here again for a stretch, and ALWAYS AT YOUR DISPOSAL, you know—just call me if you want anything.

To Ashley Brown

Of course I had every intention in the world of writing to you before I took off for New York, but as Lota has probably told you, I did it all in a great hurry, and neglected many things I should have done . . . I have heard from her about you several times now and know she's been enjoying seeing you. In fact in one letter she says, "Ashley has been so nice I'd like to do something nice to him" (her prepositions fail her in writing occasionally). I was trying to think of something to suggest—neither she nor Joanna are up to fudge cake, I'm afraid; she might pat the soles of your feet or something.

I thought I'd be coming up in October—lots of "business" going on then—but it seemed like a good idea to come sooner. I am just hoping Lota will be able to join me very soon—we don't know when, yet . . . I did go off to visit Jane Dewey and stayed two weeks, the countryside was so beautiful. I was feeling so lousy when first I got there—"exhausted," like you, plus a stupid concussion I had in Rio just before leaving. I'm still having dizzy spells from it—when I get in the sun too long, or when driving—especially on THRUWAYS. Heavens they are awful, aren't they?

I'm in Loren MacIver's studio. It hadn't really been lived in for almost two years so was, is, pretty dusty—but a convenient place to stay in. I know the neighborhood, have some good neighbors, and a few blocks away can see all the wilder aspects of the "Village" if I want to—but mostly prefer not to . . . I am so far behind with this BOOK—also have to work in the Public Library—oh dear, still not air-conditioned. I have seen one movie, *Blow-Up*, since I've been here, but must hurry up and get a bit more Culture. My publisher has now sent me all of Miss Sontag's works and I'm trying hard—think she knows too much for me, however—about Hegel and all the latest French Thoughts. I'm supposed to go to a big party for her novel next week—but again I am rather afraid of the dizzying drive to Connecticut . . .

To U. T. and Joseph Summers

Lota, having cabled that she was arriving at Kennedy Airport on Sunday, September 17, was met by EB and taken to 61 Perry Street looking "very sick and depressed . . . We were both extremely tired and went to bed early." EB was awakened the next morning by hearing Lota "upstairs here around 6:30—already almost unconscious." She had taken "an overdose of sedatives" during the night.

EB phoned Dr. Anny Baumann, who immediately called St. Vincent's Hospital and then phoned EB's friends and neighbors, Harold Leeds and Wheaton Galentine, who got there "in about 5 minutes." Lota had lapsed into a coma in which she remained for a week. In the hope that Lota would recover, EB delayed notifying

her family in Brazil of the attempted suicide—a decision which created misunder-
standing and recrimination. While Lota still remained comatose in the hospital, EB
wrote to her close friends, the Summerses.

September 23, 1967
Saturday p.m.

. . . It is very bad, I'm afraid, and please forgive me if I don't make very much sense. Lota came up last Sunday—18th? [September 17]— the plane was three hours late, and the minute I saw her I knew she shouldn't have been allowed to come—in fact I think I'll go back to Brazil and shoot her doctor. Anyway—she was exhausted—we passed a quiet afternoon, *no cross words or anything like that*—but I could see she was in a very bad state of depression and [I] didn't know what to do, really, except try to get her to rest. Well—sometime toward dawn she got up and tried to commit suicide—I heard her up in the kitchen about 6:30 —she was already almost unconscious. I thought she had taken Nembutal since she had a bottle of it in her hand—but later blood tests showed only Valium, I think. I'll not go into details except that within about 20 minutes—I don't think it was much longer than that—we had her in the ambulance and off to St. Vincent's—and they were giving her oxygen on the way there. —I never thought I'd be glad to see three cops in my bedroom but I certainly was. She has been in a coma ever since, but now they think she is *probably* going to live—although still unconscious she has opened her eyes and moved her arms and legs a bit, etc. St. Vincent's is the best place in the world probably for this kind of thing, thank God. —I haven't seen her yet—my doctor calls twice a day and this morning the news was that she seemed to keep on showing "improvement." —I may be able to see her tomorrow—although she recognizes no one of course; can't speak, etc. If her heart holds out, they think she will pull through.

I'm just stunned, that's all—this is so totally unlike the Lota of the last 15 years of my life with her.

Everyone has been awfully kind—but so many telephone calls I finally went and stayed with a friend down the street [May Swenson] for two nights—she will come and stay with me here, too—got a cot—because I dread the nights.

Thank god for our wonderful doctor.

I'm afraid Joe found me very nervous [on the phone] and unlike myself—but we have had a very bad year; I didn't want her [Lota] to come unless she was really well—and I feel now I had a certain premonition—I know I had—I have been feeling panicky ever since I got here and couldn't work, just wanted to drink, etc.— That's all for now —I wanted to tell you and please forgive my sounding hysterical— At least today I can write and read better, etc., and I have some HOPE.

I don't think I even thanked Joe for, or even noticed maybe, his beautiful little [George] Herbert book—I see it in all the shops now, too. Before Lota came I did read his introduction and thought it a beautiful job—I've been reading some of the poems again, too—some even help a bit, I think.

I'll answer your letter properly when I feel a bit better and really know Lota will get better—but oh how one dreads the next few weeks and months. It is awful—to love someone so much and not be able to do the right thing or say the right thing, apparently. One thing—I think she came because she wanted to be with me, anyway, no matter what—even if she had this in mind. But that idiotic Rio doctor! Wait till I get my hands on him. I even cabled him before she came—had written three times—not a peep . . .

Forgive me, my darlings—I'll write when I have any news . . .

To Rosinha and Magú Leão

This telegram to Lota's relatives living at Petrópolis was the first news to reach Brazil of Lota's collapse and death. EB sent it shortly after Dr. Anny Baumann came from the hospital in person to tell her of Lota's death that morning.

September 25, 1967

LOTA ILL SINCE ARRIVAL. DIED TODAY. TRYING TO TELEPHONE YOU. ELIZABETH

To U. T. and Joseph Summers

September 28, 1967

Lota died Monday morning sometime without having regained consciousness. That's about all I have to tell you now—Tuesday was taken up with all the arrangements necessary for sending a "body" (oh god) home to a foreign country—very complicated—and now I have just talked, forever, it seems, to the Brazilian Consul here (very nice, although I don't know him—he seems to have known Lota)—about what to say for the newspapers, etc. This is all a great waste of time because I gather it was in them all already and god knows what they said. However, we did our best and it may help some . . .

She was a wonderful, remarkable woman and I'm sorry you didn't know her better. I had the 12 or 13 happiest years of my life with her, before she got sick—and I suppose that is a great deal in this unmerciful world.

I just want to repeat (maybe) I was with her for only a few hours, actually, and there was no quarrel or discussion of any sort. I know of N.Y. gossip already so am dreading all this kind of interpretation. In fact her letters had been full of plans for our future together—although knowing her so well, I could see she was still very sick and trying to force herself to sound that way. Oh WHY WHY WHY didn't she wait a few days? Why did I sleep so soundly?—why why why—I can't help thinking I might have saved her somehow—go over and over that Sunday afternoon but honestly can't think of anything I did especially wrong—except that I have done many wrong things all my life. Please try to keep on loving me in spite of them, won't you? I am clinging to my friends desperately.

I wanted to go down with her but the doctor persuaded me not to— the Macedo Soares clan is very big and very famous—and I'd just be in the way. I shall have to go as soon as I feel a little better, of course—but I'll keep in touch with you . . .

To Ilse and Kit Barker

September 28, 1967

Lota died sometime Monday morning—I seemed to know this by instinct all that day but wasn't told until that evening, when Dr. Anny came personally to my friends' across the street. I was having supper with them, although I already knew in my heart she was dead. They have been angels to me.

That's all I can say now. Tuesday I got all the arrangements made —she will be flown back tonight, get to Rio tomorrow a.m. I wanted to go along too, of course, but Anny persuaded me it would be better to wait . . . Getting a "foreigner" back home in a coffin involves a great deal of papers, etc.—the undertakers (Anny's) do most of it . . .

There's nothing more I can say now. I have no idea what to do with my life any more, but I suppose with time things will somehow arrange themselves. Many wires from our best friends in Rio.

If you have written—don't worry—I'll cherish every word, even if too late. Forgive my burdening you—I wish I could talk with you, or rather just be with you and not talk, I've had to do so much talking the last ten days.

I'm only sorry you didn't know Lota when she was well. I had at least 13 happy years with her, the happiest of my life. I am just trying not to blame myself for all the wrong things I know I did. She was a wonderful, remarkable woman—and no one will ever know what really happened. She did have the best possible modern care—that and the fact that she came and *wanted* to be with me, anyway, are the only comforts I can find so far. But oh WHY WHY WHY didn't she wait a few days?

My dearest love to you and forgive my telling you all my troubles— but I think of you as my dear friends and think you would want to know and feel quite sure you love me, thank god, with all my faults, even.

To Maria Osser

Maria (Maya) Osser, a well-known Polish-Brazilian artist and architect, designed the house of her friend Mary Morse in Samambaia. She was also a close friend of both Lota and EB.

October 2, 1967

I was awfully touched—in fact I cried my eyes out later, something I hadn't done before—by your telephone call and offer of coming here to New York . . . Lota was determined to come, apparently, even against everyone's advice, and even if I knew from her letters that although she was trying very hard, *coitada*, she still was far from well. I simply couldn't write her NO—and in a way I'm glad I didn't, because she did want to be with me, at least—and that's about the only consolation I have so far. I don't think she had consciously planned this because she brought so many things—12 kilo bags of coffee, etc. We were together a few hours, really. She was exhausted, and sick, and very depressed. I think perhaps she felt some miracle would take place and she'd feel better the minute she got to New York. I'll really never know—and of course can't help blaming myself. I tried to cheer her up—had lots of lovely plans for her—promised we'd take an apartment in Venice next spring for a month or so—everything I could think of—but still feel I must have let her down badly somehow or other. *We had no quarrel*—everything was peaceful and affectionate—honestly; you MUST believe that—went to bed early, and of course I feel if only I hadn't been so tired and slept so hard I might have saved her.

The minute I found her—about 6:30 a.m.—(I heard her staggering down the stairs from the kitchen here, already almost unconscious) I got Dr. Baumann—she got Harold Leeds and Wheaton Galentine from across the street—and an ambulance and policemen, etc.—and I really think we had her over at St. Vincent's (just two blocks away, thank God) within half an hour. She was put in the brand-new wing, supposedly the very best equipped in the country for this kind of thing. Dr. B. kept in touch with the doctors at that hospital and called me every day, sometimes twice. For a few days there were "signs of improvement" and I hoped & hoped—but her heart finally just stopped, just a week after she went into the hospital . . . I never saw her again, except to identify her. I tried to find out what she had taken and how many—and finally she [Lota] said "Ten"—the last word she said before going into a coma. Her blood tests showed a lot of Valium—that's all I know so far—all I may ever know. If she had been younger, or in better health, she might have pulled through. But Dr. Anny says she might have had brain damage or paralysis—and you know how Lota would not have endured that. She was always impatient, my darling Lota—and finally, too impatient to live, I suppose.

Well—I have heard twice from Rio and a good many wires, of course—talked to Rosinha and Magú on that Monday night [September 25]. Already a few clippings from the Rio papers—I'm waiting for the mailman now, and dreading what he'll bring today. Her coffin got to Rio Friday a.m. Stella said many friends were going to the airport, "because she always liked people to meet her"—and the funeral was Friday afternoon. I asked to have her put in the tomb with her father . . . How Lota would have hated all this fuss, I know—but I wanted to do it that way—for my own sake, but also for her family, of course.

The saddest thing for me now is that I have never heard a word from Mary [Morse] (or Lota's doctor as far as that goes, but to hell with *him*). I know Mary must be suffering horribly and I had hoped that she would at last forgive me but probably she never will. She never understood me at all, anyway—and now I am horribly afraid that she is blaming me—thinks I didn't take good care of Lota, etc. . . . I am telling you because it is making me so terribly unhappy, I have to tell someone who knows us. I am very dumb about some things—this last year Lota told me Mary never *had* liked me—and since I did and do like her, even if I got drunk and was frightfully rude that one time (after 15 years of mutual forbearance and politeness, however)—this is hard for me to understand. Mary is so intensely maternal—you know she used to drive all the way to Rio [from Samambaia] just to pack Lota's bags for her when we went traveling. She could never understand, I know, that although my feelings were very different, Lota and I were extremely happy together in our own different ways—in fact I had 12 or 13 of the happiest years of my life with her, until that park started to go bad and people behaved so badly —and that is more than most people ever have, I think. I curse myself for going to Seattle, too, of course—but at the time Lota did not object —in fact went with me to have new clothes made, and so on—it was only later when she began to get sick (before I got back, I think) that she began to think of my leaving as just one more betrayal. I never meant it that way, God knows, and was terribly homesick and almost came home in midterm—but she would never believe any of this. I also bored total strangers with stories of the [Flamingo] park and photographs—and poor Lota finally thought I wasn't interested in it, or proud of her! However —those ideas seemed to have cleared up, from her letters—and she certainly said nothing about any of her old obsessions in the one afternoon [in New York] we had together. Forgive me for running on so. She had many friends here, you know, and everyone has been as kind as possible and done all they could. I still can't believe it is true, that's all—and can't imagine what I am going to do with my life now.

[*P.S. October 7*] I'm going down to Jane Dewey's farm for two weeks to try to rest a bit and even work . . . I'll go back to Rio as soon as I can to try to attend to business . . . I know Lota wanted to help provide for Mary's children, etc.—me, too, of course—but I can always manage. I'd like to hold on to the Ouro Prêto house if I can—but don't know yet if I can afford to or not . . . Please don't think hardly of me, Maya—I couldn't bear that. Much love to you and Vichek always. [*In margin*] I now have an awful feeling I wrote you ALL this before—forgive me if I did—it just shows how confused I am, I'm afraid.

To Ashley Brown

October 3, 1967

I don't believe you know, unless you heard in a roundabout way (in which case I think you would probably have telephoned—so probably *haven't* heard) the sad news about Lota. I thought of calling you but think it is easier on the whole to write. As you probably realized, I only came to N.Y. because the doctor there wanted me to get away—thought he could treat her better without me, also that I might have another breakdown myself, hadn't done any work in 18 months, etc. She wanted to come so badly, however, that instead of waiting six months, until December, as we had planned, she finally came [on Sunday] September 17. I couldn't say no to her cables—and I wrote and cabled the doctor over and over, and never got any reply. Friends wrote me they didn't think she was well at all. It was hard to tell from her letters—two or three good ones, then one very obsessive one, etc.

Well, she came—the plane three hours late—I saw at once she was very sick and depressed. We had only a few hours together that Sunday afternoon and they were thank heavens very peaceful and affectionate, and I tried to cheer her up with plans for N.Y., for Venice next spring, and so on. We were both extremely tired and went to bed early. Sometime in the night she got up and took an overdose of sedatives. I woke up and heard her upstairs here, around 6:30—already almost unconscious. Our dear Dr. Baumann went into action immediately, of course. My two friends from across the street got here in about 5 minutes—and within half an hour, I think, we had her in an ambulance, being given oxygen, and over at St. Vincent's, the nearest hospital—and actually, in its big new wing, the best equipped in the whole city for that sort of thing. She lived for a week, but never regained consciousness.

For a few days there was hope she might live, but her heart finally gave out and she died on Monday the 25th. I sent her back to Rio—where she was met by many friends, I gather—and the funeral was Friday afternoon the 29th. I asked that she be put in the Macedo Soares tomb in St. J. de Batista, with her father. (She loved him in spite of everything, I know.) I have just started to get letters and clippings—but already of course, last week, a good many wires from our Rio friends, & Lilli, etc.

I'll never know now exactly what happened, I suppose—it may have been a sudden impulse, or even a mistake—maybe she expected a miracle would take place and she would start feeling well the minute she got here. She was always too impatient, *coitada*. The doctor feels it is just as well now, since if she had pulled through she might have had brain damage or other effects—and you know how Lota would had loathed that. She would also have loathed all the fuss about a funeral—but I did it for the sake of the vast family, and also for my own.

I don't really know what my plans are now. Saturday I am going back to Jane Dewey's to try to rest up and work again for about two weeks, then back here—and then to Rio to see what I can attend to about our business there. I don't know how she left things yet, even, but shall hear fairly soon, I imagine. I don't know how long I'll have to stay in Brazil —or where I'm going after that, so far. I'd like to try to keep the Ouro Prêto house, if I can, but I don't know yet if I can afford to or not . . .

I am sorry to have to write you such sad news. I also am fairly sure that you probably didn't realize the seriousness of her condition, because even after the two or three breakdowns she had last year, she was always capable of putting on a good act with guests. She had threatened suicide—but that was over a year ago, I think, and I had hoped and hoped she was getting better and that we still had many happy years ahead of us. I was very happy with her—happier than I had ever been in my life —for about 14 years—until this wretched park business got so bad, really—and that is saying a great deal, I suppose.

[P.S.] The Brazil Consul & I decided to tell the press that it was a "cardiac collapse." One Rio paper has put it that way, at least, and it is true, more or less.

To Dr. Anny Baumann

c/o Jane Dewey
Havre de Grace, Maryland
October 11, 1967

. . . I had almost no trouble the last time I was here, but then it was warm, everything was open, and I stayed outdoors a lot. This time I find I can't sit in the living room or dining room for very long (because of the dog—and dog on the carpets) but he never comes into my room or this study of Jane's, where I work, so I can manage all right—but I am using more Isuprel than before . . .

Please excuse this letter if it is messy—I'm still not too good on the electric typewriter—although I want one for myself someday, I think— prose, at least, goes so much faster.

I can't even attempt to thank you for all your kindness to me lately —and, I think, ever since I came up in July.

I finally got a very short note from Lota's analyst saying he had done all he could to keep her from coming, and so had, I've found out now (maybe I told you), the famous neurologist he sent her to. He, Dr. Ackerman, wanted her to go to his sanitarium for a stretch (a very nice place; I've seen it) but she was *determined* to come to N.Y. I don't believe I can ever quite forgive these people, the analyst especially, for not *warning* me. I had been in a constant state of worry ever since I got to N.Y. (and now wish I hadn't taken his advice but stayed in Brazil, no matter what) and I had written him two, possibly three letters, without reply. Then Lota's cables got so pathetic I couldn't stand it any more. And you see she didn't tell me the truth—she wired once that the doctor "approved." It was then I sent him a long and really desperate cable, to see what he really thought, and again he didn't reply. Only one friend wrote that she had seen Lota two days before and felt she was in no condition to come—but I got that letter too late to do any good.

I can't help feeling that if I had been warned I might somehow have done better that Sunday—you weren't in town, or at least I thought you weren't—but surely I could have done *something*. This keeps on haunting me all the time, although what I told you was the truth—everything was peaceful and affectionate between us all that afternoon and evening. But oh—oh—if only I'd done something better, said the *right* thing, stayed up & watched her all night. I can't stop blaming myself for all the things I know I did wrong—in the past, and probably, without realizing it, on that Sunday.

I do want you to know that I had every intention in the world of going back to Lota, *with* Lota, and I hoped she'd get quite better and that we had many happy years still ahead of us. I really had no other thought in my mind. I try to remember that we did have thirteen or so happy years, at least—& remember her the way she really was . . .

To Marianne Moore

October 12, 1967

Just a note to say that I hope you are well and to thank you for all your kindness to me during the last few weeks—and please don't let Loren's basket, etc., worry you. Just let it sit there until I can get back & pick it up myself.

. . . It is very nice & peaceful here and I'll probably stay on until the 21st or 22nd. It all depends on what I hear from the Rio lawyers. I'm not yet sure when I have to return to Brazil. This is too far south to have brilliant colors, but the maple trees are all pure gold now, and there is also a dark, dark red tree—I think it's a beech but must ask Jane. It is such lovely countryside; I've always loved it. I am alone most of the time & take walks, read, answer letters, and today actually plan to get back to work—so it is a good place to be right now.

I imagine you watched all the World Series—well, so did I, or some of it. Jane's niece, who was here for two days, seemed to be a real baseball authority. (Of course I know much more, now, about *futebol*—that is, soccer.)

I do hope you are well and please don't overdo, and please eat lots and lots of nourishing food, and call dear Dr. Anny at the slightest cough, won't you? —It was so nice of you to come over that day and I shall never forget it.

To U. T. and Joseph Summers

61 Perry Street
New York City
October 19, 1967

. . . I meant to stay there [at Jane Dewey's] three weeks until this Sunday but got too much asthma because of her dog, and stayed only a week & a day. I can stay there only in the summertime, apparently, when the house is all open and I'm outdoors a lot. I don't like being *here*—or anywhere very much, at the moment—but I like that farm and usually get a lot done because I don't have to *answer the telephone*, feed myself, clean, etc.

Well, I don't know how long I'll have to stay in Brazil—there are three places [in Rio, Samambaia, and Ouro Prêto] to be taken care of, furniture moved, and so on, and some things shipped back here (I can imagine the Customs complications!) for me to use in some sort of place of my own—not furniture, but other items it would be cheaper to send than buy again. We had enough for three places, after all. Mary Morse has the country house and land—to sell—these are enormously valuable now—but will take a lot of time—and she is there for always; now has *three* adopted children, and also Lota owed her a lot of money (way back—a lot—but I don't know about that); I have the Rio apartment, and seven offices we owned, just starting to rent now; all our things in the Rio apartment, and all the "art," and things I bought for Samambaia, and all our books—about 5,000 at last count. What on earth I shall do with them I don't know. I hope to be able to finish my old Ouro Prêto house and *keep it*—certainly I'll have enough furniture and equipment for it now—but all remains to be seen. Perhaps I'll even have you to visit me there someday in that beautiful little 18th-century town—who knows? I have a few odd plans for when I get back—whenever that will be—but will let you know later if they work out at all. After November 1st, my address in Brazil is [the apartment in] Rio de Janeiro.

Right now I'm supposed to be doing my own WILL—have to make a new one immediately of course—but I am so overcome with Joe's speech, or essay, that I had to write him about it. I've only read me, so far, and most of Lowell; I shall read the rest in bed tonight. (Lowell had lunch with me, on his way to Washington for a committee on being nice to draft-card burners, I gather—he is to make a speech tomorrow. The big demonstration there is Saturday. Cal wanted to know about your piece about HIM—we are all so vain—but I told him I'd give him a report later.)

I think the beginning part about "meticulous attention, a method of escaping from intolerable pain" is awfully good—and something I've just begun to realize myself—although I did take it in about Marianne Moore long ago. (It is her way of controlling what almost amounts to paranoia, I believe—although I handle these words ineptly.) (Yes—the English edition [*Selected Poems*, Chatto] came yesterday—nice but no story ["In the Village"], and it looks so thin I think I must have cut out too much!)

October 20

A caller came then, a young man from Seattle I was going to have dinner with, so I didn't get any further . . .

I like what you say very much, Joe, and I'm going to volunteer just one or two suggestions or corrections—but you are the most accurate person on this fascinating subject I have read yet. Did I really say that about the faucets H & C? ["She sometimes feared her poetic inspiration had only two faucets, marked *H* and *C*"—i.e., for South and North.] I'm afraid I think it is quite funny, but don't remember saying it, and suspect you of making it up. Also my telling you I wouldn't read such & such books—well, that just sounds like my being rather rude, but I've forgotten what they were certainly—maybe this was at the University of Connecticut?

"In the Village" is *entirely*, not partly, autobiographical. I've just compressed the time a little and perhaps put two summers together, or put things a bit out of sequence—but it's all straight fact.

I like what you say about history & geography. There's a sentence in Auden's book—is it "Journal of an Airman"? something like that, and I can't remember the figures now; I should know it by heart. "If recorded history is——years long and the world is——miles away from the nearest planet (sun?), then geography is——times more important to us than history." That's all wrong, but the general idea. I didn't read this, however, until after I'd begun publishing poems—so can't say I was "influenced by it." I just thought, that's a silly notion but I think I agree with it . . .

Of course I'm amazed at the obvious reflection of Herbert in the "one tear" stanza [in "The Man-Moth"]. I'm sure you are quite right, but it had never occurred to me at all. I'm always delighted when people discover these things. I didn't even mind, because I suppose it is obvious, although I'd never thought of it consciously, when two different critics pointed out that "A Miracle for Breakfast" referred to the Mass. Well, I still read (or have begun again with your book lately) Herbert—he's the only poet I can bear these days, as I think I told U.T. . . . .

(Oh dear, "along with Mary McCarthy, Eleanor Clark, AND Muriel

Rukeyser"—for one year, if you want to put them all in! I had lunch with Mary two weeks ago—refused to go to the party for her—all the old *Partisan Review* "establishment" and friends of mine—but I didn't and don't feel up to parties yet. But I did want to see Mary, always prefer to see her alone, and we had a nice lunch—and imagine, she is now on her way to HANOI! I'm really pretty worried about her.)

The poem to Marianne Moore is based on a poem by Neruda— copied, almost—except that Neruda's is much more serious—and a better poem. I've forgotten to whom it is dedicated—a friend in Spain—and each stanza ends with *"Vienes volando"*—"you (or thou) come (comest) flying." I had a note saying this, to begin with, when it was first published, I think—then decided it wasn't important enough for a note. It is in *Residencia en la tierra*, I think.

(By the way—I had dinner with Meyer Schapiro two nights ago— he is as beautiful and fascinating as ever—lives right around the corner on West 4th Street.)

I studied very little with Kirkpatrick—and not very successfully, I'm afraid—but if you want to be exact, I began at the Schola Cantorum in Paris, with Kirkpatrick's old teacher, then took some lessons with K. himself in New York. I'm going to ship the clavichord back to the U.S. —it is badly in need of repairs—and TRY to take lessons all over again.

I did—do—like early Chirico—but "The Weed" was influenced, if by anything, by a set of prints I had of Max Ernst—lost long ago—called *Histoire Naturelle* (something like that) in which all the plants, etc., had been made by frottage—on wood, so the wood grain showed through. I'm perhaps saying too much—Lota always said I did—it was much better to keep people in the dark! But this has already been remarked on in that Twayne book, I think.

The "Songs" were for Billie Holiday, but very *vaguely*, and I left New York before I ever attempted to find music for them. I also like BLUES very much—no "fine collection" but do listen to them a lot when I'm "at home." No fine collection of anything. I taught my class in Seattle iambic pentameter after all else had failed by having them write blues— but this idea I got from Leonard Bernstein—a lecture of his I listened to, in Portuguese! in Brazil. He sings a couple of lines from *Macbeth* to a blues tune ("St. Louis Blues," I think) . . .

Well, no—I couldn't possibly live on my own income now—could only in the 1930s—but I've always been awfully lucky about handouts, grants and things, and so have gone on year after year in that way.

I plan to include in my next book, probably, the translations from Brazilian poets that I think came out best—or perhaps in FSGiroux's *Collected* next spring—but they are only four or five.

I use, or used, quite a lot of dream material, and one poem is almost entirely a dream—just stuck in a few extra lines—but I'm not saying which. (I'll tell you, just for fun, but please don't use it now. "The Prodigal" was suggested to me when one of my aunt's stepsons offered me a drink of rum, in the pigsties, at about nine in the morning, when I was visiting her in Nova Scotia.)

I wonder who the reviewer was who misunderstood "Manuelzinho" so—but then I've been accused of that kind of thing a lot, particularly in the social-conscious days—"Cootchie," etc., were found "condescending," or I lived in a world (I was obviously VERY RICH) where people had Servants, imagine, and so on. Actually, Brazilians like "Manuelzinho" very much. I've had several English-reading friends tell me, "My God (or Our Lady), it's *exactly* like that." And that's why Lota is supposed to be saying it . . .

If I've told you this before, please forgive me—but I'd like to have you know (I did write it to some other friends). In Lota's will, in the midst of all the legal Portuguese, she inserts a quotation from Voltaire—I think—his dying remark: "*Si le bon Dieu existe, il me pardonnera, c'est son métier.*" This and other things I have learned since makes me feel it was more or less premeditated—she couldn't face not getting well. She had asked one old friend of ours—and the same with another (dearest) friend, too, very unlike her to do so—if he believed in God, and when he said he did, she said: "Well, pray for me, Tamoyo." So my only consolation is that she did want to be with me, anyway. But oh heavens, it is still hard to believe, any of it.

. . . I have to PLAN—have even agreed to give some readings (I'll be needing the money) in the spring term here and there—only Harvard so far—but only if I can get $500 or $600. It is not worth it to me otherwise . . .

To the "Lowellzinhos"

While staying alone at the Lowells' apartment, EB drank too much vodka, fell, and broke her right arm and left shoulder.

> c/o Lowell
> 65 West 67th Street
> New York City
> Friday, November 10

I'll start a sort of thank-you letter to you both now while waiting for Dr. Baumann's Elsie to come & pick me up for X-rays. Excuse the capitals. It takes me so long to type correctly with one hand. Everything is fine & Nicole [the Lowell cook] has fed me splendidly & we got along nicely in our different languages. I saw Harriet [the Lowells' daughter] Tuesday & she was rather shy. Wednesday we had quite a long conversation . . . We discussed mostly the uses of mathematics, algebra & geometry in one's elderly years & I think I convinced her they occasionally come in useful. Nicole said I could invite a friend for dinner, so last night I did invite Margaret Miller & Nicole gave us a superb sole. I asked if she could make a Spanish *flan* (knowing M.M. loves it) and she just outdid herself with that & I feel I should pay you for an extra dozen eggs.

This place has been a godsend. So much more cheerful than Perry Street . . . I have used up all Elizabeth's five-cent stamps. I'm sorry, but it was so nice having a mail drop for a change I just wrote all my letters. I called Keefe & Keefe & find I owe you $105 for my delightful ambulance rides through the park . . .

Saturday morning

Well, X-rays fine. Dr. Carter said it was amazing how much faster I improved "at home" than in the hospital. I shall leave here Monday a.m., with Elsie's help, and pack at Perry Street. I am flying to Rio on Wednesday evening . . . If ever I do come back to N.Y. to live, I think I'll try to find a place up in this district. Comparatively much cheaper than the Village, I think, and oh, the joy of a doorman and a mail drop. I have cleaned your type, Elizabeth, and nothing—even putting all the books, upstairs & down, in alphabetical order—could begin to show my gratitude or make up for the stupidity of my behavior. Dr. Baumann bawled me out, and it got more & more monstrous with every visit. I think it was primarily due to grief & exhaustion. At least that started me off. Surely things can't ever get any worse. Anyway I do thank you both with all my heart. Welcome back.

To Dr. Anny Baumann

61 Perry Street
New York City
November 14 & 15, 1967

. . . *Of course* I know that my drinking & Cal's (& that of most of my N.Y. friends) are not in the least alike! And that his is only a small part, maybe, of the problem. However, what I wanted to say to you was that his wife & I, and two other very close friends of his, are all extremely worried about him, particularly as this dangerous season approaches. He just does TOO MUCH all the time & Elizabeth L. & I had a long talk about it the night they returned . . . That was apparently very strenuous—people and conversation constantly—and then that same evening he went off to "Poets for Peace" or something about VIETNAM & stayed up till 5 a.m., etc.—confessed to a hangover, had lunch with me down here & caught the plane to Harvard for three days of hard work, more & more people, parties & so on. Well, I do know he is pretty strong, when not sick, but one week of his present life would kill me. E. is really dreadfully upset about him & says she can't do anything at all, but wishes he would take a rest over the Christmas season, etc.—get away from the constant excitement, marches, demonstrations, drinking, and so on.

As you must know I love him, next best to Lota, I suppose—if one can measure love & affection or compare it—and since you are a doctor I don't think you'll think I'm being interfering to say these things. Two other old friends AND our mutual publisher have all said the same things to me. E.L. & I are also rather upset by the effect of all this on his recent work—done too fast, almost every day—and NOT the kind of wonderful workmanship that has made his reputation . . . But really, Anny—even for one with *my* hideous "pattern," as you call it—two or three big vodkas and a bottle of wine, alone, for lunch, is overdoing. And I'm afraid I've heard some rather sad stories about the late nights. Since you are a doctor, his now, too—maybe he might accept a warning from you—before he gets too high & stops taking his pills. Which is what he did in Rio—threw them away . . .

Please don't think I am trying to minimize my own behavior in any way! I am genuinely worried, that's all, and this time I am not just *trying* to think of something to worry about!

I was also very shocked when Louise Crane came to see me at the hospital. I hadn't seen her for six years, I think—and again I know her weight is mostly due to drink—she said so, as a matter of fact. On the 11th, my Perry St. friends [Leeds and Galentine] & I called on her & she already looked much, *much* better—said she had been "ON the wagon." You see, you see people in your office and not when they really get going, the way I sometimes do—and even allowing for malice, gossip, etc., some of the stories are very depressing.

But oh I wish you could do something about Cal. He has so much better things to give the world (as his wife said) than hasty reactions to all the pressures here in N.Y.

Harold Leeds tells me there was a N.Y. City "investigator" around asking the "super" & then Harold about what had been done with Lota's belongings. H. merely said they'd been sent back to Brazil. So they do have *this* address (I knew I gave it, and my name, too) for her—and the bill business gets more mysterious all the time. If ever I get it—of course it will come out of the "estate" eventually, anyway. I MUST PACK A LOT MORE. I do hope I've covered everything now and of course nothing can ever express my gratitude, Anny.

I'll write from Rio. Cal just called—9 a.m. from Boston, to say good-bye. He is so kind to me. Mrs. L. received a drama critic award yesterday so I must call to congratulate her.

To Harold Leeds and Wheaton Galentine

Samambaia, Petrópolis
November 23, 1967
. . . The arm is doing well. I wear a simple sling now—but am amazed at the various colors my elbow is turning. (And I still type one-handed,

as you see.) This place & house never looked more beautiful. It rained all the time in Rio, but here it has been heavenly as far as weather goes. The new couple here, with the maid, have helped a lot. We just made a cage for the two darling cats who are to go to Lilli (my Danish friend in Ouro Prêto). People who think cats aren't affectionate and don't remember are just plain stupid. Lilli has an Irish setter, but he is very gentle and she swears everyone will love each other. The couple didn't let my poor cats in the house (all peasants seem to be afraid of animals—and they do scratch the sofas—but Lota & I had put up with that for years). When I got here the poor dears rushed to their own bed immediately, then rushed to mine, of course.

What I am really writing about, only I seem to be stalling, is to try to thank you both. Only it's almost impossible. From the day I arrived until I left, I was nothing but a problem and a headache and it got worse & worse, and now I've left you with all those damned bags and things. All I can say is that I think I am somewhat in love with both of you . . .

I have seen various friends, the lawyer, etc. (I got to Rio just as everyone left for the weekend, of course.) Lota's sister is behaving in a really awful way, telling everyone many lies & so on, but so far I have managed to avoid her . . . The sister is already well known for lawsuits and general maliciousness—and Lota was clever enough to get certificates from *both* her doctors saying she was sane at the time she wrote her will . . .

It is just getting dark—almost 8—and the tree toads are starting to pipe up. The Siamese is in my lap, helping to type. This evening I plan to finish going over all the *discos* & see what old samba & jazz records —78s, etc.—some Louise Crane's—are worth saving. Please remember me to her & say I am never without my shoehorn . . .

There could never be nicer or kinder neighbors and I hope to see you both again not too far off. Now I have to stop & eat two poached eggs (which I shall poach myself, Joanna never having mastered the art) and a mango, ten inches long, huge, juicy, the most delicious fruit in the world. Oh do visit me in Ouro Prêto sometime & we shall stuff ourselves with them.

To Dr. Anny Baumann

Rio de Janeiro
December 5, 1967

. . . It seems that Lota's body arrived here with just the police report (which had to be received & signed by Marietta, the sister, as nearest of kin). This report said that death was due to bronchial pneumonia following an overdose of barbituates. Since you told me that only Valium was found in Lota's blood test—which (I believe) is NOT a barbituate—I ask you to please have copies of the blood test sent to my lawyer, Dr. José Barreto Filho, and the sister, both airmail & *registered*. You can see how important this might be. The police report was obviously based on my first statements to them, after I had found Lota with a bottle of Nembutal in her hand, and was never corrected.

From the 8th on, my address will be Ouro Prêto and I'll be leaving for San Francisco the 20th . . . I've gone down to 118 pounds but am keeping going, and *sober*, and maybe a week in Ouro Prêto will make me feel better. There are still a thousand small things to be done, and I have four days yet.

[P.S.] The sister has gone to such lengths that she had three people go to St. Vincent's Hospital in N.Y. to "investigate." It all couldn't be more unpleasant, but I expected *that*. I didn't expect to have awful troubles with Mary Morse, under the circumstances. The tale—natural, I suppose, but hard to listen to and deny calmly—that I did something so awful that day, September 17, that Lota committed suicide. If that were true, how could I possibly be here, I wonder—or still alive myself, even?

To Harold Leeds and Wheaton Galentine

December 5, 1967

I mailed you a letter—of thanks, mostly—from Petrópolis, on November 25th—but I since have had reason to think that at least one letter I mailed then didn't reach N.Y.—& maybe the whole batch was lost. Anyway, I'll write all over again. I am still in Rio but leaving the 9th for the address above [Ouro Prêto] until the 18th. Then I fly to San Francisco the 20th. The only address I have there so far is The Canterbury Hotel —even if I don't stay there, I could pick up mail there, if anything important comes along. There has been much to do, of course, and all very sad and unpleasant—but I have only four more days here & think I'll make it all right.

I do hope you have not been bothered by mail, etc.—just keep everything except important or personal-looking letters (you could send them to S.F.) until you hear from me again. I keep thinking of the many odd packages, suitcases, etc., I left behind me & I am terribly sorry to have been nothing but trouble for you both since last July. I hope very much I'll be able to return some of your infinite kindness, sometime—also be more like myself . . . I've tried to let everyone I can think of know of my changes in address, but a few always get overlooked—or high-school children want me to write them the story of my life, to read in English class—so you can open anything with suspiciously unformed handwriting & if that's what it is—throw away.

As I said before, only you may not have got that letter—I can never thank you enough for your kindness and generosity & everything else. I feel quite sure I wouldn't have survived at all without you. (And I shall dedicate something better than the poor HEN [poem, "Trouvée"] at least, sometime, to you, as one other small footnote of gratitude.)

I take my smoke machine [for curing] to Ouro Prêto Saturday—also one fresh fish (but the maid & I can't decide what kind) and a few chicken breasts, I think, in an ice bucket. I do have a couple of small presents for you you'll get eventually.

To Arthur Gold and Robert Fizdale

[POSTCARD]

December 7, 1967

I don't know whether you ever saw this night view of Lota's park ["Flamingo Park by Night"]. They actually have put up more of the lamps too. But both children's playgrounds—or at least the pavilions in them —have been turned over to the Tourist Agency! None of it bears thinking about. She worked so HARD. Going to Ouro Prêto & hope to make it to San Francisco for Christmas with friends. Hope you are being hand-pulled in carriages & sleighs.

[FIVE]

1968-1979

SAN FRANCISCO, OURO PRÊTO, CAMBRIDGE

Geography III, NORTH HAVEN, LEWIS WHARF

To Frani Blough Muser

1559 Pacific Avenue
San Francisco, California
January 4, 1968

. . . I can't remember what I told you of my plans—they were pretty vague. Anyway, I have had a young friend . . . staying with me & we have decided to try keeping house together for a while. She was married to a Northwesterner, is now divorced, and has a son aged 18 months—and wants to get away from her home town, naturally. So she came down to meet me here and we talked it over and decided to give it a try. She will be able to do quite a lot of secretarial work for me, which I've decided I've reached the age I need to have done—and also I discovered she had taken a course at some time in *haute couture* or something. Anyway, she shortened my skirts above my knees in a most professional way. She's gone back to see about her moving, pick up the child, etc. We looked at places and found a rather nice "flat" (as they call the two-floor, old houses—this is a top floor).

It's a "nowhere district" as X.Y. says—not quite *in* anything good, but almost—but has 4 bedrooms, 2 fireplaces, even a back yard—and the kitchen is certainly better than any I've cooked in for 16 years. The rooms are small, but well planned for our needs, I think. At least I can shut myself up to work at one end of it while she entertains the baby at the other—and it's very conveniently located, from what I know of the city by now. Well, I just couldn't seem to start living alone right away—and couldn't bear New York just now, and certainly not Brazil—so we'll see. I find San Francisco delightful—it has been warm and sunny. Today I went to all the "smart shops" in about half an hour—and it is fun walking around. I've seen my Irish friends and been taken to Chinatown—think New York's is better, however—and finally got around to writing notes to a couple of poets I know—or know of—at Berkeley. Do send along some "nice friends." I think I'll be feeling almost sociable again, once I get into that "flat"—between a laundry and a body works and across the street from the Cancer Society. *Back to the U.S.A.* I can't even understand X.Y.'s slang most of the time and have never seen the latest kitchen gadgets, so maybe it's about time to overhaul my vocabulary . . .

To Maria Osser

January 4, 1968

. . . My conversation with you upset me very much, you sounded so strange. If these had been ordinary days, or ordinary months, the last awful three months, I'd think it was just because I'd happened to call you at an awkward moment . . . but they haven't been ordinary months in my life and I am determined not to beat about the bush with you or anyone ever again, but to try to find out what the matter is. Something as tragic and awful as Lota's death prevents one from trying to be normal, or casual, or trying to "overlook" small things the way one usually does . . . Actually you were the last straw in a whole series . . .

My six weeks in Brazil were the very worst stretch I remember ever having gone through. New York, and Lota's coming there and dying, were terrible, of course—but somehow I got through all that and accepted it . . . You called, you remember, and made me weep by saying you'd fly over to stay with me. Then you wrote me one of the nicest letters of all, which I have saved. That all helped. When I got to Rio, however, things were very different . . . Well, at first I thought I was imagining it—but I really wasn't. There was an undercurrent of real hostility among most of the people I had thought were my best friends there . . . There were exceptions: Magú & Stella, in Rio, behaved naturally affectionately, and Stella *helped* me—almost no one else did a thing, Maya. In Ouro Prêto, Lilli and (he happened to be there, too) Vinícius de Moraes. Otherwise —no one came near me, and I spent weeks in that [Rio] apartment absolutely alone—surrounded by the accumulation of years, trying to pack it up, throw it out—all the awful business that everyone has to go through sometimes, only I'd never had to before. A few people came to call—and usually said something ambivalent or quite wrong & cruel. Marietta was putting on her act, I gathered, but I really never dreamed anyone would believe anything she said—such as that I was stealing Lota's *jewels*! . . . The story with Rosinha is too awful to go into and I am trying to forgive her because she was totally in the wrong & behaved like an idiot. Well —that's the way it was and I won't go into details, and I won't talk about my troubles with Mary [Morse]—(well, I did, some)—and there, I imagine, is where any trouble with you might lie, too. Because it was damned funny, Maya—you knew I'd just come from Brazil and you didn't ask about anything or anybody there—and it would have been only natural for you to ask, especially about Mary.

. . . I should attribute all this in Rio to their grief for Lota. However, it went far beyond that—and I have barely mentioned *some* of it—none of all the reported gossip, wild stories. Even [the doctor] Décio seemed determined to tell me anything that could make me feel worse . . . That time (and I rarely react quickly & get angry when I should) I really hit the ceiling & shouted at him . . . I only went [to New York] because he ordered me to, and I just sat in Loren's studio and moped, mostly—saw almost no one, couldn't work or sleep or eat—and just worried, as I had done for the last two or three years, about Lota. I didn't WANT to go— but Lota & I agreed it might be the right thing . . . The plan was for her to come in December—but she couldn't wait, and finally I couldn't bear to have her keep asking and wired her "Come whenever you want to, darling." In Rio I discovered that everyone *knew* Lota was sick, perhaps dying, but they couldn't keep her from coming and at last she got out of town almost secretly. I have finally decided that Dr. Anny is right—that I was being used, unconsciously no doubt, as a scapegoat. This was pretty hard on me since I am the one who suffered most of all from Lota's sickness (& I think now this had been coming on for many years, if not for Lota's whole life)—and I am the one whose life has been most affected—in fact changed forever, and whose loss is the greatest. After all, I lived with her for sixteen years, or it would have been sixteen in November—and twelve or so of them were the happiest of my life.

The misunderstanding with Mary was horrible . . . I never realized how much Mary hated me until I came back from Seattle—in fact I'd been stupid enough to think that, even if she never made any attempt to understand me, she even rather liked me! (& in fact I did like her) . . . One thing I'd like to clear up with you: Lota and I had discussed the terms of Lota's will long ago, many times, and more recently before I left, when it had become an obsession with her. I agreed to *everything*— not only in the will but in the letter. In fact I suggested many of the gifts, etc., myself when she couldn't decide. The idea of leaving Mary the house furnished was only so that she could rent it. You can see how that would be natural—and I had no objections whatever. I took Mary many things and gave more to her—all of which she accepted. I suggested that she take from the house various things she had given Lota . . . and again she accepted. (Under the circumstances I later kept some of these, but there is no point in going into that.) I had already written her twice from New York saying I understood and had long ago agreed to the will and so on, and felt that she and I would have no trouble. (!) Well—we did, the minute I asked for things—I thought according to the terms of the will —in fact I *know* according to the terms of the will! But when Mary gave me a flat *no* and would listen to no pleas whatever—I gave up right away. I don't know whether this was right or wrong, cowardly or not—but I didn't want to fight. Mary never seemed to see for one moment that anything I asked for was for its associations, pure & simple—I don't give a damn about THINGS—but she does, very much, because of her daughters. Well, now she has enough, let's hope, to equip them for life!

I have never felt such hatred in my life and I stayed *alone* up there in Samambaia (except for Joanna) for 5 days, without any means of transportation, feeling it. I thought in anything as serious as Lota's death any human being would feel some sympathy—but I received none whatever—and that goes for a good many other people I thought were my friends in Rio, too. I really didn't know I was tough enough to get through something like this, but somehow I did, without breaking down. Things disappeared from the apartment [in Rio] even while I was packing—and I knew Joanna was taking them for Mary. Why on earth couldn't she have asked me nicely? I didn't want anything that didn't belong to me. Mary had even gone over all Lota's old photographs—

childhood pictures, etc.—and left me almost nothing of any interest—this after I lived with Lota all that time—much longer than Mary did, and I never *left* Lota (*she* did, and rather decisively, you know, even if she continued to live nearby).

. . . Can you imagine arriving at the only home (forgive me for being corny, but it is true) I have ever really had in this world and finding it not only not mine—I had agreed to all that—but almost stripped bare? Friends had gone up from Rio—how soon after the funeral I don't know—and taken everything. Mary left me the linen on my bed, 2 towels, 2 plates, forks, knives, etc. This was my HOME, Maya. Do people think I have no feelings? (I'm beginning to think they do. One night, rainy, from up there I got so desperate I telephoned Isa, just to talk. She said, "You're very silent—what's the matter?" I said I felt blue. Then Isa made this really classic remark: "WHY?" Look—I knew about the will long before anyone else did and, as I said, a lot of it was my own idea—but don't you think, since the house was *not* rented, or going to be, as far as I know—it would have been more elegant to wait to collect the loot until I got there? No—(and that's another idiotic but upsetting detail—Alfredo has even taken some of MY art books—things I need for the book I'm working on. And *I* was the one who suggested he be allowed to select some of Lota's books. Well, I am utterly sick of the ironies by now.)

. . . I left Brazil with a very heavy heart and I hope never to see Rio again, although no doubt I'll have to. I'm keeping the house in Ouro Prêto and I'll go there . . . I feel now as if I'd been living in a completely false world all the time—not false, but that no one ever liked me, really, or not many people, and all of them totally misunderstood the strength of the bonds between Lota and me—or, now that she's dead, they *want* to misunderstand them. Jealousy was always there, I knew—maybe it's just that that came to the surface. I don't know. I thought you were fond of me; also that we were friends and could be better friends than I could with others in Rio because we were both intelligent, "highbrow" perhaps, etc. But, Maya, I do know something was wrong when I talked to you last Sunday. I want to clear it up now, right away . . .

I'd give everything in this world—a foolish expression but I can't think what I'd give, but "everything," certainly—to have Lota back and *well*—that is the awful thing about it all. Dr. Baumann tells me she had seen this coming for a long time, that it was "inevitable"—and I try to agree with her. It was better the way it was, I suppose—if Lota had died in Brazil I would have felt worse, probably—or if she had lived on for a few weeks in New York—that would have been worst of all. Well, when I was in the hospital Dr. Anny kept telling me every day: "Grieve if you want to now, but no more guilt. I know, we all know, you did everything you could that was humanly possible." But if only one weren't just human.

I learned a great deal in Rio that made me agree that it was "inevitable"—people seemed to enjoy telling me, I'm afraid. Please,

Maya, write to me. I am very fond of you and I don't want us to stop being friends . . . I am brokenhearted—those last years were so awful, so exhausting; I didn't behave the way I wish I could have, often, but I didn't realize for a long time . . . how desperately sick Lota was. You must believe me when I say we loved each other. Other people do not have the right to judge that. She went to sleep in my arms the night of September 17th. There will never be anyone like her in this world or in my life, and I'll never stop missing her—but of course there is that business of "going on living"—one does it, almost unconsciously—something in the cells, I think. Do you think if all the above weren't TRUE, I'd be here? . . . No—I'd be dead, too . . .

To Dr. Anny Baumann

January 6, 1968

. . . I think my experiences in Rio were not just because of people acting strangely under grief—there was more to it than that. In fact, I have such a *slow burn*—I am just beginning to see the complete lack of sympathy in those I had thought of as my "friends" and it now strikes me as an almost barbaric performance, honestly. There were exceptions—Stella (whom you don't know), Magú, and in Ouro Prêto Lilli, behaved naturally and affectionately and like civilized people. I think now that after a tragic death, like Lota's, everyone is left feeling more or less guilty—and I was a convenient scapegoat. Also, some of Lota's old friends always had been jealous of me, naturally. I had to contend with that from the very beginning—but they had shown it less and less and I thought they liked me, too. But when Lota died I suppose it could all come back to the surface over again. Anyway, it was one of the most disturbing experiences of my life and it will take a long long time to get over it. I spent the last two or three days in Rio alone in a hotel and was going to go alone to the airport in a taxi—then the poet Vinícius de Moraes (*Black Orpheus*) kindly took me. In fact he was extremely kind all along—and I had scarcely known him before . . .

X.Y. is back [at home] collecting things—she'll return the 9th, probably. Yes, she is extremely "practical" and cheerful and helpful—and types *beautiful* business letters that go out over my signature . . . She knows infinitely more than I do about things like taxes, finishing furniture, and so on, and a great deal about art, of course. She is bringing back the transcript of her college marks and may be able to get in this term at the university . . . I think it is going to work out very well.

This does not mean that I don't love Lota and always shall. There will never be anyone like her in the world, of course, or in my life. It all seems like such a tragic waste to me—and I blame her stupid, incredibly cruel parents, now . . . Backward countries produce backward and irrational people—as I certainly learned in those hideous six weeks. I'm much better now—sleeping without pills and taking the other ones all the time. I'm terribly thin—but this is all to the good . . . I am beginning to feel a bit sociable again. Forgive this self-centered letter. I do like this city so far—everyone terribly POLITE, including bus drivers, which is nice after New York and Rio . . .

Sunday morning
January 7, 1968

. . . The nephew, Flavio, will probably write me when I get an address to him—through a friend. He is on my side, so far at least—but his mother's influence is strong. I thought no one in Rio would believe anything she said but, alas, they were obviously influenced by her. I had "stolen Lota's jewelry," etc.—and also had done something so awful— the moment Lota arrived, apparently—that Lota committed suicide immediately. This was reported to me. I feel I know less & less what actually happened. IF anyone wanted to commit suicide and had a drug like Nembutal at hand—surely one would take the Nembutal rather than more Valium? At least I know I would.

. . . I didn't fight with Décio, the analyst. I went to see him—he kept me waiting an hour while he bathed and dressed, and then began by saying, "When you left Lota & went to New York to start a new life—" For once I reacted promptly—I hit the ceiling. I went because he told me to, and under protest—and you know what my "new life" was like. I had only one determination: to have Lota get WELL & to spend the rest of my life with her. Then he told me, quite unnecessarily & cruelly, it seems to me, that he had *prevented* Lota from sending me some "very aggressive" letters. Well, I have about 60 letters from Lota, written during that stretch, and perhaps two of them could be considered aggressive. I cried a lot—I was exhausted by then—and then he & his wife wanted to take me to the Country Club for dinner, to "meet some new people." I know what that is like—Lota had done it & warned me—so I balked, and didn't see him again.

Well—something more pleasant. Tomorrow I move into the "flat" —today sometime late the first of X.Y.'s trucks comes. She is actually riding down on the second one, wouldn't take the train—sometime Tuesday. She works awfully hard and is very sweet-tempered and also very entertaining. I am very lucky.

I learned in Rio that everyone had tried to keep Lota from going to New York—and that she had spent most of her time in bed, writing me letters. This breaks my heart. I wrote to her, thank god, almost every day—my letters had been burnt, however. ALL my letters, from the past, too, which seemed a bit excessive. I can't bear to think of how much she suffered these past years—and if only I had been able to do something about it. You know I tried, and tried, Anny—beginning long before I went to Seattle—to get her to give up the wicked park and go away with me to Italy or someplace for a year or so—but she wouldn't even listen.

I must change this ribbon and get down to work.

April 5, 1968

. . . The cast was taken off my right arm last week and now it is just done up in sticking plaster and I can use it a lot more. I think it has healed well—the left shoulder troubles me much more than the right wrist, still, although I do exercises every day. Then last week I had to have a large & *beautiful* impacted wisdom tooth out. This was just about the worst of my physical troubles so far—they are getting almost comic by now—but today I seem almost back to normal, I think.

On the 15th I am going to Tucson, Arizona, to give a reading, god help me. Then one at Berkeley the 28th, I think. On May 12th or around then X.Y. & I are coming to New York by way of Montreal (I have two aunts there & an old friend from Brazil). After a week or two, we'll go to Brazil. I want to see how my old house is getting along and make up my mind about keeping it. I am fairly sure I want to, but really have to go back to know.

I am terrified of reading but shall ask the doctor for some tranquillizers, I think. Also keep taking the other pills, just in case.

We have done a huge job of re-painting and re-flooring in this flat and it is at last beginning to look like something and we have done so much now I think we'll just have to keep on renting it a while longer. It is quite big, very cheerful & convenient, except for the kitchen . . . no space to work in . . . The books, silver, etc., I shipped from Brazil should arrive soon, too. I have sold the Rio apartment, but so far can't get the money into this country—very difficult. That's why I'm giving these awful readings—otherwise I don't think I'd dream of it!

I miss Lota horribly & it doesn't seem to get better at all—I see very alarming news about Brazil in the papers here—apparently Carlos has now got in on it, too—I'll try to get a *New York Times* today & see if it tells any more, and I hope friends there will send me some newspapers. Lota's nephew writes me very good, long letters. He is best at the "news."

X.Y. is very nice to me & I don't know what I'd do without her these days. I can't seem to get interested in meeting people, etc.

To Ashley Brown

61 Perry Street
New York City
June 17, 1968

. . . Emanuel Brasil was here yesterday afternoon & evening, to work on the Brazilian anthology. (I think you must know something about it

—I got involved in sending Brazilian poets to the U.S.A. for readings, and then in this anthology that Wesleyan is going to publish, and Emanuel and I are co-editors. I never wanted to get involved in *any* anthology, but couldn't seem to avoid this one.) You may have heard from him all about it already . . . Of course we want your translations of Vinícius. I don't have them with me, and can't quite remember now which ones you did —a sonnet, and the Christmas poem—and I think one other? Anyway, they could all be used, and E. and I are hoping you'll undertake to do one or two more of Vinícius for us as well, since you did those so nicely. He took our table of contents off with him—but there is one long one all about WOMAN that I think is very good, funny, and typically Vinícius (and Brazilian as well) . . . Another one we selected, more or less the same subject. These should be fairly easy—free verse. Then there is a sonnet I think I'll try to do—an old one, called something or other INTIMATE —about taking a walk in the country, chewing a straw, etc. If I get stuck I'll probably call on you for help, though.

We are trying to get very good translators—Merwin, Wilbur, etc.— and shall use those I've already done, etc. It's bilingual—and (but this part is still a secret) probably TWO volumes—one from Bandeira to Cabral and a bit later, the other the younger poets. I do hope you'll be interested in this—and I am fairly confident you will be. Vinícius writes me that he is *coming* to N.Y.—has been coming since last fall—very typical: Betty Kray sent him a pre-paid cable to let her know when he was coming, so she could arrange a reading (Academy of American Poets, the real backers of this project) and a month or so later he wrote me, from Ouro Prêto, asking me to tell her he was saving her cable to send when he really was coming.

Emanuel told me there is actually a very private restaurant here called Ouro Prêto—you have to arrange it all by telephone ahead of time—very small. Think I'll try it if it isn't too expensive. I was planning to go back—my house really almost finished now, and all my books and most of my Brazilian belongings up there—this month, but decided it was too soon. I'll probably go next fall or winter. (The two cats are there, enjoying life at Chico Rey, at last word.)

Well, my reason for having to cancel my reading engagements was really much worse than a "bad tooth," alas. I developed osteomylitis of the jaw and got off the Canadian National Railway (I'd come from Vancouver) and spent almost two weeks in Montreal, one in the hospital— had an operation, lost two more teeth, had an abscess, all sorts of highly unpleasant things—and got to N.Y. very late. However, I think I'm recovering now—but it has been a bad bone year—after breaking my left shoulder here in November (I went to Brazil and packed and moved in a huge cast some of the time), I broke my right wrist in San Francisco —very badly, too—and was just out of that cast when this tooth business began. A very dismal tale. I may come back to N.Y. next fall, but I'm not sure. I have given readings now at Tucson and Berkeley—all right, but I don't enjoy them much.

I have my young friend with me, thank goodness, through all this. We were to go to Stonington last week, too—to stay with another friend—but I expected to see Jimmy Merrill, but I wasn't up to it—we may get there yet, before he goes to Greece again . . .

I really don't know how I feel about S.F. I feel it hasn't had a chance yet, what with all the broken or infected bones—but I'll be going back the end of this month, or a bit before, and shall give it another try. I am dying to get to work. No—I haven't done *anything* on the Brazil book for months now—nothing except dictate letters, business letters, and read, mostly—but now I can type again. I found I couldn't write verse at all without a pen in my hand—but I'm hoping I'll get a lot done soon now.

. . . Just got two letters from Rio, along with yours—that is extraordinary—you know how they are about letters! But no political news, and I'd like to know how things are. Well, off to show my "secretary" the Frick and the Guggenheim. Don't know why I put it in quotes, since she really is a good one, just what I've always needed . . .

To Frani Blough Muser

1559 Pacific Avenue
San Francisco, California
September 19, 1968

. . . I've been so busy the last few weeks preparing that collected edition [1970 *Complete Poems*] that I haven't written Cynthia [Krupat, book designer, Frani's daughter] about it as I should have long ago. However, the publishers did say they'd send all material on to her—and she probably has most of it already. I had to dig up a lot of things I didn't seem to have with me . . . Also make lots of improvements, I hope. I've just discovered the Public Library here . . . With quite a good Brazilian section & a pleasant place to work. Also wonderful machines, new to me, where for a dime you can copy anything in a split second. Yesterday morning I surprised myself by going out and buying a Volkswagen, and X.Y. has driven me very cautiously to the library twice already, so we have a mileage of 17 miles. It is called "Lotus White"—white seemed safest because of the fogs. If I'd bought a 1969 model, it would have been "Toga White."

I also rented a TV just for the duration of the political conventions —but it still seems to be around and I am only hoping not to get hooked. I stay up to watch those damned old movies and then can't get up at a decent hour in the morning. X.Y.'s little boy calls it "the pee-pee"—

naturally, his vocabulary being very limited. He has a child's record player his indulgent papa bought him during the summer & the other morning he played his English muffin on it. I have also acquired a young mynah bird, since I find I miss having bird shrieks around me. We are hoping that he and the child will both learn to talk soon—or teach each other.

I am reading a wonderful book—I don't know whether you'd like it or not—it's Chekhov's *The Island of Sakhalin*—his account of his trip to the prison island in 1890. My Brazil book isn't like that at all—but if it could turn out one-tenth as good, I think I'd die happy. It came out a year ago, though, and maybe you've read it. The literary—or social—life here so far is rather skimpy, but I don't mind. I've met a number of poets but they all make me feel either awfully old-fashioned or rather new— since I think the West is in the Pound tradition, more or less (I don't really know). Oh, and I have a good clavichord teacher, from Palo Alto —she's expensive, and I don't have time to practice much—but I'll take some lessons, anyway, and it is so nice to have the thing in order again.

September 20

Well, dinner & the damned TV got me, I'm afraid—a station George [Frani's son] keeps recommending to me—and last night it *was* good, for the first time—we covered Africa. But I still shall be glad when the man comes to take it away Monday . . .

I really don't know if S.F. is my SCENE or not—but it certainly is a pretty city, and I think it was a good idea to try it for a while. I'll be in N.Y. in May to give those postponed readings—giving one at Harvard the end of next month, but I don't think I'll get to N.Y. Also one here. I loathe them, but they pay. I am really so sorry I didn't see more of you, Frani, or see Curt at all. I was feeling so awful most of the time I was there in the summer, just at the end did I begin to feel normal again. This is no proper explanation, but it did make me reluctant to go any-where. I hope you will understand this.

Robert Lowell wrote me about Mary's entertaining [Senator Eugene] McCarthy, etc.—and the FBI went all over his barn, days ahead. Castine sounds like a rather strenuous resort intellectually these days. Now that I can vote for the second time in my life, I don't want to . . .

Barbara Chesney Kennedy, who lives in Tucson, arrived here a week or so ago unexpectedly and spent two nights here. Her middle son, a medical student at Columbia, was with her & I liked him a lot—he's going to be a pediatrician like his father. (They were in Brazil a few years ago & I saw them and thought Barbara had been unusually lucky in a *mate*.)

. . . The flat is pretty big and very light & sunny. But oh lord, I get homesick for Brazil. Next June I mean to go back, to my old house, for

3 or 4 months. If Nixon gets in, maybe I'll just stay—any old revolution would be better, it seems to me.

To Harold Leeds

September 24, 1968

I am ashamed of not having written you long before now. There seemed to be so many things I should say, but mostly of course they boil down to thanking you again, for all your kindness to X.Y. & me this summer. I tried to call you yesterday and the Sunday before that, but you were out . . . I'd love to hear about your Nova Scotia trips and wasn't that card from Antigonish?—I was taken there summers once or twice, when I was very small, and remember swimming in the muddy water, but I'm sure it has changed beyond recognition now.

We are getting along all right here, or better, I think I may say— especially since we got the whole flat painted white, and took up those filthy wall-to-wall carpets the landlord was so proud of. X.Y. and a high-school boy did a lot of the painting (professional help, a Negro-Japanese, graduate of the U. of Tokyo) for one day at something over $100 and now the flat is looking quite cheerful . . . My young mynah bird . . . is too young to talk, and now he has started to molt—the book says don't try to teach them while molting!—but he is tame and funny and whistles well, at least. Well, I've met some poets and others—am giving a reading here at the museum—and so on . . . Esthetically I like the place very much. Oh—I also went out and bought a Volkswagen last week . . . We have racked up 82 miles now on trips to the Public Library, mostly, very careful trips. I do want to see some of the scenery while I'm here, and the woods and birds, & it seems like the only way . . .

Dined with some friends in Mill Valley the other night and the hostess produced a better version of ratatouille than any I've ever eaten or made—much more beautiful to look at. I'd be glad to swap recipes, dear, at any time. I've heard only once from L. & LL. They must be back in Paris and I shall write to them soon. There is a lovely Bissier show here now—perhaps it was at the Guggenheim, since it seems to be under their sponsorship. (I'm sorry I can't seem to type this morning—maybe it is too early.) Louise [Crane] told me she would probably be coming this way in August or September, but I haven't heard from her and wonder if everything is all right with her.

To Louise Crane

October 10, 1968

. . . I wrote my note to you after my first letter from Lester de Pester. On the two following days I received two more, one of 26 pages (small ones, but even so) and one of 14. These are all afterthoughts and footnotes and corrections of "inaccuracies" in his *first* letter, and they themselves are full of footnotes, asterisks, and so on—and the first contained a post-card of an aerial view of Ogunquit that shows his house, garage, and two white deck chairs—everything except the dead dog, who is also featured in each letter in the same paragraph with his defunct parents. So I think we can really assume that poor Lester is a little dingy, as X.Y. says (only I don't know how to spell it, ding-y as in ding-dong). Well, he did say that my letter to him had "reassured" him, so maybe he won't bother you any more for a while. But imagine—going 15 years without seeing Marianne, when he could have perfectly well, and then making so much fuss.

I feel a bit guilty because I hadn't known that Marianne was in the hospital and hadn't written her for some time or just sent a postcard or two. I also hadn't written Dr. Anny at length as I should have, but shall today. I am really glad to hear she was there and perhaps they took the opportunity of giving Marianne extra nourishment when she didn't know about it . . . I thought all her papers were to be left to Bryn Mawr? Well, I am so glad you are there . . . and I said in my letter to Lester that we should all be "very grateful" to you. This was before I knew he'd been bothering you last winter, of course.

I saw Ginny on my way to Tucson last April. Yes, she's one of the funniest people in the world. I hadn't seen her for ten years, I think. She was awfully funny about her adopted children—"little sex pots" she called them. But Laura Huxley—well, I see she is still at the punch-ball stage. Perhaps I shall send you her book for Christmas: *You Are Not the Target*—it is full of such "recipes" for cheering one up. I started to throw away my copy (that she sent me) in Rio once and Lota said we must never throw it away! "It is one of the great comic books of the world!" Recently she published a book about her life with Huxley and his death, *This Timeless Moment*, all about LSD, ESP, etc. This is rather embarrassing for me because we have the same publisher and of course her books SELL in many editions, and in paperback, and I think there is a record that goes with it on which she reads poems. She didn't send me that part of it. Well, I am being completely bitchy this morning, I'm afraid. I'm sorry you didn't get to San Francisco but I see you scarcely had time to in one week.

I have bought a white Volkswagen, "lotus white" . . . X.Y. drives it very cautiously up and down these terrifying hills. Now I have a little flat, little car, somebody else's little boy, and have joined the great lower-middle-class American public in spending a lot of my time looking for a place to park. It is a strange sensation. I had never been in a laundromat before. I'm getting used to it now, but at first when I went to the Super-market I spent hours because I wanted to read what it said on all the packages.

I'm not sure how long this new world will intrigue me, but it is really nice & distracting for the time being. I hope to get back to my house in Ouro Prêto sometime next spring or summer—and hope to be able to spend some months there, and one day I do hope that you and Victoria too will visit me there. I think you'd like it. X.Y. sends her regards.

To Marianne Moore

October 10, 1968

I had a letter from Louise this morning & she told me you had been in Lenox Hill for about ten days . . . I am so sorry I didn't know about this sooner; it is really my own fault because I haven't written to Anny the way I should. Louise says that you are well now, however, and at home again, and I do hope you are feeling better for your stay. I didn't mind Lenox Hill too much when I stayed there; it seemed very good for a *hospital*. And if one has Anny to defend one, one gets along very well. (I did balk at having a TV, however, and had it returned behind her back!)

I didn't tell you on my postcard that the other day I was in the Supermarket (I love to go there to read the packages, it is just like a library, really) and I saw a number of *Family Circle* with "Marianne Moore on Baseball" on the cover & of course I bought it. May Sarton, Truman Capote are also in this number. I think it must be getting to be the fashionable publication. I haven't any news, really. I am about two-thirds through the Wallace Stevens *Letters* and find them much more fascinating than I'd thought they'd be. He must have been a bit of a disciplinarian, though. I liked his saying that when he came home from the office the first thing he did was make people take things off the tops of his radiators. He enjoys everything so much, too, and I also like his preoccupation with the weather and climates.

One poet I've met here, almost a neighbor, I like very much, Thom Gunn. His poetry is usually very good, I think; he's English but has lived here for a long time. I am going to Harvard sometime at the end of this month—I'm afraid I won't be able to get to New York, however . . . But I'm coming back next May to give those readings . . .

I just wanted you to know I am thinking of you and wish I lived nearer. If there's anything I can send you from California—I can't seem to think of anything at the moment except maybe those crystallized fruits (do you like them?)—please please let me know. I'm rather disappointed in the California fruits & vegetables so far. I made lemon jelly and it had no taste of lemon. The small and warped Brazilian ones have much more flavor . . .

November 9, 1968

It was so nice to have a letter from you this morning & I do hope you are continuing to feel well, and I hope you really found enough of the fruits you liked. I don't know about the Ben Jonson but must look it up. I went to Harvard to give a reading last week—just there for two days and straight back. Robert Lowell introduced me ever so nicely & I really didn't mind it too much. Bill Alfred was extremely kind to me, too, and I liked his house very much, and all his clocks—have you seen it? I saw a cousin, and also the Gardner Museum, where I hadn't been for many years—the flowers in the courtyard were magnificent—and each corner had displays of really rare orchids. I said to a guard, "You must have a fine greenhouse," and he said, "We have six greenhouses."

I am glad to hear you are going to Thanksgiving dinner at Louise's—give her my love. We were hoping to get Tom Wanning to visit us then but no word so far—maybe he'll just arrive. This isn't much of a painting—but I have a fondness for St. George (who never existed, they say) since he is the favorite of Brazil—on every bus, taxi and truck, and in most shops, too.

I am working quite a lot these days, translating & my own work, but it goes slowly. I give one reading here, too . . .

To May Swenson

November 16, 1968

The local supermarkets, the laundromat, the weekly maid, the baby-sitters, etc.—I find them pretty strange and fascinating myself, and all pretty new to me, after almost 17 years away. I really was awfully out of touch, I find. In fact every day I get amazed over something I never knew about that is just part of daily life for X.Y. She . . . has a little boy named Googie, 2 years 3 months, very appealing, if fearfully energetic (out for the day now with his favorite sitter). I go over to Berkeley to take books out of the library once in a while . . . and tonight I am going to see *I Love You, Alice B. Toklas!*—and that is LIFE at the moment. Next week I am giving a reading at a museum here—it is given by the U. of San Francisco, which is now closed by a strike—but I presume my reading is going on, since it is not on the campus. (Mark Strand was here last week—giving 18 readings—and at S. F. State the building for readings had been closed, so he read outside on the steps in the rain, with a big crowd, but mostly strikers, he thought, not poetry lovers. A voice was heard to say: "The political content of this poetry is *nil*.")

. . . (Oh, interruption to buy two chances on a Thanksgiving turkey sold by a tiny Chinese Boy Scout named Andy Wah. When we went to vote at our local playground—the Helen Wills playground—we were the only Occidentals registered in this neighborhood.)

I like the city very much, to look at, and drive around in very cautiously in the Volkswagen. (At first we made only right-hand turns and avoided the steepest hills, but X.Y. is getting better at it all the time.) We are near the waterfront and go down every day or so, but we haven't really explored the countryside yet, and the only redwoods I've ever seen are a small grove that got transplanted to Sussex, England, in the early 19th century. I'm hoping to get out to see some of the coast when I get some more work done. I did go to Tucson last spring . . . and now I've been that far, and crossed the continent twice by train, I don't feel so guilty about it. But I'm afraid I am spoiled for scenery by Samambaia and Rio forever. I just hold my tongue. Nothing can really compare with either of them. And I am homesick a great deal of the time but try not to be—I can hardly wait to get back and see my old house in Ouro Prêto . . .

The mynah's name is Jacob. He was very young when I got him; then he molted, and only now—about 4 months old—is beginning to speak a *little* bit. His second phrase is to be: "I too dislike it." I am trying to finish up a poem about Sammy, the toucan who died several years ago now, to go in my *Collected* to be published in March—I hope I can get him in. But I really haven't written a poem since I can't remember when. However—one always does start again, it seems. Stevens says in his letters (just read them all) that translating is a waste of time—but I don't agree with him completely. It gets one to going through dictionaries, and that is a helpful activity.

To Frani Blough Muser

January 13, 1969

It is the third day of a howling rainstorm here—last year the weather was almost like summer at this time, but I was told there were apt to be week-long rains. I rather like it, also the famous fogs. It is so dark, X.Y. & son are still sound asleep, at 9:30—and I'll start the day by writing to you. George arrived Saturday evening with the record. I hadn't seen him for six or maybe seven years and, well, he has grown, naturally, and has turned out to be such a nice-looking boy . . . I offered him a whiskey (when he said he was 21) but he said Coke was more his style, so we all drank Coke for about an hour . . . He was off to "North Beach"—and we were off to a ghastly arty French movie, as it turned out. I told George he could stay here any time he wanted to—there is a guest room—and I hope he'll come back to see us, anyway; I liked him a lot . . .

I played your postcard songs through three times yesterday, paying strict attention, and I am really crazy about them. I like #2—about the snowstorm—and #5 best, I think. In fact I got so enthusiastic I started writing a few postcard-poems on my own . . . I may never finish them, but I do like the idea. That afternoon X.Y. and I had run across a junk shop called "The Salvation Navy" and had spent over an hour there—

instead of at the museum, as we'd planned—and I had gone over batches of old postcards, as it happened. There weren't any very attractive cards, so I had started reading the messages on some of them—and the fatuousness of a certain Mrs. McGuire, who went to Italy in 1909, was especially haunting . . .

The Webern I have on my "complete works" in Brazil, but the Schönberg is new to me and I'll have to try it several more times. I got us a *Wozzeck* for Christmas, along with some new Beatles & other rock & roll and some Verdi, etc.—nothing if not eclectic—and this dark gloomy p.m. I propose to listen to it once more, too. I haven't been to any live music here at all . . . Bobby & Arthur's recital last spring was canceled —the manager vanished. (This town is famous for that, it seems—the only other time in their career this has ever happened it happened here, too.) We do have quite a collection of records (X.Y. is very fond of opera), although I left almost all my monophonic ones in Ouro Prêto.

Cynthia has done some lovely typography for my *Collected*—no "Complete," FS&G is calling it, to my slight perturbation. We are sort of haggling about jackets now.

We gave a party here the 29th—the first real party—and just invited everyone we'd met and liked at all—about 30 people—and hoped for the best. Strange to say, it turned out to be a big success—about 40 people came, everyone having guests at that time of year—and song and dance went on until 3 a.m. and married couples were all dancing with each other and even, as X.Y. put it, "smooching," so it *must* have been a success. The living-room floor hasn't recovered yet, two waxings later . . . The poet Josephine Miles came. She . . . teaches at Berkeley. I liked her earlier books very much, very funny & sardonic; and she is a remarkable little creature, very badly crippled all her life, with arthritis. She has to be carried to her classes—and we got some strong young friends from Berkeley to bring her here & carry her up our stairs. She loves parties but of course can't get to them very often—and lives with an old, old mother who is, as she says herself, "vacant."

The mynah bird . . . hates Googie, who probably annoyed him once when I wasn't looking—and leaned out of his cage far enough to pull a strand of G.'s long blond hair once *hard*. Now they respect each other. He shows off so much when we have company that I have to cover him up so we can go on with the conversation. I don't know what I'm going to do with him if I really get back to Brazil for three months next summer, as I plan to do—perhaps some friend here will like him enough. A young professor & wife were planning to sublet—then we discovered that they were also planning to rent the extra bedrooms, so that's out!

Well, I spent three days in Cambridge in November—gave a reading at Harvard—and I really enjoyed myself, the only reading I've ever enjoyed—the audience was so appreciative, and Ivor Richards & wife sat up front and dropped their canes and I could hear her whispering to him loudly from time to time, waking him up, etc. I went to the Gardner Museum—hadn't been there for 20 years or so—what a crazy home it must have been—but the Vermeer and the flowers were wonderful.

I hear a shriek from the rear of the flat so think I should go kiss "Googie" goodbye. He is probably being dragged off to his workday sitter. Actually he doesn't mind it when he gets there—a big casual messy girl with a little girl of her own and another neighbor child for him to play with. He put in a brief appearance at the party about midnight wearing a pair of Uncle Sam pajamas I'd given him for Christmas, and revolving very quietly among the rock & rollers. I was afraid he'd be frightened, but he wasn't and went back to bed like an angel, too. One guest . . . said to me, "What a *glorious* child!" (he *is* awfully pretty) . . .

I was in this flat a year Friday—moved in with three mattresses, a lamp, and a coffeepot—and I suppose we have accomplished quite a bit in a year. It is looking quite furnished and even nice, some rooms . . . I think I hate California, or maybe it's mostly Reagan—but it does seem to be the place where all the awful things start and happen, and I did want to get caught up on the U.S.A.

To Arthur Gold and Robert Fizdale

San Francisco
January 29, 1969

How very nice of you to go and see my former house on White Street [in Key West]. The woman who bought it has never pruned a bush since that day, I think, and when I last saw it, in 1958, I scarcely *could* see it. I took Lota there once, too, & it was still discernible—and it used to be so nice and bare and painted. As someone said, it looked like "a famous birthplace." It is funny—I just noticed the other day I have sort of repeated my old Key West color scheme in the apartment here now—and San Francisco keeps reminding me of Key West—something about the famous light, I think. (Key West's highest point is 9 feet in altitude.) I wish I'd known you were playing a concert there.

To Louise Crane

March 10, 1969

. . . I was awfully glad to hear about Marianne's arrangements with the Rosenbach Foundation; that sounds like exactly the right thing, and surely now she'll stop worrying about money. (Or no, she won't.) I am also greatly relieved to know she has someone staying with her full-time. She has answered all my brief notes or postcards until fairly recently, and I had one long telephone conversation with Dr. Anny just before she took off for Jamaica. But oh dear—everyone seems to be going slightly mad, or getting sadly confused, these days. I almost felt that I understood people, or they me, better in Brazil than now when I'm here on the same continent with them. Marianne wrote me a very funny sentence about how she should probably leave New York & come to live here (I'd described something or other that took her fancy, I suppose) and the sentence was so characteristic I quoted it in a letter to Anny. Well, Anny wrote to me first, and then telephoned, to tell me that Marianne was in "no condition to travel," I mustn't urge her to, and so on . . . All small jokes must be labeled JOKE, I see . . .

A week or so ago I read—one of 12 poets—at a huge rally for the striking teachers of S. F. State University—because from all I know about that, I am on their side. I really went as much to see some of the other poets whom I'd never seen as for idealistic reasons. A huge audience— 2,000 or so—it dragged on and on, and the hippie poets drank wine on stage, and backstage I was offered pot done up in red cherry-flavored cigarette papers. Muriel Rukeyser, whom I hadn't seen for many years, was there and really (to be bitchy) looked just like my idea of a Mexican opera star of about 1922. One lady poet attempted a sort of cheerleading act: "Give me an S!—a T!—an R!" and so on, and the audience yelled the letters back, to spell STRIKE. This was my favorite moment, since she is very small, with a very small voice and a lisp, so it came out "Give me an ETH!"

I feel almost too well caught up with the threads of life in the U.S.A. at the moment. You asked about the U. of Cal.—I suppose that means Berkeley? There are 17 or so, and just about all of them striking and rioting now. My thoughts aren't at all original—the students have a lot of real complaints; the trustees, regents, and Reagan are incredibly stupid; the cops are ghastly (I watch them on TV and everything they say of them is true, or they are even worse). But I'm against bombs and burning libraries and all violence . . . I am one of the lucky people who wanted to learn most of what I was taught, and didn't feel I was being pushed into IBM or the Army. (One hears the planes to and from Vietnam right over the house here every night.) It is all awful, that's all.

I have Roger in his sunbonnet [photo of Louise's dog], looking so pleasant, on my table. Jacob, the mynah, is talking quite a lot. He says, "My name is Jacob," "I love you," and my favorite line from my own works, "Awful, but cheerful." I am now working on "3.1416" as a change of pace . . . I wish you had known the toucan, Sammy, I had for years in Brazil, though. They don't talk, but are really the funniest birds in the world.

I can't get any news from Brazil about my beautiful old house but hope it is more or less ready for occupancy. I also hope you'll visit me there someday, when it *is* ready. You'd like that town a lot, I think, and the house, too—if it hasn't fallen down. I'll be in New York very briefly the first week or so of May and I hope I'll be able to see you then. I hope everything goes well with you, your mama, the magazine, and so on. Let me know if there is anything I can do about Marianne (can't imagine what) and I am so relieved that you have managed everything so well.

To Lloyd Frankenberg

April 10, 1969

This will probably be the last chance this morning to do any sociable letter writing, until I get to Brazil. There is so much to be done before I can get away—packing, subletting, what to do with Jacob, dentistry, and so on & on. Many streets here are planted with flowering trees—plum, cherries, etc.—very pretty with the always brilliantly painted wooden houses. It is a pretty city—I just wish I could endure the idea of the STATE a little better, but every time I see Reagan on TV I plan to leave it immediately . . .

I have such a nice co-editor on the anthology, Emanuel Brasil. I'll be seeing him in New York and HOPE he'll have his introduction ready for me to rewrite. Well, we did have more flu—or something—this variety settles entirely in the ears. Two days ago X.Y. and I both went to an ear doctor named Morry Mink! He seems to have fixed us up—at least we can hear each other talking again.

I see lots of poets, poets, poets—yesterday Denise Levertov & her husband Mitch Goodman (who may go to jail at any minute, along with Dr. Spock, etc., if you followed that). X.Y. is doing some secretarial work for her—she announced herself on the telephone as "Miss Bishop's secretary" and poor Denise, swamped with letters, said, "Oh, I wish I had one!" So I am sort of renting her out one day a week. Denise seems very sweet—as also does Josephine Miles, whom I really like a lot. But I like Thom Gunn best, I think. But there are many of them, mostly writing what I believe is now called "flow poetry"—but that may be wrong.

Heavens, you aren't 61, are you? Well, I am rapidly getting there too, I suppose, but can't believe it. (X.Y. worries about what will happen to her when she gets to be 30—she is 26 now, I think—since she firmly believes everyone over 30, possibly excepting me, should be *put away*.) Anyway, thank you for letting me see this particular poem because it has sort of started me off again on one of my own on more or less the same theme.

Tell Loren I have a huge basket on the floor full of purple and white lilacs. We bought them for an Easter-egg-dyeing party last Sunday. It was a great success even if the flat hasn't recovered yet from the dyeing—four guests, aged 2½, 2¾, 14 months and 16 months—all dyeing eggs on the floor and all came out dark brown finally. I liked the guests' names—Julia, Juili (half Italian), and Thiago (half Portuguese)—and it was our party, of course.

Do write me in Brazil at Ouro Prêto—and let's all work hard in our SIXTIES!

To Arthur Gold and Robert Fizdale

Robert Fizdale tells this story of the painter José Aparecido: "We found a rather primitive but charming painting of a church in a small shop in Ouro Prêto and asked the owner if he had others by the same painter. He told us he would ask the painter to bring us some the next day. A small, thin child appeared with paintings (he looked less than twelve), and when we asked if his father was unable to come, he said: 'I am the painter.' Elizabeth wanted to adopt him but his family refused, even though he had nine brothers and sisters. At her suggestion, she and we gave him a scholarship (bôlsa) so that he could study in an art school. Tuition was only $100 a year, I believe."

Ouro Prêto
July 15, 1969

We had such a curious and diverting time tracking down José Aparecido that I decided to write an essay called "Looking for José Aparecido," which might even make a chapter of my future book on Brazil. We met many fascinating characters and saw hitherto unknown and unexplored rural regions of Brazil. Anyway, we *did* find him. He did get his *bôlsa*, and we have seen him several times and find him more adorable each time. We have also met a lot of his family. He is the oldest of *ten*. He is coming this afternoon at four to have his picture taken. X.Y. and I have also set up a "Fizdale and Gold *Bôlsa*"—10 new cruzeiros a week —for artist's supplies, paint, brushes, and so on. The dear little boy came one evening and we gave him the first installment. He asked immediately, "And who is responsible for this *bôlsa*?" There were some people here for the Arts Festival, one a very nice young painter with a beard and a bass voice—everyone took to José A. immediately, and the painter had a serious talk with him about drawing and so on . . . I think you'll enjoy meeting J.A.'s mother because you decided to buy that painting of his. He brought us a present of some of his drawings, very careful and architectural. He really has lovely manners. Do you suppose one of these days he will really *shoot up*?

We went into the electric company here to fight a bit about the bill —and sure enough, there were three or four of those little leather "trunklets" (that's a good name for them) hanging up, with padlocks, quite well used, and looking better than when new. I want to get back there and order a lady-sized one immediately. The little iron stand you gave me— remember?—I have now decided to paint with white enamel, have a smallish potted palm on it, and have it in the "master bedroom," on the yellow tile floor. There is hot & cold water in the kitchen and one bathroom in my house now. In fact, we have been sleeping over there the past few nights because, although it isn't exactly the Ouro Verde, it is dryer and warmer than here. Also, I'm relieved to say, much quieter in the early mornings. I think quite a lot has been accomplished since you left. I bought out the entire fittings, almost, of an old pharmacy here—five big old wooden cabinets and other stuff—good wood, glass cases on top—3 will fit together in my bedroom (3 meters high) to make bookcases; one will make a very nice dining-room armoire . . .

I have spent almost two days in bed wheezing and fuming and fretting, but got a lot of strong *calmantes* from the doctor here and now feel somewhat better. I keep thinking if only we could get into MY house everything would be better, but this is probably an idle dream. Yesterday I received your second letter, Bobby, and that cheered me a lot.

Thank you for the advice about Customs, and we are glad you had no problems. José Aparecido came to call while I was in bed—I'd like to take him back with me, if it weren't that he has such a really nice mother & 9 brothers & sisters in Ouro Branco. We have invited him to Sunday dinner. He and his mother are what I really want from here. (We didn't meet his father.)

My ceilings are mostly being re-painted; the kitchen beginning to look nice. The doctor said it was "an honor to O.P." that I bought the house, and it seems to me this is the first nice thing anyone has said to me since I got to this continent on May 16th. We see that the embassies of Canada, Czechoslovakia, France, Germany, etc., have all contributed to this Arts Festival—but not the U.S.A. WHY? I wonder . . . Maybe one should consider it all a "happening." Well maybe one should consider life itself as a simple "happening"? We almost bought a car, then didn't think it was worth it for six weeks or so. The taxi drivers are our best, our only, friends. We have grown very chummy with a half-English one named Hannibal (he appears in the search for José A.) and one named Levy, who drives C A U T I O U S L Y and keeps saying things like: "Death can strike in a split second."

Your visit was the really saving grace of the summer/winter and I am still living off it.

To Marianne Moore

Casa Mariana
Ouro Prêto
September 21, 1969

The day before yesterday I was in Belo Horizonte (the capital of this state, about 60 miles away, where one has to go shopping and buy things like doorbells, light switches, maids' uniforms, etc.—the things that seem to be necessary to finish my "home" just now) and I went into a nice little shop that makes enameled signs for doctors, town halls and so on. The enclosed is a picture of the sign they are making for me, that will be nailed to the doorpost, high up. The door frame is blue, and the door is yellow. It is a huge old door, about nine feet high, from an abandoned church—I think I'll add a picture of it, too. The little plaque is white enamel with blue letters. The girl in the shop said, "Is this to be outdoors, in all weathers?" and I said, yes, in all weathers. So maybe they bake it extra well. I think the real one is a little bigger. Already all my taxi driver friends here know the name of my house, and my favorite, intelligent one, named Hannibal, knows quite a bit about you, too, and now asks about you. It's the perfect name for here because the house is on the road to a lovely little town about 8 miles away, called Mariana, and also everyone can remember it and pronounce it.

X.Y. left yesterday, to go to San Francisco and take care of things there, then she will return here. But I am all alone for a month or two and I hope to get a lot of work done now. The summer has been unavoidably interrupted all the time, but now I am actually in the house, things are much better. It is so beautiful—how I wish you could see it.

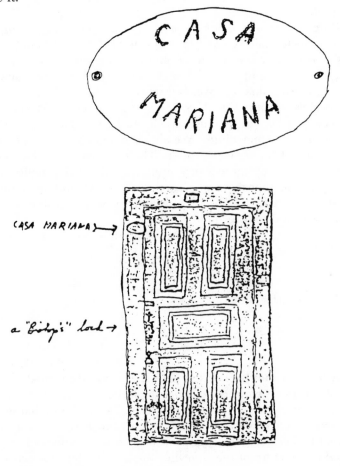

To Robert Lowell

December 15 (or 16 by now), 1969

. . . Your saying that I am "loved and revered" cheers me quite a lot. I certainly am neither here, and do wonder what on earth I am doing here and wish to God we could get away FAST. But so much to be done first. If only ONE workman knew his job and would come when he says he's coming and then not fight about the originally agreed-on pay. I am getting completely paranoid, I'm afraid—but it is true—the whole town seems out to fleece us, even 8-year-old banana sellers, etc. And our maid, I'm afraid, is not all we thought, either, in spite of our giving her new teeth for Christmas and a fortune in vitamins and shoes and so on for her & her little girl. I even have doubts about going away for a "rest" now. I don't dare leave the house in her charge. God, it is a thieves' nest. Forgive me; it is really getting to me . . .

It has been a totally wasted stretch—and had been for a long time before that, too. Oh, maybe some of it will seem comic, sometime, but if I had stayed in N.Y. or S.F. I think I might have worked on the Brazil book & even managed to say some nice things. Now I've forgotten what they were! I suppose I had Lota for so long to intervene for me, in Petrópolis, at least, and I really was happy there for many years. Now I feel her country really killed her—and is capable of killing anyone who is honest and has high standards and wants to do something good—and my one desire is to get out. But how to LIVE? . . .

Well, the carpenter did show up this a.m. but our steadiest worker fell in love (they say) and has vanished with his last pay check and the drainage system half-done. We put our garbage out as we're supposed to, and before it gets picked up, little boys throw it over the wall into my waterfall, where it hangs from the rocks and trees. Oh well, Johnson went around with garbage hanging from his hat, they say.

To Dr. Anny Baumann

December (sometime), 1969

I think I'll risk sending you this soiled old letter I've been carrying around in a pocket for weeks now. I decided it was too gloomy and weak-minded to send you and that I'd re-write it. However, on reading it through just now, I realize that the new letter would probably turn out to sound even worse, so I shall let this go, to give you a rough idea of what we have been doing here. Things are really much worse now, incredible as it seems—even the prize maid turns out probably not to be honest, either. I don't believe there is an honest soul in this town, and all seem to be out to fleece the Americans if possible. My one idea is to sell the house and get away as soon as possible.

Please do not think I am suffering from paranoia. The people of this state have a reputation for being like this . . . there is a book on the subject by a very nice man who started the museum here, and I am going to translate some bits of it in my second version of my piece on O.P.— not that I have done a line of work yet. I met him at the party in Belo Horizonte . . . He sold his house here long ago and has never come back. "It's no good," he said, in a very vulgar Brazilian idiom.

X.Y. and I are both extremely tired and just trying to hold on until we can get away. I still think my house the most beautiful in the world, and the town is beautiful, too, architecturally—but that is not enough. Don't you have a millionaire patient, slightly eccentric, who is interested in baroque architecture, or South American history, or *psychology*—who would like to buy it?—along with a lot of good 18th- and early 19th-century furniture?—I think I shall try to get myself and my 3,000 or so books back to New York. But I never felt so *poorly* in my life. I take Anorexyl, and a booster called Nardil, also a Premarin once a day, but I think Dr. Bicalho is writing you. If you have any suggestions beyond the stiff-upper-lip sort, I'd be grateful. We hope to be able to leave the child with the maid for a week and get away for a short rest after Christmas. I seem to have three lawsuits going—the neighbors hit X.Y. with a rock the other day—the police won't come, etc. etc. etc. I'll say no more except that I have never before in my life felt that I had no resources left at all, and if X.Y. weren't with me I don't think I could make it.

The sun is shining today for the first time in weeks & that helps a bit and I shall go out and take pictures of the house, to try to help sell it. The legal things will take years, no doubt, and I never expect to get very much of the money owed me. Oh well. If I get to feeling better I can teach again, I suppose.

I had a nice long letter from Louise [Crane] a short while ago with all the details of the party for Marianne, etc. Also a friend (Emanuel Brasil, whom I am doing that anthology with) took two very good, if sad, pictures of her in Washington Square in her wheelchair. She looks better than I had thought she would, I'm glad to say—even a bit fatter. When I leave I'll just take my enamel plaque off the doorpost as a souvenir. I placed it high enough so the passersby can't destroy it. We're already on the fourth doorbell and I'm going to give up when they smash this one. Louise has certainly done wonderfully well for Marianne, and I am profoundly grateful for it all.

How I wish I could talk to you. Perhaps you could make some practical suggestions! I think we are doing just about as well as we can under the circumstances, but this is certainly the worst mistake I have made in my life—I have made many but this *is* the worst. I think if I felt I could ever write again it would help. I don't even have that hope—but maybe it will come back. I have a kind of memoir of Marianne I've had in mind for years, about the periods when I knew her best, but I haven't been able to get to work on it . . .

Do you know of any other *common* drug—obtainable anywhere —that cheers one up a bit, especially in the early morning and late afternoon—? I am taking the PILLS faithfully now—have been for a long time.

Please forgive these gloomy and discouraged letters—X.Y. and I have sworn not to complain to others or to each other, even, although sometimes that gets impossible. I shall advertise the house in the cities here, also in N.Y. & London I think. Well, off to the FORUM, as they quaintly call it—where everyone expects to be *bribed* for the smallest transaction. Even the *plumber* (the fourth and most incompetent of all) knew [the amount of] my bank account here—and shouted it at me (although I didn't!).

To James Merrill

January 18, 1970

. . . Your troubles in Athens sound only too familiar. Today I have had three hopelessly lazy workmen downstairs. I have to fire them and am trying to get up my courage to. The new maid, or cook, of whom I expected great things, is having a sulking and crying fit after working here ten days, and no one can make out what the matter is. Then she broke a long thin strip—several feet—of marble off the almost brand-new kitchen sink—just *wiping* it she says. To top it all off, she is being very rude. You are right to have a room at the top of the house to get away from it all in. I haven't, and although it is a big house, for here, and I have a good study, things just seem to seep through the walls. Oh, and now the Siamese cat is howling at the study door. No one feeds him but me, and he is also lonely since Tobias, my other darling cat, died a while ago—at the amazing age, for a cat in the tropics, of 18. We have serious electrical problems, too—in fact I am re-doing most of the wiring and piping. Yes, getting away in the desert must have been wonderful. I find myself dreaming of getting away to a small flat in New York, of all places, where I might have real privacy, and no emotions brewing around me but my own . . .

I want to sell this house—although your suggestion of exchange is very appealing—but I have the same objection to it that you have: you wouldn't be there. It may never sell, or take a long time, but I am working away with this in mind, giving away hundreds of old French novels and detective stories, bad Brazilian books, and many English duplicates, etc., to lighten my freight. The house grows prettier every day, and Carnival is coming, so we hear samba music every night, and the summer rainstorm effects are superb—but somehow none of it works for me any more, and instead of being amused by the maid, the carpenter, and so on I just feel horribly weary. But of course the real trouble is, as you say, that "someone I loved very much is no longer to be seen"—and so very few things seem worth the doing any more. Forgive me, but I feel sure you are one person I can say this to (thank heavens). I don't want to go back to San Francisco very much, either. I'm hard to please!

To Frani Blough Muser

St. Valentine's Day, 1970

. . . For a long time we kept all rooms locked up. The keys are six inches long and weigh about a pound each, so this grew very taxing. And things kept disappearing, disappearing. If I complained enough, sometimes they'd re-appear where they certainly hadn't been the day before. Odd things, of no earthly use to the thieves, like pepper mills, 2 saucers, 24 old diapers that X.Y. had brought back to use as cloths. They went for good—and so on. I had a really beautiful lantern over the front door—about ten feet up—and that lasted almost a month. One morning it was gone, with wiring and all—just a hole. Now we, at last, after some fearful trials, have two servants we like and actually trust, sisters—one to cook and clean, one to be a *baba* for Googie, nice clean quiet girls, quite pretty, too—a family of thirteen, eight unmarried girls—and they have taken in three or four more children, orphans, cousins—there are about 20 people living in a very tiny crumbling mud-&-wattle house. But they don't know how to do anything *except* clean and wash clothes. I tried to teach Eva how to set the table and she said it made her nervous and she was leaving. So I do that part myself. They don't know how to use the third person. X.Y. speaks quite fluently, but I'm sure she sounds like an old miner, they all speak so badly, and with so much slang I can't understand her, and she can't understand my slightly purer Portuguese.

My birthday couldn't have been duller. Three people came over from Belo Horizonte and we split two bottles of beer. Carnival began the day before, so there was too much celebration for four nights. Even this little place has its samba schools—"Allegorical Cars" [floats] you should have seen them—and "balls." The last night we were asked to sit in the judges' stand . . . so I suppose we are members of the establishment now. Googie went absolutely wild—he liked it better than anyone else. The last night just got too much for him and he dashed off the stand and raced after a samba group with big drums, going up the hill, avoiding the policemen who tried to catch him, and doing a samba on his own. He went so fast, he vanished in the crowd. X.Y. started off in the other direction to catch him on the way around, then she didn't come back, nor did Googie. Great excitement and the judge with the loudspeaker shouted to the crowd (thousands): "Small BLOND child lost!" The blondness makes him outstanding of course; in fact I was afraid someone would kidnap him for his *beaux yeux* (blue) and fair hair (not that they wouldn't gladly bring him back in 24 hours if they did). But finally a strange lady appeared with Googie in her arms and handed him up, a little scared, to the cheers of the mob. Everyone here seems to know him. He goes out a lot to take walks with the *baba*—and when we are with him many strangers hail him by name—including all the town bums and drunks and idiots. Today the electrician has taken him home for the afternoon. The maids wanted to take him to a funeral, so we decided the atheist electrician, who has named all his sons for scientists—Marconi, Einstein, etc., and has a new baby named Oppenheimer—would provide the better social life.

Bob Giroux wired me from Union Square that I am nominated for the National Book Award [for *The Complete Poems*]. He thinks I will get it, but I think it is a case of always a bridesmaid & never a bride.

The trouble is, I really don't know where or how I want to live any more. I liked San Francisco, fairly well only—and loved the flat, but it didn't suit as a place to work in, really—now sublet to three schoolteachers. New York seems just too much to face, somehow, although I am homesick for it . . . I love this house—if ever it gets to working and we finally get unpacked, after seven months in it. No closets yet—they just don't DO things here. A beautiful big armoire for the dressing room all designed and down payment made—and then nothing. Two copies of old hanging lamps for the *sala*—one appeared four months ago, the other is still a naked bulb. Well, we finally have almost got rid of the fleas. Hens and burros had been kept in the basement for 40 years or so. And let me NOT live in a house by the side of the road. The people who come by selling vegetables and eggs are nice, but not the people who ring the doorbell and run away, and those simple souls who just come and ask for MONEY. Or "old clothes"—I said I wore mine, obviously, since we are both in rags by now and you can't buy anything here to wear—then this young lady said: "Well, just give me anything you have." They also go through my garbage every day—I think they are looking for Parker pens, probably . . .

The "old friend" who was doing the house for me is now "not speaking" & I'll probably have to go to law. The books were in such a state I had to hire a lawyer-accountant for over a month to straighten them out, and found I'd been paying for lots of things for two other houses as well (including items like cases of whiskey). Of course the "old friend" didn't like this very much, although she agreed it was a fine idea to take an accountant, to begin with. So then a lot of people stopped speaking to me. Some of them are coming around again—not that I care much one way or the other—but one really doesn't like to be treated like a dumb American millionaire. It's queer—this place is so very different from Petrópolis. I lived there mostly for over 15 years—and I was robbed just once, and come to think of it, that thief was a *Mineiro*—which proves something.

I have put ads in *The Saturday Review* and *The New York Review*— and am toying with *Previews*, but I'm afraid they're too expensive. They sent me the most amazing brochures and sample pamphlets of their "properties"—including the Duke of Windsor's French country house. We happened to be painting toilet seats when this came and I wondered if he and the Duchess got ready to sell in any such way.

Have you ever read Tomlinson's *The Sea and the Jungle*? I have just re-read most of it, trying to get going on this book, and it's really the best on the subject I know. I was also a bit cheered to read in some of Carlyle (loathe him but like those letters) that he got stuck in *The French Revolution* and "read trash for 4 weeks"—meaning novels.

It is strange to be so old. The maids regard me as a curiosity—the fact I can still get around at all—and climbing ladders! They think someone is ancient at forty.

To Dr. Anny Baumann

Washington's Birthday, 1970

I have been feeling somewhat better physically, except awfully tired and depressed all the time (which I naturally try to conceal), but Ouro Prêto is too damp, I think—lots of rheumatism & aching joints, and so on. Poor X.Y. and her son, both being blond, have troubles with fleas, ticks, insects I never saw or heard of before—they are both covered with bites all the time, *coitados* (poor things). I seem to be almost immune to all these things. But even so—X.Y. likes it here, I can't see why—well, I think she likes all this building and re-constructing—I don't; I just want things done, and peaceful, and a little *order* at last.

I had a note from Louise a few days ago, about Marianne—fairly good report. I haven't heard from Cal Lowell for months and months. I know how busy everyone in New York is, however, but I do hope he is keeping all right. Bob Giroux wired me that I am one of the nominees for the National Book Award, again. But I feel about this that I am always a bridesmaid but never a bride. The money would be nice, however—I am fearfully worried about it, and haven't earned anything in so long. This week I am going to TRY to get something ready to mail, to attempt to sell it . . .

IF I get that award, I thought it might be enough to make a quick trip to the U.S. I need some dentistry, eyeglasses, medicines, and certainly I need a change. I'm afraid X.Y. would object strenuously. Well, we'll see, and it probably won't happen, anyway. In fact, I see no end to it all. I try to keep remembering that I had about 15 really happy years until Lota got so sick—and I should be grateful—most people don't have that much, I know. But since she died, Anny—I just don't seem to care whether I live or die. I seem to miss her more every day of my life. I try hard to live in the present, as everyone always says—but the present is so hideous to me. I wish I could shake all this off and enjoy things a bit more—but

I can't seem to. I *must* get out of this country, and never come back to it. X.Y. doesn't understand this at all, of course, and I don't talk about it, naturally. I am sorry to have unburdened myself to you this way—you are the only person I can tell these things to, however. Send me some strength of character . . .

To Robert Lowell

The following letter is EB's response to Robert Lowell's three sonnets "For Elizabeth Bishop," which he had written for the revised edition of Notebook *(1970)—"Water," "Castine, Maine," and "Vocation" (later named "Calling"). After hearing from EB, Lowell composed a fourth sonnet out of the second and final paragraphs of this letter. In* History *(1973) it appears as the third poem of the quartet and is entitled "Letter with Poems for a Letter with Poems."*

February 27, 1970

It was wonderful to get your letter . . . I love the poems, of course, especially, I think, #2 ["Castine, Maine"], I suppose because it is the most personal. And the last four lines of #3 ["Do / you still hang your words in air, ten years / unfinished," etc.]. And I am always dumbfounded by your capacity for re-doing things. You say "not to lose" #1—but surely it would never be lost. I think I'll try to turn that damned "Fish" into a sonnet, or something very short and quite different. (I seem to get requests for it every day for anthologies with titles like *Reading as Experience*, or *Experience as Reading*, each anthologizer insisting that he is doing something completely different from every other anthologizer. But I'm sure this is an old story to you.) The first sonnet has the most brilliant effects, I suppose, but I do like *The Youth's Companion* (I used to take it), and the Georges. It's weird—I'd actually been contemplating a poem on George V myself all last week, because I had just re-read Max Beerbohm's account of him to his wife . . . I love the inchworm, too ["Have you seen an inchworm crawl on a leaf, / cling to the very end, revolve in air, / feeling for something to reach something?"]—except that it describes the way I feel at present only too well—and not just in respect to poetry. Oh, thank you; thank you very much—you can really never know how much this has cheered me up and made me feel a bit like myself again.

Well, you are right to worry about me, only please DON'T!—I am pretty worried about myself. I have somehow got into the worst situation I have ever had to cope with and I can't see the way out. If I could *trust* anybody in this town, I'd close up the house and leave, or leave a maid or two in it—but that would just mean coming back again, sooner or later, and although it would be a tremendous relief to get away—I don't want to do that. I am trying to sell the house, as I think I wrote you— have had several nibbles, but nothing at all certain yet. I am trying just to get everything in working order, go through all the books, papers, letters, and so on—(about 3,000 or more books here) so that I can leave if the chance comes. But it may take months or years; meanwhile it is too damned lonely and disagreeable and I have not been able to work. Just the last two weeks I've done a little, but very little—there are endless, endless interruptions, noise, confusion, thefts (you wouldn't believe how much has been stolen, a lot of it somehow right under my eyes), trips to Belo Horizonte for building materials, hiring, firing, re-hiring, re-firing. It's a terrible tale of woe. Another problem is that X.Y. likes it here and doesn't want me to sell the house—and this makes for difficulties, naturally. The saddest part of all is that I really love my house and would like to stay in it, if—if—if things were different—but the only solution seems to be to sell it and get out. The very thought of all the packing and expensive shipping makes me sick—and then, where to go? How to live? I am thinking of New York—and then Dr. Baumann writes me she thinks San Francisco is better for me! But what does she know about it? I liked the flat there—now sublet—but again, the living arrangements just didn't work, and if I go back there I'd have to find another place, or two other places, preferably. I want to live alone, dismal as it is. (But please don't refer to this when you write.) Well, all I can do is to try to get ready, and endure it here, and try to work a little while I endure, and pray to get away as soon as possible . . .

I had a slightly hysterical—no, just "excited"—letter from Bob Giroux yesterday—all about the NBA—wanting me to telephone him, then he will telephone me, and so on. I don't think he realizes it is next to impossible to telephone him from here—and I haven't a telephone, anyway. It would mean a day, or days, at the telephone company. He seems to think that you and I are the possibilities—but one never knows, and I see Rexroth is a judge and am pretty sure he dislikes me. I'm afraid my feelings about it are that I think *you* deserve it, and if *I* should get it I'd be delighted to have the money, but don't see how on earth I could make it to N.Y. All my winter clothes being in S.F., for one thing, and then doesn't one have to make a *speech*? And [Senator Eugene] McCarthy is a judge, too! All these things have so very little to do with work, and so much with personalities.

I wonder where you are going in Italy. The trip that Lota and I made there in '64 was wonderful—the last time we did anything together when she was fairly well and like herself. We had the best time of all in Venice and she wanted to go back there. I tried and tried after that to get her to give up that disastrous job and plan to go to stay in Venice for a long stretch. If only she had, I miss her more every day of my life. This is one of the reasons I want to leave Brazil (forgive me).

Also I wonder what you are going to do at Oxford?—I visited All Souls in '66—I had some friends there then—and was shown all over the place, some wonderful little garret apartments. Also—they wear such fascinating gowns. I suppose you'll be wearing one. "John Sparrow" seems always to be turning up in reference to friends—sounds so 17th-century.

Have you ever gone through caves?—I did once, in Mexico, and hated it so I've never gone through the famous ones right near here. Finally, after hours of stumbling along, one sees daylight ahead—faint blue glimmer—and it never looked so wonderful before. That's what I feel as though I were waiting for now—just the faintest glimmer that I'm going to get out of this somehow, alive. Meanwhile—your letter has helped tremendously—like being handed a lantern, or a spiked walking stick. Write when you have time—I do know how busy you are.

P.S. Having nothing of my own to send, I'll send a sonnet of Vinícius de Moraes that I did for this bloody anthology ["Sonnet of Intimacy"]. It is almost exactly like the Portuguese and rather funny, I think.

To Robert Giroux

Certain that EB would win the National Book Award in poetry for The Complete Poems, *I had written her explaining that the presentation at Lincoln Center was scheduled to take place two days after the judges' announcement, we hoped she'd attend, and that I'd phone her the minute it was announced. When I put the call through to Ouro Prêto, expecting a long delay (she had no phone and would have to be summoned), EB was already at the post office.*

March 5, 1970

I can't get over the coincidence of our meeting in mid-air like that. Perhaps it wouldn't strike you as so strange, in New York, but if you could see the circumstances here: the dismal little Post Office I just happened to go to at that time, and the two very stupid telephone girls with whom I'd been arguing for ten minutes to put through my call to you. They informed me that Oregon was a state [the FSG telephone exchange at that time was Oregon 5], and what city in Oregon did I want, and they had to be taught to pronounce Don Roberto's last name, and so on—until finally when I got into booth No. 1, they abandoned me to talk to two boy-friends, very loudly. But then I heard an English-speaking operator, I suppose in Rio, using my full name, though on this end I'd given "Dona Elizabeth," as the custom is—and I realized right away that you were calling me, and also that I had probably received the [National Book] Award. It was very nice . . . With two ex-Peace Corps workers visiting us, we all went out to dinner that evening at the best (that's not very good) restaurant here to celebrate.

After I left the Post Office the Brazilian Cultural Attaché called me, via a neighbor, and was disappointed that I already knew of the award.

He said, "Oh, you've taken the wind from my sails," and he had a car ready to send for me to make it to the plane for Rio, and reservations on a night plane to New York—all very nice of him . . . Oh, I toyed for several hours with the idea of going, but it really would have been extremely complicated and very expensive, even with the plane fare paid for me . . . I gave the Attaché my cable asking Cal to accept for me— safer than sending it from here. I thought of several witty (I thought) things to say, but then decided it was probably better to be strictly conventional. I'd love to hear about the goings-on at Philharmonic Hall [where the NBA ceremony was held] . . .

To Robert Lowell

March 5, 1970

I hope this reaches you before you take off for Italy. Such excitement here about the NBA—it was rather nice. Many wires from Bob, all weirdly misspelled by the time they got here, and then when I called him we seemed to meet in mid-Atlantic. He was calling me at the very same minute. I really wanted to go to N.Y. but it would have been an awful rush—barely 24 hours to get ready and get from here to Rio—no cold-weather clothes at all—and then, the expense, even if FSG paid the airplane fare. But I would have loved seeing you and other friends. I have never attended one of those functions and can't imagine what they are like. I remember reading parts of a speech by Updike, however, and feared that a speech might be expected. I hope my cable (Bob's suggestion) reached you, served the purpose, and wasn't an awful nuisance to you. It seems to me you are always doing things for me that I should somehow be able to do for myself, and I am really profoundly grateful. I thought of several other cables; one was "About time"—not that I'd send it. It seemed like an occasion when one should be quite square, so I hope it was all right. My stock with the Post Office, telephone company, and, I gather, the U.S. Embassy here, has gone way up. How I would love to have heard the judges' conversation—Rexroth and McCarthy especially. Well, I am sure I owe it all to you and thank you, as well as for the helping hand at the announcement ceremonies, if you were able to be there. These things make such a big impression on the ignorant—like here—it is nice.

Just made a birthday cake for the maid who is 18 today—Eva. I've never known so many Adams and Eves, seem to be the favorite names here. This girl and her younger sister have really made life much more bearable, clean and quiet—now if only they'll stay a while. The mother —they are 2 of 13—comes to the door every day or so and they go through a little ritual: "Bless me, Mother." "God bless you, my daughter," and so on. Strange little children in the street say it to me, and I feel rather foolish, "God bless thee, my child." The weather has been absolutely heavenly—such clouds, rainbows, pink rainstorms with bright green hills showing through, churches coming and going through the rain or wrapped in pale green cocoons of mist. Oh dear—I am of two minds about selling. If only things were a bit different.

We have had such a nice young man visiting, too—a former Peace Corps boy from Chattanooga, old Episcopalian family, one brother a minister, etc.—went to Harvard, where his mother thought he would become depraved. He bought a big old *fazenda* with a friend and worked it—a long story he didn't go into, but the friend committed suicide, and now this boy's legal problems are very much like mine only a great deal worse. Perhaps that has cheered me up more, too. I didn't think anyone's could be worse than mine. He hung pictures, cleaned the gramophone, sorted all the records, *knew* about electricity and plumbing—and he's coming back—I'm glad to say—because he is very much taken with X.Y., I think. I just learned today that Rothko, too, had committed suicide. I don't know anything about him, except that he came from someplace along the Washington coast—that's where he got a lot of those beautiful colors. Oh why? I wonder. Heavens, what a vale of tears it is.

I love the sonnets [about EB] and read them over and over . . .

[P.S.] Dreamed of Elizabeth last night, huddled in the middle of a group of three ladies all wearing fur coats. I suppose this is because my coat (in storage in San Francisco) was one reason I couldn't go to New York.

To Dr. Anny Baumann

[POSTCARD]

March 7, 1970

I'm sorry I wrote you such a gloomy letter recently. Things have improved a bit, and at least I have made up my mind what to do about them. Also, as you may have seen, I received the National Book Award this year—and although this doesn't really indicate much from a literary point of view it is very nice—and people here are impressed! The weather has been heavenly, too, and that helps a lot; it is "summer," but never hot like in Rio. X.Y. is putting on some sort of party tonight to celebrate the award. Our very few friends are mostly in Belo Horizonte, but some of them come over weekends—this is one—and I hope it will be successful.

I have another piece of news I'll tell you—it isn't all settled yet, so please don't tell anyone at all. I think I'm taking on the job of poetry reviewing for *The New Yorker*—something I'd really like to do. It is just 4 or 6 times a year—and one can write about what one wants to, I gather, so I think I could do it all right, and it would be a small source of "security" (much needed) . . .

To Arthur Gold and Robert Fizdale

April 26, 1970

It is 8 a.m.—a heavenly morning and we are going to Belo Horizonte to see the doctor . . . I'll mail this there and write a real letter later from home. Your painting [by José Aparecido, at art school] has been done for some time now and it is adorable, I think. I'll write about its creation in detail. It is a *present*. X.Y. may be taking Googie up to his pa, I take it, or I'll find someone going up. I propose to stay on here a while longer & work on that book—but my plans aren't very certain . . .

To James Merrill

May 5, 1970

. . . You have been so extremely kind about José Alberto Nemer— and please believe that he appreciates it very much. I have had everything except the final copying and part of the *curriculum vitae* here for months now, and thought that at any minute all would be in the mail to New York. However, the last four months—and probably for long before that, but I didn't fully realize it—my "secretary" has been very sick, and growing sicker. I didn't even know the work had not been done until the deadline came. I don't want to tell this to anyone much, but I shall tell you—she had a complete breakdown, is now in a clinic in Belo Horizonte, and the doctors and I are just hoping she'll get well enough to go back to the U.S.A. fairly soon, with her 3½-year-old son, for treatment there.

This sad business has occupied me completely for over a month now and I have had to be in Belo Horizonte much of the time. I finally got back a few days ago—with the little boy, poor child—and then I found someone nice here to leave him with—with other children—and this is the very first day I have been up to writing a letter myself, or had the time to. I'm sorry to be writing such sad things—this is the third time I have been through this with someone I am fond of in the last few years. I should really be getting used to it. My papers and letters are in complete chaos and I am hoping for a young ex-Peace Corps boy to come here fairly soon to work with me on them. I did keep your letter carefully, however, thank goodness. I'd be very, very grateful if you didn't speak of this to anyone—for the girl's sake. I am just writing to her family—or have already—and our various doctors.

So I am here quite alone—and after one more trip to Belo Horizonte,

I think I'll be able to settle down and maybe even consider some of my own work.

I told Nemer about the *next* possibility, and he is very eager to try that, too. (No, nothing got lost—I do hope John Myers didn't search too hard.) He does have a very slight chance of a *bôlsa* (scholarship) from the French Embassy—one out of 19, something like that—but he wants much more to go to New York. If by any chance the French thing does work out, I think he'd still want to go to N.Y. later (if he hasn't starved to death in France, in the meantime). I love him very much—everyone does—I'll say now that I think he is a really remarkable boy, and he has been so kind, and helped me so much throughout this last awful stretch.

The wonderful news is that you may actually be coming here . . . I still don't know what living here and working here might be like, since I don't feel as if I had really started yet. If you go to Peru—but you must go, and then come to visit me. I am all alone in a rather big house, two or three extra bedrooms, and I have a clean but somewhat incompetent maid—the best I've been able to find here, however. You can't imagine how much I would like to see you—a real representative and friend from the real world—Bobby and Arthur can tell you a bit about Ouro Prêto (I'm going to try to write to them today, too)—I think they liked it. I would show you the sights and we could rent a car and driver to go to see some even better sights, if you wanted to.

You fly from Lima straight to Rio—I've done it by day and by night—the Andes are frightening, but the day flight is worth it, I think. You'll see how exactly like some of Klee's paintings they look (rather a worn comparison now, but it is striking). In Rio you have to change airports—usually—sometimes there is a flight to Brasília that stops in Belo Horizonte. I'll write you what you should pay the cabdriver. From the airport of Galeão to the small city airport of Santos Dumont (who discovered the airplane, they say here, in case you didn't know—you must not mention the Wright Brothers). Or maybe you'd like to stop over a few days in Rio—if so, I like the Hotel Ouro Verde best. The flight from Rio to Belo Horizonte is a little less than an hour. If you know when you are coming you could wire me and I'd send over a favorite driver of my own—or you can make a bargain with an airport taxi driver, but do not pay more than *50 New Cruzeiros*. Ask for Dona Elizabetchy—or Rua Quintiliana, 546, or "Os Lages" (ledges), and stop at the big yellow door. It is also the *"Estrada para Mariana"* and my house is named for Marianne Moore and has a small plaque on the doorpost: casa mariana. You see, I have you coming in the door already.

I'm about 50 miles from Belo Horizonte, the world's ugliest city. There are very few "interesting" people here. I can think of three, but Nemer comes over most weekends and you could meet him—perhaps Vinícius de Moraes might show up, and a Rio painter I like also has a house here and is often here. Oh dear—July is the month of the "Arts

Festival"—I forgot—when the town is full of young people and, last year, looked rather like the Berkeley campus. But we could stay at home admiring the view, or go someplace else. Don't let Bobby tell you about my favorite church—I want to surprise you with it, too.

If you come, Jimmy—I seem to be putting everything in this letter —will you bring me three things I am greatly in need of? Not heavy. (1) some good TEA. I like Ridgway's—is it Queen Mary's or Queen Victoria's mix?—anyway, black tea—in a small tin box. Or Twining's Queen E.'s or Queen M.'s. I also like lapsang souchong or any good green tea once in a while. I'm all out now—and a half pound of any good tea, or quarter of a pound black, and quarter of a pound green, would be wonderful. They actually raise tea *here*, but it isn't any good. (2) Some powdered ginger. I can get the roots here occasionally, but not the powdered and, like Carlyle, my favorite food is gingerbread. A bottle of Spice Islands ginger—and (3) another of their curry (curry here, too, but not good) would brighten life a lot. THAT'S ALL. I'm really not as bad as D. H. Lawrence, am I? I don't say look in the bottom of the trunk and find the faded blue notebook and also send along the complete ms. of *Lady Chatterley*, etc.

These snapshots should go in Nemer's file, I suppose—but I just want to show you he really exists—and has more social charm than I've ever seen in such a young man. Please do visit me—I honestly think you'd like it. Bring warm clothes—it is "winter" then. I have a fireplace and an electric sheet for you.

To Dr. Anny Baumann

May 11, 1970

. . . I am afraid my news is very bad. X.Y. had a very bad breakdown and I finally got her to consent to go to a hospital in Belo Horizonte. At least, I got her as far as Belo Horizonte, and to a psychiatrist of her choice (the most famous there & head of the Brazilian Medical Association . . .).Our good friends there, and Dr. Sergio Bicalho, our medical doctor, and I all finally persuaded her to go to a hospital the night of the 28th of April. She stayed there until early morning May 10th, yesterday. I had taken over her bags and the little boy the day before, Monday afternoon. The doctor, or a very good friend of ours (I don't know which yet, but fortunately she still was liking *them* both), flew with her to Rio and saw that she got safely on the plane to San Francisco, and some member of her family was to meet her plane at San Francisco for the last flight . . . If they took Dr. Bicalho's and my advice, they took her immediately to a hospital there. I suggested the university hospital, since I know it is excellent, and they have a psychiatric floor. I am hoping very much to get a cable from her mother today or tomorrow saying that she arrived safely and where she is. I am very concerned about this, naturally, since although I have met her mother and two of her sisters, I have no idea how intelligently they might behave in a situation like this. I wrote the mother the day after X.Y. went to the hospital, and also several times more; and the Cultural Attaché (U.S.), who also acts as consul in Belo Horizonte, telephoned her last Friday night.

Well, I suppose I should have realized much, much sooner that she was really extremely sick. I don't know why one never does & especially when one is living in close contact with someone in that state. (And I have had enough experience by now, it would seem.) But about three months ago now I made up my mind that she had to leave, and also had to have some psychiatric care as soon as possible—she was obviously getting worse all the time, and even I could recognize the symptoms. Every time she seemed to be in a calm enough frame of mind I told her that when Googie (the little boy) had to go back to his father, the first part of May, I wanted her to go with him, and take a good long vacation, and see a doctor. She would apparently accept this, but then when she got worked up the next time she would accuse me of "throwing her out," etc., and refuse to go, and so on. About three weeks ago a real crisis developed in which she was more violent than ever before—fortunately, my Belo Horizonte friends were here and saw a lot of it, and one of them got Sergio to come over. (She is such a wonderful actress that I really think she might have fooled people if they hadn't actually happened on her at a bad moment.) Sergio was all for taking her away immediately —but this upset her so terribly that I said to leave her with me for a few days more and I'd get her there—which I did, somehow or other. Affection always works—or worked—much better than argument, "reasoning" certainly better than force.

Her ambivalence toward me was quite incredible—and I only really became aware of it in February, I think. I should have known much sooner—but she *is* a good actress, also concealed many, many things from me, including her own room, which she kept locked (& that didn't seem too strange, since there were a lot of building supplies in it and the Ouro Prêto workers steal a lot). Since I have got into it, I have been appalled at the accumulation, and the disorder, and the fantastic things I have found there. I think rather slowly, I know. It just came back to me yesterday how the young man who got Robert Lowell to come to Brazil treated *him*—it was exactly the same, only not quite so bad—a mixture of hero worship and incredible aggressiveness, rudeness in public, and so on. (Only in that case it was the poet who got sick, not the other person!) I think in some strange way X.Y. wanted to *be* me—and so really was trying to kill me off, to have the house, etc., all for herself. I know this sounds wild—but many, many things she did prove it, and the few good friends we have (who were here weekends) observed the same thing.

She is crazy about this house and made plans for it way beyond my means all the time. The poor girl fought with everyone in this town, I think, and has made a great many problems for me here. I am hoping if I stay on alone long enough, I can live it all down and people will realize that I didn't know about a great deal of what she was doing. I have just found out since. I have had to take a construction firm from Belo Horizonte to re-do the work on the house (it is at last *working*). She had antagonized all the workers here. (Sometimes she was right, really, because they aren't very good, and *are* dishonest.) She also went through a phase in which she thought Googie was going to be kidnapped—about 6 weeks ago. I sent them off to stay with friends in Belo Horizonte for some days that time, and Sergio saw her, took her out, etc., and she seemed a lot better when she got back—but it was very temporary.

However, since February I have just been holding on and waiting for the first of May to come, and hoping that she would hold together until then—but of course she didn't. I don't think she has touched a paper or written a letter for me for four or five months now. I've been doing what I could myself. Everything is in the utmost disorder and I am trying to get an ex-Peace Corps boy—a trained secretary—to come over from Belo H. and stay with me for a month or two. None of the work I brought poor X.Y. here to do has been touched, so far. I just tried to let her do exactly what she wanted to do, and tried to keep her happy—but it didn't work, obviously. She is a wonderful worker, when she likes what she is doing—but she got more and more obsessive about it all, every day.

Sergio tells me it is schizophrenia(?) with paranoid symptoms, too. She thought the nurses at the clinic were poisoning her, and other typical symptoms. He thinks it is very serious—but he is not a psychiatrist, of course. I have only attempted to talk to the other doctor once—and I'm very much afraid X.Y. chose him only because she knew he was the most expensive—that was another of her recent symptoms, spending my money like water, although she had always been extremely careful and honest, naturally, before. I've had to write all the banks, lawyers, etc., and send things back that she had ordered without telling me. Oh well, I suppose it is a common story.

I feel sorriest of all for Googie. When I came back here, after getting her into the hospital—he stayed those two days with our very good maid—I sent him off to play with Jair's children—you remember him? the nice restorer who worked on your little Santa Clara? Well, his wife, Zenith (! but pronounced Zen-eetchy), was wonderful with him, and with me. I told her the story, the only person I've told here, and she offered to keep Googie until he could travel with X.Y. This was much better for him than being here alone with me and the maid, I think. They have three children, the youngest a little boy just a bit younger than Googie. I saw them often, took them presents, sent them all to the circus here, etc.—and when I went to get him, early Saturday morning, he didn't want to leave. It was really awful. Zenith cried, too—and Jair was wonderful. If I could have, I think I would have left Googie there forever, to grow up in that family . . . I think he'd have more of a chance of being happy and normal. He's a beautiful little boy—4 in July—and what chance does the poor child have now? I wonder. (I don't think too highly of his father, but at least he is extremely fond of Googie.) I am very fond of him, too—although another of X.Y.'s fantasies was that I hated him.

I have written her mother just all the necessary facts—none of the details at all, to avoid distressing her as much as possible. X.Y. is so secretive about her life—I don't know but what this may have even happened to her before now. I am just afraid . . . they may have a typical "poor" reaction to this kind of thing and ship her off to a state home or something equally awful. This haunts me. I have suggested, as I said, the university hospital—but again, I don't know how long they keep patients there. Well, I just hope her mother will keep me informed. I don't think I can possibly do any more financially—at least not right away. All this has been fearfully expensive, of course. I am paying for everything at this end, and her tickets, and have paid all along for Googie. —I just found out she never wrote her family, or the child's father, once, after she came back last October. The father is supposed to send $100 a month for the child—but he didn't because he didn't know where X.Y. was. So it seems to me she should have $700 or $800 coming to her that way, and I've written to say it should be used for *her*, not sent here.

In spite of all the horrors I have been through with her here, I am still very fond of her and think I probably understand her as well as anyone does. That is not saying much, but certainly more than her family. I know she has never got along with them too well. I had to fight with the Cultural Attaché, who thinks "family" & "mother" are the same thing, I gathered—and even then he didn't say what I told him to over the telephone, so Dr. Sergio and I sent a cable saying "Advise immediate hospitalization. E. suggests university hospital" . . .

That is all, I think. I haven't had a drink for I've forgotten how many months now, Anny, and shall continue that way. I knew it was the only thing to do when things started deteriorating. I don't seem to mind being alone here and shall try to stick it out for some months and try to work, at last. I don't think I've told you but I am now the poetry reviewer for *The New Yorker*. Well, I haven't sent them my first piece yet, but I have accepted and like the idea very much. I hope I'll have some visitors. I sort of wish Louise might get to visit me this summer/winter. I'll write again. I am fine, really, just tired, but that is only natural.

To Ashley Brown

Ouro Prêto
May 20, 1970
. . . I'd like, if possible, to explain the sad business of the "baby book" [missing photo album of childhood and family pictures], for which you

have very kindly forgiven me, I think; at least you have written to me again. Well, it was missing in 1966, or maybe 1965. (I am losing track of the years.) I kept it in my study in Petrópolis, always. Lota liked the baby book very much and did take it down to her room in Petrópolis at one time. I thought I took it back up, but when she asked for it again, it could not be found. It makes me feel very bad because it has in it the only snapshots of my father I have. Oh well, I've lost a lot of old things I rather cherish. It was Lota's idea, to begin with, that maybe you had it. She was still well enough then to try to convince me about it in a logical way. I did refuse to write you, but when X.Y. took over my papers, letters, and so on, she too got the same notion. I finally weakened and wrote to you. That is the whole sad little tale. You and David Weimer were the only people I ever let work in my study. I saw him a year ago, and he is transparently good and honest and not interested in such things. I suppose if someone did take it, to make use of it, I'll be dead and gone and won't care. But I feel very bad about it.

Now that I am on this sad subject: Do *you* have any old pictures, snapshots or anything—any good at all, of Lota? I have almost nothing. I'd be extremely grateful if you have anything if you'd have copies made for me. Mary Morse went over everything in Petrópolis before I got there and took everything good. (Please don't repeat this—it is the first time I've said it, too.) I have 3 or 4 old snapshots, bad ones, and a tiny picture of Lota in the third grade, probably. Then Rosinha told me—when I was here at the end of 1967—that she was having copies made of one very good picture of Lota—taken at the Museum of Modern Art at a table, with Monroe Wheeler. It had even been used on a TV program about Lota, before I got back. The pictures never came. Somehow or other, after I returned to the U.S.A., everyone I had ever known in Rio, some friends of over 15 years (as I thought), turned against me. I saw no one —but I won't go into all that branch of my hideous affairs. I wrote to Rosinha, via Magú, who had continued to write me, occasionally, and got word back that she knew nothing whatever about this picture. An appeal to Mary Morse wasn't answered. Apparently all connections of Lota's are trying to pretend I don't exist. Well, I know that after a death like hers people do have very odd reactions. They *tried*, a few of them, the month I spent in Rio in November '67—but never a word from anyone since. To hell with them, I'm afraid is what I feel. However, since I am a social outcast here, too, it is a bit uncanny and lonely. I am not minding too much any more, however.

Mary Morse also burned all my letters to Lota, which Lota had carefully saved so that I could use them—the Amazon trip, London, all sorts of little trips when I was away from her. This is the second time this has happened to me—my correspondence over years, with an old friend, been burned by someone else who had no business to do it. The first time, the friend—whom I had never met, even—wrote me, "You'll be glad to hear—" & I should never write anything indecent—like this! Such nasty forms do unconscious jealousy, envy, etc., take. And now I have certainly lifted the lid off enough horrors for one morning.

But as you see, I have been living in an atmosphere that was not conducive to normal thinking for quite a long time. However, I am feeling better at last, all the time; in fact, in spite of the awful people here, I am feeling more like myself than I have in 4 or 5 years, I think, and it is very pleasant. I have even finished a long poem and have four more going.

X.Y. went back about 3 weeks ago to take her little boy back to his father for the summer and to visit her family. She had not been at all well, so she is having various tests made, seeing her own doctor, etc. I expect to stay on alone here now until October sometime. I've promised to read in Chicago the middle of November, and maybe I'll do a few more readings. I am NOT selling the house after all. Since I've got an honest, hardworking "firm" re-doing the plumbing, wiring, and so on (much of it for the third or fourth time), I am so cheered up about the house, and love it so much, I am going to hold on to it as long as I can—another decade, let's say. It is really getting so beautiful—and the weather is beautiful now, too. It rained all of January and nothing *worked*—I suppose that was when I almost gave up . . .

Ned Rorem—he has done another musical setting I have here of a poem called "Conversation." X.Y. sang it to me—it sounded very nice. I have written him my objections (& everybody's, I think) to "St. Elizabeths"—but he didn't answer that part of my letter . . .

I envy your going to Ireland—I had such a nice time there many years ago. But as long as I am at work again, I am happy enough here —and I do expect some visitors over the summer months.

To Marianne Moore

[POSTCARD]

June 10, 1970

I have just found a book of yours I had been hoping to find ever since I got here—the Faber *Selected Poems*. So I am feeling very cheerful and shall write you a postcard. All my other copies of your books are safe in San Francisco, but I'd lost track of this one for two years. A friend came to call the other day and noticed my little plaque on the doorpost and asked about it. So I took him into my study to show him your photograph—the George Platt Lynes one with hat & gloves, very chic. (You hang *above* Robert Lowell and to the *left* of Dom Pedro II, the last Emperor of Brazil, a nice Nadar photo that Lota found.) You three are my only photographs. It is considered very cold here today (55° Fahrenheit). All have sweaters on and go about complaining. When they stop to talk they pick hairs off each other's sweaters—the winter diversion here.

To Dr. Anny Baumann

June 17, 1970

. . . When I first realized X.Y. was sick—around Christmas—I did suggest that when she took the child back, in May, she should plan to spend the summer in the San Francisco flat, IF she'd promise to go to a good psychiatrist, or analyst, *frequently*. When she was feeling calm, she had agreed to this two or three times. Toward the end I never mentioned it again, of course; she was obviously too sick—and at any mention of the future she would insist I was "throwing her out" and so on. I believe her expression used to be that I "use up" my friends "like old gloves" and "throw them away," or drive them to suicide. You get the idea. She began finally to tell everyone we know that I overworked her terribly, never gave her a day off, or a vacation, and so on. Fortunately everyone knew better and no one believed the poor child for a moment—but maybe her mother does think I am some sort of cruel monster, who knows? Actually, X.Y. has not done one bit of work for me since around Christmas. I don't think she has even typed one letter for me in six months; I've been doing what has got done myself. She decided to help with the house remodeling, and I was so eager to have peace and quiet I just let her do whatever she wanted to—to the decided disadvantage of my poor house . . . I just don't know why it took me so long to catch on—but one day what was the matter suddenly did strike me like lightning.

One thing is that I myself have been feeling better all the time. About the time I felt like myself again (for the first time in three or four years) came the day on which I also realized X.Y. was out of her mind. My own affairs seem to be going very well in spite of all this awfulness. I have been drunk once, for a few hours, since Christmas—that's all. I have stopped smoking. I am now the poetry critic for *The New Yorker*. I told you that before, I think, and still haven't sent anything—but there is no poetry to criticize right now. And I have just—Sunday—accepted the invitation to take over Robert Lowell's courses at Harvard for the fall term, while he's in England. I want to do it, too. I went to his classes with him when I was there to read, and thought then I didn't want to teach, but if I ever had to (& I have to earn more money somehow, obviously) that was where I'd prefer to do it. I've also just sold *The New Yorker* the first poem I have been able to finish in over three years ["In the Waiting Room"] and really can't believe this. I have finished two more old ones and am well along with a brand-new one. At least I am glad to be able to give you some good news of myself.

I'm afraid the "subliminal uprush" was due to the great relief at getting poor dear X.Y. off my hands. And now that isn't solved yet. What do you think I should do, Anny? Please don't just say "Nothing. It is not your responsibility," because I am incapable of feeling like that, I'm afraid, and I am fond of X.Y. and the worse she got the more I realized how terribly lonely and friendless she is in this world and how much she needs someone to help her . . .

Postscript. I have always remembered a story you told me about a girl (the daughter of patients of yours, I think) who was also untidy far beyond the normal idea of untidiness & how she committed suicide one Thanksgiving Day. Well, X.Y. didn't show any signs of suicidal ideas at all, but the chaos she left her room in—she had kept it locked because all the "supplies" were in it—is still appalling. I get too upset when I try to clean it out, but I am doing it an hour or so a day. Before I caught on, she had bought tremendous amounts of building supplies and all kinds of tools one doesn't normally buy, and heaped them in this room: an expensive gadget that makes threads or screws on the ends of pipes, for example; two types of soldering iron, one big enough to make a battleship with, I think; sets of this and that; about $50 worth of *old* iron—a few hinges I *might* use, but not most of it, and so on. A large plumber's pump that works by electricity—somehow most of this had got into the house without my knowing it. And then the delusions got more serious—from just being suspicious (and sometimes that was justified, because the people here *are* notoriously dishonest, sort of like Naples). She suspected every-one of everything; political "spies"; kidnapping plots and so on. And since the situation is very tense here, anyway, I was terribly afraid that at any minute she'd land us into trouble with the police. I am still finding out some strange things she did—and there are still people here who won't speak to me because X.Y. fought with them, unknown to me, and they blame me for it. I just want you to get the idea, Anny, and please do not think I have been drinking or am suffering from delusions myself. I swear I have rarely felt saner.

She fought with and fired so many workmen that now I have difficulty getting anyone to work for me at all. She also fired the maids, in one hair-raising scene, shortly before she left. Then I took the best one back again, so that's all right—she seems to be staying. Oh heavens, the poor girl—what on earth can I do about her? She is so intelligent, really—and now that I see what a really ghastly family she must have, I suspect perhaps she has never been completely well, physically or mentally, in her life. I don't know if I told you—the doctors discovered X.Y. had been taking large doses of *my* stimulant medicine, Anorexyl. I wondered why it kept giving out. She was not sleeping at all, of course, & getting terribly thin. She also was obsessed about water pollution, insects, spiders—oh, the whole sad roll call.

I decided I don't want to sell the house, after all. I like it too much.

To Arthur Gold and Robert Fizdale

[POSTCARD]

July 26, 1970

I don't see how I'll ever make it until September 7, when I leave here. One week in Rio, then to San Francisco to try to wind things up there in (I hope) four days, getting to Cambridge about the 20th. Jim Merrill was absolutely the perfect guest, while I was far from the perfect hostess, being in the middle of a nervous breakdown (or something), I believe. I do hope he didn't suffer too much and I love him more than ever. I had 27 letters at the P.O. when I got there Monday and at least 20 require answers. Please find me a secretary!

To James Merrill

August 24, 1970

You must be thinking I am not only the World's Worst Hostess (& Housekeeper) but also its worst letter writer. The details would be too boring to go into—I stayed a few days with the Nemers after you left, and then came back here and actually did plunge into papers and books for a stretch. (Oh, Linda arrived at the airport just as you entered your plane; she was awfully sorry to have missed you and made the usual Brazilian remark—"Don't tell me the plane left *on time?*") Then I developed a sore throat—all Ouro Prêto had it—such as I have never had in my life. The local doctor didn't help at all so I finally went back to Belo H. and again stayed at the Nemers'. I was in bed for five days, I think, and just got back from there yesterday in time to see Lota's nephew, Flavio, for part of Sunday. I am so sorry he didn't come while you were here—he is turning out so well and I am very proud of him. He is about to publish a book of his own short stories and a large anthology of Brazilian short stories . . .

Staying at the Nemers' is a strange experience—probably like a visit to Lebanon. I find it extremely interesting, even if I say to myself every other minute, "But Lota would have *fits.*" Black olives and an extra-sumptuous kind of homemade yoghurt for breakfast, *kibbehs,* pilafs—mountains of Middle Eastern foods at all hours—and seven people all coming and going and all the younger ones busy making their fortunes. Both Linda & José Alberto start giving classes at *seven* in the morning and are rarely seen until late at night. Linda in fact has three jobs, I find . . . A terrifying huge black dog is released at night to eat up any intruders, and goes baying around the property. Their mother has never learned to read this kind of letter (is it Roman?)—just Arabic. She felt she had to sit by my bedside quite a lot and our conversations together were very odd, both being very polite but neither understanding anything the other said.

José Alberto is crazy about his little "oratorio," as he calls it, and is writing you a letter in French. For a Brazilian to get as far as *saying* he will write a letter is already something—but maybe you really will get it. Friday he received a telegram saying he had won the first prize in a huge art exposition being held in Curitiba (big city in the south) 2,000 New Cruzeiros . . . All the brothers and sisters immediately began collecting the money he owes them. He brought me home yesterday, wearing a blue shirt and purple trousers, looking like a large bunch of violets. I have yet to go to the Post Office and almost wish I didn't have to go at all, the last batch of letters was so fearful.

Again, I don't want to be boring but I am terribly terribly sorry that you came when I seemed to be going through a small—or big—nervous breakdown. It would have been sensible of me to ask you not to come, I suppose, but I did want to see you so much and I am so glad you did come even if it may not have looked that way at times. You got a very false impression of life here, I'm afraid, and I didn't—but I won't go on. You are without doubt the World's Best Guest and I never realized before how much I really love you. There. In fact I might say I adore you.

. . . It is beautiful here today and Eva had the house all shining for me when I got back and had used the stove polish very successfully on both stove & fireplace. Donald Ramos, wife, baby, and maid come the 6th, to take over. I have a great deal of preparatory work to do before then, alas—don't see how I'll ever get it done. I am typing this now with my laundress leaning on the table and smiling at me, about a foot away. She is so nice and seems to think I am lonely (which I am) and that she should come in every fifteen minutes or so to cheer me up. *Goodbye*, Jandira . . . *please*.

I haven't seen anyone here since you left, or scarcely—I had one very funny little scene when I got left alone with Lilli for a few moments. Her eyes filled with tears and she said, "But you're *suing* me," and I said, "Yes, I am," with my eyes probably filling with tears, too.

. . . The last two or three days in Belo Horizonte I was well enough to go out—once to celebrate José Alberto's prize—and discovered that there really are some quite presentable, even amusing, places in that awful city—especially one wonderful restaurant, also a place that specializes in—guess—*batidas*—of all possible flavors, where I met about seven poets at two in the morning. I somehow doubt you will return to Belo Horizonte, but if ever you do I'll be able to entertain you a bit better, I think—and frankly, didn't you find the armadillo a bit tough? . . . There was a huge roundup by the special police (DOPS) shortly after you left—over 400 students jailed, mostly released in 24 hours, but not all. They were after *maconha*, supposedly. This cartoon appeared in the paper next day— *batida* means "beaten," and a police roundup is called a *batida*, too . . .

I expect to go to San Francisco directly, about the 15th; hope to be able to finish there in four days or so, and then to Cambridge. But first, now, I must face that mail at the Post Office and I wish you were here to make your soothing and sensible (I hope you don't mind that word— but you are much more sensible than I am, I admit) presence felt . . .

P.S. I forgot to say, as I meant to, that during my stretch in bed I re-read all your book very carefully. I find that I like "16. ix. 65" very, very much—I don't think I mentioned it to you—and that I am now quite crazy about "To My Greek." It is full of beautiful images and the ending is superb. I also like especially the first section of "Flying from Byzantium." I wish you were here to tell you more—alas. Your book has made me determined to write a lot of things I suppose I just lacked the courage to before—so thank you again. Bill Alfred wrote me that Cal is in the hospital in England. This is so sad; he had kept well for such a long stretch. This certainly seems to be the year.

To Frani Blough Muser

Warren House
Harvard University
Cambridge, Massachusetts
October 1, 1970

Your letter came among some *more* bad poetry mss. (I had an awful thought as I went to the airport in Rio—"What if *no one* signs up for my two courses?" But by then it was too late to cable about this possibility & I needn't have worried—all the usual nuts and freaks seem to want to take "Advanced Verse Writing"—and yes, there *is* an Elementary or Beginners' or something Verse Writing, too). I shouldn't be so hard on the students, I suppose—that was my first impression, of the first class— when I get these mss. weeded out to the best ten, and see *them*, perhaps they won't be so bad. But why—the same thing happened in Seattle— do the hippie types just want to come to look me over and insult me, apparently? And how does one deal with them? Just interrupting doesn't stop them, oh dear. I'm the kind of teacher—when one polite boy gave me a Lily cup to put ashes in, I immediately set it on fire. But as I meant to go on saying, it was awfully nice to hear from you. Did I send you two postcards? . . . I do remember sending one, but my departure was so long & involved—I stayed a few days in Belo Horizonte, and then a week in Rio, and flights from both places were canceled and re-canceled. I finally got here at midnight the 24th or 25th.

I spent the first night with my friend Bill Alfred, of the English Dept. (*Hogan's Goat* if you remember that play), and he was terribly kind the next day—spent the whole day getting me through all the red tape. I would have been a week at it, probably, since I get lost every time I turn around, and have no gift of dealing with secretaries, etc., anyway. So now I am more or less installed, with IBM cards, a bank account, etc.—I am living temporarily in kind of an awful little bedroom and bath (and one hot plate and tiny refrigerator) at the Graduate Center—many Chinese, Hindus . . . Blacks, etc. But in a day or two I move to a *suite* in Kirkland House—two rooms and a real kitchen. I don't like this too well, but it is for such a short time, and so much cheaper than finding a furnished apt.—if I even could find one. I was offered 4-bedroom houses at $400–$500 a month, mostly . . .

I find the atmosphere of this Center very depressing—why do such places always have so many dead parlors and reception rooms, with grand-father clocks in them, reproduction antique furniture, and sets of books? Some of the sets I'd like to steal, actually. Harvard Square is not at all as I remember it from 40 years or so back—it has been re-designed entirely for automobile traffic so that it takes a long time to cross it on foot—and it is crowded with *"Eepies,"* as they call them in Brazil, or if they're not out-of-town hippies, they are hippie-ish students; and everyone seems to carry or push a baby, and also carry huge sacks of groceries. I keep wondering what I'd be like—or you—if we were students now, and asked Bill—who said I'd undoubtedly be a drop-out. I wondered why one awfully nice young ex-Peace Corps worker who stayed with me in Ouro Prêto seemed to be actually proud of having left Harvard—and now I see why. One poet friend, I'll mention no names, is demonstrating & telling classes how much more important that is than classes, and Bill—who is extremely popular here in general, was hissed at one huge lecture when he suggested they aren't here to run the country, exactly. So I may end up with no students at all, after a while. The other class—20th-century poetry up to Lowell—but I'll study only 8 poets—is much better, graduate students, mostly, and not scary like the others. Many shops still have boards in the windows, not glass—you can imagine why . . .

I shall send Cynthia [Krupat] a card and produce a present when I get to N.Y. I'm afraid I may have to go to San Francisco first, to clear out the flat there—maybe next week. Then visit my Nova Scotian aunt for her 85th or 86th birthday. Then I'll start planning for N.Y. . . . I'd love to see you. I talked with Louise Crane once on the telephone, to find out about Marianne mostly . . . What can I do about X.Y.? I'm seeing my lawyer tomorrow—she has been in touch with him. It is all dreadful. Cal had a bad breakdown in England, too, and the girl who had my Volkswagen, in S.F.—still paying on it—also wound up in a hospital and the car was found months later "in very bad condition," writes *that* lawyer. This seems to have been the year.

It was hellishly hot for the first two or three days—and of course I'd left all my little summer frocks in Rio. But now it is nice, really like "fall." I also called Dr. Baumann, who talked at great length about my more famous friends, Lowell & Moore, also her patients, and merely bawled me out when I complained faintly about the heat—so that wasn't very comforting. So I have almost decided to let the telephone alone—only answering it to try to be firm with more students, who calmly suggest that perhaps WE could work together on HIS thesis, etc. They're incredible. I had such nice Peace Corps guests—with knapsacks—and the three or four young Brazilians I like I really like a lot—so I had thought maybe I'd like the young, but now I don't know. You must know vastly more on this big subject than I do, however.

P.S. The young man I have staying in the Ouro Prêto house sent on your letter with a batch of others—and fines from the S.F. Police Dept., and so on . . . I have only two seminars—one Tuesday, one Wednesday, two hours each—that's a good arrangement. As this is a Thursday, I now have time to write a letter—and shall now go into Bonwit Teller's, I think, to buy some shoes. If I don't get lost again. But I have 5 days free—not counting for "preparation" of which I must do a lot, for a while—so I can get to N.Y. from time to time, I hope. Oh dear—the housemother or house couple or whatever they are here just asked me to read (free, I presume) *here*, and I was, I hope, most discouraging.

To Dr. Anny Baumann

Saturday morning
October 3, 1970

I had hoped to postpone the San Francisco trip for at least another week, until I really have things going here with my two seminars. I thought someone was staying in the S.F. apartment. I just found out at the lawyer's yesterday that it is now standing vacant and I am paying rent for nothing; also that it must be cleared out because the house is being sold. I returned too late last night to do anything about this . . .

If what she has written the Boston lawyer is true (he used to know her in Seattle), X.Y.'s physical health is very poor, too. The lawyer is a friend of an excellent doctor (the head of the university clinics, etc.). We agreed that if she will go to him for a check-up and be treated by him, we would *both* be willing to help with that medical expense. But nothing else—just something that could be checked up on. And I would just do it through the lawyer, of course. He is young but very bright, I think— he has handled all the trouble very well and has the advantage of knowing quite a lot about X.Y.—more than I do, probably. I am terribly sorry for her; her family is quite hopeless as far as I know—won't do anything at all—but I must avoid any communication with her, I know. It is sad, and awful. I certainly tried, but know I can't do any more.

I shall write another note to Marianne . . . On the 16th or 17th, if I'm not too weary after the S.F. trip, I may fly to Nova Scotia for two days for my remaining aunt's 85th birthday—I haven't seen her for 12 years or so. She is in much better shape than Marianne, travels all around Canada, and writes good letters—and it is a short trip from here, so I am hoping I can make it. Then after that I'll plan a New York trip—maybe for Loren's show.

I am moving to the Kirkland House address—right now, as soon as I finish packing again. I have two rooms and a kitchen—and it is cheap, for here (more expensive than N.Y.) and all I have to do is "eat with the boys" once in a while, which I don't mind at all . . .

To Loren MacIver

[POSTCARD]

Kirkland House, I–27
Harvard University
October 6, 1970

How strange it must seem to be returning to Perry Street after 12 years in France! Oh dear, I have a class on November 17th and can't play hooky. I hate to miss your opening at MoMA but I'll get to N.Y. as soon after that as I can. I hope Lloyd is all better now. Louise wrote me he'd been in the hospital in Paris, but that you are now both very well. For a scared elderly amateur "professor," I am too. Hugs and kisses.

To May Swenson

October 16, 1970

Iconographs found me here about three days ago. I had no idea (being so out of everything, most of the time) that you had produced such a large and impressive book of these poems. I didn't get any magazines all my last 18 months in Brazil (because I'd thought I was only going to stay 4 months and didn't have things forwarded or changed)—and before then I had only seen a few of them. I don't know whether I mentioned it at the time, but I liked "The James Bond Movie" very much when I first saw it—I think it is wonderful (all except the word "boobs," but I suppose I'm an old prude. No, I'm NOT!—but I don't like certain slang words for things). I'd also seen "Women," and one or two of those poems in *The New Yorker*. Is the book just out?

It is true I have been here a little over two weeks now and I am appalled by all the work I have to do. I couldn't get here earlier, as I wanted to, to prepare my courses enough in advance, so I am using my "long weekends" (Thursday through Monday) to do it. Also the last 5-day stretch I had to go to San Francisco, to clean out the flat there, put everything in storage, etc.—a very depressing task.

This is no excuse for not writing you a real letter—but I always find life in the U.S.A. too rushed, no matter how favorable the circumstances. The secretary of Kirkland House [Alice Methfessel], a very friendly girl, is about to introduce me to the mysteries of the laundry, in the basement here, and I have to buy *groceries*. (I have a small sad apartment—but very convenient for a short stay.) I thought I'd never try teaching again—but then changed my mind, and so far it really is better than the U. of Washington—two seminars a week, at least. (However, I saw the Wash. English Dept. secretary I like very much in San Francisco—she came to help me move—and they'd still like *you* there—and I think you might find one term interesting. Mark Strand goes next, I think, then Wilbur.)

In *Iconographs* you have made something a little different from the "Calligraphs"—and very different from the "Concretionists"—and I must study your NOTE some more. The Concretionists were very big in Brazil for a while—as you may know—and I finally began to see something in it and find them interesting—but of course that is a very different thing. I think John Hollander has done a book of picture-poems—but I haven't seen it, and would like to. Are they good? (Oh the bottle one is very appealing.) Well, this is something that as soon as I possibly can—(and have got through "The Comedian as the Letter C," for one thing)—I want to devote some time to, and write you properly. I hope you're still liking Sea Cliff? . . .

I have had a very bad 18 months—but things began to improve before I left Brazil, and my house is now almost "remodeled"—a Ford Fellow is staying in it for me while I'm away. I miss it very much. Tobias died . . . but he was very, very old . . . The Siamese is still there—he has never been very loved or lovable, poor little cat. I am hoping to take an Abyssinian, or something really beautiful like that, back with me . . .

To Dorothee Bowie

Dorothee Bowie, who taught in the English department of the University of Washington over thirty-five years, was assistant to the department's chairman. EB, during her first teaching job in Seattle in 1967, found in Mrs. Bowie a helpful and trusted friend.

Kirkland House I–27
Harvard University
November 2, 1970

This is just for me, selfishly, to unburden myself a little before I get up my courage to go out—and because you are the one person who will understand the awfulness of my situation here, etc. X.Y. has appeared on the scene. Just as I was beginning to relax a bit—and Wednesday the seminar had gone very well, and then on Tuesday much better, it seemed to me—and I thought I could do all right, after all. The students started out and I was gathering up my books and papers when I saw a figure standing by the door. It's a rather large gloomy old room and the doorway is dark. At first I really thought for the first time in my life I was seeing a ghost; I just couldn't believe it. But the figure didn't go away, and sure enough it was X.Y. I walked her out of there and through the campus, talking all the time so that she wouldn't talk, and got her here. She seemed pretty subdued at first, but of course soon began all the horrors she had been through in Brazil: how the doctor and two of my friends (brother & sister) had told her to get out long before she left (untrue, I'm sure); how they had tried to kill her in the hospital; how they are in a plot to get me, get my "money," my house, etc. How they had asked her about the terms of my will. (This *might* be true, I suppose, but if so it was probably to protect me from her, because toward the end they were all afraid something might happen to me.) Well, she took a bath and while she was in the tub I went down to the office here & called Bob [Bowditch], the lawyer . . . Down there I found out from the secretary, a nice friendly girl named Alice [Methfessel] that X.Y. had arrived that afternoon; had hung around—Alice and the other secretary guessed something was very wrong but didn't know what. They had given her tea—she wouldn't give her name or say what she wanted, just to find me. They knew I had a class, but didn't know where. —Well, back upstairs here Bob arrived very quickly—he thought he should come. It took us hours and hours to get her to go home with him—up till about 10 [p.m.] . . . There wasn't much noise but it was pretty touchy and I was very frightened. Then she went off with Bob—only after I had promised to see her the next day.

Wednesday . . . I went to Bob's house—he hadn't been able to go to work and one alarming thing is that I felt she had him slightly convinced. (Brazil is far away; people will believe any strange thing about it, apparently—and paranoia is awfully convincing.) . . . She stayed there [at the Bowditches'] two or three nights and drove them distracted—kept the wife up until 2 (they have three small children)—then left. Friday night I was getting ready to go to a rather fancy dinner party and she arrived—fortunately Alice spotted her and warned me and I didn't go to the door but this was just luck and would never happen again, probably. She hung around my door almost an hour—knocking from time to time—finally left. In the morning I found a letter in my mailbox. She has taken a room *right near here*—and wanted "references" to apply to go to college . . . To keep her away I did write two brief ones, saying all I could honestly say . . . And that's the way it is now and I am scared to death . . . Oh, then she somehow tracked down an English girl we know who is now working here, an occupational therapist. I saw her first and told her what was happening. She knows how things are because she visited in Brazil a year or more . . . She went to this girl's house the same Friday night and talked for over three hours to her guests—and Hilary, the girl, said that she was extremely convincing about it all. The only one who caught on was a young doctor, who recognized paranoia by the style of talking . . .

This morning I finally talked to my poor friend Bill—he is speaking to the head of the campus police . . . I am even more afraid of her showing up at my class tomorrow—all those would-be poets would just eat it up . . . X.Y. also told Bob that she knew I'd do anything he told me to because (1) I am afraid of lawyers; (2) of men; (3) *of people taller than I am.* So she is getting ready to blame him, too, for her wrongs. The stories she tells about the Brazilian clinic are hair-raising, of course. —Well, a delightful letter for you to start the week off with, & for you to receive. And I have so much work to do! God help me.

To Loren MacIver

Kirkland House
10 a.m.
November 30, 1970

I am going to write you a short note before getting going. There are unpacked bags, unopened mail, piles of books, manuscripts, shoes to be shined, bed to be made, laundry to be done, etc. etc., all about. I am sorry I felt I had to run off [in New York] to see Betty Kray like that, Loren— but she has been very patient with Emanuel Brasil and me about this anthology [of modern Brazilian poetry, sponsored by the Academy of American Poets] for two years now, and naturally she gets a lot of the boring parts of it to do. And I have done so little for her in return.

We got a taxi uptown, Emanuel and the two "young people," but it was way after 8 by the time we got there. Nevertheless we walked into the hospital boldly, and took the elevator—and I think because we had the suitcase with us, we got away with it. The nurses & orderlies thought that one of us was a patient, perhaps. Anyway we found Betty creaming her face and getting ready for bed—if you can get ready for it when you're already in it. I gave her the pear meant for Margaret—and we ate mouthfuls of it all around, out of a teaspoon.

Then I got another taxi for the long lonely ride to Kennedy—and kept thinking, if I'd had any sense, I could have taken you along for that—but then you would have had to come back alone, and perhaps you wanted to check on Lloyd before then, anyway. It was the "milk plane" or something, awful, late getting off and a long stop at Providence— arriving here at 12:45 a.m. And to my astonishment Alice, the nice house secretary, was waiting for me, her own plane having come in late. That was a great help; they take good care of me here and always seem to know my arrivals and departures somehow. So she brought me back, drank some bourbon, I drank some delicious cider (you must get some, preferably *un*pasteurized; it's better) & we discussed our Thanksgivings.

I can't seem to go to bed before 3, after my stay in N.Y. Emanuel just telephoned, the nice boy—he had called at midnight last night—and he was worried . . .

To Robert Fizdale

For New Year's weekend Gold and Fizdale had entertained EB and Emanuel Brasil at their house in Water Mill, Long Island, having driven them out in a blinding snowstorm.

[POSTCARD]
Cambridge, Massachusetts
January 8, 1971

The thank-you letter will come later. I've been up to my neck in student papers, letters, etc. One boy has given me *280 poems*, all apparently written within three months. Letter or no, it was a lovely & fascinating & surprising weekend & all your art works haunt my dreams.

Thank you for having Emanuel. It meant that we did get a lot of work done [on the anthology of Brazilian poets] & since I've been back at Harvard I've done almost all the rest.

To Loren MacIver

Casa Mariana
Ouro Prêto
March 24, 1971

. . . The dampness here raises hell with my rheumatism—but it is clearing up now—and I have been working, and going to Belo Horizonte two or three times—trying to get things a bit more ready for Frani and Curt, who arrive here the 5th, for "Holy Week." It will be awfully nice to have some company.

I'm delighted to hear about Dr. Anny. I know she is bossy, etc.—but when action is needed, she is the *cracque*, as they say here ("crack"— some kind of sporting term). I had a very nice letter from Louise [Crane] a few days ago, and then a brief note from Anny, written I think on the eve of her departure for Madeira (a place I'd love to go to myself sometime, wouldn't you? All those flowers, and old-fashioned English hotels). All Louise said was that both you and Lloyd were much better, and I do hope this is so and that you continue getting better & better. Have you been able to get back to work yet? I am trying hard to here but there has been an awful lot to do. However, I now have a youngish man, American, to come and help me with letters twice a week—he is pretty good at it— and I feel encouraged—we did 12 yesterday. Twelve more ready to do tomorrow. Where all this correspondence comes from is hard to say—but there it is.

Something called "The Living Theatre" is here—has been off & on, I gather, for some time—I never saw them in N.Y.—since then they have been wandering all over the world & somehow wound up in Ouro Prêto. They are a chief subject of conversation—called here the "Eepies." Poor things, I don't think they're making out very well in Brazil, or O.P. They gave me two plays to read—too, too reminiscent of Vassar in the '30's, for my taste. Maybe you know all about them?

I must go downtown—meat day—and I think I can now get a TELEPHONE . . .

To Frani Blough Muser

Hotel Normandy
Belo Horizonte, Brazil
April 14, 1971

I hated to leave you like that—however, waiting about in airports even with one's loved ones is a strain all around, and in that particular airport more so than usual—and I was afraid I'd arrive at the clinic & all the dentists would be out for a two-hour lunch. I hope your plane left on time, etc. The clinic and the dentist turned out to be extremely good—brand-new equipment, the *best* Belo dentist, I have learned, and he did the best he could, I think—a bit more work, too—about an hour altogether—and I paid $6. What a relief. He also gave me another "emergency kit."

Letters all safely in the Banco de Londres—the only real safety-deposit vault here, I discovered—and very British—old English ladies running in to check on their stocks (in gold mines, no doubt). Two sets Xeroxed—I found a place that does it for 10 cents a page, so it wasn't too bad—and when I finish this note I'm delivering them to the Cultural Attaché, who is sending them by diplomatic pouch for me. (He is a very Southern black—says "Goodbye now" on the telephone—Mr. *Amos*.)

Yesterday a hot and frustrating typical Brazilian day—but this morning everything started to turn out well—Mr. Amos turned up at last, and I got the call through to Rotterdam [they invited EB to a poetry festival, all expenses paid] in about two minutes. "Naturally" they're expecting me, and where are the copies of the poems? and I should get a letter in 2 or 3 days—after waiting for it almost 3 months, but I didn't say that. So it looks as if I might get to Greece and Rotterdam after all. (Wurra wurra wurra.)

Vitória has telephoned [from Casa Mariana], bless her heart, both mornings—and since they're painting the bathroom closets it is just as well I'm not there—but I'll go back this afternoon probably, unless I decide to take in another movie or two . . . Vitória, well, everyone I can think of have all said the same thing—same word—about you: "*encantadores!*" You were a tremendous success. I went to a small birthday party last night (a friend had returned from France for her birthday, bringing, of course, Camembert & pâté) & I told the story of Curt's toenails which went over BIG. So please please don't write me any thank-you letter—it should be quite the other way around. Or I should conclude with the phrase poor people always use here—"Forgive anything I did wrong."

I am dying to hear of your adventures on the Amazon. I think you are marvelous travelers and hope there were some nice passengers on the boat, etc. etc. Do let me know all about it. I realize that I am just typing on now to avoid going out in the hot sun—so shall say *até logo, com abraços fortes e*, naturally, *muitos beijos.*

To James Merrill

Hospital São Lucas
Belo Horizonte
May 8, 1971

. . . I have been feeling awful for some time and after the third or fourth *attaque* of dysentery and so on, with fever, I decided I'd better come to Belo H. and see a doctor, before starting off on my travels. It turned out that I had typhoid fever . . . not bad, second degree (there are three—and a very *stupid* thing to get here where I usually take shots every two years, am immune to lots of things by now, and so on). I came to this hospital—a pretty good one for here—and after five days the blood tests are negative, so the typhoid has stopped. I am still rather weary and have some other insignificant symptoms—so think I'll stay on two or even three more days. It is lonely and boring, but not much more so than Ouro Prêto these days—and I can certainly work here *better* than there.

I'm afraid this makes it impossible for me to leave this month when I'd planned to. Another cable from Rotterdam, and they are booking a flight for me on May 19th. That gives me barely ten days in Greece and I don't think that's long enough. So my plan now—IF this is all right with you—is to come to Athens AFTER the Rotterdam conference—that is June 8th or 9th—and—I may be able to get away before then, who knows. Now do you have other plans for that time—other guests, etc.? Please do let me know honestly—at the Ouro Prêto address. I'll be back in a few days certainly . . .

May 9th—7:30 a.m.

Up with the birds here, of course—rather with the hundred or more poor people who gather to wait on the steps of the huge Santa Casa da Misericórdia on the other side of the street, with their children and infants, while the sun is still rising . . . I will see that you are sent a cable either today or tomorrow—I do hope I haven't worried you too much. There will be time to write me at Ouro Prêto, I should think. I'll go back probably Tuesday night, the 11th—if I can finish all the things I have to do here by then.

I suppose it will be HOT after June 8th? Is there anything *I* can bring *you* from here? (I can't think of a thing, but maybe you can, and if you can I'd be delighted, of course.) As I said before—please don't think I mean to stay with you all the time—I am quite able to go off alone on cruises or whatever those island trips are called. Oh—maybe there is something you would like from the Netherlands?—cheese, chocolate, and gin are all I can think of—tell me. I am so sorry I had to postpone this visit but it is much better than coming down with typhoid in Athens, after all.

Cambridge, Massachusetts
June 3, 1971

You'll be surprised to hear from me in Cambridge & on this date (& in bad handwriting; I hope you can read it). I think you did receive the cable saying I had typhoid fever (supposedly). Well, I stayed in a Belo Horizonte hospital for eight days, went home—over the fever at least— but the "attacks" continued, and finally in despair I got to New York somehow or other ten days ago. The Belo doctor was treating me for "amoebic dysentery," but *very* casually, and it was getting worse. A specialist in tropical diseases discovered I have amoebic dysentery plus three *other* kinds, too (with marvelous names, I must say). After all these years in the tropics!

I came to Boston last Friday night to take a look at my apartment for next September, took it, but the next day had another bad attack & have been in bed ever since. I finally telephoned Rotterdam—first, saying I'd come late; this a.m. saying I couldn't come at all. The New York doctor doesn't seem to know how long it will be before I recover enough to travel. The Rotterdam people were very nice—I'm invited for the *next* conference, and just keep the plane ticket, etc.

So, dearest Jimmy, I'm afraid I can't make it to Greece. This makes me very sad & I hope to goodness doesn't upset your plans too much. There's a Western Union strike on & I can't cable you. I'm staying with my friend Alice here & she has been awfully kind—thank heaven for a good friend at such a time. Tomorrow she will bring my typewriter & I'll write again. I'm improving—I think!—but limp like a washcloth & unfit for society . . . Alice liked my fish (yours) so much I gave her one, only it is a BOTTLE OPENER.

. . . Dr. Baumann said one nice thing, after reading all the hospital reports, lab reports, etc., I brought with me from Brazil: "But these are completely *unrealistic!*" That applies to so much in Brazil, where sometimes I think that people think if they just dream up something long enough, it is true. However—Friday I began to feel much better; yesterday got up for a while, and today went out for a walk. And I feel more cheerful than I have in months—and I suspect I've had some of these weirdly named diseases, if not all of them, for months, too. Do take all possible shots for everything—but you probably do—and there isn't any against dysentery, anyway.

I think my apartment here—60 Brattle Street—will be all right when it is repainted, etc. . . . I'm staying at Alice Methfessel's now—she was marvelous with me, feeding me, in bed mostly, for a whole week, taking my temperature, everything. Now she's gone to her family for the weekend and I've had her place to myself—it is the most electrified place I have ever seen—hi-fi, radios (2), color TV, hair dryers (2), electric blanket, electric clock, electric "Water Pik," 7 lamps, and now my electric typewriter—oh well, all just normal here, I suppose, but in one huge room with all the usual electric kitchen things thrown in. I have just made a large caramel custard in an electric roaster—I just felt like it. All one sees out the many windows is treetops—very nice. I just read *The Bell Jar* (awfully good). I am terribly terribly sorry not to be going to see you in 2 or 3 days—but I never could have made Rotterdam last week—and if I sound very well now it is a sort of euphoria, because I suddenly feel so much better than I have in two months or so.

Alice wants me to stay until the end of the month, as I would have been away that long if I had made it to Europe—but I may go back a little earlier since I have really only the month of July to prepare to go away again, try to sell or rent, etc. Did I tell you that Alice and I had a trip planned—from way back, but it was a bit uncertain—for August, to the Galápagos Islands? It is more or less settled now. I'll meet her in Quito on the 1st—see it a bit—then one flies from Guayaquil—a 5-day boat cruise in the southern islands (one can go to the northern or the southern, but the southern have more birds—I *must* see a blue-footed booby before I die). Then to Lima, Machu Picchu, Cuzco, and I think we can manage two days in Arequipa—did you go there? Then back to Ouro Prêto, and back here about Sept. 2nd.

Will you give me any useful advice you can think of? I've stopped reading about Greece, alas, and now read only Darwin (again, he is one of the people I like best in the world)—guidebooks, etc. . . . Friday night, Alice informed me, she and her parents dined with a man whose Peruvian wife's family owns the Hotel Bolívar in Lima—a funny old one, I've always heard—and of course the wife's family is dying to have us stay there— so this may be a help.

I must must must stop and wash a few dishes . . . I do hope you have a brilliant, beautiful, well-behaved, and un-shy visitor en route right now to take my place—perhaps one who speaks Greek, or at least remembers all the classics better than I do.

To Arthur Gold and Robert Fizdale

Ouro Prêto
July 8, 1971

. . . First, it is wonderful about your playing in Venice and I wish I could be there. Is the concert at the Fenice, and what will you play—all Stravinsky? And oh dear, I wish I could go with you to Greece, too . . .

It seems so long ago that you were here, and how I wish you were now. I haven't attended much of the "Festival"—but there was one group singing and playing in one of the old churches the other night, "Der Fruehen Musik"—from Munich, the program said—but only the lady was German, the three men Americans. Medieval music one night, Renaissance the next—with all sorts of nice old instruments. They were really good—the best thing to come here. Tomorrow night the combined choirs of Smith & Princeton are to sing, and I must go to see all those healthy young American faces. They are also showing old U.S. comic films every afternoon (this was MY idea, from several years back, and at last someone acted on it—the nice new Cultural Attaché, Mr. Amos, I think).

I have a nice young man, José Alberto Nemer, a good friend, staying all month, so it isn't so lonely—and a French girl for a week or ten days. The man is an excellent graphic artist who wins lots of prizes—not just in Brazil—and I tried hard to get him a Merrill grant to go to New York for a year. He didn't get it, but he did get one from the French government (very hard to get too) and returned from Paris just to teach here this month. The Brazil government won't let anyone accept grants for more than a year—they want to keep everyone at home and under observation. He also plays the guitar and sings blues songs in *boites*. I do want him to get to New York sometime, though.

About August 1st I am meeting Alice Methfessel (my friend from Cambridge, you may remember) in Quito and—we're going to the Galápagos Islands. This is something I've wanted to do all my life (and Darwin is my favorite hero, almost). Then to Peru—Machu Picchu, etc., and back here for a week or ten days. I have to get to Cambridge early in September to arrange my new flat—and do some work on my new seminar, on "Letters"! Did I tell you about that? Bobby should be interested, and any ideas you have on the subject will be welcome. Just *letters*—as an art form or something. I'm hoping to select a nicely incongruous assortment of people—Mrs. Carlyle, Chekhov, my Aunt Grace,

Keats, a letter found in the street, etc. etc. But I need some ideas from you both—just on the subject of letters, the dying "form of communication."

Oh, our protégé, José Aparecido, appeared! He got a scholarship from Ouro Prêto for this July. I heard about this and thought the scholarship would cover everything; turns out he has to pay 30 cruzeiros—that is, one a day for the month, or six U.S. dollars. So, since he's as sweet and polite and calmly conversational as ever, I gave him a piece of apple pie I'd just made—it baffled him but he congratulated me on it—and a check for the added charge. He finishes the "technical school" this year, and then wants to study architecture at the university in Belo Horizonte. It's probably a good choice of career for him here, and his drawings seem to show he likes buildings! I *think* puberty has set in at last—he is about an inch taller and his face is fuzzy—not pretty, but he is still adorable.

If you know of anyone—professor, writer, painter, etc.—preferably with wife & family/or friend—who would like to RENT (and preferably BUY) this house, please let me know immediately. I am frantic about what to do with it when I go to Cambridge. I've advertised and am asking $300 a month—but would take less IF I could find someone really reliable, who liked beautiful objects of art. All equipped. I had luck last fall. Maybe you've read about "The Living Theatre" here—all in jail now . . .

To Frank Bidart

Frank Bidart's collected poems (1965 to 1990) appear in the recent volume In the Western Night. *He teaches at Wellesley College and at Brandeis University. He worked closely with Robert Lowell in his last years and became an intimate friend of EB, who designated him as her co-literary executor with Alice Methfessel.*

Ouro Prêto
July 27, 1971
. . . I am so pleased that you liked "In the Waiting Room." *The New Yorker* had kept it for over a year, and by the time the poor poem appeared I feel only fatigue & impatience when I look at it (tenses)—anyway, I can't decide whether I like it at all or not, and therefore your reaction— almost the first—was really very cheering. (I think Cal did see a bad copy of it at Christmas time—and I did a rough translation aloud for a friend, in Portuguese. Her reaction was very nice, however: she got goose-flesh on her arms and told me her first experience of the same sort—when she looked in a mirror. (Other people have told me the same thing—5 years old, brushing his teeth, etc.) Well, it is almost a true story—I've combined a later thought or two, I think—and—because you might like this kind of information—I did go to the library in N.Y. and look up that issue of the *National Geographic*. Actually—and this is really weird, I think—I

had remembered it perfectly, and it was all about Alaska, called "The Valley of Ten Thousand Smokes." I tried using that a bit but my mind kept going back to another issue of the *National Geographic* that had made what seemed like a more relevant impression on me, so used it instead. Of course I was sure *The New Yorker* would "research" this, or "process it" or something—but apparently they are not quite as strict as they used to be—or else are sure that none of their present readers would have read *National Geographics* going back *that* far.

Well, thank you so much for writing—it arrived at just the right minute.

I'm sorry I can't seem to type this morning. This machine has just come back from being repaired—not too well—and I'm not used to it yet . . . I am trying rather frantically to get away Monday—August 2nd—on the trip to Ecuador & Peru, and the Galápagos. Three weeks, then back here. Alice is coming back with me, for about a week. I'd like to return [to Cambridge] when she does, Sept. 1st or so, but it all depends on whether I've found someone to stay in this house by then or not. I've had three possibles, I think—but haven't heard definitely yet—and I don't see how I can go to Cambridge at all, unless I find someone reliable to leave here.

So—although I probably asked you—I ask everyone I meet who has any discretion at all—if YOU know of a reliable person who'd like to live in Ouro Prêto for 5 months (or longer—but I could get back if necessary in January)—please please let him or her, and me, know. In my two ads I asked $300 a month rent—a fair rent, I think—but of course if an ideal tenant appeared I'd make it much less. It's really a beautiful house, I think—and there are 4 bedrooms, study, 2 *salas*, fireplace, stove in study, all conveniences, and it's completely equipped . . . Not luxurious, but comfortable—for here, anyway. Thousands (alas) of books and a hi-fi in pretty good shape. 5 minutes' walk from the main square. Magnificent views of the whole town. No garage, but a walled garden (not gardened much yet, except for some flourishing herbs and salad beds)—and one can lock a car inside.

A good place to WORK—writer, painter, thesis, so on—and I'd take a small infant, or well-behaved older children—the garden is a safe place to play. My maid—rough, but very good, for here—and cheerful and obliging (& likes Americans) would stay on, I'm sure—and a lazy but sweet yard boy, if needed.

Well—I am doing all this very late & have one prospect in Rio that sounds good—but I'll just keep on asking everyone until I'm sure of somebody. Forgive the real estate paragraph.

The *Hermit Hamburger* sounds rather sad—everyone eating his hamburger in an individual booth? And then you add the word "monkish" too. I hope you have a good summer there and do write me again when you can. Please give my love to Thom Gunn if you see him, and also to

Josephine Miles. I think I forgot to tell you about one young couple I like very much who live in Berkeley—and the awful part is I can't remember the husband's last name.

Please, Frank, surely you can call me Elizabeth? (As you see by the poem, that's what I call myself.) Please be good and happy and industrious—and have a nice time as well. See you in Cambridge.

To Dr. Anny Baumann

16 Chauncy Street
Cambridge, Massachusetts
September 9, 1971

. . . I've been back about a week now and I am staying with Alice Methfessel until I can move into my new apartment. It has been painted—last touches today—and I am now waiting for furniture, etc., to arrive from San Francisco. I'll probably be moving in a few days . . .

It seems horribly hot, after the coolness of the tropical countries and the equator!—I seem to have some bronchitis—we both picked up awful colds on our travels—and I'm going now to the Harvard clinic to get some medicine for it. I just cough, and of course wheeze, too (& I stopped smoking a month ago).

We had a wonderful trip—I sent you postcards several times along the way and I wonder if you will have received one or two I mailed from the one post office in the Galápagos Islands? I felt that the young postmaster probably just read all postcards and never mailed anything. The islands were absolutely marvelous—sort of like one's idea of Paradise. The animals and birds are tame—not afraid of human beings—and come right up to you and sit on you, or peck your sneakers. The mother seals show their babies and flop down beside you on the sand when you go swimming.

We were on that cruise for 5 days—wanted to do the whole 9-day tour but there were no vacancies. It is very well run, a nice ship (Greek), mostly foreign passengers—French & Italian—50 or so—and 8 Americans, I think. Alice's "slides" have just come back from the Kodak company and I am keeping myself from looking at them until she gets home from work, although I am dying to see how the Blue-Footed Boobies and the Albatrosses came out.

Machu Picchu was the other high point. I don't care for Lima, however—and I had to stay there three times on the trip. Then we spent a few days in Rio, to show Alice the sights—then back to Ouro Prêto for 5 days or so. My house is NOT rented, or wasn't when I left—but Vitória, my clever maid, had a couple of American ladies coming to see it the day I left—and other possibilities—I didn't want to leave it like that, but felt I should get here early, to move into my flat, and work on the other *course*—the other one besides the verse-writing one, that is.

I hope you had a wonderful holiday and rested some and didn't climb mountains ALL the time. Louise Crane called up yesterday—but she hadn't much news of our mutual friends that I didn't already know— except that Marianne's brother is getting sick, too.

I must walk over to my apt. and see what "Charlie" (my Harvard-boy painter) is up to—and then do a bit of marketing, and then on to the clinic. I expect to be coming to New York fairly soon . . .

To Frani Blough Muser

> 60 Brattle Street
> Cambridge, Massachusetts
> October 23, 1971

. . . At present I'm too occupied with other people's LETTERS for my seminar—and the hopeless red tape that I didn't know about, of a "Reserve Desk"—ye gods! Last weekend I did go up to Vermont for overnight, to see the "colors"—and they were marvelous, too—went up miles & miles in a ski lift, and then walked down . . .

Do you know about the week of CULTURE at Vassar?—starting the 26th, I think, with a panel on "The Artist as Social Critic"—with Mary McCarthy *and* Muriel Rukeyser. I was asked for this but have my seminars on Tuesdays and Wednesdays, so couldn't go. Imagine! I told Nathalie Rahv on the phone and she said, "Oh, Muriel will be *raped*." I had promised to give a reading sometime, so they are combining me with the general culture & I'm going there Wednesday evening. I am trying not to think about it. Perhaps *you* could get to that "panel"? I bought *Without Marx or Jesus* yesterday, to prepare myself for conversation—but don't know when I'll be able to read it.

Friday night I have tickets to see all the Olympic champion figure skaters—with [Dick] Button presiding. I rather nervously asked Nathalie if she'd like to see this with me (I remember her & you skating away at college) but she seemed to like the idea. I MUST get out and go to Boston (on that "subway") to go shopping, having no clothes at all—and having to face Mary in her Givenchy-s, no doubt . . . I must mail a silver rattle to Robert Lowell's new son.

To May Swenson

> November 7, 1971

. . . I'm glad you wrote me about the Ann Stanford anthology . . . It does sound like a good anthology—but I'd refuse, anyway, May. I thought at some time in the past I must have told you that I have always refused to be in any collections, or reviews, or special numbers of just women? *Always*—this has nothing to do with the present Women's Lib Movement (although I'm in favor of a lot of that, too, of course). I see no reason for them and I think it is one of the things to be avoided—and *with* "Women's Lib" perhaps even more so. WHY "Women in Literature"? No—it's *The Women Poets in English*, I see. But still, WHY? Why not *Men Poets in English*? Don't you see how silly it is? (But please don't tell Ann Stanford just how silly & wrong I feel it to be—and always have. I am writing her a gentle note.) Literature is literature, no matter who produces it. Probably it's true that some of the earlier women poets and writers have not been brought to people's attention enough—men's & women's attention. I have a student here who's preparing a paper on this for another class . . . BUT I don't like things compartmentalized like that, and in this case I think it defeats the very purpose it's supposed to be for. I like black & white, yellow & red, young & old, rich & poor, and male & female, all mixed up, socially—and see no reason for segregating them, for any reason at all, artistically, either. Well, that's enough. I hope Ann Stanford will understand—but I wouldn't want to say very much & perhaps make her uncomfortable with her project—so you see, I'm no crusader.

Seven readings! How do you do them? I should do a few more this year (for the money) . . . A high-powered agency was after me for years (the one Auden uses) but I knew the pace would be too much for me. I read at Vassar two weeks ago & am going to the U. of Virginia soon. I've never been there & would like to see it. But I'd do two or three more if they paid enough—before I have to go back to Brazil . . .

I can't imagine what translations you saw in Ohio! Emanuel Brasil (I think you've met him) was here last weekend & we worked on galleys and now the first vol. of the Brazilian anthology is rolling, I hope. The second, if there is one, will be even harder. I don't like anthologizing—but am more pleased than I thought I'd be with the first volume.

To Lloyd Frankenberg

Late in October at Vassar, EB experienced a terrible asthma attack, brought on by a sheepskin coat in her host's car, requiring shots of adrenaline before her reading on the 27th. Not fully recovered, she then collapsed. At Peter Bent Brigham Hospital in Boston she was "black and blue all over" from injections, and then went back to the infirmary for three more weeks until December 6.

Stillman Infirmary (Room 5)
Cambridge, Massachusetts
December 2, 1971

You are being honored with my Letter #2 [from the hospital]. #1 I wrote yesterday to my auntie. Louise Crane telephoned a few days ago & just now I called Margaret Miller—first long-distance call from here;

it made me *sweat*, but was very enjoyable. So now I know you are at home
. . . I'm so glad you're OUT & now I'm IN—like those little weather-
figures & their houses—but I hope to get out in another week now, maybe
sooner. This is a very nice place, however, and I don't mind being here
at all. It was heaven to get back here after Peter Bent Brigham
Hospital—the famous Boston place I was at for a week. This is all very
modern—Sert (architect)—and I actually have one of my classes on the
seventh floor (the hospital is the fifth). My dear students are going right
on being prolific & meeting *without* me—probably having much more
fun that way—and yesterday I woke up from a doze to find three huge,
bearded, long-haired boys at my bedside, eager to tell me all about *their*
class. They're *sweet* . . . I wonder if you've read all of Raymond
Chandler?—I like him *better* than Dashiell Hammett—real poetic, sometimes. Did you get the batch of books?—and had you read them all? I
hope not.

Tell Loren it took 5 or 6 days for her card to get from P. B. Brigham
to here! And tell her to write AGAIN. Oh! 10 a.m.—time for *Sesame Street*,
my favorite TV show. Yesterday's was especially good. I get a bit tired of
learning my alphabet, but I adore Bert & Ernie & the *Cookie Monster* &
recommend them highly. Get well *quick*. We both *must*, having many
fish to fry, between us. Much love.

To May Swenson

6 a.m.
December 5, 1971
You so beautifully got the point (I've been re-reading Henry James's
letters, for my seminar—as you might guess) of the "Crusoe" poem
that I want to write you a note to thank you. (I'm afraid it *isn't* very
good.)

I was hoping that Ms. or is it Miz (Harvard has adopted this, but I
still don't know how to say it) Stanford would *quote* me, or my refusal—
but I suppose that was a bit naïve of me—& of course although I feel my
own argument is invulnerable, I didn't really want to disturb her about
her anthology.

Almost since writing you, I've been sick, really awfully sick. I was
here (Stillman Infirmary), then in Peter Bent Brigham Hospital 8 days,
then back here—well, I've lost track, but it is almost a month now. But
tomorrow I *may* go home. (Oh—it was a bad asthma attack—worst I've
ever had.) This means I've missed two seminars each four times—but
maybe I can make some up in the January "reading period." The verse-
writing class has been marvelous—meeting anyway, all by themselves
. . . And the quantities of Xeroxed poems on hand—I have a market bag

full! The poets meet in this same building & they *drop in*—when allowed to. It is a very nice hospital & since I've got back here I've almost been enjoying myself.

I may be coming to New York the 17th—and shall stay at the Cosmopolitan Club for a week or ten days—probably back here for New Year's but I don't know yet. Just possibly you may get to town, before Florida, & come to call? I'm weak like an overcooked noodle, but I'd love to see you . . .

To Arthur Gold and Robert Fizdale

> Cosmopolitan Club
> New York City
> December 20, 1971

This paper knife (admittedly very ugly) comes from a German lady (Jewish) who lived in what is now Tanzania for many years & has been helping an order of nuns there distribute the native handicrafts. I think you may like the music it is wrapped in better than the handicraft—so I include it in my grab bag of Christmas presents.

I hope to see you both again very soon, or talk to you at least—so please send some sort of itinerary—*including* your stay in Italy. If I can afford the proper clothes for the Pavilion [part of the Villa Albrizzi in Este, where the pianists were to stay], I'm determined to visit you there.

P.S. Aksakov's *Years of Childhood* is out of print. I've been talking to the Oxford University Press & telling them to get it back in right away. It's a *small* blue Oxford Classic book, thin paper—if ever you spot a second-hand copy. I know you'd love it. (And I'm loving the Turgenev. —You've read Henry James's letters about T., haven't you? They're wonderful, too.)

P.S. 2—(The season's getting me.) That gold ring I usually wear says inside (or did I show you?) "Lota—20-12-51." Twenty years ago was the day I told Lota I'd stay in Brazil & she had [the ring] made for my birthday that next February. —I think I miss her more in New York than any place. She liked it so much & had such good times here—and with you.

To Frani Blough Muser

> 60 Brattle Street
> Cambridge, Massachusetts
> January 5, 1972

Never have I seen a more passionate tea strainer. Perhaps it was intended for an absinthe dripper, or for opium, as in *The Opium Eater* —the latter, probably, since it is a poppy. (I forgot to close one of the dozens of levers on this marvelous machine.) I do like the little patch-box. I examined it with a magnifying glass and see that the sheep's eyes are really little black bulges—a fantastic-looking little sheep. Thank you very much . . . Cynthia sent me a box of wonderful apples—an assortment—all good except the "Delicious-es." I can't stand them, but don't tell her. Emanuel Brasil spent two days with me, over Christmas, and we had some baked and some raw. Yesterday I made applesauce, too—it's supposed to be good for this disease we've all had and Alice was coming to dinner—she'd had it, too. It consists mostly of throwing up a lot—in the middle of the night, mostly—but lasts only 48 hours . . .

I hope you all had a fine Christmas in spite of the general grimness. I went up to Jackson, N.H. for the New Year's weekend, but the skiing was only possible one day—after that, it was all ice or water—beautiful to look at, but too dangerous, for me, anyway. It was a lovely place and I'd like to go back. I'm coming to N.Y. next week for two days only, probably—it is the National Book Award. I'm on the "translations" committee—and never again, I must say—unless it proves to be better when we actually meet. But they do pay one's fare, etc., and that is nice—will even pay mine from Seattle in April for the final meeting . . .

I wonder if you've had time to read any of the Quentin Bell book—probably not. I finally got Vol. 2 but the first vol. is better, I think. However, I do think it's a good book and I feel much more sympathetic to V. Woolf since reading it. For one thing, I never knew she had had so many breakdowns. It is an awful story. And the Bloomsbury group seem much more hard-headed, somehow, considering the period they grew up in, than I had thought them before.

I see out the window that the Loeb Theatre has just opened its box office so I must go out and try to get a ticket for the Balinese dancers on Wednesday—I think I'd like to see them. I would have liked to have seen the Moscow Circus & the Chinese acrobats, alas—neither are coming to Boston, I'm afraid. It's nice not to be teaching at last—but I do have one exam to think up—I think I'll make it terribly hard. But I've liked most of the students a lot this year—in fact, I'm going to give a party for the writing class on the 18th. I wish you could attend; some of them are adorable. I have to give a $100 prize each time to that class & this time I am going to surprise the very superior Ph.D.'s in it & give it to a darling freshman—an Irish boy who looks like the sun—he really does—he cheers one up just to look at his round pink face & when he reads his poems (which are very funny) he breaks down in fits of the giggles.

Emanuel Brasil & I dined Christmas Day with the master of Kirkland House—that wasn't such a good idea—a wildly assorted group, from the French *au pair* girl to the sister from Tasmania, etc. And everyone had had much too much to drink before we got there. At one point the master started to fall down, and Em., who goes to acrobatics class every night, made a marvelous catch and saved him by the belt—ice cubes flying through the air, etc. The rowing coach, also present, cried out,

"Good save, Brazil!" All a bit athletic—so afterwards we went to *Chloe in the Afternoon* just to forget. But it isn't very good—or I didn't think so.

This machine types faster than I can think and I'm afraid this shows it. But I just wanted to thank you and wish you a good new year—with a lot less drudgery in it, I hope.

January 8, 1972
(post-telephone conversation)

I cut this out of the *Harvard Gazette* to send you and forgot to enclose it of course. I really think that old "absentminded professor" stuff is no joke—it is too true. I am getting worse & worse—or maybe it is just age. The other day the missing reading glasses were only discovered when I noticed the butter dish sitting on the coffee table in the living room. So —naturally the glasses were *in the refrigerator*.

The thermometer has gone up to 6°. Mrs. Murphy is cleaning for me—first time. She has worked for Bill Alfred for many years and seems very nice. She works from 7 to 3 at an Old Folks Home here—and if they're all like her, the attendants, it might not be so bad—maybe I'll look into it. I keep seeing ads for a really elegant-sounding one near here—and I figured out that a room with bath would be about $1,500 a month. My goal is to somehow achieve that income before retiring to it —but how on earth to? Harvard has given me a "term appointment" for 4 years—that's up to retirement age—or so I've been told over the telephone. I'll believe it when I get an official letter, but not before. As far as I can see, the academic world is a bloodthirsty jungle one . . . The girl who drove me to Brown was full of grim little tales and began by saying, "Hear what happened at M.I.T. today?" I hadn't. "Eight heads lopped." And so on. And how she got fired—or the places she'd been fired from —I didn't like to ask the reasons. But she did seem a bit paranoid, I'm afraid.

I should be writing that exam—I think I'll make it terribly hard. One boy—young man, actually, 25, I think—told Alice that my course was the hardest he'd ever taken! I was amazed—it seemed too easy to me, and he is very bright and wrote a good paper. But I think I was pleased, too, since I really don't know whether anyone learns anything at all— from me, that is. And now dear Mrs. R. is due—she is quite a good novelist, very funny—but decided she wanted to try writing poetry, for which she has no talent at all, but a lot of enthusiasm. She has no *rhythum*, I guess—none at all.

To Lloyd Frankenberg

[POSTCARD]

January 8, 1972

. . . This is to thank you & Loren for your nice letter & her card— *think* I have them in the right order & I do admire the way you WRITE —I mean instead of using a typewriter. It is partly because of rheumatism and partly because of illegibility & partly because of a (false) idea of "time" that I type. I don't really burble on nearly as much when I write with a pen.

I've been reading about the movie of *A Clockwork Orange* in the papers—at first I thought it sounded much too violent for me—but apparently it is done in lovely colors & with a ballet-like style. Maybe I'll see it, rapes & all. The same was true, they tell me, of *Bonnie and Clyde* which I also refused to see, but shall next time it comes around. This p.m. I am going to see *The Last Picture Show*, recommended by students & others—we'll see—maybe just another exercise in nostalgia.

P.S. Speaking of George Herbert, I wanted my writing class to read "Love unknown," one of my favorite poems of his, for certain *points* I was trying to make, and being lazy I asked my dear John Peech to read it aloud—out of an old edition Cal gave me. He didn't know about the old English *f* being used instead of *s*—and he began:

> *Deare Friend, fit down, the tale is long and fad*

and of course we all started laughing. Poor boy, he just couldn't read it, so I had to do it myself.

To Ashley Brown

January 23, 1972
Sunday a.m.

I've just finished reading the last paper in my "letters" class— pretty awful—last year's class wrote like moderately educated people; I don't know why these 9 or 10 can't write *at all*—hanging participles, "one," "you," "we" all at once—oh well, the works. I'm depressed by them . . .

But now I'll write to you as I've been meaning to for several months. First, thank you for being so nice—according to Betty Kray—about accepting some changes in your translations. I think they were mostly in one poem of Cabral de Melo's—and a *very* difficult poem. The book should appear now in March, I think—late March or early April. I hope we can go on with Vol. II—it apparently depends on how well this one goes, or is up to Wesleyan, I don't know. Emanuel just telephoned—he wants to give up his apartment—it's much too expensive—and live in a room, and eventually give up his UN job to just *write*. But how will he live? & I think he sends money to his family in Rio.

Oh—I feel especially grateful for your having accepted my tinkering with your verbs, etc., in the translation, because we had a bad time with R. Eberhart (of course). He really takes the cake for nastiness—and I've had a series of notes & cards from him (after 20 years or more of silence) telling me of his successes and *who* read to thousands and got "standing ovations" & kissed *him* on both cheeks, at Dartmouth; then on to the U. of Washington, where "hordes" are trying to get into his classes. And always signed with love, etc. However, I think perhaps he is genuinely naïve, and all these insults come from the unconscious—BUT is that any excuse?

A friend of mine—Joe Summers—passed through Cambridge Thursday & told me that Anthony Hecht was leaving for one of those State Dept. lecture tours in Brazil yesterday. I tried to get a telephone number he gave me—friends of Hecht's in Rochester—to send a message to him, but couldn't reach them. I wanted to give him your address, for one thing, and also tell him that if by any chance he was lecturing in Belo H. and got over to Ouro Prêto he could stay at my house, or at least drop in on it. However, I imagine you know him already?—or you'll meet him through the Fulbright, the Embassy lady, or something?—Anyway, if by chance you see him after you get this—please tell him I did try to get some information about Brazil to him, and extend the hospitality of my house. I met him only once, long ago, and liked him.

Is there any chance (where did I get this idea?) of your wanting to stay in Ouro Prêto for a while sometime?—and when would it be? Of course I'd be very pleased and just hope the house and Vitória are still there and in working order. I am writing you first, because it's easier; then, right now, to Linda, José Alberto, Vitória, and Lilli—and two or three banks, and one lawyer—in Portuguese. I've had quite a few messages from J.A. and Linda about the house—but I am way behind with my answers and really don't know what is going on. I don't know when or if I have to go back—or anything—I'd really like to stay on here and WORK—my own work—for a few months if possible. I get homesick for O.P. but know that soon after I get there I'll be bogged down in housekeeping and maintenance, and also dying of isolation and boredom and finding it hard to work—this is what seems to happen there. I can work all day alone—but around five I'd like a little company. Perhaps if Lilli (*coitada*) had not bought that huge hopeless TV and become an addict, my situation in O.P. wouldn't be so bad! (I have one here, I must admit—small, brightly colored—but there are occasional good things every week—and the reception is almost perfect.) . . .

Anyway—will you please write me and forgive my long silence. Oh—I don't approve of health talk in letters—but it's true I was hideously sick from the end of October through all of November—in the hospital all that time. Two hospitals ("intensive care"—I was really pretty far gone—asthma—and thought my day had come) then 3 weeks in the Harvard Infirmary. I've never had an attack like that. Thank heavens for Blue Cross—and the fact I was a member of the Harvard Faculty at the time—otherwise my three weeks would have cost over $60 a day (as it was, *free*) and my eight days at P.B.B. would have cost *$2,500*. After January 29th I won't even dare get a cold.

But I am very well now—trying to cut out the cortisone—I even took up cross-country skiing last weekend—bought skis & boots yesterday—and am going back to New Hampshire to do it again next weekend. This is getting to be an awful fad here, too—like everything—however, I still think it's nice to get outdoors and exercise . . . and exercise—I have a ping-pong table instead of a dining table . . . (but I'm bad at ping-pong). This apartment is pleasant—I wish it were higher up, but otherwise I like it—and I need more furniture. My first serious entertaining will be to have the Robert Fitzgeralds to dinner—on the ping-pong table . . .

To Frank Bidart

February 1, 1972
Monday morning
. . . I had a long talk with [poet] Lloyd Schwartz—who sounds so like you it is uncanny—does he come from the same place in California or what? and he was very nice—is calling your mamma and Bob. The college pharmacy proved to be most obliging—I never dreamed they'd offer to mail the drugs to you [in England]—but they did, before I'd mentioned it, airmail and special delivery, too . . . But please, you must return early enough on the 7th to come to my first party. Everyone has accepted so far—but only three ladies—me and that Miss Lawner and Alice—and maybe Alice will get cold feet because of all those poets, but I'm hoping she'll come. I just talked to her and Stowe is out for the long weekend—all booked up already, oh dear—but we'll probably have some other plans. I think we're going back near Putney this coming Sat. & Sunday—unless the weather changes. It was so marvelous yesterday, and we drove around a bit and found a very nice place to stay at Newfane . . . a beautiful old New England town . . .

Your news, Cal's news, is terribly sad [one of Caroline's daughters had been badly burned in an accident] . . . WHY hospitals have to be so rough I don't understand—Cal said they were to the parents, not so bad to the children or patients themselves. (After my stay in P. B. Brigham I'll believe almost anything of them—but I've never told you some of the more painful details. And as Cal says, it is mostly *unnecessary*.) Anyway —I'm sure Cal is glad to have you there during this bad time. Write me if you have time and feel like it. I think you must have got most of the "work" done before this tragedy happened.

I just talked to Bill Alfred—I haven't seen him in ages—since before Christmas, I think. He is coming the 7th. I told him what you'd just been telling me over the telephone and of course he was full of dismay and sympathy. He had just started to write a play—or *the* play—this morning, I think. Marks were in Friday. I failed one student. Should have failed some more, but he really was by far the worst. In his "paper" he said that Lady Mary W. Montagu "should be cut up in little pieces and burned alive," etc.—because of her frivolity and indifference to ethnic problems, I suppose. Now he'll probably attempt to do this to me if I don't watch out. Anyway—it is nice to feel relatively "free." I don't know how much longer I can stay on here but hope I can for a while.

. . . Alice took me to what they call the "Stolen Rug Store"—do you know it? Really marvelous bargains—and I bought something large and expensive (being put together now) for the living room—of *flax*—really beautiful. So—housekeeping goes apace. Your tiger will figure largely in the decorations for the party—if I can manage the other details. I had a dinner menu all planned for tonight for you—it's merely postponed now.

Thursday I am going to read in Philadelphia—and spend a night there. I don't know anyone there at all.

Sat. afternoon I went to the first wedding of my life—in a church & *all like that.* I found it pretty depressing, I must say. Do you know that little J. who worked in Kirkland House? She was the bride—the one with bright red hair. Her sister, 16, who looks exactly like her only younger & bigger, has red hair, too—only a prettier shade (I adore red hair). Almost the best thing about the wedding was when they were all standing up in the front of the church—and the afternoon sunlight came in and lit up the sister's hair—a wonderful, almost blinding glow of red hair, almost through the ceremony. But it all took about 15 minutes. Seems shocking to me. Then a country club. All salt-of-the-earth New Englanders, I'm sure. Slight differences in caste between the parents of the bride and those of the groom—from Texas & slightly "poorer." *That* mother-in-law looked stiff & papery, just like poor Mrs. Nixon . . . We hadn't cared for the Putney Inn the night before, so ate at a Howard Johnson's on the way back—dozens of skiing (I think) families and innumerable children, all guzzling french fried potatoes with ketchup and gigantic mounds of ice cream and whipped cream and so on—revolting but fascinating. But yesterday was really heavenly—deserted fields, huge rolling fields, soft snow, not too cold, and bright sunlight—everything dazzling. The snow sparkles like diamonds, with colored lights—but then when you ski into the shade of the woods the dazzle doesn't stop—just turns to fewer but more intense glints of bright blue and purple. It was lovely. I fell down only once and I must confess to feeling pleased when Alice—who was trying to "show off," I fear—also fell down once. I thought I'd be lame, but I'm not.

END. I loathe these airmail-letter forms. Now to see if I can fold it. With love to you all—and do get enough sleep—and we'll see you soon.

To Selden Rodman

February 11, 1972

I was surprised to hear from you from Brazil. I didn't know that you were planning what must be your second trip there?—or had even been to my house the *first* time. Perhaps Lilli told me, but if she did she probably didn't remember your name!—this happens quite often, so I have to guess what "Americans" (sometimes English or something else) *might* have visited Ouro Prêto in my absences. I must have been here when you visited Octavio Paz—this is the second fall semester I've taught at Harvard and I'm going to do it again next fall. I have a small apartment here now. I'm not sure when I'm returning to Brazil. I certainly have to sometime, because of the house and all my worldly goods there. I am crazy about my house—but find Ouro Prêto a bit isolated—and I never intended to live there all the time when I bought the house in 1965. It was to be for vacations and a sort of hobby, remodeling it (which took about 5 years; it was literally falling down).

I have just got to know Octavio Paz and I enjoy him & his wife both very much. They're amusing and unpretentious and nice. I went to his first lecture—a course in Spanish American poetry—yesterday, and to my surprise understood every word. I'd thought my Spanish hopelessly drowned in Portuguese by now. Octavio—well, you must know—is giving the Charles Eliot Norton lectures this year.

You didn't enclose the clipping about João Cabral de Melo. I had a wonderful letter from Vinícius a while ago, still in Bahia—and I'll write him soon. The first volume of the anthology of Brazilian poetry should be out at the end of March, I think. I haven't seen your book about the poets of S.A. Yes, Flavio's death was ghastly. I'd known him since he was a child of 8 or 9. He was bringing out a book of Brazilian short stories —a collection going back to old ones I'd never heard of—also a book of his own. I have no idea what has become of them—or if they were ever published. He wrote some good lyrical poems—I have quite a few of them and there are probably more. I don't really know what happened to him; I saw him at the very end of September 1970, when I was on my way here, and he seemed in wonderful shape that one evening in Rio. I have not seen his widow and she didn't write me. He was an extremely bright boy; it is heartbreaking.

I came back from N.Y. two days ago, from attending Marianne Moore's funeral. But that death was really to be desired, she had been sick for so long. If you are not still in Brazil, you'll probably never receive this!

P.S. If you know of anyone who'd like to rent my house—or buy it —be sure to let me know, please.

To Louise Crane

March 2, 1972

. . . I think they *have* increased my capital—perhaps doubled it, I'm not sure—but that has been over 40 years. As you see, I owe them a lot of money—$22,000 to be exact. This is not all debt—I invested about $15 or $16 thousand in Brazil—and get income there from some little offices that Lota and I bought. It's enough to live on there, modestly—but even so it is absurd to be spending $100 a month or whatever it is, in $$$$, on the interest. It is a long story—actually I showed great force of character not to have *more* money invested in Brazil. I'd like to get that debt paid off, but I probably never will be able to—unless I write another *The Group* or something.

I'll probably go back to Brazil around June 15th—stay 6 weeks, and then, if I have any money, take a trip in August before returning here in September. I'll probably be able to sublet this place to someone in summer school. I'm going to write [about selling Marianne Moore's letters] right now. I've put it off because I hate to sound so mercenary—nevertheless, I do have to think of old age and a slightly higher-class Old Ladies Home . . .

Did I tell you there is supposed to be gold hidden in my Ouro Prêto house—or in the garden? I've even had the cellar broken into, and holes dug in the walls and floor—maybe that would be the solution to all my problems—finding a hoard of gold. There is even a map—but I suspect that if there ever was gold hidden there it was dug up long ago . . . There was a fire in a bakery on the main street a few years ago. When they started to dig into the chimneys, to re-build the ovens, gold coins literally fell out of the old chimney in a stream. But the government gets almost all of it, if they hear of it.

Octavio Paz's lecture last night was better than the first one I heard—but his accent is terrific. The same little party after every one, apparently—only the address changes and maybe the food is better at one than the other—and there is always a large poodle weaving in & out.

I must write two letters in Portuguese, oh dear.

P.S. I'd be very happy to have an elephant-hair bracelet—anything at all [as a Marianne Moore memento]. Or if the Mexican toy chest turns up, I'd like that, too. She used to keep it in the hall in Brooklyn for years—and I saw it in N.Y.—but maybe it is now in Philadelphia. There's an Emily Dickinson room here in the Houghton Library—I've never had the courage to go to see it.

To Harold Leeds

March 7, 1972

. . . That sad day in Brooklyn [at the memorial service for Marianne Moore] you and Bob [Giroux] were certainly looking very well. So was Dr. Anny—quite beautiful & I wondered at her—then I realized that all the last times I've seen her was to have dinner with her after she'd put in a long day at the office. No wonder she looks healthier & more glamorous at 11 a.m.! Louise telephoned me this morning & we were talking about Marianne's belongings, the Rosenbach "room" [in Philadelphia], etc.—and I think we should all feel very grateful that Louise has been on the job about Marianne's affairs these last years, thank goodness.

And now I'm writing to ask a favor of you, or for some information, that is. Now that I'm through my classes, just staying on here for a few months, I'm trying to get this apartment furnished a bit more. You are probably familiar with this chair. I can buy it here in Cambridge (the high-backed model) for $210, I think it is. I found it at this Scandinavian store in N.Y.—East 5th St.—for about $30 or $189 less—everything is extra-high in Cambridge. But with freight, etc., it would be almost the same thing. They said they call it the "Cloud Chair" (!) but by prying and poking at the one in Cambridge, I discovered the label, *West Norway Factories, Ltd.* What I want to know is—could I write directly to them and order a chair that way, and if so, do you know where the "factories" are? I can't even think what the capital of Norway is at the moment. Oh, Oslo.

I'd like to get the high-backed chair and the footstool if I can afford it, and Alice Methfessel wants a chair, too. It may be impossible to order directly, but I thought you'd know.

. . . I've taken up cross-country skiing, in a mild way—it is wonderful, when the snow is good. One advantage of Boston is that it is easy to get out of and to New Hampshire or Vermont in an hour or so. I went last weekend to *Newfane*—dead, almost no inhabitants, but the most beautiful New England architecture—a huge courthouse, two or three churches, Greek column houses, a large green, and elm trees. It snowed all Saturday night and Sunday morning seemed like 1872—even people *walking* to church. But alas, around the hills of Putney one could hear the occasional snowmobile roaring & grinding away. (Anny approves of this sport skiing—*she* used to cross-country ski. I also have a ping-pong table instead of a dining table—I must tell her, because I'm sure she'll approve of that, too.)

Remember me to Wheaton, and I hope to get to New York for long enough to see you both sometime. Now that I'm a member of that genteel Cos Club, maybe you'd dine with me—Sunday nights there's a buffet and wonderful roast beef.

[P.S.] Loren has sounded much better when I've talked to her recently—and I hope Lloyd is. I brought back two of her paintings my last trip—beautiful ones, I think. I don't imagine you've ever seen either of them: *The Waters* (c. 1939) and *Floorscape* ('43 or '44).

To Robert Lowell

March 21, 1972

I've been trying to write you this letter for weeks now, ever since Frank [Bidart] & I spent an evening when he first got back, reading and discussing *The Dolphin*. I've read it many times since then & we've discussed it some more. Please believe I think it is wonderful poetry. It seems to me far and away better than the *Notebooks*; every 14 lines have some marvels of image and expression, and also they are all much *clearer*. They affect me immediately and profoundly, and I'm pretty sure I understand them all perfectly. (Except for a few lines I may ask you about.) I've just decided to write this letter in two parts—the one big technical problem that bothers me [concerning the "plot"] I'll put on another sheet—it and some unimportant details have nothing to do with what I'm going to try to say here. It's hell to write this, so please first do believe I think *Dolphin* is magnificent poetry. It is also honest poetry—*almost*. You probably know already what my reactions are. I have one tremendous and awful BUT.

If you were any other poet I can think of I certainly wouldn't attempt to say anything at all; I wouldn't think it was worth it. But because it is you, and a great poem (I've never used the word "great" before, that I remember), and I love you a lot—I feel I must tell you what I really think. There are several reasons for this—some are worldly ones, and therefore secondary . . . but the primary reason is because I love you so much I can't bear to have you publish something that I regret and that you might live to regret, too. The worldly part of it is that it—the poem—parts of it—may well be taken up and used against you by all the wrong people —who are just waiting in the wings to attack you. —One shouldn't consider them, perhaps. But it seems wrong to play right into their hands, too.

(Don't be alarmed. I'm not talking about the whole poem—just one aspect of it.)

Here is a quotation from dear little Hardy that I copied out years ago—long before *Dolphin*, or even the *Notebooks*, were thought of. It's from a letter written in 1911, referring to "an abuse which was said to have occurred—that of publishing details of a lately deceased man's life under the guise of a novel, with assurances of truth scattered in the newspapers." (Not exactly the same situation as *Dolphin*, but fairly close.)

"What should certainly be protested against, in cases where there is no authorization, is the mixing of fact and fiction in unknown proportions. Infinite mischief would lie in that. If any statements in the dress of fiction are covertly hinted to be fact, all must be fact, and nothing else but fact, for obvious reasons. The power of getting lies believed about people through that channel after they are dead, by stirring in a few truths, is a horror to contemplate."

I'm sure my point is only too plain. Lizzie is not dead, etc.—but there is a "mixture of fact & fiction," and you have *changed* her letters. That is "infinite mischief," I think. The first one, page 10, is so shocking—well, I don't know what to say. And page 47 . . . and a few after that. One can use one's life as material—one does, anyway—but these letters—aren't you violating a trust? IF you were given permission—IF you hadn't changed them . . . etc. But *art just isn't worth that much.* I keep remembering Hopkins's marvelous letter to Bridges about the idea of a "gentleman" being the highest thing ever conceived—higher than a "Christian," even, certainly than a poet. It is not being "gentle" to use personal, tragic, anguished letters that way—it's cruel.

I feel fairly sure that what I'm saying (so badly) won't influence you very much; you'll feel sad that I feel this way, but go on with your work & publication just the same. I also think that the thing *could* be done, somehow—the letters used and the conflict presented as forcefully, or almost, without changing them, or loading the dice so against E. It would mean a great deal of work, of course (but you're a good enough poet to write *anything*—get around anything—after all)—and perhaps you feel it is impossible, that they must stay as written. It makes me feel perfectly awful, to tell the truth—I feel sick for *you.* I don't want you to appear in that light, to anyone—Elizabeth, Caroline—me—your public! And most of all, not to yourself.

I wish I had here *another* quotation. [Henry] James wrote a marvelous letter to someone about a *roman à clef* by Vernon Lee—but I can't find it without going to the bowels of Widener, I suppose. His feelings on the subject were much stronger than mine, even. In general, I deplore the "confessional"—however, when you wrote *Life Studies* perhaps it was a necessary movement, and it helped make poetry more real, fresh and immediate. But now—ye gods—anything goes, and I am so sick of poems about the students' mothers & fathers and sex lives and so on. All that *can* be done—but at the same time one surely should have a feeling that one can trust the writer—not to distort, tell lies, etc.

The letters, as you have used them, present fearful problems: what's true, what isn't; how one can bear to witness such suffering and yet not know how much of it one *needn't* suffer with, how much has been "made up," and so on.

I don't give a damn what someone like Mailer writes about his wives & marriages—I just hate the level we seem to live and think and feel on at present—but I DO give a damn about what you write! Or [James] Dickey or Mary [McCarthy]—they don't count, in the long run. This counts and I can't bear to have anything you write tell—perhaps—what we're really like in 1972—perhaps it's as simple as that. But are we? Well—I mustn't ramble on any more, I've thought about it all I can and can't reach more lucid conclusions, I'm afraid.

Now the absurd. Will you do me a great favor and tell me how much you earned for a half-term, or one term, I guess it is, when you left Harvard? They have asked me to come back—when I was so sick I didn't think it through very well—for the $10,000 I got last year & last fall, and a "slight raise." (This may be $500 I learned from Mr. B.) Of course I should have insisted on some sort of definite contract then & there but I didn't even think of it until later. I have rented this place for a year and another year—but I must plan ahead and I am getting fearfully old and have to think of what I'm going to do in the future years, where I'm going to live, etc. At present I'm afraid even to get a cold because I have no hospital protection—thank god I did have when I was very sick. The Woman's outfit—whatever it is here—has been after me, too—asking me if I am getting the same salary that you got, and I don't know. This sounds very crass—but it's true I could earn more at other places—but prefer to stay here if I can. But I must have some sort of definite contract, obviously. Forgive my sordidness (as Marianne would call it).

I had a St. Patrick's Day dinner for Bill Alfred—a few days late— and Octavio Paz, etc.—very nice . . . Now I have to go to the dentist and I'll send this without thinking. Otherwise I'll never send it.

The Dolphin is marvelous—no doubt about that. I'll write you all the things I like sometime! I hope all goes well with you and Caroline and the little daughters and the infant son.

[*EB enclosed a full page of queries ("petty comments") and added another sheet to conclude her letter.*]

Somewhere—I can't find it right now—you wrote "with my fresh wife"—that seemed just too much, somehow—the word "fresh" again had a sort of Hollywood feeling I'm sure you didn't intend—you've avoided it almost completely. Well, I could go on, of course. Most of these are trivialities & some I forgot to mark as I read through the book—many times, now. You know I am quite fiendish about trivialities, however. But right now they don't seem worth it. I am having trouble trying to decide how to divide this letter, but I think I'll put all my technical remarks on these pages. *This is the one big criticism I'd make:*

As far as the *story* goes—of course you haven't stuck exactly to the facts & didn't have to. But starting about page 44 I find things a little confusing. Page 44 is titled "Leaving America for England"—obviously about the idea of that. Then 47, "Flight to New York." (I wonder if "Flight" is the right word here even if you do fly.) Then New York, and Christmas—"swims the true shark, the shadow of departure." That's all about that. (The N.Y. poems in themselves are *wonderful*.) (Can the line about the "play about the fall of Japan" *possibly* be true?!) But after the "shadow of departure" comes BURDEN—and the baby is on the way. This seems to me a bit too sudden—there is no actual return to England—and the word BURDEN and then the question "Have we got a child?" sounds almost a bit Victorian melodramatic. This is the only place where the "plot" seems awkward to me, and *I* can fill it in of course—but I think it might baffle most readers.

The change, decision, or whatever happens between page 51 and 52 seems too sudden—after the prolongation of all the first sections, the agonies of indecision, etc. (wonderful atmosphere of life's *stalling* ways).

You've left out E.'s trip to London?—that's not needed perhaps for the plot—but it might help soften your telling of it?—but I somehow think you need to get yourself back to England *before* the baby appears like that. (Frank Bidart took violent exception to the word "bastard," I don't know why—I think it's a good old word and even find it appealing & touching. He must have worse associations with it than I have.)

April 10, 1972
(Monday?)

I have two letters from you here now—and I was so relieved to get the first one, especially. I was awfully afraid I'd been crude, rude, etc. Look—I do see how when you have written—one has written—an absolutely wonderful, or satisfactory, poem—it's hard to think of changing anything. However, I think you've misunderstood me a little.

I quoted Hardy exactly, and the point was that one *can't* mix fact & fiction. What I have objected to in your use of the letters is that I think you've changed them—and you had no right to do that.

April 12

Well, I was interrupted and have stayed interrupted for two days, apparently. It was—is—as I was saying—the mixture of truth & fiction that bothers me. Of course, I don't know anything about your possible agreements with E. about this, etc., and so I may be exaggerating terribly.

To drop this painful subject and go on to the rest. I think the rearrangements you are thinking of making will improve the last part of the poem enormously—and I see what a lot of hard work they entail, too. The idea of the italics—and your saying some lines—sounds fine.

I am so glad Harriet's visit apparently went off so very well. After all, she has two very bright parents and so must have inherited a good deal of intelligence!

I am getting ready to go to New York; the Brazilian anthology (or Vol. I of it) is to be launched tomorrow at a huge, I gather, party, and I must be there. I don't want to be especially, but must. This is no real answer to your letters—and thank you for being so frank about the poems.

. . . I read your Berryman piece with sadness—also wonder that you

could do it all so fast and spontaneously. I have the new book [*Love &*
Fame] here but haven't had time really to study the poems yet. It is awful,
but in general his religiosity doesn't quite *convince* me—perhaps it
couldn't quite convince him, either. He says wonderful little things, in
flashes—the glitter of broken glasses, smashed museum cases—something like that.

I am still struggling to put down all my Marianne Moore recollections.
I've also done a couple of poems—one a pretty long one, still being
furbished a bit—the first of this batch maybe I'll enclose. It is very old-
fashioned and umpty-umpty, I'm afraid—but I'm grateful to get anything
done these days and one usually starts me off on two or three more, with
luck. Frank has also asked me for a blurb and I struggle with the phrases
for that in between everything else. It is terribly hard. His poem is so
personal, so conclusive—so definitive, almost (for Frank). I don't see
where he can go after that, really. I wish he'd try something easier. He
has such amazing taste and sensitivity about other people's poetry. I wish
he were a happier young man. I do think we've become very good friends,
however.

The Pazes have also been very friendly and we had—I had—an
Easter breakfast party—a great success, I think, with Frank doing best
at egg dyeing, and Octavio madly searching my bedroom and bathroom
for eggs—all brand new to him, these Easter rites—

It's spring—first one I've seen in many years. I had one wonderful
last skiing weekend in Stowe—unbroken fields & mountainsides of
snow—and then back here where everything looks very bare and still
brown—and the brick walks are still bleached white by all that salt they
use in the winter.

[P.S.] Just received an ad for a book about you called *Everything to
Be Endured.*

To Loren MacIver

April 21, 1972

I certainly hope you are feeling better—and that something can be
done about your "corset" so that you can use it without its hurting. I
haven't any news—except that after a snowstorm yesterday it is again a
beautiful spring day and the lilacs under my bedroom window—the
neighbors'—still seem to be growing—green buds. I haven't seen a Northern spring for so many years I don't really know how fast things open up,
or if one snowstorm will kill them, etc. I have no views here at all—the
only thing really wrong with this apartment—but for a week or two I
should have a *sea* of lilacs out the bedroom window, at least. Did I tell
you that the super has a huge black cat named Midnight? He's very

friendly and nice and sits quite a lot in our hideous glass-brick lobby, on a red plastic sofa.

The super—Joe MacGrath—came in to fix the broken Venetian blind in the kitchen last night—broken rope. He is ENORMOUS—and growing, I think—and very very Irish. After 6, he smells of booze. When I got back from the hospital he held my hand for a long alcoholic greeting, in the glass-brick lobby. He also took a great fancy to Alice and detained her in a sentimental way one night for a long time . . . I was trying to cook dinner while he worked on the blind—and he couldn't grasp the principle of the thing—the rope fell all the way out, finally, and then he had to thread it back through all the slats—this took about an hour. I gave him a drink. When he left, he left the blind tied up in several large knots— it won't go up or down now. (I knew how to do it, but didn't have the heart to show him.) And he said as he left, "I'll get someone who knows how to fix the shitty thing." I was very surprised.

I am making a batch of cookies to send to E.—hadn't made any for several years but thought it was a good idea. I think I'll call tonight.

It occurred to me the other day that you simply must paint a picture of a Boston Garden Swan boat. You'd do a lovely one. Did I send you one of those postcards? If you could get over for a short visit, when it is warmer, we'd go & take a ride on them.

Tell A.F. that if she ever comes this way (unlikely), I'd like to talk with her about Lloyd's book. I do hope he's feeling better; his voice certainly sounds brisker on the telephone. Well—remember my condescendingly good advice and be patient and understanding with all our peculiar friends . . .

[P.S.] Frani took me to the Storm King Art Center. Thirteen David Smiths dotted around the grounds, among other things—a very funny and nice *The Lady Artist* of David Smith—do you know it?

To James Merrill

May 12, 1972

It was lovely to arrive home after an extra-long session with the dentist and find the pot of lilies of the valley at my door. Did you know—how did you know?—they are one of my favorite flowers, almost the *very* favorite. I used to raise them from bulbs in the closet, in New York, but they're hard to grow—usually come out very spindly. These are lovely— including the little green lawn around them—& are smelling up the whole room beautifully. I have a poem—the one about the dead baby, you may remember it—in which my mother lays him out and I put a lily of the valley in his hand. Well, it was quite true—she had sort of framed him in lilies of the valley—*her* favorite flower—although where they got them in Nova Scotia in the winter I don't know—probably someone had raised them at home. Mary Chess used to make a lovely *muguet* scent—but her flower scents aren't what they used to be when she was alive.

I wish you'd had more time and our lunch could have lasted longer. I didn't say a quarter of the things I wanted to about *Braving the Elements*, for one thing. I also meant to ask you about "Claire / Coe in 'Tehuantepec' "—in the "Banks of a Stream" poem, I suppose *rivière* is a diamond necklace, isn't it, of course. "Strato in Plaster" is very sad & good. There are *beautiful* images in every poem, etc. etc. I envy you your industry and application and discipline.

Well, Linda called again last night to say she isn't coming now until the end of the month or the first part of June. She is "taking a course" in Chicago. I couldn't understand how, but it seems there's a Brazilian (in exile, no doubt) there giving a series of lectures, in Portuguese, that she *has* to hear . . . I suspect they are on guerrilla warfare or something like that but I'll probably never know. I am a bit suspicious of her friends' activities in Chicago, her friends in Mexico, and so on, and only hope she won't get in trouble. She says she is going to take a course in English, too—and that's a good idea. This works out better for me because now I am free to go back to the Phi Beta Kappa poem for a while—and probably we can fly back to Brazil & to Belo Horizonte—together, which is more pleasant than doing the trip alone.

Tonight I'm going to hear Beverly Sills in *La Traviata*—with Alice and her father & mother. I've invited them to dinner. They don't like "spices," just plain, wholesome food—this cramps my style. Do I dare to put anise seeds on the roast of pork or not? Better not.

The weather is cold but beautiful since you left—what a pity you had such an awful day. As soon as it warms up and the lilacs open a bit more, I'm going to the Arnold Arboretum.

With much love to you—and please remember me to Grace Stone, and her daughter. I found [E. F. Benson's] *Miss Mapp* and *Trouble for Lucia* at a drugstore here—but think I've missed an important one—her husband must have died and Georgie proposed somewhere along the line.

[P.S.] I bought a simple B.A. gown at the Coop yesterday—it is so cheap and flimsy—it looks exactly like a child's witch costume for Halloween. But when I received my one honorary degree my hat was much too big and the gown reached the floor & covered my hands. Another recipient, an actress, had had the forethought to get a really *mini*-gown, above the knees, and she got the biggest hand and the rest of us felt jealous. So I thought I'd take one that more or less fits this time. It *zips* —shades of Edward III!

To Aunt Grace

On December 2, 1956, EB had written Aunt Grace she had begun a new poem, "The Moose," and would dedicate it to her. Finished sixteen years later, it becomes the Phi Beta Kappa poem at Harvard.

> June 15, 1972
> Commencement Day here

. . . I must get all my papers, letters, etc., back into this country as soon as possible. I must sell them—to support me in my old age—and the sooner this is done the better. (I have a big collection of letters from Marianne Moore and other now "famous" friends—and I can sell them—to a library here or to two or three others. This may make all the difference between a poorhouse or a fairly comfortable nursing home for my declining days!)

What has really prevented me from coming [to Nova Scotia] was that I had to give the Phi Beta Kappa poem here this year—that was day before yesterday—and I had to get the damned poem *written*, first. This is a very long one, about Nova Scotia—the one I said was to be dedicated to you when it is published in a book. It is called "The Moose." (You are *not* the moose.) It was very successful, I think—it was broadcast here some- time yesterday [the broadcast done from a tape made at the ceremony] —I missed it, thank goodness—and will be in *The New Yorker*. I'll send you a copy. But it took me weeks to get it done and I almost had a collapse worrying for fear it wouldn't be done on time. Well—I seem to be blowing my own horn this morning—but you see I also got two honorary degrees this year—one at Rutgers University (New Jersey) and one at Brown. I enclose the clipping from *Time* about Brown—can't find the first one. This meant two trips away and very boring receptions, processions, etc. —I now have three "hoods"—I don't know what to do with them. A famous lawyer here, also receiving a degree, has *12* hoods and told me he was thinking of having a *quilt* made of them. The picture from yes- terday's *Globe* is terrible. The black man, in *Time*, was my "partner" in the academic procession at Brown (Providence). He has a white beard now, and is very very talkative, but quite amusing. They made us walk *miles* to the "Old Meeting House" . . .

I find my airplane ticket is wrong—have to go and change it; get a haircut; get traveler's checks; go to Boston and buy shoes and some un- derwear & get to a luncheon. I'm skipping the exercise here, having seen two already this year—buy a few little presents to take to Brazil, including blue jeans for the maid—etc. etc. etc.—and hope to God I get away by Sat. Oh, and see the lawyer about a new WILL, and tomorrow, one final dentist appointment—also in Boston. It's hot and muggy. I am sick of that Boston subway! Well, it will be *cold* in Ouro Prêto . . .

I'm also sorry to sound so conceited—but you can see how busy I've been. These honorary degrees are rather silly, but I think they may help me get a permanent job here—and the "fringe benefits" that now I only have when I'm actually teaching. So I went through with it all, even if it is nonsense.

To Frani Blough Muser

Ouro Prêto, Brazil
June 26, 1972

I found this rather damp block of airmail paper here—and a whole carton of Lucky Strikes, left in the cupboard last August. The cupboard must have worked fairly well as a humidor—the cigarettes are a bit limp, but perfectly good. This is fine—since the booze & cigarettes purchased at Kennedy got left behind in the Santos Dumont Airport. (I *told* Linda I wouldn't trust them with anyone) & heaven knows if they'll ever turn up. She . . . had Varig reservations for Tuesday & I thought how lucky that was, because of the strike on Monday. Nevertheless, we discovered we'd been bounced—probably someone bribed Varig. Anyway, it has been getting worse & worse every trip, so in a pet, I switched over to Pan Am and it wasn't crowded at all, and much more efficient and didn't charge any overweight. (And Linda, like all visiting Brazilians, must have had 100 lbs. or so of odd items, mostly from drugstores.)

I came straight through here—no one home—dank and cold and half the light bulbs burned out. However, Vitória showed up after a few hours and all is in pretty good shape. My biggest problem was that there were no matches in the house and I had about 5 in one last paper holder. There was a large bottle of *cachaça* in the kitchen and I used that to start two fires—worked beautifully, lovely blue flames. Airing, cleaning, polishing going on at a great rate. The weather is perfectly beautiful—bright sunshine, just crisp enough—such a relief after the awful rainy days in N.Y. And I, too, am going through papers and burning large baskets full. I thought I'd done most of this last year, but keep finding more bundles of letters and old checks—only somehow or other *I* did all this, in past years, all by myself . . .

Well, it was lovely seeing you and the house in ?—is it Sakonnet Point? It seems so green and lush and peaceful, looking back, here in the dry season, with that awful "festival" about to begin, and the poor little town looking beautiful but filthier than ever. However, I won't be lonely—several callers already—and Emanuel is supposed to come the middle of the month to work with me. I've already written to the *Previews* representative in Rio—and only hope he is still there. I wish I could keep the house (and maybe I'll have to) and I wish you could keep yours—I can't quite remember the name, all that comes to me is "Peascod" and that isn't right. "Peasefield"??

I'm reading that huge Craft book on Stravinsky—it is fascinating—and then there will be an *"omnibus"* of all those little books (I have two or three in paper). I wonder how accurate Mr. Craft is? He spares no one, certainly. What do you think? (You are my authority in everything musical.) Just before I left Cambridge I was listening to some radio music and thought it was wonderful, whatever it was—and at the end the announcer said it was Ruggles, but didn't say what.

Oh—the Phi Beta Kappa affair went off all right, I think—the head of the law school, who was running it, introduced me (every fact wrong) and then said, "The title of Miss B.'s poem is 'The Moose,' " and then (I suppose so that the audience wouldn't think I was going to deliver a *mousse* recipe) he spelled it out—"The M-O-O-S"—and sat down. Then the audience thought I was going to read in Dutch, maybe. This led to a great deal of very academic merriment later. The glee club sang several selections, right in our ears, behind us. One of the singers lives in Kirkland House and Alice asked him how the ceremony had gone. The boy said he thought they'd been off-key, and that some woman had read a poem. A. asked innocently how that had been, and the boy said: "Well, as far as poems go, it wasn't bad." I consider that a great compliment.

Please give my love to the members of your family and I'm sorry I didn't get to see any of them before I left. I really adore your grandchildren. Thank you for your hospitality. I wonder if wild roses would grow here or do they need salt air? I've brought a lot of flower seeds—the kind of thing, like Vinca, that usually will grow anywhere—and V. has kept the thyme, parsley and chives going—also *plenty* of kale. I should be writing business letters; I'm putting off struggling with a couple in Portuguese . . .

I'm going to try to get back August 1st.

To Frank Bidart

July 11, 1972

. . . I think I'm only going to be here 17 or 18 more days—then back to Cambridge, briefly. At last word from Alice, our trip is getting "finalized" or "formalized"—and we may be able to take the mailboat we wanted to take, up the coast of Norway. I don't see why you couldn't join us, anywhere along the line of our travels, and of course for as long as possible—we'd love to have you, you know. I just don't want you to spend your money recklessly . . . (a lot of money). I wrote Alice maybe she'll soon send you our itinerary.

The letter *E* fell off my electric typewriter (those damned Coronas) Sunday, and it has gone to Belo Horizonte to be soldered. Thank heavens I had this old Royal, non-electric, here. It was less embarrassing—after all, *E* is the most-used letter in the English language.

It's Wednesday today, but I feel that the weekend is just over, and it was rather hectic. José Alberto Nemer, Linda's youngest brother (25, I think) is staying here, giving an art class for the July Festival, and Linda and a friend came Friday evening. I didn't go out "on the town" with them nights, I find it too cold and grim and boring—all those dirty "ippies," as they call them. One sordid little bar I rather liked, but now find I really only must have enjoyed it when I was drinking *cachaça*—it is necessary to my *nostalgie de la boue*. There are OLD Brazilian movies every afternoon—I went once—very amusing, but I haven't the time to go—and there has been some good music. I liked best a group, "Quinteto Violado," from the northeast—2 guitars, bass, drums, and a flute—the flautist is 13 years old, very good, too. Popular music, and then a lot of "cowboy" ballads, etc., from the northeast—lovely stuff, really. I'm bringing back 3 or 4 new records—are there any you want especially?

Monday, after gorgeous weather, the fog closed in, mingled with downpours and thunder & lightning, so Linda and friend stayed on until yesterday—the road was too dangerous. It's rather beautiful—most of the time I can't see a thing out of the windows, then the fog shifts, and a church or a palm tree appears mysteriously. Thank goodness I have a stove and a fireplace . . . Yesterday the new (very young) Cultural Attaché and his even younger wife came over from Belo H.—stayed to lunch and—I can't believe it—ALL my papers can be sent back via APO (Army—U.S. Post Office)—straight to Cambridge. I haven't heard a word from Emanuel, but even if he doesn't come I can manage, I think—get what's left here ready, and just hire a car to go to Belo and the bank, and transfer everything to the USIS office. So don't worry about not being able to help . . .

I've made lots of changes in "The Moose" & think it is vastly improved. However—I got the proof & they want to run it (*New Yorker*) July 15th—and I'm afraid they'll run the original version, oh dear—unless my corrections get there in time.

To Dr. Anny Baumann

[POSTCARD]

Helsinki, Finland
August 11, 1972

When I got back from Brazil, you were off on vacation. I was told you'd be back in N.Y. the 14th. Alice & I left Boston August 6th. Three days in Stockholm, which I loved, then here. Sunday we go to Leningrad for four days. Then back to Bergen (Robert Lowell may join us) & on the 20th we sail twelve days up & down the coast of Norway on a mailboat . . . This is a "nice change" from Brazil!

To Arthur Gold and Robert Fizdale

Helsinki, Finland
August 18, 1972

Just back from four days in Leningrad. I can't remember whether you've been or not—anyway I wouldn't advise it much. Finland looked pretty *triste* (like Nova Scotia) on the way over; on the way back, it looked absolutely beautiful, the flower of cultivation and civilization, and still does . . . Helsinki is pretty charm-less, but there are wonderful shops & I spent most of my money on fabrics & a work of art. (Lota would have loved it here, so much "Swedish modern," which she adored.) On Sunday off for twelve days up the coast of Norway on a mailboat—WHEE!

60 Brattle Street
Cambridge, Massachusetts
September 28, 1972

. . . Yes, I did get the James Schuyler book and I meant to write you about it right away. I hadn't read his poetry until last year when James Merrill recommended it—someone lent me *Freely Espousing* and I like some of those poems a lot. But this book is much finer, I think—some really lovely poems—and nice love poems, which are very rare. Thank you very much and if you see him give him my congratulations . . .

Where are you going to publish your translated story? I have here a large collection of my works in Italian—it came a week ago and I haven't even looked at most of them yet. I can make out *some* Italian but not very much—but I love being called "La Bishop" in the Introduction. I think I should have an Italian who knows English (idiomatic, *spoken* English) very well go over it for me—and I suppose there must be some such here at Harvard, but I don't know anyone. Do you? At the same time a lot—almost the works—has been done into French by a lady at Wellesley who translated some of Marianne—years ago. I had my doubts about its tone—it seemed much too formal to me, but my French is not all that good & I know no slang to speak of, etc. But Octavio Paz's French wife, Marie Jo (a darling—I liked them both best of all here last year & miss them now they've gone back to Mexico), has just returned it to me, all corrected—and I haven't had time to look through that yet, either. It was awfully kind of her. It's more fun to appear in Italian, though—*everything* sounds beautiful. I'm glad you liked "The Moose." I had another small poem in last week's *New Yorker*—and two more to come soon, one a fairly good one, I think.

Alice & I shall be at the concert on November 18th. She has never heard you play, of course, and is eager to. We're trying to get tickets to go to the matinee that day of *No, No, Nanette* but I'm not sure we'll be able to . . . I'll probably be at the Cosmopolitan Club. It would be wonderful if you had any spare hours for lunch, tea, breakfast, anything at all—but I imagine you'll be far too busy?—and in demand.

Classes began this week—one Tuesday, one Wednesday—I should feel flattered & gratified, etc. About 40 people or more trying to get into the writing class (of ten) and I think about 60 showed up for the "Modern Poetry" one yesterday—but somehow I just feel tired although that's a word I don't think one should use, especially after 60. But the thought of reading about 40 batches of poems, mostly bad—and then a lot of little essays on "The Emperor of Ice Cream" this weekend. (I think I thought up that test walking through the Square on my way to the class yesterday—it was very hot and *everyone* was eating ice-cream cones—it's a kind of Harvard obsession, anyway.)

To James Merrill

October 12, 1972

. . . I could weep myself to think of Mr. [Chester] Kallman's weeping over "The Moose." Did I tell you that I visited my aunt in Nova Scotia two or three weekends ago? I was taken on drives to see the "fall colors"—better there than anywhere else—graveyards, old places where I used to live long ago, etc. But one thing struck me—calling on the woman who now lives in my grandparents' house. She was entertaining the lady who runs the village telephone switchboard for tea—so there were five ladies, with my aunt, cousin and me. They ALL, except me, did that queer thing with the indrawn breath, saying "ye-e-es" to show sympathetic understanding. I wish I could imitate it better—it is almost an assenting *groan*. Well, that is about the only poem of mine that branch of my family has really taken to. (One second cousin or something—not really related—had just taken out his Moose License for the season. I asked my cousin what on earth one would do with a shot moose and she replied, "Roast it!")

After some initial *bad* troubles with a psychotic (I think) black man, my reading-poetry class is doing very nicely and one little freshman . . . wants to write her term paper on *you*. I also have one frighteningly good young man in the writing class. He knows all about euphonics? philology? and those phonetic marks I have never been able to master. I have also not mastered this new typewriter yet—it is so *sensitive*. Perhaps it will write some poetry on its own.

I shouldn't be writing to you at all, but to *Previews*, the bank, my income tax man, and of course my innumerable fans. (I get some pretty odd letters, too—but "The Moose" has brought letters from some nice elderly people, I think they are, from Maine & Canada, etc.) Sunday after this I'm going to lunch at John Brinnin's & Mrs. Vendler will be there.

I don't know her but she called to offer me a lift and went on *some more* about your book (I had assumed she knew you, too).

This doesn't count as a letter—that will follow sometime. I am dying to come to Greece. Remember me to Rollie McKenna.

To Dr. Anny Baumann

December 6, 1972

. . . The Dexamyl situation has been changed and Dr. Wacker here (head of the Harvard Medical Service) now provides me with a monthly prescription. Robert Lowell did *not* join us in Helsinki or Bergen. A young friend of his & mine, Frank Bidart, who was working with Cal in England, did, for 3 days, and we all had a wonderful shopping spree. The thing I bought—well it is a ceramic plaque, tiles, painted and otherwise, that turned out to be by Arabia's most famous designer, one Rut Bryk ("Ruth," I think). I saw it the first minute I entered the shop & took a fancy to it —it was very expensive & I kept going in to look at it and think about it. Finally the last day in Helsinki I bought it. It is very bright and cheerful. But it wasn't until they made out the sales slip that I discovered the plaque has a title: EASTER. That makes it all the nicer. Now after three months' waiting, it is here in the living room, but I can't hang it up until I've bought a gadget at the hardware store that detects studs in the wall— because it is pretty heavy. I do hope you can see it sometime.

Well, the less said about Cal's visit the better, I think. He was in Cambridge 4 days and I saw a lot of him and gave a dinner party for him and Caroline & the Fitzgeralds (poet & his wife—I like them very much & they had been old friends of Cal's). The party went on until 2 a.m., so I think it was successful. But Cal and Caroline were of course exhausted by their awful stay in N.Y.—and I & other friends were exhausted when they left, I'm afraid. And we are all dreading the publication of the *three* collections of "sonnets," old & new. I don't think he should publish them and have written him so and told him so—but nothing makes any impression on him. I'm afraid they are going to do him great harm, as well as being unbelievably cruel to Elizabeth. The baby seemed very nice, the 15 minutes I saw him, and Caroline does love children and was very nice with him—that was the best 15 minutes of the visit.

I was told last night that yesterday the English Dept. voted on my being given a "term appointment"—that's what they call something permanent for me, and I had said I had to have it or I'd go somewhere else, because I couldn't go on in this *ad hoc* way year after year, etc. Well, it seems they voted to do it—unanimously, I mean—but it still has to pass "Administration." I don't know what this means exactly, but I think it is pretty sure to. I was afraid—and so were friends—that Cal's returning next fall would mean I wasn't wanted—but apparently not. There are so many poets around, however, that I have said I'd teach in the spring term next year. Perhaps I'll be able to get some work of my own done for a change. I am going back to Seattle about March 20th—one term only. I don't want to, but they pay very well (better than Harvard—most places pay better than Harvard!) . . .

I had Thanksgiving dinner for 6—my biggest cooking effort in some time—and *that* party lasted from 3 p.m. until 2 a.m., so must have been successful, too. I don't think I'll come to N.Y. this Christmas—Christmases there get more & more dismal—but I do have to be in N.Y. twice, I think, in January . . . Now I must get ready for the 2 p.m. seminar—look up all the words in the dictionary so that *I'll* know them when the students don't & they'll think I'm awfully smart. I can't say I like teaching much, but this time I am lucky and both groups are very nice—some adorable students. I'm going to give a mixed ping-pong and poetry party for the writing class sometime in January. Oh, today I am also going to take a "flu shot." I wonder if they really do any good?

To James Merrill

January 8, 1973

Alice just telephoned me from her office and read me out of *The N.Y. Times*—about your receiving the Bollingen [Prize], and a few nice remarks you made, too. So I am hastening to send you my congratulations. That's wonderful. I'll see the paper later—it is too cold to go out to buy one—5 degrees at the moment, with frost on the windows, for the first time—and Mrs. Murphy is here to clean for me, also for the first time, so I'd better stay around to supervise a bit. At present she is sitting in my rocking chair drinking a cup of tea, but I *believe* she plans to go on with the cleaning some more.

I have meant to write to you for 2 or 3 days—a young lady finally telephoned me from the Y.M.H.A. [Poetry Center]. (I am gradually making an important discovery—at least, I think now I *have* made it—that is, if you don't answer letters, sooner or later the unanswered person telephones you. At first this just made me feel guilty, but now I am beginning to think it is the only sensible way to deal with a great proportion of one's correspondence.) Well—WE are now going to read on April 11th—if that is all right with you? (Maybe she's telephoned you, too?) I have to be in N.Y. for the Book Award thing on the 12th . . .

May I go first? Read, I mean? I don't really mind too much any more—but I think I'd mind a lot less, and enjoy your reading more, if I had my own over with. It's nice—only about 25 minutes each, I should think. The only other time I was part of a team was with Richard Howard. He wanted us to alternate poems—I can't imagine why—and I put my foot down firmly on that idea. I think you and I will make a much better couple, somehow, than Richard & I did. WE promised to laugh at each other's funny lines, though SOMEONE has to start a laugh, I think—or no one ever does.

I recently went to Brown and no one cracked a smile, even. However, that may have been because of a very odd introduction. I don't want to be mean about Mr. Honig because I like him—and he was so upset he probably didn't realize quite what he was saying—but he introduced me by saying he'd spent the whole day with a graduate student who'd gone mad, trying to get him to go to a hospital, I think. To *calm* him, he had read him my poetry. Well, that was all right, I suppose, but then Mr. Honig added that the young madman had become convinced that *he*—the madman—had written my poems. Then "Ladies & Gentlemen, Miss B." and I said, "Thank you, Mr. H.," feeling that if only I were quick-witted there was probably a wonderful remark to be made—although it scarcely seemed the occasion for humor.

The girl from the Y.M.H.A. seemed very excited at the prospect of you and me. Someone—I don't know who—had sworn to her I'd *never* accept. People make these dogmatic statements about me behind my back—who are they? Miss Geffen of the Institute also telephoned once and said someone had told her I *never* answered my telephone. I seem to be talking about myself an awful lot, for a letter supposed to be congratulatory for your work . . . Anyway I think you deserve the prize & I'm very pleased.

Cal Lowell is here, or en route—I'm having dinner with him. He came over for the Pound "Requiem" affair Friday night in N.Y. I refused to participate. He was here for some days (was it in November?) with new wife, baby, nursemaid, etc. I saw just a little of the baby, who is walking & looked large & strong and very nice, as year-old infants go.

I adored your postcard of the "Drown." Also—is that Greek the word for AIRMAIL? I had a large collection of old postcards—but alas, most of them got destroyed, I'm afraid, in Brazil. My house is now listed with *Previews*, at vast expense—they are preparing a "pamphlet"—I'm afraid at any minute I'll weaken and decide not to sell it—but know I mustn't —I CAN'T live there, really—architecture is not enough. (And I'm awfully sick of looking at the Loeb Theatre. Where to go?) With lots of love, Jimmy, and write some more poems right away. (Alice took me to the airport once and I said oh dear, I have nothing to read on the plane. She replied, unfeelingly, "Well, write a poem and read it.") I am actually *planning* to now that classes are over—have a long, long one about my dead toucan, Uncle Sam—maybe it will be done by April 11th . . .

To Dr. Anny Baumann

March 19, 1973

I thought that I was the one who owed a letter, so it was a pleasant surprise to hear that you were feeling a little guilty—because I usually am feeling awfully guilty these days. I am writing to you in a great hurry now because on the 22nd I'm starting off for Seattle (by train—or by air to Chicago, and from there by train)—and of course there are a thousand things to do before I can leave . . .

Well, I wasn't at all sure until two days ago about that "term appointment." I gathered that the English Dept. had voted for me, but I had yet to hear from the Board of Governors, who do the final deciding—and it looked rather unpromising to me at times. I heard that 11 of the younger English teachers had been dropped. However, I finally got a very impressive, diploma-like paper, addressing me as "Madam" this time—Harvard is learning; everything used to be addressed "Sir" before—and I have been appointed for four years. This is wonderful—that is, if I can survive teaching one more half-year & three full years—because that will bring me up to retirement age. I'll have taught enough terms to be entitled to medical care for the rest of my life—whee! However, I must really check on this & see that it is quite true. Of course I don't *want* to teach two terms a year—but I think it is certainly worth it, if I can hold out.

You will be pleased to hear, I think, that I have been doing quite a few readings—and I DON'T like to, but wanted to earn some more money, to be able to do my own work. I read at Bryn Mawr; went to Oklahoma for four days and read there (and had a wonderful time there, too); at Wellesley again; and recently at the University of Virginia. I have two readings arranged for out in the Northwest, too. Then on April 11th (I may have told you this already) I'm going to read in N.Y. at the Y.M.H.A., with an old friend, James Merrill. This doesn't pay much, but I stood them up there once years ago and felt I should—and with Jimmy it will only be for half an hour & should be easier. You are on my guest list for this affair—or at least for the party being given for us afterwards. I'm afraid I don't really recommend either the reading or the party—but I do hope I'll have a chance to see you . . . I'm getting much less nervous about the readings—but find the further away from home, the better I seem to do—Oklahoma was the best so far, I think—a wonderful audience.

My other big piece of news is that I have started buying an apartment here, in Boston that is. *Only please don't tell anyone about it just yet*—I may tell my friends when I get to New York in April. It is really very exciting—it is on a wharf—Lewis Wharf—right in Boston Harbor. I heard about it and went to see it and made up my mind in about 5 minutes—even if I go bankrupt trying to pay for it. (It is terribly expensive.) The wharf or warehouse was built in 1838, an enormous granite building, really beautiful, and in wonderful condition. One of the best Boston architects, Karl Koch, is doing the whole thing—all re-done inside of course—and everything so far is exactly what one would like. In fact, Mr.

Koch will be my next-door neighbor. I'm on the 4th floor, overlooking part of the harbor, with a verandah, 6 by 12 feet—a bit bigger—and I can see the ships (not that there are very many these days) and watch the tide rise & fall, at least. At nights there are still lots of smelt fishers—fishing with gasoline flares, very pretty. High beamed ceilings; exposed brick walls, a fireplace, oh all sorts of things and luxuries I've never had before—like doormen & elevators & air conditioning. The whole Boston waterfront is being renovated and it is the *one* beautiful place to live. After the grand scenery I have been used to in Brazil, it has been a comedown to look out on a dirty street for two years. And getting in at the beginning like this I've been able to arrange the walls more the way I want them—one large bathroom and a big closet instead of two small bathrooms, etc.—and one bedroom larger and the other, or study, smaller. About as much space as I have here—although the ping-pong table will have to go, I'm afraid. Of course I'm so spoiled I'd like something three times as big—but only millionaires can afford space in this country. If I can sell the Ouro Prêto house, all will be well—but I suppose I shall sell it, sooner or later. If not—well, off to the poorhouse. But it is, nevertheless, *a good investment*—I've been assured of this by an architect friend here, and also my lawyer, or rather the lawyer in my lawyer's firm who specializes in condominiums. I'll try to mail you a brochure before I leave —even if it is a bit exaggerated, probably—and I never quite believe in architects' dreams. It's curious but true that ships from Nova Scotia used to dock here—perhaps even my great-grandfather's—and that all the granite was quarried in Quincy, the home of my ancestors on the *other* side of the family—near Boston. I think I fell in love with the building —it is just too handsome for words; walls 18″ thick—the brickwork is beautiful, and I even like the rusted iron bolts and bars they've left in the walls, and the two uprights that will be in the study. Well, I mustn't write any more, but I do hope you can see it one of these days. It won't be ready for occupancy until the end of September. So I'll keep this place on until then—and I'll probably have to go to Brazil sometime before then. I hope to be able to send up a few favorite pieces of furniture.

A friend will be staying here while I'm in Seattle, probably, and that will help with the rent.

I had two slight attacks of the "flu"—the vomiting kind—everyone had one or the other—but since then I've been fine. We only got cross-country skiing twice this year—no snow—and even those two times weren't as good as last year. I take 16 or so Ecotrins a day—and with them my joints don't hurt too much. My 84- (or 86)-year-old aunt was just here for 5 days—I thought it was for overnight, but she stayed *on!* Except for her eyesight, she seemed in fairly good shape—but oh dear, I hope I don't live to that age.

To Arthur Gold and Robert Fizdale

University Motel
Seattle, Washington
April 25, 1973

I am appalled to realize I haven't yet thanked you for the lovely, adorable [gold laurel] wreaths [presented to EB and James Merrill to wear at the Y.M.H.A. poetry reading]. We didn't quite dare to wear them on the platform, but at the party at John Hollander's afterwards . . . (the party was roaring away when we got there), we decided to make an entrance, and adjusted our wreaths in the hall mirror before going in. Maybe it's just my natural modesty, but I felt a wreath was more becoming to Jim. There were a great many people there—I don't think I ever saw Jim again after our grand entrance. And Frank Bidart & I had to catch a late plane back to Boston.

My excuse for not having thanked you before is, well, two excuses. I was very upset by an insistent photographer who just wouldn't leave me alone. After saying she wouldn't, I could see her actually snapping away from the wings and once lost my place—also I could hear a tape recorder going. So I think I've tried to obliterate the whole thing from my mind —except for the wreaths & notes. The other excuse is that one has to work awfully hard here—7 classes a week, instead of 2 seminars, as at Harvard, and the classes are much bigger—17 poets all producing a poem every day, it seems to me—and the other huge class all totally baffled so far by Marianne Moore, etc. In despair I finally just tell them anecdotes.

Then you see above [letterhead drawing of motel] my "lovely home"—comfortable enough, except for taking the garbage down 3 flights—but I walk to work, something over a mile & back—and estimated that I climb about 500 steps a day—everything seems to be on the third floor (back, in the motel). I know I take it all too hard—I don't know why I can't relax about it a bit more. But one feels one *must* enlighten these children somehow.

I can't even sleep—here it is 6 a.m. Well, the flowers are beautiful all around—and yesterday at least ten robins arrived all at once—that loud cheerful song before dawn was unmistakable. Lots of birds.

Alice tells me you are going to Paris & will be back in June. Don't you sometimes tire of it? I know when I think I've decided—or was invited—to teach three, no four, more years at Harvard. Oh dear, oh dear!

But did she tell you I am buying an apartment down on Lewis Wharf? . . . I have a real verandah, looking over the harbor and up the Mystic River—and although Boston is a rather dead port these days, enough ships go by to make it interesting—and it is beautiful at night . . . Well, you must see it, that's all. IF I sell the Ouro Prêto house, all is well . . .

I must concentrate on E. E. Cummings for half an hour or so—and I don't think I really like him a lot. Yesterday I attempted to explain, quite unsuccessfully, I think, [Marianne Moore's poem] "Marriage" [to the students]. No one thought it was funny—no, one girl laughed.

Thank you again for the wonderful and surprising wreaths—so well made, too.

To Dr. Anny Baumann

60 Brattle Street
Cambridge, Massachusetts
June 14, 1973

I got back from Seattle, by way of San Francisco & a visit to friends in Palo Alto, about a week ago. Just now I had a telephone conversation with Louise . . .

I am very glad Seattle is over and I won't consider teaching there again; it is really too much. However, they seem to approve of my old-fashioned kind of teaching & have asked me back next May to give the Theodore Roethke Memorial Reading. I'm the first woman who's been asked for this, so I thought I'd better say I'd come.

I hope to stay here all summer and do some work of my own—as I may have told you, I have promised to read a paper on Marianne Moore sometime early in September here . . .

It didn't seem so extraordinary this morning, but after I talked to Louise, it did: last night I had a wonderful dream, a cheerful dream for once. I seemed to have acquired a "town house"—it looked like San Francisco—three or four floors, with a garden on one side and a view of the bay on the other. I was first in a downstairs room, welcoming guests; then I went upstairs to a large dining room with a round table, elegantly set for eight people—outside there were peonies in the garden & petunias & a fountain. I was bringing James Merrill into the room. And you—you were pouring CHAMPAGNE into the glasses around the table. This seems to me to be such an unusually optimistic dream, and something so unlikely for you to do—that I thought I'd tell you about it!

One year ago today I had to read that Commencement poem here —what a relief not to have to attend the ceremonies this year!

To Ashley Brown

September 17, 1973

Thank you for your letter & card from Ireland—I even had some intention of writing you in Ireland, but I seemed to be so absorbed by that "paper" I was writing [about Marianne Moore] that weeks went by without my thinking of anything else. I did get it done and read about 15 pages of it at that Institute affair—now I am re-copying ALL of it. It is quite long and I hope to sell it somewhere, of course. It was fun, really, once I got going—but it is very simple, I'm afraid.

No, I haven't bought the whole warehouse. It is HUGE—but I am buying an apartment in it; slowly and fearfully (and they just lost my first big check—oh dear) . . . The view can scarcely compare with Rio, but it is certainly better than Brattle Street—and it's a wonderful old part of town, right down below Faneuil Hall and the markets, etc.—and the aquarium almost next door. Terribly extravagant of me—but one is only old once.

Cal is here for this term—he came about a week ago, I think—but I have been in the hospital for a week with a slight case of pneumonia and pleurisy. I've been out for 3 days and am all right, just languid. Peter Taylor, whom I like very much, is also here. I'm seeing him today—and Octavio Paz and his wife are back, and I adore both of them. I am glad they are back and I think he'll be coming back for several half-years now, like me. However, I've been quite out of social life lately, either at home typing or in the infirmary coughing . . .

Oh dear—you say a librarian at Vassar was helping someone with a "dissertation" on me—how I wish they could vanish forever. One really nice little high-school boy has dug up some perfectly god-awful poems I had almost forgotten about.

The Ouro Prêto house is listed with *Previews* and I must get back there sometime—I'm not sure when—probably this fall sometime . . . I hope they can sell it soon—but first I must take out some pieces of furniture, etc. I am dreading this trip very much, but it can't be avoided.

I haven't seen Emanuel for a long time and wish I had—we do talk on the telephone once in a while. A man named Dean, U. of Wisconsin, wrote quite a nice little pamphlet about translating and the anthology—have you seen it? He said very nice things about your translations.

Well, Cal is considering buying a house *here*—and the Pazes are buying an apartment—seems to be the thing to do these days . . . I feel the time is approaching when I must give a PARTY. I usually enjoy my own very much, but the prospect seems too much right now—probably it's because every time I laugh, I get an awful stitch in my side . . .

To Loren MacIver

[POSTCARD]

October 1973

Forgive me for hanging up so abruptly last night. Actually I'd been meaning to for some minutes—fearing for your telephone bill. Alice and a friend of hers, both too youthful to have seen the original movie showings (unborn, probably), were attending a Katharine Hepburn show right down the street—a week of *her*—so I'd asked them to come in for a drink on the way home. The friend is a Canadian—an extremely bright girl on all kinds of scholarships. And this reminds me!—if you get a chance to see a French-Canadian movie called *My Uncle Antoine*, you should see it—it is slow to begin with and extremely sad—but really wonderful . . .

Well, I've been watching some baseball, too, tell Lloyd—and have become an ignorant fan of the Mets. It's the one game I know the rules of, and I *loathe* football. And on a color TV (mine was just repaired and the color is staggering), it's wonderful. I have nowhere near the interest in this "boy's game" that Marianne had—but I've watched it twice now & last night was fun. Tonight might decide everything. But the new costumes shock me a bit—it's almost *too* colorful . . .

Nova Scotia was awfully nice. We went to Great Village and Muir MacClachlan in the MacClachlan General Store remembered me and he looks just as he did, aged 6 in "Primer Class," except for being bald.

To James Merrill

The postcard view was entitled "Tidal Bore, Nova Scotia—One of the Greatest Natural Wonders of the World."

[POSTCARD]

November 2, 1973

I think *I* am about to become a Tidal Bore with my repetitive complaints about not having time to write letters. I hope you remember back to my Brazilian period, when I think I did write you long letters . . . Not teaching doesn't seem to help at all—I'm still behind and obsessed. Octavio Paz (I think you met him here, didn't you?) and I were complaining to each other [about correspondence] & he said, "And none of it is *poetry*!" and his wife said, "I know, you and Elizabeth should start a Poets' Lib movement." I must say my glimpse of *his* desk & study—after he had lived in their new apartment for 2 weeks—helped me a lot. It looks even worse than mine does after 2 years here—but then, he's a *very* important gentleman.

Anyway—you must be coming to Stonington soon; and yes, I'll be delighted to read with you in Washington—and yes, I did receive your two wonderful long poems and I have read them both several times. I especially like the one for the godchild's party, and was it *really* like that?

This is a souvenir of a recent trip to Nova Scotia—view from a nearby motel called "Tidewater," I think.

To Loren MacIver

January 1, 1974
New Year's morning

Thank you for being so patient with my ridiculous gloom last night. Here is a wretched copy of the short sad poem I mentioned ["Five Flights

Up"]. I can't find the good carbon paper (can't find anything, actually). It began with a dream—a few of the first lines—about Alice's apartment, where the view does include these odd things and the weird man who raises Corgies, I think, shouted at them one day last summer when I was working there, with the windows open: "You ought to be ashamed of yourselves!" . . .

However, I'm at last going on with a long one about Sam, the toucan I used to have. It's sad, too, but fairly funny, I think—since *he* was so funny.

Now I must clean house. I think my adorable Diana (my Argentine painter) comes tomorrow. "Cleaning woman"—that's what she said she was on the telephone, to friends' surprise. I think she's a really talented painter, too—here studying at the Museum of Fine Arts, etc. But I can't have her find things in such disarray.

My love to you both and all best wishes—you do sound splendid these days.

To James Merrill

[POSTCARD]

Ouro Prêto
April 2, 1974

I'm in Ouro Prêto & THINK I've sold the house—heavens, I can't believe it! I'll see you before you see this, probably—or at least on the 15th. Dan Halpern is making reservations for you—or did I tell you? I am quite gaga with packing, etc. Anyway—greetings, and this is a Rio view ["Chinese Pagoda with Sugar Loaf in Background"] I don't think you saw. I read from the *Yellow Pages* to my class!

To John Malcolm Brinnin

[POSTCARD]

Rio de Janeiro
April 4, 1974

My address book is in my suitcase, which is in the baggage hold, and I can't get it out until my plane leaves for Belo Horizonte. So I hope this reaches you, since I don't know how to spell Caesar / Ceaser—all look wrong [street address in Duxbury]. This card shows—to the left of the white streak of light—the *beginning* of Lota's park. It goes on for two miles—and lots more trees, etc., further on. Rio is hot, hazy but beautiful, even if I hate it. It's the end of "summer" here. I'm at the Airport Santos Dumont (HE invented the airplane, not the Wright brothers, didn't you know?) . . .

To James Merrill

60 Brattle Street
Cambridge, Massachusetts
April 20, 1974

. . . It's a beautiful day & I took a stroll through the North End [of Boston]—heresy, but I like it better than Cambridge. Wonderful Italian butcher shops, bakeries (macaroons), fruit shops, etc. I bought a can of a new kind of coffee, ten cents cheaper than Medaglia D'Oro—KITTY MIA—and can scarcely wait to try it.

No, I am very glad you wrote what you did about "Crusoe [in England]." I don't get much criticism, perhaps because of my gray hairs (or else just nasty remarks, like James Dickey's)—and I'm really grateful. Actually, there was quite a lot more in the last two or three parts of that poem. Then I decided that it was growing boring (this may be one bad effect of giving "readings"—the fear of boring), and that the poem should be speeded up toward the end and not give too many more details—so I cut it quite a lot—the rescue to one line, etc. If I can find the original ms. here (under the ping-pong table, no doubt) I might be able to put back a few lines about Friday. I still like "poor boy"—because he was a lot younger; and because they *couldn't* "communicate" (ghastly word) much. Crusoe guesses at Friday's feelings—but I think you are right and I'll try to restore or add a few lines there before the piece gets to a book. In fact, now that I think of it, I can almost remember 2 or 3 lines after "we were friends"—that's where something is needed, probably.

I saw the tapestries—or most of them—but very hurriedly & through thick crowds. I have a painter friend in Seattle who is going to have a show sometime in Santa Fe—I forget the name of the gallery. (*His* name is Wesley Wehr—Norwegian.) Perhaps you could give me David's address & if he goes to Santa Fe they might meet sometime. Wesley is older, but a very curious, odd & interesting painter & person—so mad about fossils the university has given him some sort of position telling *them* about fossils.

That's my next trip—to Seattle, in May—but I am rather looking forward to it. I'm going to take ten live lobsters and some New England clams and have a Maine lobster party for the few people I like there. Most of them think that frozen lobster tails (crawfish, really) from Australia are the *real thing*.

I am looking forward to the Ouija-board poem—even if I don't believe in the Ouija board. (Last night I watched a bit of Virgil Thomson on TV—the interviewer was so stupid I gave up—but he did say good things about G. Stein—Virgil did, that is. And when he was asked if he had got along without money in Paris he replied, "I always et." The interviewer was baffled by this, and V. added—"I thought if I was going to starve, I might as well starve where the food was good" . . .)

Mark Strand was here yesterday, house-hunting—he might even take this place—for his year as Fannie Hurst Prof. of Poetry at Brandeis. It is odd to think of Fannie Hurst reading poetry all her life—one gathers she did, from her bequests . . .

To Ashley Brown

(New address after July 1)
437 Lewis Wharf, Atlantic Avenue
Boston, Massachusetts
June 11, 1974

. . . I taught this last term and it seems to grow harder rather than easier. I also ran around giving some readings here & there—the last one out to Seattle for four days, for the Roethke reading. Now I am trying to get the apartment finished and get moved—I hope by the end of this month. However, the bookcases are still to be built—and since if I build as many as can be squeezed in, they will hold only 1,750 books, and I have approximately 3,500, I think I'll be giving a series of book-selling parties this fall—maybe some book Giving-Away parties.

I can't remember if I sent you a card from Ouro Prêto or not—I was there for 8 days only in April. I meant to spend—and needed to spend—a month, after Christmas, but fell downstairs, stupidly, and broke my right shoulder and spent most of the holidays here in the infirmary. I got quite a lot done during my week—I think—but still haven't sold the house, although there are three or four fairly good prospects now. Transportes Fink (remember them?) are supposed to be shipping all the books and some furniture—but I haven't heard a word from them since I left. They are a very good & reliable firm, though, so I am trying to believe everything is all right.

After this note to you I MUST write Vitória—also send more *cruzeiros*—and where oh where is the Banco de Minas Gerais checkbook, and what is the *cruzeiro* at now? These are the things that haunt me night and day—and all I really want to do is go off quietly and polish up my piece on Marianne Moore. I've read *parts* of it twice now (here & in N.Y.) but there are other parts I still want to do some work on. It is very simple indeed—not critical.

. . . I wonder if you'll get to Ouro Prêto, or to Bahia? I have some very nice young doctor friends now working in Bahia—except that they're about to come back here to report or something—the tropical medicine exchange—but you could look up a Dr. Ken Mott . . . Well, if he's there he'd be at that gray & white hospital in the middle of Bahia, where they study tropical diseases.

I *don't* think Octavio Paz is "red-faced"! Cal does see people oddly sometimes! But he *is* very friendly—and I am very fond of him and his wife, Mariejó—in fact, I adore them, and I am so glad he'll be back here next fall. Perhaps I miss the Latin temperament sometimes—at least they are the only people, or almost, with whom one can have "fun" here. The rest aren't "white-faced & hostile"—or maybe they are. I know very few people, really. Cal tried to make me accept a large, heavy, high-relief(?) silvery head of him, hung on a red ribbon—did you see that? I think it was given him at Columbia—but I refused it. I think he has now decided to come back for next spring term. You certainly seem to have had a lot of poets, etc.—well, here, too—but so much goes on here that I miss a great deal of it—or avoid it when I can. Yes—Alex Comfort. I saw him on the morning news TV a while ago—it is a strange metamorphosis, certainly. But perhaps we should all write sex books and insure ourselves wealthy old ages. Perhaps pornography is the only way I'll ever pay for Lewis Wharf.

I wasn't in Brazil long enough to feel much of the atmosphere—and just in Ouro Prêto. Lilli seems better than she has for some years. There's a nice painter living near her—Carlos Bracher. I think he was traveling when you were there before—if you go there, you'd like him, I think. Scliar arrived a day or two before I left. But I did nothing except pack and label, etc. I was amazed at how well everything did work out, within one week. And the town looked beautiful—better painted than usual.

I've been translating some of Octavio's poems—one long one (not one of his best, but he did it by request), about Joseph Cornell, will be in *The New Yorker* soon now. *Alternating Current* is awfully good—what I can understand of it. He is a really charming man, and we commiserate with each other about teaching. Do you really like it? It seems to me when I do get to know a teacher he always confesses that he really hates it. But *some* must like it; Roethke obviously did.

I'm going down to Duxbury tonight with a friend. John Brinnin has kindly lent us the use of his house there for about a month—it's nice; right on the bay. I'm going to take nothing but the Marianne Moore piece and 3 poems . . . and hope to get my mind on higher things than marks and bills for a few days. Do let me hear from you from Brazil.

To Loren MacIver and Lloyd Frankenberg

[POSTCARD]

North Haven, Maine
July 30, 1974

And so it is [referring to caption, "A ferry from Rockland serves this ISLAND PARADISE"]—but not a bit like this picture! This is the village

—one general store—the rest is fields and woods, very much like Nova
Scotia—and birds & wildflowers. Alas, we have to go back in a few days.
I hope you are both keeping well & I gather it hasn't been *too* hot. I'll
try to send you a small flower collection. I'm crazy about the "Lesser
Stitchwort"!

To Frani Blough Muser

> 437 Lewis Wharf
> Boston, Massachusetts
> October 1, 1974 (8:30 a.m.)

. . . It's a beautiful clear morning, tide coming in. The view really
makes up for everything—not that there's too much to complain about
now; they finally have been correcting all the drafts, light plugs, leaks,
etc., and today a strenuous-looking couple are coming to clean the floors
so I can put down the rugs, at least. But until the things from Brazil get
here I don't dare hang anything up—and have no desk, or dining table,
etc.—back to using packing boxes as furniture—and the wood dust (from
sand-blasting the beams) has been fierce. Well, eventually it will be nice,
I think—picturesque at least. (Some tenants have lowered their ceilings
—to cover up the beams!)

That wonderful laundry list!—it has made a great hit with my
friends—I must show it to John Brinnin, too. I forgot to take it last
Saturday when I went to Duxbury. In May, when we had his house, Alice
planted a dozen or so tiny tomato plants and they and we have been
swamped by tomatoes—they did entirely too well. Two weeks ago I made
a large batch of piccalilli with green ones—another bag of green ones
waits for me now, in the kitchen. Since John B.'s mother is from Nova
Scotia and he was born there, too, we all share a passion for piccalilli &
chow-chow (& kippered herrings)—so I must get to chopping.

Gretchen Keene Smith is in Boston and is coming to dinner—you
may not remember her—a classmate & friend of Margaret's & mine at
Vassar, very nice. She lives in Seattle & said she was dying for some
Eastern seafood—she came from Boston. So I'm going to buy two Maine
lobsters—the store is almost next door. I thought I'd never eat city-bought
lobster again after the two weeks at North Haven. There we just had to
telephone and a man caught them that morning, "hauled" them, rather,
and we ate them that night—they are infinitely superior. But two months
have elapsed, so my lobster connoisseurship may have dulled a bit. I love
marketing around here—when you next come here I must take you to
the Toscana butcher shop—and the Caffè dello Sport. If I go in blue
jeans, they're very nice to me. I was only insulted once, when wearing a

dress—when I asked for almond paste in a pastry shop, the woman told me to try S. S. Pierce's—and I'm so slow I didn't realize until I got home that I'd been insulted.

I'd love to hear some of the Ives. I don't think I'll get to N.Y. at all, though—except for reading at the Morgan Library on Dec. 4th. You'll get an invitation but I don't recommend it—same old stuff, mostly. Well, no—Octavio is going to introduce me and that part of it will be nice, I think.

I seem wound up this morning and I *must* get to work here. I'm still unpacking books from Brattle St. I'm afraid you are a more efficient unpacker and goer-over of boxes than I am. I hope you're all well and when is that next trip?—not until some time in the winter, I think. Oh, I'd like to rush up to the Museum of Fine Arts and see what Mexican things they have. However, closets, the shutter man, and piccalilli are calling.

October 15, 1974
Tuesday a.m.

. . . I have to stay home for my disagreeable but expert "cleaning couple" this a.m. and go to a memorial service for Anne Sexton this p.m.—and, I think, since Curt's birthday has gone by, that one more day won't matter now. I'll mail [the book] from Cambridge, where there are mailers and a post office at hand, tomorrow morning. I hope you could *tell* him about his present—and that he'll tell *me* just how authentic the material is.

I think you must be deep into "Mini-Ives"—I read about it in *The N.Y. Times* every day now. My music for the week was one visit to Mabel Mercer (over 75, I think, but still a great pleasure) and listening to *The Daughter of the Regiment* last night on TV—very entertaining. Maybe you'd like a visit to Boston this year to coincide with one of Sarah Caldwell's operas—and if I can find the program I'll send one—she's *attempting* some quite interesting things.

I was sent a book by Jean Valentine & observed that Cynthia did the jacket—which is *very* nice. By chance, Jean V. was here & telephoned me, and told me Cynthia also did the very nice typography . . .

I was in Duxbury for the weekend and yesterday went to a little place called "Edaville," nearby, where they run a little narrow-gauge train through the cranberry bogs—to show how cranberries are harvested, etc.—about 5 miles, very pretty. Unfortunately, apparently cranberries *straight* weren't enough for the many child passengers, so they have put up awful figures along the route—a sort of introduction to Disneyland, I think—and the children confuse cranberries with Peter, Peter Pumpkin-eater, and Santa's Candy Shop—the biggest hit, I fear—that, or "There's Daddy's CAR!" on the return trip. However, it's a nice ride to take the grandchildren on sometime.

I *must* get to work. The postcard of the 1938 hurricane is won-derful—to think I weathered it on the dunes on Cape Cod and didn't even know I'd been through a hurricane until two days later—when I went to town and found telegrams from frantic friends and aunts, etc.

It's beginning to get nice in this apt.—but it takes forever. Please wish Curt many happy returns for me—a bit late—and I hope he enjoys the book—also a bit late.

To Lloyd Schwartz

Music and poetry critic Lloyd Schwartz has two books of poems, These People *and* Goodnight, Gracie. *Co-editor of the well-known anthology* Elizabeth Bishop and Her Art, *he also wrote the 1991* New Yorker *profile about Brazil's posthumous interest in EB. This letter records EB's reactions to his poem "Who's on First?"*

October 21st, 1974

Since I don't know when I'll ever have time to talk to you properly about "work," I think I'll send this back to you now with a few comments, and I hope you won't mind them . . . I know that Frank [Bidart] thinks it's your "best poem"—and I myself think it is a very economical and acutely put description of a contemporary situation—moving, *awful*, de-pressing in the extreme, etc.—but I'm still not sure whether one could call this prose dialogue a poem. Of course I am hopelessly old-fashioned and perhaps I don't like things expressed so openly and nakedly, I don't know.

. . . I can't bear to have my friends run themselves down. Even if I read it in a magazine and didn't know you, I think I'd wonder at the exposure. (There is a piece, a sort of prose-poem fantasy by James Schuy-ler in that book of stories by poets, edited by Howard Moss [*The Poet's Story*], that I really rather liked. It may be about an even worse situation—I gather from the ending—but the details, the hilarity, some-how make it more acceptable—at least, to me.)

Well, perhaps because I am so utterly depressed by "Who's on First?"—maybe it is good after all. One phrase I can't abide—it may be what everyone says at present, but it always offends me—that is "to have sex." (Even Isherwood has used it.) If it isn't "making *love*"—what other way can it be put? (I first heard it years ago when the famous fan dancer ??? was talking about her pet snake—maybe that prejudiced me.) (Oh—*Sally Rand!*) It seems like such an ugly, generalized sort of expression for something—love, lust, or what have you—always unique, and so much more complex than "having sex" . . .

And those are my thoughts on this bright and beautiful but freezing cold morning . . . Remember me to Sucio [cat]—lots of love.

To Frank Bidart

EB gave a reading, under the joint auspices of the Academy of American Poets and the Pierpont Morgan Library on December 4, introduced by Octavio Paz.

Cosmopolitan Club
New York City
December 5, 1974
10 a.m.

You & Alice must have got home safely, I think—or surely I'd have heard something by now.

I'm sorry that in the flurry of flattery, kisses, black ties, lamé gowns, etc. (& *did* you meet Mrs. Hugh Bullock & enjoy her elegant dinner party?), I forgot to thank you for the roses. I think you probably ordered "yellow," didn't you?—since I've said I like yellow roses. Well, they aren't yellow—they're a really marvelous pale apricot color, and strange to say that's the color scheme of this room. Yellow walls & sofa, curtains, bedspread, etc., mixed yellow, pale green & exactly the same shade of apricot. (Not that I think much of this club's décor.) But this room is better than usual & the sun is coming in & I have a nice rock-&-roll station & the roses are slowly opening. AND that reading's over with, thank heavens!

Just found a brand-new book of [Julio] Cortázar stories in the hall (another nice thing—there are bookcases all over the place here) and I think I'll go back to bed for a while & indulge in some useless *reading* . . .

To Frani Blough Muser

60 Brattle Street
Cambridge, Massachusetts
December 14, 1974 (2 p.m.)

I'm at my old home this nasty rainy afternoon. When Alice gets back from two *exams*, we're supposed to go to a cocktail party in Brookline. I'm early and I'll write you a note [about Galápagos]—it will be a mess, I'm afraid—I can't seem to understand the workings of this typewriter . . . *Darwin's Island* is rather dry and technical, as I remember it. On the other hand, the Sierra Club's two books—did you tell me you *had* those, with all the color photographs?—are a bit too much. The actual colors *are* extraordinary, depending on the time of day, maybe—but I haven't been able to read Beebe with any pleasure for years! I wonder if the islands will look different in Jan. or Feb. from the way they looked in August? And which you'll get a chance to see. Academy Bay, of course, where the Darwin Research Center is—unfortunately it isn't at all beautiful like some of the islands.

It was on Charles Island, where we went swimming—a nice beach, flamingoes & a lagoon in back of it—and where I had my one triumph. *I* saw the first—and only, I think—Vermilion Flycatcher. Everyone had been trying to see one every day, with all their elaborate glasses and zoom lenses, etc. It is very tiny, bright red & black, really ruby-like—and quite tame, so it flew along beside us from tree to tree and obligingly let itself be seen by the eager fellow passengers when we got closer to them. At Academy Bay there's a Post Office. The stamps are very nice and we bought cards and stamps—rather high—but the Post Office man wouldn't let *us* lick them or put them on ourselves—with the result that the stamps & cards were never seen again—so be prepared. (He spoke Spanish.) There's also a school—I found it very depressing—and the strange man who has land iguanas in his house & tries to sell you his paintings. We had better luck with the "Post Office" on Charles's "Post Office Bay"— I put a note in the barrel for Alice, directed to Cambridge, and when she got back two weeks later there it was. A couple from Salem had picked it up & mailed it.

I do hope you get to Hood—that's where the Blue-footed Boobies and the Albatrosses are—but the Albatrosses wouldn't be mating at the time of year, or *courting*—they hadn't got around to the actual mating. But we did see a pair of sea lions mating on James, I think that was— great lava grottoes, with clear blue water where the *fur* seals live, mostly (good for swimming, too). The seals were almost under water, and an excited bevy of young-lady seals surrounded them helpfully— it was an extraordinary sight and really beautiful—went on for a long time.

I found my diary of the trip but it's rather sketchy—in a notebook provided by our "cruise." If I find anything useful in it when I get home I'll add to this or maybe telephone.

I love the *Robinson Crusoe Pop-Up*! The pictures are wonderful (the text isn't so wonderful, I'm afraid) and I have a strange feeling *I've seen it before*—maybe there were some ancient Pop-Ups at my grand-mother's—I feel sure I have. I wrote that poem two years before I went to the Galápagos, however—and I was glad to hear the tortoises hiss the way I'd said they did. (I wrote a poem about the Amazon before I went there, too—and altered one line a year later. Maybe I'd better start poems about all the other places I'd like to go to, since a poem seems to bring on the trip, sooner or later.)

I'm sorry I didn't have time to talk to *anyone* properly at the Morgan Library affair. It was also a little dismaying NOT to recognize a good many people I hadn't seen for 20 years—or more, some of them. Oh dear. I'm glad it's over.

I left "work" and came over here thinking I'd listen to *Jenufa* on Alice's very superior radio—now it turns out to be *Death in Venice*. Well, I'll try it, I suppose.

To Robert Lowell

437 Lewis Wharf
Boston, Massachusetts
January 16, 1975

I think I sent you a postcard from Florida, but did I really? Anyway—I had a wonderful time there; went on a 3-day sailing trip with old friends; went to a marvelous wildlife sanctuary; went swimming almost every day; got very *tan*—and so on. And came back feeling much much better than when I left bleak Boston. I just got my mail yesterday & it included a letter from you, dated Dec. 18th—I left Dec. 27th—it's odd I didn't get it before I left—but no, I suppose not—the Christmas mail.

Now I have just talked to Frank [Bidart], who says he talked to you and that you may get here before you get this. Well, I'll proceed with it anyway. Frank says that you have been having arthritis(?) in your back —between the shoulders. I'm sorry to hear that. I have it rather badly, too, and a touch of it in that spot, although my hands are the worst. The only thing for it is ASPIRIN—in huge doses. I go occasionally to the Robert Brigham Hospital (nothing *but* arthritis there) but have almost stopped going because with aspirin one does as well as one possibly can, apparently. Also—hot water, and exercise. But all that aspirin upsets the stomach—or gives you ulcers—so I take a coated kind, ECOTRIN, that works very, very slowly, but doesn't produce a bellyache. (There are other brands. I take from 12 to 16 every day & don't have much pain, actually. But after seeing most of the patients at Robert Brigham I usually think I don't have arthritis at all.)

I am now going to be very impertinent and aggressive. Please, *please* don't talk about old age so much, my dear old friend! You are giving me the creeps. The thing Lota admired so much about us North Americans was our determined youthfulness and energy, our "never-say-die"ness —and I think she was right! In Florida my hostess's sister had recently married again at the age of 76, for the third time—her second marriage had been at 67—and she and her husband, also 76, went walking miles on the beach every day, hand in hand, as happy as clams, apparently, and I loved it. (A very plump, pretty, sweet lady—as naïve as a very small child.) Of course—it's different for a writer, I know—of course I know! —nevertheless, in spite of aches & pains I really don't feel much different than I did at 35—and I certainly am a great deal happier, most of the time. (This in spite of the giant oil tankers parading across my view every day.) I just *won't* feel ancient—I wish Auden hadn't gone on about it so in his last years, and I hope you won't.

However, Cal dear, maybe your memory *is* failing! Never, never was I "tall"—as you wrote remembering me. I was always 5 ft. 4 and ¼ inches—now shrunk to 5 ft. 4 inches. The only time I've ever felt tall was in Brazil. And I never had "long brown hair" either! It started turning gray when I was 23 or 24—and probably was already somewhat grizzled when I first met you. I tried putting it up for a very brief period, because I like long hair—but it never got even to my shoulders and is always so intractable that I gave that up within a month or so. I think you must be seeing someone else! So please don't put me in a beautiful poem "tall with long brown hair"! What I remember about that [first] meeting is your dishevelment, your lovely curly hair, and how we talked about a Picasso show then on in N.Y., and we agreed about the Antibes pictures of fishing, etc.—and how much I liked you, after having been almost too scared to go—and how Randall and his wife threw sofa pillows at each other. And Kitten, of course, *Kitten*. You were also rather dirty, which I rather liked, too. And your stories about the cellar room you were living in and how the neighbors drank all night and when they got too rowdy, one of them would say, "Remember the boy," meaning you. Well, I think I'll have to write *my* memoirs, just to set things straight.

It will be nice to see you. Caroline and I had a "real nice visit" as they say in Florida and I'm looking forward to seeing her again. Alice is at B.U. Business School, poor dear, and will soon be coming for dinner after her class on "Taxes"—which she insists she *loves*. So I must stop and slice some green beans— See you later, alligator, as they also do say in Florida.

To Frani Blough Muser

January 22, 1975

I can't remember the day you're supposed to return—but at least I can have a thank-you note waiting for you when you do, I hope. (I mean I hope the note will be there, but also *naturally* hope for your safe return.) Your cards have been alarming, to say the least—alarmingly interesting, as Henry James might say, or maybe horrendously interesting.

And—Christmas presents! You went too far—the records came, was it before I went away?—and the same evening I had Frank ("musical") and Alice to dinner and we played them. Gottschalk I knew . . . We tried hard with the computer music. I think Alice, who dropped that course last term but is taking it again this one, gave out on that first. I try again from time to time when alone. Did I tell you what happened to A. and her computer? (Excuse me if I did; I think it's so good I tell everyone.) She was trying to work the thing and make it answer whatever her problems were and kept getting wrong answers time after time. Finally the computer got so cross with her it ordered, "Have a shitty day!"

And *then* I got the brown jacket, which is very nice and just right for some brown pants I have . . . My almost three weeks in Florida did all of me a world of good except my memory. We went on a three-day sailing trip, for one thing—wonderful—and to a place called Corkscrew Swamp

Sanctuary, also wonderful, full of "wildlife" including nesting storks, and where all the wildlife was almost as used to people and as tame as in the Galápagos. You & Curt may have to go there to observe it close to . . .

The Pazes are leaving next week for Mexico. We, Alice & I, discovered that neither of them has ever seen anything north of Boston. Octavio did go to *one* "New England" place but can't remember which—so we are taking them to see the "country" and snow, we hope, tomorrow. We're spending one night at Newfane and one at Woodstock, nice places to stay at both, and beautiful churches, covered bridges, etc. They have been telling all their friends about this as if we were taking them to Hudson Bay, at least. I was told they refused a dinner invitation tonight because they are getting ready to go to *Vair-mont*. Since they both hate the cold, I am a bit nervous about it all. It was 22° below in Vairmont last night— but that was exceptional & I think it's warmed up a lot already.

My belongings from Brazil are actually in New York—unloaded by now, maybe. I can't believe it . . .

That's really enough for today, but I must tell you what I also got in the mail yesterday besides your second installment of the gunboat story. Judy Flynn (I wrote her two Christmases ago, I think, but had no reply) sent me a very nice note and a whole batch of *Blue Pencils*, 1928–29 [student magazine at Walnut Hill School], also two or three "comic" poems I'd apparently sent her a bit later. I haven't re-read them all yet —in fact I seemed to remember everything in them all too well after one glance. Ye gods! what awful poetry I wrote then. (I hope to god I'm not deceiving myself if I think I've improved.) And you have a story that begins "Life was very hard for Bridget O'Neill." And a *long* poem called "Nightmare." I don't think you were nearly as corny as I was. We were very strong on sonnets. My "comic" poems are a lot better—couplets— but I haven't the faintest recollection of having written them . . .

To James Merrill

March 28, 1975

It was nice to hear your voice [from Greece] so improbably close last Sunday—and I'm sorry you can't come to B.U. for that term—it would also be awfully nice to have you in the neighborhood.

I know I have a long letter from you here that I've been meaning to answer but I am not going to look for it now, even. (I have a young carpenter here banging in the brackets for the bookshelves—the original *real* carpenter didn't hammer them in hard enough, with disastrous results—two shelves flew across the room [I was at the opera, fortunately], books everywhere, and lots of broken *objets d'art*—but mostly, fortunately, things I should have got rid of anyway.) Also a young lady who doesn't know how to clean house *at all* & she is singing & doesn't know how to do that, either.

But I'm writing you this morning because last night Frank Bidart telephoned me to tell me that Reuben Brower had died, rather suddenly—and I thought you'd like to know. You may already know, of course, by the time you get this letter, because you probably had many friends in common—but I thought I'd write you anyway. He had a "massive heart attack" the day before & was in intensive care and they thought he was doing very well and would recover, but he didn't . . . My last conversation with him was a very cheerful one, about 2 months ago—he had managed to get a young Brazilian friend of mine accepted as a Junior Fellow, and he was so happy about it—because the boy (Ricardo O'Reilly Sternberg) . . . is a *poet*—quite a good one—the son of old friends of mine. They scarcely ever take poets, it seems, preferring scientists, and Reuben didn't think he'd make it, but he did.

How awful! I remember now that your last letter was mostly about the details of Chester Kallman's death and strange funeral. Well, I might as well go on with the fearful tolls of mortality, I suppose. Loren MacIver has been in St. Vincent's for six weeks or more with a broken right wrist and arm and right hip—she's about ready to leave now, but the problem is where she should go next. She's adamant about a convalescent home, and that studio is impossible for her without a lot of help. In the meantime, Lloyd Frankenberg (who'd been woefully sick for several years now & not getting any better) took sleeping pills and died. I think this was a wise decision for him, really.

To turn to the world of the living—I'm about to go out and buy some lamb for a small Easter lunch I'm giving. The North End is hung with dead lambs, or their skins, also goats. Goat seems to be the Italian Easter dish. But I saw such youthful lambs yesterday—tiny chops—well, maybe a small saddle would do. Peter Taylor & his wife are coming—I wonder if you know her poetry? She is really pretty good—and has a third book ready for the publisher now. I've just written to John Hollander saying I can't read in N.Y. in June or July—he hopes you can. Maybe you could visit me in North Haven Island for a July weekend? It's *beautiful*.

To Miss Pierson

The identity of Miss Pierson, obviously a stranger to EB, is unknown. The editor is grateful to James Merrill, who came into possession of this letter in Amherst at a book-signing event, where he was given a copy by a man who disappeared before explaining how he acquired it. It bears EB's full signature.

May 28th, 1975

I am answering you because (1) You enclosed a stamped, self-addressed envelope. (This happens very rarely.) (2) You think that poetry discussion groups are "a bloody bore"—and, although there are exceptions, in general I agree with you completely. [*In margin:*] But perhaps by (3) you meant the "family" poem—about one's grandfather or how one broke away from Mother, etc.? I am a bit tired of those.

I think you have set up difficulties for yourself that perhaps don't really exist at all. I don't know what "poetic tools & structures" are, unless you mean traditional forms. Which one can use or not, as one sees fit. If you feel you are "moralizing" too much—just cut the morals off—or out. (Quite often young poets tend to try to tie everything up neatly in 2 or 3 beautiful last lines, and it is quite surprising how the poems are improved if the poet can bear to sacrifice those last, pat, beautiful lines.) Your third problem—why shouldn't the poet appear in the poem? There are several tricks—"I" or "we" or "he" or "she" or even "one"—or somebody's name. Someone *is* talking, after all—but of course the idea is to prevent that particular tone of voice from growing monotonous.

From what you say, I think perhaps you are actually trying too hard—or reading too much *about* poetry and not enough poetry. Prosody—metrics—etc. are fascinating—but they all came *afterwards*, obviously. And I always ask my writing classes NOT to read criticism.

Read a lot of poetry—all the time—and *not* 20th-century poetry. Read Campion, Herbert, Pope, Tennyson, Coleridge—anything at all almost that's any good, from the past—until you find out what you really like, by yourself. Even if you try to imitate it exactly—it will come out quite different. Then the great poets of our own century—Marianne Moore, Auden, Wallace Stevens—and not just 2 or 3 poems each, in anthologies—read ALL of somebody. Then read his or her life, and letters, and so on. (And by all means read Keats's Letters.) Then see what happens.

That's really all I can say. It can't be done, apparently, by willpower and study alone—or by being "with it"—but I really don't know *how* poetry gets to be written. There is a mystery & a surprise, and after that a great deal of hard work.

P.S. If you don't have a poetry library at hand—I recommend the five small volumes edited by Auden and Pearson, with very good introductions, *Poets of the English Language*. They come in paperback now. [*Handwritten:*] This is a borrowed machine; please forgive the untidiness.

To James Merrill

Duxbury, Massachusetts
June 10, 1975

. . . Alice and I went to *I Capuleti e i Montecchi*, with Troyanos as Romeo and Sills as Juliet, on Thursday night and loved it. I gather that you did, too? All that lucious Bellini music. I had no idea what was going on most of the time—no "plot" given anywhere—but I didn't really care . . .

Frank sent down, by Alice, his book and yours, and yesterday Tony Hecht came for dinner (he gave the Phi Beta Kappa poem at college this morning) and gave me three poems. I am overwhelmed and cast into gloom by such prolific—whatever the noun of that word is.

I started reading [the typescript of] *The Book of Ephraim* two nights ago, rather late, and although I can't say I stayed up all night, I almost did —I think it was 4 a.m. when I turned off the light. I'll have to go over it all again, especially the last third, when I *was* getting a bit weary—but I found it *fascinating*, of course. There are many really lovely, ravishing passages, for one thing. I've marked them all, also some questions. There are a lot of things I don't know about in it—and then, of course, I have to keep my disbelief in abeyance as someone has surely said—but I didn't find that hard, at 2 a.m. in the complete silence and slight spookiness here, alone.

I wish (as I say to my students) you'd numbered the pages. Then I could compliment you more easily on this and that page. One thing that struck me very much was how easily you went from one form to another—the variety is there, but it doesn't sound difficult—as if you found rhyme or assonance the easiest thing in the world.

Frank & I had a phone conversation about *Ephraim* & agreed we wished the "Dramatis Personae" were a bit fuller. I like very much the return to the house in section G. The mirror part in Q. I didn't know who "Maisie" was. Well, it is all much too big for me to write about in one letter, or on this one morning when I have to start cleaning house to get ready to leave here. I don't think we have ever talked of Maya Deren. I didn't know you knew her so well, apparently. I didn't—except that I heard a lot about her in, and after, Haiti—and read something she wrote about Vodun. Also saw her husband's movie, *The Life of a Cat*—which I liked very much, and then I went to one party there—a very strange affair.

The book should certainly make a profound impression. When I remember the three or four new books I get every week of my life, with 14 or so tiny, repetitive little poems in them, frantically trying for effect by using dirty words, etc.! Now this will show people (those who read) what it is to *work* . . .

I'll take the book to Maine, where I'll have more collected thoughts, I hope. Thank you so much for sending me a copy.

To Frani Blough Muser

> Sabine Farm
> North Haven Island, Maine
> July 9, 1975

I'm afraid I find Mexico City very much like hell these days—traffic as bad or worse than Rio (though not quite as fast) & pollution the worst

I've ever tried to breathe—but you know all this. (I hadn't been there for 32 years—it has grown from 1 million then to almost *11* million now.) Alice had only 4 days, so first thing Sat. a.m. we went off to the Archaeological Museum—only to find it closed for the day because the Prime Minister of Sweden was being given a very grand luncheon there. That was a blow; we went to the park and up to the Castillo, etc. (she'd never been to Mexico before). The Pazes have a wonderful apt. right in the city—or near the "Angel"—a penthouse, filled with things from India—and lots of trees & plants. They have rented a house in Cuernavaca, and we went there for the night—I never would have recognized that town at all. (I spent 2 or 3 months there before.) I never did like C.—but the house (rented from rich Americans) was very agreeable. (I started to read a book and a bill for "One mink jacket, $1,999.00" fell out.) We did get to Teotihuacán—and that is many times bigger, and better excavated & restored, etc. Had a Coke with our nice driver, Jesus, in *La Gruta*. (We had two drivers; one came to the hotel and said, "My name is Angel. Jesus will be along in a few minutes.") I was in Cuernavaca twice—second time we went to Tepotzotlán and the convent—this was almost as I remembered it; the only thing that was. There really wasn't time to go to Oaxaca as I wanted to—and after the TV day—I really wanted to take a NAP. Which I did, at length, in Cuernavaca. We were 4 languages: Octavio, Joseph Brodsky, Vasko Popa (his language is Serbo-Croatian) & me—it was very weird. Fortunately no one ever watches these programs, I gather—they are done to prove to the backers that TV has a cultural side or something—it was all very interesting and novel, to me, and went on for *hours*.

At midnight there was a huge dinner party—I have no idea who most of the hundred or so people were—at a nice old inn I remembered—a suburb . . . I was interviewed once by a young lady (all the young ladies connected with the TV wore false eyelashes & gobs of makeup) who asked me tragically why I didn't write about "*L-o-vv*" (rhyming with *of*). I was also interviewed by another young lady—in a group—whose name is *Ulalume*—her parents admired E. A. Poe—who gave me her collected poems (I'd just met her that minute) already signed "With love, Ulalume." Well . . . I felt I really wasn't up to the three gentlemen poets, who had *said* they weren't going to argue or discuss "theories" and then did, vehemently—for 2 hours. (This tape will be cut, I presume.) Of course the *real* news all that week was the Women's "Conferencia" in one part of town & the rival Women's "Tribuna" in another part . . . The *Zona Rosa* didn't exist when I was there before—and now the Zócalo-downtown is so terribly run-down and abandoned. But that is more than enough about my-week-in-Mexico. Oh, Alice did get to the museum for an hour on Sunday—and I got back to it for a long time alone on Tuesday. It certainly is impressive and (as I tried to remember all the cultures) I was lost in admiration for Curt's having mastered them all.

I probably told you about *this* place, which is approximately my idea of heaven. I'm here two weeks earlier this time—the barn swallows are just about to fly away from their overcrowded nest on the porch, instead of sitting wobbling on the telephone wire. I want to catch the first flight & keep running to look at them instead of working. They're all—4, maybe 5—standing up shoving & pushing—it looks rather like an overcrowded box at the opera. There is a magnificent view of Penobscot Bay and islands, and those schooners that now take people on cruises sail by from time to time—very Marin-ish. (He painted around here, so that's to be expected, I suppose.) If you ever get to this part of the U.S., please come out to North Haven. There's a ferry from Rockland three times a day. This place is called Sabine Farm because Mrs. Pettit's husband's first name was Horace! We figured this out by reading the dedications, etc., in all the books—mostly very highbrow . . .

To Ashley Brown

> 437 Lewis Wharf
> Boston, Massachusetts
> August 5, 1975

Your letter came this morning & I'm writing you right away—a note of sympathy more than anything else. What an awful time you have had! I think I am more afraid of having something wrong with my eyes than of anything else. I've gone to hear Ella Fitzgerald twice now—she sings every year at Symphony Hall for the benefit of the Retina Foundation—I think it's called—because she has had several eye operations here, and always makes a speech thanking one doctor in particular. (But no doubt Atlanta has good doctors, too!) And then she goes on to sing as energetically as ever.

In the last *N.Y. Review* I see a long interview with Sartre, on his 70th birthday—perhaps you've seen it? I'd already read it in a French magazine a few weeks ago—and whether one likes him or not, he says some really interesting things about his life, friends, approaching *blindness* & so on. (Apparently he is almost blind—but of course has had only one eye all his life, to begin with.) But can you imagine a worse fate for your declining years than being read aloud to by Simone de Beauvoir? Always loyal—nevertheless, he does say she *"reads too fast." Coitado!*

I got back to Boston from North Haven Island the night of July 31st—almost wept to leave. I adore that place . . . I'd probably rent it for *two* months, except that the family who owns that house and two or three others and a great deal of land reserves it for members of the family, usually, for one month. It's a beautiful island—the few "summer people" have mostly gone there for years & years, are all fearfully rich, dress in rags, and the houses are far apart. I can't see another one from "Sabine"—just fields down to the water, fir trees, wildflowers, and a vast view of Penobscot Bay, islands, schooners, and so on—and it is *silent*, except for bird songs . . .

No—I haven't sold the Ouro Prêto house, and I HAVE to—I'm working on some other projects for it now, since *Previews* does absolutely nothing. A young Brazilian friend & his American wife are staying in it right now for a week or so—he's the son of old Brazilian friends of Lota's & mine; his father has been a professor at Berkeley now for some years. This young man, Ricardo Sternberg (father's name: Hilgard O'Reilly Sternberg—very Brazilian, *não é?*), writes very good poetry and was just made a Harvard Junior Fellow—a great honor . . .

To Dr. Anny Baumann

November 29, 1975

It was good to hear your voice just now. If I take the nine o'clock shuttle plane I can be at your office easily by 11. I might fly over the night before—but either way I'll be there—and sober. Please don't worry about that! . . .

What I'm writing to ask you is this—*please* don't just discuss drinking with me, or scold me for any past lapses, *please*. There were two or three bad days about two weeks ago now—and I have talked & talked with Dr. Wacker (head of the Harvard Med. services) about this. OF COURSE I know I shouldn't drink, and I try hard not to. I have missed only one class in five years because of this and I have NEVER taken a drink before a class. I feel I simply can't bear to hear another word on the subject. I last drank because of other problems—and they are really very difficult and sad ones—and I think you might help me with the worst of them, possibly—if anyone can. That and my physical state of decay, or whatever it is, are what I want to see you about. I feel I can't bear to be made to feel guilty *one more time* about the drinking. There *are* things that are worse, I think, and I hope you can help me with them. At least I am sure you are a more thorough and careful and smarter doctor than anyone I know here, nice as they've been to me, and—as you said—you do know all my past history far, far better. (I also like you a lot better.)

December 5, 1975

The radiologists were both awfully nice and we looked at my insides together—what a mess, but apparently nothing seriously wrong. I didn't know what the word "neoplasm" meant, but since one of them seemed to know I teach at *Harvard*, I didn't like to confess my ignorance but looked it up in the dictionary when I got back. None of those, either, they said.

I haven't had time to read Mrs. [Candace] MacMahon's bibliography carefully yet, just glance at it. It represents a great deal of work, I know (the kind of work I've never been able to do in my life!). I'll send it back to you in a few days—on Monday or Tuesday. She sent a copy of two chapters of a Twayne book by Anne Stevenson (you certainly don't have to read *that*). It is so badly written, out-of-date, and full of mistakes—although I sent her lots of information and even visited her in England in 1964—that for Mrs. MacMahon's benefit, I'm going to correct *some* of it for her. It would be impossible to correct it all.

I hope this improvement will last—and that your thoughts about the future will prove to be right. It was just plain stupid of me not to come to see you long before. The Harvard Infirmary is a pleasant place to be able to stay—and FREE—and the nurses & doctors are all very nice, but—how much more *sensible* it would have been of me to come to see you earlier, before they started their rather casual experimenting with anti-depressants, etc.!

. . . This is just to say thank you, with all my heart, and I shall—no, will—try to be less "paranoid" and I hope what you said about my saddest problem will prove to be true.

[P.S.] It is just getting dark—late sunset here—and if you *squint* a little, looking across the mouth of the Mystic River here, to all the brick and green buildings in the Charlestown Navy Yard—it looks almost like the Grand Canal in Venice—really.

To Frani Blough Muser

[POSTCARD]

December 7, 1975

I have only the vaguest idea of the present state of our "relationship" except that I know I feel *greatly in your debt*. It was so nice to be told NOT to write & I'll limit myself to a card, as I do only too often these academic years. I've been very "poorly" for two or three weeks. Finally, like an idiot—I should have done it a month ago—I made a flying trip to N.Y. Thursday to see Anny, taking my Harvard X-rays along—and my burden of complaints.

Now everything's much better. It is pretty certain I'm having—have had a long time—a recurrence of some of the kinds of dysentery that did me in 3 years ago—and the Harvard Infirmary didn't spot this at all—so soon everything will be fine again, I trust. I took the nine o'clock shuttle over & the three o'clock back. Had to hear Octavio read that night—so didn't attempt to call you . . .

To Dr. Anny Baumann

c/o Russells
Fort Myers, Florida
December 24, 1975

I'm sorry I wrote you such a gloomy note before leaving. I don't know how things will turn out, but at least I am feeling much better here, *away* from it all for a while, and getting some rest, etc. It is cold, unfortunately, but the sun is shining. However, it is too cold & windy to take a cruise as we'd planned to do over Christmas. I'm taking the Russells out to dinner instead. They are as nice as ever, but Charlotte is not well at all, poor dear, and I want to cook all the dinners she'll let me, here, to save her some work . . .

Yesterday I actually got out my watercolors and designed my own book jacket for the book of poems that will come out, I hope, next fall. It's to be called *Geography III*, and looks like an old-fashioned schoolbook, I hope. I've brought two long poems to finish, and—the Marianne Moore piece. But first—today—I must get off *five* Guggenheim recommendations—this is rather a lot and awfully hard to do discreetly, etc.

The Boston airport was closed the day I left—the second day of the 3-day blizzard there—but they had one runway open for two hours and I was one of the lucky ones who got away—only three planes left that day. It was a bit scary and we had to be defrosted for an hour or so—but once up, all went well, and I even made connections at Atlanta, although my bags didn't come until the next day . . .

A very nice old, old friend comes here the 29th for 10 days—she's a good sailor, too, and I hope we'll get in a cruise then. (I'm afraid I feel a bit nervous about going out any distance with *two* bad hearts. Although I used to be a good sailor, I don't have the muscles I once had and the boat is a bit too big for one person to handle.)

I'm now going to take a long walk on the beach. Perhaps I'll even send you a more cheerful poem before I leave here. One of the things I didn't get into the villanelle ["One Art"] that I feel I've also lost, and that I really regret most of all, is that I don't think I'll be able to go back to that beautiful island in Maine any more—this is too complicated to go into, but it really breaks my heart . . .

I don't think you got our 18 inches of snow or whatever it was—and I expect you keep right on working through this holiday season—as I shall try to do, too.

January 10, 1976

. . . The weather has not been good—sunny, usually, but cold—I've only been swimming once and we couldn't take the 3-day cruise we'd planned, over New Year's, because it was too cold and windy. We had only one afternoon's sailing—my friend is an old sailor, too—and we loved that . . . The Russells, who have been extremely kind as always, are going on a long race—16th to 20th, more or less—and I'll be completely alone—feel as if I am already. Charlotte is *wonderful* with Stephen—infinitely patient—and asks me to dinner, but I can't bear to go *every* night.

I wrote you a rather long letter two days ago and then rather sensibly, for me, tore it up. I don't think that your idea of being cheerful, ignoring everything, and pretending that nothing is wrong is going to work at all—you are much too optimistic! Also—I don't think you really got the situation very accurately. However, I won't go into any of it now except to say I am desperately unhappy; can't work, can't sleep—and can't *eat* (which is all to the good, I suppose!). I managed to keep up a good front *most* of the time, not all, and now I am quite alone for 10 days I'll try hard to WORK—but I just can't seem to concentrate.

Two or three of my Boston friends have been awfully kind and telephoned frequently—they don't know the story, or perhaps *do*, intuitively, I don't know.

I wanted to come back by way of New York to get prescriptions from you, mostly—also see Dr. Cahill and go to that dentist, Dr. Hudson, I didn't get to see last time. (I'll make these calls today.) I think Dr. Cahill just wants another sample, or whatever one calls it. While here a few teeth fell out, of course—and I went to Charlotte's dentist. He stuck them in again much better than before, I think, and also said that I *didn't* have to have all my upper teeth pulled out. *He* wouldn't let anyone do that— there are enough good ones & enough healthy roots (?) to last some time more. You said to get a "second opinion" and now I'll go to Dr. Hudson, who I know is a fine dentist, and get a third. The dentist here's remarks were the brightest spot in my life, I'm afraid, for about four months . . .

January 15, 1976

The other page or so of that letter was too stupid to send you. I have just called your answering service to say that I won't be coming to N.Y. on the 21st—I think (or rather Charlotte thought for me; I don't think I *think* any more) that getting to N.Y. and seeing three doctors in one day would be too much at present. I'm now going back the 19th, to Boston. I can get over to N.Y. at a later date. I have also changed my mind about taking a term off—going away wouldn't really help, I know; I'd be even lonelier and more unhappy away than back in Boston & Cambridge, I suppose. At least there I do have a few friends & having to work 2 or 3 days a week may help, who knows. IF they'll take me back—after Dr. Wacker so kindly got me out of it!

. . . The Russells go away on a race today sometime—but say they'll be back to put me on the plane the 19th. My friend Frank [Bidart] will meet me, I think. (Alice seems to have gone to *Maine*. I really don't know quite what she's doing—or I understand some of it and forgive it, certainly, but don't see why she has to be so inconsiderate about it all—that's what really hurts, believe it or not.)

I'm afraid I've been an awful fool and I hope you will forgive me. I'm pretty sure your advice didn't—or won't—work, but I'll try to keep on living, at least. I have a kind of "nurse" staying (at $1,000 a day, no doubt)—but can't bear to be completely alone. What I'll do when I get back I just don't know. Anyway, as I said, please forgive me if you can.

To Frani Blough Muser

March 10, 1976

My foot (I must have told you about it) is getting better rapidly. I went down & got my mail myself for the first time, just now. I still haven't tried a shoe on it but shall tomorrow. I gave a reading last Thursday at that St. Botolph Club I may have mentioned—and had a wheelchair & crutches. The audience was *very* appreciative but the next morning I realized I hadn't explained what was wrong to *everybody*—just people at my table for dinner and the two or three I happened to know—and maybe the audience thought I was a hopeless cripple and were just being kind, oh dear.

Tomorrow night I'm going to hear John Ashbery read at Wellesley —and I think he will be going to Oklahoma with me on April 8th [for the presentation of the *Books Abroad*/Neustadt International Prize for Literature, given to EB at the University of Oklahoma]. I'm pleased he said he would . . .

"The Executive Suite"
University of Oklahoma
Norman, Oklahoma
April 10, 1976

. . . Before the ceremony Alice & I went to a very bad Chinese restaurant across the street from the Public Library, and this is the message I found in my Fortune Cookie: "*Your financial condition will improve considerably.*"

And so it has. Yesterday was the big day, or evening, from 6 p.m. on—and on. I gave out about eleven o'clock their time—twelve mine. Oklahomans are all so *very* friendly—in fact I really like them—even if a good many have come here from other places. Ivar Ivask made at least five speeches—one at every opportunity, and we finished the various events at his house . . . I have a diploma in red leather—it is about two feet by three feet—I hope it will go into my suitcase. And the Eagle Feather—which is over a foot long, and must weigh 3 or 4 pounds, in a velvet-lined box of solid walnut, like a small coffin. The feather, on further study, is actually quite nice—I met the young sculptor, who made it after a lot of ornithological studies.

The Neustadt family, who give all this money, was present in force. Mrs. Neustadt—a widow, the matriarch of the clan—about 80, I was told, although appearing much younger—very chic, too, and what pearls! Her son, two daughters and about eight granddaughters—all extremely handsome . . . One granddaughter had just got a contract to sing in the opera in Munich; she's 21. Well, I finally began to think that Mrs. N. had done the University of Oklahoma a great service. She must have given an awful lot of money to bring jurors from Algiers, Norway, Turkey, etc. The faculty families take turns "hosting" (as they say). It's quite surprising to find these nice Midwesterners familiar with Francis Ponge and Giuseppe Ungaretti, and so on. Perhaps you haven't been to receptions at Harvard? I have—and the contrast is enormous. Everyone here is "natural"—no cryptic remarks, no eccentricities, no showing off or upmanship. (However, I'd hate to have to live here.)

I didn't mean to rattle on—but you are the first person I've talked to since the events of yesterday. What I meant to say, in Cambridge, and forgot to while you were there playing with the grandchildren, Bob Giroux phoned. I discussed my idea of a book jacket [for *Geography III*] with him, and said I'd written to Cynthia a few days earlier. I wish you could have heard how flattering he was about Cynthia's work—said *of course* she'd know how to make the jacket I have in mind, if anyone did, and what good work she does, etc. etc.

. . . Oh heavens, now John Ashbery and I have to go and have an "intimate" lunch with Ivar Ivask. I wanted to go home today but couldn't get out of it . . . This "executive" SUITE—well, no one could believe it. The wall-to-wall carpet, very shaggy, looks exactly like chopped red cabbage and it runs from the wall right up the front of the BAR, to meet the padded leather top! Large dark chartreuse armchairs, plush, and everything—tables, etc.—*octagonal*. It seems to be the theme here . . . Well, that's enough!

[P.S.] It's HOT here—but was below freezing when I left Boston!

To Robert Giroux

April 19, 1976

Here is ["One Art"] the villanelle [for the new collection, *Geography III*]. *The New Yorker* has had it for three months or so now & I'll speak to Howard [Moss] about printing it before long. I do have a "gentleman's agreement" with them, about a six-month wait being the limit. I still have hope of getting three or four more done before it is too late. The longest is almost done—about two pages. I'll do my best to make it by the end of this month.

Dear Mr. Oberdorfer (lawyer) and I seem to have had a hard time getting together, but the contracts *shall* be in the mail this afternoon.

Thank heavens, it is a bit cooler today. I mailed all the material I wanted Cynthia to look at to her last week and I hope to hear from her today, too.

To Frank Bidart

Stafford Hotel
St. James's Place
London
June 14, 1976

I feel like writing you a letter this morning—or *telephoning* you even (you are probably still UP), but I mustn't do that again. I should be going to Rotterdam but I am going a day & a half late—mostly because I think I should see the editor at Chatto's & tonight I may go to the theatre—by myself—if they (the porter) can get me a ticket for the play I want to see. The first day I was here in London I had had asthma, a cough & so on. I think HEATHROW did me in. It is pure hell, isn't it?—although I hadn't much to carry or rather to *push* (on a trolley labeled "For the use of the infirm & elderly only") & I did have a porter when the suitcase arrived —in fact I've had porters every little trip, by luck.

I had a very nice time at the Barkers'—saw several other old friends down from London, etc.—slept a lot; and that's when my chest finally cleared up completely. I'm now using that new (in the U.S.) English "preventative" medicine. Kit Barker gave me 50 more—he gets it free, of course, and so far so good. But it has been HOT—a bit better the last four days. London was 85°—and London at 85° is like New York or Boston at 105°—I suppose because of the closeness together of everything, no cross ventilation, almost no air conditioning. I saw the Heilmans (Seattle)—a nice lunch party—Bea Roethke (now Lushington) was there & I liked Mr. L. very much, etc. Also Henry R.—had dinner with him too—a wonderful place.

Then Saturday & yesterday at [the Lowells'] Milgate Park. Well, maybe sometimes you are right about how being so fearfully, automatically "observant" can be a "Calvary"? Anyway it was somewhat as I'd imagined, but raised to the fifth power. Cal, however, seemed and looked awfully well—younger, even. Yesterday I read all, I think, of [his new book] *The Day* & liked many poems *very much*— better than the "sonnets." But oh, if only he'd stop harping on old age! Sheridan is adorable, as you said—extremely pretty—filthy dirty—and speaking very clearly.

[Caroline] . . . was very friendly & *talkative* (maybe not "afraid" of me any more?)—but doing all the cooking, I discovered. No help at all except "Ernie." Well, this [end of airmail notepaper] looks like goodbye.

June 15, 1976
10 a.m. here (5 a.m. there?)

I have this "air letter" left & I might as well send it to you—that doesn't sound nice!—I mean, *to whom else* should I send it?

I think when I got back from the theatre last night that depression overcame me, for the first time in a long time—and I thought it was 6 p.m. your time—a good time to call. But I shouldn't have left word with your answering service, and this time I really *insist* on paying for that call a short time ago—PLEASE!

I'd been told it was the "best thing in London"—the play—and it was too dreary & glib for words. That on top of my weekend visit—well, I shouldn't have said as much as I did. Cal went to Aldeburgh yesterday, I think, or today. Benjamin Britten has set parts of *Phaedra* [in Lowell's translation] & it's to be given as the last item, I think. Something is *wrong*, really. I've read about this in the *Times* almost every morning—an *American* homage by Britten (who is extremely sick, etc.)—and *Phaedra*, but Cal's name has never been mentioned—odd, isn't it?

Well, I must pack up again & go to meet Mrs. Norah Smallwood [at Chatto's]. I have no idea what I can say to her!

Cal really looked very well. In fact, Ilse Barker said, on the telephone yesterday, that he looked much younger than she'd thought he would. Alas, he seems to attribute his recovery to—acupuncture.

To Frani Blough Muser

Lewis Wharf
Boston, Massachusetts
July 21, 1976

. . . One can get phone calls at the Harvard Infirmary, but I wasn't there—and I didn't arrive on a stretcher, at least (I couldn't have lain down, anyway) but in a wheelchair & was met by an ambulance. Poor Frank rode with me, weeping (I didn't have enough wind to tell him I really *wasn't* dying), and after a couple of hours at the Infirmary they sent me to Cambridge Hospital. The Infirmary doesn't have all those weird oxygen machines, etc.

The Cambridge H. people were really wonderful with me. I never had so much attention in my life and they got me over it much better than Peter Bent Brigham & with considerably less pain, too . . . I got home Saturday—limp & covered with bruises but fine otherwise. And the trip wasn't really "ruined" at all. Poor Alice, our flight back must have been hell for her—but it had its funny moments. We stopped briefly at one of the tiny Azores (I think), Santa Maria—& the Portuguese airline had *two* doctors waiting, in white jackets, syringes at the ready, to hop on & shoot me up & of course the passengers & crew were all very thrilled & talkative & I couldn't have cared less or been less embarrassed. Well, this is almost a Victorian health letter so far—excuse it.

We came back on the 6th to see the "Tall Ships" . . . Boston Harbor is really too small for those ships (after Rotterdam it looks like a duck pond) and so they came in under power, mostly—but they all did have to come up as far as my side of the building & turn around, etc.—and from all reports Lewis Wharf got very gay . . . Alice smuggled a TV—medium-sized one—into the hospital for me (against the rules, and those they rented were about 2″ × 4″) so I did see the replay of some of the ships on Sunday and spent all the rest of Sunday with the QUEEN. It all went off very well and she made rather a good speech and Boston seemed quite crazy about her—and one ancient poet I know slightly read a *sestina* to her. (One end-word was "connection"—not very poetic, somehow.) From time to time a friend would telephone me from *my* party and then say something like "Oh, I can't talk now—here comes the *Constitution!*"

Your Dutch boats sound awfully nice. It's odd—one thing I meant to find out while I was there was the purpose of those "side pieces," as you called them—and I forgot to ask. I seem to have been the only poet who wanted to see the famous harbor—so I got sent with someone's daughter, Magreet, aged 17, whose English was *extremely* limited . . . It is incredible, but maybe you've seen it—almost 400 of those stork-like cranes, and hundreds of other weird gigantic elevators, drydocks, ships from all over the world—and those wonderful Dutch barges that go very fast—hung with flags—and then at the stern always lace curtains and geraniums in the cabin windows. I had rather a good time after I got going there—and liked a few of the poets a lot—three "Iron Curtain" ones especially—and a very nice Jewish-Dutch girl, or young woman who has translated a lot of my works—and had a Brazilian lover, born in Petrópolis! (We had dinner in Amsterdam at the *highest point* in the Netherlands, the top—23rd story—of a new Japanese hotel.) Oh—I was reviewed in the Rotterdam paper very favorably, except they felt it was unfortunate that I had a "Texas accent"! My Amsterdam friend said she'd "get" the critic for that—he's never even been to the U.S. Amsterdam looks down on Rotterdam as very provincial and after 6 days there I saw what they meant . . .

Portugal. I really don't know what to say—we saw almost everything we meant to, except Minho, the north. We liked Óbidos and Tomar and *Sagres*—especially—where Henry the Navigator started off all the voyages but never set foot on a ship again after one trip to Africa (Lota said this was because he got so seasick). A magnificent coast—but the eastern part of the Algarve is horrid—all hotels, hippies, trash, etc. . . .

To Ashley Brown

. . . I do thank you very much for putting me up, making my break-
fasts, and arranging for all the drives, the fancy lunch, and everything
else. I'm sorry I didn't have time to take my sheets, etc., off & fold them
up neatly. I did manage to at Miss Brée's, thank goodness, but there I
did leave behind a perfectly horrid detective story called *How Some People
Die* and I hope she doesn't think it typical of my taste. (I sometimes read
them on plane trips, especially taking off & landing, to take my mind off
things.) It was nice to see you "at home" after many years of hearing
about it & I love the Peruvian rug, and the de la Monica, and many other
items. But please do invest in a humidifier and a hygrometer! I'm watching
mine now—but it's warmer and awfully damp, and with the window open
the humidity is up to 55°—well within the safety zone.

I think the nicest part of the trip was dinner at Celso's—I'll write
him next. And I forgot to thank Bernadette for the pressing job—but I
will. . . . When I got back last night I learned that James Dickey's wife
had died—the same day I was there, I think. He put himself out so to be
nice to me—to my amazement—and he certainly was sober enough. I
feel awfully sorry and I'll write to him, too—something I never would
have thought I'd be doing a week ago.

I'm still wishing I hadn't read so much of A. Huxley's life—I'll never
get caught up on sleep. Germaine Brée had equally fascinating books in
her guest room, too. Everyone was very nice to me there and entertained
me all over the place, and it is very pretty—the various Reynolds
estates—& Germaine & I took a long walk in the woods. I liked her very
much. I'm sorry to say that the audience there was *much* better than in
South Carolina—I don't know why. I've had three readings in my life
that I enjoyed completely and that seemed to get better & better as they
went along, and that was one of them. I felt I let you down awfully in
Columbia—but the audience felt *dead* to me. I'm sure you must know
that feeling—and then one gets tired, and hears one's voice getting tired,
and it is awful. Of course I should have "programmed" you to laugh
loudly when I winked or something . . .

To Frani Blough Muser

. . . I bought myself a small oven a while ago—a little thing that sits
on the kitchen counter and can toast, bake, de-freeze frozen dishes,
etc.—mine also can broil but I think I'll get the broiler-less model for
Margaret. As I remember, the stove at Knickerbocker Village is *gas* (I
haven't been there for 20-some years) and I hate to think of all the lighting

of matches, etc.—and this gadget is so easy to use—and keep clean, etc. . . .

Friday night I went to hear *The Messiah* at Symphony Hall. It was packed, and really great fun—and Susan Wyner was the soprano soloist—a very good tenor, too. She had to sit there for 45 minutes before she could begin, poor thing—but did beautifully with "I know that my Redeemer," etc.

The Academy thing [EB had just been elected to the fifty-member American Academy of Arts and Letters] is just due to my longevity, I'm afraid—& the fact that someone else died. I was about to resign if they didn't put me in it, anyway! There are so many *creeps* (as Alice would say) in it already, but they're the people who live around N.Y. and are very *active*, etc. After last May's "ceremonial" I thought I'd never go back again, it was all so sad and dreary.

Oh—I received three copies of the book [*Geography III*] three days ago—and I think it is extremely pretty—cloth cover, pages, everything, except the fact that it is glued, not sewn. But that isn't Cynthia's fault and she has done a lovely job—everyone who has seen it says so, too. I've written Bob Giroux to say I'd like some books on sale at the Americana Hotel [in New York, where the annual convention of the MLA was to be held, at which papers on EB's poetry and a reading by EB were to be given on December 28]. The talks are to take place in the "Imperial Ballroom" that seats 13,000! You don't have to attend any of this of course. My plan for the 28th is to leave when the "papers" begin and go to the Stage Delicatessen across the street and eat corned beef hash (the best I've ever had in my life, there) until it is time to return to the Americana. Maybe you could join me there?

I envy you very much, going to Egypt. Well, next year with luck I can take half a year off and maybe get there, or somewhere . . .

To Loren MacIver

January 5, 1977

. . . Did I tell you of Edna's wonderful remark after the Elliott Carter music [settings for EB's poems] last Tuesday night? She was sitting by Margaret Miller, who hated it & wanted to leave & complained, etc., & asked Edna what *she* thought of the music. Edna was very canny. She said, "Well, I suppose it's *good publicity.*" I love that.

Yesterday and the day before were beautiful here—lots of snow (12 inches while I was away), but sunny and not too cold and the harbor a pale, pale milky blue. Seven ducks seem to be wintering here. I walk to my allergy doctor for a weekly shot—about a mile, I suppose—along the waterfront. Yesterday I walked back the long way, around by "Copp's Hill" graveyard—very ancient, and very beautiful—all the faint, slatestone angels eyeing one out of their depths in the snow. I'm afraid I do like Boston—better than New York.

I never got into the Matisse gallery. I tried the Calder—it (or the lobby of the Whitney) was jam-packed with young people in skiing clothes & backpacks—just like Harvard—so I bought the catalogue and left . . . I do wish you could get up and exercise your little limbs from time to time. I *know* you have pain, etc.—but you are too valuable to take to your bed like a character in Proust!

[P.S.] I remembered finally the wonderful misunderstanding of English idiom that I tried to tell you about my French friend. She had seen an ad in the Boston subway of these new milk-&-alcohol drinks: "Our Hereford Cows are not a bum steer" and, as I said, she knew things like "bullshit" but telephoned to ask what on earth a "bum steer" was.

To Dr. Anny Baumann

February 10, 1977

. . . The spring vacation for Harvard is from April 2nd until April 11th, the day after Easter. That would be a very good time for you to come . . . The weather should certainly be fairly pleasant by then, and Alice & I have already discussed what things you'd like to do best here —of course there are at least three fine museums—but there are other and less exhausting amusements as well.

Robert Lowell is here again, for the spring term, and he likes the idea of seeing you, too. Classes began this week. He came alone—he's living in a college house for the term. A day or so after he got here, he had what the doctors called a "slight congestive heart failure." He had been complaining of shortness of breath—when he was here in December & November—and it got much worse. He was in the Phillips House here for just a week, I think it was, with oxygen, no liquids to speak of, etc.— but got out yesterday, and even went to one of his classes. Of course if he could only stop smoking—but he says the doctor says it's too late to stop—but must restrict liquids to 2 quarts a day. I haven't seen him for 2 or 3 days—talked to him on the telephone—just now—again. Saw him in the hospital several times.

My "allergist" is very nice and so far all has gone very well. I am almost off the prednisone, thank goodness. I hate it; I can't even get my ring on, scarcely my shoes. But I haven't had any asthma at all, and now go for shots every two weeks—soon once a month, I think.

I have made two, maybe three (I've *forgotten*—too much going on) trips to New York but never for more than a day—once overnight, I think. Now I'm through with that committee, thank goodness. The other trips were very hasty ones too—for 2 interviews and a radio—tape—reading & interview with WBAI. I don't know when that will be heard—they said they'd let me know. The reviews [of *Geography III*] so far have been embarrassingly good—but of course someone is bound to *attack*, sooner or later! The *N.Y. Times* daily review was better than the long one two Sundays ago—it was full of foolish mistakes—I don't think the reviewer had read very carefully.

I read in the Boston Public Library on the 2nd—quite successful, I gather—at least the place was full and a very responsive audience and a very nicely assorted one—a lot of my students, the Brazilian wife of the French Consul, my next-door neighbor here at Lewis Wharf, a notorious lady who owns, and sings at, a nightclub called "Bette's Rolls-Royce" ... etc. (The Rolls, yellow, antique, is parked under my window.) I suppose I should enjoy all the fuss about that very thin book—but on the whole I am *very* glad I was out of the country every time a book was published before.

Loren telephoned yesterday and sounds much, much better—a new young couple, brother & sister, taking care of her. Please just let me know when you'd like to come. (I can't believe it!)

To James Merrill

> March 11 (?), 1977
> Friday night

I think I'll just give up on that half-written airmail letter I started to you some months ago. After I stopped writing it, it seems to me now that many events of interest and importance to us both came along and now for the life of me I can't remember what they were ...

I'm awfully sorry I couldn't see you the other day. It's true—I have something called a "hiatal" (?) hernia—usually I'm not even aware of it but once in a while it gives one a fearful bellyache, etc. Since I found out about this a year or so ago I've learned it's very common. It is better today, and tomorrow I'm going to Washington to read for an organization called A.W.P. You may know about it; I know almost nothing, but I haven't seen the Hirshhorn collection or museum yet, and I'd like to see some more art there again so I thought this was the opportunity. (Something wrong about that sentence. Since I started teaching "Intermediate Prose" this term, I find I can't write even the cat is on the mat without worrying about it. However, to go on with that thought—I have some very good students & one young man wrote a story about his mother—Polish, a concert pianist, who was giving a recital—a Brahms something-or-other—in Symphony Hall just before he was born. His birth was so imminent that she played right through labor pains & couldn't manage a bow—and he appeared 2 hours later at Mass. General!)

I saw (heard) [Glinka's] *Russlan and Ludmila* Tuesday night & only compared notes with Frank on Wednesday. I enjoyed a lot of it. I like fairy tales—but I always seem to give out at Sarah's productions about 40 minutes before the end. Then there are tiny matters of taste: I didn't like the witches' hair standing up—or the high center to the king's crown—or the blue swamp with white trees. However, that's nothing musical. The *N.Y. Times* review was much better than Dick Dyer's here. Frank tells me that the next section of *Ephraim* is better than the first. I'm sure you had a lovely poetical time—and Frank's book is out—or maybe you already have a copy. He seems quite delighted—except for that teensy-weensy line of white paper that shows on the jacket. Oh dear. But today he even sounded cheerful about that. I hope to god he gets some nice reviews.

To Loren MacIver

June 21, 1977

. . . As I think you know, I've really been awfully sick and I'm still very *feeble*. It was idiotic of me—I should have guessed what the matter was, probably—but by the time I could get an appointment with a doctor, I was missing 60% of my red corpuscles and had lost something like two and a half quarts of blood. (I didn't know I had that much to begin with!) It was a relief to know something was really wrong. I'd just been feeling guilty about being "lazy," etc. I was sent to "Emergency" for blood transfusions without even going home first, and the doctor complimented me by saying he'd never known anyone to come into the office with so little red blood "under their own steam." I am feeling a lot better now, of course, but taking lots of iron pills I hate—and awfully languid, etc. I don't want to talk about health, it's very boring—but maybe that will explain a bit more why I may have sounded cross and also why I am reluctant to take on any extra writing except what I have planned—and some of it I *have* to do this summer—that is, July & August . . .

Alice & I went to Maine last weekend to take a lot of stuff over to North Haven—then Sunday went on an Audubon Society trip ("birding," it's called) to see PUFFINS, mostly—way out on an island of sheer rock —all day. It was really fun—and funny. We were supposed to see something called "The Sooty Shearwater" (& did) & Alice had promised to call out, "Oh—there's a Shitty Sorewater!" She really did say this to our GUIDE but apparently he didn't notice anything & just said "Where?" . . .

I don't think I've told you about my New York job for next year? Two days a week at New York University [at Washington Square]—and an *apartment thrown in*—two bedrooms, etc. One term only, but I think it may be fun, if I can take all those bus rides. I'll be here [Boston] until June 29th—then Sabine Farm, North Haven, Maine, for eight weeks.

To Mary McCarthy

EB's refusal of Mary McCarthy's request to visit her at North Haven (see paragraph 2) was, in the novelist's words, "because you had got the notion that I had put you and Lota in The Group*" as lesbian characters. McCarthy's denial, written much later in Paris (October 28, 1979), never reached EB, who had died earlier that month. The relevant passage of McCarthy's letter is given below.**

Sabine Farm

North Haven, Maine

Early July 1977

I've just written Cal & I hope both notes will make the mail this morning. (The R.F.D. man is named Colon Winslow. He used to weigh 300 lbs. and since he now weighs only 200 he is called "Semi-Colon.")

I told Cal that I was awfully sorry but I'd be grateful if you *didn't* come over—at least not this summer. Maybe next, if I can manage to come back here. (This is the fourth summer I've been here and I am very fond of it.) Somehow everyone seemed to come visiting in July and all last week there were eight or nine people here, including a year-old baby (charming, but noisy)—and when they finally all left Sunday, I began working at last—first time since last summer—and the French friend who's here also started working, with a sigh of relief—Celia Bertin, I think she met you long ago in Paris.

Also, as Cal may have told you, I've really been rather sick lately— just got out of the hospital before I came here. I'm a lot better now, thank goodness, but still can't manage the bicycle & have to have blood tests every week . . .

I hope you'll understand—and I hope to see you next time. Frani & Curt come the 8th and I hope to finish a couple of poems before then. I imagine they'll be driving up to Castine to see you.

[P.S.] I've heard from Cal about the Hannah Arendt book. I'm so

---

* *Mary McCarthy's letter:* "Now that Cal is dead, I feel at liberty to tell you something he told me that last summer [of 1977], i.e., that he was convinced you had called off the projected trip to North Haven because you didn't want to see *me*. Because you had got the notion that I had put you and Lota in *The Group*. I'd had no inkling of that before, not a suspicion. Lying isn't one of my faults, and I promise you that no thought of you, or of Lota, even grazed my mind when I was writing *The Group*. The character Lakey owed a little something to Margaret Miller but only in her appearance—the Indian eyes and the dark hair—and in her Fine Arts studies. There was also something of Nathalie [Swan] in her—a kind of hauteur or fine anger maybe or fathomless scorn. As for the Baroness, I can't remember where I got her if she came from real life at all . . . I can see how someone could imagine that you, as a Vassar contemporary, might be expected to figure in *The Group*. It's perhaps even strange that you didn't, but that is the fact. I'm highly conscious, normally, of where the bits and pieces of a book come from—the Baroness seems to be an exception—and they identify themselves to me by a physical trait, which may at times be vocal . . . Well, this is a bore for you, and I won't say more. But please do believe me."

sorry I didn't see her before she died. She had written me a very nice note.

To Frani Blough Muser

July 18, 1977
Monday morning

. . . Sneakers are decidedly *in* in North Haven this season—mostly the newer types with stripes of blue, red, etc., but any old sneaker will do. For the past years it has been "Top-Siders" and although I've now had a pair for three years, they never seem to look aged enough for here. Anything you have in rags is good, too. Our neighbor, Emily Lattimore —you'll meet her, daughter-in-law of Owen, and our landlady's niece— a bit eccentric, mother of six—but we rather like her—says that if we come here 12 years we *might* get invited to a cocktail party (not that I want to be). I was delighted when this season (4th) IRMA (I type large because she is impressively so in the grocery, etc.) remembered me and actually said, "Hi! How are you?" So I hope you don't expect much social life. The Lamonts are said to have moved here from Bar Harbor because they couldn't stand the social life there any more . . .

They now think people—pre-Indians, whoever they were—have been coming here for at least 6,000 years—and Emily turned up a grinding stone or something in her lettuce bed . . . We can take a walk to "Turner Farm"—a place I didn't discover until last year & then just by chance, on the east side of the island. I won't tell you about it, but surprise you. But that is where the U. of Maine is *digging* now.

Alice & I have just entertained two complete strangers over Sat. & Sunday—Jack Unterecker, who wrote a huge biography of Hart Crane, for one thing, and a very young man, Roger Conover, who writes poetry, knows friends of mine in Cambridge & has moved there with his wife recently. Well, Jack (as I now call him) is doing a "monograph" or something on me—he'd written & telephoned to Boston—then was coming here, or just down the coast, for a wedding, and asked to come over. Fortunately they both turned out to be very nice—and Jack knows Cynthia. . . . Anyway—he admires Cynthia's work. Roger went jogging and got lost—we thought he'd never show up and when he did we figured out he'd jogged 14 or 15 miles. We also just discovered he left his bathing trunks in one room and the clothes he arrived in in another.

Yes, I thought the *Newsweek* piece was good, too. Margo Jefferson, who wrote it, flew over from New York to talk to me. She seemed very smart and I liked her a lot—and she obviously *had* read my *oeuvre* (not a very big task).

As you may know, liquor is very cheap in New Hampshire, and very expensive (& just gone up) in Maine. So perhaps you could bring a supply

of your favorite tipple with you, and a half gallon of Old Crow for us. Also
—the Sunday papers if you have them, and a Maine TV guide—there's a
newspaper shop right near the ferry landing for that. (We've only seen one
newspaper since we've been here.) And—if you see any nice *fresh* vegetables and fruit along the way—I'll reimburse you for all this, naturally.

P.S. Do you intend to go and call on Mary McCarthy at Castine?
Cal threatened to bring her over, but I wrote him & I don't think he will.

August 23 (I think), 1977

Mary [McCarthy]'s house sounds quite beautiful—at least those stair-
cases do. I've rather lost track of company, but Frank Bidart came—two
or three days—then went on to Castine, where they (the Lowells & he)
were not invited to dinner because Mary didn't "have enough room."

I wish you'd been here yesterday—we were invited out on a boat—
friends of the Thatchers . . . —a 40-foot sloop. There was a good wind
and we went all around this island to North Harbor, no—Winter
Harbor—on Vinal Island. That island is completely different—it's a
"granite island." We sailed about 5 hours & I think you would have liked
it very much. Then three of us came back by outboard motor through a
narrow passage, under a bridge, "Mill River," into the sunset and back
to the old ferry landing. I do wish you'd been here, it was so nice.

Friday we're going out again—on a lobster boat, I think—with our
landlady, to visit—can it be Buckminster Fuller?—one never knows who's
going to be on these islands. Anyway—I'm sorry when you were here our
social life was so dull. (It's been much duller before!) I'm glad you seem
really to have liked this place that was found entirely by chance. And
sleep—well, I slept off & on for 4 days, I think—and I'm a very parsi-
monious sleeper. I really thought you looked *much* better when you left
than when you arrived—a nice pale tan, and sort of (as they say) relaxed.

Margaret telephoned, to my surprise, two days ago. She sounded very
cheerful and I hope this is true . . .

I called N.Y.U. at last this morning & find I have to be there the
19th—well—maybe I'll be able to have you & Curt to dinner sometime
this fall—even a "party." I was awfully glad you could get here.

To James Merrill

August 27, 1977

. . . This summer things seem a bit clearer and I have *again* said I'd
read for Marianne's birthday in New York, November 15th. (I went and
gave a reading at Bryn Mawr early last spring sometime—an enormous
audience in a kind of cathedral—but you've probably been there?—and
afterwards I discovered all three of Marianne's nieces had been in the

audience . . .) When she asked me—Barbara Thatcher, I mean—for suggestions, I'm afraid I immediately thought of you, and I am very sorry but I
certainly hope you'll accept. No one will take more than ten minutes. I
think I've convinced them NOT to play a tape recording of Marianne reading (in fact I said I'd walk out if they did that). Ex-Mayor Lindsay (M.M.
liked him a lot) will preside—refreshments first, I gather. Oh dear god,
why do I let myself in for these things, and now you, too? But it may not be
so bad after all. I've had an idea for a black singer M. liked a lot—one of
the last times I "went out" with her was to hear him sing some Ives songs
she'd never heard. He is very good, and if I can track him down and he
remembers the songs—that might make a pleasant break.

It has been a beautiful summer but mostly I've been too poorly to
enjoy it properly. The last few weeks have been better, though. Frank
came for 3 days, I think—and it was really nice to see how he *cheered
up*. Then he went on to Castine to visit Cal . . .

I am DREADING leaving, the 29th, and beginning at N.Y.U. the 19th.
My one desire is to retire. This is no doubt due to lack of vitamins or
something—but tonight we have our last Maine lobsters—thrashing
around in a bucket now . . . Forgive a stupid note and I hope to see you
in New York & do forgive my getting you into this M.M. thing. You can
perfectly well refuse.

To Dr. Anny Baumann

January 7, 1978
. . . I don't sleep well, but mostly because I can't get comfortable—
feeling, as I do, that my poor old body is one huge HERNIA. But that
doesn't matter, since I don't do anything but lie around and read, anyway,
most of the time. I have to give five or six readings—mostly in April, I think
—and shall need badly to earn the money. I've just GOT to get to feeling
better, somehow. I think I really am *sick*—and I have been a little frightened by Dr. Briggs's (I like him very much, however) apparent indifference
as to whether I have shots or not. Dr. Foster, here, too, seemed totally indifferent to my troubles the last time I saw him—probably in May or June.
You know I'm really not a hypochondriac and I also try not to complain too
much—but I am at my wits' end & want badly to feel enough better to get
some of my own work done. This N.Y.U. thing has been a nightmare—but I
accepted before I felt so badly & then felt I couldn't get out of it. Alice has
been wonderful—she's done nothing, really, but look after me for months now.

I remember in the past you & I had several theoretical discussions
about what a patient should be told about his state & what he shouldn't.
(You may not remember this but I do—on one endless drive to Congonhas,
in Brazil.) You have said you didn't believe in telling the worst, or giving
up hope, etc., because medical "miracles" or unexpected changes did

take place. However, I am one of those people who much prefer to know the *truth*—if there is any "truth" to be known. Since I seem to be getting worse rather than better—I must know what you—and Dr. Briggs, if he has any opinion—*really* think. *Will you please tell me?* I really can't bear to go on living like this any longer. (I am NOT "depressed," however!—that was *one* episode in my life, over two years ago now.) . . .

I must get ready to leave for New York.

To Dorothee Bowie

437 Lewis Wharf
Boston, Massachusetts
January 26, 1978

This long silence is due to several impediments (as Miss Moore would have put it). I *hated* N.Y.U., and the going back & forth (although I didn't do it every week) was exhausting. Then I gave two, no three, I think, readings, etc.—and then I got sick again, exactly like last spring, so that I barely made the last two classes, then went the next day straight to the hospital—this time in New York. Medical talk is the most boring I know, except for talk of diets—and now I'm engulfed in both. After taking iron pills all summer and feeling horrible and getting nothing done but one poem in 10 months—my blood count went down, down, down. Then I ate a half pound of liver a day for 10 days—same thing. Then, being in N.Y., Dr. Baumann sent me to a hematologist and I had iron shots for over 2 months—the blood went up a bit, then down a bit. Apparently I can't absorb iron and there's none in my bone marrow. (Although how the marrow makes blood & gets it out of your bones into your bloodstream has never been satisfactorily explained to me.) So then I went to Lenox Hill Hospital, more transfusions, etc.

Fortunately Alice had driven me over for the last stretch of classes, so she was in N.Y. in the rather large, super-deluxe, motel-style apartment they provide with that wretched job. (I never would have taken it if I'd realized how bad the students are and how disorganized the place is—and of course if I'd known I would get more anemic all the time.) This all comes from the huge hiatal hernia—which came, or has got bigger and worse, because of all the cortisone various dumb doctors here have given me. Dr. Baumann and the other two doctors involved don't want to operate (although it would be a relief, in a way) because it is dangerous to operate on asthmatics. So—I am on a diet of skimmed milk, or Jell-O, or consommé, every hour and Gelusil or something like that every half hour. Yesterday I was allowed a pear—and I never tasted anything so delicious in my life—so it is going to be nice to re-discover the simple things of life bit by bit—like food. And that's more than enough about that.

You've probably read about our terrific snowstorms in N.Y. and even more, here. I overlooked Park Avenue from my hospital room and it was very strange to see people skiing down Park Ave. The whole city was closed down. The TV announced, "The slopes are very good on Murray Hill." We came back the 24th—the highways are clear but the cities are in a mess. Then it poured all day yesterday, so now most of the snow has gone—now we have floods—and it is starting to freeze so there'll be skating in the streets next. When I watch "weather" on TV (A.'s favorite program) I always notice what's going on in [the state of] Washington—and I think you've been having floods of rain. Well, what a relief it is to be home—even if I have a five-foot stack of mail to be dealt with . . .

I was trying to remember your E.B. cozy-corner and I'm not sure whether you have—or if you don't, if you'd care for—one of my genuine primitive paintings. I'll be glad to send you my next work of art— and surely, now I'm not teaching for a while, I'll have time to paint some pictures—even think of a poem, possibly. And then—I am coming to read in Oregon at Eugene, Portland and Corvallis the last week of April. I could bring lobsters that far with me and fly them to you . . .

I do want to see you, and your house and garden—if you'll be there. The allergies seem to get worse rather than better (after endless series of shots and cortisone the dumb allergist gave me, that really did me in). In N.Y.—in the vast "complex" of apartment houses where most of the N.Y.U. people seemed to live—there was a crippled man, badly crippled, in an electrified wheelchair, down the hall from me—an endless, narrow, dark-blue hall. He had two cats—and kept his door open when he was at home (someone came to cook dinner for him, etc.—and he actually worked at N.Y.U.—lecturing on I don't know what). Well, he had 2 cats, a yellow one and a darling black and white one, quite youthful. They would come out and just sit in the middle of the hall, looking for some excitement. The little black & white one was quite friendly—it started coming to call on me. She also sat by the mail drop and when every once in a while a letter would drop down it—*that* was the thrill of her life. I wish I could have a cat! a dog!—"not even a canary," the doctor says. Well, I'm lucky to be feeling so much better and this weird diet will make me pure and ascetic.

To Ashley Brown

March 1, 1978

Robert Fitzgerald has just telephoned me—mostly to tell me what a nice time he had with you, what a good host you were, etc. So much has been happening here that I'd forgotten he was going to Columbia. I'll be seeing him this afternoon. It is Robert Lowell's birthday and *in memoriam* I'm going to read at Harvard—half Cal, half me. I did exactly the same thing at the Guggenheim in late November. Then tomorrow there's a memorial service in the Harvard chapel—with some music—Bach on the organ and two arias—I hope it's a good singer. Caroline Lowell has come, and Elizabeth Hardwick is coming tomorrow—and there are even more such complications. I wish the next two days were over with! There's also an exhibition of Lowell papers at Houghton Library—*two* receptions, at least, and a dinner (I'm skipping that) . . .

I haven't written for a long time—not to *anybody*. That Berg affair at N.Y.U. was a very bad idea—in all respects, except that it provided a large & well-equipped apartment. But I got to feeling worse & worse and went straight to the hospital after my last class. (Robert may even have mentioned this—he takes my health very seriously—although I'm sure my troubles can't compare with his.) Anyway my "acute iron deficiency" is a lot better and at the moment I feel better than I have in two or three years. And now—as for you—I do wonder how you are and how your eyes are.

Now I'm going to ask you for a favor, or at least some advice. Maybe I told you that one of the Harvard Jr. Fellows (now in his last year as such) is Ricardo Sternberg—Brazilian, from a family I knew in Brazil, an extremely nice and intelligent family. His father has been a prof. at Berkeley now for many years—geography, or geography-history—and I knew Ricardo when he was a small boy in Rio. He is now writing his Ph.D. thesis on Drummond de Andrade—two-thirds done, I think he is quite bilingual, actually got the fellowship for his poetry in English (a very rare event—they're usually historians, economists, etc.) and I think has a lot of talent. He has published a few poems here & there but not a book yet. He's a very charming young man, I think . . . Well, since you do know so many Brazilians and probably know much more about possible jobs for Brazilians—I just thought I'd ask you what you think, at least. He's very bright and works hard. I am very fond of him—& I am very fond of his parents, too. You might know of other possibilities that he doesn't. He might get his thesis done by June, I think he said.

A terrible translation of Drummond de Andrade in the last *American Poetry Review*. Well, everybody's doing it. Ricardo and I put on a small show for a friend who teaches at Bristol Community College—Brazilian popular songs & sambas. There are mostly Portuguese-speaking students there, and actually four or five were Brazilians. I gave English versions, Ricardo gave Portuguese, then we played recordings. It was very simple but rather fun.

I've got myself into a reading schedule I can't believe—but I did cancel one endless trip to Oregon. (These places keep adding "work-shops," extra readings, celebrations of somebody or other's birthday, etc.)

This weekend I go to Washington, in two weeks or so to Durham, and from there to Arkansas—then Storrs, Conn., and later on Bennington. This is all to earn $$$, I'm afraid—because I'm not teaching now—and hope never to again! If I get a Guggenheim (I think I may) I can probably just make it for a year—and then I hope "something will turn up." I want desperately to do some work of my own.

My Brazilian lawyer actually showed up in Boston a while ago—and my affairs there are more or less straightened out. I *think* he even has someone in mind to sell the Ouro Prêto house to—that would solve my problems for a long time.

There's supposed to be another snowstorm today—and a Cambridge minister (I dislike the race), just called and murmured away about taping this reading for posterity. I'm about to take 2 sedatives and suck some cough drops. Pray for me.

To Jerome Mazzaro

Jerome Mazzaro is the author of Postmodern American Poetry *(1980) and* The Figure of Dante: An Essay on the "Vita Nuova" *(1981). He teaches at the State University of New York at Buffalo.*

April 27, 1978

. . . You say you are "reading about wasps"—in reference to my poem "Santarém." Now if I'd written "beehive"!—I *have* read about bees, but know nothing of wasps except for being stung once. "Santarém" *happened*, just like that, a real evening & a real place, and a real Mr. Swan who said that—it is not a composite at all.

Your piece about my "Recent Poems" fascinates me. I never dreamed of *Alice in Wonderland* in connection with "Crusoe in England." I don't believe I ever read *The Little Prince* & when I wrote the poem I hadn't re-read *Robinson Crusoe* for at least 20 years.

I never heard of Katherine May Peek and many other writers you mention—or haven't read them, not even Virgil's *Eclogues*! You reduce me to illiteracy! In the Duxbury poem ["The End of March"] the water *was* the color of mutton-fat jade; I wasn't aware of any echo until you pointed it out. And my feelings are hurt by your thinking I'd *gulp* "grog à l'américaine"!

Well, it takes an infinite number of things coming together, forgotten, or almost forgotten, books, last night's dream, experiences past and present—to make a poem. The settings, or descriptions, of my poems are almost invariably just plain facts—or as close to the facts as I can write them. But, as I said, it is fascinating that my poem should arouse in you all those literary references!

To Loren MacIver

[POSTCARD]

May 28, 1978

I haven't heard from you for some time & I hope all goes well. I think I've talked with you since that trip—two trips joined by one flight, really—in North Carolina & Arkansas, haven't I? Then I did one last reading, at Bennington, a short time ago. I hadn't been to that part of Vermont in years. It is really lovely, although spring hadn't quite arrived then. Readings, etc., take place there in what was a stable—a huge room, with a balcony on three sides—but obviously a stable. There are chairs, like any auditorium, on the floor—but the students also sit on the balcony floor, high up, all around—and it was very odd to look up and see a hundred or so pairs of dangling legs on three sides.

Monday Alice & I made a trip to the Arnold Arboretum. The day before had been "Lilac Day"—but Monday just as good and fewer people. We walked miles—but what you would have liked especially was this "lilac path"—actually a path through a whole big hillside of lilacs. Imagine the wonderful smell . . . I'll be away from June 14th to 24th, visiting assorted friends. July 1st Alice and I go to Maine for two months—North Haven.

To Dr. Anny Baumann

June 30, 1978
9 a.m.

. . . Alice and I had a lovely time, visiting three—or three sets, I should say, of elderly people—one wonderful lady who comes from Prince Edward Island, where my grandfather Bishop came from, and has a large & very lovely house on Lake *Memphremagog*, in Quebec. Then on to northwest Mass. for 2 or 3 more days at two places. All the hostesses very erudite—one, a very old friend of mine, is Russian. One of the best features of the trip was when crossing the wilder sections of Maine we saw TWO moose. A deserted forest road—the second moose was lying beside it, in a nice grassy ditch. Alice stopped the car, and the moose got up very slowly, walked across in front of us, and then stood behind a tree on the other side of the road—thinking she was hidden, but wanting to study us some more.

I feel fine and very energetic. (I've just packed up all the papers I mean to work on the next two months—we leave at 8 a.m. tomorrow.) In Maine I am going to lead a life of *blameless purity* and hard work, I hope. We have very few guests coming, only one for any length of time, and she works, too—and the house is big enough so that I have a "study" to myself and can shut myself in every morning for as long as I want. In spite of what you think about North Haven—there *is* a resident doctor and also a *summer* doctor (last summer a young man from Cambridge– Harvard, etc., who certainly seemed intelligent) . . .

After telephone calls to several friends here, much drama, etc., Candy [Candace W. MacMahon] did receive my "Foreword" [to *Elizabeth Bishop: A Bibliography 1927–1979*] and yesterday wrote me it was "perfect." (It's very *short*.) There wasn't all that rush about it anyway, I find.

To Dorothee Bowie

July 4, 1978

The fireweed has been burning away for over a week now & of course it makes me think of you . . . I seem to have had a real BLOCK so far this summer, about any kind of writing, including letters, diary, anything . . . And the "news" is scarcely lively: today we go to the "store," and— if we get there before two—we can go to the ladies' cake sale at the church. Also, we can go to buy some lettuce, etc., at a sort of farm a young girl and her husband are running this season. The last time we went there a very grande-dame-sort-of-summer-resident, with large hat & basket, said to me, "Tomorrow we can probably buy green beans; won't that be fun?" So you see how hectic things are here. "Down" is going northeast. It's "up" to Boston.

We're going to the cake sale to lay in some cake or brownies for *teas*—because tomorrow Kit & Ilse Barker & Thomas (15 or 16 years old now) are coming for five days, and I think they must have their teas— especially Thomas. They are old friends at whose house I met Leslie Norris, in Sussex. I've probably spoken of them—I've known them since 1950. They are on a charter-flight trip, rather short, and are winding it up here. Leslie is visiting again in the Cranberry Isles—north of here. I think he visited there last year—the Mannings, editor of *The Atlantic Monthly*. They have a boat & there was a rumor they might sail up to North Haven—it's quite near by boat and very far by land—but nothing came of it . . . I'm engaging Joe Brown to take us all out on his lobster boat on Tuesday, if it's fine, for a trip around the islands—only he referred to it as a "sail." Can he be *that* old?

We've been very quiet—by choice. A couple here just over the 4th —he left us a kite. Then my old friend Rhoda (of 51 years) was here for ten days, a very nice woman (wonderful, in fact, and very funny) with five children, many family troubles, etc.—and she's no trouble at all. She sent Alice another kite—purple (A.'s favorite color) of something superior called MYLAR (semitransparent) . . . Anyway, they are both long, long "dragon" kites, and look lovely up in the sky, wriggling away—especially the purple one. Then we had two elderly (*I* say!) professors—a sort of duty invitation—for 3 days—and that was rather hard going since one of them, particularly, was inclined to argue about *everything*. Then nobody except maybe John Brinnin, and Frank Bidart may come for a weekend . . .

I don't imagine you know about Bill Read? Possibly I did tell you he had cancer? This was discovered definitely last September—and it was pretty hopeless then. (We are sure it had begun at least 2 years earlier, when he was very poorly and coughed, etc., and no doctor could—or would—find out what was wrong.) Well, things got worse & worse; John took the year off. Bill—quite sensibly, I think—refused to go to a hospital, and kept going somehow, until the day he died, at home, in June. They made trips to Venice, Paris, and to the Stratford Theatre (in June). Of course this was hell for poor John. Bill liked you a lot—always asked about you . . .

When are you going to make that trip to Boston?—September? October? You and T.J.?—any later it's apt to be *cold*, as I'm sure you remember. Please come and we'll try to show you a better time than last time—there's the new Quincy Market right next door, and thousands of old books for T.J.

I had to go to Rockland on the ferry last week and listened in on a long conversation—narcissistic monologue, rather—by a rather handsome young painter (bad painter, from what I saw when I peeked into his van). He's been coming here since childhood, but . . . talked away about Puget Sound, Seattle, and where he teaches art (I don't know where). He also *runs*. I was very tempted to enter into his monologue but just eavesdropped for an hour while he went on & on about the difference in ART on the East Coast & the West Coast.

We'd love to see you, both Alice & I—and hope we shall fairly soon. I'd love to hear any news from there, too. *Lots* of blueberries this dry summer—and raspberries . . .

To Frank Bidart

> Sabine Farm
> North Haven, Maine
> July 9, 1978

Here's that poem ["North Haven—In memoriam: Robert Lowell"]— the first I ever read over a telephone, I think! There are still a few bad spots, I know—& maybe the whole poem is bad—I can't really tell, and I hope you'll be very *honest* with me about it. I do think the "idea"—perhaps not the most important thing—is rather good, though. The first stanza I wanted to give a feeling of an intensely quiet meditation (?)—something like that—and probably there should be two such stanzas, I don't know. Either more, or not at all, perhaps. I don't like the word "given" and will change it. "Daisies pied" and "to paint the meadows with delight" are straight from the summer part of the song in Shakespeare—you know the other part, "When icicles hang by the wall"? . . . The "incandescent stars"

I'm pretty sure are from Marianne's "Marriage"—but that isn't too important. (I think I felt the more literary the better!) "Mystic blue" is I think a steal from Cal, isn't it?—also more or less on purpose.

Well, it needs more work—and also may be absolute *corn*—I wish you'd tell me. The flowers & birds parts are actually the best—and totally lost on you, Frank dear, I'm afraid! There should be a wider space after the first stanza—the others equal spaces. Oh dear, oh dear—I just don't know—I am now doing two [poems] at once. "Sammy" (the toucan), and a very slight affair about the Carlyles I started long ago—it's almost done.

We didn't go out in a lobster boat today because the captain thought it was too foggy. I hope we can tomorrow because that's the Barkers' last day. I think they really like it here & Kit has been doing a lot of water-coloring. Oh, I wish I had another month! I feel I've just got going and now there are only 18 more days . . .

[P.S.] I'd rather you didn't show this effort to anyone until I think it's really finished.

To Frani Blough Muser

[POSTCARD]

437 Lewis Wharf
Boston, Massachusetts
November 2, 1978

I wanted desperately to get to that Indian show, also to see the Pazes. But after the sprained ankle, I had to read in Rochester and still have other engagements. Next week I'm reading in Virginia, Boston College, and *Dallas*. I'm also reading at Vassar. This awful program is to make all the money possible before the end of the year—and the $—because *not* teaching makes me poorer, and I hope NEVER to have to teach again . . . A friend who'd been at the Paz lecture said it was "very dense"—but perhaps that means that *he* is. I've just glimpsed the Dallas–Ft. Worth airport on TV—the world's biggest; it looks ghastly. But Alice & a friend from Dallas are going with me and we *think* we're going to have *fun*. This card [photos of American buffalo] is from the Eastman Museum in Rochester. I loved it; lots of buttons to push, etc. Well, I've eaten armadillo at a game restaurant in Brazil, and boar, and, long ago in Nova Scotia, bear.

To James Merrill

[POSTCARD]

Duxbury, Massachusetts
November 20, 1978

Letter-writing seems to be my lost art. Well, and so is poetry-writing, I'm afraid, or almost. There is always too much to say. Well, I learned a week or so ago, as I gave lunch to the president of Bryn Mawr ("Pat" to me), that you are at home—at least in the U.S.A.—and that you are going to give the reading there next April 3rd. I'm some sort of consultant there now, and I'll be going down on April 2nd to consult and staying over to hear you read. Have you seen the Barnes Collection? If not, would you like to attempt to see it with me? I have failed to twice, but maybe "Pat" could arrange it for us. I have meant to write you for 4 months or more since I've been reading your Volume I. It is a great performance—it dazzles me, and some parts are too philosophical for my literal mind, but I keep trying. I'm at John Brinnin's house; he's at St. Thomas for a long time.

To Frani Blough Muser

437 Lewis Wharf
Boston, Massachusetts
December 12, 1978

HAVE I written you since Dallas, etc.? I can't seem to remember— how I saw Elizabeth Bell Higginbotham, and how she kept asking about you—just you—a good many times? And how I was so glad I did have the courage to look her up because she is just as nice as ever, very good-looking, and a really public-spirited fine citizen. She was on jury duty but had Alice and me and two friends who come from Dallas and they went with us—to Sunday breakfast, with English muffins she'd made herself, etc. I hadn't seen her since 1932, I think, and a man, also from Dallas, arrived, too—and I hadn't seen him since 1949. It always surprises me when people turn out so well—but then, perhaps they don't change much. What idiotic thoughts I'm having! I think it's because I've just realized it is *the twelfth of December*. Oh—she also appeared at the reading, at Southern Methodist University (called SMOO). Have you ever been to Dallas? I found it extremely depressing.

. . . I'll be mailing you a very small gift, for you and Curt, tomorrow, I hope—something I get from Seattle once in a while . . . Since you did seem to like the Brazilian bell (I must find out its real name) last year— I had plans to get you a much more picturesque and colorful instrument—to hang on a wall, maybe—but it hasn't got here yet and may never get here—in which case a friend will bring me back one next summer. Please, please don't give me anything but *History Today*. I love it dearly, but it is too expensive, I think. I'll even send for their binders —since I never remember history very well, I can easily read them over & over & over.

I gave five readings, I think, last month and I was supposed to go to

Vassar on the 28th—but we had a snowstorm here the 27th and the morning of the 28th there was a pea-soup fog, plus an icy airport, and I was afraid of flying in the 12-passenger commuter plane to Poughkeepsie. They were a bit cross but then wrote to apologize, saying they hadn't realized how bad the Boston weather was. And how bad it will be for several months to come, I hate to think.

I am sorry I didn't get to New York in October . . . I've been thinking about the Hawthorne story—or was it stories? Margaret telephoned me, to my great surprise, earlier today. The turtle has been very sick, but is recovering—he was in a coma . . .

Elizabeth (as we now call each other) lives in the *best*, I imagine, section of Dallas, and it's called "Turtle Creek" (you see how my mind is making connections in a weary way). But that city!—when I drew back the curtains at the Ramada Inn the first morning I really almost cried. Did you know that Texas is bigger than France? That the airport is the biggest in the world—bigger than *Manhattan Island*? Well, Turtle Creek was certainly pleasanter than most of the rest of it. My friends drove us to "East Texas" for overnight—the saddest little towns—but the scenery improves a little toward Louisiana; at least there were hills and pine forests. All the lakes except one—half of it in La.—are artificial . . .

To Robie Macauley

Robie Macauley, author, teacher, and editor, came to Boston from Chicago in 1977 to join Houghton Mifflin as an executive. When he learned that he was living in the same building as EB, he asked her advice about local stores, cleaning women, and other resources. The result was this famous letter.

[undated, 1978]
Wednesday afternoon

I've talked to Mary (Whelan) who comes to me at about 8 Wednesday mornings. She seems quite willing to work for you, too—but I'm not sure how much time you would want her to spend. She has been at my apt. from 8 to 1—at $3.50 an hour, that makes $18.00—(with 50¢ for carfare—I've told her she should get the "Senior C's" card, and then she can ride for 10¢ a ride—she is *quite* senior, but keeps that a secret). I'm beginning to think this is a bit too much for me; also now that I'm home at last I don't need quite that much help. So—we talked about it and she said she'd be willing to work for me for 3 hours and for you for 2—if that would be all right with you. She is not wonderful—except for her age, the 13 children, the hopeless, cranky "Joe," etc.—but she is by far the best cleaner I have had here. And she has the gift for making things *look* tidied up and dusted, at least. Well, you can tell me what you think and if you want to try her you could lend me a key and I'd escort her there next Wed.—also tell me what you want done especially.

A few addresses: My favorite drugstore is Tony Accaputo, Jr.'s—Commercial Wharf Pharmacy—the small one with an entrance across from the Rusty Scupper, also through on the next street—NOT the new, big pharmacy across Atlantic Ave. Tony—or both Tonys—are very nice and obliging—even drove off in a storm once to Mass. General to get me some drug or other— (2) You know about the Toscana Meat Market (their sausages are good). (3) Guiffre's Fish Market—on the end of Salem Street, or corner, before the expressway. They're very nice there, too. (4) Halfway down Parmenter St., on the left—between Hanover & Salem, is a nice vegetable store. On that corner of Salem St. is Polcari's Coffee Shop (not a café)—where you can get all kinds of things—teas, coffees, spices, etc.—jars of a wonderful Italian mixture of chocolate & hazelnuts, for desserts for friends with a sweet tooth, etc.— (5) Also on Salem St. —one of the Martignetti's—booze and groceries—their soda, Coke, etc., is the cheapest. (6) Drago's Bakery—1st left off Fleet St.—North St.— the round breads aren't so good, but the long ones, *flutes*, etc., are the best—but they're apt to be all sold out by four o'clock. Between 12 & 1 they also sell freshly made pizza, by the square—good, but not as good as some others. (7) Fleet Market, to the right on North St.—go in the back door—is an old wholesale house that hasn't a retail store any more—but sells to ordinary customers. It's worth going to if you need quite a lot of things—usually very fresh—for one or two items the Parmenter St. shop is quicker & more agreeable. (8) Off Hanover to the left—Prince St.—the first little bakery, on the left, is one of the best although it doesn't look it. (The one across the street is not good.) Their cannoli are good—ask them to give you the filling separate & put it in before serving. Also—they usually have *soft* macaroons. Down Hanover on the right—Trio's Ravioli Co.—make their own noodles, etc.—green noodles very good. Also Italian sauce—I sometimes buy it and just add meat or whatever— All kinds of spices there—and beans, etc.

There are two cafés on Hanover St. I sometimes go to. (1) Caffè dello Sport—the most famous; rather grim—maybe North Italian? Across the street (right side) Café Pompei—more cheerful—maybe Neapolitan?— But now cappuccino's gone up to a dollar! Also—this café makes—or did last year—the best spumoni I've ever had—the owner makes it and if he's there he'll sell you sections to take out, or a whole one. (The sons or whoever they are are apt to be disagreeable about this.) When I gave "dinner parties"—which I must take up again soon—I used to buy spumoni—or sometimes cannoli from the Prince St. shop. I think you have a liquor store that delivers so I won't go into that.

Did your friend George tell you about what they call "sticky stamps" (!)? You can buy parking tickets—to give friends who come in cars—from Pilgrim Parking, Inc.—607 Boylston St.—02116—for 25¢

each—booklets for $25.00. Then you give 1, or 2, or 3 (the most) to your friends as they leave and this saves them several $$$ for parking here. I don't recommend the florist in the building—very expensive & not very good. Harbor Greenery *was* better—but I haven't been there since they moved. Around the corner from Guiffre's—I don't know the name of that street—there's a small cheese store, nothing but—and they have very good cheeses, many kinds, fresh fonduta, etc.—much, much cheaper than in Quincy Market, say. In the warm weather Salem St. is fun on weekends—everything out in the street, no cars—fresh mint, basil, etc. —bins of olives.

Oh—Toscana sells very good olive oil—big bottles—also much cheaper than well-known brands at the markets—their eggs are good, too. (They also advertise "Custom Made First Communion Dresses." Must be Charlie's mother or wife.) That's all for today.

[P.S.] I forgot the Galeria Umberto—left side of Hanover St. just beyond the Caffè dello Sport. A big bare room—filled with schoolchildren after school—nothing but pizzas & other Italian delicacies, very cheap— calzoni, etc.—soft drinks and wine (if you ask for it), no coffee—a loud jukebox, loud arguments, but it is fun for a quick lunch. All these cafés have lots of tourists on weekends.

To Ashley Brown

January 8, 1979
. . . One thing I wanted to ask you about—and forgot—was that young man, Paulo Costa Galvão, from Rio. About his dissertation—I don't think there's too much to say about me *in Brazil*—just those poems, and a few Brazilian ones since. There's another Ph.D.-er, an American girl, who has the same idea, I think—and I've been trying to discourage her, on the whole. Her idea was to go to Brazil (with husband!) for a year, look up all my "old friends" (and enemies, I gathered, too) and so on— this is some sort of translingual (?) project—she has studied Portuguese. I think it is all very cooked-up and suspect. The few friends I had are mostly dead—or wouldn't remember me—or have actually turned against me.

Also—I really had almost no "literary" life in Brazil—and made no *impact*! I have a rather ghastly Carnival poem ["Pink Dog"] that will be in *The New Yorker* at Carnival time. It may turn out to be one of a group about Brazil.

In the Travel Section of yesterday's *N.Y. Times* there was an article, "Flannery O'Connor Country." Did you see it? I'd like to hear Flannery's comments on that. And by the way—I have a good friend here, quite young, who suffers from lupus—apparently now pretty well under control. She says that it is *not* hereditary—that Robt. Fitzgerald really did a disservice in his Introduction by saying that it is an inherited disease. There is a lupus society in Boston! I think my friend has a lot of pain—but apparently it can be slowed down, if not ever cured completely . . .

To Dorothee Bowie

February 9, 1979

. . . I have the most beautiful bouquet of "spring flowers" I have ever seen—honestly. If I had my paints with me I'd even attempt to do you a small watercolor or gouache of them—and I still may if I can get them home safely tomorrow. Daffodils, small iris, daisies (two kinds and sizes), yellow snapdragon, pink snapdragon, and eight rose-red tulips, just now opening. It is really lovely. I HATE birthdays, or mine, that is—but I have to admit I've almost enjoyed this one. Alice had seven to dinner on the 7th—another friend's birthday is then (he is exactly *forty* years younger than I am, but I tried not to think about that too much). Seamus Heaney (Irish poet and his wife now here for a term—nice and *very* Irish), Frank, Jerry, etc.—anyway, we had a very gay & lively time.

I haven't any news really. I have to go to N.Y. for that National Book Award thing—have read at least 200 books of poetry, mostly bad, and don't expect to enjoy these meetings in the slightest—however, I may be surprised.

I'll really try to find you that Japanese book that caught my fancy so much—perhaps silly to send it before you go to *China*, so I may wait— they didn't have it at my favorite bookshop near Alice's here. I've written to get copies from the Ecco Press of "*Helena Morley*" & shall send as soon as they come—they are a bit slow, I'm afraid. I find—from Blackwell's—that the price of the OED, 13 volumes, is *more* in England than here! I'll wait, anyway. I have a grim long poem in the Feb. 26th *New Yorker*—two more coming, I'm not sure when . . .

My god (as you'd say!) it's AWFUL to be so old—it seems all of a sudden, although of course it couldn't be! Thank you for the beautiful, lovely flowers—they at least are young!

To Robert Giroux

February 21, 1979

Thank you for the Flannery O'Connor Letters. I can't stop reading them—have until 2 a.m. for two nights now, to the detriment of my daily life, since an ex-student has been coming early for three days to re-arrange my "library" for me—an awful job. The letters are wonderful, aren't they, and make me feel bad even more that I never got to Milledgeville. (I think I was *afraid* of Flannery!) I get bogged down, naturally, in some of the Catholicism—and feel that perhaps some of the letters to a Dr. Spivey, etc., could have been cut—but never mind—what an admirable and amazing young lady she was! I never dreamed of all that revising and re-writing and accepting of advice that went on.

I gave a reading in Dover, New Jersey (wherever it was), last week & there seemed to be a supply of books on hand; in April at the U. of Penn.; and in early May at Vassar. Toward the end of May I'm at last going on one of those Swan's trips in Greece for two weeks—something I've wanted to do for years. I hope I'm not too decrepit to clamber around in temples and theatres.

A *Vassar Quarterly* came yesterday with a very pleasant interview with me by a young Vassar graduate—we spent an afternoon together last June. Unfortunately I didn't realize I was to appear in the same issue with another interview, with Muriel Rukeyser. Her life is one heroic saga of fighting for the underdog: going to jail, writing about silicosis, picketing alone in Korea, also thinking very deeply about POETRY & motherhood. In comparison I sound about like Billie Burke. I could at least have said I was an industrial worker for the Navy during World War II & cleaned binoculars. Oh dear.

. . . An unknown man who signs himself just "John" dropped off—in person, I gather—three quite mad letters to be forwarded to me by FSG. I have no idea who he is; the handwriting isn't that of any John I know. He seems to think I live in New York, thank goodness. They aren't threatening—to me, at least—but he seems to want to enlist my help against the "feminists" who are injuring him in some way—and does go on & on . . . As long as he doesn't know where I live, it doesn't worry me, but I am curious as to who he is. I've received mad letters before and I felt rather relieved when I read a letter or two of Flannery's telling someone about the same problem . . . I wonder if something should be done about this man? He *writes*, I gather.

To Ashley Brown

March 1, 1979
. . . Flannery's letters are wonderful and I've been completely ab-sorbed in them—but I do think (as an ignorant pagan, I suppose) that some of the Catholic essays go on a bit too long and give an impression of her being a bit too dogmatic. However, perhaps I'll get the point of the stories better for it all. You appear a good many times, of course—and you and Caroline Gordon. (I *must* read her novels—I never have—or Tate's one, either.) Once she says you're going to Africa. (I don't know about that period of your life!) . . . I wish more than ever I'd got to visit her.

. . . Well, the Lowell poem (mine) ["North Haven"]—I just made it up as I went along, as far as the occasional rhymes, or off-rhymes go. It took me almost all summer. There's another by Derek Walcott in the last *Paris Review* that I think is very good—as far as I've studied it now. Someone is printing a broadside of mine, with a drawing of North Haven at the top by Kit Barker—who visited me there last summer and did lots of sketches & watercolors. I don't care for broadsides much, but I think this one might actually be nice. (They are called something else in England, apparently—Kit wrote me this sounded like a "naval battle off North Haven.")

To return to Flannery—of course I am very curious to know who the friend "A" is—but I suppose it's none of my business & maybe she's well known as a writer by now.

Well, I meant my Carnival poem was "ghastly" as to subject matter—not such a bad poem!—["Pink Dog"] at least I hope not. I have two or three more equally "ghastly" I feel I must publish sometime.

Seamus Heaney is at Harvard this term—perhaps you know him. I'd met him here before & I like his poetry a lot. He's here with a charming wife and 3 children & has been giving readings . . . He's reading at Harvard next week. Jimmy Merrill on the 13th, too. I avoid readings whenever I can, but I did like Heaney's reading—the one I heard two years ago . . .

I made madeleines in Petrópolis a few times—and must have left my pans behind. They were very tricky as I remember. I've been making a wonderful chess pie version—perhaps you know it?—Lemon Chess Pie. I like it better than the brown sugar kind—very lemony. I'll send recipe if you want—but you probably know all about it. Eleanor Taylor certainly did!

To Dorothee Bowie

Duxbury, Massachusetts
May 7 (I think), 1979

We received your postcards from China with joy . . . I hope you kept a diary?—a very *full* diary. I've wished for many years I'd gone to Peking when I could have gone—long ago, pre-all-revolutions—even if it had meant taking a lot of *capital*—which we New Englanders never do.

Alice & I aren't going to the Galápagos!—much as I'd like to go there again—we're going to GREECE. Not for very long, though. It's a "Swan's Cruise"—an English outfit that's been running for ages—two weeks, with professors from Oxford, Archbishops, and whatnot along—giving constant lectures. Very educational and very strenuous. (I expect to die about at Patmos.) Alice took one in 1966 when she was even younger and *more* vigorous, and that almost did her in. But they are very good, everyone says. John Brinnin has done it *three* times. There are various routes and I think we have one of the best. We sail from Venice—return to Dubrovnik—where we meant to spend a day at Kotor—which just fell into the sea, or the highway to it did, because of the earthquake . . . Then back to London by air. We leave Boston the 17th—leave for Venice the 24th—return from the trip the 7th of June, visit the Barkers, and back to Boston the 10th—and on the 11th I go to Princeton for one of those honorary LL.D.'s.

I'll be mortally glad when it's the 13th, I think. (I would *never* have started these LL.D. things except that Dr. Baumann kept boasting about how many Miss Moore had so I sort of felt I had to accept. But this week I'm going for another, to Dalhousie U.—Halifax, N.S.—and for some reason this one rather pleases me—not that any of my relatives ever went there!)

July 1st—back to North Haven for 8 weeks—I can't seem to stop going there even if it's extravagant. And that's my future—the immediate past was three days at Vassar—very nice, rather to my surprise—the new president was extremely nice. Alice went with—*drove* me, I should say —in her brand-new *Honda Accord deluxe*—*bronze*. We both like it very much and it has so many gadgets you can't believe it—cassette player, a place for coins for tolls—air conditioning, and so on—but you know those clever Japanese. She saw in the paper today that there's a year's waiting list for them now, and also the price has gone up—so it's good she bought the last one in Cambridge when she did . . .

Yes—you must go to the Galápagos if you can—that and my Amazon trip were the best of my life so far . . . In the winter they take longer, so it isn't so strenuous—and you see the northern islands we didn't get to see. But—the Blue-Footed Booby!—and the Albatrosses' courting dance! I think I'll go back and be a squatter at Academy Bay—there *is* a sort of hotel there.

John Brinnin has bought a house in St. Thomas, V. I.—very famous and elaborate—although he's renting parts of it. This place is rented for the summer—I suppose he'll sell it eventually. He's coming up next weekend and we're bringing him down for two days—how I can take the time I don't know—there is so much to do to get ready for this trip—also some more shots . . . another typhoid—and one doctor said cholera, but Dr. B. said no . . .

I wish I could see your garden. I don't think I'll even have time to go to the Boston Arboretum this spring—in about a week all the lilacs will be in bloom there and it is heavenly . . .

To Dr. Anny Baumann

[POSTCARD]

London
May 22, 1979

Alice is sending you a more up-to-date picture of this hospital [St. George's], where she spent 2½ days. It was scary at first—we thought we'd have to give up the trip. It has turned out all right & it was very interesting to see an aspect of English life we'd never seen. (*Tea* for patients at 11 p.m., etc.) Alice made friends with her *eleven* wardmates, of course. For the Barkers' tomorrow & the next day off to Greece.

To Loren MacIver

[POSTCARD]

Mykonos, Greece
May 28, 1979

The island of Delos this a.m. & here this p.m.—now at sea again. Delos is superb—and Delphi & the ruins of Apollo's temple even better. But Mykonos is the Provincetown/Haight-Ashbury of the Aegean, I'm afraid. Still back streets & flowers are nice. The temperature has been just right. The trip is handled awfully well but I don't like *quite* that many English at the same time! Alice finds the Mykonos pelican "icky" but I like it.

To James Merrill

[POSTCARD]

S.S. *Orpheus*
June 3, 1979

Approaching Santorini (with dread—but I think I'll stay at ocean level, since mules give me asthma & my knees have stopped working— 588 steps—there goes a dream of my life). If I were you I think I'd live on the top of Patmos—or in Thassos, which I loved too, even if there was a cloudburst & everyone almost drowned. Knossos this a.m.—the museum wonderful when one can see through the mob & really hear our really wonderful Greek guide. It's a curse not to be tall.

To Dr. Anny Baumann

[POSTCARD]

Isle of Kos, Greece
June 4, 1979

This [photo] is the passageway in the hospital, dedicated to Asclepius on the isle of Kos, where the patients walked back to their dormitories. They were given a little *opium* & walked through here to the sound of running water & then were supposed to sleep a lot & to have helpful *dreams.* It all sounds very pleasant. There were mud baths too for arthritis. Everything is going well & we're having a wonderful trip.

To Ashley Brown

> 437 Lewis Wharf
> Boston, Massachusetts
> June 25, 1979

Infância was one of the first books I struggled through my first year or two in Brazil. I still think it's a marvelous book and can't understand why you couldn't (as I think you told me) get it published in the U.S.A. In fact, although I'd just returned from my trip to Greece, I couldn't stop reading it over again, much too late that first night—with jet lag. Your introduction is very nice. You don't seem to mention much about his imprisonment. Another thing I read, very early on in Brazil, were his "Prison" volumes—all four of them—awfully good, I think. I've gone over what I have here. Oddly, I don't have *Infância*—but I do have *Angústia* and almost everything else—mostly lovingly dedicated to Lota.

Perhaps I told you that once Octavio de Souza & his wife (our summer neighbors and awfully good friends) brought him to call on us? He was very sick then. Although we couldn't talk much—and I was afraid to say a word in Portuguese—he was awfully nice. I liked him a lot, I remember . . .

I'm about to go to North Haven, Maine, for July & August. I just got back 10 days ago from my Swan's trip to Greece. It was marvelous & I'd like to take another, a slightly different set of islands, next year, but I'll never be able to afford to . . .

To Robert Giroux

> June 30, 1979

I have lived on handouts for so long that I hesitate to send you this [announcement of National Endowment for the Arts $15,000 fellowships to "individuals who have made an extraordinary contribution to American literature over a lifetime of creative work"]. However, I hope you'll be willing to recommend me. I'm afraid I live beyond my means in Massachusetts & should probably move to Utah or Florida—but I don't want to! I'll be extremely grateful if you'll recommend me. I've also asked Helen Vendler, who was very nice about it.

I *do* have a job next term teaching once a week at M.I.T. I can't imagine what that poetry course will be like! Tomorrow I'm going to Maine—North Haven island—and I only hope I'll get a lot of work done there . . .

North Haven, Maine
July 20, 1979

Thank you very much for writing that recommendation for me. Also for your other suggestion. I rather feel I've had my share—but I also feel the nursing home creeping on. [EB was not awarded the fellowship.]

It is beautiful here, as beautiful as ever, and hard to work, what with one aspect of Nature or another. We spend a lot of time looking things up in various Peterson Guides, etc.

I'd be delighted to have you visit for a weekend if you ever wanted to. It *is* a long way off from New York, but one can shuttle to Boston and then take Downeast airlines to Rockland (about 45 minutes, I think) & from there the ferry comes to North Haven three times a day—an hour and fifteen minutes, if the weather is good. Let me know. It is usually cool & the view is magnificent.

To Harold Leeds

August 15, 1979
Wednesday morning

We are having our annual mowing, to keep down the spruce trees, and one huge tractor is being run by an 80-year-old man whose name I forget and the other by Dick Bloom, the crabmeat winner. I hurried out early to keep them from mowing the large upland cranberry patch—they mowed around me as I picked. Now I'm making quite a batch of lingonberry sauce.

The "cocktail" wasn't bad. "Pinky" was actually quite pleasant. It seems they have dammed up a brook on their estate, making a rather big pool—at the edge of the bay—and now we've been invited to go swimming. This is pretty good—it only took six summers (Emily said any social contacts would take twelve). But it's much too cold, and threatening to rain again—after only one of the typical, gorgeous, photogenic sunsets you never saw . . .

Thank you for the wonderful bowls . . . We feel bad about leaving already—and are packing a lot of heavy things for our friend Frank, who comes tomorrow . . . Then Aileen Ward for two days—and then a very bright but slightly mad young lady of 17 who just got into Yale. We are fond of her mother (Polish—*very* Polish) . . .

Down to the mailbox before it pours again . . .

To Frani Blough Muser

Lewis Wharf, Boston
August 30, 1979

The only thing I can think of to say is "I don't know where the summer's gone to." At least I've kept *meaning* to write you, but I didn't write anything except the most necessary business replies. I think one reason for the general indolence & forgetfulness was that it was the foggiest summer ever on record. (One man said, "No, '63 was a little worse.") Such fogginess seems to make one sleepy, lazy, and extra-remote.

Last Sunday we had a very different hymn-singing, at Barbara Thatcher's (I don't think you met them—Bryn Mawr trustee, etc.—her cousin married an Episcopalian minister), over for church. We sang a lot of nice hymns, but there weren't enough of us and either the piano was tuned an octave too high—or I can't get any higher than middle C any more. With all the fog & rain, there were hundreds of chanterelles [mushrooms]—but I've decided they aren't as good as other kinds. Back here last night; to Memphremagog tomorrow, and back for good (& M.I.T.) Tuesday. I hope you'll forgive my silence & let me hear from you soon. I *was* tired after the Swan's trip—but it certainly was worth it. Oh, I read *When the Tree Sings* by Stratis Haviaras. I thought it was awfully good . . .

To Her Poetry Students

EB had classes scheduled at M.I.T. for September 30 and October 1, 1979, which she was unable to attend because of illness. She wrote out the following in her own hand in block capitals, and it was posted on the classroom door. She could not keep her promise to return on October 7; she died in her apartment at Lewis Wharf on October 6, 1979.

MISS BISHOP IS IN [HOSPITAL] & IS
VERY SORRY SHE WILL BE UNABLE TO MEET
HER CLASSES THIS WEEK. SHE *WILL* MEET THEM
ON OCTOBER 7TH AND 8TH.

1. WILL ENGLISH 285 PLEASE CONTINUE STUDYING
ALL THE [THEODORE] ROETHKE POEMS IN THE
NORTON ANTHOLOGY.

2. THE LIST OF STUDENTS FOR ENGLISH 582
WILL BE POSTED HERE BY NOON ON OCTOBER 7TH.
IN THE MEANTIME, PLEASE TRY TO FINISH A
BALLAD (AT LEAST 8 STANZAS). IT CAN RHYME
A-B-C-B OR A-B-A-B.

To John Frederick Nims

Poet John Frederick Nims, the editor of Poetry *magazine, had written EB about a few footnotes to her poems that he wanted to use in the college textbook he was editing*, The Harper Anthology of Poetry, *covering English verse from medieval times to the present. On the day she died, EB typed out and mailed this friendly letter. Her closing word, "Affectionately," is proof that her goodwill and good manners persisted to the end.*

437 Lewis Wharf
Boston, Massachusetts
October 6, 1979

. . . I'm going to take issue with you—rather violently—about the idea of footnotes. With one or two exceptions (I'll mention them later) I don't think there should be ANY footnotes. You say the book is for college students, and I think anyone who gets as far as college should be able to use a dictionary. If a poem catches a student's interest at all, he or she should damned well be able to look up an unfamiliar word in the dictionary. (I know they don't—or most of them don't—but they should be made to, somehow. The [historically] earlier poems you are using of course may require some help—but mine certainly don't!) "Isinglass" is in the dictionary; so is "gunnel" (see "gunwale"); so is "thwarts" [these three words occur in "The Fish"].

One of my few exceptions is the ESSO-Exxon note to "Filling Station," because I'm not sure how long ago now that happened, but a good many years. Also, I'd let students figure out—in fact, I TELL them [in the poem]—the cans are arranged to say so-so-so, etc., so I don't think *that* has to be explained. However—most of them might well not know that so-so-so was—perhaps still is in some places—the phrase people use to calm and soothe horses. All flower names can be looked up, certainly—some students even SEE flowers still, although I know only too well that TV has weakened the sense of reality so that very few students see anything the way it is in real life.

In "The Moose" I'd prefer to have you use just the first sentence of the note—on page 1226. (!) I don't think page 1227 needs any notes at all, nor does 1228. Please leave all that out! (A Japanese anthology quoted another poem in which I mentioned the Port of Santos—and that footnote said, "Port—a dark red wine." Also—the Norton Anthology is full of such stupid remarks—they locate St. John's [Newfoundland] in the Caribbean somewhere, and so on & so on.) "Macadam" is in the dictionary. And—a lot of the poem is about "childhood recollections"—I almost say it in so many words. If they can't figure that out, they shouldn't be in college—THERE!

You can see what a nasty teacher I must be—but I do think students get lazier and lazier & expect to have everything done *for* them. (When I suggest buying a small paperback, almost the whole class whines, "Where can I find it?") My best example of this sort of thing is what one rather bright Harvard honors student told me. She told her roommate or a friend—who had obviously taken my verse-writing course—that she was doing her paper with me, and the friend said, "Oh don't work with *her*! It's awful! She wants you to look words up in the dictionary! It isn't *creative* at all!" In other words, it is better *not* to know what you're writing or reading. Perhaps my class at M.I.T. has embittered me—but so did N.Y.U. and some of the Harvard classes—although there have been good students and a few wonderful ones from time to time. But they mostly seem to think that poetry—to read or to write—is a snap—one just has to *feel*—and not for very long, either. Well, I could go on and on—but I won't! Two or three years ago I was talking away about "The Quaker Graveyard" and when I asked a question the whole class responded in chorus with what I discovered (I was using my own book) were the footnotes from the Norton anthology —some right, in that case, but again some wrong. We finally all got to laughing—but that was an unusually bright class.

Of course I am writing this just about my own inclusions—and "The Moose" may well be too long. And of course there are many [historically] early poems I can see the necessity for notes for. If "The Moose" is too long, I'd suggest another from *Geography III*—any you like. I do hope I haven't offended you now—but I think the teaching of literature now is deplorable—and if you can get students to *reading*, you will have done a noble work. Affectionately . . .

NOTES AND ACKNOWLEDGMENTS

INDEX

Notes and Acknowledgments

After David Kalstone's death in 1986, Alice Methfessel, the executor of Elizabeth Bishop's estate, asked me to take on the job of editing the poet's letters, a task for which David had contracted a few years earlier. I agreed to do this, even after I discovered that almost the only letters of Elizabeth's that David had been able to collect were those to Marianne Moore and Robert Lowell, required for his marvelous study of Elizabeth's poetic development, published posthumously as *Becoming a Poet*. When I started to collect the rest of Elizabeth's correspondence, I was astonished to find how much there was and how wide-ranging her letter writing had been. I finally had more than three thousand letters from which to make a selection. Who knows how many other letters still repose in unknown hands? Some of them may yet turn up, unlike her letters to Lota, almost all of which were burned, shockingly enough, even though, as Elizabeth wrote, "Lota had carefully saved [them] so that I could use them," in the unfinished book about Brazil.

As edited, this book contains 541 letters written to more than fifty correspondents. Elizabeth was such a good letter writer and there were so many letters to choose from that the job of selection was far from easy. My editorial rationale had three aspects: readability, intrinsic interest, and as complete a picture of Elizabeth's life and work as a single volume could provide. It was obvious that the selection would have to be substantial, like the edition of Flannery O'Connor's letters, *The Habit of Being*, edited by Sally Fitzgerald, which Elizabeth admired. To achieve this, and in order to save space, I made several editorial decisions: (a) to omit all salutations and closings, with only a few exceptions (like her first letter addressing Miss Moore as "Marianne," or the closing of her last letter, which was mistakenly described in one biography as a "business letter"); (b) to omit addresses in any sequence of two or more letters written from the same place, except in the opening letter; (c) to indicate my editorial interpolations by putting them in brackets, so that all words in the main texts that are in parentheses are EB's; (d) to correct errors (unless intentional) in spelling, titles, attributions, dates, or other lapses of memory or diction. Elizabeth was aware that her handwriting was often illegible and required a magnifying glass to decipher it; only one or two words, as I recall, proved in the end to be impenetrable. Her mother's family name was spelled both Bulmer and Boomer, but, as is evident from her dedication of "The Moose" and her letters, Elizabeth always used Bulmer and I follow her usage.

This is not a facsimile edition; it is an edited selection, and the three dots of elision indicate the deletion of words, sentences, and paragraphs, to avoid an excess of repetitions—or of occasional *longueurs*. She deserves a multivolume edition of all her letters and I hope it may be available some day.

I have had the generous help of many of Elizabeth's friends, starting with Frani Blough Muser, who provided me with copies of all the letters Elizabeth wrote her, beginning in 1928, when they were at the Walnut Hill School, and ending with the poet's death. Painter Loren MacIver, whom I had the pleasure of meeting and interviewing with Cynthia Krupat on several occasions in her studio on Perry Street, provided me with copies of Elizabeth's letters and with little-known details of their lifelong friendship. Harold Leeds, who had met Elizabeth through his friend Louise Crane, was helpful in many important ways, especially with an accurate account of Lota's suicide. I am grateful to Pearl Kazin Bell and to Robert Fizdale for straightening me out on details of the Brazilian years at Rio, Samambaia, and Ouro Prêto.

Among others to whom I owe thanks for letters—not all of which I was able to use—are Keith Althaus, Dorothee Taylor Bowie, Emanuel Brasil, Edward Burns, Nora Riley Fitch, Dana Gioia, William Goodman, Daniel Halpern, Ivar Ivask, Barbara Chesney Kennedy, David Lehman, William Logan, Sandra McPherson, Agnes Mongan, Charles North, Gloria Oden, Chester Page, Ned Rorem, Charlotte and Charles Russell, William Jay Smith, Willard Spiegelman, David Staines, Donald E. Stanford, Hilgard O'Reilly Sternberg, May Swenson, Tamara A. Turner, Wesley Wehr, and Robert A. Wilson.

For special help while working on this book, I am grateful to William Alfred, Michael Anderson, Ilse Barker, Frank Bidart, Jane Bobko, John Malcolm Brinnin, Lisa Browar, Ashley Brown, Catharine Carver, Ross Claiborne, Paul Elie, Jori Finkel, Harry Ford, Kerry Fried, Jonathan Galassi, Carmen Gomezplata, Elizabeth Hardwick, Michael Hathaway, Dorris Janowitz, Alfred Kazin, Judy Klein, James Laughlin, Robie Macauley, Candace MacMahon, J. D. McClatchy, Hugh James McKenna, Rollie McKenna, James Merrill, Leonard Millberg, Herbert Mitgang, John Frederick Nims, Octavio and Marie Jo Paz, Alice Quinn, Claudia Rattazzi, Selden Rodman, Lloyd Schwartz, Eileen Simpson, Joseph and U. T. Summers, Peter and Eleanor Taylor, Helen Vendler, Arthur Wang, and Lynn Warshow.

The following curators and librarians provided copies of Bishop letters and other assistance for which I am grateful: John Lancaster, Amherst College Library; Leo Dolenski, Bryn Mawr College Library; Timothy Murray, University of Delaware Library; Rodney Dennis, Curator of Manuscripts, and Melanie Wisner, Houghton Library, Harvard University; Francis O. Matson, Berg Collection, New York Public Library; Walter Litz and Patricia Marks, Princeton University Library; Leslie Morris, Rosenbach Museum and Library; Kathleen Manwaring, George Arents Research Library, Syracuse University; Nancy S. MacKechnie, Curator of Rare Books and Manuscripts, Vassar College Library; Holly Hall, Rare Books Division, and Kevin Ray, Curator of Manuscripts, Washington University at St. Louis.

Finally I want to thank Alice Methfessel for asking me to edit Elizabeth Bishop's letters and for her generous help at every point; Charles Phillips Reilly for unswerving support at difficult junctures; and Cynthia Krupat, who designed this book and is very much *in* it, for her sensitive and creative assistance from the beginning.

R. G.

Index

Klee, Paul, 96, 97, 291, 442, 521

Klein, Melanie, 371, 411, 451, 452; *Envy and Gratitude*, 371

Knopf, Alfred A., 460

Knopf (publisher), 86, 283

Koch, Karl, 577–78

Kraft, Victor, 226, 227, 250

Kray, Betty, 494, 538, 554

Krupat, Cynthia (Muser), 99, 441, 495, 502, 533, 552, 588, 605, 606, 610, 615

Kunitz, Stanley, 363, 366

"Labors of Hannibal, The," 58

Lacerda, Carlos, 242, 251, 288, 299, 309–10, 311, 327, 359, 373, 390–91, 392, 394, 398, 401, 410, 415, 417, 421, 422, 425, 426, 428, 430, 438, 446, 459, 493

La Fontaine, Jean de, 158, 160, 181, 207, 245, 297, 300

La Guardia, Fiorello, 424

Lahey, Gerald F., 20

Larcom, Lucy, 407, 409; *A New England Girlhood*, 407

Larkin, Philip, 363, 406

Lattimore, Emily, 615

Lattimore, Owen, 615

Laubers, Mr./Mrs., 90

Laughlin, James, 59, 80, 86, 88, 98, 101, 110, 336; and "Peonies of Sympathy," 59

Lautrec, *see* Toulouse-Lautrec, Henri de

Lawrence, D. H., 16, 37, 150, 434, 522; *Lady Chatterley's Lover*, 522

Leão, Magú, 472, 488, 491, 506; EB letters to, 469

Leão, Rosinha, 241, 291, 322, 331, 354, 368, 380, 472, 488, 506; EB letters to, 469

Leavis, F. R., 225

Lee, Vernon, 562

Leeds, Harold, 465, 467, 471, 481; EB letters to, 404–5, 464–65, 481–82, 483–84, 497, 560–61, 636

Léger, Alexis, *see* Perse, St.-John

Le Monde, 425

"Letter to Two Friends," 348

Levertov, Denise, 505

Levin, Harry, 384

Lewis, John L., 89

Lewis Wharf, 577–78, 579, 581, 585, 587, 589, 601; EB letters from, 587–89, 592–96, 599–601, 607–13, 618–24, 625, 626–32, 635, 636–39

Library of Congress, 147, 175, 180, 186, 187, 281, 297, 300, 325; Dylan Thomas recordings, 199, 200, 281; EB at, 180, 181, 185, 188, 193, 194–205, 206, 209, 281, 325; Robert Frost recordings, 297

Liebling, A. J., 373

Life and Letters Today, 35, 38, 41, 46, 47, 70*n*

Life magazine, 74–75, 174, 399, 400, 401, 402, 403

"Life of the Hurricane, The," 128

Lindsay, John, 617

Lindsey family, 83, 84, 121

Listener, The, 249

Literary Society, 407

Littlefield, Lester, 113, 117, 497–98

Living Theatre, The, 540, 545

Livy, 165

Lockwood, Miss (teacher), 18

Logue, Christopher, 406

London Review, 291

London *Times, The*, 395, 607

Longworth, Alice Roosevelt, 37, 196

Longworth, Nicholas, 37

Loofy, Dr. Laf, 353

Looker, Miss, 200

Lorca, Federico García, 332

"Love Poems," 270; *see also* "Four Poems"

Lowell, Caroline, *see* Blackwood, Lady Caroline

Lowell, Elizabeth Hardwick, *see* Hardwick, Elizabeth

Lowell, Harriet, 345, 363, 366, 388, 394, 396, 406, 412, 479, 564

Lowell, James Russell, 125, 142, 256

Lowell, Robert (Cal), 146, 164, 344–45, 515; *Benito Cereno*, 432; "Calling," 515; and Carley Dawson, 156, 158, 164, 165, 179; "Castine, Maine," 348, 515; "Commander Lowell," 350, 351; on cover of *Time*, 464; "David and Bathsheba in the Public Garden," 408–9; *The Day*, 606; description of, 168, 175, 241, 277, 432, 480, 606; *The Dolphin*, 561, 563; "The Drinker," 386; EB friendship with, 167, 173, 174, 177, 178, 187, 191–92, 206, 269, 284, 326, 363, 391, 392, 400, 409, 415, 433, 435, 459, 462, 476–77, 481, 500, 514, 518, 527, 548, 554, 571, 574, 576, 581, 586, 624, 631–32; EB letters to, 146–48, 151–55, 159–63, 166, 168–69, 170–72, 180–83, 193, 196–98, 202–5, 212–13, 218–19, 221–23, 224–26, 318–20, 322–24, 332–34, 339–40, 346–53, 361–63, 364–67, 370–72, 381–85, 386–88, 394–96, 405–9, 416–18, 420–22, 439–40, 479–80, 515–17, 518–19, 561–65, 592–93; and EB's "In the Village," 408, 431; "Falling Asleep over the Aeneid," 151–52, 153; "The Fat Man in the Mirror," 147; "For Elizabeth Bishop" sonnets, 348, 515, 521; *For the Union Dead*, 408; and Frank Bidart, 545, 556; health of, 358, 411–12, 458, 532, 533, 607, 611; *Imitations*, 394; "Jonathan Edwards in Western Massachusetts," 409; letter to EB, 344–46; *Life Studies*, 349, 364, 369, 562; *Lord Weary's Castle*, 408; and Mary McCarthy, 423, 496, 614, 616; memorials to, 620, 624, 631–32; "The Mills of the Kavanaughs," 161–62, 170, 212, 213; *The Mills of the Kavanaughs*, 218; "Mother Marie Therese," 171, 219, 226; "My Last Afternoon with Uncle Devereux Winslow," 350; *Near the Ocean*, 459; "91 Revere Street," 332, 340; *Notebook*, 515, 561; "The Old Flame," 409; *The Old Glory*, 439; *Phaedra*, 394, 412, 607;

"The Quaker Graveyard in Nantucket," 147, 639; and Randall Jarrell, 201, 312, 313, 434; recordings by, 149; reviews *North & South*, 146 and *n*; "Sailing Home from Rapallo," 350; Santayana piece, 240; "The Scream," 408; "Skunk Hour," 348, 350; in South America, 411–12; "Terminal Days at Beverly Farms," 350; "Vocation," 515; "Water," 408, 515

Lowell, Sheridan, 606

Lucan, 371

Luce, Clare Boothe, 371

Lynes, George Platt, 31, 32, 33, 527

MacArthur Fellowship, 215

McBride, Katherine E.: EB letters to, 217–18, 223–24, 238–39, 254

McCarthy, Sen. Eugene, 496, 516, 518

McCarthy, Senator Joseph, 298, 300*n*

McCarthy, Mary, 37, 68, 69, 345, 384, 496, 614 and *n*, 616; and *Con Spirito*, 8; EB letters to, 614–15; EB's early friendship with, 6, 7, 9, 14, 15, 21, 24, 25, 26, 28, 29, 31; and Edmund Wilson, 98, 120; *The Group*, 289, 320, 416, 419, 423, 428, 614 and *n*; and James West, 405, 416, 423; views of, 239, 268, 289, 320, 323, 375, 416, 419, 423, 428, 476–77, 548, 562

Macaulay, Thomas, 151, 192

Macauley, Anne, 387

Macauley, Robie, 387, 388; EB letters to, 627–29

MacClachlan, Muir, 582

McCullers, Carson, 242, 271

McCurdy, Miss (teacher), 15

Macdonald, Dwight, 408, 415

Macedo Soares, Maria Carlota Costellat de (Lota), 235, 240, 243, 252, 263, 266, 268, 274, 278, 279, 280, 281, 283, 290, 292, 293, 311, 313, 314, 317, 318, 325, 328, 340, 341, 348, 357, 364, 365, 372, 380, 382, 383, 387, 389, 390, 414; aftermath of suicide, 482–83, 488–93, 509; and Brazilian politics, 271, 288–89, 299, 391, 426, 427, 438; early friendship with EB, 226, 231, 233; EB describes illness to Dr. Baumann, 445–46, 448–53, 456–59; EB letters to, 455–56; EB relationship with, 238, 239, 249, 256, 258, 259, 261–62, 275–76, 277, 280, 345, 346, 368, 388, 435–36, 439, 453, 461–62, 465, 475, 491, 493, 516, 551; and EB's Seattle trip, 440, 441, 444, 457, 460, 472; family of, 260, 275, 287, 289, 292, 315, 321, 326, 331, 346, 354, 355, 356, 358, 371, 373, 384, 393, 482, 488, 492; friendship with Carlos Lacerda, 242, 373, 392; friendship with Gold and Fizdale, 262, 263, 367, 551, 572; friends of, 271, 275–76, 291–92, 323, 488, 491, 526; health of, 419–21, 453, 454, 456, 457, 459, 462, 464, 465–66, 475, 491, 492–93; as homebuilder, 234, 241, 244, 246, 252–53, 256, 257, 259, 264–65, 267, 272, 282, 286, 290, 305, 316, 359, 377, 391; as landowner, 234, 236, 264, 317, 365–66, 392; and Marianne Moore, 333, 363, 447; and Mary Morse, 226, 472, 476, 488, 489–90, 526; park project, 392, 393, 394–95, 396–97, 398, 400, 404, 410, 413–14, 415, 417, 419–20, 422, 424, 426, 429, 430, 432, 436, 438, 440, 445, 452, 472; personality of, 258, 278, 330–31, 384, 428, 437; suicide of, 467–74; in *Time* magazine, 430; travel abroad, 277, 284, 288, 332, 335, 342, 343, 349, 354, 374, 378, 380, 391, 392, 399, 400, 401, 425–26, 438, 448, 454, 461–62, 516; and U.S., 337, 339, 340, 344, 348, 592

MacGrath, Joe, 566

MacIver, Loren, 77, 78, 79, 80, 81, 83, 85, 90, 112, 117, 122, 136, 150, 169, 173, 175, 178, 181, 238, 253, 258, 294, 305, 338, 354, 358, 368, 392, 401, 436, 464, 465, 466, 467, 475, 488, 505, 560; *Acropolis* (painting), 338; EB letters to, 157, 179, 184–85, 186–93, 194, 195–96, 200–1, 207–8, 209–10, 214–15, 232–33, 255, 304, 306, 309–10, 402, 415–16, 423–24, 443, 535, 538–39, 539–40, 565–66, 581–82, 582–83, 586–87, 610–11, 613, 622, 634; *Floorscape* (painting), 561; *Hellenic Landscape* (painting), 338; *Rue Mouffetard* (painting), 338; *The Waters* (painting), 561

Mack, Gerstle, 278

McKenna, Rollie, 329, 574; EB letters to, 329

MacLaughlin, Mr./Mrs., 140

MacLeish, Archibald, 201, 205; *Poetry and Opinion*, 205

MacLeod, Mr., 147

MacMahon, Candace W.: *Elizabeth Bishop: A Bibliography*, 601, 623

Macmillan, H. F.: *Tropical Gardening and Planting*, 117, 120

Macmillan (publisher), 104, 160

MacNeice, Louis, 73, 319, 436

Macpherson, Winifred Ellerman (Bryher), 61, 63, 70

Magazine, The, 16

Mailer, Norman, 562

Mallarmé, Stéphane, 94, 97, 213

"Man-Moth, The," 477

Mann, Thomas, 350

Mansfield, Katherine, 68

"Manuelzinho," 315, 320, 321, 330, 479

Marchand: *Memoirs of Napoleon*, 324

Marlowe, Christopher: *The Jew of Malta*, 7

Marlowe, Sylvia, 447, 460

Marshall, Margaret, 31, 37, 220–21, 284

Massachusetts Institute of Technology: EB teaches at, 635, 637, 639

Mather, Cotton, 10, 16

Maugham, W. Somerset, 350

Mazzaro, Jerome: EB letters to, 621

Meigs, Mary, 222

Melo Neto, João Cabral de, 422, 494, 554, 558

Melville, Herman: *Moby Dick*, 419

"Memories of Uncle Neddy," 406; *see also*
"Uncle Artie"
Mercer, Mabel, 588
Mercury, The, 24
Meredith, George, 6*n*; *Diana of the Crossways*, 6
Merlin, Frank, 21, 26
Merrill, James, 248, 302, 329, 495, 530,
572, 577, 580, 632; "About the Phoenix," 303; "Banks of a Stream Where
Creatures Bathe," 567; *The Book of
Ephraim*, 597, 613; *Braving the Elements*, 567; "The Cruise," 303; EB
compares with Henry James, 302–3; EB
letters to, 302–4, 444–45, 511–12,
520–22, 530–32, 541–44, 566–67,
573–74, 575–76, 582, 583, 584–85,
594–95, 596–97, 612–13, 616–17,
625–26, 634; "Flying from Byzantium,"
532; "The Greenhouse," 302; "A Narrow Escape," 302; *Nights and Days*,
444; *Short Stories*, 302–3, 304;
"16.ix.65," 532; "Strato in Plaster,"
567; "To My Greek," 532; "The Wintering Weeds," 303
Merrill grant, 544
Merton, Thomas, 171
Merwin, W. S., 494
Methfessel, Alice: EB designates as literary co-executor, 545; EB relationship
with, 542, 543, 544, 556, 557, 560,
567, 572, 576, 583, 590, 591, 594, 596,
597, 604, 613, 615, 617, 618, 622, 623,
624; as Kirkland House secretary, 536,
537, 538–39; travels with EB, 547, 570,
571, 598, 604, 608, 632, 633, 634
Mexico, 107–12, 597–98
Miles, Josephine, 502, 505, 547
Millay, Edna St. Vincent, 272, 408
Miller, Henry, 175, 336
Miller, Margaret, 7, 8, 9, 14, 15, 21, 23,
24, 25, 26, 27, 29, 30, 31, 34, 35, 38,
43, 44, 65, 70, 72, 79, 92, 101, 110,
117, 129, 141, 173, 186, 187, 189, 222,
354, 464, 480, 549, 587, 609, 610, 614*n*,

616; and car accident, 60–61, 62, 64;
EB letters to, 74–76
Miller, Mrs., 14, 24, 25, 28, 29, 31, 61,
64, 71, 76
Milton, John, 175, 407, 408
Minahan, Miss, 270
Mindlin, Henrique: *Modern Architecture in
Brazil*, 311
Mink, Morry, 505
"Miracle for Breakfast, A," 54, 55, 57, 58,
59, 61, 477
Miró, Joan, 90
M.I.T., *see* Massachusetts Institute of
Technology
Mitchell, Margaret: *Gone with the Wind*,
263
Mizener, Arthur, 143; EB letters to, 143–
44; reviews *North & South*, 144*n*
MLA convention, 610
Modern Architecture in Brazil, 311
Mongan, Agnes, 297, 298, 392
Monroe (Harriet) Award, 123, 124
Montale, Eugenio, 395, 396
Monteverdi, Claudio, 347
Moore, Henry, 285
Moore, Janet, 165, 169
Moore, Marianne, 20, 76, 146, 181, 315,
378, 460, 461, 579, 580, 596, 633;
"Anna Pavlova," 310; "Apparition of
Splendor," 334; and baseball, 499, 582;
birthday commemoration, 616, 617;
"Camellia Sabina," 20; Casa Mariana,
508, 521; "Crossing Brooklyn Bridge at
Twilight," 466; death of, 558, 559, 560;
description of, 17, 21, 277, 333, 347,
361, 365, 416, 477, 563; EB friendship
with, 22, 23, 28, 158, 160, 166, 168,
169–70, 174, 175, 182, 187, 196, 205,
224, 256, 263, 325, 328, 338, 348, 431,
462, 478, 503, 504, 505, 510, 514, 533,
535; EB letters to, 20–21, 27, 29–30,
31–33, 33–34, 38–39, 40–43, 44–49,
53–55, 56–59, 60–65, 66–68, 69–71,
72–74, 76–81, 85–86, 87–90, 91–93,
94–97, 100–6, 107–12, 112–20, 121–

22, 123–24, 126–27, 128–29, 139–41,
206–7, 235–38, 244–45, 256–57,
279–82, 296–98, 299–300, 304–6,
310–11, 334–35, 353–54, 356–57,
357–59, 392–93, 409–10, 429, 447–48,
466, 475–76, 499–500, 507–8, 527–28,
595; and EB poetry, 55, 122, 135; EB
recollections of, 565, 579, 585, 586, 602;
EB to review poems of, 223, 225; "Elephants," 117, 119–20; in *Family Circle*,
499; "Four Quartz Crystal Clocks," 89,
104; "The Frigate Pelican," 54; "A
Glass-Ribbed Nest," 89–90, 109; health
of, 370, 372, 402, 498; "He 'Digesteth
Harde Yron,' " 102; "In Distrust of
Merits," 113, 128; introduces EB in
Trial Balances, 29, 58; *Like a Bulwark*,
354; "Logic and 'The Magic Flute,' "
334, 335; and Lota, 333, 363, 447;
"Marriage," 580, 625; "The Mind Is an
Enchanting Thing," 119, 120; *Nevertheless*, 119, 124; in *The New Yorker*, 364,
374; "The Pangolin," 104; *The Pangolin
and Other Verse*, 41, 42; "The Paper
Nautilus," 89–90; "Pigeons," 38; "The
Plumet Basilisk," 63n; *Predilections*,
310; "Propriety," 121; reviews "*Helena
Morley*," 376; reviews *North & South*,
142; "Spenser's Ireland," 101; "The
Sycamore," 334; in *Tiger's Eye*, 153;
view of Summers's *George Herbert*,
300–1; "Virginia Britannia," 38; *What
Are Years*, 101, 104; "What Are Years?,"
89; "The Wood-Weasel," 120
Moore, Merrill, 76
Moore, Mrs., 17, 22, 27, 33, 47, 77, 80,
108, 119, 127, 139, 447
"Moose, The," 320, 334, 568, 570, 572,
573, 638, 639
Moraes, Vinícius de, 455, 488, 491, 494,
523, 558; *Black Orpheus*, 491; "Sonnet
of Intimacy," 517
Moravia, Alberto, 387
Morgan (Pierpont) Library, 588, 590,
591

Morison, Samuel Eliot, 203
"Morley, Helena," 270, 314, 316, 342,
348, 357–58; *see also The Diary of "Helena Morley"*
Mormons, 220–21
Morse, Mary, 252, 255, 263, 267, 274,
278–79, 330, 379, 381, 397, 420, 421,
456; after Lota's death, 472, 476, 483,
488, 489–90, 526; description of, 263,
278; and EB, 292, 368, 472, 476, 483,
488, 489–90, 526; and Lota, 226, 233,
239, 240, 242, 380, 457; trip to U.S.,
374, 375, 377, 378
Moss, Howard, 187, 294, 335, 336, 589,
605; EB letters to, 335–36, 357, 363–
64, 373–75, 385–86; "The Feast," 386;
The Poet's Story, 335, 589; "A Song
Struck from the Records," 385; "Tourists," 385; *The Toy Fair*, 294
Mott, Dr. Ken, 585
Moulton, Dr., 340
Moulton de Hegermann-Lindencrone, Lillian, 446; *In the Courts of Memory*, 446;
The Sunny Side of the Diplomatic Life,
446
"Mountain, The," 256
movies and plays: *Baboons*, 30, 31; *Black
Orpheus*, 374, 381, 382, 491; *Blow-Up*,
467; *Bonnie and Clyde*, 554; *Chloe in
the Afternoon*, 553; *A Clockwork Orange*,
554; *The Cocktail Party*, 203; *The Dog
Beneath the Skin*, 41, 42; *8½*, 421;
Faustus, 57; *Horse Eats Hat*, 45; *I Love
You, Alice B. Toklas!*, 500; *Jeux Interdits*,
287; *King Solomon's Mines*, 212; *The
Last Picture Show*, 554; *The Life of a
Cat*, 597; *The Mating of Millie*, 163; *A
Member of the Wedding*, 203; *Moulin
Rouge*, 278; *Murder in the Cathedral*,
41–42; *My Uncle Antoine*, 582; *Porgy
and Bess*, 306; *Potemkin*, 42; *Quo Vadis*,
287; *Rashomon*, 267; *Romeo and Juliet*,
31; *Son of Mongolia*, 48; *Women in
Fury*, 436
"*Mrs. Beeton's*" cookbook, 389

Mumford, Lewis, 415, 424; *The Condition of Man*, 376
Murray, Gilbert, 10, 15
Muser, Curt, 3, 84, 85, 320, 496, 539, 541, 588, 594, 626
Muser, Cynthia, *see* Krupat, Cynthia (Muser)
Muser, Frani Blough, 8, 16, 78, 320, 419, 539, 614; EB letters to, 3–8, 9, 14–15, 16–18, 21–22, 23–24, 25–26, 28–29, 30–31, 33, 34–38, 39–40, 43–44, 65–66, 68–69, 71–72, 74–76, 84–85, 86–87, 93–94, 99, 423, 427–29, 440–41, 487, 495–97, 501–3, 512–14, 532–34, 540–41, 548, 551–53, 569–70, 587–89, 590–91, 593–94, 597–99, 601, 604–5, 607–8, 609–10, 615–16, 625–26, 626–27, 636–37; "Experiment in Objectivity," 15; "Nightmare," 594
Muser, George, 496, 501
Museum of Fine Arts, 583, 588
Museum of Modern Art (New York), 28, 82, 83, 85, 89, 97, 173, 199, 201, 261, 535
Museum of Modern Art (Rio), 316, 417
Museum of Natural History, 57
Mussolini, Benito, 76
Myers, John, 521
My Life As a Young Girl, 260, 269, 270; *see also* Black Beans and Diamonds; The Diary of "Helena Morley"

Nabokov, Nicolas, 406, 410, 411, 412, 413
Nabokov, Vladimir, 384
Nation, The, 48, 85; Marianne Moore in, 47, 117, 142, 257, 305; and Mary McCarthy, 31, 37; review of *North & South* in, 142, 305
National Book Award, 302, 335, 382, 445; EB and, 552, 575, 630; EB wins, 513, 514, 516, 517–18, 519
National Endowment for the Arts, 635
National Gallery, 198, 325

Nemer, José Alberto, 520, 522, 530, 531, 544, 555, 571
Nemer, Linda, 530, 555, 567, 569, 571
Neruda, Pablo, 107, 108, 137, 138; *Residencia en la tierra*, 478
Neustadt family, 605
Neustadt International Prize for Literature, 604
Neutra, Richard, 377
Neway, Patricia, 368
New Directions, 57, 60
New Directions (publisher), 86, 331
New Leader, The, 443
New Letters, 66
New Republic, The, 9, 87, 97, 98, 101, 225, 241, 383
News for Women, 82
New Statesman and Nation, The, 249, 259, 300, 333
Newsweek, 615
New World Writing, 61, 242, 251, 274, 309
New Yorker, The, 15, 120, 186, 286, 338, 375, 387, 589; Brendan Gill book, 596; Charles Pearce at, 86; EB relationship with, 127, 134, 142, 143, 165, 182, 221, 222, 247, 251, 254–55, 259, 268, 313–14, 323, 327, 378, 382, 545, 546, 605; EB to be poetry critic, 519, 525, 528; Howard Moss at, 335, 357, 374; Katharine White at, 330, 414, 415; and Marianne Moore, 87, 88, 89, 245, 364; and Mary McCarthy, 416; and May Swenson, 361, 535; Pearl Kazin at, 193, 254, 296, 313–14; publishes "The Bight," 184; publishes "The Burglar of Babylon," 431; publishes "Cirque d'Hiver," 85, 86; publishes EB translation of Octavio Paz, 586; publishes "Gwendolyn," 240, 254–55, 266, 269, 271; publishes "In the Village," 242, 249, 254, 271, 273, 280, 285, 289, 291; publishes "In the Waiting Room," 545–46; publishes "Manuelzinho," 315, 320; publishes "The Moose," 568, 572; pub-